1

AA

KEYGUIDE

PORTUGAL

CONTENTS

KEY TO SYMBOLS

- ✚ Map reference
- ✉ Address
- ☎ Telephone number
- 🕓 Opening times
- ✋ Admission prices
- Ⓜ Underground station
- 🚌 Bus number
- 🚆 Train station
- ⛴ Ferry/boat
- 🚗 Driving directions
- ℹ Tourist office
- 🎫 Tours
- 📖 Guidebook
- 🍴 Restaurant
- ☕ Café
- 🍸 Bar
- 🏬 Shop
- ① Number of rooms
- ❄ Air conditioning
- 🏊 Swimming pool
- 🏋 Gym
- ❓ Other useful information
- ▷ Cross reference
- ★ Walk/drive start point

112

128

269

220

CONTENTS PORTUGAL

3

U IDERSTANDING PORTUGAL

Understanding Portugal is an introduction to the country, its geography, economy, history and its people, giving a real insight into the nation. Living Portugal gets under the skin of Portugal today, while The Story of Portugal takes you through the country's past.

UNDERSTANDING PORTUGAL

Portugal has many faces—underdeveloped and unspoilt regions coexist with sophisticated coastal resorts that have been firmly on the tourist map for more than 40 years. Lisbon, the capital, happily combines modern development with old-fashioned, idiosyncratic charm, while regional capitals, such as Porto, Coimbra and Évora, each have their own distinctive personalities. But it's the coast and sea that define Portugal both physically and historically. In short, wherever you go, you will find variety and interest; there are truly many Portugals to discover.

LANDSCAPE

Portugal is a small country (89,106sq km/ 34,404sq miles), but it enjoys immense geographical diversity. North of the Rio Tejo, the hills and upland areas are a continuation of the meseta, the block of high plateau and mountains that occupies much of the Iberian peninsula. The climate here makes for a green, cultivated and heavily populated landscape, particularly in the Minho and Douro, though much of remote, mountainous Trás-os-Montes is good for little but sheep-grazing. Farther south in the Beiras, Estremadura and Ribatejo, the countryside is predominantly fertile and undulating, rich in woodlands, vines and olives.

South of the Tejo, the vast, sun-drenched and empty Alentejan plains are Portugal's granary, where huge wheat fields are interspersed with cork oak stands, olive groves and plantations. To the south, passes through the low hills lead to the fertile Algarve and the coast. This is a sinuous 1,793km-long (1,114-mile) ribbon that includes vast sandy beaches, dramatic cliffs, headlands and hidden coves, dunes, pinewoods and marshland.

ECONOMY

At the time of the 1974 Carnation Revolution, Portugal was economically at least 50 years behind the rest of Europe, thanks to the policies of Salazar. Since then, enormous strides have been taken, particularly since the country's entry into the European Union (EU) in 1986. For much of the 1990s, Portugal's economic growth was well above the EU average; in recent times, its GDP has stood at around 70 per cent of those of the leading EU economies.

Portugal is the world's largest cork producer and among the largest producers of wine. Its leading industries include textile and footwear manufacture, papermaking and engineering. Tourism is increasingly important, while agriculture is notoriously inefficient. Many farms are little more than minute smallholdings.

POLITICS

Portugal is a republic. Administratively, the mainland is divided into 18 districts, responsible for their own health, education and financial affairs. Municipal power is in the hands of 305 *concelhos*, similar to district councils (boroughs), which are elected every four years. Madeira and the Azores are autonomous regions.

DEMOGRAPHY AND RELIGION

Portugal's population stands at around 10.5 million; the birth rate, unlike that in many other southern European countries, is rising, albeit by a very low percentage (0.4 per cent). Most Portuguese still live on the land or in small towns, mainly close to the coast, with population levels highest in the Minho and lowest in the Alentejo.

The Portuguese are fervently Roman Catholic; although it is falling, church attendance is much higher than in many other European Catholic countries. This is reflected in the large numbers of festivals, processions and religious pilgrimages that are still an integral part of daily life.

PORTUGAL'S REGIONS

LISBON

Lisbon is packed with history. Its main sights are its castle and Alfama area, the elegant Baixa, Chiado and Bairro Alto districts, Belém and the superb Mosteiro dos Jerónimos, the sleekly modern Parque das Nações complex, and some fine museums, like the Museu Calouste Gulbenkian and the Museu Nacional de Arte Antiga. Shopping and nightlife, which should include an evening of *fado*, Portugal's soul music, add another dimension to any visit.

Opposite *Porto and the D. Luís bridge seen from the Douro*
Right *The manicured gardens of Solar de Mateus in Trás-os-Montes*
Below *You can buy a host of gourmet delights in Porto's old stores*

AROUND LISBON

Around Lisbon on either side of the Tejo estuary, there's the option of relaxing on the coast or visiting some of Portugal's finest royal palaces. The most important of these are at Sintra, a cool hillside oasis where you'll find the medieval Palácio Nacional and the 19th-century Palácio da Pena. There's another palace at Queluz, and one more at Mafra. From here, it's a short drive to the coast and Cabo da Roca, the westernmost point of mainland Europe. South are the fashionable resorts of Cascais and Estoril, while, across the Tejo, the dunes curve along the Costa da Caparica to remote, windswept Cabo Espichel.

THE MINHO AND TRÁS-OS-MONTES

The Minho region is considered by many Portuguese to be the most beautiful and varied part of the country. Here you'll find the fertile river valleys of the Minho and Lima, expansive stretches of lovely sandy beaches along the Costa Verde, and the spectacular gorges and mountains of Peneda-Gerês, Portugal's only national park. The largest towns of the Minho, historic Guimarães and Braga, Portugal's ecclesiastical heart, lie in the south of the region. The main coastal resort is Viana do Castelo, while Barcelos is famed for its exuberant weekly market, one of Europe's largest. Both river valleys are home to a string of attractive small towns, and the area is particularly noted for its huge variety of traditional crafts.

PORTO AND THE DOURO

Porto is Portugal's second-largest city, an unabashedly commercial hub near the mouth of the Rio Douro. Huge urban redevelopment has spruced up this once shabby city, and Porto today has plenty to offer in the shape of its historic riverside Ribeira area, Romanesque Sé (cathedral), clutch of fine buildings, good museums, and excellent shopping and entertainment. On the Douro's opposite bank is Vila Nova de Gaia, whose history is inextricably linked with the port trade and where you can learn about and sample the fortified wine that is undoubtedly Portugal's most famous export.

The Douro region lies on the north bank of the Rio Douro, a magnificent river that gives the area its name and cuts through some of Portugal's most impressive scenery. The landscape encompasses both rolling hills and steeply terraced vineyards dotted with port lodges, while the main towns include beautiful Amarante and the buzzing coastal resorts of Póvoa de Varzim and Vila do Conde.

THE BEIRAS

The Beiras region is divided into three parts—the Beira Alta to the northeast, the Beira Baixa in the southeast, and the Beira Litoral along the coast. The Beira Alta and the Beira Baixa are the least visited of Portuguese regions, with wonderful countryside including the Serra da Estrela, mainland Portugal's highest mountain range, the lovely Serra da Arrábida and splendid, remote villages, such as Almeida, Belmonte, Trancoso and Monsanto. The main towns of the region are Guarda, at an altitude of more than 1,000m (3,280ft), and Viseu, birthplace of Grão Vasco, Portugal's greatest Renaissance painter. To the west, the Beira Litoral is dominated by the great university city of Coimbra, from where you can reach the Roman site of Conímbriga, Montemor-o-Velho and its castle, and the ancient forest of Buçaco. North from here is Aveiro, an estuary city surrounded by canals and lagoons; from Aveiro, a long sandy coast stretches north and south—head for the resort of Figueira da Foz to enjoy it at its best.

ESTREMADURA AND THE RIBATEJO

Estremadura and the Ribatejo are both packed with delights. Architecturally, Alcobaça and Batalha should be high on any visiting list, as should Tomar and the historic former headquarters of the Knights Templar (later the Order of Christ). East across the Serra de Aire lies Fátima, one of the Catholic church's most important shrines. North is the elegant inland town of Leiria. From here, it's a short hop to the coast, where a string of pretty resorts stretches south towards Lisbon. Pick of the bunch are Nazaré, Peniche—from where you can visit the offshore islands of Berlenga—and Ericeira. Inland gems include medieval Óbidos, the castle at Almourol, set on an islet in the Tejo, and pretty town and castle of Abrantes.

The Trás-os-Montes, 'beyond the mountains', is remote and sparsely populated, unofficially divided into the southern and fertile Terra Quente (Hot Land), and the climatically extreme north, the Terra Fria (Cold Land), where life is hard. The fortified frontier towns of Chaves and Bragança are the main northern bases, with Vila Real, the nearest town to the landmark Solar de Mateus manor house, dominating the southwest. Away from these, the main draws are the small towns and villages, such as Miranda do Douro on the Spanish border, and the magnificent countryside, where the way of life still seems relatively unchanged. The region has three natural parks: the Serra de Alvão in the west; the Parque Natural de Montesinho on the northern border with Spain; and the Parque Natural do Douro International, which straddles the Spanish border in the east.

THE ALENTEJO

The Alentejo region falls into two parts, Alto (Upper) and Baixo (Lower). It's a vast agricultural area, its rolling plains dotted with cork plantations and scattered towns and villages. Évora, one of Portugal's most attractive towns, is the main draw in the north, while Beja, once an important Moorish settlement, commands the south. The Alto Alentejo is home to some of the country's most picturesque hilltop towns, among them Elvas, with its superb fortifications, and Monsaraz, Marvão, Castelo de Vide and Évoramonte, all with fine medieval buildings. Lively Estremoz, famed for its market, and Vila Viçosa, seat of a royal palace, lie east of Évora, while the road west leads through picturesque Alcácer do Sal to the coast. South in the Baixo Alentejo, Serpa is also pleasant, as is Mértola.

THE ALGARVE

The Algarve is Portugal's holiday playground. To the east of Faro the coast is fringed by long, sandy offshore islands, while to the west, bays, coves and cliffs predominate. The main towns are Faro, Portimão and Lagos, but in tourist terms, these are outshone by resorts such as Albufeira, Carvoeiro, Praia da Rocha and Vilamoura, and the sporting enclaves of Vale do Lobo and Quinta do Lago. To escape the crowds, you'll need to head towards Sagres and the western coast around Cabo de São Vicente, or take in low-key Tavira in the east. The interior still has relatively untouched towns, such as Silves, and picturesque villages like Alte, Castro Marim and Estoi. For scenic beauty the Serra de Monchique hills take some beating, while, on the coast, the Parque Natural da Ria Formosa shouldn't be missed.

GETTING THE MOST FROM YOUR STAY

Many visitors to Portugal come for the sun, sea and beaches, but, given the country's relatively small size, it's quite possible to focus on more than one region or type of holiday. This is best done by car, as public transportation, though more than adequate for day-to-day use, can be patchy. Exploring some of the inland and more remote regions gives a whole new perspective and a far better insight into the country, with the chance to sample the delights of the more old-fashioned aspects of Portuguese life. From the Algarve resorts, a few hours' drive north opens up the sparsely populated Alentejo region, while Lisbon lies only a relatively short motorway drive away.

From the capital, it's easy to head into the Beiras, Ribatejo and Estremadura, home of many of the country's great towns and monuments. Visitors to the north can combine the buzz of Porto with time spent in the beautiful Douro and Minho regions, while the remote wilderness of the Trás-os-Montes lies a relatively short drive to the east. Time anywhere away from Lisbon and the Algarve will give you a taste of the 'real' Portugal, and a chance to experience the sincere, welcoming kindness of the Portuguese themselves.

Above *In one of the sheltered bays of the Algarve, the golden sands of Praia de Dona Ana near Lagos are backed by spectacular cliffs and rock formations*

LISBON

Alfama (▷ 70–71): Wander through the picturesque streets of Lisbon's medieval quarter.

Bairro Alto (▷ 69): Spend an evening eating, drinking and listening to *fado*, Portugal's unique soul music with a tradition all of its own.

Belém (▷ 73–76): Visit some of the capital's most significant monuments and important museums.

Castelo de São Jorge (▷ 78): Enjoy the space, the shady greenery and the great views of the city you get from its one-time citadel.

Chiado (▷ 69, 92–95): Browse around some of Lisbon's most stylish shops.

Hotel As Janelas Verdes (▷ 104): Recover from a day's sightseeing as you relax in this elegant 18th-century mansion overlooking the Rio Tejo.

Museu Calouste Gulbenkian (▷ 80–82): Enjoy a world-class collection of art from every century, spanning East and West.

Parque das Nações (▷ 85–87): Take in the Oceanário, stroll the riverside gardens and indulge yourself shopping.

Ribeira Market (▷ 83): Give your taste buds a treat as you browse this great food market.

AROUND LISBON

Cascais (▷ 109): Indulge in some chic retail therapy in this popular holiday resort.

Costa da Caparica (▷ 109): Catch the little train and hop off at one of the relaxing beaches.

Sintra (▷ 112–113): Visit two of Portugal's royal palaces—the Palácio Nacional de Sintra and the extraordinary neo-Gothic Palácio Nacional da Pena.

THE MINHO AND TRÁS-OS-MONTES

Barcelos (▷ 127): Buy a ceramic cockerel at the Thursday market—the essential Portuguese souvenir.

Bom Jesus do Monte (▷ 129–131): Climb the steps of Portugal's great baroque architectural set piece.

Citânia de Briteiros (▷ 133): Visit one of Portugal's most impressive archaeological sites, with extensive Celtic remains.

Guimarães (▷ 134–135): Head for a café table in the splendid Praça de Santiago and watch life go by.

Miranda do Douro (▷ 136): Stand above the Douro river and look across the dramatic gorge to Spain.

Parque Natural de Montesinho (▷ 136–137): Walk, drive or cycle through this unspoilt rural area.

Solar de Mateus (▷ 142): Stroll through the glorious formal gardens here, the finest in Portugal.

Taberna do Valentim, Viana do Castelo (▷ 151): Eat the freshest of fish or try the best of Minho regional cookery amid simple, rustic surroundings.

PORTO AND THE DOURO

Café Majestic, Porto (▷ 172): Pause to drink a coffee and eat a pastry served by uniformed waiters at this elegant café.

Cais da Ribeira (▷ 159): Explore the maze of narrow alleyways leading through old Porto down to the riverside.

Casa da Calçada, Amarante (▷ 174): Luxurious surroundings, superb service, great riverside views and beautiful gardens—these all add up to the perfect overnight stop.

Fundação de Serralves (▷ 161): Come here for exciting, cutting-edge modern art in Porto.

Ponte Dom Luís I (▷ 159): Walk across Porto's celebrated two-tiered bridge for great river and city views.

Torre dos Clérigos (▷ 160): Climb this tower in Porto for bird's-eye city views.

Vila Nova de Gaia (▷ 164–165): Find out about the story of port and enjoy a tasting at one of the port lodges.

THE BEIRAS

Almeida (▷ 179): Walk the 4km (2.5 miles) around the grassy walls for glimpses of town life from above and superb views across the plateau.

Coimbra (▷ 182–185): Visit the famous complex of the Velha Universidade.

Conímbriga (▷ 186): See the best of Portugal's Roman past at the archaeological site and museum.

Palace Hotel do Bussaco (▷ 206): Indulge yourself with a stay at this luxurious hotel, an ex-royal hunting lodge in the heart of the national forest near Luso.

Parque Arqueológico do Vale do Côa (▷ 189): Discover 20,000-year-old art etched into the rock.

Serra da Estrela (▷ 191): Mainland Portugal's highest mountain range—dramatic scenery and crisp air.

A Taberna, Coimbra (▷ 204): Enjoy the best of traditionally cooked local dishes in the university city.

Viseu (▷ 193): Take in masterpieces by Grão Vasco, Portugal's greatest 16th-century painter.

ESTREMADURA AND THE RIBATEJO

Alcobaça (▷ 212–213): Spend a few hours at this great monastery, one of Portugal's finest Gothic buildings.

Batalha (▷ 214–217): Marvel at the Manueline stonework in the Capelas Imperfeitas.

Castelo de Almourol (▷ 211): Take a tiny ferry across the Rio Tejo to visit the fairy-tale castle on its river island.

Ericeira (▷ 211): Sample superb lobster and super-fresh fish in this fishing port north along the coast from Lisbon.

Estalagem de Santa Iria, Tomar (▷ 233): Escape the crowds and enjoy perfect peace at this hotel on a river island.

Fátima (▷ 217): Join the pilgrims at the country's greatest shrine.

Óbidos (▷ 218): Spend a night in this walled medieval town after the daytime crowds have gone home.

Peniche (▷ 219): Catch a boat to view the vast numbers of sea birds on the Ilha Berlenga.

Serras de Aire (▷ 219): Visit dramatic limestone caves.

Tomar (▷ 220–222): Explore the Convento de Cristo, once the headquarters of the successors to the Knights Templar.

THE ALENTEJO

Alcácer do Sal (▷ 237): Spot the storks' nests in this laid-back riverside town.

Arraiolos (▷ 237): Shop for local rugs and carpets.

Beja (▷ 237): See some of Portugal's finest azulejos (tiles) at the Convento de Nossa Senhora da Conceição.

Estremoz (▷ 239): Visit the Saturday market in the Rossio before exploring the Vila Velha (Old Town).

Évoramonte (▷ 239): Climb up to the castle for superb views across the Alentejo.

O Fialho, Évora (▷ 254): For the best in Alentejan cooking.

Vila Nova de Milfontes (▷ 246): Join Portuguese holiday-makers for a fabulous stay by the sea.

THE ALGARVE

Almancil (▷ 261): Visit the church of São Lourenço to see some of Portugal's best blue azulejos (tiles).

Carvoeiro (▷ 266): Take a boat trip to see the fabulous hidden coves and rock formations.

Faro (▷ 263–265): Explore the old town before indulging in some of the central Algarve's best shopping.

Parque Natural da Ria Formosa (▷ 267): Find out about the Algarve's environment.

Portimão (▷ 268): Shop where the locals shop.

Sagres (▷ 269): A great base from which to explore some unspoilt areas.

Silves (▷ 270): Spend time exploring this historic town, once the Algarve's Moorish capital.

Tavira (▷ 270): Enjoy the fine architecture and gentle pace of life.

Opposite *The imposing Ponte do 25 de Abril suspension bridge crosses the River Tagus at Lisbon*

Below *The Rossio, the main square of Lisbon's Baixa quarter*

TOP EXPERIENCES

Visit a port lodge and sample a few varieties of vintage port—try the delicate *porto branco* (white port) as a chilled aperitif.

Above *The beach at Praia da Rocha, one of the Algarve's finest*
Below *Colourful glazed plates are typical of the decorated pottery made throughout Portugal*

Take a cruise up the Douro valley, the best way to appreciate this lovely area.

Eat a *pastel de nata*, a super-sweet, flaky-pastry custard tart, whose recipe is still a closely guarded secret, at the Antiga Confraria de Belém in Lisbon (▷ 98).

Visit the market at Barcelos for a real taste of rural Portugal.

Listen to *fado* at a *fado* house in the Bairro Alto in Lisbon, or in Coimbra, its other home.

Go to a soccer match at Lisbon's Estádio da Luz or Porto's Estádio das Antas.

Splash out for a night in one of the historic *pousadas*, maybe in a castle or former convent.

See the world-class treasures at the Museu Calouste Gulbenkian in Lisbon.

Shop for local artisan work—there's a huge range of crafts in every region.

Visit Coimbra, a buzzing riverside university city that combines fine medieval buildings, churches and monuments with great shopping and eating opportunities.

LIVING PORTUGAL

LANDSCAPE AND NATURE

Portugal can be divided into a number of distinctive geographical zones, but overall the Atlantic is the predominant influence. This means much of Portugal enjoys a mild, rainy climate. In the Minho region bordering northwest Spain, climate variations are similar to those of northern Europe. The Peneda-Gerês National Park—once the home of the brown bear—still shelters predators, such as the wolf and the Imperial eagle, as well as the rare Gerês fern. The highland plains and mountains extend into Spain, but gradually give way to lush pasture in central Portugal. South of Lisbon, the endangered Iberian lynx roams the remoter parts of the arid Alentejo plains. This zone is at increasing risk of turning to desert in what is one of the world's most serious environmental problems. The Algarve, though, has a milder, more Mediterranean climate. More than 3,000 hours of sunshine a year help to warm the Atlantic waters as they round Cape St. Vincent and flow towards the Mediterranean. Farther north, the seas are cold and can be treacherous. Vineyards make their mark on the landscape in 30 different wine-growing regions, from the stepped terraces of the Douro valley to Dão high in the mountains of Beira Alta, the Alentejo plains and, overseas, the volcanic islands of Madeira and the Azores.

WINE COUNTRY

Portugal has a wealth of indigenous grape varieties and pioneering wine-makers. A number of mainland Portugal's finest grape varieties were wiped out by the devastating phylloxera outbreaks that spread across Europe in the 19th century. Now, however, these varieties have been re-created and are flourishing under the direction of a new generation of internationally trained wine-makers.

Over the last 20 years Portuguese wines have been redefined, modern technology has arrived and been embraced and quality has now taken over from quantity as the prime concern, creating an altogether more sophisticated product. Admittedly, much still needs to be done in promoting this relatively unknown treasure on the international market but as more quality estate labels flourish so too, hopefully, will customer confidence abroad.

Above *A verdant landscape of hills and trees surrounds the village of Monsaraz in the Alentejo*
Opposite left *Alqueva barrage, part of the massive hydro-electricity in southern Portugal*
Opposite right *The mighty Vasco da Gama bridge in Lisbon*

WORLD FIRST

Environmental issues have not always been high on the Portuguese agenda, but the focus is gradually shifting towards preserving the country's natural landscapes and resources.

Starting production for the national grid in 2008, the Central Solar Fotovoltaica de Amareleja is said to be the largest solar energy power station in the world. Extending over 250ha (618 acres) outside the sunny town of Amareleja, in the southern Alentejo the plant comprises some 2,500 revolving panels which follow the course of the sun throughout the day.

When full output is reached by the end of 2008, it is hoped that Central Solar Fotovoltaica de Amareleja will supply energy for more than 30,000 homes. In addition to providing a clean and renewable source of energy, the investment of around 240,000 euros is hoped to inspire the creation of additional such plants across other parts of southern Portugal.

WATERY GRAVE

Europe's largest hydroelectric dam and reservoir, built to irrigate sun-baked southern Portugal, has paradoxically split the local community. The Alqueva floodgates were closed in 2002, damming the Guadiana river and creating an artificial lake covering 250sq km (96sq miles). Before the dam could be built, though, the village of Aldeia da Luz—and its graveyard—had to be relocated. A collection of Stone Age rock paintings and a Roman fort were also submerged.

Humans were not the only species to have relocation forced on them. Imperial eagles, Iberian lynx, black storks, wild boar and bats all lost their habitats in the area, along with some rare plant species. The government says the reservoir will boost agriculture, watersports and tourism, but it remains to be seen whether the benefits to farmers will outweigh the devastating impact on the environment.

SPACE AGE SOLUTIONS

Forests and woodland cover some 9 per cent of the Portuguese countryside and the government is working hard to protect these natural habitats. But the forest fires that raged during the 2003 heat-wave devastated vast tracts of woodland and eroded topsoil.

In 2003, European space agency satellites sent images to firefighters in Portugal, showing the spread of the blazes, thus helping the rescue services. the Portuguese are now simply better prepared for such an emergency; in 2004, prevention plans included forestry patrols, with around 26,000 soldiers and engineers drafted in to create firebreaks.

Despite these efforts, fires (often started intentionally) continue to devastate large tracts of forest each summer, as fire prevention plans and the funding necessary to put these plans into action fail to reach affected areas.

VASCO DA GAMA BRIDGE

Opened in 1998, the Ponte Vasco da Gama is Lisbon's newest bridge and the longest in Europe. Nearly half of its 16km (10-mile) length spans the Tejo estuary. The vast cable-stayed bridge enables north–south traffic to bypass Lisbon, alleviating the rush-hour congestion suffered by commuters on the older 25 de Abril Bridge and improving the air quality in the capital. It is now a landmark in its own right.

Despite its benefits, the project was not unopposed, particularly by ornithologists who were worried about the effect building work would have on the nearby bird sanctuary. In response, the Lusoponte consortium formed to build the bridge agreed to take special steps to avoid disturbing the flamingos, egrets and cormorants that feed in the area, and a great deal was done to minimize the impact on the local environment.

LIVING TRADITIONS

The towering statue of Cristo Rei (Christ the King) looking out over the Tejo estuary from Cacilhas serves as a constant reminder of Portugal's Catholic heritage. Although statistics suggest the Church's influence is in decline among the young, the crowds of pilgrims at the shrine of Fátima suggest little, if any, loss of faith. Go into a Portuguese home and you may come across an ornamental cockerel, the national symbol. These cockerels come from Barcelos, where legend has it the miraculous crowing of a dead cockerel saved a pilgrim from the gallows five centuries ago. For all that time, the country was a monarchy, though it has now been a republic for nearly 100 years. Despite this, the claimant to the throne is a popular figure. Many other customs and traditions have similarly survived or adapted to meet the test of time, as is the case with local fairs and markets. In remote Trás-os-Montes, the ever popular *Festa dos Rapazes*, celebrated around the time of the winter solstice, is firmly rooted in ancient pagan rites of passage, as masked men prove their bravado by leaping over raging bonfires; in Ponte de Lima, the still thriving 12th-century market also clearly shows that tradition in Portugal lives on.

THE ALTAR OF PORTUGAL

The shrine of Fátima is the religious heart of Portugal and a place of devotion for Catholic pilgrims from all over the world. It receives some 2 million visitors every year.

The year 2007 brought exceptional numbers of visitors as Fátima marked the 90th anniversary of the apparitions of Our Lady. Rector Monsignor Guerra invited Pope Benedict XVI to attend the closing ceremony of these celebrations on 13 October and to preside over the inauguration of the new and controversial Church of the Most Holy Trinity, a concrete basilica that sits somewhat incongruously alongside the old one. The year was also the 100th anniversary of the birth of Sister Lúcia who was buried alongside her two cousins in the Chapel of Apparitions in 2006.

Above *A beautiful decorated* azulejo *(tile) from Lamego*
Opposite top *A university student from Porto wearing traditional celebratory dress*
Opposite bottom *Duke Dom Duarte of Portugal and his wife, Duchess Dona Isabel Bragança*

UNIVERSITY LIFE

Held every May, the *Queima das Fitas* is the culmination of a set of university rituals that begin on enrolment day. They include the *latada* (baptism), when new students are given outrageous haircuts and embarrassing forfeits to carry out in public.

The best place to see the *queima* is in Coimbra, the home of Portugal's oldest university. The tradition gets its name from the symbolic burning of a *fita* (narrow ribbon) by students about to start their final-year examinations. Only after the ritual has been observed may finalists decorate their traditional folders with ribbons representing their particular faculties. The partying continues for a week, reaching its climax in a carnival-style procession through the city's streets—the last chance to let off steam.

AZULEJOS

The patterned glazed tiles that decorate the façades and interiors of many Portuguese buildings are the product of centuries of artistic tradition. At the Museu Nacional do Azulejo (National Tile Museum) in Lisbon, you can see murals that depict panoramic views of the capital before it was devastated by the great earthquake of 1755.

To see contemporary *azulejos*, take a trip on the Lisbon metro which is decorated with tiles created by Lisbon-born artists Maria Keil and Rolando Sá-Nogueira. Keil's design at Intendente station is considered to be a masterpiece of tile art. For a different approach, head to Laranjeiras station, where Sá-Nogueira has used photo-realism to create mouthwatering depictions of ripe oranges—the fruit after which the district is named.

THE HOUSE OF BRAGANÇA

When you think of the royal houses of Europe, you may be forgiven for leaving Portugal off the list. But Dom Duarte Pio de Bragança is internationally recognized by monarchists as the rightful king, representing the nation at royal gatherings throughout Europe. Pretender to Portugal's abolished throne—a revolution in 1910 deposed the monarchy—Dom Duarte was born in exile in 1945. The family returned home five years later when the law banning the former royals was abolished. Married to Portuguese commoner Isabel de Heredia, the 24th Duke of Bragança now has three young children— eldest son and heir Afonso, Maria Francisca and Dinis. They are cherished by many Portuguese supporters, who regard them as living representatives of centuries of history, and who continue the campaign to see the monarchy restored.

PORT

Port has been produced in the Douro valley since Roman times, although it did not really make an impact outside Portugal until the British began importing it in quantity from 1703.

Despite its popularity, the demands of today's competitive drinks market have forced the Portuguese to rethink port's image. Once deemed old-fashioned, this sophisticated fortified wine is now staging a comeback, particularly among younger people. Exports to North America are rising steadily, while the British are experimenting with alternatives to the classic vintages. Lower-alcohol white port is perfect as a chilled aperitif, while cocktail lovers might like to try an Autumnal Equinox: Mix two measures of port to one of Grand Marnier and a half measure of an almond-based liqueur. Serve over ice and join the new wave of port enthusiasts.

THE SEA

Portugal's history has been inextricably linked to the sea since the Moors crossed the Strait of Gibraltar. They occupied the 'Al-Gharb'—the Moorish name for what is now the Algarve—for 500 years until the 12th century. Portuguese expansion began some 400 years later when the great explorers, such as Vasco da Gama, set sail, rounding the Cape of Good Hope and opening up new trade routes to the east. Today, the sea continues to define the nation. The crowded, though beautiful, beaches of the Algarve stretching along the southern coast are a crucial source of tourist revenue. In contrast, the stormy seas of the Atlantic coast to the north are one of Europe's most important fishing areas, also making a vital contribution to the economy. The sea provides the Portuguese with a staple part of their diet; only Japan and Iceland consume more fish per capita than Portugal. To best enjoy the Portuguese fish experience, head to any fishing village and order your choice of fish grilled with potatoes, salad and a generous dose of olive oil.

'365 WAYS TO COOK SALT-COD'

Dried salt-cod, or *bacalhau*, is arguably Portugal's most famous national dish. A popular saying states there is a different salt-cod recipe for every day of the year, and a glance at the average menu certainly seems to uphold this claim—the ubiquitous *bolinho de bacalhau* (codfish croquette) appears in restaurants throughout the country and is a tasty snack.

The story starts in the 1500s, when sailors learned to salt cod on their epic voyages, drying it out on deck until it was stiff as a board. On the beaches of Nazaré you can still see racks of fish drying in the sun the traditional way. What has changed, however, is that salt-cod now accounts for a quarter of Portugal's fish imports, as fishermen struggle to keep up with demand.

Above *Fishermen mend their nets on the beach at Figueira da Foz as the sun sets*
Opposite left *Justin Mujica cuts a dash through the surf*
Opposite right *Natural erosion by wind and water has created the rock formations at Ponta da Piedade*

SEA ARCHES

On the southern Atlantic coast at Ponta da Piedade, near the picturesque town of Lagos, there is a headland of sculptured cliffs comprising what may well be the largest collection of sea arches in the world. The rock is riddled with grottoes, deep holes and natural tunnels, all the hallmarks of centuries of natural erosion.

Lagos town council decided to take action to protect this much-visited beauty spot. The lighthouse, cliff path and deep sandy creek—supporting countless forms of marine life—attract large numbers of tourists every year. The funds raised were used to prevent further erosion by regenerating the vegetation, for the building of designated paths and viewpoints for visitors, and for improved traffic controls and parking facilities. Alternatively this natural phenomenon can be viewed from the sea with companies offering excursions in Portuguese schooners or in smaller dinghies which allow closer inspection.

PLENTY MORE FISH?

The Portuguese eat an annual average of 70kg (154lb) of fish (the European average is 22.5kg/ 50lb). This makes them the third-highest consumers of fish in the world.

All along the coast there are numerous sea-dependent communities regularly landing mackerel and sardines, but Portugal's fishermen are finding it hard to meet the demand in the country for these fish. They currently catch only 68 per cent of Portugal's fish supply—many sardines are now imported from Russia and cod mainly comes from Norway.

Concerns about the rapid depletion of fish stocks in the North Atlantic have also led to cutbacks in quotas across the European Union, and Portugal's fishermen are suffering the consequences. The fishing fleet—local, coastal and offshore—is being downsized and the fisheries have agreed to maintain current landing levels in an attempt to aid stock renewal.

WHALE-SPOTTING

The Azores archipelago is one of the best places in the world to spot whales. Sperm whales thrive here, coexisting with the 24 other sea mammal species registered on and around the islands. When Europhlukes—a project funded by the European Commission—set to work compiling the largest whale and dolphin database in the world, Whale Watch Azores (WWA) jumped at the chance to become involved in this ambitious project.

WWA, which also runs whale-spotting tours around the islands, already has the largest sperm whale register in Europe. It has identified more than 1,500 examples, along with blue, sei, killer and pilot whales. Now the Europhlukes database is fully up and running, anyone can submit photographs to the website and discover whether their particular whale, dolphin or porpoise has been spotted elsewhere.

WORLD-CLASS WAVES

Hotshot Tiago Pires is Portuguese surfing's most famous export. This rising star has been winning competitions on the world circuit ever since he was crowned rookie of the year in 2000.

But it is at home in Ericeira that you will find one of Tiago's best-loved surf spots. Known simply as The Reef, this finger of lava, sticking out at the southern tip of Ribeira Bay, is not for the inexperienced. Swells come in from the deep Atlantic, folding over the rocks into what Tiago warns is one of the fastest—and most dangerous—tubes in the world.

In January 2005 Tiago towed into the biggest waves ever surfed in Portugal, just off the coast of Cascais. The day was one that went down in the annals of Portuguese surfing history and is still talked of today among surfing aficionados.

THE MODERN ARTS

Portugal is not renowned for its contribution to the arts, but it can still claim its fair share of famous painters, poets, writers, musicians and dancers. Since the Middle Ages, a number of classic works have come to stand as cultural landmarks on the Portuguese arts scene. Figurative art in Portugal can be traced back to Stone Age rock paintings and the *berrões*—roughly carved granite bulls and boars—probably used in fertility rituals as early as 4000BC. Literature, however, lagged behind. It was not until the 16th century that a poetic masterpiece was to appear. *The Lusiads*, an epic account of the voyages of discovery by Luís de Camões (*c*1524–80), records the transition from medieval to Renaissance times. His portrait of Vasco da Gama rivals that of Virgil's Aeneas, while the theme he chose stands up to comparison with Homer's Odyssey. In the 20th century, another Portuguese poet, Fernando Pessoa (1888–1935), made his mark. By creating a series of alter egos and publishing works under their names, he created a literary genre all of his own.

LISBON FASHION WEEK
ModaLisboa—first held in 1991—is Portugal's answer to the catwalk shows of London, Paris, New York and Milan. Lisbon is working hard to promote itself as a capital of fashion and its fashion week is rapidly achieving international status. More than 20,000 people now attend this event every year, and it has become a showcase for the talents of fashion designers and models alike.

At the cutting edge is Ana Salazar, considered to be the leading light of Portuguese fashion. Her contribution was recognized when she was awarded the Order of Infante D. Henrique by the president. Lisbon fashion week is a launching pad for new talent, propelling contemporary designers such as José António Tenente, Lena Aires, Fátima Lopes and Maria Gambina onto the international fashion scene.

Above *Pianist Valentina Igoshina performing at the Sintra Festival of Music*
Opposite top A Viagem do Elefante, *published in 2008, by 1998 Nobel Prize winner José Saramago*
Opposite bottom *Portuguese* fado *singer Mariza Nunes in performance*

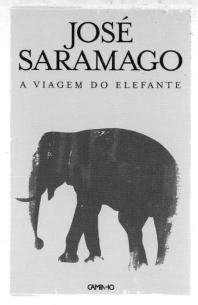

JOSÉ SARAMAGO
A VIAGEM DO ELEFANTE

CAMINHO

FADO DIVA

Hailed as the new Amália Rodrigues—Portugal's legendary *fadista*, or *fado* soloist—Mariza Nunes stands out from the crowd in more ways than one. *Fado* is Portugal's take on the blues, and Mozambique-born Mariza has both the voice and the looks to carry it off. Her peroxide crop may shock, but her vocal skills never fail to impress.

Fadistas are expected to stand stock still as they sing to hushed audiences in the bars and clubs of Lisbon and Coimbra. But Mariza defies convention. Always moving to the jazzed-up rhythms that set her style apart, she brings elements of gospel, soul and rock to this traditional song form that is unique to Portugal.

In 2004, Mariza recorded a duet with international popstar Sting for the Olympic games in Athens and 2008 saw her successfully complete an extensive European tour with a large number of US dates planned in 2009.

MUSICAL OASIS

On a farm in Castelo Branco, Maria João Pires has realized a life-long dream. The Portuguese piano virtuoso has opened a retreat where musicians can work in an environment perfectly in tune with their artistic needs. It took a great deal of work to get the project off the ground and turn Maria João Pires' dream into a reality. Lack of funding meant things got off to a shaky start, but the Portuguese government came to the rescue. Today, the Belgais Centro for the Study of the Arts has a concert hall with fantastic acoustics and a studio where Maria João Pires recorded *Moonlight*, her reinterpretation of the Beethoven sonatas that launched her career. Since then this musical oasis has gone from strength to strength, running courses for students from all over the world, and in 2008 their wonderful children's choir represented Portugal at the Zaragoza Expo.

NOBEL LAUREATE

When José Saramago won the 1998 Nobel Prize for Literature, he famously joked that 'this prize is for all speakers of Portuguese, but while we're on the subject, I shall keep the money'. Born in 1922 in Azinhaga, Portugal's greatest living author is still writing novels, plays, short stories, poetry and non-fiction. Many of his novels present alternative versions of historical events—what historians call counterfactuals— often with an intriguing supernatural twist.

A long-standing member of the Communist Party of Portugal, Saramago has also turned his attention to contemporary politics. The Stone Raft—a tale about Portuguese and Spanish society—follows four people whose lives are thrown into turmoil when the Iberian Peninsula breaks away from mainland Europe, spinning through the Atlantic towards the United States and triggering a geopolitical crisis.

SINTRA FESTIVAL OF MUSIC AND DANCE

Running now for more than 40 years, this festival, held during June and July every year, has a firm following among the region's arts lovers. Chamber music, piano recitals and ballet performances are staged either in the Olga Cadaval cultural centre or in fantastic venues such as the Pena, Regaleira and Queluz palaces, top estates and local churches.

Aiming to promote up-and-coming artists, the festival often showcases young talent as it did in 2008 with piano recitals by Denis Matsuev.

Born in Siberia in 1975, Denis Matsuev was catapulted to stardom at the 1998 International Tchaikovsy Competition in Moscow and has been in much demand as an international concert pianist ever since. His memorable Rachmaninoff performance in Sintra was justifiably much praised by critics in the local press

ECONOMY AND POLITICS

Portugal has come a long way since 1986 when it joined the European Community. At the time it was seen as Spain's poor relation, but EU membership soon paid off for the country. Fast forward a few decades and you find a nation that has organized an international Expo, hosted a European football championship and been actively involved in European politics. In 2007 European leaders descended on the capital amid tight security to formalize the controversial Treaty of Lisbon with former Prime Minister José Manuel Durão Barroso leading them as the President of the European Commission. Not so long ago it would have been hard to imagine Portugal achieving so much. However, despite these high-profile events Portugal, like the rest of the world, has suffered in recent years from soaring food and fuel prices and consequentially, some argue, from rising crime rates. Lisbon police complain about the summer spate of pick-pocket attacks on tourists, the daily media report a rise in armed robbery and Portuguese grumble among themselves about poor wages, high prices and soccer. But Portugal is resilient and when the world economy allows it to do so, it will undoubtedly pick itself up and continue on its road to recovery.

ECONOMIC GOALS
Braga municipal stadium is an architectural triumph. Built specially for the Euro 2004 football championships, it was carved out of the mountainside on the site of a former quarry. But this is not the only Euro 2004 success story. Although many critics said that in the midst of recession the government should be investing in hospitals rather than sport, Portugal now has seven new stadiums costing a total of 500 million euros to build. If this sounds like a lot of money, compare it with the 800 million euros the new Wembley stadium in London will have cost in total. There is still more of which the Portuguese can be proud. Three of the sites have been awarded UEFA's highest, five-star, rating, rivalling the best stadiums in Western Europe.

Above *The grand entrance to Palacio de Sao Bento in Lisbon, the home of the Portuguese parliament*
Opposite left *Porto's new metro, a symbol of urban regeneration*
Opposite right *Farming in Portugal has problems to overcome*

PUT A CORK IN IT

Generations of families in the Alentejo region of southern Portugal have earned their living as cork-makers. Portugal is the world's leading supplier, producing 50 per cent of all cork stoppers.

The industry currently keeps 15,000 people employed, but these jobs are coming under threat from a new trend in wine-bottling, with retailers opting for plastic- and screw-top alternatives to traditional corks. And there is another side to the story. According to the Worldwide Fund for Nature, it is not only Portugal's economy that could suffer. The harvesting of cork is environmentally friendly and, if the cork forests are not managed responsibly, they eventually could turn into desert. This would spell more trouble for many endangered species—such as the Iberian lynx—that are already battling for survival.

FARMING QUOTAS

Portuguese farmers suffered a bad year in 2003 when they lost out because Portugal was the only EU member state to vote against the reform of the Common Agricultural Policy. The agriculture minister said the resulting EU cuts in milk quotas for dairy farmers in the Azores—one of the poorest regions of Europe—would cripple the islands' economy.

But quotas are not the only problem. High land prices mean most of Portugal's farms cover less than 5ha (12 acres), making it all but impossible for farmers to sell their livestock and produce at competitive prices, or to create opportunities for young people to join the industry. The reforms in Brussels have done little to address these concerns. Many of the country's farmers hope that the trend towards organic farming will save the day.

JOB CREATION

High unemployment has blighted Portugal's economy in recent years, with 2007 figures the highest since 1987. But a new masters course in business start-up and management, run by the ISCTE Business School in Lisbon, has already had a positive impact on the job market. One of the first students to graduate in 2003, Helena Serdoura, came from a business background as a partner in one of the few recruitment agencies for domestic workers in Portugal. The course helped her broaden and fine-tune her business skills through the study of marketing techniques and effective administration. On graduating, Helena Serdoura set up Housekeeping, a school where domestic staff can improve their knowledge of cookery, flower arranging, etiquette, babysitting and first aid. Its doors opened in 2004 and, in just a few months, 70 people had completed training courses.

REGENERATION

While holidaymakers may enjoy taking the old-fashioned trams down Avenida do Boavista to the seafront district of Foz do Douro, commuters in Porto had long been yearning for a quicker, smoother ride to work. Drivers crossing the river from Vila Nova de Gaia also longed for a day when traffic jams would be a thing of the past.

Their wish came true in 2002 with the opening of the Metro do Porto—the largest transport project under way in the EU—which now carries 60 million passengers per year. Architect Eduardo Souto de Moura designed the 66 stations and engineer Adão de Fonseca built the Infante D. Henrique Bridge, which spans 371m (1,217ft) over the Douro. The system has five colour-coded lines intersecting at the central station of Trinidade, dramatically cutting journey times for commuters and easing the city's traffic congestion.

FACES OF PORTUGAL

Perhaps as a result of Portugal's small land mass and population, its people have always been united by three factors: a common language, their Catholic faith and the sea. This cohesion helped Portugal become the first unified nation-state in Western Europe. Despite this, the Portuguese can chart their ancestry back to a variety of ethnic groups. In the north, many families trace their roots back to the early Celtic tribes who settled in the area long before the Romans arrived. In contrast, the south bears witness to five centuries of Moorish occupation, particularly in the Algarve region. The language itself contains corruptions of Moorish expressions in words like *oxalá*, which means 'if only' in Portuguese and comes from the Arabic *Inshallah* (Allah willing). In modern Portugal, regional differences owe more to tradition and climate than they do to wars and battles with prospective occupiers. The popular saying 'while Lisbon plays, Braga prays and Porto works' supports the theory that life up in the north has always been more conservative and devout than in the warmer, easy-going south.

MOORISH LEGACY

In the small town of Arraiolos near Évora in central Portugal, local carpet-weavers make wall-hangings and floor-coverings using traditional Moorish techniques handed down from mother to daughter for more than 500 years. The authenticity of each *tapete de Arraiolos* (needlework rug) is guaranteed by the Arraiolos Producers' Association.

The roots of this flourishing art form can be traced back to the Inquisition, when the Moors, Jews and anyone else who was not a God-fearing Catholic were persecuted or forced to flee the cities. Some of the Moors sought refuge in the Alentejo plains, where they set about making rugs. Their legacy lives on to this day in Arraiolos, where it has spawned a prosperous cottage industry.

Above *The church and monastery of San Gocalo in Amarante is the focus of a lavish festival in June*
Opposite top *Tomar is the host to one of Portugal's liveliest traditional festivals*
Opposite bottom *A young girl in elaborate folk costume*

BULLFIGHTING COUNTRY

Vila Franca de Xira, north-east of Lisbon in the heart of Portugal's bullfighting country, has an unrivalled reputation for bull rearing. Twice a year visitors gather here for the running of the bulls. For several days each July during the Festa do Colete Encarnado (Red Waistcoat Festival), there are bullfights and bull runs, when the young bulls are turned loose and the hot-headed, drunk or just plain misguided attempt to dodge them as they thunder through the streets.

The festival gets its name from the traditional outfits worn by the *campinos* (cowboys), who watch over the bulls on the Ribatejo marshlands. The courageous Lusitano stallions traditionally ridden by Portugal's bullfighters are also bred in the area. Unlike his Spanish counterpart, the aim of the Portuguese *toureiro* is not to kill the bull, but rather to show off his horse's high standard of schooling.

HISTORIC RIVALRY

Relations between Portugal and Spain, its only neighbour, have always been characterized by intense rivalry. A popular saying states that from Spain the Portuguese can expect 'neither a good wind nor a good marriage'.

The town of Olivença in the Alto Alentejo is a living reminder of this centuries-old aspect of Portuguese life. Both the town and 600sq km (231sq miles) of surrounding countryside were annexed by the Spanish in 1801 and, although Portugal has never got the land back, it has not stopped trying. The Grupo de Amigos de Olivença—Friends of Olivença—campaigns ceaselessly to end what it regards as the illegal Spanish occupation.

Other locals, however, take things much more philosophically. They boast that the women of Olivença are unique by virtue of their combination of classic Portuguese beauty and Spanish grace.

FEAST OF SÃO GONÇALO

The church of São Gonçalo in Amarante is the most famous building in this pretty town on the banks of the Tâmega river to the east of Porto. On the first weekend of June each year it becomes the focus for the Feast of São Gonçalo, the patron saint of the town. São Gonçalo is also important locally because he is in charge of marrying off single women.

Just as in the rest of Portugal, folklore here goes hand in hand with the Roman Catholic faith, in which it usually finds a basis and inspiration. As part of the festivities, each young couple who live in or come from Amarante exchanges lupin seeds—an ancient Portuguese fertility symbol—or phallus-shaped cakes, thus incorporating a pagan custom into the saint's day celebrations. These fascinating little tokens represent the couple's mutual love.

RURAL V URBAN

The village of Casais in the hill-country of Monchique in southern Portugal offers visitors a taste of the peace and tranquillity typical of rural life. But behind this seemingly idyllic façade, the reality is somewhat different. It seems that the lure of urban living may one day put an end to this pastoral existence and to the regional culture that accompanies it.

Abandoned farms and overgrown fields are both increasingly common sights throughout the *serra*, the mountainous border that separates the Algarve from the Alentejo.

The lack of economic prospects is forcing many families to head for the towns and coastal areas in search of jobs that can guarantee them better living standards. Today, the rural population of Monchique stands at just 17 people per square kilometre (0.3sq miles).

SPORTING LIFE

Portugal is a proud soccer nation with a world-class pedigree—the skills of 1960s player Eusébio, the 'black panther', rivalled those of Brazil's Pelé. It again confirmed its credentials when FC Porto romped to victory in the 2004 Champions League. And the eyes of the world remained fixed on the country as it hosted the third-largest sports event in the world. The national team made it through to the final of Euro 2004 and, although they were beaten by Greece, the smooth running of the tournament made the host nation a winner. But there is much more to sport in Portugal than 'the beautiful game', even though football-crazy Portuguese might disagree. From stunning championship golf courses to world-class surfing beaches and great facilities for extreme sports, the possibilities are endless.

Above left *Cristiano Ronaldo in action during the 2006 World Cup*
Above right *Windsurfing is particularly popular in Portugal*

ABOVE PAR

Golf is big business in the Algarve, where, for many years, local courses have been designed on purely commercial grounds. However, growing concerns about the impact this has had on the local environment are now being taken seriously.

Vila Sol Golf Resort near Almansil, which has played host to two Portuguese Opens, has made high environmental quality a key selling point to the increasing numbers of golfers who are concerned about the long-term effects of their sport on the environment. At Vila Sol, treated waste water irrigates the course and much of the original forest has been retained in the roughs. There are sizeable populations of wild birds and reptiles, including ocellated lizards and chameleons, all of which make the resort an extra-special destination.

SPORTING CHANCE

Named World Player of the Year by Fifa, soccer's governing body, in 2003, Portuguese midfielder Luis Figo is arguably one of the world's all-time great footballers. At the time of his signing by Spain's Real Madrid in 2000, he was the world's most expensive player, having been the subject of a 55-million-euro transfer fee.

Figo has never forgotten his childhood in the working-class Lisbon suburb of Cova da Piedade. In 2003 he set up the Luis Figo Foundation, which aims to give needy children some of the opportunities that Figo had enjoyed. The foundation promotes sports initiatives to help keep youngsters off the streets. Although concentrating its initial efforts in the Lisbon area, the foundation has plans to expand the project and help many more deprived children throughout the rest of the country.

THE STORY OF PORTUGAL

As part of the Iberian peninsula, Portugal shares much of its ancient history with Spain; indeed, it is hard to disentangle the two until the 12th-century creation of an independent Portuguese kingdom when the Christians drove out the Moors. Cut off from the rest of Europe by the northern mountains, this was a land apart. Early settlers had occupied parts of the country as far back as 5500BC, but the historical dawn really broke with the establishment of a Celtic culture in the north around 700–600BC. Farther south, by 300BC, Phoenicians and Carthaginians, two great trading nations, had settled in turn around modern Lisbon. They were followed by the Romans, who arrived in 210BC. In the fifth century AD, as the Roman empire fell apart, Vandals, Alans, Suevi and Visigoths crossed the Pyrenees from the north and settled in the area between the Douro and Minho rivers. By the sixth century, the Visigoths had gained the upper hand over their main rivals, the Suevi. They ruled from Toledo in modern Spain and had little interest, and less influence, in what was to become Portugal. In the eighth century AD their lack of cohesion resulted in one faction asking the North African Moors for aid. By 711, however, the Muslim forces had turned on the Visigoths and were sweeping through Iberia.

THE LIVING LEGACY

There are no great Roman sites in Portugal, but, around the world, more than 200 million people daily commemorate the Roman occupation every time they speak. Portuguese is a Romance language, evolved from Latin, which developed over the seven centuries of Roman occupation. It is very similar to Galician, the language spoken in Spain's northwest corner. Over the years, words have crept in from the north, from Arabic, and from India and China, but Portuguese remains a Latin-based tongue, even though it sounds more like something from eastern Europe. Portuguese is the official language of Portugal's historic colonies, with Brazil leading the field, and ranks seventh among the most spoken languages worldwide.

Above *The Temple of Diana at Evora is the best-preserved evidence of the Roman occupation of Portugal*

PAVED STREETS AND PLUMBING

Scattered throughout the Minho are more than 40 *citânias*, fortified hill settlements constructed by the Iron Age Celts who arrived in Portugal from northern Europe around 700–600BC. By far the finest site is at Briteiros, where the paved streets, drainage and circular huts are superbly preserved.

The Roman historian Strabo left a vivid account of the lifestyle of Portugal's Celtic inhabitants of around 20BC. They lived simply, drinking water and eating acorn bread. Beer and wine were saved for special occasions, when the whole community would assemble to dance to traditional music. On a more primitive note, the Celts also carried out mass human sacrifices, casting their auguries by inspecting the entrails of their still-living prisoners.

VIRIATUS—A HERO OF HIS TIME

In 193BC the Lusitani, a tribe based between the Tejo and Lima rivers, rose up against the Romans. This marked the start of a 50-year struggle against the might of the Roman empire.

In 147BC Viriatus emerged as the rebel leader, raising an army, gaining territory and defeating the Romans time after time. The frustrated Roman Senate sent an army to put down the revolt once and for all, but Viriatus promptly succeeded in trapping its legions and forcing them to surrender. Cunningly, he used his prisoners as a bargaining tool, gaining Roman recognition for his rule. In 139BC, however, the Roman emissaries, ostensibly sent to negotiate with Viriatus, assassinated him. His followers were crushed by the legions and subsequently enslaved.

BRIDGING THE GAP

In Chaves in the Trás-os-Montes you can walk across a bridge that's been standing since the end of the first century AD. Chaves was a military town, swarming with troops, and an important metal-trading hub. Such was its importance that the Roman Emperor Trajan commissioned the construction of a 12-arched bridge, 140m (460ft) long, that was strategically positioned on the road linking Braga and Astorga.

Two columns, inscribed with the names of governors and generals, still stand, along with milestones showing distances to towns along the road. The bridge has carried heavy traffic ever since and has been strengthened many times. With the building of a new bridge upriver, the original bridge looks set to stand for a few more centuries.

DIVINE SWINE

Prehistoric peoples focused their fertility rites on some pretty odd objects, and none more so than the pig. Held in reverence by the Celtic tribes, there are more than 200 sturdy granite pig statues in Trás-os-Montes, all of which are well over 2,000 years old. Crudely carved, but very definitely porcine, the *porcas* measure as much as 2m (6.5ft) in length and were probably worshipped as much for their strength and power as for their fertility and rich meat.

They were originally placed in sacred enclosures, usually circular, but have migrated over the years, and are now proudly displayed in village squares, local museums and along roadsides. The biggest and best of the *porcas* can be found at Murça, between Vila Real and Mirandela.

Right *A Roman mosaic floor in Vilamoura*

Below *Prehistoric stone pigs, called* porcas, *can be seen throughout Trás-os-Montes region*

THE MOORS AD711–1249

The damp green hills of northern Portugal held little attraction for the Moors, who were happy to concentrate their efforts on the well-watered Tejo valley, the rich lands of the Alentejo and, above all, the Algarve. By the ninth century AD, the Algarve was a rich and important kingdom in its own right, entirely independent of neighbouring al-Andalus. Xelb, modern Silves, was its glittering capital, from where tolerant laws were issued to the *Moçárabes*, the Christians subject to Moorish rule. Agriculture and scholarship flourished, with towns growing up across the Moorish holdings. Meanwhile, the Christians were regrouping up in the north in what they christened Portucale, the lands between the Minho and Douro. Portuguese victory against the infidels at Ourique in 1139 was a major blow for the Moors; by 1148 Lisbon was in Christian hands and Afonso Henriques' title as first king of Portugal had been confirmed by the treaty of Zamora. The following century saw steady Christian expansion; in 1249 Faro fell to them and Christian Portugal was established.

AN EASTERN INFLUENCE

The Moors inhabited Portugal for more than 500 years. They made their mark in scholarship and science, shipbuilding and construction, and, most lasting of all, in agriculture. They irrigated the land, damming and channelling water for use in irrigation and to power water mills. They practised crop rotation, introduced oranges and lemons, planted almond and fig groves, and raised cotton and rice. Their love of sweet things put sugar firmly on the Portuguese menu, while their spices pepped up the national diet.

The Portuguese landscape, particularly in the Moors' stronghold of the Algarve, would look extremely different today without their legacy.

Above *The 10th-century castle at Guimarães was a stronghold of Afonso Henriques*
Opposite top *The Moors introduced irrigation to Portugal, leaving wells such as this as a legacy*
Opposite bottom *An imposing statue of Afonso Henriques, sword in hand*

THE BATTLE OF OURIQUE

It was from Portucale that Afonso Henriques launched his push southwards to drive out the infidels. According to legend, God was certainly on Afonso's side at the battle of Ourique in 1139. The legend has it that Christ appeared to Afonso in a vision immediately before the battle encounter and blessed Afonso's shield.

Guarded by this blessing, Afonso took on no fewer than five Moorish kings in single combat. He and his forces won a decisive victory, and he went on to become Portugal's first king.

His deeds are commemorated on the national flag, which has five shields on it. Some argue that the number represents the Moorish rulers Afonso defeated, some that it symbolizes the five wounds of Christ on the Cross.

QUEEN OF THE SOUTH

Showpiece of the Moorish *al-Gharb* (Algarve), Xelb (modern Silves) was a thriving capital, with a population of more than 30,000, a huge castle and a stock of architectural treasures. In 1189 it was besieged by Sancho I, son of Afonso Henriques, looking for easy loot. The castle's water supply held out throughout the summer, but when the cisterns finally ran dry, the Moors were forced to surrender, encouraged by Sancho's promises of clemency.

What followed, though, was mayhem and massacre, with more than 6,000 slain. In 1191 the Moors retook the city, but in 1249 Xelb became permanently Christian. A long period of decline followed—by the 1500s the population was just 140.

ANCIENT HONOURS

Warriors were needed to oust the Moors, and in 1166 Afonso Henriques raised an élite force of knights that was to become the great military *Ordem de Avis* (Order of Avis). Like the Knights Templar, it was a fighting monastic order, its members taking vows of poverty, chastity and obedience. Its prime obligation was to fight the Moors whenever the king should command it.

The order was given the town of Avis as its headquarters, and later monarchs donated vast tracts of the reconquered lands to the knights.

In 1789 the order was secularized, though its members still came from the aristocracy. It still exists and is one of the oldest surviving orders of chivalry in Europe, with Portugal's president as its head. Membership is conferred on army officers who have outstanding military careers.

THE FIRST KING OF PORTUGAL

Born in 1109, Afonso Henriques was the son of Henry of Burgundy and Tareja, the illegitimate daughter of Afonso VI, King of Léon and Castile of Spain. Henry died in 1114, leaving Tareja as regent of the embryonic kingdom.

By the time he was 30, Afonso Henriques had wrested power from his mother, established his capital at Guimarães, won a stunning victory over the Moors at Ourique, repudiated his vassalage to Léon and declared himself King of Portucale. In 1143, Léon, although reluctant to relinquish its influence over the kingdom, recognized Afonso's right to the throne. Papal approval quickly followed. Afonso went on to drive the Moors out of Santarém and Lisbon. By the time of his death in 1185, only the Alentejo and the Algarve remained in Moorish hands.

With its borders settled and a stable monarchy on the throne, Portugal's main worry for the next 150 years or so was Castile, its powerful and territorially ambitious neighbour to the east in Spain. The heroic Dom Dinis (reigned 1279–1325) got Castile to recognize Portugal's borders in 1297, but it was only Portuguese victory at the battle of Aljubarrota in 1385 that eventually led to a lasting peace. With Castile put firmly in its place, it's hardly surprising that the thoughts of maritime Portugal turned seawards. The following century saw an unprecedented age of discovery and exploration. Prince Henry the Navigator, the son of João I and Philippa of Lancaster, founded the School of Navigation at Sagres in the Algarve. Between 1419 and 1497, Portuguese seamen discovered Madeira and the Azores, opened up the west coast of Africa, rounded the Cape of Good Hope, and found a sea route to India and beyond. As a result, Portugal became the world's premier trading nation. In 1494 Portugal and Spain signed the Treaty of Tordesillas. Negotiated by the Pope, this gave Portugal Brazil and the Orient. The Spanish took the rest of the Americas.

A BATTLE AND A PROMISE

João I's proclamation as King of Portugal in 1385 led to an immediate confrontation with Castile, which backed the rival claimant to the throne. Juan I of Castile invaded the country at the head of a 30,000-strong army.

On the eve of battle, João vowed to build a great abbey in honour of the Virgin Mary if he was victorious. The two armies clashed at Aljubarrota and, undoubtedly helped by England's timely loan of 500 archers, the Portuguese captured the Castilian standard within an hour. Juan was chased back into Castile, and Portuguese independence was secured for the next 200 years. Three years later, João kept his promise to the Virgin and the building of the great abbey at Batalha began.

Above *João and Henry IV of England at dinner*
Opposite top *Henry the Navigator inspired the Portuguese to become successful explorers*
Opposite bottom *The great compass rose at Sagres*

DEFENDING THE FRONTIER

Dom Dinis inherited a country newly reconquered from the Moors; he also inherited one that needed stabilizing and strengthening. The biggest threat came from Castile in the east, and Dinis set about negotiating at once with his powerful neighbour. In the Treaty of Alcañices in 1297, he got the Castilians to recognize Portugal's frontiers, but he took the precaution of backing this up with something more concrete. The result was a chain of more than 50 great castles along Portugal's eastern border. Many still stand, among them superbly sited Monsaraz; Belmonte, guarding the Serra da Estrela; Marvão and Castelo de Vide, within a stone's throw of Spain; and ancient Leiria in the east, though Dinis later rebuilt it as a royal residence.

INTO THE 'SEA OF DARKNESS'

In the early 15th century, rounding Cape Bojador on the west African coast was the ultimate challenge. The southernmost point on sea charts, it was the edge of the world, beyond which lay a 'sea of darkness'.

It was hardly surprising that sailors were scared of this stretch of water and its approaches. Between 1421 and 1433, no less than 14 expeditions failed to round the cape, and Henry the Navigator was losing patience with his lily-livered captains. In 1434 he dispatched the explorer Gil Eanes with instructions to round the cape without fail, promising him rich rewards if he succeeded. Eanes sailed south, doubled back from the Canaries and rounded the cape. The deadlock of superstition was broken and the way south was opened.

THE ENGLISH CONNECTION

When the English nobleman John of Gaunt sent his archers to aid João I on the battlefield of Aljubarrota, it was a move that paved the way for one of Europe's oldest alliances. Suitably grateful for English help, João concentrated on cementing the ties between the two countries. In 1386 he signed the Treaty of Windsor, and in 1387 he married Philippa of Lancaster, the daughter of John of Gaunt. They had five sons; their third son was the inspirational Henry the Navigator—a notable half-English prince.

Henry IV, Henry V and Henry VI of England successively ratified the Treaty of Windsor. Henry IV made João a Knight of the Garter, England's highest order of chivalry, to reward his loyalty.

SLAVE TRADE

From the 1440s, Portuguese merchant ships were sailing west to the Atlantic islands and south down the west coast of Africa, and then eastwards to India and other parts of Asia. Raid and trade was the name of the game, as the demand for labour to work the new sugar plantations in the Azores and Madeira grew.

Slavery had been a fact of life on the Iberian peninsula since Roman times, but figures rocketed in the 1450s, with slave numbers increasing by the year. North- and west-coast Africans were no longer domestic slaves, but worked as field hands, paid for in goods and shipped in often appalling conditions to the Azores, Madeira, Cape Verde and São Tomé. By the 1460s Madeira was the largest sugar producer in the western world.

SPANISH DOMINATION 1520–1640

By 1520 Portuguese wealth and power may have been at its zenith, but with such a far-flung empire, there were hidden problems that were soon to bubble up to the surface. Very little of the money flowing into the country filtered down to the people at large, and there was no developing entrepreneurial class to handle the national finances. After the expulsion of the Jews and the establishment of the Inquisition, Portugal was left with a huge commercial empire, but not the financial expertise to run it. By 1580 the money coming in from the empire was no longer enough to maintain it, and debts and costs were rising. Something had to give—and what gave was the monarchy. Three years after Dom Sebastião's death, his uncle, Philip II of Spain, moved in, defeated the Portuguese at Alcántara and had himself crowned king in 1581. After a rosy start, Spanish domination brought few advantages. By 1640 the Portuguese had had enough. Conspirators threw out the Spanish governor and popular pressure persuaded the reluctant Duke of Bragança, head of Portugal's most powerful noble family, to take the throne as João IV.

OVERSTRETCHED

Portugal ran its empire via the *feitorias* (factories), a series of fortified coastal trading posts that stretched round Africa to India and the Far East. Well fortified and easily resupplied by sea, the *feitorias* lulled the Portuguese into believing that they could maintain a grip on their possessions with minimal effort.

For years, the system worked well enough, but by the mid-16th century it became clear that relying on 10,000 men to maintain this huge empire was simply not enough. The vital resupplying became more difficult and more expensive—the sea passage to Goa in India alone could take up to 18 months, and it was as far again from Goa to Macau. The rewards, once so great, could no longer keep up with the expense.

Above *Philip II of Spain took the Portuguese crown in 1581*
Opposite top *A caravel, the ship that helped the Portuguese to carve out an empire*
Opposite bottom *A Portuguese fortification in Morocco where the crusade against the Moors ended*

DISASTER IN MOROCCO

Things may have been going badly at home, but the deeply religious and equally bloodthirsty Dom Sebastião (reigned 1557–78) was determined to resurrect the glory days of the Christian reconquest. Obsessed with war and bored with matters of state, Sebastião's ambition was to launch nothing less than an all-out crusade against the Muslims in North Africa.

In 1578, Sebastião managed to assemble a 14,000-strong army and set sail for Morocco. Near Alcázarquivir he met 40,000 Muslims who overwhelmed the Christian forces, killing Sebastião and 8,000 of his followers. Only three years later, the remnants of the Portuguese army were to stand little chance against Philip II of Spain when he marched into Portugal to claim the throne.

DIAMOND TRADE

Until they were discovered in Brazil in 1725, diamonds came from India, with the Portuguese being the most prodigious shippers. Portuguese-Jewish diamond merchants settled in Antwerp in the early 16th century, where they mastered the technicalities of the trade, including the cutting and polishing of the stones. They were more than ready to handle the imports that poured out of India and through Lisbon to the north of Europe.

Most of the diamonds, along with sapphires and amethysts, originated in southern India, where the fabulous Koh-i-noor diamond was later found. Local Indian rulers acted as middlemen between the prospectors and the Portuguese merchants, often keeping the largest and most valuable stones for themselves.

THE PORTUGUESE INQUISITION

Auto da fé, trial by fire, is not a Spanish phrase —it is Portuguese. The Inquisition in Portugal was just as feared and just as active as it was in Spain. It was set up in 1531 primarily to deal with those Jews who had supposedly embraced Christianity and so were allowed to remain in the country after the mass expulsion of 1496, though its brief was broadened to investigate and punish all forms of heresy.

Its investigations were basically unjust. Prosecutors, often acting on anonymous denunciations, were free to arrest anyone they chose, while the accused had no right to legal counsel or to question the accuser face to face. Known criminals often gave evidence unchallenged. Nor was there any right of appeal. Burning at the stake was the ultimate punishment.

A PORTUGUESE ODYSSEY

Luís Vaz de Camões, Portugal's greatest literary figure, was born in 1525 and died in 1580. Outside Portugal, his fame rests on a single work, *Os Lusíadas (The Lusiads)*. This epic poem, glowing with patriotic fervour, celebrates Portuguese achievements in the great age of discoveries through the medium of Vasco da Gama's voyage to India. Da Gama is the poem's hero.

Camões was ideally placed to write about the East. His father had died in Goa and he himself spent 16 years travelling abroad. He lost an eye in Morocco, escaped shipwreck, was several times thrown in jail and enjoyed a passionate love affair with a local girl.

He returned to Lisbon in 1570, where he published *Os Lusíadas* unsuccessfully in 1572. He died eight years later in poverty.

With the house of Bragança installed on the throne, relations with England back on course, and the discovery of gold and diamonds in Brazil, things were looking up. Money poured into the royal coffers, and just as quickly poured out again, as João V (reigned 1706–50) embarked on an orgy of spending, squandering vast sums on lavish building schemes. His son, José I (reigned 1750–77), was fortunate to have as his chief minister the Marquês de Pombal, a believer in enlightened despotism who dealt with the great Lisbon earthquake of 1755 and launched a massive modernization drive. The rise of Napoleon led to a major new threat for the country. Lisbon was captured by the French in 1807, João VI fled to Brazil, and Portugal found itself embroiled in the Peninsular War. Two British generals, the Duke of Wellington and Lord Beresford, played the major role in expelling the French, but things remained unsettled until 1820, when Portuguese liberals drew up a new constitution. On his return from Brazil, the king accepted it, but his queen and younger son, Miguel, had other ideas. They led a reactionary movement that, after João's death in 1826, was to set the monarchy on an inexorable, though slow, slide to its eventual overthrow early the next century.

A NICE CUP OF TEA

Nearly 5,000 years ago, the Chinese were the first to enjoy a cup of tea, but it was only in 1560 that a European first sampled it—the first person to try this new beverage was a Portuguese Jesuit called Jaspar da Cruz. Within a century, Portugal was importing tea from China to Lisbon. They called it *chá*.

The Dutch caught the taste for tea as well, and it was in the Netherlands that a young exile, later Charles II of England, started to drink it. In 1662 Charles married the Portuguese Infanta Catherine of Bragança, also a confirmed *chá* drinker. In England, where king and queen led, the country followed. The royal stamp of approval was all it took to make tea as much enjoyed in England as it was in Portugal.

Above *Port casks ready for shipping*
Opposite left *The Convento do Carmo in Lisbon was destroyed in the 1755 earthquake*
Opposite right *The Marques de Pombal saved the people of Lisbon from starvation after the earthquake*

THE MARQUIS DE CAMPO MAIOR

With the royal family safely in Brazil, two British generals were the prime movers in the campaign to push Napoleon out of Portugal and Spain. They were Sir Arthur Wellesley, the future Duke of Wellington, and William Carr, Viscount Beresford.

Carr first encountered the Portuguese as governor of Madeira; it was love at first sight, and he immersed himself in learning the language and studying the country. It stood him in good stead in 1809, when he was given the task of reorganizing the Portuguese army, a task he achieved brilliantly, turning it into an effective fighting force fit to take part in the battle of Buçaco in 1811. He was made Marquis of Campo Maior and remained in Portugal as the country's administrator until 1821.

THE LISBON EARTHQUAKE

On 1 November 1755, as Lisbon churches were packed for the annual Mass for the dead, disaster struck in the form of a catastrophic earthquake, the aftershock of which was felt as far away as North Africa.

For six minutes the ground heaved, while roofs and domes collapsed, killing hundreds of people, and a tidal wave swept in from the Tejo river, engulfing much of the lower part of the city. Candles, lit for the feast day, ignited fires that would burn for days.

The chief minister, Sebastião José de Carvalho e Melo, later the Marquês de Pombal, stepped in, advising 'bury the dead, feed the living'. Thanks to him, nobody starved, there were no epidemics and, within 20 years, the Baixa, the historic heart of the city, had been triumphantly rebuilt.

RED, WHITE AND RUBY

Britain's on-and-off wars with France between 1679 and 1714 made port big business. French wine imports slumped, leaving a gap in the market that enterprising merchants quickly filled. Port flooded into Britain, encouraged by the Methuen Treaty of 1703, which lowered the import duty on it to a third of that on French wines. British entrepreneurs began establishing wine estates along the Douro, and names like Sandeman, Croft, Cockburn and Graham appeared. By 1756 the British had a stranglehold on the trade, and were passing off less-than-average port as the real thing. This led to the establishment of restrictions on what was port and what was not. The rules are still in force.

THE BRAZILIAN QUESTION

With Napoleon's troops massing for invasion in 1807, the royal family, court and government hotfooted it across the Atlantic to Brazil and Rio de Janeiro. It was a bad move for the mother country; by 1815, Portugal, now administered by Beresford, was far weaker than Brazil, its most important colony.

Trouble, in the shape of the liberals, loomed at home, and in 1821, João VI, weak, indecisive and suffering from piles, set sail for Lisbon with 4,000 officials and plenty of cash purloined from the Bank of Brazil. He left his son Pedro behind as regent. The next year, Pedro refused to return to Portugal. In 1822, he declared Brazilian independence. Portugal had lost its largest possession.

TOWARDS A REPUBLIC 1826–1910

When João VI died in 1826, his son and heir, Pedro, emperor of newly independent Brazil, installed his brother Miguel as regent in Portugal—but only on the condition he accepted a new, more liberal constitution. Miguel agreed, but once in power, promptly restored absolutist rule. Britain, Spain and France backed the liberals, who finally succeeded in installing Pedro (who had abdicated in Brazil) as king in 1834. The rest of the century saw a constant tug of war between those who supported Pedro's 1826 constitution and the liberals, who clamoured for a return to the 1820 version they had devised, which was more democratic. By the 1850s, the two factions had settled into a fairly stable two-party system. The monarchy, meanwhile, now virtually bankrupt and humiliated as stronger European powers embarked on a scramble for territory in Africa, became increasingly unpopular and there was a growing surge of republicanism. Dom Carlos (reigned 1889–1908) clung to outdated ideas of kingship, attempting to rule dictatorially. In an attempted coup in 1908, he and his eldest son were assassinated. His successor, Manuel, hung on for another two years, until he was forced off the throne and into exile when the army and navy revolted.

LIBERTADOR AND USURPADOR

In February 1828, Pedro IV's brother Miguel, having promised to uphold the new constitution, arrived in Portugal. By July, he had overthrown it and had himself crowned king.

The move was not unpopular in Portugal itself, but Pedro, back in Brazil, saw it as a usurpation of his daughter Maria's rights— she had been married to Miguel at the age of seven. Pedro abdicated in Brazil and sailed for the Azores, where, in 1832, he set up a government-in-exile. From here, he captured Porto, but could get no farther until, with the help of the Duke of Terceiro's forces marching from the south, Lisbon fell to him in 1833. When Pedro died in 1834, Maria was put on the throne and Miguel went into exile.

Above *The state opening of the Lisbon to Porto railway in 1856*
Opposite top *Manuel, Portugal's last king, was forced off the throne by a revolution in 1910*
Opposite bottom *Pena Palace, Victorian Gothic architecture at its most exuberant*

THE SAXE-COBURG-GOTHA CONNECTION

Pedro IV, king of Portugal and ex-emperor of Brazil, died in 1834, leaving his daughter Maria to inherit the throne. Her second husband died; in 1836 she married Ferdinand of Saxe-Coburg-Gotha, a cousin of Queen Victoria's adored consort, Prince Albert.

Ferdinand was to be an equally devoted husband. Like his cousin, he dabbled in the arts, helping to design the neo Gothic Palácio da Pena at Sintra in the 1840s. He also had a hand in restoring the treasures of Mafra and Alcobaça, both of which had been damaged by anti-clericals, and still found the time to father 11 children. Ferdinand's eldest son, Pedro V, came to the throne when he was only 16, Ferdinand having served as regent for the previous two years.

RETREAT FROM AFRICA

From the 1860s Portuguese explorers were penetrating inland Africa from the coast, but so were the British, the French and, later, the Germans. Trouble loomed over rival territorial claims, and the 1884 Berlin Conference attempted to sort this out by partitioning the continent. Portugal was awarded Mozambique, Angola and Guinea, but only on condition it occupied the territories effectively.

Back in Africa, Portugal soon clashed with the British in the form of Cecil Rhodes in a disputed area of territory between Mozambique and Angola. Portugal protested at Rhodes' incursions; Britain claimed that the local chiefs had recognized its rights. Faced with the prospect of a war that would have been disastrous, Portugal climbed down in 1890.

THE IRON ROAD

Portugal may have been a latecomer to the railway age, but the second half of the 19th century saw construction of lines all over the country. Track laying started in 1852 under British supervision with the construction of the Lisbon–Porto line, which was opened in 1856. This was soon followed by additional lines running to the east and south.

By the 1880s, Portugal was linked to the north and east with Spain by rail. In 1890 Lisbon's Rossio station opened, and both Lisbon and Porto acquired their own urban lines.

By 1915, a network of tracks, some of them scenically stunning and still in use today, had opened up all but the most isolated parts of the country.

THE FALL OF THE MONARCHY

By 1910, following years of mounting republican agitation, revolution was in the air. It came at dawn on 4 October, when units of the army and navy rose, backed up by civilians. Lisbon's Rotunda was occupied and two warships bombarded the king's residence. By mid-morning, the republican flag flew above the city and Manuel left for Mafra.

The following day, fishermen shipped the royal family out to their yacht, which sailed for Gibraltar. Before he left, Manuel wrote '…I am Portuguese and always will be…Viva Portugal'. He lived out his exile in England, dying at Twickenham in 1932, and was buried in the royal pantheon in the church of São Vicente de Fora, Lisbon.

Between 1910 and 1926 the new Portuguese republic was in chaos; 45 governments came and went, and there were military risings, financial meltdown and growing hostility to the politicians throughout the country. Things came to a head in 1926 with the military-backed suspension of the republican constitution and the installation of General Carmona as president—he was to remain in office until his death in 1951. The stage was set for the rise of António de Oliveira Salazar, a one-time economist from Coimbra University who was to control the country until 1968. In 1928 he was installed as finance minister, becoming prime minister—and dictator—in 1932. He balanced the books, but at a huge cost. Portugal's political, economic and cultural life was stifled for almost 40 years. Foreign investment was discouraged, censorship was absolute, agriculture stagnated and the poor were kept illiterate. The idea was to keep the masses in their place with a diet of '*fado*, Fátima and football'. In a changing world, there were demands for greater democracy at home, while resisting independence in the colonies impoverished the country further. The result was revolution.

THE IRON HAND

Salazar may have spurned the pomp and the rhetoric of fascism, but he admired Hitler and Mussolini—even keeping a photograph of the latter on his desk. Following the Nazi example, he set up the deeply feared PIDE *(Polícia Internacional e de Defesa do Estado)*, a special police force modelled on and initially trained by the Gestapo. Backed by a vast network of paid informers, the PIDE managed to permeate every aspect of Portuguese society.

In 1936 Salazar set up a military-style youth movement, the *Mocidade Portuguesa*, and the paramilitary, extreme right-wing *Legião Portuguesa;* both adopted the Nazi salute and survived right up to the 1974 revolution.

Above *A colonial statue pulled down by the UNITA movement in Angola*
Opposite left *Celebrating the overthrow of the Caetano regime*
Opposite bottom *The children whose claim to have seen visions of the Virgin Mary made Fátima famous*

WORLD WAR II

It took a fine balancing act to keep Portugal out of World War II. Salazar, despite his admiration for Hitler and Mussolini, knew that neutrality was essential for his country. In 1939 he signed a mutual protection pact with the Franco regime in Spain to ensure this.

Portugal became a base for the rich, political refugees, spies and exiled royalty. The Germans were kept happy with supplies of tungsten, a vital mineral for war production, and the British by being allowed to set up military bases in the Azores. The Portuguese themselves were mainly pro-Ally, demonstrating their loyalties by drumming their feet or coughing loudly whenever Hitler or Mussolini appeared on cinema newsreels. The sight of George VI or Winston Churchill on screen was greeted with shouts of 'Viva... Benfica'—there could have been no greater compliment than to compare the two men with Portugal's best-loved football team.

SALAZAR'S FINAL YEARS

In August 1968, while enjoying the summer at Estoril, Salazar fell heavily from his canvas director's chair, striking his head on the tiled floor. The blow had no immediate effects, but by September crushing headaches proved to be the symptoms of a brain haematoma. The operation to drain it was successful, but it was followed by a massive haemorrhage on the other side of his brain. Marcelo Caetano took over as premier, but, such was the fear that Salazar inspired, nobody dared to tell him that his days of power were over. He lived for another two years, receiving ministers and even journalists, believing to the end he still had absolute control over Portugal. He died in July 1970, leaving Caetano to continue his authoritarian, right-wing policies of the Estado Novo. It was only the 1974 Carnation Revolution which was able to break this legacy, although its influences can still be felt.

THE CARNATION REVOLUTION

Opposition to Marcelo Caetano, Salazar's successor, crystallized in the army with the formation of the *Movimento das Forças Armada* (MFA), a group of young officers disillusioned with the wasteful colonial struggle and conditions at home. After one abortive attempt, things came to a head in April 1974 under Major Otelo Saraiva de Carvalho. Just after midnight on 25 April, the start of the revolution was heralded by the radio broadcast of a banned protest song. Things went like clockwork, and by 3am Lisbon was secure. At 8am the MFA made its first broadcast, and within hours red carnations, the seasonal flowers, sprouted from rifle barrels all over the country—this became a symbol of revolution and regained freedom.

THE END OF EMPIRE

By 1960 Portugal faced growing colonial problems. In 1961, India marched into Goa, dramatically ending more than 400 years of Portuguese rule. In Africa, Salazar attempted to defuse the freedom movements by combining a determined hearts-and-minds campaign with a ruthless military clampdown on the guerrillas.

After the 1974 revolution, though, popular opinion at home was pressing for granting the colonies their independence. Exhausted by long years of war, the Portuguese withdrew from Angola in 1975, leaving the liberation movements to battle it out for power. Thousands of Angolans were killed in the ensuing war. In 1976 Portugal withdrew from East Timor, the result being more than two decades of bloody Indonesian rule.

The 1974 revolution heralded the start of Portugal's emergence as a democracy onto the world stage. Portugal's entry into the European Community in 1986 was a move that brought unprecedented economic growth. Portuguese self-confidence boomed with the huge success of Expo '98 in Lisbon, the problems of the last colonies were laid to rest, and inflation, infant mortality and illiteracy were tackled. The euro replaced the escudo as the national currency in 2002, and in 2004 the European Football Championships, held in the country, introduced yet more foreigners to the charms of Portugal as a tourist destination. Problems remain, but Portugal faces the future with growing optimism.

Above left *Vasco da Gama mall in Lisbon*
Above right *Cable car at the site of EXPO '98 in Lisbon*

A DEMOCRATIC STATE

Despite teething troubles in the 1970s and early 1980s, modern Portugal is a fully fledged democracy, ruled by a government elected by citizens over the age of 18. It has a president, who is commander-in-chief of the armed forces, a prime minister, a council of ministers, an assembly (parliament) and an independent judiciary.

The president is elected for five years and is advised by a 16-strong council of state. Guided by the assembly election results, the president appoints the council of ministers, who present their programme to the assembly for debate.

Portugal has two autonomous overseas regions, Madeira and the Azores. Macau, Portugal's last dependency, reverted to Chinese rule in 1999.

TOURISM

Tourists discovered the Algarve in the 1960s and, boosted by the opening of Faro airport, it did not take long for it to become a major holiday destination for foreign visitors. Today, tourism accounts for more than 25 per cent of Portugal's foreign investment and nearly 10 per cent of its GDP. Visitors now regard Portugal as much more than a sun, sand and sea destination, with increasing numbers visiting Lisbon and exploring the country's interior. Badly planned coastal development was curbed when it became clear that it was destroying the very qualities that attracted visitors, and moves are being made to develop a greener and more sustainable tourist industry that helps to preserve the environment.

ON THE MOVE

On the Move gives you detailed advice and information about the various options for travelling to Portugal before explaining the best ways to get around the country once you are there. Handy tips help you with everything from buying tickets to renting a car.

ARRIVING BY AIR

Most visitors to Portugal arrive by air, with numbers rising every year as the choice of budget airlines operating into the country expands and weekend breaks grow in popularity. Mainland Portugal has three international airports: Lisbon, Porto and Faro, serving respectively the central part, the north and the south of the country. If you're flying in from another continent, you'll arrive at Lisbon, the only airport with direct scheduled flights from the USA. Porto, in the north, is the gateway to Portugal's most heavily populated area, constantly busy with business travellers and a good jumping-off point for the Minho, Douro, Trás-os-Montes and the Beiras. Faro, serving the Algarve, is the busiest in terms of holidaymakers, and also makes a good entry point if you're planning to explore the southern third of the country. Some visitors to Portugal choose to fly to Spain and pick up an air, train or bus connection into Portugal from there.

LISBON

Lisboa Portela lies 7km (4 miles) north of central Lisbon. It's a busy, crowded airport, with two terminals: Terminal 1 is on three levels, arrivals on the ground floor and check-in and departures above. International check-in desks are located behind and to the right of the shopping area on the second level, with a flight information board to the right of the main entrance. Allow plenty of time when departing, as the airport layout is confusing and check-in and security can be slow. Terminal 2 is a two-minute bus transfer to the west and is for domestic services.

Portela has an airport information desk (check-in level), visitor information office (arrivals hall), hotel reservation desk, car rental desks, shops, a bank, restaurants, snack bars and coffee shops, post office, lost luggage office and left luggage facilities. There is easy access to the surrounding motorway system from the airport.

GETTING INTO CITIES AND TRAVELLING ON FROM AIRPORTS

AIRPORT (CODE)	LISBON (LIS)	PORTO (OPO)	FARO (FAO)
DISTANCE TO CITY	7km (4 miles)	11km (7 miles)	4km (2.5 miles)
TAXI	Price: €15–€20 Time: 20–30 min	Price: €15–€18 Time: 30–45 min	Faro €10–€12 (15 min), Albufeira €41–€49 (30 min), Carvoeiro €59–€70 (45 min), Portimão €63–€75 (50 min), Lagos €78–€93 (60 min), Vilamoura €28–€35 (25 min), Vila Real de Santo António €57–€70 (55 min)
TRAIN/METRO	Nearest metro station is Areeiro or the Gare do Oriente at the Parque das Nações (2.8km/1.7 miles); not recommended	Metro. Violeta Line (E) Time: 25–35 min. Frequency: every 20 min 6am–1.30am. Price: €1.35	N/A
BUS	Aerobus No. 91 to Avenida da Liberdade, Rossio, Praça do Comércio and Cais do Sodré. Frequency: every 20 min 7.45am–8.15pm. Price: €3.35 (valid all day on all public transportation) www.carris.pt Additional Carris buses to the central area: 5, 22, 44, 45, 83. Frequency: every 20–30 min. Price: €1.40	STCP buses to central areas: 601 every 30 min 6am–12.30am; 602 every 20 min 6am–12.45am; 604 every 20 min 6am–1am. Price: €1.30 www.stcp.pt	EVA buses to central Faro. Frequency: daily every 30 min 7.08am–9.17pm. Price: €1.65
CAR	Central Lisbon: at airport roundabout take Avenida Almirante Gago Coutinho all the way to Rossio Other directions: North: take A1 signed Porto Northwest: take 2nd circular north (direction Porto) then IC17 to A8 South: take 2nd circular north to Ponte Vasco da Gama or south to Ponte 25 Abril via Eixo Norte-Sul Cascais/Estoril: take 2nd circular south then A5	Central Porto: take IC1 and follow signs to city Other directions: North: take A3 (IP1) to Braga South: take A1 signed 'Porto/Lisboa' East: take A4 (IP4) to Vila Real/Bragança	Central Faro: take N125-10 link road, then N125 Other directions: take N125-10 link road, then either N125 east or west, or A22 (IP1) motorway east or west

PORTO

Aeroporto Francisco Sá Carneiro is 11km (7 miles) north of central Porto. Completed in 2006, the airport terminal has undergone major expansion, providing a greater range of facilities in spacious surroundings. Porto handles Portuguese domestic and European flights from its one terminal and classes itself as an international airport.

Airport services include tourist information desks and car rental.

FARO

Aeroporto de Faro is 4km (2.5 miles) west of central Faro. This modern airport handles international scheduled and charter flights and Portuguese internal flights. The airport can be extremely busy, particularly on weekends in the July and August high season; check-in and security can be slow, especially for charter flights.

Services include banking, a visitor information office, car rental desks (mainly located outside the terminal), self-service restaurant, snack bars, shops and a post office.

FROM OUTSIDE EUROPE

If you're flying to Portugal from another continent, Lisbon is your arrival point. It is the only Portuguese airport, for instance, with scheduled flights direct to and from the USA—and these are limited in number. Continental has only one flight from Newark to Lisbon a day, as does TAP.

For US visitors, the alternative to flying direct is to fly to one of Europe's main hub airports, such as London Heathrow, Amsterdam Schiphol, Paris Charles de Gaulle or the Lufthansa hub, Frankfurt am Main, and then pick up a connecting flight with a European carrier from there. Obviously, this extra leg will add to the journey time—it's therefore sensible to plan flight connections so that you have limited stop-over time. Alternatively, you could plan things so that you can spend some time sight-seeing in your stop-over point.

AIRLINES		
UK		
BMI Baby	tel 0871 224 0224	www.bmibaby.com
British Airways	tel 0844 493 0787	www.ba.com
British Midland	tel 0870 607 0555	www.flybmi.com
Easyjet	tel 0871 244 2366	www.easyjet.com
Flybe	tel 0871 700 0535	www.flybe.com
Monarch	tel 0870 040 9040	www.monarch.co.uk
TAP Air Portugal	tel 020 7630 0746	www.flytap.com
USA		
Continental	tel 800 231 0856	www.continental.com
TAP Air Portugal	tel 0845 601 0932	www.flytap.com

COPING WITH A DELAY

» In the high season, flight delays are inevitable, particularly at Faro, which has to cope with an exceptionally high volume of holiday flights.

» If your flight is delayed, the best plan is to stay landside for as long as possible.

» If the weather is fine, you could pass the time on the outdoor public terrace bar, which has an excellent view across the lagoon to the Praia de Faro beach.

» If the delay is longer than a couple of hours and you have checked in your bags, you could take a taxi to the beach itself for a last meal or swim.

USEFUL AIRPORT CONTACTS		
General		www.worldairportguide.com
Lisbon	tel 218 413 500 (general)	www.ana.pt
Porto	tel 229 432 400	www.ana.pt
Faro	tel 289 800 800	www.ana.pt

ARRIVING BY ROAD

Driving to Portugal takes time, so, if you are thinking of doing it, weigh up the pros and cons carefully. If you are coming from the UK, you can ferry your car to northern Spain. From elsewhere in Europe, though, you drive through several countries to reach your destination.

BY CAR

If you are driving to Portugal, you will need the following documents:
» Valid driver's licence.
» Original vehicle registration document.
» Motor insurance certificate (at least third-party insurance is compulsory).
» Passport.

From the UK, you can cross the Channel either through the Channel Tunnel (Eurotunnel UK, tel 0870 535 3535; www.eurotunnel.com) or by ferry (see below).

The major routes south to Portugal will take you through France and across Spain. There are two main options: both start south down the west coast of France on the E5, crossing the Spanish border at Irún. If heading for central or northern Portugal, from Irún head west across to Bilbao then through Valladolid and Salamanca to the border at Vilar Formoso. From there head west on the A25 for Porto and the north or head southeast on the A23 for central areas and Lisbon. For southern destinations the quickest route is still via Bilbao, then Burgos, Madrid and Badajoz. Head west on the A26 to Lisbon or take the A6 followed by the A2 for the south and Algarve.

BY BUS

International bus services to Portugal from the UK are operated by Eurolines, the foreign arm of National Express (tel 08705 143219; www.eurolines.com).

Destinations include Lisbon, Porto, Coimbra, Bragança, Guarda, Viseu, Beja, Faro and Portimão, with a return (round-trip) adult fare to Lisbon costing around €200; under-12s travel half-price, senior citizens at a discount.

Passengers from the UK have to change buses in Paris, which sometimes involves a lengthy wait; it may be simpler to travel independently to Paris. Journey time is around 40–45 hours, depending on your destination.

BY FERRY

If you're driving to Portugal from the UK, you can cut down on the driving time slightly by taking a ferry to northern Spain. The main international ferry access points are Santander and Bilbao, from where it is still a long day's drive through most of Spain to reach Portugal. There are no scheduled direct ferry services between Portugal and elsewhere in continental Europe, the UK or North America.

USEFUL WEBSITES

Useful journey planning information can be found at:
» www.theAA.com
» www.autoroutes.fr
» www.autopistas.com
» www.brisa.pt

FERRIES FROM THE UK

PLYMOUTH (UK) TO SANTANDER

Brittany Ferries (tel 44 (0) 08709 076 103; www.brittany-ferries.com) operates a twice-weekly service from Plymouth from 30 March to 28 October with a journey time of 20 hours 30 minutes. All passengers are obliged to book either a cabin or seat. Ferries dock in the heart of Santander. For the road route into Portugal from there, see above.

PORTSMOUTH (UK) TO BILBAO (SANTURTZI)

P&O Ferries (tel 44 (0) 08716 645 645; www.poferries.com) runs a year-round service to Bilbao with a journey time of 35 hours. Passengers must pre-book cabins. The service runs every three days, except in January, when there are two sailings only. Ferries dock at Santurtzi, 15km (9 miles) northwest of the city. From the port, follow the A8 west to Santander, then south to Bilbao and one of the routes above.

TRAVEL TIPS

» If you are travelling overland, pack a small bag with everything that you'll need for the journey easily to hand.
» Keep documents and money safely out of sight, especially if you're likely to fall asleep on a bus or train.
» If you're travelling with children, make sure you have plenty to keep them amused.
» Make sure you have change for the automatic motorway tolls, or buy a pass in advance.

ARRIVING BY TRAIN

Though it takes time—and fares are quite high when compared to the cost of budget flights—travelling by train to Portugal can be quite an experience. The service itself is first rate.

From the UK you can travel by train to Portugal via Paris. The other rail option is to enter Portugal by train from Spain—a good choice if you want to experience another European country during your visit. Journey times are long (25–28 hours from London to Lisbon), though, and fares are quite high compared with those of budget and charter flights. The main route from Paris to Lisbon runs via Bordeaux, Biarritz, Irún, Donostia, Salamanca and Guarda; change at Irún for the Lisbon train and again at Guarda for connections to Porto and Coimbra. Travelling from Spain (Madrid), the rail route will take you through Cáceres to Marvão-Beirã, Abrantes, Entroncamento and so to Lisbon. From Lisbon you can connect with Porto, Coimbra and the south.

From the UK, it's best to use Eurostar via the Channel Tunnel as far as Paris, from where trains south are fast and frequent. Eurostar trains depart from St. Pancras Station and take less than three hours. You must check in at least 30 minutes before departure and you are allowed to take two suitcases and one item of hand baggage on board, all of which should be clearly labelled with your name, address and allocated seat number. You will need to show your passport to clear immigration and customs.

RAIL PASSES

Portugal is a relatively small country with a somewhat fragmented rail system, and train travel is not expensive. In view of this, a rail pass makes sense only if you're visiting Portugal as part of a longer trip to Europe. If you're planning to make only one or two train journeys during your stay, it will probably work out cheaper to buy individual tickets as you need them.

Inter-Rail passes are valid for one month's or 22 days' unlimited train travel within a specified zone, or for 5 days' travel in 10 days, or 10 days' travel in 22 days; you have to be a European citizen or have lived in Europe for six months to be eligible. The full fare for a month-long Global pass is currently around €599, or

€399 for those aged under 26; the ticket gives discounts on the cross-Channel services, including Eurostar. Portugal is in the same zone as Spain and Morocco.

For more information see www.interrailnet.com.

Eurail passes are available for North American visitors, and must be purchased before arrival in Europe. They allow several days' consecutive travel, or journeys on a certain number of days within a fixed time period, in up to 20 countries. If you're planning to travel only within Portugal, a Eurail pass is unlikely to pay for itself. For more information see www.raileurope.com.

If you are 65 or older you are entitled to a 50 per cent discount on most train fares on production of ID.

ARRIVING VIA SPAIN

If you want to combine visits to Portugal and Spain, there are easy connections from and to Madrid, Seville and Santiago. Direct train connections link Madrid and Lisbon (10 hours), Seville and Ayamonte on the Portuguese border (2 hours 30 min) and Vigo in Galicia and Valença on the border (45 min). Combining Portugal and Spain is also a good idea if you're renting a car, but check whether your rental agreement allows you to take the car from one country to the other.

TRAIN INFORMATION AND TICKETS

EUROSTAR

EPS House, Waterloo Station, London SE1 8SE, UK tel 08705 186186

www.eurostar.com

RAIL EUROPE

179 Piccadilly, London W1V 0BA, UK; International Rail Centre, Victoria Station, London W1V 1JY, UK tel 08705 848848

www.raileurope.co.uk

EUROSTAR AND FAST EUROPEAN TRAINS

FACILITIES	JOURNEY TIMES AND PRICES
»1st- and 2nd-class seating.	» Total journey time from Waterloo to Lisbon is around 25–28 hours.
»Bar/restaurant cars.	
»Trolley service on day trains.	» Total journey time from Madrid to Lisbon is around 10 hours.
»Baby-changing facilities on day trains.	
»Air conditioning.	» Return (round-trip) ticket prices range from around €212–€514 (Waterloo–Lisbon) and €89–€300 (Madrid–Lisbon).
»Telephone kiosks.	
»Toilets in each carriage (car).	
»Toilets for passengers with disabilities.	

GETTING AROUND

GETTING AROUND IN LISBON

Carris runs Lisbon's public transportation system, an integrated network that includes buses, trams and funiculars, or street elevators, all of which are frequent, inexpensive and reliable. You will be able to see everything you want by using just a few routes—but make sure they include a tram ride, just for the experience.

BUSES

» *Autocarros* (single-decker buses) cover the whole city, and can be crowded. There are few seats, so be prepared to stand, and, although Lisbon has a low crime rate, watch your pockets and belongings.

» *Paragens* (bus stops) show the route number and list the stops along the line. The stop where you are is indicated inside the bus.

» Board at the front and validate your ticket. Exit towards the rear.

NIGHT BUSES

Carris operates a *madrugada* (night service) along the main routes; buses run between 11.45pm and 5.30am, depending on the route.

TRAMS

Lisbon's wonderful *eléctricos* (trams) are worth taking for the pleasure of the ride. They run along five routes and climb some of the steepest city gradients in the world.

Nos 28, 12 and 25 are traditional trams that cover the heart of the old city. Beware of pick-pockets on these tourist routes. No. 18 runs west to Belém, while No. 15 is a 'supertram' along the river from Cais de Sodre through Belém to Algés.

ELEVADORES

Three useful funiculars are Bica, Glória and Lavra, providing quick routes from the Baixa up to Bairro Alto. The walkway from Santa Justa elevator links the Baixa with the Carmo church and Largo do Carmo above. The ride is a pleasure in itself.

METROPOLITANO

Lisbon's metro is a slick and efficient way of getting around. There are four lines, with interchanges at Baixa-Chiado, Marquês de Pombal, Alameda and Campo Grande.

» Trains run 6.30am–1am.

» Entrances are marked with a white 'M' on a red background.

» Tickets cost: Zone 1 80¢, Zones 1 & 2 €1.10 per journey or €7.30 for a *caderneta* 10-trip ticket in Zone 1, €10.40 for Zones 1 & 2, or buy a combination '7 Colinas' ticket valid on metro, bus and trams.

» Validate your ticket in the box next to the entrance barrier.

» Information boards (green, blue, yellow or red according to the line) indicate direction of travel by the name of the station at the end of the line.

» Metro maps are available at main stations.

LOCAL TRAINS

If you're visiting Cascais, Estoril, Queluz or Sintra, you can travel there by local train. Trains run from Cais de Sodre to Estoril and Cascais, and also stop at Belém. For Queluz and Sintra, catch the train at Rossio station.

The Lisbon Card also covers travel on these trains.

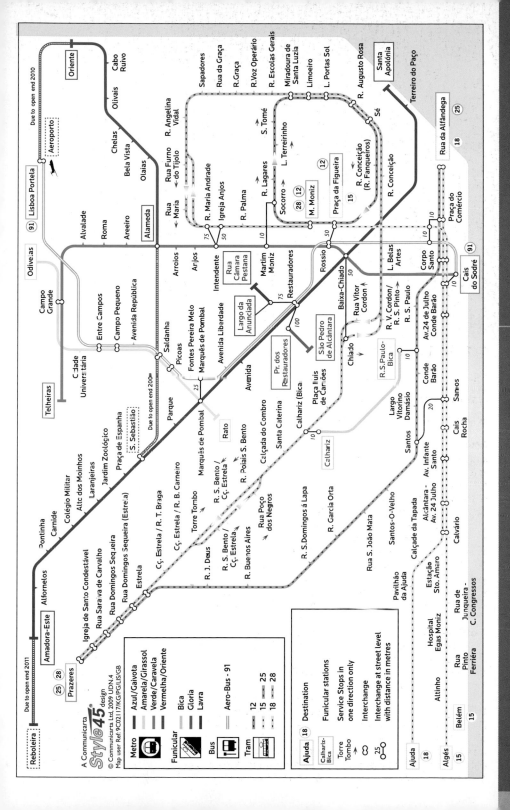

CARRIS INFORMATION

You can get information on Carris services by telephoning 213 613 000 or on their excellent website: www.carris.pt, at the company's kiosks in Praça da Figueira, Restauradores and Cais de Sodre, or at any tourist office. Travel details, ticket information and free maps of the transport system are available. For tourist services contact the Carristur office on Praça do Comércio (tel 213 582 334; www.carristur.pt).

TICKETS

Buy *bilhetes* (tickets) before boarding at the Carris kiosks and at shops and kiosks displaying the Carris logo. Single-journey tickets can also be bought on board for €1.40.

Bilhete1dia Carris/Metro

1-day travel pass (€3.70) valid from purchase time until midnight on buses, trams, *elevadores* and metro.

Bilhete de Bordo

Single-journey ticket (€1.40) available on board and valid in only one zone.

BUCs

Single tickets in blocks of 10 (€7.51 for Zone 1, €11.48 for Zones 1 and 2), available from kiosks. Books of two or five tickets also available.

All combination tickets are now also sold in the form of an electronic card called '7 Colinas' (seven hills). The card is bought separately for 50¢ then charged with the desired tickets. This is known as 'zapping'. Values of between €1.50 and €10 can be added to your card and used on metro and bus networks. If you have any sort of combination ticket, it must be validated the first time you use it by passing it through the machine next to the driver when you board.

Above *Bus timetable on a Lisbon tram stop*
Below *Train at Lisbon's state-of-the-art Oriente station*

FERRIES

Ferries across the Rio Tejo leave from various points throughout the day. Fluvial river station, near the Praça do Comércio, links Lisbon with Cacilhas, Montijo and Barreiro; there's also a service from the Parque das Nações to Cacilhas, and from Belém to Trafaria. Buy your tickets at the ferry point; single tickets 81¢–€2.10.

SIGHTSEEING TOURS OF LISBON

Carris Tramcar Tour

Complete tour of Lisbon's central tram routes in a traditional tram with multilingual headphone commentary. Departures every 30 min from Praça do Comércio, €17.

Cityline-Sightline Tour

City tour that includes Belém. Apr–end Oct every 30 min (every 20 min Fri–Sun and public holidays); Nov–end Mar every 60 min from BUS terminal (metro: Marquês de Pombal). Adults: €15; child (6–11) €7.50, under-5s free.

Transtejo

River cruises with English, French and Spanish commentary. Two departures from Fluvial daily Apr–end Oct, at 3pm. Adults €20; children (5–12) €10; under-5s free.

TAXIS

Lisbon taxis are cream or occasionally black and green. A green light indicates the taxi is occupied. All have meters—check to ensure yours is switched on; tips are discretionary. Taxi stands in the city include those at Rossio, Fluvial, Praça da Figueira, Chiado, Largo da Misericórdia and Avenida da Liberdade.

Taxis themselves are inexpensive, even though fares rise after 10pm, at weekends and on public holidays. You can telephone for a cab:
Autocoope tel 217 932 7560
Rádio Táxis tel 218 119 000
Teletáxis tel 218 111 100.

TIP

If you're planning a lot of travel and sightseeing in Lisbon, consider investing in a *Cartão Lisboa* (Lisbon Card). This gives unlimited travel on buses, trams, *elevadores* and the metro, along with free—or greatly reduced—entry to many main sights (1-day €15, 2-day €26, 3-day €32). For more information see the Lisbon tourist office website: www.askmelisboa.com.

GETTING AROUND IN PORTO

Porto has a comprehensive public transportation network, which includes STCP buses and trams and an expanding, partly underground, state-of-the-art metro system. Most main sights, however, are within the compact heart of the city, easily reached on foot, and so it's unlikely that you'll need to use many public transportation routes.

BUSES

An extensive bus service operates throughout Porto from 6am to 9pm; this reduces between 9pm and 1am, when the *madrugada* (night service) covers the principal routes until 5am. Buses can be crowded and there are few seats.

All tickets must be validated on boarding by stamping them in the machine at the entrance.

Bus stops show the bus number, destination, zone and whether it is a day, evening or night service.

METRO

Construction started on Porto's metro system in 1999. It comprises five lines covering 60km (37 miles) and with 69 stations. The Linha Azul (Blue Line) was opened in 2002 linking Trinidade in central Porto to Senhor de Matosinhos in the northwest. It was extended in 2004 in time for the Euro 2004 Football Championships linking Trinidade to the Estádio do Dragão in the southeast.

Trains run 6am–1am. Entrances are marked with a stylized wavy blue 'M' on a white background. Tickets cost between 95¢ and €1.95 depending on travel zones covered. Visit www.metrodoporto.pt.

TRAMS

There are two short tram routes, worth experiencing for their old-fashioned charm. No. 1 runs the 4km (2.5 miles) between Passeio Alegre and Infante, and No. 18 the 1km (half a mile) between Masserelos and Carmo. Single tickets (95¢) can be purchased on board; all travel cards include tram rides.

TAXIS

There are taxi stands in most of the main squares. Prices are low (€4–€5 for most central destinations). Ordinary taxis are metered; those distinguished by an 'A' (*carros de aluguer*) do not run on a meter and are best used for longer distances; negotiate a price before you ride.

You can call a taxi by telephoning:
Rádio Táxis tel 225 073 900
Táxis Invicta tel 225 076 400
Rádio Táxis Os Unidos tel 225 029 898.

FERRIES

A ferry service crosses the Douro between Passeio Alegre (next to the lighthouse) in Porto and Afurada in Vila Nova de Gaia, departing every 5 minutes from 7.30am–9pm. A single ticket, bought on board, costs €1.

TIP

The Porto Card, a 1-, 2- or 3-day combined travel and museum card, gives unlimited travel on the bus, tram and most of the metro system, free entrance to many museums and monuments, and discounts on other attractions, including river cruises and city tours. For more information see www.portoturismo.pt. Buy it at the tourist information offices at Fenianos, Ribeira or Casa da Câmara (old city hall by the Sé). It costs €7.50 (1-day), €11.50 (2-day) or €15.50 (3-day). There is also a 1-day walker card giving discounts but no travel.

TRAVEL INFORMATION

The main place for transportation information is the Loja de Mobilidade (tel freephone 800 220 905; www.cm-porto.pt), the transportation shop in the visitor information office at Rua Clube dos Fenianos 25 (currently manned afternoons only due to staff shortage; check at the tourist office in the same building). It provides information on all forms of city transportation, including timetables and an excellent free booklet and map. There's another STCP office on Praça Almeida Garrett, opposite São Bento station.

TICKETS

You can buy *bilhetes* (single tickets) on the buses (€1.50) or booklets of 2 or 10 tickets from STCP kiosks, newsstands and shops displaying the STCP logo. Pre-purchased tickets are considerably cheaper, costing €1.65 for 2 trips or €7.05 for 10 in the central zone. Metro tickets are available from automatic machines in the stations; they all combine with the STCP system and cost 95¢ for 1 journey and €9.50 for 10 (+1) in the central zone.

Travel passes

» Andante Tour 1 is valid for unlimited travel on bus, tram, metro, train for 24 hours starting when first used (€5).

» Andante Tour 3 is valid for unlimited travel on bus, tram, metro, train for 72 hours starting when first used (€11).

» Andante 24 is valid for one day on both the bus and metro system (€3.35 in the central zone, or €6.85 for all 6 zones).

Validate your ticket when you board the first time you use it.

CRUISES ON THE RIVER DOURO

Porto is the starting point for many of the river cruises up the Douro. They range from a 1-hour cruise around the city area to 7-day luxury cruises with visits to historic *quintas* (country estates) and fine dining included. Prices range from €10 for an hour's excursion to €945 for a 7-day luxury cruise along the Douro into Spain. The main operators are:

» Douro Azul tel 223 402 500; www.douroazul.com.

» Rent Douro tel 224 646 352; www.rentdouro.com.

CAR RENTAL IN PORTUGAL

If you decide to rent a car in Portugal, where rental rates are among the lowest in Europe, there's a wide choice. The major chains are all represented and have offices at airports, train stations and downtown in the major cities. You are likely to find the best value if you shop around beforehand, and book in advance before you leave home. The Algarve has numerous smaller, local and reasonably priced companies, but you may be unable to book them in advance from your home country. The solution is to travel from Faro airport to your destination by public transportation or taxi, completing your car rental deal on the spot on arrival. If your trip to Portugal is being organized by a specialist tour operator, it will be able to arrange car rental for you when you book your holiday or flight.

» Before you leave home, check your insurance to see if you will need any additional cover. You will generally be offered the option of a collision damage waiver, which is advisable in Portugal.

» You will need your credit card as a deposit when you pick up the car, and it's rare to pay additional charges for car rental with anything other than a credit card.

» Drivers of rented cars must be over 23 and carry a valid driver's licence.

» Photographic proof of identity is a legal requirement in Portugal; even if you have a new driver's licence with a photo it is best to keep your passport/national ID card with you at all times as this is required by law. Some police will accept just a driver's licence, others will not.

» If there is to be more than one driver, you must specify this when you collect the car; the additional driver/s will also have to sign the rental agreement. If you intend to drive off public roads, check that the insurance covers this.

» Before you set off, thoroughly check both exterior and interior of the vehicle for any damage. If you find any, report it at once and get a company representative to look at it and make a note.

» You will generally be given the choice of returning the car with or without a full tank of fuel; it is cheaper to fill it up yourself just before you return it.

TIPS

If you're picking up a rental car in Lisbon with the intention of driving on, try to avoid an early morning or evening collection time. Traffic in and around the city is extremely heavy during the rush hour, when the main roads and the Tejo bridges can get clogged for hours.

CAR RENTAL COMPANIES

Book your rental car before you leave home, either by phone or online. Major international rental groups are listed below.

	TELEPHONE UK	TELEPHONE US	WEBSITE
Alamo	0870 400 4562	800/462-5266	www.alamo.co.uk www.alamo.com
Avis	08700 100 287	800/331-1212	www.avis.co.uk www.avis.com
Budget	0844 581 2231	800/527-0700	www.budget.co.uk www.budget.com
Hertz	08708 448844	800/654-3131	www.hertz.co.uk www.hertz.com
National	0870 400 4560	800/227-7368	www.nationalcar.co.uk www.nationalcar.com
Thrifty	01494 751500	800/847-4389	www.thrifty.co.uk www.thrifty.com

DRIVING

Up until the 1990s, Portugal had one of Europe's least developed road networks, with just one (incomplete) motorway open between Lisbon and Porto. Since then, a massive injection of European Union funding into road construction has given the country a network of motorways and main highways that has provided faster and easier access to main towns and cities as well as to previously remote areas. Portugal is now served by an adequate road system, with dual carriageways (divided highways) and motorways linking the main cities and towns, and minor roads connecting smaller towns and villages.

Driving makes sense if you are concentrating on smaller cities and towns and rural areas. But be aware that Portuguese roads are of variable quality and are sometimes in bad condition. You may encounter winding roads with poor surfaces and maintenance, bad illumination and signing, and heavy and slow-moving traffic.

The sharp rise in car ownership has brought congestion problems, particularly in and around cities and on smaller roads. In addition, Portuguese driving has a justified reputation as being among the worst in Europe; statistically, Portugal is consistently number one in terms of traffic accidents and deaths per capita, and also leads the field in the number of pedestrians being run over. Much is being done to tackle the problem, with better policing and prosecution and a concerted effort to educate drivers. Portugal is one of the few European countries where driving tips are a daily feature of morning TV news.

The best bet is to stick to motorways for long journeys and try and steer clear of cities, particularly Lisbon and Porto. One-way systems, narrow streets, heavy traffic and lack of parking make city driving stressful, and even smaller towns are best avoided during the busy morning and early evening periods. Be prepared for exceptionally heavy traffic on summer weekends, when roads and motorways around big cities are heaving, and the roads in the Algarve, Portugal's major holiday playground, have to contend with a massive influx of both Portuguese and foreign drivers.

DOCUMENTS

Carry documents with you whenever you are driving; if you are stopped, the Guarda Nacional Republicana (GNR) will want to see them. Both UK and US driver's licences are valid in Portugal, but it is recommended that you also carry a translation. For UK drivers, the new licences with photographs and the pink, EU-style ones include a translation; if you hold an older, green licence, it is a good idea either to update your licence or apply for an International Driving Permit. Holders of US driver's licences should also apply for an International Driving Permit. Though these permits are not compulsory, they can smooth out problems and also act as another form of identification. Permits can be obtained from many national motoring organizations including the AA and AAA.

RULES OF THE ROAD

Some of the following rules of the road are flagrantly ignored by most Portuguese motorists. They are the law, and foreign drivers should observe them.

» Drivers must be at least 18 years of age and hold a full driver's licence.
» Drivers who have held a licence for less than a year must not exceed 90kph (55mph) or any lower speed limit.
» Drive on the right.
» Unless otherwise indicated, give priority to all vehicles approaching from the right at intersections.
» Vehicles already using a roundabout take priority over those entering it.
» Seatbelts are compulsory.
» Children aged under 3 are prohibited from sitting in the front seat unless in an approved child seat.
» All children between 3 and 12 must use an approved restraint system wherever they are sitting.
» Speed limits: built up areas 50kph (31mph); outside built-up areas 90kph (55mph) or 100kph (62mph); motorways (autoestradas) 120kph (74mph). Minimum speed on motorways is 40kph (24mph).

BRINGING YOUR OWN CAR

Before you leave:	You will need:
» Have headlights adjusted for driving on the right.	» A valid driver's licence; Portuguese law requires everyone to carry photographic proof of identity at all times. If you have an old-style licence without a photo, make sure you have your passport with you when you're driving.
» Contact your motor insurer or broker at least one month before taking your car to Portugal.	
» Have your car serviced.	» Vehicle registration document.
» Check the tyres and tyre pressures.	» Motor insurance certificate; third-party insurance at least is compulsory.
» Make sure both wing mirrors (side mirrors) are properly adjusted.	» A first-aid kit, fire extinguisher and spare bulbs.
» Ensure you have adequate breakdown cover (AA European Breakdown 0800 085 7253; www.theAA.com).	» It is compulsory to carry a warning triangle, to display a nationality sticker or Euro-plates and to carry a fluorescent vest to wear if your car breaks down.

» You must use dipped headlights in poor daytime visibility, in tunnels and on zero-tolerance IP roads at all times.

» Drinking and driving: For levels of alcohol in the blood from 0.05 to 0.08 per cent, penalties include a fine and withdrawal of driver's licence for one month to one year; for more than 0.08 per cent, a fine and withdrawal of licence from two months to two years.

» Non-residents have to pay all road fines on the spot to the police officers concerned. If you refuse to, or cannot, pay, you will be asked for a deposit based on the maximum fine for the offence committed. If you refuse to pay that, your vehicle will be impounded by the police and not released until you pay in full.

WARNINGS AND SAFETY

» Be aware constantly of overtaking vehicles, especially on corners, double white lines and on your right.

» Some roads (usually IP numbers) are classified as zero tolerance. If they display blue signs showing dipped headlights, this is a mandatory instruction no matter what the weather. If you drive without lights on these roads, you are liable to be stopped by the traffic police and will receive an on-the-spot fine of €25 (Portuguese citizens lose their licence for one month).

» Speed limits and other road rules are enforced by radar traps and unmarked police cars.

» Beware of radar-controlled traffic lights in smaller towns and villages, where green lights will change to red if you're over the speed limit (50kph/31mph). The threat of this often leads to erratic driving by local motorists. Such traffic lights are usually signified by a warning sign: *velocidade controlada* plus the speed limit.

» Roads and non-motorized vehicles (e.g. bicycles, donkey carts) are not well lit at night, so drive with caution, keeping a special eye-out for pedestrians, who often wear dark clothes.

» Be patient on rural roads, where there are sometimes horse-drawn vehicles, donkeys and farm animals.

» Watch out for drivers of cars and agricultural vehicles in both remote areas and the city; they don't always signal their intentions.

» Drivers will often get far too close to the car in front, even on motorways.

» Traffic signs and signposts can often be difficult to spot.

» Never leave any property visible in the car when you're not using it and always lock the car when you leave it, if only for a few moments.

» Lower the aerial (antenna) and tuck in the side mirrors when you park.

MOTORWAYS

Portugal's motorway *(autoestrada)* system is built and run by private companies, Brisa being the major one (freephone 808 508 508; www. brisa.pt). Motorways run from north to south of the country, from Valença on the Spanish border to Lagos in the Algarve. They link the cities of Braga, Aveiro, Coimbra, Leiria and Lisbon with the Algarve, and there is a further network around Lisbon. In addition, the A23 runs northeast from Entroncamento to Vilar Formoso on the Spanish border; the A6 links Lisbon with Badajoz in Spain; and the A22 runs from the western Algarve to the Spanish frontier at Vila Real de Santo António.

All motorways are signposted and approached via slip roads leading, in most cases, to the toll booths. Take the ticket from the automatic booth on the left of the car and the barrier will lift. Keep your ticket safe while you're on the motorway, as you will need it to pay when you come off it. Cash payment is made to the official in the booth at the exit; the amount due is displayed on a screen outside the payment window.

All toll booths have a Via Verde (Green Channel), controlled by CCTV, that enables tolls to be automatically deducted from your bank account. This channel is available only if you have previously registered with Via Verde and obtained a green channel identification box. You can find out more about the scheme on www. viaverde.pt (Portuguese only).

Slip roads onto and off Portuguese motorways are sometimes short and you may have to stop and wait before you can join the main carriageway. Watch for drivers coming up fast and driving close behind you; Portuguese drivers will often pull out suddenly with no warning.

Autoestradas have service areas approximately every 50km (30 miles) with fuel stations, bar/restaurants, rest areas, shops and toilets. Some of them also have hotels.

Toll charges on motorways are relatively high; the cost of travel from Lisbon to Porto, for example, will be around €19.

PROBLEMS

If your car breaks down, turn on your hazard warning lights, put on a fluorescent vest and place the warning triangle 50m (55 yards) behind the vehicle. If you're driving your own car, you can get help from ACP (Automóvel Clube de Portugal; www.acp.pt), which has reciprocal breakdown assistance arrangements with overseas motoring organizations. It provides 24-hour help: tel 707 509 510. Many

---

TIPS FOR TOWNS

» Study a city map before you reach your destination, so that you can recognize major landmarks that will help you orientate yourself (e.g. a castle, cathedral, river, major boulevard).

» Work out by which road you are entering the town to help you decide on left and right turns.

» Remember to watch for badly placed signs.

» Be aware that traffic lights are often small and poorly sited.

» Slow down, take your time and watch for other drivers.

» If you make a mistake, remember that most drivers are used to dealing with the unexpected and will eventually make room or give way to you.

car insurance policies will cover your car in Portugal, but it's worth taking out extra insurance in case of breakdown.

If you have an accident, call the police (tel 112) but do not admit liability. Witnesses should remain at the scene to make statements, exchange details (name, address, car details, insurance company's name and address).

If the Guarda Nacional Republicana (GNR) stop you, they will want to see your personal and car documentation. They may give no reason for this, but you are most likely to have been pulled over for speeding or some other infringement of the law, such as driving without lights on a zero-tolerance road. The officers will calculate an on-the-spot fine for non-residents from the official police highway code book, and will issue a receipt for the money. Most police patrolling major roads speak English, so do not attempt to plead ignorance. Remember that the Portuguese have a high respect for all officials; the more polite and helpful you are if stopped, the quicker you will be on your way.

PARKING

Parking in Portugal's bigger towns and cities is difficult. Traffic is heavy, streets are congested and often medieval, and picturesque towns were not built to accommodate modern vehicles. Only top-rank hotels have private parking, and you can spend hours trying to find central parking anywhere. The smaller much-visited historic towns and villages, such as Évora, Beja and Marvão, have good-sized parking areas on the outskirts, and are small enough for the old hearts of the towns to be easily accessible on foot from these. In larger places, you may have a long walk in from the parking area. Coimbra is one of the few places to have instituted a 'park and ride' system; this may be copied by other towns.
» Unemployed men sometimes earn a little money by pointing out empty

parking spaces to drivers. In return for a tip of around 50¢, they will keep an eye on your vehicle for you.
» The best time to arrive in a town is during the lunch hour, when streets are quiet and there may be more spaces.
» Prices in downtown parking areas are generally very reasonable, though some can get quite busy, especially during festival times.
» If you can find metered parking, it's good value.
» If you arrive at night, check your chosen parking street has no restrictions that will come into force before you return the next morning. Cars may be towed away to make space for weekly markets.

BUYING FUEL
» Fuel stations are generally open from 7am until midnight; some remain open 24 hours.
» The types of *gasolina* (fuel) normally available are *gasolina 95* (95 octane unleaded), *gasolina 98* (98 octane unleaded) and *gasóleo* (diesel).
» Fuel is currently priced around €1.52 per litre for unleaded and €1.42 for diesel.

» Some fuel stations still have an attended service. For a full tank, ask for *cheio, se faz favor*.
» Less common are 24-hour pumps which are sometimes automatic. These take cards and occasionally €5, €10 and €20 notes (bills) and will dispense fuel until the money runs out. They can be temperamental, however, and will often reject all but the most pristine notes.

MOTORCYCLES AND SCOOTERS
If you're staying on the coast, particularly in one of the Algarve resorts, you may be tempted to rent a scooter or 80cc motorcycle to get around. These are readily available, but take things easy if you have little or no experience, or have not ridden one of these vehicles in Portugal before: Be extremely wary of other road-users. That said, a motorcycle or scooter is economical, fun and easier to park than a car.

You'll need to be at least 18 (over 23 for motorcycles exceeding 125cc) and to have held a full motorcycle licence for at least a year. Rental starts at around €25 a day and usually includes third-party insurance, helmet rental and locks.

BICYCLING

Bicycling is a great way to see some areas of Portugal, but it is not recommended away from quiet country roads, or in the busy and hilly northwest. Remember, too, that Portugal can get very hot in high summer. Tourist offices can help you with tracking down rental outlets—rental rates start at around €10 a day—and may also have information on routes, although designated bicycle routes are virtually non-existent. Bicycles may be taken on local trains for a small fee.

ROAD CLASSIFICATION

EM—Estradas Municipais
These vary in width and condition, but are usually fairly narrow, with few markings or guardrails.

EN or N—Estradas Nacionais
Two-lane roads where the width may vary. They normally have horizontal and vertical markings and signs, although these can be in poor condition. Some of these roads, such as the N125 in the Algarve, have a notorious reputation for accidents.

IC—Itinerários Complementares
Can have either two or four lanes, and often pass through populated areas.

IP—Itinerários Principais
Controlled-access three- or four-lane roads linking major towns and cities, characterized by heavy traffic and impatient drivers. The IP5, linking Aveiro with the Spanish border, has a particularly bad reputation, as does the Amarante–Bragança IP4.

A—Autoestradas
Toll motorways, all built within the last 20 years.

The chart below lists major points on Portugal's road network. Use the chart to gauge the distance in miles (green) and duration in hours and minutes (blue) of a car journey.

The distance/duration chart is a triangular matrix with the following diagonal headings:
Aveiro, Beja, Braga, Bragança, Chaves, Coimbra, Évora, Faro, Guarda, Guimarães, Leiria, Lisboa, Miranda do Douro, Portimão, Porto, Sagres, Valença do Minho, Viana do Castelo, Vila Real de Santo Antonio, Vilar Formoso, Viseu.

Upper-right triangle (reading by row):

601	202	531	441	104	521	826	308	211	204	436	558	821	123	914	331	235	835	359	137
909	1023	1037	518	123	233	639	1056	356	312	1001	524	810	309	1017	922	213	730	732	
410	223	307	745	1038	441	024	429	635	540	1032	059	1126	123	121	1038	533	347		
147	538	859	1256	344	341	659	837	130	1250	407	1344	534	532	1235	435	407			
438	913	1209	435	247	559	737	317	1203	304	1257	345	347	1247	503	304				
438	722	246	255	121	259	542	717	208	810	416	320	731	337	134					
356	516	932	317	226	838	632	647	725	854	758	336	607	609						
912	1329	601	416	1234	118	939	212	1146	1051	057	1059	905							
418	407	545	322	907	351	1000	605	603	852	051	131								
417	623	604	1324	047	1417	145	144	1306	509	323									
232	704	605	330	658	537	441	609	458	255										
907	410	536	504	758	756	524	636	432											
1229	537	1323	704	702	1214	306	421												
934	054	1141	1045	215	1053	859													
1027	207	112	939	442	220														
1234	1139	308	1147	952															
056	1146	656	510																
1051	654	332																	
943	943																		
222																			

Lower-left triangle (reading by row):

337																			
114	513																		
309	582	234																	
263	595	134	100																
60	297	175	316	260															
300	78	435	504	517	260														
473	143	596	725	681	413	221													
176	373	263	209	257	155	295	516												
122	613	22	207	156	164	535	756	241											
116	221	251	392	336	76	184	337	231	240										
258	179	369	483	427	167	136	239	322	358	142									
335	562	318	84	184	320	484	705	189	340	396	511								
468	303	591	720	676	408	366	73	511	751	341	234	700							
78	458	55	231	172	120	380	541	216	44	196	314	315	536						
518	177	641	770	726	458	416	123	561	801	391	284	750	50	586					
197	577	78	312	210	239	499	660	341	19	315	447	396	655	119	705				
145	525	76	310	212	187	447	608	339	97	263	445	394	603	67	653	52			
481	124	596	706	717	421	202	53	497	735	345	303	686	126	541	176	660	608		
224	421	311	257	283	203	343	616	48	289	279	370	174	611	264	661	389	387	545	
91	423	212	231	172	88	345	509	85	190	164	255	244	504	131	554	290	198	545	133

TRAINS

Trains in Portugal are operated by CP—Caminhos de Ferro Portugueses (tel 808 208 208; www.cp.pt). Its network, augmented in some areas with connecting buses, covers much of the country, and includes some wonderfully scenic lines. There are different types of trains and services. Local trains can be snail-like, and so you may find some destinations easier and faster to reach by bus, although trains are sometimes cheaper. Full timetable information may be hard to track down if you want to get from one part of the country to another, although train timetables for individual lines are sometimes available at main stations. The best policy is to plan your journey in advance, using the excellent English-language website.

DIFFERENT TYPES OF TRAIN

» Both Porto and Lisbon have a local network of commuter trains; the Cascais and Sintra lines out of Lisbon are useful for visitors.
» Some minor lines have been replaced by buses operated by CP; train tickets and passes are valid on these.
» Narrow-gauge lines still exist in the north and are part of the network. The Tâmega, Corgo, Tua valley and Douro, all superbly scenic lines, fall into this category.
» Stations can be some distance from the town or village they serve; connecting transportation is not guaranteed.

STATIONS

Lisbon and Porto have more than one estação de comboios (station), each with amenities such as bars, cafés, newsstands and left-luggage facilities. In the rest of the country, major cities have one station. Smaller stations generally have little more than a ticket office and waiting room; some may even be unmanned. Some Portuguese stations are decorated with azulejos (tiles) showing local scenes.

TICKETS

» Portuguese trains have first- and second-class bilhetes (tickets), which can be purchased online (www.cp.pt) and at train stations. Different price structures exist for different train categories, with regional trains being the cheapest. Overall, rail travel is relatively inexpensive.
» Rail-pass holders must pay supplements on the faster services, such as the inter-regionales, intercidades and the Alfa between Lisbon and Porto.
» Groups of 10 or more are eligible for bilhetes de grupo (combined tickets) on regional services. This usually gives reductions of between 20 and 30 per cent but must be applied for four days in advance, and discounts are calculated case by case (tel 808 208 208).
» The Cheque Trem (Rail Cheque), obtainable in two different values, can be in an individual's name or a company's name and has no time limit; it gives a reduction of 10 per cent and can be used for purchasing tickets at the normal price and for many other railway services. Check the CP website for more information about tickets.

» There is a 10 per cent reduction for ida e volta (return, or round-trip journeys) on trips of more than 91km (56 miles).
» Children between 4 and 11 pay 50 per cent of the full price; under-4s travel free.
» Senior citizens (over 65) are entitled to a 50 per cent discount on production of proof of age.
» Passengers travelling without a ticket will incur an on-the-spot fine payable to the conductor.
» Some country stations are unmanned; in this case, you can buy your ticket on the train without a penalty.

AT THE STATION

» Every station has a bilheteira (ticket office) or máquina de bilhetes (ticket machine), which will accept notes (bills) as well as coins in payment. At the ticket window, prices are displayed on a readout at the cash register—useful for establishing the cost if you don't speak Portuguese. Check your tickets if you want a return (round-trip) ticket to make sure that you were understood properly and have been issued with the correct type.

RAIL PASSES

INTER-RAIL PASS

(for European residents)
Valid for one month's unlimited train travel within a specified zone. Unless you are going to be making a lot of train journeys, you will almost certainly be better off buying individual tickets. For information: www.interrailnet.com.

EURAIL PASS

(for non-European residents)
Valid for first-class train and ferry travel on Eurail group transportation for periods of 15 or 21 days, or 1, 2 or 3 months. Useful if you're visiting Europe for a long trip and planning to travel around a lot. For information in the US: tel 888/382-7245; www.raileurope.com/us.

EURAIL FLEXIPASS

(for non-European residents)
As Eurail Pass, but valid for 10 or 15 days within a 2-month period travelling first class.

In Portuguese a one-way ticket is *ida*, and a return *volta*.

» Major stations have information screens giving travel details of arrivals and departures; if you can't see your train on the board, point at the ticket and ask the way to the appropriate *plataforma* (platform).

» Timetables are normally posted on the walls inside the station; if you have to make a connection, use these to find the time and platform of your next train.

» For lost property, call the station at either your arrival or departure point.

TYPES OF TRAIN

REGIONAL AND INTER-REGIONAL

Most Portuguese trains fall into these categories. They run throughout the country, using both first- and second-class carriages (cars) with an acceptable level of comfort. Regional trains stop at most stations; inter-regional ones are faster, stopping only at major stations. On-board facilities are basic, but do include toilets.

INTERCIDADES

These are fast, comfortable intercity trains, on which advance reservation is advised; this adds around 60 per cent to the price of a normal ticket. On-board facilities include bar/café, telephones and toilets. Both first- and second-class seats are available. Such trains link: Lisbon–Porto–Braga; Lisbon–Guarda; Lisbon–Covilhã; Lisbon–Evora; Lisbon–Algarve. A second-class return (round-trip) ticket between Lisbon and Porto costs €39.

ALFA

This fast, luxurious service operates between Lisbon and Porto, with stops at Coimbra and Aveiro. Advance reservation is recommended, and some Alfa trains are made up of first-class carriages (cars) only, with all the facilities to be expected on a premier service. A second-class return (round-trip) ticket between Lisbon and Porto on the Alfa costs €55.

The chart below shows the duration in hours and minutes of a train journey between these destinations in Portugal.

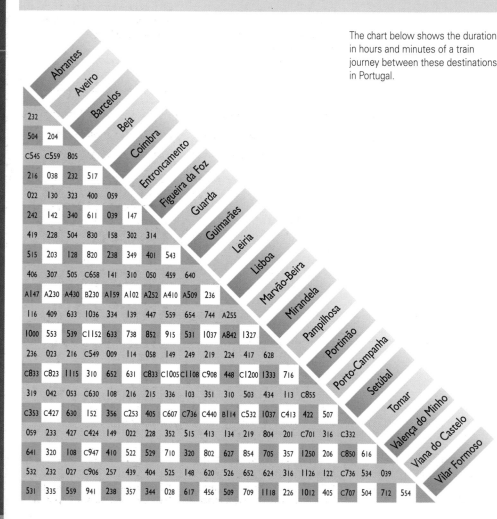

BUSES

Portugal has a good bus network at local, regional and national level. You should be able to travel almost anywhere using buses, which are often faster than the equivalent trains.

» Buses in Portugal are operated by various different companies, all private, mainly running services within their own region. Privatization has led to hot competition between operators, with a proliferation of more frequent services on the more popular routes, and the inevitable cutbacks or even cessation of many local services.

» There is no national long-distance bus company. Portugal's network of long-distance express buses is run by many different companies, although these do combine their timetables and fare structures. Although not obligatory, it is often best to reserve in advance,

especially at busy times of the year. For information and reservations, tel 969 502 050 (some operators may speak English). You can also check times, and book and pay for tickets, online at www.rede-expressos. pt (Portuguese only, but simple to operate). Express buses are comfortable, with air conditioning; smoking is not permitted.

» From larger towns and cities, services may be run on identical routes by several different companies; these will all leave from different bus stations, depending on the operator—Porto alone has nearly 20 companies, each with its own dedicated terminal.

» In smaller towns, *estação de camionetas* (local bus stations) are the places to get information and book tickets.

» Be aware that companies, routes, addresses and timetables may change every year; check with local tourist offices for the latest information.

» Local services are geared to the population's needs, so many buses operate to suit working, market and school hours.

» Bus services are far less frequent, and sometimes non-existent, on Saturdays and Sundays.

TAXIS

Taxis are available in cities and towns, including some surprisingly small places. Fares in Portugal are relatively low by European standards. If you don't have a car, this makes taxis a good option for getting around in rural areas, especially as, away from the major towns and cities, it is acceptable to negotiate for a few hours' hire.

» Portuguese taxis are generally metered, with a minimum fare of around €1.50.

» Any luggage carried in the boot (trunk) is charged for as an extra.

» Additional charges are made between 10pm and 6am.

» Taxi hire in the Algarve is the most expensive in the country.

» Tipping is not obligatory, but 10 per cent of what is on the meter is appreciated—Portuguese taxi drivers are often very helpful.

» Check that the meter is switched on and set to minimum fare before you set off.

» If there's no meter, agree the price with the driver before you drive off.

» After paying, check your change.

» At airports and train stations, wait at the official stand, sometimes controlled by an official.

» It's sometimes easier to telephone for a taxi or go to a stand than to rely on flagging one down on the street; bus and train stations are also good places to find taxis.

INTERNAL FLIGHTS

As a small country (Lisbon and Porto are only 300km/185 miles apart), Portugal has little in the way of internal flights, although there are regular services to both Madeira and the Azores.

Lisbon is connected to Porto and Faro by air, but there are no direct mainland flights from Porto to anywhere other than Lisbon.

TAP AIR PORTUGAL
Reservations: tel 707 205 700
www.flytap.pt. Services include:
Lisbon to Porto;

Lisbon to Funchal and Porto Santo;
Lisbon to Faro;
Lisbon to Azores (see below);
Porto to Funchal and Azores.

GETTING TO MADEIRA AND THE AZORES FROM PORTUGAL
TAP Air Portugal operates flights from Lisbon and Porto to Madeira,

and from Lisbon to Ponta Delgada on São Miguel and to the islands of Terceira, Faial and Pico in the Azores. SATA Air Açores connects both Lisbon and Porto to Ponta Delgada, from where it runs inter-island flights to the other islands in the group.

» SATA Air Açores: www.sata.pt
» TAP Air Portugal: www.flytap.pt

VISITORS WITH A DISABILITY

In Portugal, the major problems for people with a disability often lie not so much in the transportation, accommodation and public buildings as in the actual nature of the old cities and towns. Things are progressing, but disability facilities in Portugal overall still lag behind those in northern European countries and North America. This is partly offset by the helpfulness of the Portuguese themselves, who will make great efforts to render your visit as stress-free and uncomplicated as possible.

» If you have a disability, plan your trip carefully in advance. Aim to travel with able-bodied friends, or consider booking via a specialist tour operator. Contact both your departure and arrival airports and the airline you are flying with in advance of your date of travel to let them know what assistance you will need. It can be a problem getting this organized without advance notice.

» Taxis can take wheelchairs folded and stored in the boot (trunk), but Portuguese taxis are normal saloon (sedan) type cars, and so getting in and out of them may be difficult.

» Dial-a-ride bus services exist in Lisbon: tel 213 613 141, or log on to www.carris.pt. The service operates Mon–Fri 6.30am–10pm, Sat–Sun 8am–10pm and each trip costs €1.40. Rides require one day's notice, but before using the service you must present a medical certificate, ID and a photograph at the Carris headquarters in Santo Amaro so that a user's card can be issued.

» Buses do not have wheelchair access.

» Dogs for the blind travel free.

» Drivers from the UK can use a disabled person's parking badge in Portugal.

» You should be aware that many streets in old quarters of towns and cities are cobbled. They are often very steep.

» Official buildings tend to have good access.

» Major museums are making headway in providing wheelchair access, but coverage is patchy.

» Access steps are the major problem in cathedrals and churches, especially in rural areas.

» Reserve well ahead and be specific about your requirements.

» For a relaxed holiday, steer clear of big cities and use a car to explore rural areas, the coast and the smaller towns and villages.

USEFUL CONTACTS

Accessible Portugal
www.accessibleportugal.com
This is the only Portugal-based company to offer inclusive trips designed specifically for people with restricted mobility, wheelchair users and their families. Choose from short tours and city breaks, cruises, adventure trips or longer and more in-depth journeys covering Spain and Portugal; or opt for a customized tour tailored to your personal needs and preferences. Check the website for full details. The organization provides transportation in specially adapted vehicles and it can supply comprehensive nursing care upon request.
✉ Rua João Freitas Branco 21D, 1500-714 Lisboa
☎ 217 203 130 or 926 910 990
🕐 Mon–Fri 10–7

Holiday Care
www.holidaycare.org.uk
This organization provides useful publications and information on accessibility for visitors with disabilities.
✉ Tourism For All, The Hawkins Suite, Enham Place, Enham Alamein, Andover SP11 6JS
☎ 0845 124 9971

Secretariado Nacional de Reabilitação
www.inr.pt
This government-run site provides information on transportation facilities (Portuguese only) and publishes the *Accessible Tourism Guide*, with comprehensive listings of hotels, travel agents, restaurants and clubs.
✉ Conde de Valbom 63, 1069-178 Lisboa
☎ 217 929 500

Society for Accessible Travel and Hospitality (SATH)
www.sath.org
Lots of tips for travellers with mobility or visual impairment can be found here.

Wheeling Around the Algarve (Rodando Pelo Algarve)
www.player.pt
A highly personal company in the Algarve, this organization will arrange everything from airport transfers and villa rentals to wheelchair rental and sporting and leisure activities, and is contactable 24 hours a day, 7 days a week.
✉ Rua Casa do Povo 1, Apartado 3421, 8135-905 Almancil
☎ 289 393 636

REGIONS

This chapter is divided into eight regions of Portugal (▷ 7–9). Places of interest are listed alphabetically in each region.

Portugal's Regions (▷ 62–290)

LISBON

Known as the city of seven hills, Lisbon overlooks the broad Tagus estuary and this, combined with its extraordinary light makes it one of Europe's most beguiling capitals. It is a city of contrasts, maintaining its distinct, tight-knit neighbourhoods with their decrepit, paint-peeling dwellings, cobbled streets and tight lanes, while embracing modernity and change. Its sense of history is preserved through its planning and architecture; from the Moorish Alfama and its 12th-century Sé; through the golden-age, Manueline masterpieces of Belém and the meticulously planned 18th-century Baixa, to the ultra-modern Parque das Nações on the city's northeastern edge.

In addition to its history and architecture, Lisbon possesses some great museums, the Gulbenkian, the Museu de Arte Antiga, the Berardo Collection at the Centro Cultural de Belém and its most recent addition, the Museu do Orient, one of the world's primary collections of Asian *objets d'art*. Those in search of retail therapy will not be disappointed by period speciality shops with original interiors, chain stores and colossal malls; nor the food lover, by the wide range of cuisine available.

Lisbon is not a large city and one of its greatest pleasures is simply to walk its streets. Take time to sit at pavement cafés in imposing squares, hop aboard historic 19th-century trams which trundle up hills at precipitous gradients; savour newspaper-wrapped roasted chestnuts in season or custard tarts at Belém at any time of year; and enjoy the river, endearingly referred to by locals as the *mar de palha* or sea of straw, a reference to its shimmering golden water as the sun sets over it to the west.

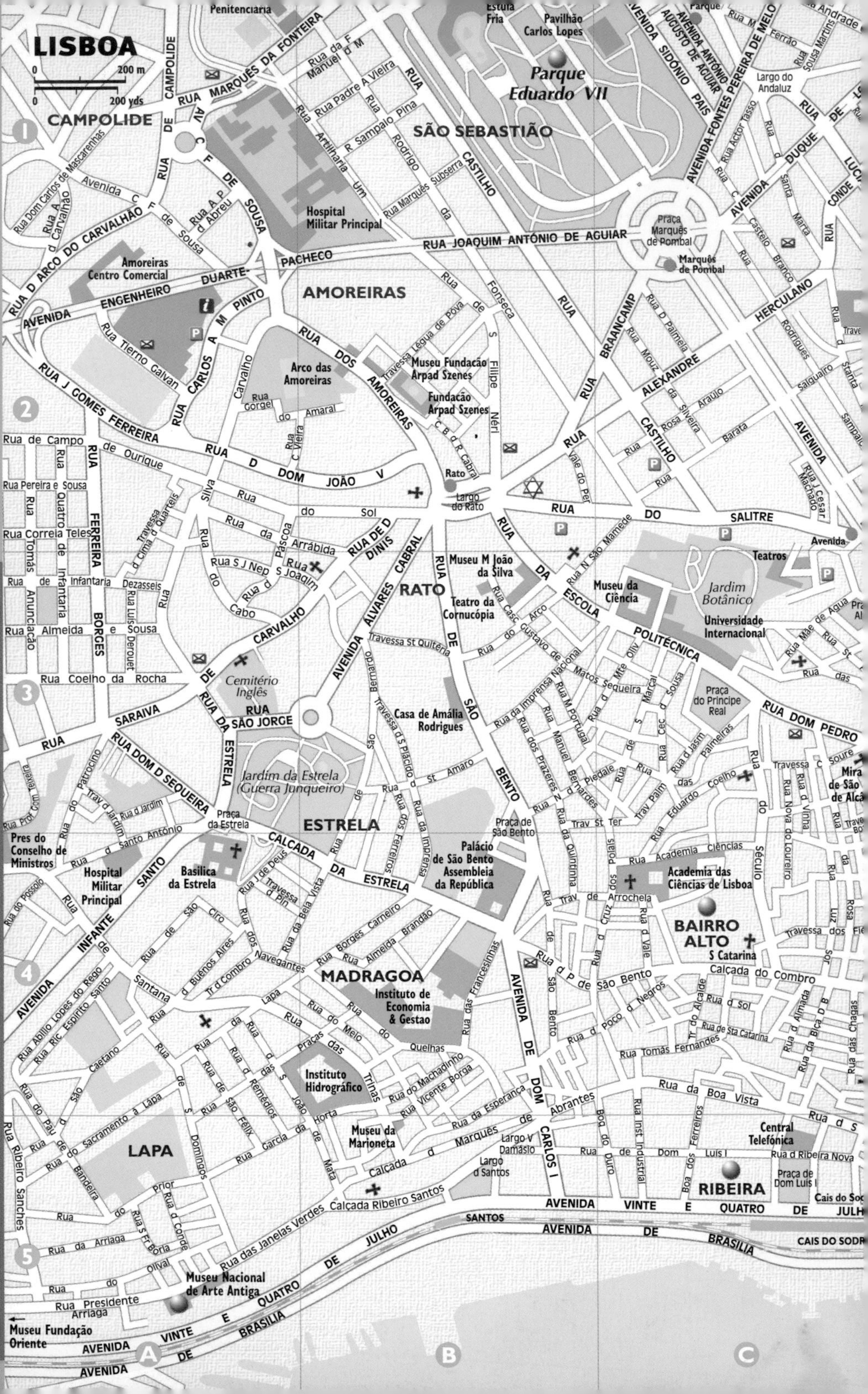

LISBOA

0   200 m
0   200 yds

Penitenciária

Estufa Fria

Pavilhão Carlos Lopes

Parque Eduardo VII

Largo do Andaluz

CAMPOLIDE

SÃO SEBASTIÃO

Hospital Militar Principal

RUA JOAQUIM ANTÓNIO DE AGUIAR

Praça Marquês de Pombal

Marquês de Pombal

Amoreiras Centro Comercial

AMOREIRAS

Arco das Amoreiras

Museu Fundação Arpad Szenes

Fundação Arpad Szenes

RUA DOS AMOREIRAS

RUA D DOM JOÃO V

Rato

Largo do Rato

RATO

RUA DA ESCOLA POLITÉCNICA

Museu M João da Silva

Teatro da Cornucópia

Museu da Ciência

Jardim Botânico

Universidade Internacional

Teatros

Praça do Príncipe Real

RUA DOM PEDRO

Mira de São de Alca

Casa de Amália Rodrigues

Cemitério Inglês

RUA DA ESTRELA

Jardim da Estrela (Guerra Junqueiro)

Praça da Estrela

ESTRELA

Academia das Ciências de Lisboa

BAIRRO ALTO

S Catarina

Praça de São Bento

Palácio de São Bento Assembleia da República

Pres do Conselho de Ministros

Hospital Militar Principal

Basílica da Estrela

MADRAGOA

Instituto de Economia & Gestao

Quelhas

Instituto Hidrográfico

Museu da Marioneta

Central Telefónica

LAPA

Largo V Damásio

Largo d Santos

RIBEIRA

Praça de Dom Luís I

Cais do Soc

AVENIDA   VINTE   E   QUATRO   DE   JULH

SANTOS

AVENIDA   DE   BRASILIA

CAIS DO SODR

Museu Nacional de Arte Antiga

Museu Fundação Oriente

AVENIDA   VINTE   E   BRASILIA

AVENIDA   DE   BRASILIA

A   B   C

BURACA

RADIAL DA BURACA

ALFRAGIDE

Forte de
Monsanto

IC19

Palácio dos
Marquêses
de Fronteira

SETE RIOS

Museu Calouste
Gulbenkian

ARCO
CEGO

OLAIAS

PICHELEIRA

PORTELA

MONSANTO
Parque Florestal
de Monsanto

CAMPOLIDE

ESTEFÂNIA

BAIRRO
LOPES

Hospital
Miguel
ombarda

CASELAS

Estoril

A5

CAMPO DE
OURIQUE

RATO

GRAÇA

Castelo de
São Jorge

ital de
Marta

CARAMÃO

A2 IP7 E90

ESTRÊLA

BAIRRO
ALTO

ALFAMA

ital de
António
apuchos

RESTELO

AJUDA

SANTO
AMARO

ALCÂNTARA

LAPA

Tejo

PEDROUÇOS

BELÉM

AVENIDA DA ÍNDIA

PONTE DO
25 DE ABRIL

Setúbal

Parque das
Nações

0   1 km

0   1 mile

a   b   c

ANJOS

Miradouro Nossa
Senhora do Monte

GRAÇA

Hospital de
São José

Museu Ethnológico
da Sociedade de Geografia

Martim
Moniz

Convento Nossa
Senhora da Graça

Rua Leite de Vasconcelos

Coliseu

Miradouro
da Graça

Igreja
de Graça

Campo de
Santa Clara

Panteão Nacional
de Santa Engrácia

Praça dos
Restauradores

Palácio
Foz

Restauradores

Teatro Dona
Maria II

São Vicente
de Fora

SANTA
APOLÓNIA

ESTAÇÃO CENTRAL
DO ROSSIO

Largo São
Domingos

Rossio

MOURARIA

Castelo de
São Jorge

ALFAMA

Museu Nacional do Azulejo,
Igreja da Madre de Deus

Museu de
Arte Sacra
Igreja de
São Roque

Largo D
Cadaval

Rossio

Praça Dom
Pedro IV

Largo S C do
Castelo

Museu-Escola
de Artes
Decorativas

Santa Luzia

Miradouro
de Santa Luzia

Santa
Apolónia

Museu
Nacional Militar

Museu
Arqueológio
do Carmo

Elevador de
Santa Justa

Largo do
Carmo

Baixa-
Chiado

Santo António
de Lisboa

Largo
São Miguel

Alfândega

Museu e Casa
do Fado

CHIADO

Teatro Nacional
de São Carlos

BAIXA

AUREA

Nossa Senhora
Conceição Velha

Sé
(Catedral)

Casa dos
Bicos

Doca do Terreiro
do Trigo

Largo da
Biblioteca Pública

Museu do
Chiado

Praça do
Município

RUA DA ALFÂNDEGA

AVENIDA

Jardim
do Tabaco

Ministérios

Ministérios

Doca da Marinha

Ministério

Welcome
Center

Cais das
Colunas

Praça do
Comércio

Terreiro do Paço

AVENIDA DA RIBEIRA DAS NAUS

Estação Fluvial
Terreiro do Paço

Gare
Fluvial

Tejo

D   E   F

LISBON STREET INDEX

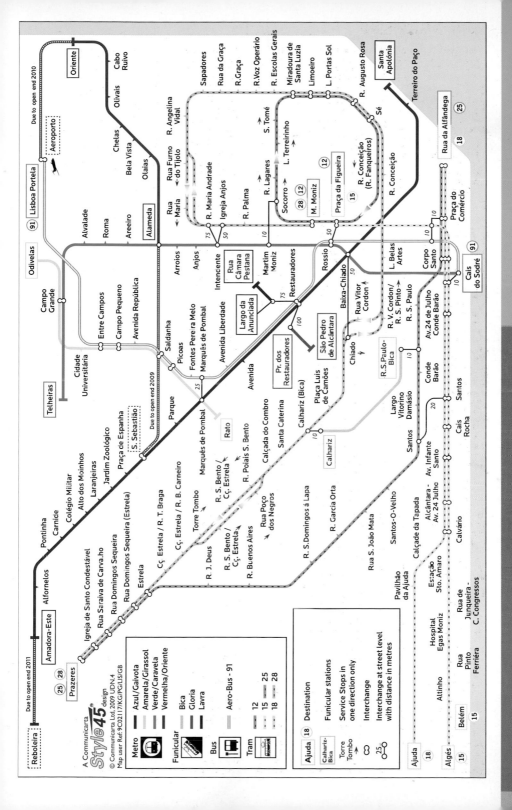

BAIRRO ALTO AND CHIADO

The narrow streets of the Bairro Alto are where you'll find some of Lisbon's best nightlife, while Chiado has traditional shops, stylish cafés and elegantly restored buildings.

BAIRRO ALTO

First laid out in the 1500s, Bairro Alto by day is a quiet residential area that's home to a broad cross-section of *Lisboetas*. It has three pleasant squares: the Largo de Trindade Coelho, bordering the upper Chiado; the Praça Luís de Camões, a square at the southern end of the *bairro* (district); and the Jardim de São Pedro de Alcântara, a garden *miradouro* (viewpoint) with great vistas over the Avenida da Liberdade district. These squares are linked by a maze of alleys and streets, where it's as easy to get lost as in the Alfama (▷ 70–71). Here you will find some of the city's quirkier shops—alternative fashion outlets, music shops and second-hand booksellers near the Trindade. By night it's very different, as thousands of people throng the streets, bars and restaurants. The Bairro Alto is also one of the traditional strongholds of *fado*, Portugal's unique contribution to popular song, and the area still has more than 20 *fado* clubs, some aimed at tourists, others packed with intently listening Portuguese.

CHIADO

This district's focal point is the Largo do Carmo and the main streets of Rua Garrett and Rua do Carmo, which are both lined with some sumptuous stores. Big international names stand alongside traditional Portuguese shops selling luxury goods of all kinds, as well as the pick of the pan-European chain stores and an elegant mall at the bottom of Rua Garrett.

MUSEU ARQUEOLÓGICO DO CARMO

The museum is in the ruins of the Gothic Convento do Carmo, which was destroyed in the 1755 earthquake. The entire nave is open to the sky, with tombs on either side of the main altar. One is the resting place of Ferdinand I; nearby lies Gonçalo de Sousa, chancellor to Henry the Navigator, who is commemorated by a statue on top of his tomb. Among the rest of the eclectic collection, look out for the pre-Columbian mummies, an Egyptian sarcophagus, Iron Age flints and arrowheads, Roman coins and ancient ceramics.
✠ 65 D4 ✉ Largo do Carmo, 1200-092 Lisboa ☎ 213 478 629 ⏰ Apr–end Sep Mon–Sat 10–7; rest of year Mon–Sat 10–6 💷 €2.50

TIP
» Use the *elevadores* to get up the hills.

Above The Igreja de São Roque
Opposite Decorated building in Chiado
Below Typically narrow Bairro Alto street

REGIONS LISBON • SIGHTS

ALFAMA

INFORMATION

www.visitlisboa.com

➕ 65 F4

INTRODUCTION

Although buses and trams serve the area, walking is by far the best option—the labyrinth of narrow alleys cannot be accessed by vehicles in many parts. Begin at the Sé (cathedral), then walk up the hill towards the Graça, before cutting down past Igreja de São Vicente de Fora to explore Lisbon's oldest district. There is plenty to see along the way, including some great photo stops at the *miradouros* (viewpoints). These are also good for a refreshment pause, though you might want to wait and find somewhere for lunch in the Alfama itself. Give yourself the time to explore the district to the full and to take in its buzzing street life.

Under the Moors, this was the grandest area of the city, and this continued during the early years of Christian rule, but a succession of earth tremors caused the nobility to move away, leaving the Moorish character of the district untouched. This can be seen today in its labyrinthine streets, their twists and turns designed to confuse enemies, and the distinctly Arabic latticed window shutters on many houses. Because it is built on rock right against the castle hill, the area suffered relatively little damage in the 1755 earthquake. It still remains a vibrant, heavily populated blue-collar district, though Lisbon's young professionals are starting to snap up top-floor apartments and the number of visitors continues to rise.

WHAT TO SEE

THE SÉ

Lisbon's cathedral—the Sé—stands on the site of the city's main mosque. It was founded by Afonso Henriques in 1150. Like the other great Portuguese Romanesque cathedrals in Évora (▷ 240–243) and Coimbra (▷ 182–185), it's a fortress-like building, redolent of the troubled times when it was constructed. It has been damaged over the centuries by earthquakes, the worst occurring in 1755 when the south tower collapsed and the chancel, chapels and high altar suffered structural and fire damage. Restoration continued on and off into

Above *The red rooftops of Alfama seen from Portas do Sol*

the 19th century, resulting in a building whose Romanesque appearance was virtually lost under baroque and neoclassical additions. This was put right in the 1930s, when the baroque trappings were removed and the rose window and squat towers were restored. Off to the right, you'll find the treasury and cloisters. The latter were built in the 13th century. Traces of Roman Olisipo, Visigothic remains and sections of the mosque's walls have been found here.

🕆 65 E4 ✉ Largo da Sé, 1100-585 Lisboa ⊙ Cathedral: Mon–Sat 9–7, Sun 9–5. Museum and cloisters daily 10–5 ✋ Museum and cloisters: €2.50 🚌 37; Tram: 28, 12

MUSEU-ESCOLA DE ARTES DECORATIVAS

www.fress.pt

Founded in 1947 by the banker Ricardo do Espírito Santo Silva, the Museum of Applied Arts is home to both a great furniture collection and working craft studios—you can buy their products in the museum shop. The collection is beautifully displayed in a series of reconstructed rooms, lavishly decorated with contemporary tiles and *objets d'art*. Other highlights include early Chinese export ware, and some exquisite silverware—don't miss the travelling toilet case, inspired by those in the French court at Versailles, but made in Lisbon.

🕆 65 E4 ✉ Largo das Portas do Sol, 1100-411 Lisboa ☎ 218 881 991 ⊙ Daily 10–5 ✋ €4; 20 per cent reduction with a Lisboa Card 🚌 37; Tram: 12, 28

IGREJA DE SÃO VICENTE DE FORA

A church dedicated to St. Vincent, patron saint of Lisbon, was first built on this site in 1147; in 1580, Philip II brought in his architect Juan Herrera to build something more in the Italian Mannerist style. Severely damaged in the 1755 earthquake, the church was restored and is now one of Lisbon's finest examples of baroque architecture. The soaring nave, with a fine coffered vault, leads the eye up to the gilded high altar with its *baldachino* (canopy), while the walls are decorated with superb tiled panels. In the cloisters, you will find still more tiles decorated with court and hunting scenes from La Fontaine's fables. The refectory is the pantheon of the Bragança dynasty.

🕆 65 F3 ✉ Largo de São Vicente, 1100 572 Lisboa ☎ 218 824 400 ⊙ Church: Tue–Sat 9–5, Sun 9–12.30. Cloisters: Tue Sat 10–5, Sun 10–11.30 ✋ Church: free. Monastery and cloisters: €4 🚌 37; Tram: 12, 28

MORE TO SEE

CASA DOS BICOS

A 1523 merchant's house built by Brás de Albuquerque. Though not open for visits, the house is worth seeing for its façade, which is decorated with *bicos* (pyramidal spikes), after which it is named. When it was restored in 1983, Roman and Moorish remains were found underneath.

🕆 65 E4 ✉ Rua dos Bacalhoeiros 10, Campo das Cebolas, 1100-070 Lisboa
🚌 28, 35, 39, 745, 746, 759, 794

IGREJA DE SANTO ANTÓNIO DE LISBOA

This small baroque church replaced one destroyed in 1755 and reputedly stands on the site of the birthplace of St. Anthony of Padua in 1195. There is an adjoining museum packed with mementoes of the saint.

🕆 65 E4 ✉ Largo de Santo António da Sé, 1100-401 Lisboa ☎ 218 869 145 ⊙ Daily 9–12.30, 3–7 ✋ Free 🚌 37; Tram: 28

PANTEÃO NACIONAL DE SANTA ENGRÁCIA

This church was designated the national pantheon in 1916. There are great views over the Alfama and the Tejo from the dome. The *Feira da Ladra*, Lisbon's flea market, is held outside on Tuesdays and Saturdays.

🕆 65 F3 ✉ Campo de Santa Clara, 1100-471 Lisboa ☎ 218 854 820 ⊙ Tue–Sun 10–5 ✋ €2.50 🚌 Tram: 28

TIPS

» If you get lost in the Alfama don't worry. Simply head downhill to get your bearings; you'll eventually emerge near the waterfront.

» Pickpockets can be a problem, so keep a close eye on your bag, wallet and camera. Narrow, ill-lit and deserted streets and alleys are best avoided after dark.

» It is advisable to catch the tram up to the Graça and walk downhill to avoid having to walk uphill.

Below *Founded in 1150, Lisbon's fortress-like cathedral looks almost as it did in medieval times*

BELÉM

INTRODUCTION

The suburb of Belém, 6km (4 miles) west of central Lisbon, has enough to keep you busy for a whole day. Its monuments and museums are scattered around a fairly wide area beside the Tejo, with views across the river and a plethora of spacious promenades, gardens and water features. The best way to get there is on tram 15 from the middle of the city; or you could take the train from Cais do Sodré on the Cascais line. Remember that almost everything is shut on Mondays and that Sundays, when entrance to some sites is free, can be very busy. Leave time to stroll along the waterfront and enjoy the plants and flowers in Belém's two parks, the tropical Jardim do Ultramarino and the Jardim Botânico da Ajuda.

The area of Belém was once a maritime settlement that was situated right on the water. It was known as Restelo and was quite separate from the city of Lisbon. Manuel I changed its name to Belém in the early 1500s, by which time the district was synonymous with maritime exploration. In 1493 Columbus paused here on his way back to Spain from the Americas, and in 1497 it was the starting point for Vasco da Gama's journey to discover a sea passage to India. The Mosteiro dos Jerónimos was built over the course of the 16th century to give thanks for da Gama's successful voyage.

The Salazar regime revamped the waterfront and laid out the pools and gardens fronting Jerónimos. The Padrão went up in 1960, and in 1992 the Centro Cultural de Belém (▷ 76) was built to mark Portugal's presidency of the European Union. Little remains of old Belém except for the houses on the Rua de Belém, but the area attracts thousands of visitors who come to enjoy the monuments and museums.

WHAT TO SEE

PADRÃO DOS DESCOBRIMENTOS

www.padraodescobrimentos.egeac.pt

The idea for a monument commemorating the great age of Portuguese discoveries was first mooted in 1940 during the Exhibition of the Portuguese World, for which the Belém area was radically reconstructed. The first Padrão was temporary and the swooping white edifice you see today was erected in 1960. The jutting pediment resembles the prow of a Portuguese caravel, with a trio of curving forms behind the wind-filled sails. Its hard lines are softened by the figures crowded on the sloping prow. Dominating them is Henry the Navigator (1399–1460), holding a ship in his hand. Behind him, the 32 other figures include Manuel I, whose reign (1495–1521) coincided with some of the greatest voyages, and Luís de Camões, Portugal's most famous poet. You can take an elevator to the top for great estuary views; the exhibition space inside stages temporary shows on aspects of Lisbon's history. The pavement in front combines a design of a compass and a world map showing the great Portuguese voyages and their dates, making it possible to trace their steady progress south, east and west. It was a gift from South Africa to commemorate the quincentenary of Henry the Navigator's death.

✉ Avenida de Brasilia, 1400-038 Lisboa ☎ 213 031 950 ⏰ May–end Sep daily 10–6.30; Oct–end Apr Tue–Sun 10–5.30 💶 €2.50; free with Lisboa Card and on Sun 10–2 🚌 28, 714, 727, 729, 751; Tram: 15 🚃 Linha de Cascais to Belém ▢

TORRE DE BELÉM

www.mosteirojeronimos.pt

Built between 1515 and 1519, the Torre de Belém, one of Portugal's most potent national symbols, originally stood well out into the river, a fortress

Opposite *The stunning memorial to Portugal's greatest explorers*
Below *Built to guard the approaches to Lisbon, the Torre de Belém now stands at the edge of the Tejo*

designed to safeguard the western approaches to Lisbon's harbour. The great earthquake of 1755 substantially altered the course of the River Tejo, and the Torre today stands on the water's edge, though still surrounded on three sides by the sea. It was designed for Dom Manuel I by Francisco de Arruda, who had previously worked on Portuguese buildings in Morocco, and the Moorish influence is evident in much of the architectural detail, seen at its best in the turrets with their rounded domes. The combination of these elements with Gothic, Venetian and Byzantine touches makes it unique. It is also the only complete example of the Manueline style to survive in Portugal, the others being remodelled earlier buildings or completed at a later date.

Look out for the armillary spheres in the decoration, which represent navigational instruments and were Dom Manuel's personal badge, and the cross of the military Order of Christ of which he was the Grand Master. Don't miss the intricate stone ropework, so typical of Manueline decoration, or the first European sculpture of a rhinoceros under the northwest corner watchtower. There's a serene Gothic statue of the Virgin of Calm Voyages set in a niche on the second-floor terrace—from here, steps lead up to the top of the tower with wide views across the Tejo. You can reach the terraces via the surprisingly plain and unadorned interior, whose chief point of interest is the 'whispering gallery', the acoustics of which amplify the tiniest whisper.

✉ Avenida de Brasília, 1400-038 Lisboa ☎ 213 620 034 🕐 May–end Sep Tue–Sun 10–6.30; Oct–end Apr Tue–Sun 10–5 (last entry 30 mins earlier) 🖐 €4; joint Torre de Belém/Mosteiro dos Jerónimos ticket €8; free with Lisboa Card and on Sun 10–2 🚌 28, 714, 727, 729, 751; Tram: 15 🚉 Linha de Cascais to Belém 🎁 Poor selection of expensive souvenirs

MOSTEIRO DOS JERÓNIMOS

www.mosteirojeronimos.pt

The Mosteiro dos Jerónimos is both the triumphant symbol of Portugal's great seafaring age and Lisbon's finest monument. It was built on the site of an earlier church founded by Henry the Navigator, where Vasco da Gama spent his last night on shore before setting out on his voyage east. Dom Manuel I vowed to erect a larger church if the voyage was successful, though it took until 1551 before the entire complex was more or less complete. The main architects were Diogo da Boitaca, pioneer of the Manueline style, and João de Castilho, a Spaniard. The west door, by Nicolas Chanterene, shows Manuel and his second wife, their patron saints, the four evangelists and the apostles. Look for the Manueline details here and throughout the church and its cloisters. You will also see these on the south entrance, the work of da Boitaca and de Castilho. The central statue is of Prince Henry the Navigator, the bearded figure.

Inside, heavily decorated columns soar towards the superb rib-vaulted ceiling. Under the gallery to the left, you will find the tomb of Vasco da Gama, while that of the poet Luís de Camões lies across the aisle. Da Gama's sarcophagus is supported by lions and decorated with his coat of arms, ropework and six-sailed caravels. Touchingly, he wears a beret with a pompon on top, and his shoes have pompons.

The double-floored cloister is reached by exiting the church. The combination of different architectural influences, the Gothic and Renaissance contrasting with innovative touches such as the recurring anchors, ropes and maritime motifs, makes it a perfect example of Manueline style. The upper floor, besides being the best place to get an overview of the cloister, gives access to the church's organ gallery, well worth taking in for its superb view over the interior of the church and for a close-up of the carving on the columns.

✉ Praça do Império, 1400–206 Lisboa ☎ 213 620 034 🕐 May–end Sep Tue–Sun 10–6; Oct–end Apr Tue–Sun 10–5 (last entry 30 mins earlier) 🖐 Church: free. Cloisters: €6 or €8 for joint Mosteiro/Torre de Belém ticket; free with Lisboa Card, free on Sun until 2pm 🚌 28, 714, 727, 729, 751; Tram: 15 🚉 Linha de Cascais to Belém 🎁 Sells expensive museum reproductions, china and T-shirts from all over Portugal, plus some books (but no guides)

Below *The twin-towered entrance to Museu da Marinha*

MUSEU DA MARINHA

www.museu.marinha.pt

Lisbon's Naval Museum is in the west wing of the Mosteiro dos Jerónimos, to which it moved in 1962 following a fire in its original home in the Arsenal. It's among Europe's finest maritime museums, with a huge collection. In the sections relating to the age of discoveries, you will find fascinating models, globes and maps, as well as the museum's oldest treasure, a polychrome wooden carving of the Archangel Gabriel said to have accompanied Vasco da Gama on his great voyages. The Oriental room also contains astrolabes and instruments for navigating by the stars. Heavily gilded royal barges contrast with deep-sea fishing equipment, and the flying boat flown by two Portuguese pilots across the Atlantic to Brazil in 1922. In the adjoining children's museum, the Museu das Crianças, there are plenty of interactive displays to keep children entertained.

✉ Praça do Império, 1400–206 Lisboa ☎ 213 620 019 🕐 May–end Sep Tue–Sun 10–6; rest of year Tue–Sun 10–5 💷 €3; 25 per cent reduction with Lisboa Card; free on Sun 10–1 🚌 28, 714, 727, 729, 751; Tram: 15 🚊 Linha de Cascais to Belém 🍴 Moderate–expensive 🛍 Expensive museum reproductions, china and T-shirts from all over Portugal, some books (but no guides)

MUSEU NACIONAL DOS COCHES

www.museudoscoches-ipmuseus.pt

Once the Royal Riding School, this richly decorated 18th-century building is now the National Coach Museum. It forms part of the complex of the Palácio do Belém, the official residence of the Portuguese president. Carved gilded wood, painted panels and opulent hangings adorn a huge collection of vehicles. There are also equally impressive displays of sedan chairs, cabs and prams. Examples to look out for include the 18th-century coaches built for the Marquês de Frontes, Portugal's ambassador to the Holy See, a carriage sent by Philip III of Spain in 1619, and a 19th-century English coach, built in London and last used for Queen Elizabeth II's state visit to Portugal in 1957.

✉ Praça Afonso de Albuquerque, 1300–044 Lisboa ☎ 213 610 850 🕐 Tue–Sun 10–5.30 💷 €4; free with Lisboa Card and on Sun 10–2 🚌 28, 714, 727, 729, 751; Tram: 15 🚊 Linha de Cascais to Belém 🛍 Sells expensive museum reproductions, china and T-shirts from all over Portugal, plus some books (but no local guides)

Above *The tranquil and ornate cloisters of the Mosteiro dos Jerónimos are two-floored*

MORE TO SEE

CALOUSTE GULBENKIAN PLANETARIUM

www.planetario.online.pt

Informative shows about the stars and heavens are presented here. Some are slanted towards the use of celestial navigation during the age of discoveries.
✉ Praça do Império, 1400-206 Lisboa ☎ 213 620 002 🕐 Shows: Wed–Thu 4, Sat–Sun 11, 3.30 💰 Adult €4, child (under 17) €2; €2 reduction with Lisboa Card 🚌 28, 714, 727, 729, 751; Tram: 15 🚉 Linha de Cascais to Belém

CENTRO CULTURAL DE BELÉM

www.ccb.pt

A modern cultural venue that stages exhibitions, concerts and live entertainment, the CCB is also home to the Museu Colecção Berardo. This internationally renowned collection includes a permanent exhibition of some 800 works of modern and contemporary art including pieces by Miro, Mondrian, Warhol and Picasso, among others (www.berardomuseum.com; Sat–Thu 10–7, Fri 10–10; free).
✉ Praça do Império, 1499-003 Lisboa ☎ 213 612 400 🕐 Mon–Fri 8–8, Sat–Sun 10–7 💰 Varies according to exhibitions and performances 🚌 28, 714, 727, 729, 751; Tram: 15 🚉 Linha de Cascais to Belém

JARDIM BOTÂNICO TROPICAL

www.iict.pt

Tucked away up a side street to the east of the Jerónimos Monastery is this little-known garden. Established in 1906, it houses a fine collection of tropical and subtropical plants and trees. A good place for a relaxing break from Belém's attractions.
✉ Largo dos Jerónimos, 1400-209 Lisboa ☎ 213 620 210 🕐 May–end Oct Mon–Fri 10–5.30, Sat–Sun 11–5.30; rest of year daily 10–4.30 💰 Adult €1.50, child (8–17) ¢75 🚌 28, 714, 727, 729, 751; Tram: 15 🚉 Linha de Cascais to Belém

MUSEU NACIONAL DE ARQUEOLOGIA

www.mnarqueologia-ipmuseus.pt

For those interested in Portugal's Roman heritage, there are Roman mosaics, sarcophagi and sculpture from all over the country.
✉ Praça do Império, 1400-206 Lisboa ☎ 213 620 000 🕐 Tue–Sun 10–6 (last entry 5.45) 💰 €4; free with Lisboa Card and Sun 10–2 🚌 28, 714, 727, 729, 751; Tram: 15 🚉 Linha de Cascais to Belém

Above *One of the many opulent coaches on display at the Museu Nacional dos Coches*

THE BAIXA

In 1755 Lisbon suffered one of Europe's most catastrophic recorded earthquakes, which killed thousands and destroyed much of the historic heart of the city, including the entire area behind the waterfront. The Marquês de Pombal, Portugal's first minister, decided to rebuild in the style of the time. The result is the Baixa, a carefully planned network of 18th-century streets lined with elegant classical buildings. The main axis is the Rua Augusta, a straight thoroughfare of tiled façades, mosaic pavements and idiosyncratic shopfronts.

PRAÇA DO COMÉRCIO

Rua Augusta leads south through an over-the-top monumental arch, the Arco Triunfal, finally completed in 1873, to the Praça do Comércio, a vast waterfront square that stands on the site of the Terreiro do Paço. Pombal wanted a square that would rival any in Europe, and this space was the result. Lined on three sides with arcades, its fourth side is open to the Tejo, Lisbon's sea gateway.

PRAÇA DOM PEDRO IV

The district's other great open space, the Praça Dom Pedro IV, known simply as the Rossio, owes much to Pombal's 18th-century remodelling. The grand building on the north side is the Teatro Nacional de Dona Maria, built in the 1840s on the site of the old Inquisitor's palace. The statue in the middle is of Dom Pedro IV.

   The Rossio opens out to the northwest into the Praça dos Restauradores and the neo-Manueline façade of Rossio station. At the top you will find the Elevador da Gloria, a ramshackle funicular that links Restauradores with the Bairro Alto.

ELEVADOR DE SANTA JUSTA

Just off the Rua do Ouro, you will find the Elevador de Santa Justa, one of Lisbon's best-loved landmarks. Opened in 1901, the 45m-tall (147ft) elevator was constructed to link downtown Baixa with the Largo do Carmo above. It was designed by Raul Mesnier de Ponsard, a disciple of Gustave Eiffel. The ride up in the elevator gives fantastic views over the Baixa, and the viaduct at the top brings you out beside the ruins of the Convento do Carmo.

TIPS

» Street vendors sell roast chestnuts here in winter.

» Late afternoon is a good time to explore the area and see the streets at their liveliest.

Below *Vast Praça do Comércio stands on the Tejo waterfront*

INFORMATION

www.castelosaojorge.egeac.pt

✚ 65 E3 ✉ Castelo de São Jorge, 1100–129 Lisboa ☎ 218 800 620 ⊘ Tickets: Mar–end Oct 9–8.30; rest of year 9–5.30. Castle and Olisipónia: Mar–end Oct daily 9–8.30; Nov–end Feb daily 9–5.30. Câmara Escura: Mar–end Oct daily 10–5; Nov–end Feb daily 11–2.30 (weather permitting) 💰 Castle: €5 (includes Olisipónia and Câmara Escura); 30 per cent reduction with Lisboa Card 🚌 37; Tram: 28, 12 🍴 Casa do Leão: an elegant and expensive restaurant in one of the surviving rooms of the Alcáçova ☕ Small self-service café with hot and cold drinks, snacks and ice cream 🛍 Small shop with a limited selection of souvenirs

TIPS

» The castle and its gardens are a great place to spend a couple of hours during the hottest part of the day.
» The paving is uneven, so watch your step and wear comfortable, flat shoes.

Below *The view over Lisbon and Castelo São Jorge is spectacular from Esplanada da Igreja da Graca*

CASTELO DE SÃO JORGE

The birthplace of the city is an oasis of peace and cool greenery with superb views over the busy streets and the River Tejo below. If you have time after visiting the Castelo, explore the medieval quarter of Santa Cruz within the outer walls.

The Castelo de São Jorge has long been a defensive stronghold—a fort stood here even before the coming of the Romans in 138BC. They built a citadel on the site of the present castle, from which the Roman city spread down the hill. The Moors built a castle over the earlier Roman fortification with the Alcáçova in the middle—the palace that still stands today. Portugal's kings lived here from 1279 to 1511, moving out only after the construction of the Palácio de Ribeira.

THE RAMPARTS, WALLS AND GARDENS

Topped with battlements and crowned with 10 towers, the inner walls surround two courtyards, from which stairs provide access to the wall-top walkways. Walk along the castle's ramparts for some of the best views over Lisbon and its river. From these you can climb the towers, one of which contains the Câmara Escura, an old-fashioned camera obscura. This gives bird's-eye views of the streets and people far below. More stairs lead down the hill to the outlying Torre de São Lourenço. The entire complex had a thorough facelift before Expo '98, as did the surrounding gardens, and it is now one of the best-kept parts of central Lisbon.

THE ALCÁÇOVA AND OLISIPÓNIA

The Alcáçova was the original Moorish palace, which served as the royal residence from the 14th to the 16th centuries. Little of it remains today and what there is has been heavily restored, but you will get a good idea of its original size and state in the series of chambers now housing the Olisipónia, a multimedia exhibition focusing on the history of the capital.

A series of screens and sound effects leads you through a 25-minute rundown of the city's past, with some good information on Portugal's golden age in the 15th and 16th centuries and some insights into the great earthquake of 1755. Unusually for Portugal, there is an English audio commentary.

CENTRO DE ARTE MODERNA

www.camjap.gulbenkian.pt
Lisbon's modern art complex is part of the Fundação Calouste Gulbenkian (▷ 80–82). You can walk through the grounds from the Gulbenkian Museum to reach it, taking in the outdoor sculpture collection, including works by Henry Moore, along the way. The light and airy modernist building is the perfect setting for the 20th-century art by Portuguese artists, including works by José de Almada Negreiros (1873–1970); look out for his *Self-Portrait* (1925), showing him and friends in the Café A Brasileira in Lisbon. Other artists of note are the Futurists Amadeu de Sousa Cardosa and Guilherne Santa-Rita, and Paula Rego, a contemporary painter.
✚ 65 B1 ✉ Rua Dr. Nicolau de Bettencourt, 1050-078 Lisboa ☎ 217 823 474 ⏰ Tue–Sun 10–6 (last entry 5.45) 👆 Adult €4; museum and temporary exhibitions €5, Modern Art and Gulbenkian (▷ 80) museums plus temporary exhibitions €7; free on Sun 🚇 Praça de Espanha or São Sebastião 🚌 746

MUSEU CALOUSTE GULBENKIAN
▷ 80–82.

MUSEU DO CHIADO
www.museudochiado-ipmuseus.pt
Founded in 1914 as Portugal's national museum of contemporary painting and sculpture, the Museu do Chiado was totally revamped after the Chiado fire of 1988. Reopened in 1994, with a contemporary facelift by the French architect Jean Michel Wilmotte, it now concentrates on Portuguese art between 1850 and 1950. The collection covers every movement, from romanticism, naturalism, modernism and surrealism to abstractionism. Artistically, works such as *A Sesta* by Almada Negreiros and *O Desterrado* by Soares dos Reis are the best, but most visitors will find scenes of Lisbon, such as Carlos Botelho's *Lisboa e o Tejo*, more interesting.
✚ 65 D5 ✉ Rua Serpa Pinto 6, 1200-444 Lisboa ☎ 213 432 148 ⏰ Tue–Sun 10–6

Above *Exhibits at the modernist Centro de Arte Moderna*

👆 €4; free with Lisboa Card 🚇 Baixa-Chiado 🚌 758, 790; Tram: 28

MUSEU NACIONAL DE ARTE ANTIGA
www.mnarteantiga-ipmuseus.pt
Portugal's national art museum is located in a beautifully converted 17th-century palace with a pleasant tranquil garden.
   The Museu Nacional de Arte Antiga is the place to come to see the best of Portuguese painting, enjoy an overview of other European painting schools, and take in a comprehensive collection of furniture, textiles and objects from all branches of the decorative arts. The museum's strengths are its Portuguese paintings and the Far Eastern collections, particularly the examples of late 16th-century Japanese Namban art, dating from the time the Portuguese were in Japan. They arrived there in the early 1500s and stayed until the Japanese closed the country to Europeans.
   Portuguese Painting—Floor 3. This covers the 15th- and 16th-century schools, when Portuguese painting was heavily influenced by Flemish artists such as Jan van Eyck and Rogier van der Weyden. The big names are Nuno Gonçalves, Grégorio Lopes and Frei Carlos. Gonçalves' star piece is the São Vicente Polyptych, a six-panel altarpiece showing a crowd paying homage to St. Vincent, Lisbon's patron saint.
   European Painting—Floor 1 (Ground). The Flemish and German schools are strong here, the Temptation of St. Anthony by Hieronymus Bosch being an outstanding example of that artist's surrealistic style. Look out, too, for works by Cranach, Dürer, Raphael and Zurbarán.
   Far Eastern Art—Floor 2. This is an outstanding collection of decorative art, including porcelain and metalwork, dating from the colonial period in Africa and the Far East. The ceramics and silverware rival the exhibits in the Gulbenkian (▷ 80–82), particularly the Chinese porcelain and the huge steely and lustrous 1756 silver dinner and decorative table service by F. T. Germain of Paris. The 16th-century Japanese screens depict the arrival of the Portuguese in Nagasaki; they are full of quirky European figures with long pointed noses and stork-like legs.
✚ 64 A4 ✉ Rua das Janelas Verdes, 1249-017 Lisboa ☎ 213 912 800 ⏰ Tue 2–6, Wed–Sun 10–6 👆 €4; free with Lisboa Card 🚌 60, 713, 727; Tram: 25

MUSEU CALOUSTE GULBENKIAN

INFORMATION

www.museu.gulbenkian.pt

✚ 65 B1 ✉ Avenida de Berna 45A, 1067-001 Lisboa ☎ 217 823 000

⏰ Tue–Sun 10–6 (last entry 5.45)

🖐 Adult €4; museum and temporary exhibitions €5, Gulbenkian and Centro de Arte Moderna (▷ 79) plus temporary exhibitions €7; audio guide €4; child (12–18) €2, under-12s free ⓜ Praça de Espanha, Saõ Sebastião 🚌 746 🍴 Self-service restaurant serving mediocre food and snacks throughout the day 🍵 Café serving coffee, drinks and snacks; part of the restaurant 🛍 Shop selling a wide selection of art books, almost exclusively in Portuguese, and some good-quality and expensive museum reproduction souvenirs. Some smaller, less expensive objects aimed at children. Postcards and guidebook available.

INTRODUCTION

Lisbon's only world-class museum, housed in a sleek building in lovely gardens, is home to a comprehensive but compact collection of great art, with examples from every century and from all over the world. The Museu Calouste Gulbenkian is part of the Fundação Calouste Gulbenkian, a few minutes' walk north of Parque Eduardo VII. The collection is relatively small, but every exhibit is a superlative example of its type. There is a free leaflet with a floor plan and an audio guide for rent. A complete guidebook can be purchased in the museum shop. The exhibits are clearly laid out in geographical and chronological groups: there are two main sections, one of which is devoted to European art and the other to the art of the ancient and oriental worlds. All the exhibits are labelled in Portuguese and English.

The museum is part of the Fundação Calouste Gulbenkian, a cultural foundation that funds the art collections, the Centro de Arte Moderna (▷ 79), an orchestra, a choir and a ballet company, and runs three concert halls and two exhibition galleries in Lisbon. The foundation is active throughout Portugal, funding museums and libraries and giving charitable grants to a huge range of projects. This is all possible thanks to Calouste Gulbenkian (1869–1955), an Armenian-born oil magnate, who made millions in the Middle East. Art collecting was his passion, and the Museu Calouste Gulbenkian is the result of years of astute buying and a deep pocket. During World War II the British seized control of his assets, and it was neutral Portugal that provided one of the most important 20th-century cultural patrons with a home.

WHAT TO SEE

EASTERN ISLAMIC AND ARMENIAN ART—ROOMS 4 AND 5
Two interconnecting galleries hold the Eastern Islamic and Armenian collections, providing an overview of all that's best from these regions, with particular emphasis on works from the 15th to 17th centuries. The silk and wool carpets, some laid flat, others used as wallhangings, are a high point, as are the numerous examples of wall tiles from the Ottoman Empire—one particularly beautiful 15th-century panel of *faïence* tiles with a turquoise, blue and white underglaze stands out.

Don't miss the Persian and Turkish ceramics, especially the mainly blue-and-white Turkish Izmet bowls. These have a definite Ming influence, probably owing to traders' contact with China as Chinese pottery started to travel west along the so-called Silk Road. An entire case is filled with exquisite Egyptian glass mosque lamps made in the 14th century—gilded, translucent and iridescent, they represent staggering technical expertise for the period in which they were created.

FAR EASTERN ART—ROOM 6
The exhibits include deep Ming bowls with a translucent celadon green glaze, though more eye-catching by far are the Chinese porcelain vases and covered pots, mainly dating from the 17th and 18th centuries. Two outstanding sets are made of enamelled porcelain, one decorated with chrysanthemums in clear pink, turquoise and green on a white ground, the other with pink and green flowers and natural motifs on a black glaze. On the right as you leave the gallery, don't miss the intricate 14th-century Chinese coromandel screen, inlaid with lacquer and paper designs.

EUROPEAN ART—ROOMS 7–17 PAINTING
Highlights from the painting collection include Ghirlandaio's *Portrait of a Young Woman*; she is wearing a pink dress with green sleeves, while her coral necklace draws attention to the delicate wisps of hair around her face. More pretty girls feature in a trio of portraits by the English artists Gainsborough, Romney and Lawrence, while Rembrandt's *Pallas Athene*, a dark depiction of the goddess with a superb shield and plumed helmet, is more sombre. Rubens is represented by a sympathetic portrait of his second wife Helena Fourment, and there is an atmospheric Turner, *The Mouth of the Seine*, all swirling water and pearly tints.

Venice fans shouldn't miss the side room devoted to Guardi—19 real or imagined Venetian scenes, including one showing Palladio's design for the Rialto bridge. Corot, Monet, Renoir and Degas represent the French Impressionists; outstanding here are two winter scenes, a Millet pastel of *Snow-Covered Haystacks* contrasting finely with Monet's *Ice Floating*.

SCULPTURE, FURNITURE AND PORCELAIN
The museum's sculpture collection includes a 15th-century Luca della Robbia medallion from Florence, a Rossellino bas-relief of the Madonna and Child, and Houdon's marble *Diana* (1780).

The French Louis XV and Louis XVI furniture is superb and includes chairs, cupboards, sideboards and inlaid tables, set off by wallhangings and tapestries. There's more French pre-Revolutionary opulence in the shape of silver and gold tableware, together with a large display of Sèvres porcelain, some with a blue and some with a green background glaze.

RENÉ LALIQUE
The final room is devoted to work by the art nouveau jeweller and designer René Lalique, and includes 169 pieces of his jewellery, intricate and sinuous designs embellished with enamel, gold, diamonds, pearls and other gems.

TIPS
» Allow around 2–3 hours for a leisurely visit.
» Leave time to enjoy the fine gardens that surround the Fundação Calouste Gulbenkian's buildings.
» Combine visiting the Gulbenkian with the Centro de Arte Moderna (▷ 79), which is also part of the foundation and situated nearby.

Opposite *The gallery of 18th-century French decorative arts is full of treasures*
Below *Nicholas Houdon's impressive marble statue of* Diana

GALLERY GUIDE

1. Egyptian art
2. Graeco-Roman art
3. Mesopotamian art
4. Oriental-Islamic art
5. Armenian art
6. Art from the Far East
7. Work in ivory; Illuminated manuscripts
8. 15th-, 16th- and 17th-century painting and sculpture
9. Renaissance art
10. 18th-century decorative art: France
11. 18th-century painting and sculpture: France
12. 18th- and 19th-century silverwork: France
13. 18th- and 19th-century painting: England
14. Paintings by Francesco Guardi
15. 19th-century painting and sculpture: France
16. and 17. Works by René Lalique

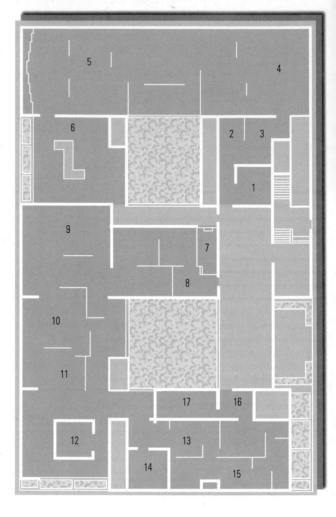

Egyptian Art—room 1

A small collection of superlative quality—look for a 16th-century BC carved ivory spoon; a relief stela, showing an offering being made to the Pharaoh (1580BC); and bronze cats (664–525BC).

Graeco-Roman Art—Room 2

Highlights here are an Attic Greek vase (450BC) decorated with scenes of chariots and games, the Roman iridescent glassware, a Greek silver pitcher (third century BC) and intricate Roman jewellery (second century BC– fourth century AD)

Mesopotamian Art—Room 3

Look out for an Assyrian bas-relief from the palace of Assurbanipal in Nimrud showing a bearded warrior wearing a feather-trimmed cape (ninth century BC).

Ivories and Illuminated Manuscripts—Room 7

Medieval Books of Hours, missals and gospels, all lavishly embellished and decorated.

Left Decorated tiles adorn the gardens of Palácio dos Marquêses de Fronteira

MUSEU FUNDAÇÃO ORIENTE

www.museudooriente.pt

Behind the imposing 1940's façade of the renovated Pedro Alves Cabral building is a collection dedicated to the Portuguese presence in Asia and the breathtaking Kwok On collection. Comprising more than 12,000 pieces, the Kwok On focuses on performing art forms from across Asia and includes masks, shadow and puppet theatres, costumes and musical instruments.

🚇 Off map 64 A5 ✉ Avenida de Brasília, Doca de Alcântara, 1350-362 Lisboa ☎ 213 585 200 🕐 Wed–Mon 10–6 (last entry 5.30), Fri 10–10 (last entry 9.30) 💷 Adult €4, child (6–12) €2, under 6 free, family €9; free Fri 6–10 🚌 12, 28, 714, 738, 742; Tram 15, 18 🚆 Linha de Cascais to Alcântara

MUSEU NACIONAL DO AZULEJO AND IGREJA DA MADRE DE DEUS

www.mnazulejo-ipmuseus.pt

The museum traces the history of the *azulejo* (tile) from the 15th century to the present day. Highlights include the Lisbon cityscape, prior to the 1755 earthquake. There are more stunning *azulejos* in the adjoining church.

🚇 Off map 65 F4, 65 C1 ✉ Rua da Madre de Deus 4, 1900-312 Lisboa ☎ 218 100 340 🕐 Tue 2–5.30, Wed–Sun 10–5.30 💷 €4; free with Lisboa Card 🚇 Arroios then 🚌 794

PALÁCIO DOS MARQUÊSES DE FRONTEIRA

This small, pink country house was originally built in the 1670s, more than 130 years after St. Francis Xavier supposedly said Mass in the chapel before his voyage to India. The palace was damaged in the 1755 earthquake, so what you see today dates from the late 18th century. It's particularly noted for its *azulejos* (tiles), which decorate both the interior of the house and the gardens. The big attraction inside is the Sala das Batalhas, where tiled panels illustrate battles against the Spanish during the 1640–68 Wars of Restoration. The gardens are laid out in the Italian Renaissance style, with parterres, topiary and fountains.

🚇 65 B1 ✉ Largo de São Domingos de Benfica, 1500-554 Lisboa ☎ 217 782 023 🕐 Palace: guided tours only. Jun–end Sep 10.30, 11, 11.30, noon; rest of year Mon–Sat 11, noon. Gardens: Mon–Sat 2.30–4.30 💷 Palace and gardens: €7.50. Gardens: €3 🚇 Sete Rios then 🚌 70

PARQUE EDUARDO VII AND THE ESTUFAS

www.cm-lisboa.pt

There's no better place to spend tranquil hours than in Lisbon's main park, the Parque Eduardo VII, at the northern end of the monumental Avenida da Liberdade. It opened in 1903, the year Edward VII of England visited Portugal to reconfirm the Anglo-Portuguese alliance (in existence since 1382), and was named in his memory. The layout is formal in the extreme, revolving around two broad mosaic-paved walkways, intersected by minor paths, lined with trimmed hedges. The big neo-baroque building by the eastern entrance is the Pavilhão Carlos Lopes, a sports pavilion renamed in memory of Portugal's marathon champion. Walk north from here for some great city views and to explore the *estufas* (greenhouses). Three interconnect, the *estufa fria* (coldhouse), the *estufa quente* (hothouse) and the *estufa doce* (containing plants that thrive in arid conditions). Opened in 1930, they are crammed with flowers, shrubs and trees, planted around ponds and fountains.

🚇 126 B1 ✉ Praça Marquês de Pombal 1070-099 Lisboa ☎ 213 882 278 🕐 Estufas: May–end Sep daily 9–5.30; Oct–end Apr daily 9–4.30 💷 €1.61 🚇 Marquês de Pombal 🚌 All Avenida da Liberdade services

PARQUE DAS NAÇÕES

▷ 84–87.

RIBEIRA MARKET

www.espacoribeira.pt

You will get a real taste of Lisbon life around the Ribeira market and Cais de Sodré—everyone shops here. Cais de Sodré is a main transport hub. From here you can take a train to Estoril and Cascais, the metro or a ferry across the Tejo. The station is opposite Ribeira market, Lisbon's main food market. The best range of goods is on show in the late morning when the food market is still in full swing and the flower sellers are setting up.

West of the market, much of the waterfront has been redeveloped, and the trendy bars and restaurants are popular with joggers and skateboarders. A couple of blocks away, you will find the Bica, with its stylish eateries and food stores. Take the Elevador da Bica from the Rua de São Paulo in Santos to Calçada do Combro in the Bairro Alto before strolling to Miradouro da Santa Catarina, a popular meeting place, with wonderful views.

🚇 64 C5 ✉ Avenida 24 de Julho, Cais de Sodré, 1200-479 Lisboa ☎ 213 244 980 🕐 Mon–Sat 5am–2pm 🚆 Cais de Sodré

PARQUE DAS NAÇÕES

INTRODUCTION

It's an easy journey by metro to the state-of-the-art Oriente station in the Parque das Nações, from where you have only to walk through the huge and tempting Vasco da Gama shopping mall to reach the park itself. The site is rambling, and distances can be deceptive, but judicious use of the miniature train and the cable car will help you to get around. Aim to visit the Oceanário before the queues build up, then spend the rest of the day exploring everything else. Although the crowds are thinner during the week, the atmosphere is best at the weekends when thousands flock here to enjoy the attractions and wander along the waterside promenades. You can also visit the park without going into Lisbon, as it's easily accessible from the motorway system.

Until the early 1990s the area now containing the Parque das Nações was an industrial wasteland, scarred by derelict warehouses, an oil refinery and the municipal abattoir. The site was chosen as the hub of Expo '98, Lisbon's international World's Fair, which launched the country firmly into the European mainstream. The fair ran from May to September 1998 and was a huge success, attracting many thousands of visitors.

Once Expo closed, the site was reopened as an urban district and given its present name. Construction around the park is ongoing, with the ultimate aim of creating a large-scale and well-planned residential and business zone, focused around the existing park and its huge riverside gardens. The area contains two of Lisbon's largest concert venues and a multitude of shops, cafés and restaurants. It is served by excellent public transport links via Santiago Calatrava's stunning Estação do Oriente rail, metro and bus station.

WHAT TO SEE

OCEANÁRIO

www.oceanario.pt

Designed by the American architect Peter Chermayeff, the Oceanário opened in 1998 as part of Expo '98. Its role was to provide Lisbon with a permanent reminder of the Expo by linking the country's maritime past with the future role of the oceans. The building crouches on the water's edge like some futuristic underwater machine, but it's the marine life inside that attracts the crowds.

INFORMATION

www.parquedasnacoes.pt

➕ Off map 65 C1 ✉ Alameda dos Oceanos, 1990-223 Lisboa ☎ 218 919 333 🚇 Oriente line to Oriente 🚌 28

Above *Oriente station was built for Expo '98*

Opposite *Some of the inhabitants of the Oceanário*

The huge central tank, visible from two levels, contains more than 7 million litres (1.8 million US gallons) of salt water and is inhabited by a range of fish and sea creatures from the world's oceans—sharks, rays and great schools of smaller fish living at different depths. This is surrounded by four areas representing various oceanic ecosystems: the Atlantic, the Antarctic, the Pacific and the Indian. These exhibits have both above- and below-water habitats, allowing visitors to see birds, animals and vegetation typical of these zones above ground as well as the marine life under the water. The puffins and guillemots in the Atlantic zone are very popular, as are the Magellan penguins hopping around the snow in the Antarctic zone and the fish-eating sea otters of the Pacific. All these creatures can be viewed underwater once you reach the lower level, where sunlight filters through the water onto the weeds and coral, and shoals of fish glide by.

Additional tanks cover sea habitats as diverse as living coral reefs to mangrove forests. Highlights here are the Australian dragon fish, their camouflage so perfect that they're almost impossible to detect against the seaweeds they live in; the luminous tropical jellyfish; vivid anemones and an astounding range of crabs. There are more than 15,000 animals and plants here, with around 450 different species represented. Educational interactive exhibits include information on sea fishing, ocean products, currents, winds, tides and conservation. Everything is clearly labelled in both Portuguese and English.

✉ Esplanada D. Carlos 1, Doca dos Olivais, 1990-005 Lisboa ☎ 218 917 002/6 ◷ Summer daily 10–8 (ticket office closes at 7pm); winter daily 10–7 (ticket office closes at 6pm). Summer/winter schedules change with the hour change ◷ Adult €11, child (4–12) €5.50, under-4s free, family €26.50; tickets can be booked online ◷ Oriente ◷ 28 ◷ Illustrated floor plan in English free ◷ Excellent shop selling a wide range of ocean-related books, souvenirs, stationery and stuffed toys

PAVILHÃO DO CONHECIMENTO—CENTRO DA CIÊNCIA VIVA
www.pavconhecimento.pt
This is another great attraction for families. It's a science park that aims—and succeeds—in getting the message across to ordinary people that science and technology are fun. There are plenty of permanent interactive exhibits, ranging from how holograms work to technology in everyday life, while children can spend hours in the cybercafé with its free Internet access.

Run by the Portuguese Ministry of Science and Technology, the site also has thematic exhibitions, drawing on the resources of the world's major scientific institutes. Highlights among these are the Unfinished House, designed by the Cité des Sciences in Paris, San Francisco's Exploratorium, and the See, Do, Learn display jointly conceived by the universities of Cardiff and Helsinki. All of these are interactive exhibits and learning zones where visitors can enjoy a real hands-on experience of science at its liveliest. Everything is clearly labelled in both English and Portuguese.

✉ Alameda dos Oceanos, Parque das Nações, 1990-223 Lisboa ☎ 218 917 100 ◷ Tue–Fri 10–6, Sat–Sun 11–7 ◷ Adult €7, child (7–17) €4, (3–6) €2.50, under-2s free, family €15 ◷ Oriente ◷ 28 ◷ Explanatory English leaflet €1.50 ◷ Good book and gift shop with plenty of reasonably priced souvenirs

THE WATERFRONT AND GARDENS
The Tejo is up to 10km (6 miles) wide here and walkways, planted with shrubs and trees from Portugal's former colonies, run all along the water's edge from west of the Oceanário to beyond Ponte Vasco da Gama. At weekends, thousands of locals flock here to relax and enjoy the fine views; during the week, though, it's one of the city's most peaceful areas. Don't miss the Jardim da Agua, where ponds are linked by stepping stones and jet fountains spray cooling water.

Below The striking Sun Man *sculpture by Jorge Viera*

MORE TO SEE

ARCHITECTURE

Parque das Nações has several buildings of architectural note. Don't miss Siza Viera's Pavilhão de Portugal with its hanging cement awning meant to resemble a sheet of paper or the mushroom-like Pavilhão Atlântico.

CABLE CAR

A cable car runs the length of the waterfront between the Oceanário and the Torre Vasco da Gama, with a bird's-eye view of the park.

✉ Parque das Nações, 1990 Lisboa 🕒 Jul–end Sep daily 11–8; rest of year daily 11–7
🖐 One way: adult €3, child (4–13) €1.65, under-4s free. Round trip: adult €6, child (4–13) €3.30, under-4s free

JARDINS DA ÁGUA

To the west of the Oceanário is this charming water garden where a series of walkways and bridges takes you past trickling streams, water channels, fountains and jets.

✉ Passeio de Ulisses, Parque das Nações, 1990-288 Lisboa 🖐 Free

PAVILHÃO ATLÂNTICO

www.pavilhaoatlantico.pt

This is Portugal's largest indoor arena, used for sport, conferences and concerts.

✉ Rossio dos Olivais, 1990-231 Lisboa ☎ 218 918 409

TEATRO CAMÕES

www.cnb.pt

Home to Portugal's Companhia Nacional de Bailado (national dance company), this very modern theatre offers a varied programme. Check at the box office.

✉ Passeio de Neptuno, 1990-193 Lisboa ☎ 218 923 477

Above *The oceanarium, built for Expo '98 and one of the world's finest*
Below *Torre Vasco da Gama observation tower marks one end of the waterfront cable car*

THE CHIADO AND BAIRRO ALTO

On this varied walk in and around the Alfama quarter of the city, you'll take in some of Lisbon's ritziest stores as well as getting the chance to ride on the celebrated funiculars.

THE WALK
Distance: 2.4km (1.5 miles)
Time: 1 hour without stops, 2–2.5 hours with visits
Start/end at: Praça dos Restauradores

★ Start in Praça dos Restauradores with the Palácio Foz on your left and walk round the corner to the Elevador da Gloria.

❶ The *elevador*, opened in 1885 as the second funicular railway to be built in the city, links the Bairro Alto with downtown Lisbon. Take your seat for a real Lisbon experience and turn left at the top of the steps when you get off.

Walk straight down Rua de São Pedro de Alcântara, keeping the side wall of the Igreja de São Roque to your left.

❷ The opulent Church of São Roque, with its sumptuous painted wooden ceiling, was built in the late

16th century by the Jesuits. The most ornate of the side chapels is the one dedicated to St. John the Baptist, which was built in Rome and shipped to Lisbon after receiving a special papal blessing in 1749.

Turn left in front of the church and walk around the square to the far corner, where you'll see a flight of steps. Go down these, then take the second turning right along the Rua da Condessa, a quiet street with small workshops and a couple of bars. This street leads onto Largo do Carmo.

❸ Largo do Carmo is an attractive square with benches and acacias, and is home to the Museu Arqueológico do Carmo.

Walk through the square and head down Calçada do Sacramento until it meets Rua Garrett, where you turn right.

❹ Rua Garrett is one of Lisbon's ritziest shopping streets. Walk uphill, taking in the wonderfully traditional shopfronts along here and the elaborate façade of the Basílica dos Mártires across the way.

Just past the Mártires is Rua Serpa Pinto. You could detour right down it to visit the Museu do Chiado, or stay in Rua Garrett and pause for a drink or coffee at the Café A Brasileira at No. 120, famous for its literary associations (▷ 99).

With the café behind you, cross the road, walk through Largo do Chiado and head along Rua Duques de Bragança. A short way along you'll see Largo São Carlos below you on the left. Take the steps down to the square, which is dominated by the façade of the Teatro Nacional de São Carlos.

❺ The Teatro Nacional de São Carlos is Lisbon's opera house, built in the late 18th century and taking La Scala in Milan as its architectural model. It has a marvellous rococo interior, which you can experience during the winter opera season (▷ 95).

Past the theatre, continue straight ahead down Rua do Capelo, then turn left onto Rua Ivens, a fine street lined with harmonious early 19th-century buildings. This will take you back to the Rua Garrett. Turn right and you'll see the modern Chiado shopping area ahead.

❻ The Chiado shopping area was built during the reconstruction that followed a catastrophic fire in 1988. The design of the rebuilt district is by Alvaro Siza Vieira, a Porto-based architect who succeeded admirably in retaining a touch of tradition in this historic neighbourhood.

Turn left at the bottom of Rua Garrett and walk down Rua do Carmo, another classy shopping street. The viaduct of the Elevador de Santa Justa can be seen overhead.

❼ The Elevador de Santa Justa is a street elevator, designed in 1901

by a follower of Gustave Eiffel, the builder of Paris's Eiffel Tower, to link the Baixa with the Largo do Carmo above. The walkway from the elevator to the square was reopened a few years ago, and when you take the elevator up there are some great views—turn right down the steps to the entrance.

At the bottom of Rua do Carmo, bear right onto the Rossio. You can simply walk up through the square to return to your starting point, bearing left past the station, or lengthen the walk by turning right and crossing Rua Aurea, Rua dos Sapateiros and Rua Augusta to reach Praça da Figueira. Turn left here and walk through the square, then take another left turn to bring you back onto the Rossio—and thence back to Praça dos Restauradores.

WHERE TO EAT
A Brasileira, on Rua Garrett, is great for snacks (▷ 99), while Cervejaria Trindade on Rua Nova da Trindade is good for prawns and ice-cold beer (▷ 99).

WHEN TO GO
During shopping hours is a good time for the walk as some of Lisbon's best shops provide temptation en route.

PLACES TO VISIT
IGREJA DE SÃO ROQUE AND MUSEU DE ARTE SACRA
✉ Largo Trindade Coelho, 1200-470 Lisboa
☎ 213 235 381 ⊗ Church: Mon–Fri 8.30–7, Sat–Sun 9.30–5. Museum: Due to reopen after refurbishment early 2009

MUSEU ARQUEOLÓGICO DO CARMO
(▷ 69)

MUSEU DO CHIADO
(▷ 79)

Above *Interior of the church of São Roque*
Opposite *Stylish art deco shopfronts in the Baixa*

THROUGH LISBON'S ALFAMA DISTRICT

On this varied walk in and around the Alfama, Lisbon's oldest quarter, you'll have the opportunity to visit several historic churches as well as enjoying some of the city's best views.

THE WALK

Distance: 3.7km (2.3 miles)
Time: 1–1.5 hours without stops, 2–4 hours with visits
Start at: Praça do Comércio
End at: The Sé

★ Set off in Praça do Comércio with your back to the water, and turn left in the far right-hand corner to walk up Rua da Prata. Take the first right down Rua do Comércio and cross Rua dos Fanqueiros. Then take the first left and second right (following the brown signpost) uphill. You'll see the church of La Madalena on the right; follow the curve of the street up to the right onto Rua de Santo Antonio da Sé.

Straight ahead you'll soon see the façade of the Sé (▷ 70–71). The cathedral's oldest parts date from 1150, when building on it started. Keeping the cathedral on your right, continue to walk uphill following the path of the tramlines along Rua da Augusta da Rosa.

❶ On Rua da Augusta da Rosa, the high wall on your right conceals the Law School, part of the University of Lisbon.

Continue uphill through Largo de São Martinho onto Rua do Limoeiro, then climb up the steps on the right next to the grassy bank to reach a *miradouro* (viewpoint) with a splendid view.

❷ The Miradouro de Santa Luzia takes its name from the tiny church of Santa Luzia, whose exterior is decorated with 18th-century *azulejos* (tiles). Look out for the scene depicting Praça do Comércio. From the viewpoint, the domes and spires to the left are those of the Igreja de São Vicente de Fora (▷ 71). The steps opposite lead up to the Castelo de São Jorge (▷ 78).

Continue round the left-hand side of the church and walk up to Largo das Portas do Sol, home to the Museu-

Escola de Artes Decorativas, housed in what was once a 17th-century palace (▷ 71), another *miradouro* with river views, and a statue of St. Vincent. Follow the road—and the tramlines—uphill, forking right and keeping to the cobblestones until you see a brown *miradouro* sign pointing to the right up Calçada da Graça. This street climbs fairly steeply to the Igreja da Graça, from where there's an outstanding view of the city below.

❸ The Graça church was founded in 1271 to house a sacred image of the Virgin, and enlarged in the 16th century. The great Lisbon earthquake of 1755 destroyed the original church; the present one is late 18th-century rococo. It's a real neighbourhood church, the scene of fervent Lenten processions. Have a peep inside before enjoying the views, which take in the castle, the River Tejo and its bridges, and the rooftops of the Baixa. The façade of

Rossio station is easy to pick out, and you'll notice the easy-to-spot dome of the Estrela church on the skyline.

With the Graça church behind you, walk along the south side of Largo da Graça and take a right, down the steps and onto Rua da Voz do Operário—look for the tramlines again as a guide. Walk downhill along the street until you get to the Igreja de São Vicente de Fora to the left.

❹ The Church of São Vicente de Fora is dedicated to Lisbon's patron saint. According to legend, this fourth-century AD figure was martyred in Spain and his body found its way to Portugal in a boat guided by two ravens, making landfall at Cabo de São Vicente in the far southwest. His remains were brought to Lisbon in 1173.

Continue downhill, following the tramlines round to the right. About 300m (330 yards) on, where the road swings right, cross over and walk down the Escadinhas das Escolas, a long flight of steps. At the bottom of the steps turn right onto Largo do Salvador, where you fork left and head downhill. These steep, narrow streets penetrate right into the heart of the historic Alfama district (▷ 70).

❺ The Alfama is Lisbon's oldest quarter, Moorish in appearance and consisting of a warren of alleyways called *becos* and *travessas*. It is full of vibrant life, much of it played out in the streets and squares.

Continue down to a tiny square with the Centro Paroquial de Alfama across the corner on the right; turn right next to this and head along a row of shops. You'll emerge onto Largo São Miguel.

❻ Largo São Miguel is another small square, with a church on the right and a solitary, lofty palm tree planted in its middle.

Walk across the square, keeping the church on the right, and carry straight ahead onto Rua de São Miguel. This becomes Rua de São João da Praça, named after the unpretentious 18th-century church along it. Bear left along the side of the church, gradually heading uphill. In a few minutes you will emerge along the southern side of the cathedral.

WHERE TO EAT
There is lots of choice, but try Lautasco in the Beco do Azinhal, with its lovely shaded patio, or Malmequer-Bemmequer in the Rua São Miguel.

WHEN TO GO
This is a good walk at almost any time in daylight hours, except perhaps in the middle of the day. Many people claim the *miradouro* at the Graça is the best place in Lisbon from where to enjoy the sunset.

PLACES TO VISIT
IGREJA DE SÃO VICENTE DE FORA
(▷ 129)

IGREJA DA GRAÇA
✉ Largo da Graça, 1170-165 Lisboa
☎ 218 873 943 🕐 Tue–Fri 9.30–12.30, 3–6, Sat–Sun 9.30–12.30, 3–8 ✋ Free

Opposite *A tile detail from Santa Luzia shows pre-earthquake Lisbon*
Below *Lisbon's great medieval cathedral*

WHAT TO DO

SHOPPING

A CARIOCA

This superb coffee house opened its doors in 1936 and is, to this day, one of the city's best. Behind its original façade and fittings, it sells all manner of coffee, freshly ground or as whole beans, plus some fine teas and a tempting selection of quality chocolate products.

✉ Rua da Misericórdia 9, Bairro Alto, 1200-270 Lisboa ☎ 213 420 377 ⏰ Mon–Fri 9–7, Sat 9–1 ⓜ Baixa-Chiado

ALFAIATARIA NUNES CORRÊA

Named after its founder, and opened in 1856, this classic men's outfitter clothed the men of Portugal's royal family for more than half a century and dictated fashion among high society. Come here for quality off-the-rack and bespoke suits and shirts.

✉ Rua Augusta 250, Baixa, 1100-056 Lisboa ☎ 213 240 930 ⏰ Daily 10–7 ⓜ Rossio

ANA SALAZAR

www.anasalazar.pt

Probably Portugal's best-known fashion designer, Ana Salazar set up her own label in the 1980s and opened a Paris showroom in 1985.

Her designs often make intriguing use of stretch fabrics in neutral tones of grey, earthy browns and soft maroons.

✉ Rua do Carmo 87, 1200-093 Lisboa ☎ 213 472 289 ⏰ Mon–Sat 10–7 ⓜ Baixa-Chiado

AZEVEDO RUA

The place for hats of every kind. A family business since 1886, this Baixa institution has original wood cabinets, stuccoed ceilings and a vast inventory, including Panamas, straw hats, berets, bonnets, tams and bowlers. It is one of the few remaining hatters to make tri-horned bullfighter hats.

✉ Praça Dom Pedro IV 69–73, Baixa, 1100-202 Lisboa ☎ 213 427 511 ⏰ Mon–Fri 9.30–7, Sun 9–1 ⓜ Rossio

CASA DAS VELAS LORETO

This shop has been selling candles since 1789. The small, teak-and-mahogany interior is lined with glass cabinets full of every size and shade of candle: religious, moulded, scented, large and small. All are produced on the premises.

✉ Rua do Loreto 53, Bairro Alto, 1200-241 Lisboa ☎ 213 425 387 ⏰ Mon–Fri 9–7, Sat 9–1 ⓜ Baixa-Chiado 🚋 Tram 28

Above *Coliseu dos Recreios*

CASA HAVANESA

Despite its inconspicuous façade and dated interior this tobacconists and gift shop has been a reference point since its opening in 1861. Frequented by the most refined and the most humble of Lisbon clientele, it features in novels by Eça de Queiros' and Ramalho Ortigão. For many years it acted as an informal bank offering loans alongside its cigars. In 1876 the Bank of Portugal is said to have turned to the Havanesa to exchange bank notes for gold. Today, among other things it sells hand-rolled cigars and fine smoking paraphernalia.

✉ Largo do Chiado 24, Chiado 1200-108 Lisboa ☎ 213 420 340 ⏰ Mon–Fri 10–7, Sat 10–1 ⓜ Baixa Chiado

CENTRO COMERCIAL AMOREIRAS

www.amoreiras.com

The oldest of the city's malls is housed in the post-modern Torres das Amoreiras. Despite there now being many malls, it remains popular with Lisboetas, who think it is more refined than the newer mega-malls. It also has a multiscreen cinema.

Avenida Duarte Pacheco, 1070-103 Lisboa ☎ 213 810 200 🕙 Daily 10am–11pm 🚇 Marquês de Pombal, Rato 🚌 48, 53, 58, 83, 711

CENTRO COMERCIAL COLOMBO
www.colombo.pt
To the north of the city, this terracotta temple to modern consumerism stands opposite the Benfica stadium. When completed in the late 1990s, it was the biggest mall in Portugal and Spain housing three floors of shops, galleries, food halls and entertainments, including a roller-coaster.
✉ Avenida Lusíada, 1500-392 Lisboa ☎ 217 113 600 🕙 Daily 9am–midnight 🚇 Colégio Militar

CENTRO COMERCIAL VASCO DA GAMA
www.centrovascodagama.pt
At the Expo '98 site east of the heart of the city, the Vasco da Gama mall has all the main chain stores, plus a few smaller names. Avoid weekends when it gets really crowded.
✉ Parque das Nações, Avenida Dom João II, 1990-094 Lisboa ☎ 218 930 600 🕙 Daily 10am–midnight 🚇 Oriente

CONFEITARIA NACIONAL
Founded in 1829 and selling all kinds of delicious confectionery, this store is worth a visit just for its interior. The wood-and-glass cabinets and antique mirrors make the perfect setting for the rows of tempting goodies made to traditional recipes. The tasty almond cookies are particularly good.
✉ Praça da Figueira 18-B, 1100-241 Lisboa ☎ 213 424 470 🕙 Mon–Sat 8–8 🚇 Rossio

EL CORTE INGLÊS
www.elcorteingles.pt
The gigantic El Corte Inglês department store, part of the Spanish chain, offers a full range of quality and designer items: clothing, accessories, perfumes and cosmetics, electrical appliances and household goods. In the basement there is a gourmet delicatessen section, restaurants and a

multiscreen cinema showing films in their original language.
✉ Avenida António Augusto de Aguiar, 1069-413 Lisboa ☎ 213 711 700 or 707 211 711 🕙 Mon–Thu 10–10, Fri–Sat 10am–11.30pm 🚇 São Sebastião 🚌 2, 12, 746

FEIRA DA LADRA
This is the city's main flea market, selling the usual junk: old record-players, car stereos and old trinkets passed off as genuine antiques. It also has records, CDs and lots of South Americans selling their crafts.
✉ Campo de Santa Clara, Graça, 1100 Lisboa 🕙 Tue 8am–1pm, Sat all day 🚋 Tram 28

JOSÉ ANTÓNIO TENENTE
www.joseantoniotenente.com
After working under Ana Salazar, Tenente opened his own store in 1990. Since then he has become one of the country's leading international designers. His cotton shirts and suits are popular, thanks to their sleek, innovative design, as is his fabulous selection of stylish accessories.
✉ Travessa do Carmo 8, Chiado, 1200-095 Lisboa ☎ 213 422 560 🕙 Mon–Sat 10.30–7.30 🚇 Baixa-Chiado

LIVARIA BERTRAND
www.bertrand.pt
This bookstore, Portugal's oldest, was founded in 1773 and still retains much of its 19th-century interior. Most books are in Portuguese, but it's a good place to find coffee-table picture books on a variety of Portuguese themes that make excellent gifts or souvenirs.
✉ Rua Garrett 17, Chiado, 1200-203 Lisboa ☎ 213 476 122 🕙 Mon–Sat 9am–10pm, Sun 11–8 🚇 Baixa-Chiado

LUVARIA ULISSES
Opened in 1925, this tiny shop retains its period interior and the personal service of days gone by. It has a fine selection of gloves in leather, silk, satin and cashmere.
✉ Rua do Carmo 87a, Chiado, 1200-093 Lisboa ☎ 213 420 295 🕙 Mon–Sat 10–7 🚇 Rossio

MANUEL TAVARES
www.manueltavares.com
On the southeast corner of Praça da Figueira, this traditional grocery store and deli has been in business since 1860. The original decorative wooden shelves are crammed full of products from around the country: cheese, wine, dried fruits, Madeira honey cake and a very tempting counter loaded with elaborate confectionery.
✉ Rua da Betesga 1A, Baixa, 1100-090 Lisboa ☎ 213 424 209 🕙 Mon–Sat 9.30–7.30 🚇 Rossio

MERCADO ABASTECEDOR DA RIBEIRA
Lisbon's largest covered market is just down from the Cais do Sodré station and is one of the city's most important fresh fish outlets. It is also excellent for a range of other fresh produce, including fruit, vegetables and regional cured meats and cheeses.
✉ Avenida 24 de Julho, Cais do Sodré, 1200-479 Lisboa ☎ 213 244 980 🕙 Mon–Sat 6am–2pm 🚇 Cais do Sodré

OURIVESARIA W. A. SARAMENTO
Often known by its old name of Rua do Ouro (Gold Street), this street was traditionally home to jewellers and goldsmiths. W. A. Saramento, founded in 1870, is still producing fine filigree and stonework, and has some exquisite pieces of jewellery on display.
✉ Rua da Áurea 251 (also known as Rua do Ouro), 1100-062 Lisboa ☎ 213 426 774 🕙 Mon–Fri 10–1.30, 3–7, Sat 10–1 🚇 Baixa-Chiado

PARIS EM LISBOA
In the exclusive Rua Garrett in the Chiado, it is hard not to notice the sinuous and wonderful art nouveau exterior of this textile shop, which is just as grand inside as it is out. In business since 1888, it now specializes in quality towelling products made in factories in northern Portugal.
✉ Rua Garrett 77, Chiado, 1200-203 Lisboa ☎ 213 424 329 🕙 Mon–Sat 10–7 🚇 Baixa-Chiado

RETROSARIA BIJOU

This lovely art deco shop offers a glimpse of how shopping for haberdashery once was, with its old wooden counters and personal service. Founded in 1922, it stocks buttons, ribbons, cords and threads.
✉ Rua da Conceição 91, Baixa, 1100-152 Lisboa ☎ 213 425 049 🕐 Mon–Fri 9.30–7, Sat 9–1 🚇 Baixa Chiado

ROSA AND TEIXEIRA

Amid the stylish designer shops of the Avenida da Liberdade, this popular boutique is one of the most highly regarded classical menswear stores in the city. In addition to their own-label off-the-rack clothing, they offer bespoke tailoring and a long line-up of designer names.
✉ Avenida da Liberdade 204, 1250-147 Lisboa ☎ 213 110 350 🕐 Mon–Sat 10–7.30 (Aug Mon–Fri only) 🚇 Avenida

SANTOS OFÍCIOS

www.santosoficios-artesanato.pt
This shop, opened in 1995 to promote quality, hand-selected crafts, is housed in an 18th-century stable. Representing all regions of Portugal, it stocks an eclectic mix of pottery, rugs, embroidered linens, figurines, tiles and sculptures. A full shipping service is available.
✉ Rua da Madalena 87, Baixa, 1100-319 Lisboa ☎ 218 872 031 🕐 Mon–Sat 10–8 🚋 Tram 28

SOLAR

Rua Dom Pedro, leading into Rua do Alecrim, is home to many antiques shops; one of the best known is Solar, with a fine collection of salvaged, hand-painted tiles, some of which date back to the 15th century. There is also good furniture and pewter ware.
✉ Rua Dom Pedro V 68–70, Bairro Alto, 1250-094 Lisboa ☎ 213 465 522 🕐 Mon–Fri 10–7, Sat 10–1 (Jul–end Aug Mon–Fri only) 🚇 Restauradores then Gloria elevator 🚌 758, 790

VISTA ALEGRE

www.vistaalegre.pt
Producing exquisite porcelain since 1824, Vista Alegre is renowned for its high-quality, classic designs. Its luxury headquarters spotlights them in a lavish setting composed of polished marble and glass. There are also smaller branches in all the major city malls.
✉ Largo do Chiado 20–23, Chiado, 1200-108 Lisboa ☎ 213 461 401 🕐 Mon–Sat 10–7 🚇 Baixa-Chiado

VIÚVA LAMEGO

www.viuvalamego.com
To buy similar *faïence* tiles to those that grace many façades, try the central outlet of the Sintra-based Viúva Lamego tile factory. They specialize in the reproduction of 16th- to 18th-century motifs.
✉ Largo do Intendente 25, 1100-285 Lisboa ☎ 218 852 408 🕐 Mon 12–7, Tue–Fri 10–7, Sat 10–1 🚇 Intendente

ENTERTAINMENT AND NIGHTLIFE

BUDDHA

www.buddha.com.pt
If you are dining or drinking at one of the Doca's restaurants and bars, this club across the road is a convenient place to end the evening. Housed in a 1940s' maritime terminal the décor is of Asian influence with lots of exotic wood, low tables and Buddhas. Deep house music leads to chilled sounds in the lounge.
✉ Gare Marítima da Alcântara 30, Docas, 1350-049 Lisboa ☎ 213 950 555 🕐 Tue–Thu 10pm–4am, Fri–Sat 10pm–6am ✋ Charge at discretion of doorman 🚌 28, Tram 15

CASINO DE LISBOA

www.casinolisboa.pt
Opened in 2006, this is the latest addition to Lisbon's busy nightlife scene. Situated opposite the Oceanarium in the Parque das Nações, its minimalist architecture makes it hard to miss. Choose from around 1,000 slot machines, game floors, theatre, music and dance shows, bars and restaurants.
✉ Alameda dos Oceanos, Parque das Nações, 1990-204 Lisboa ☎ 218 929 000 🕐 Fri–Sat and day before national holiday 4pm–4am, Sun–Thu 3pm–3am 🚇 Oriente 🚌 28

CHAPITÔ

http://chapito.org
This relaxed restaurant and outdoor bar just below the castle has exceptional views over the city. Next door is a circus school, so there are often juggling, tap-dancing and clowning shows as well as live bands from 11pm Thursday to Saturday.
✉ Rua Costa do Castelo 1–7, 1149-079 Lisboa ☎ 218 855 550 🕐 Bar (Bartô) Tue–Sun 10pm–2am. Restaurant (Restô) Mon–Fri 7.30pm–2am, Sat–Sun 12pm–2am 🚌 37; Tram 12, 28

COLISEU DOS RECREIOS

www.coliseulisboa.com
Opened in 1890, this was one of the first public buildings in Portugal to use wrought iron, both in its structure and as an architectural feature. A little faded yet still grand, it frequently hosts ballet performances and contemporary music concerts.
✉ Rua Portas de St. Antão, 1150-269 Lisboa ☎ 213 240 585 🕐 Box office: Mon–Sat 1–7.30 or until half an hour after start of performance 💰 €20–€100 🚇 🚇 Restauradores 🚌 36, 44, 91, 709, 711, 732, 745

DOCA DE ALCÂNTARA

This converted dockside warehouse under the 25 de Abril bridge houses a selection of restaurants and bars, with terraces looking over the marina. Try Doca de Santo, which has live music from Sunday to Thursday nights.
✉ Alcântara, 1350-352 Lisboa 🕐 Restaurants: 12–2.30, 7.30–10.30. Bars: 9pm–2am or later at weekends 🚇 Alcântara 🚌 28; Tram 15

EL CORTE INGLÊS

www.uci.pt
A cinema complex in the basement of the huge department store shows all the latest blockbusters in their original language. A small supplement buys a VIP ticket, which entitles you to a pre-film drink and priority seating.
✉ Avenida António Augusto de Aguiar, 1069-413 Lisboa ☎ 707 232 221 🕐 Ticket

office: daily 1.30pm–12.30am 🖑 €5.70, VIP €7.50 🚇 ⬛ Ⓢ São Sebastião 🚌 2, 12, 746

FUNDAÇÃO CALOUSTE GULBENKIAN
www.gulbenkian.pt
The most important cultural venue in the country, the Gulbenkian Foundation has its own orchestra and choir, which stages regular performances throughout the year. It also hosts national and international art exhibitions.
✉ Avenida da Berna 45A, 1067-001 Lisboa ☎ 217 823 030 🕐 Box office: Mon–Fri 10–7, weekends of performances 1–start of performance 🖑 €10–€60 🚇 ⬛ Ⓢ São Sebastião 🚌 746

HOT CLUB
www.hcp.pt
Opened more than 60 years ago, the Hot Club is Lisbon's best choice for dedicated jazz enthusiasts. With live shows every week, many great names have played gigs here.
✉ Praça da Alegria 39, 1250-004 Lisboa ☎ 213 467 369 🕐 Tue–Sat 10pm–2am 🖑 €7–€15 (concert days) Ⓐ Avenida

INSTITUTO DA CINEMATECA PORTUGUESA
Housed in a late 19th-century house just off the Avenida da Liberdade, Portugal's national film theatre screens contemporary Portuguese films and international classics.
✉ Rua Barata Salgueiro 39, 1250-042 Lisboa ☎ 213 596 262 🕐 Mon–Sat 12.30pm–12.30am; tickets 2.30–3.30, 6–10 🖑 €2.50 🚇 ⬛ Ⓐ Avenida

LONDRES
www.castellolopescinemas.com
If you are fed up with multiplexes and in search of a taste of yesteryear try to catch a film at Cinema Londres. Choice will be limited with only two screens but Hollywood's best offerings pass through and there are some excellent neighbourhood cafés for after-movie snacks.
✉ Avenida Roma 7A, 1000-010 Lisboa ☎ 707 220 220 🕐 Ticket office daily 2.30pm–12.30am 🖑 €5.50 Ⓡ Roma

LUX
www.luxfragil.com
Just past the Santa Apolónia train station, this nightspot is one of Lisbon's hippest. It attracts a mixed but sophisticated crowd as its three different floors each play their own style of music. In summer there is an open terrace overlooking the River Tagus.
✉ Avenida Infante D. Henrique, Armazém A, Cais da Pedra, Santa Apolónia, 1950-376 Lisboa 🕐 Tue–Sat 10–6 🖑 Charge at discretion of doorman 🚌 745, 759, 781, 794

PAVILHÃO ATLÂNTICO
www.pavilhaoatlantico.pt
Built for Expo '98 within the Parque das Nações complex, this blue, mushroom-like pavilion plays host to big international stars, rock concerts, Broadway shows and international sporting events.
✉ Rossio dos Olivais, Parque das Nações, 1990-231 Lisboa ☎ 218 918 409 🕐 Box office: daily 1–7 or until half an hour after start of performance. Tickets also available at FNAC stores around the city that accept credit cards, and ABEP and Alvalade (▷ 311–312) 🖑 €20–€120 depending on show 🚇 Estação do Oriente 🚌 28

SÉTIMO CÉU
Always keeping up with the latest trends in both interior decoration and music, Sétimo Céu is one of the most popular gay bars in the city. It specializes in excellent Brazilian *caipirinha* cocktails—*cachaça* (sugarcane liquor), sugar and limes on ice.

✉ Travessa da Espera 54, Bairro Alto, 1200-176 Lisboa ☎ 213 466 471 🕐 Mon–Sat 10pm–2am 🚇 Restauradores then Glória elevator 🚌 758; Tram 28

SOLAR DO VINHO DO PORTO
www.ivp.pt
This 18th-century mansion is home to the Port Wine Institute, established in 1933 to control port quality and promote the drink around the world. Its club-like atmosphere makes it an ideal place to try the many ports on offer. You can take a tutored tasting of port wine, or choose your own to sample.
✉ Rua de São Pedro de Alcântara 45, Bairro Alto, 1250-237 Lisboa ☎ 213 475 707 🕐 Mon–Sat 11am–midnight 🖑 Prices per glass start at €1 🚇 Baixa-Chiado, Restauradores then Glória elevator

TEATRO NACIONAL DE SÃO CARLOS
www.saocarlos.pt
The Teatro Nacional de São Carlos opened in 1793. The splendid gold leaf and red auditorium has been the stage for the country's most prestigious opera productions and major symphony concerts ever since it opened.
✉ Rua Serpa Pinto 9, Baixa, 1200-442 Lisboa ☎ 213 253 045 🕐 Box office: Mon–Fri 1–7 or until half an hour after start of performance. Opera season: Sep–end Jun 🖑 €20–€100 🚇 ⬛ Ⓢ Baixa-Chiado 🚌 758, 790; Tram 28

Below *Browsing at Ladra flea market*

SPORTS AND ACTIVITIES

CARRIS-TUR

www.carristur.pt

Take a panoramic, open-top bus ride around the city's main sights, starting on the eastern side of the Praça do Comércio. Or try one of their lovingly restored, early 20th-century wooden trams, complete with their original brass fittings, which will take you along the city tram routes.

✉ Praça do Comércio, 1100-148 Lisboa ☎ 213 582 334 🕐 Departure times are regular but they do vary. For tickets and information see the above address or go to the tourist information office 🚇 Baixa–Chiado

CITYLINE

www.cityline-sightline.pt

The most frequent and comprehensive city tours are offered by multinational giant Cityline, starting at its Marquês de Pombal terminus by the park. Some of the more popular routes are the Avenida, Baixa, Belém and Estrêla, before returning to the Marquês de Pombal.

✉ Avenida Duque d'Avila 116B, 1050-084 Lisboa 🕐 Apr–end Oct, every 30 min between 9 and 6; Nov–end Mar departures every 60 min between 10 and 5, Fri–Sat departures more frequent 🖐 Adult €15, child (6–11) €7.50, under-5s free 🚇 Marquês de Pombal

CLUBE DE GOLFE PAÇO DO LUMIAR

www.golfepacodolumiar.pt

If you don't want to leave the city to tee-off then this course, to the north of the city centre, offers nine holes as well as a driving range. Its attractive clubhouse is home to an elegant restaurant overlooking the course which serves traditional Portuguese cuisine.

✉ Quinta dos Alcoutins, Rua Principal, Lumiar, 1600 Lisboa ☎ 217 591 719 🕐 Mon 10–7, Tue 8.30–8, Wed and Fri 8.30am–9pm, Thu 8.30am–10pm, Sat 8–8, Sun 8–7 🖐 18 Holes €35 weekday, €40 weekend, club rental €20, buggies €25 🚇 Lumiar then taxi or bus 3 to Estrada Velha do Paço de Lumiar

ESTÁDIO DE ALVALADE

www.sporting.pt

Home ground to Sporting Lisbon, this green-and-white-tiled stadium seats 54,000. The complex includes restaurants, bars, a bowling alley and cinemas. For match information see the local press or the club's official website.

✉ Sporting Clube de Portugal, Edifício Visconde de Alvalade, Rua Professor Fernando da Fonseca, 1600-616 Lisboa ☎ 707 204 444 🕐 Ticket office: daily 12.30–7.30, match days 10am–half time 🖐 €12–€40 for standard games 🚇 Campo Grande 🚌 78, 767

ESTÁDIO DA LUZ

www.slbenfica.pt

The Estádio da Luz (Stadium of Light) is the home of Benfica soccer club. For match information see the local press.

✉ S. L. Benfica (club), Avenida General Norton de Matos, Benfica, 1501-805 Lisboa ☎ 707 200 100 (general and tickets) 🕐 Ticket office: daily 10–7, match days 10–half time 🖐 €15–€40 🚇 Colégio Militar-Luz 🚌 3, 750, 767

PRAÇA DE TOUROS

www.campopequeno.com

For a chance to appreciate the renowned horsemanship of Portuguese bullfighters, the restored 19th-century neo-Moorish bullring at Campo Pequeno is worth a visit in season. Note that in Portugal, unlike in Spain, the bulls are not killed in the ring, but are skilfully wrestled to the ground.

✉ Campo Pequeno, Avenida João XXI– Avenida da República, 1969 Lisboa ☎ 217 820 575 🕐 Season: May–end Sep. Bullfights: Thu 10pm 🖐 €20–€50 according to the line-up 🚇 Campo Pequeno 🚌 36, 108, 732, 745

TEJO BIKE

www.parquedasnacoes.pt

A great way to get around the Parque das Nações is by bicycle. Rent one from outside the Pavilhão Atlântico or the Oceanário. Children's equipment is available.

✉ Rossio dos Olivais, Parque das Nações, 1990-231 Lisboa ☎ 218 919 333

🕐 15 Apr–15 Sep daily 10–8, 16 Sep–14 Apr Mon–Fri 12–6, Sat–Sun 10–6 🖐 Adult €2.50 for 30 min, €4 for 1 hour, child €2 for 30 min, €3 for 1 hour 🚇 Oriente 🚌 28

TRANSTEJO

www.transtejo.pt

These river cruises take two-and-a-half hours and are a superb way of seeing the city from a different perspective. The fabulous view of Lisbon's hills, dotted with churches and the castle, is especially good in late afternoon, when the light is generally fantastic. The commentary on the boat is in English, French and Spanish.

✉ Estação Fluvial do Terreiro do Paço, Praça do Comércio, 1100-148 Lisboa ☎ 808 203 050 or 218 824 671 🕐 Apr–end Oct daily 3pm 🖐 Adult €20, child (5–12) €10, under-5s free 🚇 Baixa-Chiado 🚌 9, 45, 732, 746, 759

HEALTH AND BEAUTY

FOUR SEASONS HOTEL RITZ LISBON SPA

www.fourseasons.com

The Ritz has one of the most luxurious spas in the city. It offers a full range of treatments including salt and oil scrubs, facials and wraps. There is also a pool, sauna and Turkish bath.

✉ Rua Rodrigo da Fonseca 88, 1099-093 Lisboa ☎ 213 811 400 🕐 Daily 6.30am–10.30pm, treatments 8–8. Reserve in advance 🖐 Varies depending on treatment. Salt and oil scrub €80, facials €120–€160 🚇 Marquês de Pombal

FOR CHILDREN

FUNCENTER

www.funcenter.pt

If the weather is poor and children need entertaining the Funcenter could be a good option. Housed on the top floor of the gigantic Colombo shopping mall (▷ 93) it offers a 24-lane bowling alley, soft-play area, snooker, arcade games and an indoor roller-coaster.

✉ Loja A-206, Centro Comercial Colombo, Avenida Lusíada, 1500-392 Lisboa ☎ 217 113 700 🕐 Sun–Thu noon–midnight, Fri–Sat noon–2am 🖐 Each activity is individually priced 🚇 Colégio Militar

JARDIM ZOOLÓGICO

www.zoolisboa.pt

Home to some 400 species, Lisbon zoo is set in lovely gardens and has a variety of attractions to entertain children. There are dolphin and sea-lion shows, a birds of prey and macaw presentation, hands-on farm animals and a cable car.

✉ Praça Marechal Humberto Delgado, Sete Rios, 1500-423 Lisboa ☎ 217 232 910 🕓 Apr–end Sep 10–8; Oct–end Mar 10–6 👆 Adult €15, child €11.50, under-3s free 🚇 Jardim Zoológico 🚌 16, 54, 70, 746, 758, 768 🚉 Sete Rios

OCEANÁRIO

www.oceanario.pt

This cleverly designed oceanarium (▷ 85–86), one of the largest in Europe, is not to be missed. It has a huge central tank that can be viewed from two different floors, and is home to countless sea creatures, such as manta rays, sharks and eels. Four smaller tanks house more species from four different oceans.

✉ Esplanada D. Carlos 1–Doca dos Olivais, Parque das Nações, 1990-005 Lisboa ☎ 218 917 002 or 218 917 006 🕓 Summer 10–7; winter 10–6 👆 Adult €11, child (4–12) €5.50, under-4s free, family €26.50; 1 free visit with Cartão do Parque 🚇 Oriente 🚌 28

TELEFÉRICO

www.parquedasnacoes.pt

Running about 20m (65ft) above the ground from the Torre de Vasco da Gama towards the Oceanário, Lisbon's cable car gives amazing views of the river, the Ponte Vasco da Gama and the whole of the Parque das Nações. You will see the Torre Vasco de Gama stretching up 140m (458ft) into the sky, Lisbon's tallest building.

✉ Parque das Nações, 1990 Lisboa ☎ 218 919 333 🕓 Jul–end Sep daily 11–8; rest of year daily 11–7 👆 Adult one way €3, return €6, child (5–15) one way €1.65, return €3.30, 1 return trip free with Cartão do Parque 🚇 Oriente 🚌 28

Right *A model shows clothes by designer Osvaldo Martins at the Lisboa Fashion Week, Modalisboa, in March*

FESTIVALS AND EVENTS

FEBRUARY
CARNAVAL

Celebrated throughout Portugal with fireworks and parades, Carnaval in Lisbon is based around the Avenida da Liberdade, where a long-planned parade of bright costumes, samba dancers and decorated floats makes its way along the avenue.

☎ 210 312 810 (tourist office) 🕓 Date varies

MARCH
MODALISBOA

www.modalisboa.pt

Held in various venues around the city, this is Lisbon's most important and spectacular fashion event. Shows and other fashion-related activities are spread over several days, attracting all the top national designers and international models and celebrity names from New York, Paris, Milan and London. This event is also held in October.

☎ 213 213 000 🕓 Dates vary, usually end Mar (check website)

APRIL
ESTORIL OPEN TENNIS CHAMPIONSHIPS

www.estorilopen.net

Held at the Jamor sports venue, to the west of the city, the Estoril Open is Portugal's top tennis competition, attracting many international players.

✉ Club de Tenis do Complexo, Desportivo do Jamor, 1495 Cruz Quebrada ☎ 800 211 010 🕓 Early Apr

MAY
ROCK IN RIO LISBOA

This is Lisbon's largest and longest running summer music festival held at the Parque de Belavista and attracting big international names such as Amy Winehouse, Bon Jovi and Rod Stewart.

🕓 Last weekend May–first weekend Jun 👆 Daily tickets include several stages and line-ups €53 🚇 Belavista 🚌 22, 794

JUNE
FESTAS DOS SANTOS POPULARES

These are some of the city's traditional festivals. Alfama, Mouraria and Madragoa are decorated with bunting and host all sorts of events.

☎ 210 312 810 (tourist office) 🕓 Jun

SANTO ANTÓNIO

Held in honour of Lisbon's patron saint and marking the beginning of the Festas dos Santos Populares; Alfama's streets are decorated and host sardine barbecues.

🕓 12–13 Jun

DECEMBER
LISBON MARATHON

www.lisbon-marathon.com

Approximately 3,500 runners embark on a circuit around the city, starting and finishing in the Praça do Comércio. The half-marathon runs on the same day. You must register in advance to participate (tel 213 616 160).

☎ 210 312 810 (tourist office) 🕓 Date varies, usually at beginning Dec

EATING

z

RESTAURANTE ⬇

PRICES AND SYMBOLS

The restaurants are listed alphabetically. The prices given are the average for a two-course lunch (L) and a three-course dinner (D) for one person, without drinks. The wine price is for the least expensive bottle. All the restaurants listed accept credit cards unless otherwise stated.

For a key to the symbols, ▷ 2.

ALI-À-PAPA

With a warm candlelit interior, somewhat reminiscent of a Bedouin tent, the Moroccan Ali-à-Papa offers a limited but quality menu late into the night. *Tagine moderbel*, made with lamb and fried aubergines (eggplant), is always in great demand, as is the exotic *couscous tifaya*, made with lamb and raisins and spiced with cinnamon. For vegetarians, the vegetable and chickpea couscous is an excellent choice. To finish, you could try the yoghurt mousse with condensed milk, lemon and strawberries. It's advisable to reserve during the summer months.
✉ Rua da Atalaia 95, Bairro Alto, 1200-038 Lisboa ☎ 213 474 143 ⏱ Wed–Mon 7–midnight 🍴 D €17, Wine €10 🚇 Baixa-Chiado

ANTIGA CONFRARIA DE BELÉM

www.pasteisdebelem.pt
A visit to Belém would not be complete without stopping at this nationally famous establishment for a coffee and *pastel de nata* (custard tart). Not even the owners of this cake shop know the secret recipe that produces the crisp pastry for these egg-custard-filled tarts, which has been guarded by the master pastry-makers since 1837. Served warm out of the oven, the tarts should be liberally sprinkled with the icing sugar and cinnamon provided.
✉ Rua de Belém 84–92, Belém, 1300-085 Lisboa ☎ 213 637 423 ⏱ May–end Oct daily 8–noon; Nov–end Apr Mon–Sat 8–11, Sun 8–10 🍴 €1.50 for custard tart and coffee 🚌 28, 714, 727, 729, 751; Tram 15 🚊 Belem

ANTIGO 1° DE MAIO

The menu of this informal regional eatery changes from day to day, but often includes *açorda* (bread-based stew), fried squid or fresh tuna. Finish with caramel cream or forest-fruits tart. The service is friendly and the selection of wines good.
✉ 1° de Maio, Rua Atalaia 8, Bairro Alto, 1200-041 Lisboa ☎ 213 426 840 ⏱ Mon–Fri 12–3, 7–10.30, Sat 7–10.30.

Above Customers at A Brasileira café in the Chiado district

Closed first 3 weeks in Aug 🍴 L €15, D €20, Wine €8 🚇 Baixa-Chiado

BICA DO SAPATO

www.bicadosapato.com
Bica do Sapato is one of the trendiest of Lisbon's trendy restaurants, at a prime dockside location just across from the Santa Apolónia train station. With its inviting riverfront terrace and its super-modern interior, Bica do Sapato encompasses three varied and different eating areas: the restaurant, offering the popular *sugestão da semana* (dish of the week); the café, serving traditional Portuguese dishes; and the sushi bar, where on Wednesday the fixed-price *dia dos sabores* (day of flavours) menu is good value.
✉ Avenida Infante Dom Henrique, Armazém B, Cais da Pedra, Santa Apolónia, 1900-001 Lisboa ☎ 218 810 320 ⏱ Restaurant: Mon 8pm–11.30pm, Tue–Sat 12–2.30, 8–11.30. Café: Mon 5pm–1am, Tue–Sat 12–3.30, 7.30–1. Sushi bar: Mon–Sat 7.30pm–1am 🍴 L €30, D €50, Wine €12 🚊 Terreiro do Paço 🚌 745, 759, 781

A BRASILEIRA

This Chiado café is one of Lisbon's most venerable coffee houses, complete with original wooden and mirrored interior. Once the retreat of artists and writers, such as 20th-century poet Fernando Pessoa (whose statue stands outside), the café continues to serve excellent coffee and cakes. The terrace is a good place to watch the world go by.

✉ Rua Garrett 120, Chiado, 1200-024 Lisboa ☎ 213 469 541 🕐 Daily 8am–2am ✋ €9 for light snack and drink 🚇 Baixa-Chiado

BÚFALO GRILL

www.bufalogrill.com.pt

Meat-lovers should not miss a visit to this excellent Brazilian *rodízio*, where every possible cut of prime South American beef is brought in a constant flow to your table. There's also an amazing hot and cold salad bar, as well as a dessert buffet of tropical fruits, cakes and sweets. Frequent live music shows add to the Brazilian atmosphere.

✉ Rossio dos Olivais, Parque das Nações, 1990-231 Lisboa ☎ 218 922 740 🕐 Daily 12.30–3, 7.30–12 ✋ Full *rodízio* with salad buffet €18.95; dessert buffet €4.50; weekdays lunchtime *rodízio* €14.30; desserts €3.30, Wine €11 🚇 Oriente

CASA DA COMIDA

www.casadacomida.pt

From outside, the 'House of Food' seems somewhat unimpressive, but pass the doorman and descend the wooden staircase and you enter a sophisticated eatery. In the dining rooms the food is traditional Portuguese with a French twist. Clam soup, anglerfish with leek and lemon, or duck with olives are all regulars. The wine list is good and the place serves delicious desserts.

✉ Travessa das Amoreiras 1 (off Avenida Alexandre Herculano), 1250-025 Lisboa ☎ 213 885 376 🕐 Tue–Fri 1–3, 8–11, Sat and Mon 8pm–11pm ✋ L €26, D €35, Wine €14 🚇 Rato 🚌 758, 709

CASA DO BACALHAU

If it's a *bacalhau* experience you want, try the former brick-vaulted stables of the count of Lafões just beyond the Santa Apolónia train station. There are more than 20 salt-cod dishes to choose from. Start with a *bacalhau* broth or a plate of *pataniscas* (salt-cod fritters) then move on to *bacalhau* with corn bread. There is a good selection of *bacalhau*-free desserts as well, such as the *sericaia com ameixas* lemon and cinnamon cake from the Alentejo served with Elvas plums.

✉ Rua do Grilo 54, 1900-706 Lisboa ☎ 218 620 000 🕐 Mon–Sat 12–3, 8–11 ✋ L €25, D €30, Wine €8 🚌 742

CASANOVA

In a converted warehouse, across the road from the Santa Apolónia train station, this genuine Italian eatery is an inexpensive alternative to a characterless fast-food joint. There is an extensive range of pizzas on offer, all thin crust and cooked in a traditional pizza oven in front of you. You can also enjoy fine crostini, bruschettas and other traditional Italian dishes, such as Neapolitan sausage with beans, or mozzarella with aubergine (eggplant).

✉ Avenida Infante Dom Henrique, Armazém B, Cais de Pedra, Santa Apolónia, 1900 Lisboa ☎ 218 877 532 🕐 Tue–Sun 12.30pm–1am ✋ L €14, D €18, Wine €8 🚇 Terreiro do Paço 🚌 745, 759, 781

O CASEIRO

This restaurant near the Jerónimos monastery is attractive yet unpretentious. Simply grilled fish and meat, or more elaborate dishes such as oven-roasted lamb or *açorda de marisco* (bread stew with prawns), come in generous portions. Try the almond pudding to finish.

✉ Rua de Belém 35, 1300-083 Lisboa ☎ 213 638 803 🕐 Mon–Sat 12–3, 7–10.30. Closed Aug ✋ L €16, D €22, Wine €9 🚌 714, 727, 732, 759; Tram 15 🚆 Belém

CERVEJARIA TRINDADE

www.cervejariatrindade.pt

In business since 1836, this restaurant and beer hall is one of the city's oldest. The food here is nothing particularly out of the ordinary—grilled beef fillets, omelettes and fresh, though somewhat overpriced, seafood. However, the place itself is a classic Lisbon landmark. Housed in what was once a convent, it has vaulted ceilings, magnificent tile panels and noisy crowds that make it worth a visit, even if it's just for a quick, ice-cold *imperial* (a small glass of beer). There is a non-smoking section.

✉ Rua Nova da Trindade 20c, Bairro Alto, 1200-303 Lisboa ☎ 213 423 506 🕐 Daily midday–1am ✋ L €13, D €23, Wine €6.50 🚇 Baixa-Chiado 🚌 758, 790; Tram 28

CHÁ DA LAPA

This is an ideal place for a quiet lunch or afternoon tea if you are visiting the Museu Nacional de Arte Antiga (▷ 79). It is half tea room, half belle époque restaurant, decorated with red velvet sofas, wood panelling and printed wallpaper, where everything is freshly made. At lunchtime they offer a couple of *pratos do dia* (dishes of the day), and there are mouth-watering cakes and desserts. The apple pie and cheesecakes are particularly worth trying.

✉ Rua do Olival 8–10, Lapa, 1200-742 Lisboa ☎ 213 900 888 🕐 Daily 9–7. Closed last 2 weeks in Aug 🚌 60, 713, 727; Tram 25 🚆 Santos 🚌 Turn right out of museum then left up right side of square. At top turn right. Chá da Lapa is on the left

A CHARCUTARIA

The owner-chef of the Charcutaria started cooking originally for friends but was persuaded to open to the public. Natural tones with light wooden panelling, brick arches and basketware chairs create a calming atmosphere. Choose from game dishes, such as miniature partridge pies and hare with beans, or stick to old stalwarts like *carpaccio de bacalhão* (salt cod). Finish with the highly prized *doces conventuais*—desserts with eggs and lots of sugar, originally made in convents.

✉ Rua do Alecrim 47A, Bairro Alto, 1200-014 Lisboa ☎ 213 423 845 🕐 Mon–Sat 12.30–3, 7.30–11 ✋ L €25, D €35, Wine €12 🚇 Baixa-Chiado 🚌 758, 790

CLUBE DE JORNALISTAS

This restaurant, with its verdant flower-filled patio, provides some of the best outdoor dining in the city. The terrace is open for lunch and light snacks throughout the day while the two indoor dining rooms serve a Mediterranean menu emphasizing local seasonal produce. Begin with *pão com azeite*, large slices of rustic bread with a splash of olive oil, then try duck with air-cured ham and *fines herbes*. The *delirium de chocolate* for dessert lives up to its name.

✉ Rua das Trinas, 129-r/c (ground floor), Lapa, 1200-857 Lisboa ☎ 213 977 138
🕐 Mon–Sat 12.30–3, 7.30–12 🖐 L €36, D €44, Wine €10 🚌 60, 727; Tram 25
🚋 Santos

COMIDA DE SANTO

www.comidadesanto.com.pt
Off the Rua da Escola Politécnica, this lively Brazilian restaurant brings a touch of the jungle to the Lisbon scene. It specializes in deceptively powerful *caipirinha* cocktails made with limes and *cachaça* (sugar-cane liquor). Brazilian dishes, such as chicken *muquecas*, cooked in coconut milk, and delicious *feijoada* (pork and black bean stew) accompanied by toasted manioc and orange, are served in generous portions. Try fresh mango and papaya to finish. There are only 12 tables, so reservations are essential.

✉ Calçada Engenheiro Miguel Pais 39, Rato, 1200-172 Lisboa ☎ 213 963 339
🕐 Daily 12.30–3.30, 7.30–1 🖐 L €20, D €35, Wine €8 🚋 Rato 🚌 758

CONVENTUAL

On one of the prettiest squares in town, this place offers some of the best dining in the city. Decorated with antique and modern sacred art, it continues the religious theme in the names of some of its dishes, such as Pope of Avignon snails, and its excellent *doces conventuais*, egg and sugar puddings traditionally made by convent nuns. The *arroz de pato* (duck with rice) is superb.

✉ Praca das Flores 44–45, Rato, 1200-192 Lisboa ☎ 213 909 246 🕐 Tue–Fri

12.30–3.30, 7.30–11, Sat, Sun, Mon and national holidays 7.30–11. Closed Aug
🖐 L €25, D €35, Wine €10 🚋 Rato
🚌 758

ENOTECA – CHAFARIZ DO VINHO

www.chafarizdovinho.com
Off the Praça da Alegria, Chafariz do Vinho is an excellent place for a tapas-style meal of cured ham, spicy sausages, cheeses and a good bottle of wine. Alternatively, there's the *menu de prova*, which offers a choice of three dishes plus dessert.

✉ Rua Mãe d'Água/Praça da Alegria, 1250-000 Lisboa ☎ 213 422 079
🕐 Tue–Sun 6pm–2am. Closed 23 Dec–10 Jan 🖐 D €25, Wine €14 🚋 Avenida

GAMBRINUS

www.gambrinuslisboa.com
In a street packed with restaurants, Gambrinus is the best and most expensive. With its comfortably sedate interior, it's popular with politicians, journalists and other Portuguese celebrities. Sit at the bar or in one of the two dining rooms and choose from a huge selection of seafood, fresh fish, meat and game.

✉ Rua Portas de Santo Antão 23, Baixa, 1150-264 Lisboa ☎ 213 421 466 🕐 Daily noon–1.30am 🖐 L €35, D €50, Wine €18
🚋 Restauradores

EL GORDO

For a taste of neighbouring Spain try this informal place with its café-style tables and classically Mediterranean ochre walls. A long tapas menu includes all the expected delicacies, such as tortilla, stuffed peppers and green asparagus. Galician influences such as squid risotto, *octopus à Galega* and an excellent *escabeche de perdiz* (partridge) also appear.

✉ Rua São Boaventura 16–18, Bairro Alto, 1200-409 Lisboa ☎ 213 424 266
🕐 Thu–Tue 5pm–2am 🖐 D €25, Wine €8
🚋 Baixa-Chiado

MARTINHO DA ARCADA CAFÉ

This old coffee house, founded in 1782, was a gathering place for Lisbon's literati—it was here that poet Fernando Pessoa enjoyed a daily glass of absinthe. The

restaurant is fairly expensive, but the bar, with its fine wood-panelled counter, is still a good spot for a coffee and light snack. Try the Algarve *cataplana* (clam stew).

✉ Praça do Comércio 3, Baixa, 1100-148 Lisboa ☎ 218 879 259 🕐 Bar: Mon–Sat 7am–11pm. Restaurant: Mon–Sat 12–4, 7–11 🖐 €7 for drink and snack in bar
🚋 Baixa-Chiado

MEGAVEGA

For a light option head to the Baixa to this ultra-modern eatery promoting healthy living. Make your selection from a wide choice of vegetarian dishes, cold salads and fresh fruit juices all aimed to be rich in vitamins, minerals and fibre. There is also a take-away service for a picnic, and there is a non-smoking section. The small health food store sells organic wine, olive oil, jams and tea. Credit cards are not accepted.

✉ Rua dos Sapateiros 113, 1100-577 Lisboa ☎ 213 468 063 🕐 Mon 11–7, Tue–Sat 11–10 🖐 L €10, D €15, Wine €8
🚋 Baixa-Chiado

NICOLA CAFÉ

This city landmark dates from 1777 and gained its fame as one of the café haunts of the literary and liberal set. Its fine art deco interior boasts huge mirrors. The location makes it a popular café, although the service is not particularly attentive. Diners can enjoy light and unimaginative meals on the busy pavement terrace.

✉ Praça Dom Pedro IV 24, Baixa, 1100-200 Lisboa ☎ 213 460 579 🕐 Mon–Sat 8am–10pm, Sun 9–7 🖐 €10 for light snack and drink 🚋 Rossio

PAP' AÇORDA

In a converted bakery in the Bairro Alto is this fashionable restaurant. Choose from oysters, mussels or a variety of *açordas* (thick bread-and-egg stews to which prawns and lobster are added). The chocolate mousse is wonderful.

✉ Rua da Atalaia 57–59, Bairro Alto, 1200-037 Lisboa ☎ 213 464 811 🕐 Tue–Sat 12–2, 8–11. Closed first 2 weeks of Jul and Nov 🖐 L €33, D €45, Wine €14
🚋 Baixa-Chiado

LA PAPARRUCHA

www.lapaparrucha.com

As would be expected of an Argentinian restaurant, beef features heavily on the menu. Served with potato, grill-roasted corn and black beans, the high-quality selection of beef cuts grilled *a la parilla* is reason enough to come here, but what sets La Paparrucha apart from other Argentinian restaurants is its magnificent terrace and view. With its late opening hours it attracts the younger partying set.

✉ Rua de Dom Pedro V 18–20, Bairro Alto, 1250-094 Lisboa ☎ 213 425 333 🕐 Daily 12–3, 7.30–2am 🍴 L €20, D €25, Wine €8 Ⓜ Baixa-Chiado 🚌 758, 790

PAVILHÃO CHINÊS

One of Lisbon's eating eccentricities, this café-cum-cocktail bar is worth popping into just for a look. Every available inch of wall space is covered with an eclectic selection of bric-à-brac, collected by Luis Pinto Coelho, the place's owner, from around the world. The result is a mishmash of fine oriental porcelain hanging alongside tin soldiers, iron helmets, fans, statues and dolls. It will certainly keep you entertained while you enjoy a cup of coffee or an aperitif.

✉ Rua Dom Pedro V 89, Bairro Alto, 1250-093 Lisboa ☎ 213 424 729 🕐 Mon–Sat 6pm–2am, Sun 9pm–2am Ⓜ Baixa-Chiado or Restauradores, then Gloria elevator

PORTUGÁLIA RIO

www.portugalia.pt

Part of a chain of *cervejarias* (beer houses) dotted around the city, Portugália Rio has one of the best positions of them all, right on the riverfront. These establishments have limited menus of steaks, served with chips and rice, prawns and, of course, beer. They are good places for a quick, reasonably priced meal late into the night, but are not a viable option for vegetarians.

✉ Cintura do Porto de Lisboa, Doca de Santos, 1200-109 Lisboa ☎ 213 422 138 🕐 Sun–Thu noon–1am, Fri–Sat noon–2am 🍴 L €16, D €22, Wine €6.50 🚌 Cais do Sodré Ⓜ Cais do Sodré

LA RÚCULA

www.larucula.com.pt

Pizzas, pasta, or a selection of great starters—such as rocket (arugula) soup, bruschetta, or fresh mozzarella and mushrooms—are just a few of the menu options. Sit in the airy dining room or on the terrace outside and enjoy the amazing views over the Tagus.

✉ Rossio dos Olivais, Parque das Nações, 1990-231 Lisboa ☎ 218 922 747 🕐 Daily 12.30–3, 7.30–11.30 🍴 L €15, D €20, Wine €4.85 Ⓜ Oriente

A SEVERA

www.asevera.com

Named after the gypsy singer and Portugal's first great *fado* performer Maria Severa, who died in 1836 at the age of only 26, this restaurant serves traditional Portuguese cuisine accompanied by live folk dancing and *fado* shows. Don't be put off—it has a great atmosphere and the professionally staged shows contribute greatly to what will prove a fun evening. Interesting *fado* paraphernalia decorate the alcoves.

✉ Rua das Gáveas 51–61, 1200-206 Lisboa ☎ 213 428 314 🕐 Thu–Tue 12–3, 8pm–3am 🍴 L €18, D €40, Wine €14 (D prices include an €18 charge for the *fado* and folk show) Ⓜ Baixa-Chiado

SOLAR DOS PRESUNTOS

www.solardospresuntos.com

This is among the best of the many restaurants that line this popular street. You will recognize it by the air-cured hams hanging on display in the window; inside, the walls are covered with football memorabilia and tributes to the restaurant from famous patrons. The kitchen specializes in traditional Minho dishes, including roast kid and, when in season, highly prized fresh lampreys. Excellent fresh fish and seafood is stewed in a *caldeirada* or simply grilled. Service is friendly and, at the same time, highly professional.

✉ Rua das Portas de Santo Antão 150, 1150-269 Lisboa ☎ 213 424 253 🕐 Mon–Sat 12–3.30, 7–11. Closed Aug 🍴 L €16, D €25, Wine €8.50 Ⓜ Restauradores

OS TIBETANOS

www.tibetanos.com

In the Buddhist Centre off the Avenida de Liberdade, Os Tibetanos is the best vegetarian restaurant in the capital. Dining rooms are spread over several floors, with views over the city and an interior patio. The menu is extensive and inexpensive, and includes such dishes as fresh cheese lasagne, vegetable curry and *momos Tibetanos* (Tibetan pasties). Credit cards are not accepted.

✉ Rua Salitre 117, Rato, 1250-198 Lisboa ☎ 213 142 038 🕐 Mon–Fri 12–2, 7.30–9.30 🍴 L €12, D €16, Wine €8 Ⓜ Avenida or Rato

VALLE-FLÔR

For a special occasion, it is worth splashing out on a meal at Lisbon's most luxurious restaurant. In what is now the Pestana Palace Hotel (▷ 104), the nationally acclaimed Valle-Flôr has polished wooden floors, high gilded ceilings and period furniture. The French chef creates exquisitely elaborate tastes and textures from traditional ingredients, varying the menu on offer with each week and season.

✉ Pestana Palace Hotel, Rua Jau, 54 Santo Amaro, 1300-314 Lisboa ☎ 213 615 600 🕐 Daily 12.30–3, 7 10.30 🍴 L €40, D €60, Wine €15 🚌 738; Tram 18

XL

XL is around the corner from the National Assembly building, with a closing time that makes it a good late-night dining spot. The restaurant is decorated with ochre-painted walls, rustic furniture and antique curios, and it has an exceptional cellar. Soufflés are the kitchen's particular forte. Also worth trying are the Camembert in breadcrumbs with raspberry sauce and the traditional Portuguese dishes, which include good salt cod. Finish off the meal with a dessert of delicious crêpe or crème brûlée.

✉ Calçada da Estrela 57, Estrela, 1200-661 Lisboa ☎ 213 956 118 🕐 Mon–Wed 8pm–midnight, Thu–Sun 8pm–2am. Closed 3 weeks Aug 🍴 D €35, Wine €15 🚌 727; Tram 25, 28

STAYING

PRICES AND SYMBOLS

The prices are the lowest and highest for a double room for one night including breakfast, unless otherwise stated. All the hotels listed accept credit cards unless otherwise stated. Note that rates can vary widely throughout the year.

For a key to the symbols, ▷ 2.

ALBERGARIA SENHORA DO MONTE

www.maisturismo.pt/sramonte.html
In a prime location up in the quiet Graça district, this hotel has uninterrupted views of the city. The rooftop breakfast bar looks across the river Tagus to the Christ statue and Ponte 25 de Abril. It's worth paying extra for a south-facing room with a terrace. It's a short tram ride to the heart of the city.
✉ Calçada do Monte 39, Graça, 1170-250 Lisboa ☎ 218 866 002 💶 €95–€130
ⓘ 28 (4 with terrace) 🅿 🚇 Martim Moniz 🚋 Tram 28

HOTEL AVENIDA PALACE

www.hotel-avenida-palace.pt
Built in 1892, this was the first luxury hotel in the city. It still provides palatial opulence in the heart of cultural and business

Lisbon, having maintained its characteristic romanticism from the days of the belle époque. The bedrooms and public areas are lavishly decorated and packed with 18th-century French and Portuguese Empire-style furniture, and all rooms are equipped with modern facilities, including triple-glazing. Especially enchanting are the fairy-tale black and gilded staircase, magnificent salons and wood-panelled breakfast room with enormous, delicate chandeliers and views up the Avenida da Liberdade.
✉ Rua 1° de Dezembro 123, Rossio, 1200-359 Lisboa ☎ 213 218 100 💶 €195–€215
ⓘ 65 rooms, 17 suites 🅿 🚇 Rossio

BAIRRO ALTO HOTEL

www.bairroaltohotel.com
Acclaimed by the international press and in the heart of the upmarket Chiado area, this classic 18th-century façade hides an interior of understated elegance and luxury. Try one of the Deluxe rooms, which offer a dual aspect of Praça de Camões and Rua das Flores with the Tagus in the distance. As well as a restaurant and bar there is a panoramic terrace which serves light snacks and drinks; this is a great

Above *Lisbon has many stylish hotels*

place for lunch. At the end of a day of sightseeing head to the Wellbeing Centre for a welcome and relaxing massage.
✉ Praça Luís de Camões 2, 1200-243 Lisboa ☎ 213 408 288 💶 €340–€480
ⓘ 55 🅿 🚇 Baixa-Chiado

HOTEL BORGES

www.hotelborges.com
This hotel in the exclusive Chiado district, next to the art nouveau A Brasileira café (▷ 99), with its statue of Fernando Pessoa sitting outside, is good value for money. Don't be put off by the mirrored lobby with its dated furnishings, as most rooms have been refurbished and are now freshly carpeted and well coordinated. Light sleepers should avoid the front rooms, especially at the weekend, when the café stays open late.
✉ Rua Garrett 108–110, Chiado, 1200-205 Lisboa ☎ 213 461 951 💶 €85 ⓘ 96
🅿 🚇 Baixa-Chiado 🚋 Tram 28

HOTEL BRITANIA

www.heritage.pt
For fantastic art deco architecture, this is the place to stay, just off

the Avenida da Liberdade. It was built in 1944 by modernist architect Cassiano Branco and, though restored, retains all its charm. Rooms are large and well decorated; facilities include a safe and Internet connection. Notice the superb 1940s chandeliers in the polished marble entrance hall, and the symmetry of the breakfast and reading rooms.
✉ Rua Rodrigues Sampaio 17, 1150-278 Lisboa ☎ 213 155 016 💶 €201–€265 excluding breakfast (€14) 🛏 32 (non-smoking available), 1 suite 🔖 💻 Avenida

HOTEL DUAS NAÇÕES
www.duasnacoes.com
In the middle of the pedestrian Baixa shopping district, Duas Nações represents good value for money. Set in a chic 19th-century townhouse with a solid marble and stone entrance, it has simply furnished rooms, some of which share bathroom facilities. All of them, however, have been refurbished and, while modest, are kept impeccably clean. A buffet breakfast is served in a large, bright dining room decorated with tile panels and furnished in dark wood.
✉ Rua da Vitoria 41, Baixa, 1100-618 Lisboa ☎ 213 460 710 💶 €35–€75 🛏 69 (74 with shared facilities) 🔖 💻 Baixa-Chiado

HOTEL HERITAGE AV. LIBERDADE
www.heritage.pt
As the latest addition to the Heritage group of hotels, this 18th-century building has been lovingly restored and painted an eye-catching shade of blue. The bright, period exterior leads to a contrasting, contemporary interior decorated with gentle hues, elegant furniture and fine fabrics. Rooms are fully equipped with CD, DVD, wireless Internet connections and satellite TV. There is a relaxing lounge area in which to enjoy a coffee and plan your day before heading straight out onto the city's main Avenida.
✉ Avenida da Liberdade 28, 1250-145 Lisboa ☎ 213 404 040 💶 €206–€315 excluding breakfast (€14) 🛏 41 rooms, 1 suite 🔖 🏊 Indoor 💻 Restauradores

HOTEL IBIS LISBOA LIBERDADE
www.ibishotel.com
Part of a large French-owned chain, Ibis hotels can be found around the country, and while all rooms look the same and are far from inspiring, they offer excellent value for money and are a comfortable, functional place in which to spend the night. This particular Ibis branch is completely non-smoking, which makes a most welcome change in Portugal. The hotel will also serve breakfast from as early as 4.30am should you need your coffee before that early-morning flight home.
✉ Rua Barata Salgueiro 53, 1250-043 Lisboa ☎ 213 300 630 💶 €65–€75 🛏 70 🔖 💻 Avenida or Marquês de Pombal

HOTEL JORGE V
www.hoteljorgev.com
In a 1960s building just off the Avenida da Liberdade is this well-established hotel. The bedrooms are not big and the furniture is not particularly modern—the patterned carpets can clash a little with the riotous curtains and bedspreads—but all have modern marble bathrooms, a safe and some have small balconies. A buffet breakfast is served in the ground-floor dining room and there is 24-hour bar service. Most importantly, the hotel staff are friendly and helpful.
✉ Rua Mouzinho da Silveira 3, 1250-165 Lisboa ☎ 213 562 525 💶 €75–€95 🛏 43 rooms, 6 suites (non-smoking available) 🔖 💻 Avenida

HOTEL LISBOA PLAZA
www.heritage.pt
Off the Avenida da Liberdade, the Plaza was built in 1953 and elegantly updated in 1988 by Graça Viterbo, one of Portugal's most famous interior designers. The large, modern rooms are decorated in warm tones with sumptuous fabrics. All are equipped with Internet connection. The public areas feel like private sitting rooms, with book-filled cabinets, pictures and ornaments. The restaurant, which serves all meals, including breakfast, has

buffet and à la carte menus. Guests can swim at the nearby Sheraton.
✉ Travessa do Salitre 7, 1269-066 Lisboa ☎ 213 218 218 💶 €160–€240 excluding breakfast (€14) 🛏 94 rooms, 12 suites (non-smoking and anti-allergic available) 🔖 💻 Avenida

HOTEL LISBOA REGENCY CHIADO
www.regency-hotels-resorts.com
The Regency Chiado is in the exclusive Chiado shopping district, inside the reconstructed Armazens do Chiado buildings that were destroyed by fire in 1988. Its main attraction is the awe-inspiring view over Lisbon and its castle from public areas and the private terraces of superior rooms. Decorated according to feng shui principles, the bedrooms are a fusion of Portuguese and oriental design, using rich tones of red, deep greens and dark woods; they also have Internet connection. The breakfast buffet is lavish.
✉ Rua Nova do Almada 114, Chiado, 1200-290 Lisboa ☎ 213 256 100 💶 €175–€285 🛏 38 rooms, 2 suites 🔖 💻 Baixa-Chiado

HOTEL MÉTROPOLE
www.almeidahotels.com
An imposing, elegant hotel, the Métropole has a prestigious location on the western side of the Rossio. It opened in 1917, and a complete refurbishment in 1993 restored many of the original features. The best rooms are on the top floors facing the square, as they have great views of the castle. All the bedrooms are elegantly furnished in 1920s style and have double-glazing so you sleep easier.
✉ Praca Dom Pedro IV 30, Rossio, 1100-200 Lisboa ☎ 213 219 030 💶 €134–€190 🛏 36 🔖 💻 Rossio

HOTEL VIP INN VENEZA
www.viphotels.com
Housed in what was a palatial 19th-century townhouse, the façade has Moorish-influenced arches. The interior is lavishly decorated with wrought iron, polished wood and stained glass, while bright murals of Lisbon adorn the monumental

staircase. Some of the 37 rooms overlook the Avenida da Liberdade.

✉ Avenida da Liberdade 189, 1250-141 Lisboa ☎ 213 522 618 ♿ €113 excluding breakfast (€8.50) ⓘ 37 🚇 Avenida

AS JANELAS VERDES

www.heritage.pt

This 18th-century mansion, near the Museu Nacional de Arte Antiga, provides personal service in intimate surroundings. The sumptuous public rooms could easily be mistaken for those of a private house, and the home-away-from-home feeling is encouraged further by the self-service honour bars and the extra-friendly staff. The well-equipped rooms have Internet connection. In summer, breakfast is served on an ivy-clad patio, and on the top floor the library and terrace offer uninterrupted views over the Tagus.

✉ Rua da Janelas Verdes 47, Lapa, 1200-690 Lisboa ☎ 213 968 143 ♿ €195–€298 excluding breakfast (€14) ⓘ 29 (non-smoking available) 🚇 🚌 60, 727; Tram 25 🚉 Santos

LAPA PALACE

www.lapapalace.com

Converted from what was once the 19th-century residence of the Count of Valença, and set amid tranquil gardens overlooking the River Tagus, this is one of Lisbon's plushest and most expensive hotels. At the time of writing, it is the only one with a heated outdoor pool. Inside, the original opulence has been lovingly restored, especially in the frescoed Columbano room and the luxurious Count of Valença suite. Others are decorated in art deco, belle époque and oriental styles; their facilities, somewhat incongruously, include Internet connection.

✉ Rua do Pau da Bandeira 4, Lapa, 1249-021 Lisboa ☎ 213 949 494 ♿ €365–€575 ⓘ 89 rooms, 15 suites 🚇 🚌 Indoor and outdoor 🚋 🚌 713, 773; Tram 25 🚉 Santos

PALÁCIO DE BELMONTE

www.palaciobelmonte.com

If money is no object, take the opportunity to stay here, at the 500-year-old home of the earls of Belmonte. This national monument has undergone a US$24 million restoration using ancient building methods alongside state-of-the-art energy-saving systems. The bedrooms are peaceful, simple and dressed in rich silks, with great views of Lisbon or the gardens. Even the outdoor pool is lined with black marble. Take your breakfast on the terrace.

✉ Páteo Dom Fradique 14, Alfama, 1100-624 Lisboa ☎ 218 816 600 ♿ €300–€1,200 ⓘ 11 suites 🚇 🚌 Outdoor 🚌 Tram 28

PENSÃO ALEGRIA

www.alegrianet.com

Set in a pleasant square off the Avenida da Liberdade, this lemon-painted *pensão* provides fairly basic, though friendly, service. All the rooms have been redecorated and have private facilities. The wooden floors and furniture are simple, but fabrics are coordinated and everything is spotlessly clean. The dining room offers breakfast, but no other meals.

✉ Praca de Alegria 12, 1250-004 Lisboa ☎ 213 220 670 ♿ €58–€73 ⓘ 35 🚇 Avenida

PENSÃO LONDRES

www.pensaolondres.com.pt

In the famous area of Principe Real on the northern fringes of the Bairro Alto, this *pensão* is housed in what was once a town mansion. It is good value for money—and is also gay-friendly. The rooms are pleasantly furnished with slightly old-fashioned pieces; those on the fourth floor have good views over the Castelo de São Jorge and Ponte 25 de Abril. Breakfast is served in a sunny dining room at the back.

✉ Rua Pedro V 53, 1st–4th floors, Bairro Alto, 1250-092 Lisboa ☎ 213 462 203 ♿ €50–€80 ⓘ 40 🚇 Rossio then Glória elevator 🚌 758, 773, 790

PENSÃO RESIDENCIAL ROYAL

Pensão Royal offers one of the best budget deals in town. Its rooms are simple, yet freshly painted and decorated with attractive fabrics; all have their own bathroom. Breakfast is now served, though there are plenty of cafés to explore right on the doorstep. If the Royal is full, try Pensão Galicia upstairs, which is run by the same family. No rooms have private bathrooms, although some have a shower, but it is clean and friendly (€35–€50, tel 213 428 430).

✉ Rua do Crucifixo 50, 3rd floor, Baixa, 1100 Lisboa ☎ 213 479 006 ♿ €45–€70 ⓘ 6 🚇 Baixa-Chiado

PESTANA PALACE HOTEL

www.pestana.com

About 5km (3 miles) west of the city, this fabulous 19th-century palace has been restored to its former Romantic Revivalist glory. Most rooms are in modern wings that blend effortlessly into the extensive gardens. The chandeliered public rooms are particularly opulent, as are the four suites in the main palace building. The hotel's Valle-Flôr restaurant serves outstanding international cuisine (▷ 101).

✉ Rua Jau 54, Santo Amaro, 1300-314 Lisboa ☎ 213 615 600 ♿ €180–€290 ⓘ 173 rooms, 17 suites 🚇 🚌 Indoor and outdoor 🚋 🚌 738; Tram 18

POUSADA DE JUVENTUDE DE LISBOA

www.pousadasjuventude.pt

Lisbon's 176-bed youth hostel has double rooms with private facilities as well as dormitory accommodation. The rooms are simple, youth-hostel style; if you are sharing a dormitory, remember to bring a padlock for your locker. The bar is open from 6pm to midnight.

✉ Rua Andrade Corvo 46, 1050-009 Lisboa ☎ 213 532 696 ♿ €43 for double with private facilities, €16 in shared dormitory ⓘ 176 beds (including 13 doubles, 1 with wheelchair access) 🚇 Picoas 🚌 36, 44, 727, 738, 745

RESIDÊNCIA ROMA

Off the Avenida da Liberdade, Residência Roma is unbeatable value if you are visiting in a group and are prepared to self cater. Standard rooms are available, but, for the same price and a walk up an extra flight or two of stairs, there are apartments for up to five people that come complete with a fully equipped kitchenette. The deal is great value for money for stays of three days or more. The interiors of the apartments are simple and slightly old-fashioned, but nevertheless the place is spotless. ✉ Travessa da Gloria 22a, 1° (1st floor), 1250-118 Lisboa ☎ 213 460 557 ✋ Rooms or apartments (up to 5 people, extra person €15) €50–€80 🛏 28 rooms, 12 apartments 🔄 🚇 Avenida

RESIDENCIAL AVENIDA PARQUE

www.avenidaparque.com

On the east side of the Parque Eduardo VII, this unpretentious *residencial* provides efficient service and good value for money. Rooms are comparable in standard to those in many 3- and 4-star hotels, with modern light wood furniture and double-glazing. Breakfast is served in the ground-floor dining room. ✉ Avenida Sidónio Pais 6, 1050-214 Lisboa ☎ 213 532 181 ✋ €53–€85 🛏 44 🔄 🚇 Parque, Marquês de Pombal

RESIDENCIAL CAMÕES

www.pensaoresidencialcamoes.com

In the heart of the Bairro Alto, this well-priced *residencial* has simple, somewhat dated furniture, but is friendly and clean. Some rooms have private shower facilities and others have sink and bidet combinations with shared toilets. From Thursday to Saturday night the street-side rooms are noisy owing to late-night revellers. Credit cards are not accepted.

✉ Travessa do Poço da Cidade 38, 1° Esq (1st floor, left-hand door), Bairro Alto, 1200-334 Lisboa ☎ 213 467 510 ✋ €40–€50 Apr–end Sep including breakfast; €30–€35 Oct–end Mar excluding breakfast 🛏 10 rooms with private facilities, 8 rooms with shared facilities 🚇 Baixa-Chiado 🚌 758, 790

SOLAR DO CASTELO

www.heritage.pt

This 18th-century palace shares its ancient walls with the Castelo de São Jorge, and its many medieval elements have been made into interesting architectural features. With only 14 intimate rooms and discreet service, it feels like a private home. Bedrooms are decorated in warm tones with fine fabrics in a mix of modern and classical styles, and the Pombaline-style windows look out onto an attractive tiled patio where a good breakfast is served in warm weather. ✉ Rua das Cozinhas 2, 1100-181 Lisboa ☎ 218 806 050 ✋ €230–€340 excluding breakfast (€14) 🛏 14 rooms (non-smoking available) 🔄 🚌 37; Tram 12, 28

SOLAR DOS MOUROS

www.solardosmouros.pt

Below the Castelo de São Jorge, inside a bright yellow, steeply perpendicular building, this hotel is decorated in wild shades and outlandish modern paintings adorn the walls. The rooms are starkly modern with minimalist furniture, bright art and African sculptures. Some rooms have steep spiral staircases (which may be a problem for small children or people with disabilities) and loft-style ceilings.

The breakfast room has great views over Lisbon and the river. ✉ Rua do Milagre de Santo António 6, 1100-351 Lisboa ☎ 218 854 940 ✋ €119–€259 🛏 12 🔄 🚌 37; Tram 12, 28

VIP EDEN APARTHOTEL

www.viphotels.com

This pink art deco building was once one of the city's best-known cinemas. Redeveloped in 1996, it now provides quality self-catering accommodation in studios and apartments, which sleep two to four people each. All are modern and functional, with fitted bathrooms and fully equipped kitchens. The roof terrace and outdoor swimming pool look straight out onto the Castelo de São Jorge. Breakfast is available on the terrace at an extra charge. ✉ Praça dos Restauradores 24, 1250-187 Lisboa ☎ 213 216 600 ✋ Studios €110–€177, apartments €156–€185, excluding breakfast (€8.50) 🛏 34 studios sleeping up to 2 people, 56 apartments with 2 rooms sleeping up to 4 people 🔄 🚕 Outdoor 🚇 Restauradores

YORK HOUSE

www.yorkhouselisboa.com

It is essential to reserve in advance if you want to stay in this tranquil and elegant 17th-century former Carmelite convent tucked away in a discreet location in classy Lapa. Seven of the bedrooms are decorated in traditional style, while the rest have been given the minimalist-chic treatment. On sunny days, you can eat your breakfast under the huge palm in the courtyard. A first-rate restaurant, frequented by many non-residents, serves a refined version of traditional Portuguese cuisine. ✉ Rua das Janelas Verdes 32, Lapa, 1200-691 Lisboa ☎ 213 962 435 ✋ €65–€250 excluding breakfast (€15) 🛏 32 🔄 🚌 60, 727; Tram 25 🚊 Santos

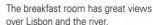

Left *An elegant public room at Hotel Lisboa Regency Chiado*

AROUND LISBON

Though the immediate city of Lisbon is surrounded by sprawling, high-rise suburbs, push farther afield on either side of the Tagus to discover breathtaking coastal drives, clifftop walks, glorious beaches, dramatic promontories and verdant hills.

For spectacular cliff scenery, drive from Cascais around the coast, through the Parque Natural de Sintra-Cascais to the windswept Cabo da Roca, where the Atlantic mercilessly pounds below. For a gentler, but no less exhilarating experience, head south of the Tagus and take the sweeping coastal road from Setúbal through the Parque Natural da Serra da Arrábida, to the fishing village of Sesimbra.

The mossy Sintra hills offer scenic drives through forests and awesome views over the whole region including the chic resort towns of Cascais and Estoril to the south. Here the visitor is spoiled with modern luxuries such as five-star hotels, elegant shopping and fine restaurants; and families can enjoy the gentle beaches. For more beach options, look across the Tagus to the Costa da Caparica, an uninterrupted swathe of sand which stretches south for some 25km (15 miles).

Lovers of palaces and monuments should take time in Sintra. Friezes and tiles at the Palácio Nacional, rambling ramparts of the Moorish Castle, the eccentricities of the Pena Palace and mystical gardens at Regaleira are but a few of its highlights. Time permitting, the monolithic palace at Mafra with its 880 rooms and 4,700 doors and windows and the delicate rococo palace at Queluz are also worth a visit. For time out choose between a glass of chilled wine and a *queijada* in the square in Sintra or a fresh, grilled-fish lunch in Sesimbra.

CABO ESPICHEL

www.visitcostaazul.com

A lonely road runs through villages and windswept country to Cabo Espichel, where a lighthouse looms above the pounding sea. To the right stands a baroque church fronted by a large square, lined with shabby 18th-century pilgrim lodgings.

The church is dedicated to Nossa Senhora do Cabo (Our Lady of the Cape), patron saint of fishermen. In its gloomy interior, candles light the gilded surround of the image of Ave Maris Stella (Our Lady Star of the Sea). Large crowds gather here for the feast of Nossa Senhora do Cabo on the third Sunday in September, when fishermen pray for safety and good catches. This remote cape was also one of the locations in Wim Wenders' film *A Lisbon Story*.

➕ 330 A10 ℹ️ Largo da Marinha 26–27, 2970-635 Sesimbra ☎ 212 288 540

CABO DA ROCA

www.estorilcoast-tourism.com

The headland of Cabo da Roca lies at the end of the Serra de Sintra. Wild and rugged, with spectacular views, it's the westernmost point of continental Europe. There's little to see apart from the lighthouse and a monument inscribed with words by Luís de Camões, Portugal's national poet. The tourist office will sell you a certificate to prove you have stood this far west, but time is better spent admiring the coastal views. Unspoilt beaches lie north and south: Praia Grande to the north and Guincho, popular with surfers, to the south. North is the picturesque village of Azenhas do Mar, its rows of cottages seemingly tumbling down the cliffs to the seawater swimming pool below.

➕ 330 A9 ℹ️ Cabo da Roca, Azoia, Colares 2705-001 ☎ 219 280 081 🚉 Sintra or Cascais, then bus 403

CASCAIS

www.estorilcoast-tourism.com
www.cm-cascais.pt

Cascais, popular with Portuguese, expatriates, and foreign visitors, is both a holiday resort and a busy

Above *The Costa da Caparica has many uncrowded beaches*
Opposite *Floral Cascais is a busy fishing port as well as a popular tourist resort*

fishing village. Fishermen's boats are still drawn up on the sand of one of the beaches and early risers will see the boats chug out at dawn. The bulk of the Cidadela fortress, built in the 16th century to protect the bay and the Lisbon approaches, dominates the waterfront, behind which lie the narrow streets of the old town. The streets form a flower-hung maze, lined with chic shops, bars and restaurants. In the evenings head for the newer quarter around the pedestrianized Rua Federico Arouca to the east.

Cascais is well endowed with parks and gardens—the attractive Parque Municipal da Gandarinha contains the mansion of the counts of Guimarães, now a museum with an eclectic, mainly 19th-century collection (tel 214 815 304; Tue–Sun 10–5; free). Across the park is the Museu do Mar (tel 214 815 906; Tue–Sun 10–5; €2.04), which is crammed with sea-related exhibits, such as model boats, old fishing lines and nets, mariners' clothes and equipment. The town has three beaches and a swanky yacht marina, but bathing is not recommended, so, if you want to swim, head west and north towards the beach at Guincho. You can rent bicycles at Guia (▷ 118). Be prepared for big summer crowds in Cascais, particularly at the weekends, when it's packed with visitors from Lisbon.

➕ 330 A9 ℹ️ Avenida Combatentes da Grande Guerra, 2750-326 Cascais ☎ 214 868 204 🚉 Cascais

COSTA DA CAPARICA

www.visitcostaazul.com

If you're looking for a typical Portuguese beach resort, head for the Costa da Caparica, the largely unspoilt stretch of coastline running south from the Tejo estuary. It's easily reached from Lisbon by car, by bus from Praça de Espanha in central Lisbon, or by taking the ferry from Lisbon to Cacilhas, from where there are regular bus connections to Caparica itself. Vast beaches stretch down the coastline from this lively resort. They are linked by a miniature railway running through the dunes, which stops 18 times between Caparica and Fonte da Telha to the south. The railway provides easy access to the beach, which grows increasingly wilder and more deserted the farther south you head, but you will find wooden beach bars and restaurants at every stop.

Families tend to stick to the northernmost areas, the well-heeled young head for the stretch between Praia da Riviera and Praia do Rei, and the southernmost beaches are reserved for nudists. The sea is clean, but remember that undertows can be dangerous, particularly for small children, so take extra care if you plan to swim. To catch a glimpse of the unspoilt beauty of this coastline, take the train at least as far as Praia da Mata (stop 8), the first point with little building except for the occasional beach bar.

➕ 330 A10 ℹ️ Avenida da República 18, 2825-399 Caparica ☎ 212 900 071

ESTORIL

www.estorilcoast-tourism.com

Classy Estoril gained its reputation after World War II, when it became a bolt-hole for rich expatriates and exiled royalty. It's still a smart resort, with plenty of grand hotels and exclusive villas within a stone's throw of its long sandy beach. This is backed by a promenade running west; you can stroll all the way to Cascais in half an hour or so, pausing at one of the pleasant waterfront bars. The town's main attractions are its golf course and the casino in the Parque do Estoril, planted with tropical trees and scattered with fountains.

🔲 330 A9 ℹ️ Arcadas do Parque, 2765-267 Estoril ☎ 214 663 813 🚉 Estoril

MAFRA

www.cm-mafra.pt

Gold from Brazil paid for João V's astonishing architectural legacy. Built between 1717 and 1755, the Palácio e Convento de Mafra (Wed–Mon 10–5.30; last admission 4.30; €5, Sun free until 2pm) is modelled on Madrid's El Escorial. Its focus is the magnificent basilica, flanked on either side with wings containing the royal apartments and backed by monastic quarters. More than 50,000 builders were employed on site, constructing a building 220m (720ft) long and 68m (220ft) high, with 880 rooms, 4,700 doors and windows and 29 courtyards. The basilica's dome is one of the world's largest, and its possession of six organs unique, while its bell towers contain 114 bells—free bell-ringing concerts are held every Sunday at 4. Palace tours take in the royal apartments, including the Hunting Trophy Room, where all the furniture is made of deer antlers and upholstered in deerskin; and the library, a rococo showpiece with elaborate stuccowork and a chequered marble floor. Mafra also hosts an autumn International Festival of Music, with baroque and contemporary concerts in the basilica and library.

🔲 330 A9 ℹ️ Palácio Nacional de Mafra, Torreao Sul, Terreiro Dom João V, 2640-492 Mafra ☎ 261 817 170

PALÁCIO NACIONAL DE QUELUZ

www.ippar.pt

This elegant, pink-washed palace started life as a hunting lodge until Dom Pedro III embarked on its rebuilding in 1747. This transformed the lodge into a palace, now the country's finest example of rococo architecture, with rambling 18th-century formal gardens. In 1760 Dom Pedro married his niece, the future Queen Maria I who spent 27 declining years here, driven mad by grief following the death of her son. More renovations followed her death and Queluz eventually became state property in 1908. Today, it's preserved as a museum portraying 18th-century aristocratic life, decorated with fine pieces from the former royal collections. The mirror-lined Throne Room, the elegant public rooms and the Ambassador's Chamber, where visiting diplomats and foreign dignitaries were received, trace the development of Portuguese taste from the rococo to the neoclassical. Don't miss the gardens, where the pools, fountains terraces and parterres form the perfect background to the palace itself. The Royal Guards palace is now a luxury *pousada* hotel.

🔲 330 A9 ✉️ Largo do Palácio, 2745-191 Queluz ☎ 214 343 860 🕐 Palace: Wed–Mon 10–5 (last admission 4.30). Gardens: May–end Sep Wed–Mon 10–6; Oct–end Dec Wed–Mon 10–5; Jan–end Apr 🎟️ Palace: €4, free Sun until 2pm. Gardens: free. Royal Palaces ticket (€6) includes the palaces at Sintra, Mafra and Ajuda 🚉 Queluz-Belas 🍴 Cozinha Velha, in palace's original kitchens; open for lunch and dinner 🔲 🔲

SESIMBRA

www.visitcostaazul.com

Encircled by cliffs, Sesimbra is a beguiling resort. Historically, it was the site of a Moorish settlement, and you can still visit the Moorish castle (daily 7–7; free) high on a hill behind the town. Around the narrow streets and *praça* (square) of the old town, apartment blocks and hotels spread across the hillside, while the palm-lined promenade is thronged with visitors enjoying fresh fish at the café-restaurants.

Follow the signs to the Porto do Abrigo and you leave the holiday industry behind—this is a serious fishing port with its ocean-going trawlers. Both sides of town come together in the early morning, when beach and streets are thronged with fishermen maintaining their nets.

🔲 330 A10 ℹ️ Largo da Marinha 26–27, 2970-657 Sesimbra ☎ 212 288 540

Left *The beach and town of Sesimbra*
Opposite *Strolling along the tree-lined promenade at Estoril*

SINTRA

INFORMATION

www.cm-sintra.pt

✚ 330 A9 ℹ Praça da República 23,
2710-616 Sintra or Estação de Sintra,
Avenida Dr Miguel Bombarda, 2710-590
Sintra ☎ 219 231 157 or 219 241 623
🕐 Jun–end Sep daily 9–8; rest of
year daily 9–7 🚂 Sintra 📖 Ilustrated
leaflets (free) available for both palaces
in Portuguese, English, French, German,
Spanish, Italian and Japanese. General
guidebooks available at souvenir shops in
Portuguese, English, French, Spanish and
German, prices vary

Above *The imposing exterior of the
Palácio Nacional da Pena*

INTRODUCTION

The summer residence of the kings of Portugal and of the Moors before them,
Sintra is beautifully set in wooded mountains with wonderful views out to sea.
It is now a World Heritage Site with a wealth of outstanding palaces, gardens
and museums.

Sintra is made up of three separate villages, spread out over lush, wooded
hills and along valleys. This makes driving the best way to explore all the sights
quickly, though a half-hourly tourist bus links all the main attractions. Trains from
Lisbon arrive in Estefânia. Sintra-Vila, where you will find the Palácio Nacional
de Sintra and the Quinta da Regaleira, is a short walk uphill, while the third
village, São Pedro de Sintra, is 20 minutes on from there. The Palácio Nacional
da Pena is on top of a hill some distance away from Sintra-Vila. Visiting the
gardens of Monserrate and the Convento dos Capuchos means taking a taxi,
unless you prefer a 9km (5.5-mile) hike through the hills.

Sintra also has excellent sports facilities, with golf, tennis, horseback riding
and swimming on offer in the area (the sea is within easy reach for swimming
and watersports). Its arts scene is lively—the Festival of Music and Dance
(Jun–Jul, ▷ 21) is one of Portugal's most prestigious events. São Pedro
de Sintra is a good place for antiques and boutique shopping and holds an
excellent market every second Sunday.

The Romans used Sintra as a defensive post, but it was the Moors that
fell in love with this green, well-watered spot, building a palace here before
the 10th century. It fell to the Christians in 1147, and Sintra palace became
the property of the kings of Portugal, a situation that remained unchanged
until the monarchy was overthrown and the last king exiled in 1910. The kings
used the palace both as a hunting base and a refuge from Lisbon's summer
heat, enlarging it and laying out gardens. Wealthy aristocrats followed in the
royal footsteps, and by the 19th century the Sintra hills were dotted with vast
mansions and huge villas; some are still privately owned.

WHAT TO SEE

PALÁCIO NACIONAL DA PENA

www.ippar.pt; www.parquedesintra.pt

There's been a building on the site of the Palácio Nacional da Pena, high above Sintra-Vila, since the 14th century. It was originally a chapel with an adjoining late-Gothic cloister, which fell into disrepair after it was damaged in the 1755 earthquake. In 1836, Queen Maria II married Prince Ferdinand of Saxe-Coburg-Gotha, an enthusiastic Romantic. He commissioned the German architect von Eschwege to design today's extraordinary palace, which fortunately has been preserved despite the overthrow of the monarchy in 1910.

What you'll see is a fantasy of neo-Gothic, an over-the-top combination of Manueline decoration, Germanic embellishments and Moorish features. There are turrets, cupolas, domes and battlements everywhere, and the interior is no less bizarre, a celebration of late Victorian taste where every surface is lavishly decorated. It's been described as 'a textbook of 19th-century decorative arts and the Belle Époque in transition to the 20th century', and bears more than a passing resemblance to the fantasies of Ludwig II, the 'mad king' of Bavaria, who was responsible for the castle at Neuschwanstein. Highlights include some remarkable stuccowork, splendid bathrooms and kitchens, and some mildly erotic unfinished paintings by Carlos I, the last king of Portugal. Don't miss the wooded garden below the palace, an oasis of verdant shade and soothing water.

✉ Estrada da Pena, 2710-609 Sintra ☎ 219 105 340 🕐 May to mid-Sep park daily 9.30–8 (last entry 7), palace daily 9.45–7 (last entry 6.15); rest of year park daily 10–6 (last entry 5), palace daily 10–5.30 (last entry 4.45) 🖐 €11 park and palace all areas; free with Lisboa Card; Mon certain outdoor areas only €7.50, Sun free until 1pm 🚌 Sintra then Scotturb bus 434

PALÁCIO NACIONAL DE SINTRA

www.ippar.pt

A pair of extraordinary conical chimneys surrounded by a riot of decorative architecture dominates the heart of Sintra-Vila. This is the Palácio Nacional de Sintra, a summer pleasure palace built largely during the late 14th and 16th centuries by Dom João and his successor, Dom Manuel. Stylistically, it's a happy blend of Gothic and Manueline styles with plenty of Moorish touches. There's a set route through the palace, taking in all the main rooms, with tantalizing glimpses of hidden courtyards and superb views over the

TIPS

» Use the 434 bus to get around; a hop-on-hop-off Sintra ticket costs €4.50, while a day rover includes all Scotturb bus routes and costs €10. Use it to go on to Cascais via Cabo da Roca, returning to Lisbon on the Cascais line (www.scotturb.com).

» If you take a taxi to Monserrate or Capuchos check the price first with the driver as meters aren't always used; the price should be approximately €12. Taxis wait outside the station and in the Praça de República in Sintra-Vila.

» Reserve ahead if you want to stay in Sintra.

» Visitors interested in gardens may wish to purchase the '4 Parks' ticket (€12) which includes Pena, Castelo dos Mouros, Monserrate and Capuchos.

Below left *View over the Palácio Nacional de Sintra summer palace*
Below *Balustrades and domed turrets add to the Moorish feel of the Palácio Nacional da Pena*

surrounding landscape. Pause first in the Hall of Swans, the magnificently tiled hall whose ceiling is decorated with painted swans, adorned with golden necklaces. During João I's reign it was the main reception chamber and is the largest room in the palace. It overlooks a central patio, with a stucco-embellished grotto, which once acted as a cooling fountain.

Steps lead up from here to the Hall of Magpies, a private antechamber. Here both frieze and ceiling are painted with a flock of jaunty magpies, each holding in its beak the legend 'Por bem' ('For the best'). It was reputedly painted on the orders of Dom João to put a stop to the gossiping of the court ladies—Philippa of Lancaster, João's wife, had found out from this about the king's affair with one of her ladies-in-waiting.

From here a succession of smaller rooms and corridors leads to the stupendous Hall of Stags, lined with blue *azulejos* (tiles), its coffered ceiling displaying the armorial bearings of 72 noble families. The views towards the sea are fabulous—it is said that the kings could watch their fleets setting out to Africa, Brazil and India from here.

✉ Largo Rainha Dona Amélia, 2710-616 Sintra ☎ 219 106 840 🕓 Thu–Tue 10–5.30 (last entry 5) 👋 €5; free with Lisboa Card 🚉 Sintra

QUINTA DA REGALEIRA

The Quinta da Regaleira, a short walk from Sintra-Vila's main square, is an elaborate private estate that achieved World Heritage status in 1995. It's a fine example of turn-of-the-20th-century revivalist neo-Manueline architecture, built by the wealthy landowner António Carvalho Monteiro (1850–1920) and designed by the Italian architect Luigi Mannini (1848–1936), who was also responsible for Buçaco (▷ 179). The extraordinary main house, all towers and ornate stonework, has some elaborate rooms—look out for the rococo wooden ceilings and incredibly detailed mosaic floors.

It's the gardens that steal the show, a maze of paths on a steep hillside planted with camellias, hydrangeas and tree ferns, and dotted with lakes, fountains, terraces and statuary. They are full of Masonic themes and imagery, the highlight being the Initiation Well, inspired by the Freemasons and Knights Templar, which you approach through a revolving stone door. Moss-covered steps lead to the foot of the well and through an eerie tunnel.

✉ Rua Barcosa du Bocage, 2710-567 Sintra ☎ 219 106 650 🕓 Apr–end Sep daily 10–8 (last entry 7); Feb–end Mar, Oct daily 10–6.30 (last entry 6); rest of year daily 10–5.30 (last entry 5); guided visits (reserve in advance) 👋 Unaccompanied €5; guided visits (must be pre-arranged) €10 🚉 Sintra

Right *Statuary is a feature of the magnificent Quinta da Regaleira gardens*
Below *A detail of the imaginative exterior of the Palácio Nacional de Sintra*

MORE TO SEE

CASTELO DOS MOUROS

www.cm-sintra.pt

www.parquesdesintra.pt

The ruins of the Moorish castle consist of two defensive positions, set on rocky crags, with a mosque between them.

✉ Parque de Sintra, 2710 Sintra ☎ 219 107 970 🕐 May to mid-Sep daily 9.30–8; rest of year daily 10–6 (last entry 60 mins earlier) 💰 €5 🚉 Sintra

CONVENTO DOS CAPUCHOS

www.cm-sintra.pt

www.parquesdesintra.pt

An evocative hermitage around 9km (5.5 miles) from Sintra, the cells here are cut from the rock and lined with cork from the woods. It was occupied from the mid-16th century to 1836.

✉ Serra de Sintra, 2710 Sintra ☎ 219 289 621 🕐 May to mid-Sep daily 9.30–8; rest of year daily 10–6 (last entry 60 mins earlier) 💰 €5 🎫 Guided tours €10, reserve ahead by phone 🚉 Sintra

MONSERRATE

www.cm-sintra.pt

www.parquesdesintra.pt

A vast garden just outside town is planted with subtropical trees and plants.

✉ Est. de Monserrate, 2710-405 Sintra ☎ 219 107 806 🕐 Gardens: May to mid-Sep daily 9.30–8; rest of year daily 10–6 (last entry 1 hour before closing). Palace: May to mid-Sep 10–1, 2–7; rest of year 10.30–1, 2–5 (last entry 30 min before closing). For Palace visits, call 219 237 300 to reserve a tour. 💰 Gardens and part of palace: adult €5, child (6–17) €3 🚉 Sintra

MUSEU DE ARTE MODERNA

www.cm-sintra.pt

www.berardocollection.com

A huge collection of modern art is displayed at this modern art museum. Exhibits change every two months.

✉ Avenida Heliodoro Salgado, 2710-575 Sintra ☎ 219 248 170 🕐 Tue–Sun 10–6 (last entry 5.30) 💰 €3; €2.10 with Lisboa Card; free Sun 10–2 🚉 Sintra

Above *Moorish Castelo dos Mouros watches over the town of Sintra*
Below *The architecture of Palácio Nacional da Pena shows a mastery of elaborate detail*

EXPLORING THE PARQUE DA PENA

This is a waymarked circular walk through the wooded grounds of the Parque da Pena. Perfect on a hot summer's day, the route winds downhill through cool, shady woods, giving tantalizing views and taking in an exotically planted valley and four bird-haunted lakes.

THE WALK

Distance: 3.3km (2 miles)
Time: 1 hour or 1–2 hours if visiting the Palácio da Pena en route
Start at: Main entrance
End at: The bottom gate near the fourth lake

★ Walk through the main entrance and follow the green signs uphill along the tarmac path. Shortly you'll see a sign for the Picadeiro at an intersection.

❶ The Picadeiro was once a venue for small bullfights and still retains its original shape.

As the path reaches the road, walk straight across and up the steps if you're visiting the Palácio Nacional da Pena (▷ 113).

❷ From outside the Palácio Nacional da Pena, there are wide views over a jumble of pinewoods and granite outcrops to the sea,

scenery that typifies 19th-century Romantic taste and is perfectly in keeping with the excesses of the palace itself. Built over the ruins of a 16th-century monastery, the palace was the brainchild of Ferdinand of Saxe-Coburg-Gotha, the German husband of Dona Maria II. Helped by fellow-German architect Baron Eschwege, Ferdinand built a mock medieval extravaganza that, to today's eyes, is a masterpiece of kitsch.

Leave the palace and walk back downhill through the approach tunnel to the main road. Cross the road and walk down two steps to turn left onto the waymarked path—there's a green arrowed sign marked *'caminho pedonal'*. At the next sign ('Alto de Santo Antonio') bear right to walk along the tarmac path through some heavy vegetation of pines and laurels. The path swings left to an intersection, where you

follow the green arrows left along a gravel path. Where the path branches, fork right and follow the arrows straight ahead.

❸ In the depths of the park you can see how the inspiration for the design of the landscape came from the notion of combining elements of northern forest with typical Mediterranean and Asiatic plantings. One of the park's original purposes was for use as an acclimatization garden for the constant stream of new discoveries being brought back from China and the Far East by 19th-century plant hunters.

At the next intersection you could detour right to the *miradouro* (viewpoint) or continue the walk by following the sign (in English) to the Giant.

❹ The Giant is an outlandishly large statue of a man perched on a granite outcrop above the path at 490m (1,600ft) above sea level.

Continue downhill to the intersection and bear right following the signs to the Alto de Catarina. En route, a small path goes up to the left to the Cruz Alto, the highest point in the park; do not follow this, but instead stick to the sandy path that wends its way through thick cover to an intersection with a tarmac track. Follow the signs downhill to the Queen's Fern Valley until you come to a clearing with a small pool surrounded by tree ferns. Leave the track here and take the two steps through the gap in the wall on the right onto a cobbled path.

❺ The Queen's Fern Valley is one of the loveliest parts of the park, an area thickly planted with tree ferns, some of them reaching as high as 6–7m (20–23ft). Shelter for these delicate species is provided by mature beech, chestnut and oak trees, and by thickets of camellias. As the path gently meanders downhill you're accompanied everywhere by the rush and gurgle of the tiny streams that tumble through the valley. You will see a maze of little paths, so follow your

nose downhill, being sure to watch your footing as the cobbles can sometimes be slippery.

At the bottom, the path rejoins the main track near a magnificent red cedar. Turn right here and walk the 50m (55 yards) to the Fonte dos Passarinhos, a Moorish-style tiled pavilion with benches and a fountain inside. Keep the pavilion on your right and continue downhill, following the signs to *lagos* (lakes). When you reach the lakes, follow the path down with the water on your left.

❻ There are four man-made lakes, edged with walls and boulders and fed by the water from the Queen's Fern Valley. They're home to various waterbirds, including a pair of black swans. The largest is the bottom lake, where there's a monument to Dom Fernando II, the initiator of the plantings here in 1839. Don't miss the duck houses, complete with crenellations, Moorish flourishes and ramps to give the ducks easy access to the water.

Leave the park through the bottom gate; a tourist bus runs from the stop just up to the right.

WHERE TO EAT

There is nowhere to eat in the park itself. Either take a picnic, or try a restaurant in Sintra town before or after the walk.

WHEN TO GO

With its shady paths and easy downhill walking, this walk is particularly enjoyable on hot summer afternoons.

PLACES TO VISIT
PALÁCIO NACIONAL DA PENA
(▷ 113)

Opposite *The palace of Pena emerges from densely wooded slopes*
Below left *The park combines European and Asiatic plantings*
Below right *Woods stretch into the distance from the Moorish palace*

Above *The stylish resort of Estoril has plenty to offer visitors*

CARCAVELOS

CARCAVELOS SURF SCHOOL
www.windsurfcafe.pt
Surfing is big in Portugal, and Carcavelos beach is popular with both pros and beginners. If you're a beginner, you could arrange lessons with a professional teacher. These are available at the Windsurf Café, the hippest of the Carcavelos beachfront bars, set mid-way along the beach.
✉ Windsurf Café, Praia de Carcavelos, Avenida Marginal, 2775 Carcavelos ☎ 962 850 497 or 966 131 203 ⏰ Wed–Fri 5pm–7pm, Sat–Sun 11–1, 4–6. Closed Aug ⚐ Registration €10; 1 lesson €25; set of 4 lessons €75

CASCAIS

BAR DO GUINCHO
www.bardoguincho.pt
Overlooking the pounding Guincho surf, this is a good place for a snack lunch or full meal. It is also a hot nightspot, snug with a log fire in winter and cool and breezy in the summer. During weekends, it hosts live bands and karaoke.
✉ Estrada do Abano, Praia do Guincho Norte, 2750-715 Cascais ☎ 214 871 683 ⏰ Sun, Tue–Thu noon–2am, Fri–Sat noon–4am 🚌 415, 405 from Cascais

BICAS
For getting around town pick up a bicycle free of charge outside the station in Cascais, or if you fancy a ride out to the Guincho beach along the cycle track then pick one up at the kiosk at the Cidadela forte or at Guia. (You must show ID or a passport.)
☎ 214 868 204 (tourist office) ⏰ Daily 9–5

BOCA DO INFERNO
The 'Mouth of Hell', where surf rushes into a crevasse in the rocky coastline, is Cascais' most popular attraction. Around it a small craft market has grown up, which offers a good selection of pottery, woollens and textiles.
✉ Estrada da Boca do Inferno, 2750 Cascais ☎ 214 868 204 (tourist office) ⏰ Daily 10–7

CASCAISHOPPING
www.cascaishopping.pt
Since it was extended in 2003, this mall now has around 160 shops housing branches of major international stores, such as FNAC, Mango, C&A, Benetton, Zara and many more. It also has two large food halls and multiscreen cinemas.
✉ Estrada Nacional 9, 2645-543 Alcabideche ☎ 210 121 628 ⏰ Daily 10am–11pm 🚌 417 from Cascais

CASCAIS MUNICIPAL MARKET
The municipal market lies behind the Cascais Villa Shopping Mall. Although the inside stands are open all week, the best days to come are Wednesday and Saturday, when the central courtyard is filled with stalls selling fresh local produce.
✉ Avenida 25 de Abril, 2750 Cascais ☎ 214 868 204 (tourist office) ⏰ Wed and Sat morning 7–1

CENTRO CULTURAL DE CASCAIS
www.cm-cascais.pt
At the heart of cultural activities in Cascais is the CCC, housed in funky renovated buildings near the castle. A full line-up of events includes classical music, dance, theatre, exhibitions and, in summer, live performances held in the Largo de Camões.
✉ Avenida Rei Humberto II de Itália, 2750-641 Cascais ☎ 214 848 900 ⏰ Tue–Sun 10–6 ⚐ €5–€10, although many events are free 🚭 📱

CENTRO HÍPICO DA QUINTA DA MARINHA

www.quintadamarinha-centrohipico.pt
Horse-racing began here in 1924 and today this venue is one of the largest and best equipped in the country, with paddocks, show grounds, outdoor arenas, a racing track and horses to rent by the hour.
✉ Quinta da Marinha Areia, 2750-004 Cascais ☎ 918 140 674 or 918 139 434 ⏰ Daily 9–1, 3–7 💶 €30 per hour

COCONUTS

www.nuts-club.com
Cascais' best-known club is perched on the rocks above the ocean, just past the marina. With several bars and lounge areas, it plays club sounds from top DJs.
✉ Avenida Rei Humberto II de Itália 7, 2750-461 Cascais ☎ 214 844 109 ⏰ Jun–end Sep Tue–Sat 11pm–6am; Oct–end May Fri–Sat; nights before a national holiday 11pm–6am 💶 Usually €10 (includes drinks) but can be as high as €250 to discourage undesirable patrons

JARDIM DA GANDARINHA

This large park is great for kids when it's time to relax and take a break from shopping or the beach. As well as grassy lawns, there are adventure playgrounds with slides, swings and climbing frames, a lake with ducks and swans, dirt tracks for bicycle riding and an aviary. Peacocks wander freely through the park.
✉ Parque Municipal da Gandarinha, 2750-475 Cascais ☎ 214 868 204 (tourist office)

OITAVOS GOLFE

www.quintadamarinha-oitavosgolfe.pt
www.portugalgolf.pt
Designed by Robert Trent Jones and considered one of the best courses in Europe, Oitavos has 18 holes and a par of 71. The chic clubhouse, with outdoor terraces and panoramic views, looks out over the ocean.
✉ Quinta da Marinha, Casa da Quinta 25, 2750-004 Cascais ☎ 214 860 600 ⏰ May–end Oct daily 7.30am–8.30pm; rest of year daily 7.30–7 💶 Jul–end Aug and 15 Nov–15 Feb €75 18 holes; rest of year €150 18 holes; club rental €40; electric trolley €18; buggy €55

JUNE–JULY
FESTIVAL DE MÚSICA E DANÇA

This music festival (▷ 21) is held mainly in the Centro Cultural Olga Cadaval in Praça Francisco Sá Carneiro and is the highlight of Sintra's cultural calendar, attracting world-class dance and classical music performances.
✉ Sintra ☎ 219 231 157 (information from the tourist office at Praça da República) or 219 107 117 (Centro Cultural Olga Cadaval at Praça Francisco Sá Carneiro) ⏰ Mid-Jun to mid-Jul

JULY
ESTORIL JAZZ FESTIVAL

This laid-back festival brings top international jazz names to perform in Estoril throughout July. Weekend performances are held in several venues, so for full details contact the tourist office, opposite the train station on Avenida Marginal.
✉ Estoril ☎ 214 663 813 (tourist office)

JULY–AUGUST
FEIRA DO ARTESANATO

Held during the summer, this crafts fair sets up daily in the area beside the casino. It offers a selection of regional crafts, as well as paintings, handmade jewellery, leather goods and other souvenirs.
✉ Estoril ☎ 214 663 813 (tourist office) ⏰ Summer daily 6pm–midnight

ESTORIL
CASINO ESTORIL

www.casinoestoril.pt
The casino at Estoril has more than 1,000 gaming machines, as well as traditional gaming tables. The show rooms offer dancing girls and top musical entertainment, the gardens flash with lasers and the Chinese restaurant is one of the best in the whole country.
✉ Praça José Teodoro dos Santos, 2769-327 Estoril ☎ 214 667 700 ⏰ Daily 3pm–3am, floor shows Mon–Sat 11pm, Sun 10pm

CLUBE DE GOLF DO ESTORIL

www.portugalgolf.pt
Designed by Mackenzie Ross in 1945, this club underwent changes when the Cascais highway was built in the 1960s. But it remains a great par-69 course, with the 16th hole considered by many golfers to be Portugal's best.
✉ Avenida da República, 2765-273 Estoril ☎ 214 680 054 or 214 660 367 ⏰ Daily 7.30–8 💶 18 holes Mon–Fri €65, Sat–Sun reserved for members; club rental €35; hand trolleys €4 🚌 Take Estoril/Sintra turn-off from the A5 highway. Turn right on the EN9 towards Sintra. The course is 200m (218 yards) on the left

SINTRA
MUSEU DO BRINQUEDO

www.museu-do-brinquedo.pt
In a converted fire station, this museum has more than 20,000 toys, including clockwork trains.
✉ Rua Visconde de Monserrate, 2710-591 Sintra ☎ 219 242 171 ⏰ Tue–Sun 10–6 💶 Adult €4, child (3–16) €2

PIRIQUITA

Piriquita started making its famously delicious *queijadas* (cheesecakes in a pastry shell) in the 1860s. It is also known for its almond *travesseiros*.
✉ Rua das Padarias 1–7, 2710-603 Sintra ☎ 219 230 626 ⏰ Thu–Tue 9am–10pm. On Wed Periquita II is open just up the road

SINTRA TUR HORSE AND CARRIAGE RIDE

www.sintratur.com
To see Sintra by horse-drawn carriage, rent one by the *pelhourino* (pillory) just below the National Palace, or from the entrance to the Parque da Liberdade. It's worth checking prices at the tourist office.
✉ Sintratur, Rua João de Deus 82, 2710-579 Sintra ☎ 219 241 238 or 219 231 157 (tourist office) ⏰ May–end Sep 10–6; rest of year 11–5 💶 €30–€90

Above *One of Sintra's relaxing bars*

PRICES AND SYMBOLS

The restaurants are listed alphabetically. The prices given are the average for a two-course lunch (L) and a three-course dinner (D) for one person, without drinks. The wine price is for the least expensive bottle. All the restaurants listed accept credit cards unless otherwise stated.

For a key to the symbols, ▷ 2.

All listings in Cascais, Carcavelos and Estoril can be reached from Lisbon by train from the Cais de Sodré station. Listings in Guincho are best reached by taxi from Cascais (approximately €6), although bus numbers from Cascais are given. Listings in Sintra can be reached from Lisbon by train from the Rossio train station.

CASCAIS

CARVOARIA

Just beyond the Visconde da Luz garden, this is a great option if you're looking for plainly grilled, reasonably priced fresh fish. You can choose from a selection of sea bass, bream, or whatever has been freshly caught that day, all cooked over hot coals as the restaurant's name implies—*carvoaria* means

coalhouse. For dedicated meat-eaters, there are cuts of beef and pork, which are also served grilled. ✉ Rua João Luís de Moura 24, 2750-387 Cascais ☎ 214 830 406 🕓 Sun–Fri 12–3, 7–11, Sat 12–3. Closed first 2 weeks Apr, first 2 weeks Oct 🖐 L €12, D €15, Wine €7.50 🚌 Cascais

CASA DA GUIA

www.casadaguia.com
Out on the Guincho road, the group of eateries is a great place for lunch or afternoon tea. Choose from pastries and quiches at Confeitaria do Monte, or sample a slice of cake at Chá da Guia and watch the sun set over the ocean. At night, you could try Dom Grelhas or Prazeres da Carne for grilled fish and meat. ✉ Estrada do Guincho, 2750 Cascais 🕓 Daily 10–10 🖐 L €10, D €20, Wine €7 🚌 415, 405 from Cascais

ENOTECA DE CASCAIS

www.enotecadecascais.com
Situated in the centre of Cascais, this place is a wine lover's dream, with more than 400 wines, 50 available by the glass. The menu is varied and includes fine cheeses and cured meats, wild boar with apple and mango chutney and bream with

spinach. It may be best to try one of their set menus for two in order to sample a variety of the great dishes on offer (€55–€60 for two). ✉ Rua Visconde da Luz 17 ℹ j-3, 2750-415 Cascais ☎ 214 822 328 🕓 Sun–Thu 7.30–1am, Fri–Sat 7.30–2am 🖐 L €25, D €35, Wine €10

FORTALEZA DO GUINCHO

www.guinchotel.pt
Perched above the ocean in a 16th-century fort, this Michelin-starred restaurant looks onto the ocean and the cliffs. The prices are high, but reflect the quality of the experience and the impeccable service. Try gilt-head sea bream with stewed fennel and anise, or their roast partridge, and, for dessert, chocolate truffles with lemon sorbet. There's an extensive list of Portuguese and foreign wines. ✉ Estrada do Guincho, 2750-642 Cascais ☎ 214 870 491 🕓 Daily 12.30–3, 7.30–10.30 🖐 L €50, D €75, Wine €15 🚌 415, 405 from Cascais

MELTING POT

In downtown Cascais above the Largo de Camões, this candlelit restaurant serves a set menu of 10 courses. Dishes vary daily and all are expertly prepared and deliciously cooked. A typical menu is salad, breaded grilled cheese with wild berries, and stewed partridge. Credit cards are not accepted.

✉ Rua Nova da Alfarrobeira 4A, Cascais ☎ 214 820 627, 919 916 123 ⊙ Tue–Sat 7.30–10 ✋ D €30 inc. wine 🚆 Cascais

PEREIRA

This simple eatery serves traditional cooking with few frills. Food arrives on metal serving platters in large portions, so ask for a half-serving or share. Roast kid and duck with rice are popular, as are the other meat dishes, which are served with chips and rice. For dessert, the *leite creme* (crème brûlée) is good. Credit cards are not accepted.

✉ Rua Bela Vista 92, 2750-304 Cascais ☎ 214 831 215 ⊙ Fri–Wed 12–3, 7–10.30 ✋ L €12, D €17, Wine €6.50 🚆 Cascais

PORTO DE SANTA MARIA

www.portosantamaria.com
One of the most respected fish restaurants along this windswept Atlantic coast road, award-winning Porto de Santa Maria is set above the ocean with views of the *serra*. After a glass of champagne, choose from the seafood and fresh fish on offer, which is simply grilled over hot coals, or lightly fried. When it comes to dessert, soufflés are the house forte.

✉ Estrada do Guincho, Guincho, 2750-640 Cascais ☎ 214 879 450 ⊙ Tue–Sun 12.30–3.30, 7.30–10.30 ✋ L €40, D €55, Wine €11 🚌 415, 405 from Cascais

SOMOS UM REGALO

The best grilled chicken restaurant in Cascais, this restaurant has large conical chimneys. Order your chicken with or without *picante* (spicy piri-piri sauce) and accompany it with rice, fries, a large tomato salad and pitcher of sangria. A good option for kids, and the staff are helpful.

✉ Avenida Vasco da Gama 36, 2750-509 Cascais ☎ 214 842 109 ⊙ Thu–Tue 12–2.30, 7–10 ✋ L €12, D €16, Wine €8

COLARES

MOINHO DOM QUIXOTE

If you are driving from Cascais to Colares and Sintra via Cabo de Roca, this is a superb place for lunch or afternoon tea, especially in good weather. The Moinho is a converted windmill with beautiful terraced gardens and magnificent views over the Sintra hills and the coastline. The salads and hamburgers are equally excellent, and the bar attracts a lively crowd in the evening.

✉ Rua do Moinho, Azoia, 2705-001 Sintra ☎ 219 292 523 ⊙ Daily noon–2am ✋ L €12, D €20, Wine €8 🚌 403 from Sintra or Cascais station 🚗 Take the Cabo da Roca turn-off from the main Cascais–Colares coastal road and then second left, signed to Moinho

ESTORIL

AL FRESCO

Although situated in a somewhat unattractive shopping mall just up from the casino, this restaurant serves genuine Italian cuisine as opposed to the fast-food variety. You could start with delicately seasoned carpaccio, then move on to one of the many delicious pasta dishes. It was its superb risottos that put this restaurant on the map, and there are several varieties to choose from, including *funghi porcini* (dried mushrooms) and prawns with mint.

✉ Centro Comercial Estoril Parque, Lj 45 (shop 45), Rua de Lisboa 5, 2765-240 Estoril ☎ 214 676 770 ⊙ Tue–Sun 12.30–3.30, 7.30–11.30 ✋ L €15, D €22, Wine €8 🚆 Estoril

ESTORIL MANDARIN

The classy Mandarin Sol offers some of the best Chinese food in the country. Housed within the Estoril casino complex, it has great views down the length of the park to the sea. At night, the trees and fountain are lit up and lasers flash (there's a laser show nightly at 9.30pm). The dining rooms are large and airy, and the menu is predominantly Cantonese. Dim sum and Peking duck are popular choices. Finish off with banana, apple and pineapple *fasi* (fritters).

✉ Praça José Teodoro dos Santos, Casino do Estoril, 2769-237 Estoril ☎ 214 667 270 ⊙ Wed–Mon 12–3, 7–11 ✋ L €25, D €30, Wine €10 🚆 Estoril

PRAIA DO TAMARIZ

A good spot for lunch along the seaside promenade from Cascais to Estoril, the place where exiled European monarchs, political refugees and spies took up residence during the 1940s and 1950s. Set above the sandy Tamariz beach, the place provides quick snacks as well as more substantial meals for the visitors and locals who come to enjoy the beach and ocean views from its terraces.

✉ Praia do Tamariz, 2765-289 Estoril ☎ 214 681 010 ⊙ Apr–end Sep daily 9–12; Oct–end Mar Wed–Mon 9–6 ✋ L €12, D €22, Wine €7 🚆 Estoril

SINTRA

LAWRENCE'S HOTEL

www.lawrenceshotel.com
This fine 17th-century building was patronized by Lord Byron, Eça de Queiroz and other prominent literary figures of the 19th century. You can eat in one of the the classic dining rooms or on the terrace, with its views of the *serra*. Try the salt cod à la Lawrence's, or the delicious fish soup served with a puff pastry crust. (▷ 123 for accommodation details.)

✉ Rua Consigleri Pedroso 38–40, Vila Velha, 2710-550 Sintra ☎ 219 105 500 ⊙ Daily 12.30–3, 7.30–10 ✋ L €35, D €50, Wine €14

TACHO REAL

This restaurant is situated in the historic heart of Sintra. It offers traditional Portuguese dishes, including salt cod, squid, *caçao* (skate) on a bed of clams, prawn curry and beef medallions Tacho Real style. For vegetarians there is a good selection of roasted vegetables. The pears stewed in red wine make a great finish.

✉ Rua da Ferraria 4, Vila Velha, 2710-555 Sintra ☎ 219 235 277 ⊙ Thu–Tue 12–3, 7.30–10 (Nov–end Feb Mon 12–3 only; months may vary) ✋ L €25, D €30, Wine €16

STAYING

PRICES AND SYMBOLS

The prices are the lowest and highest for a double room for one night including breakfast, unless otherwise stated. All the hotels listed accept credit cards unless otherwise stated. Note that rates can vary widely throughout the year.

For a key to the symbols, ▷ 2.

AZÓIA
CONVENTO DE SÃO SATURNINO
www.saosat.com
Clinging to the hillside overlooking the Atlantic, this 12th-century convent is an oasis of calm, just the place to relax after a busy day touring. In the bedrooms, the atmosphere created by the combination of old ceiling beams and beautiful fabrics is unbeatable. Breakfast is served in the converted kitchen and chapel, or on sunnier days on the shady terrace. Dinner can be ordered in advance and eaten while admiring the sunset. Beside the swimming pool is a pavilion where an open fire is laid on cooler days.

✉ 2705-001 Azóia ☎ 219 283 192
🖐 €140–€190 🛈 6 rooms, 3 suites
🏊 Outdoor 🚌 403 from Cascais 🚗 Turn off the main Cascais–Colares road at the left turn signed 'Cabo de Roca'. Take the second left, go past Moinho de Don Quixote and look for the sign for the *convento* on the left-hand side

CASCAIS
CASA DA PÉRGOLA
www.pergolahouse.com
This *casa* in central Cascais is easily recognized by the vivid blue, white and red decorative tiles adorning its façade (not to mention many local postcards). The interior is fairly formal, while the bedrooms have carved wooden beds, stucco ceilings and beautiful old light fittings. The hotel is closed from 1 December to the end of February.

✉ Avenida Valbom 13, 2750-508 Cascais
☎ 214 840 040 🖐 €99–€131 🛈 8

ESTALAGEM SENHORA DA GUIA
www.senhoradaguia.com
Some 3km (2 miles) from Cascais, on the Guincho road, this fine 1970s

Above Hotel Tivoli Palácio de Seteais in Sintra is an 18th-century palace

building was once the country retreat of the Sagres brewery family. As a hotel it's impressive, offering some of the most sophisticated accommodation in the area, with immediate access to the sea and several golf courses. Set in pretty gardens with a panoramic saltwater swimming pool and large restaurant terrace, the hotel is tastefully furnished with both period and contemporary pieces.

✉ Estrada do Guincho, 2750-642 Cascais
☎ 214 869 239 🖐 €150–€300 🛈 40 rooms, 1 suite (non-smoking available)
🅿 🏊 Outdoor 📺

ESTALAGEM VILLA ALBATROZ
www.albatrozhotels.com
Set right above Cascais bay, this delightful 18th-century villa was built by the dukes of Palmela, and at one time was frequented by novelists and poets. It now offers some of the most stylish boutique accommodation in Cascais. Rooms

in this 5-star hotel are fresh and airy, and are decorated in a Dona Maria style with exquisite fabrics and prints. The equally elegant restaurant serves both national and international cuisine.

✉ Rua Fernandes Tomás 1, 2750-342 Cascais ☎ 214 863 410 🖐 €177–€385 🛈 11 ♿

FAROL DESIGN HOTEL
www.farol.com.pt
Close to the marina and the Boca do Inferno, this 19th- century building was once the home of the Count of Cabral. It has now been stylishly refurbished and a modern wing has been added. Seven of the rooms were designed by well-known Portuguese fashion designers, some using vibrant hues and others soft pastel shades. An outdoor saltwater pool and full spa facilities add to the pleasures of this fabulous homage to design. The ultra-modern black, white and shocking-red restaurant, the Rosa Maria, has sea views and a menu of dishes described as 'Mediterranean fusion'. A summer bed terrace and ocean terrace are both perfect for evening drinks. In fact, they boast that you can 'practically touch the sea' from here.

✉ Avenida Rei Humberto II de Itália 7, 2750-461 Cascais ☎ 214 823 490 🖐 €130–€300 🛈 33 ♿ 🏊 Outdoor saltwater

HOTEL ALBATROZ AND ALBATROZ PALACE
www.albatrozhotels.com
The oldest and architecturally most impressive part of this hotel, which is made up of four buildings set on the rocks above the beach, is the duke's palace, dating from 1873. Here, neo-Manueline meets neo-Gothic with a hint of Arab influence. The design of the spacious interior shows great attention to detail. The terrace bar is a great place to watch the sun set and the restaurant offers a fine international menu.

✉ Rua Frederico Arouce 100, 2750-353 Cascais ☎ 214 847 380 🖐 €275–€365 🛈 48 rooms, 11 suites (located in palace) ♿ 🏊 Outdoor

VILA BICUDA
www.vilabicuda.com
If you are looking for a self-catering option Vila Bicuda is a great choice as it is centrally situated between Cascais town centre and the Guincho beach to the north. The resort offers all the amenities of a hotel with the added independence of private accommodation, ideal for those travelling with children. There is child care available on site. A car would be useful.

✉ Rua dos Faisões, Vila Bicuda, 2750-689 Cascais ☎ 214 860 200 🖐 Studio apartments €90–€300, 1 bedroom apartment €150–€375, 2 bedroom apartment €180–€450, 3 bedroom apartment €250–€600 🛈 78 studios, villas and apartments ♿ 🏊 Outdoor

ESTORIL
HOTEL PALÁCIO DE ESTORIL
www.palacioestorilhotel.com
This hotel was opened in 1930 as part of a plan to encourage tourism in the area, and during World War II it became a haven for many well-heeled refugees from across Europe, including several exiled monarchs. From those who had escaped to safety but had run out of cash, the understanding hotel management accepted payment in diamonds, rubies or gold. Thankfully, much of the hotel's old-world charm remains intact. Its splendid Pompeian public rooms and intimate salons lead to Regency-style bedrooms, many with superb views.

✉ Rua Particular, 2769-504 Estoril ☎ 214 648 000 🖐 €350–€380 🛈 130 rooms, 30 suites ♿ 🏊 Outdoor

SINTRA
HOTEL TIVOLI PALÁCIO DE SETEAIS
www.tivolihotels.com
Set in classically landscaped gardens surrounding the pool, this 18th-century palace is a relaxing haven. The public rooms, furnished with period furniture and elaborate hand-painted murals, once hosted parties in honour of the royal family, who used to spend the summer at nearby Sintra. Sash-windowed

bedrooms are all lavishly furnished with period-style furniture, and the grand marble staircase descends to the Panoramic restaurant, decorated with 18th-century-style murals. The covered terrace beyond overlooks the gardens. Staff are friendly and helpful, and there is a tennis court.

✉ Rua Barbosa do Bocage 8–10, 2710-517 Sintra ☎ 219 233 200 🖐 Closed for refurbishment until early 2009. Call for latest information 🛈 29 rooms, 1 suite ♿ 🏊 Outdoor

LAWRENCE'S HOTEL
www.lawrenceshotel.com
Opened in 1764, this inn claims to be the oldest hotel on the Iberian peninsula, and soon became a haunt of such 19th-century literary figures as Lord Byron. Closed for many years, it was restored to its former state in 1999 and is often referred to as a 'restaurant with rooms'. The wood-panelled library has an open fire, and there are welcoming bedrooms, hand-painted walls and breathtaking views. The superb restaurant serves modern Portuguese cooking (▷ 121).

✉ Rua Consigliéri Pedroso 38–40, 2910-550 Sintra ☎ 219 105 500 🖐 €205–€256 🛈 11 rooms, 5 suites ♿

QUINTA DA CAPELA
www.quintadacapela.com
This one-time ducal home on the mossy country lane linking Sintra with Colares was practically destroyed in the 1755 earthquake. The façade you see today dates from the 18th-century rebuilding, when the chapel was lined with fine decorative tiles. Rooms are furnished with a mixture of antique and country-style pieces; breakfast is served in the attractive dining room looking out over the quiet gardens. Modern additions include a pool, gym and sauna, but the quinta still remains the epitomy of a Sintra country house. Closed November to end February.

✉ Turismo de Habitação, Estrada Velha de Colares, Monserrate, 2710-502 Sintra ☎ 219 290 170 🖐 €150–€160 🛈 9 🏊 Outdoor 🐾

THE MINHO AND TRÁS-OS-MONTES

These neighbouring regions offer stark contrasts. One is heavily inhabited, given to manufacturing and agriculture and vying for predominance with the Atlantic to its west; the other is natural, indomitable with wide open moorlands, towering valleys and a sparse population. What does unite these two northern regions is granite. Whether used in construction or still sitting in monolithic boulders, this grey rock is ubiquitous. On rainy days, when the sea and hill mists roll in, it can appear dour and forebidding, but catch it on a sunny day and its crystal grains glisten adding a sparkle to the verdant landscape.

The remoteness of Trás-os-Montes has ensured the preservation not only of its rugged granite geography but of its ancient traditions. There are medieval, ritualistic festivals such as that of the *Rapazes* in Miranda do Douro; gastronomic delicacies like the highly prized *alheira* (smoked sausage) which dates from the Inquisition; and scattered over the hills the 19th-century, white-washed *pombais* (dovecotes), now being restored and promoted as a tourist attraction. If visiting in the early spring there is the added bonus of seeing the steep river terraces covered in almond blossom.

Where Trás-os-Montes appears to be at nature's mercy, the Minho has been reigned in and domesticated. Below its uplands, the granite boulders have been broken down to build its towns. Viana do Castelo bustles with traditional commerce and has 16th-century, Flemmish-influenced architecture. On alternate weeks, Ponte de Lima hosts Portugal's oldest market, established by royal charter in the 12th century, while Barcelos' weekly *feira* is great for pottery and the emblematic cockerel. Braga has its churches and Guimarães its historic squares. Thanks to frequent rain and an abundance of springs, the land is fertile and heavily cultivated. Be sure to notice the granite-supported vines of the must-try, regional *vinho verde* (slightly fizzy, young wine).

BARCELOS

www.rtp.pt

Try to visit Barcelos on a Thursday, when this attractive town bursts with vibrant life during its vast weekly market, or *feira*, which is one of the largest in Europe. Here you can buy anything from fruit and vegetables, grown by farmers on the surrounding smallholdings, to live rabbits, sportswear, clothes and CDs, as well as the wonderful handicrafts for which the Minho is famous. It's also the place to pick up a red-and-black ceramic cockerel, the town's emblem. Legend has it that a Santiago pilgrim, wrongly accused of theft, declared that the judge's roast chicken dinner would stand up and crow if he was sentenced to hang. The cock crowed, the pilgrim was set free and a monument was erected in memory of the miracle, which you can still see in the archaeological museum in the ruins of the old ducal palace. The palace stands high above the River Cávado and is backed by the beautiful 13th-century Igreja Matriz, whose interior, rich with blue *azulejos* (tiles), glitters with gold. There are more tiles and ceramics in the Museu de Olaria, which has a huge range of Minho examples. Another of the town's highlights, the 1704 Templo de Bom Jesus da Cruz, overlooks the Campo, site of the *feira*. Its white and granite exterior sets the standard for church design all over the Minho. Take time to stroll through the tempting shopping streets and walk along the riverbank.

✚ 326 B3 🛈 Torre de Menagem, Largo da Porta Nova, 4750-329 Barcelos ☎ 253 811 882 🚊 Barcelos

BRAGA AND BOM JESUS

▷ 128–131.

BRAGANÇA

▷ 132.

CAMINHA

www.rtam.pt

Caminha, a relaxed river port and historically important frontier town, stands at the confluence of the River Coura with the mouth of the Minho. The town still guards the border between Portugal and Spain, and you can take a ferry across the river to the Spanish town of La Guardia. It's a peaceful place to stop if you're heading south, with a clutch of monuments around its spacious main square, the Praça Conselheiro Silva Torres. Here you will find a fine 16th-century granite fountain, a stately town hall and a clock tower that once formed part of the 14th-century fortifications.

The road through the arch leads to the town's main attraction, the magnificent Igreja Matriz. Built between the 15th and 16th centuries, at the height of the town's prosperity, the Renaissance building's carved south door is framed by pilasters supporting a gallery with statues of St. Peter and St. Paul. Inside, there is a superb maplewood ceiling, a fine carved pulpit and intricate decorative *azulejos* (tiles).

✚ 326 B2 🛈 Rua Ricardo Joaquim Sousa, 4910-155 Caminha ☎ 258 921 952 🚊 Caminha

CHAVES

www.rt-atb.pt

For centuries the town, only 12km (7.5 miles) from the Spanish border, was fought over by the Spanish and Portuguese. Today, things are more peaceful, and modern Chaves is proud of its links with Spanish Galicia, celebrated during the *Festas da Cidade* in July. A market town and capital of the northern Trás-os-Montes, Chaves is also well known for being a spa resort—the hot springs bubble up from the ground at 73°C (163°F) and have valuable therapeutic properties. The area also produces gastronomic delights, including some of Portugal's finest hams, sausages and red wines.

The old quarter stands just above the River Tâmega, with the spa to the west below the old walls. The area is dominated by two 17th-century fortresses, the Forte de São Francisco, now a luxury hotel, and the Forte de São Neutel, where concerts are sometimes held. There's an interesting museum, the Museu da Região Flaviense in the Praça de Luis Camões (tel 276 340 500; Mon–Sun 9–12.30, 2–5.30; €1), which traces the history of the town from its foundation as a Roman spa—a good place to visit once you have seen the Ponte Trajana, named after Emperor Trajan. The main churches, the Igreja da Misericórdia with its huge tile panels, and the severe Igreja Matriz, its apse still proudly retaining its Romanesque elements, are both worth a visit.

✚ 326 D2 🛈 Terreiro de Cavalaria, 5400-531 Chaves ☎ 276 340 661

Opposite *Torre de Menagem, part of the Barcelos fortifications, houses the tourist office*
Below *The picturesque old quarter of Chaves clusters around the Roman bridge*

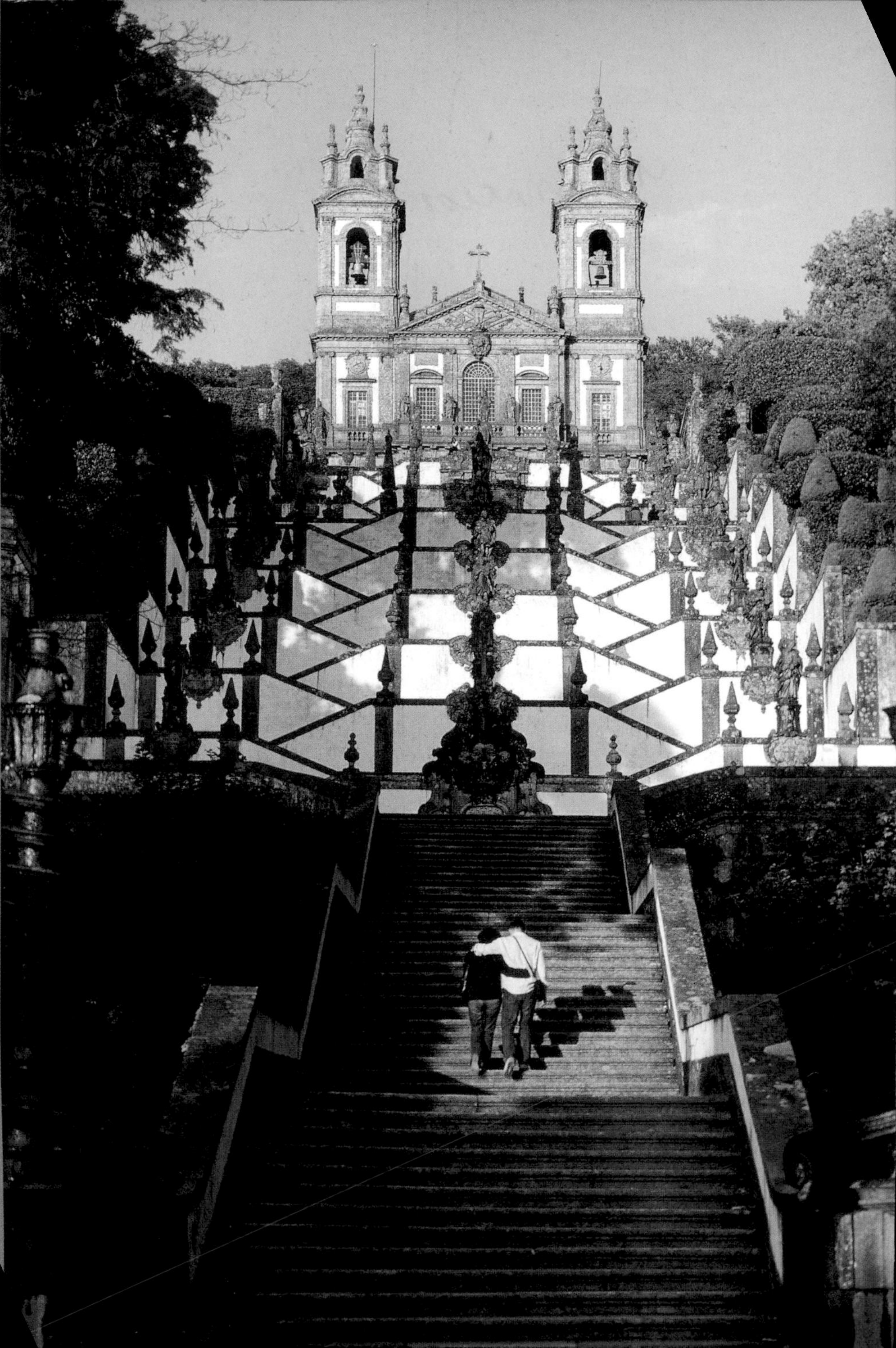

BRAGA AND BOM JESUS

INTRODUCTION

Braga makes a good base if you are touring the southern Minho, particularly if you are relying on public transport. If you are simply making a brief visit for a few hours, start exploring from the Praça de República, an arcaded square at the top of the old town. From here, follow Rua do Souto downhill; Braga's highlights are on or around this lively shopping street, which runs down to the Porta Nova and traverses the whole of the old city. The baroque staircase and pilgrim church of Bom Jesus do Monte are on a hillside 5km (3 miles) east of the city; you can drive right up to the church near the top of the hill, or alternatively there are regular buses from Braga to the foot of the staircase at the bottom of the hill, where a funicular runs up to the church.

Braga, Roman Bracara Augusta, has a long history, much of which is entwined with that of the Catholic Church in Portugal, starting from the time of the Christian reconquest of the 11th century. The city was probably a Celtic foundation. After a long period of Roman occupation, it fell to the Suevi and then to the Visigoths before being captured by the Moors. Recaptured by the Christians in 1070, its archbishops pressed hard for recognition as the Primates of the Spains, Iberia's most important religious position, against the rival claims of Toledo and Tarragona.

Eventually, Braga's name became synonymous with Catholicism in Portugal. The Portuguese saying 'while Coimbra studies and Lisbon plays, Porto works and Braga prays' neatly sums up its traditional position in Portuguese life, as demonstrated by the city's many fine examples of Renaissance and baroque buildings, erected at the most potent time in Portugal's ecclesiastical history. The superb ornamental stairway of Bom Jesus do Monte, just outside the city, is a splendid example of the architectural achievements of the period.

Braga is still the seat of the Portuguese archbishops, and the religious processions and celebrations here are among the most fervent in the country. Over the past decades, however, the city has been keen to shake off its traditional conservative and religious image and has been working hard to promote more commercial assets, particularly the thriving industries on the outskirts. The prominent role Braga played in the 2004 European Football Championships certainly brought the city's secular side well to the fore. Its

INFORMATION

www.cm-braga.pt

✚ 326 C3 ℹ️ Avenida de Liberdade 1, 4710-305 Braga ☎ 253 262 550 🕐 Jun–end Sep Mon–Fri 9–7, Sat–Sun 9–12.30, 2–5.30; rest of year Mon–Fri 9–12.30, 2–6, Sat –Sun 9–12.30, 2–5.30 🚆 Braga

Above *The baroque façade of the Hospital de São Marco in Braga*
Opposite *The double stairway leading to Bom Jesus do Monte has more than 1,000 steps*

TIPS

» Driving into and out of Braga is confusing—arrive either early or during the middle of the day when there's less traffic.

» There's a large underground parking area below the Praça de República on the Avenida Central, a few minutes' walk from the highlights.

» Braga's most important festivals celebrate *Semana Santa* (Holy Week, the week before Easter), the *Festas de São João* (the Festival of St. John, 23—24 Jun) and *Bom Jesus* (Sacred Jesus, six weeks after Easter at Whitsun). It's a wise precaution to reserve accommodation well in advance if you are planning to stay in the city during these times.

» Bom Jesus is very crowded at weekends.

Below *The fine granite and whitewash exterior of the Bom Jesus do Monte church, Braga*

continued diversification demonstrates that Braga is much more than simply a deeply religious and politically reactionary town.

WHAT TO SEE

SÉ

www.se-braga.pt

Braga's cathedral was founded immediately after the Christian reconquest in 1070 on the site of a Moorish mosque. Little remains of the original French-influenced Romanesque building, but the south doorway on the side wall to the right of the main façade is decorated with quirky scenes from the legend of Renard the Fox. The main east front has a portico with Gothic arches, built in the 16th century for Archbishop Diogo de Sousa by Basque workmen. As you approach, it's more likely your eye will be drawn to the cathedral's roofline, topped with pinnacles and balusters. This, too, was commissioned by the Archbishop and is the work of João de Castilho, who was to go on to work on Lisbon's Mosteiro dos Jerónimos (▷ 74), one of the greatest of all Manueline buildings in Portugal.

The interior is surprisingly small, a plain nave contrasting with the rich baroque woodwork and a Manueline font, with its elaborate, twisted carving. Walk down the nave to the crossing, with its 1970s stained glass, for a close-up of the high altar, where the plain granite walls provide the perfect backdrop for a lovely 14th-century statue of the Virgin and an altar carved with scenes from the Ascension. The *azulejos* (tiles) in the chapel to the left date from the 18th century. Turn your back on the altar for a view of the ornate double baroque organs in the Coro Alto, a masterpiece dripping with gold and covered with trumpets and angels.

A door below the Coro leads into the cloisters, giving access to a courtyard surrounded by three chapels. The Capela dos Reis, where you will find the 16th-century tombs of the cathedral's founders, Henry of Burgundy and his wife Tareja, the parents of Afonso Henriques, the first king of Portugal, is the most important. From the cloisters, stairs lead up to the Treasury, one of the richest in Portugal, where the compulsory guided tour whisks you past treasures spanning 800 years of masterful craftsmanship. There's a plethora of vestments, plates and reliquaries; highlights include a 10th-century Mozarabic ivory chest, a stupendous 18th-century silver-gilt monstrance studded with diamonds, and a rock crystal cross from the 14th century.

✉ Rua Dom Paio Mendes, 4700-424 Braga ☎ 253 263 317 🕓 Museum: Jun–end Aug Tue–Sun 9–12, 2–5.30; rest of year Tue–Sun 9–12, 2–6.30 ✋ Museum and chapels €3, chapel and choir stalls €2

BOM JESUS DO MONTE

The church and ornamental approachway of Bom Jesus, one of Portugal's most famous buildings and a triumph of baroque architecture, were commissioned by Archbishop Maura-Teles in 1723 and completed in 1783. A harmonious mix of whitewashed plaster and granite, the double staircase leads up to a grandiose church, commemorating through simple allegory at each landing the life and sacrifice of Christ. You can approach the church up the stairs, or by the Via Sacra, a sacred path lined with chapels whose wooden tableaux show scenes from the Passion of Christ. Each landing of the staircase has a fountain which is intended to recall the five wounds of Christ, the five Senses and the three Virtues. Pilgrims crawl up the steps on their knees, but most visitors come simply to enjoy the surrounding woods and gardens and the superb views. There are even finer vistas at the Santuário do Sameiro, about 2km (1 mile) farther on, a shrine built in the 1830s. Its vast 1950s concrete esplanade and heavy statuary bear witness to the importance given to the shrine by the Salazar regime.

✚ 326 C3 ☎ Bom Jesus do Monte 🕓 Church: daily 8–8 ✋ Funicular €1

MORE TO SEE

ANTIGO PAÇO EPISCOPAL
This huge fortress-like building consists of three blocks, dating from the 14th, 17th and 18th centuries. They now contain the municipal library and some of the university faculties. The medieval north wing has a fine reading room with a gilt coffered ceiling. The palace overlooks the pleasant Jardim de Santa Bárbara.

✉ Largo do Paço, 4700-415 Braga ☎ 253 601 187 🕐 Mon–Fri 9–12, 2–5.30 ✋ Free

MUSEU DOS BISCAÍNHOS
www.ipmuseus.pt
An absorbing museum of the decorative arts housed in the 17th- and 18th-century bishops' palace. Rooms are filled with contemporary furniture, paintings, carpets and sculpture, all in keeping with the date and style of the building. The ground floor retains its original flagstones, laid to allow carriage access to the stables. Behind the palace are tranquil green gardens.

✉ Rua dos Biscaínhos, 4700-415 Braga ☎ 253 204 650 🕐 Tue–Sun 10–12.15, 2–5.30 ✋ €2

PRAÇA DE REPÚBLICA
The main square connects the old and new city, overlooked by two linked arcades sheltering several wood-panelled historic cafés, once the meeting points for Braga's intellectuals. Behind stands the Torre de Menagem, once part of the defensive wall system. The square also has a superb trio of modern fountains.

Above *Detail of the opulent gold and frescoed interior of Braga cathedral*
Below *The tomb of Dom Henry, founder of Braga Cathedral*

INFORMATION

www.cm-braganca.pt
www.bragancanet.pt/braganca
✚ 327 F2 ℹ Avenida Cidade de
Zamora, 5300-111 Bragança ☎ 273 381
273 🄯 Oct–end Apr Mon–Fri 9–12.30,
2–5, Sat 10–12.30; May–end Sep
Mon–Fri 10–12.30, 2–6.30, Sat 9–12.30,
2–5, Sun 9–1

TIPS

» Winters in the Terra Fria area of Trás-
os-Montes are bitter and summers are
scorching; aim to visit Bragança in spring
or autumn.
» If time is short, concentrate on the
Cidadela, and, to get a real sense of the
place, perhaps return in the evening when
the crowds have left.
» The heart of old Bragança is remarkably
compact, so park your car and explore the
city on foot.

BRAGANÇA

The medieval city of Bragança is named after the Bragança dynasty, which
acquired the dukedom in 1442. During the 17th-century Spanish occupation,
it was the Braganças who became dominant; João IV gained the throne in
1640, and the family remained the Portuguese ruling house until the fall of the
monarchy in 1910. In recent years Bragança has benefited immensely from EU
funding, while, thankfully, retaining its old spirit.

THE CIDADELA

On a hillock to the east of the town is one of Portugal's most evocative sites,
a circle of medieval walls that encloses a clutch of whitewashed houses over
which loom a massive castle and keep. The huge Torre de Menagem, built in
1187, dominates the open space at the top of the hill—33m (108ft) high with
15 turrets around its walls. Inside, the two halls are lit by Gothic windows and
there are superb views from the top of a small military museum. Opposite
this is the Igreja de Santa Maria, a Romanesque church remodelled in the 18th
century, when the doorway niches and vaulted painted ceiling were installed.
Squashed up beside the church is the Domus Municipalis, built in the 13th
century as a council chamber and one of few surviving Romanesque civic
buildings in Europe. Pentagonal in shape, it has an arcaded first floor and an
underground reservoir beneath. It was here that the *homens bons* (good men)
met to dispense justice. Wrongdoers could have found themselves in the
pelhourinho (pillory) near the castle—it's supported by a prehistoric granite pig,
thought to be a fertility symbol and one of more than 200 found in the region.

MUSEUMS

The quality of the exhibits in Bragança's Abade de Baçal museum in Rua
Conselheiro Abílio Beça (tel 273 331 595; www.rpmuseus-pt.org; Tue–Fri
10–5, Sat–Sun 10–6; €2) reveals the role the town played as an administrative,
fiscal and judicial capital. In a sensitively converted 18th-century palace, once
the bishop's home and backed by splendid gardens, the museum focuses
predominantly on Celtic art from the surrounding area, but some rooms contain
sculpture, religious art and fine textiles as well. There's also an appealing
collection of local costumes and topographical paintings of the Trás-os-Montes.
    Also worth a visit is the Museu Ibérico da Mascara e do Traje at Rua D.
Fernão Mendes 24. Opened in 2007 it houses a collection of masks and
costumes as used by the *rapazes* during religious festivities (tel 273 381 008;
www.mascaraiberica.com; Tue–Sun 10–12.30, 2–6; €1).

Above *The vast Cidadela dominates the
medieval city of Bragança*

CITÂNIA DE BRITEIROS
www.guimaraesturismo.com

The Minho is scattered with the remains of *citânias*, Celtic hilltop settlements, and none is better than Citânia de Briteiros, which occupies a superb position in the oak-forested hills between Braga and Guimarães. These Iron Age villages were mainly established between 600 and 500 BC and remained occupied through to the third century AD.

Briteiros, one of Portugal's most impressive archaeological sites, is thought to have been the last stronghold to fall to the Romans, and it provides an insight into a forgotten way of life. Excavations here began in the 1870s and still continue today. Paved streets run through the settlement, with hut outlines on either side. A couple have been reconstructed to show the stone benches that hugged the circular walls and the central pillar that supported the thatched roofs. At the communal bathhouse, below the main settlement, are tanks and an ancient oven, once used for heating water to produce steam.

🚩 326 C3 ℹ️ Guimarães tourist offices: Alameda de São Dâmaso 83, 4810-286 Guimarães or Praça de Santiago, 4810-300 Guimarães ☎ 253 412 450 or 253 518 790 🕐 Alameda office: Mon–Fri 9.30–12.30, 2–6.30; Praça de Santiago office: Mon–Fri 9.30–6.30, Sat 10–6, Sun 10–1

COSTA VERDE
www.rtam.pt

The Costa Verde, the Green Coast, runs north through the Minho from Porto to the Minho river and the Spanish border, a stretch that includes beautiful beaches and a clutch of lively resorts. The main holiday towns are Viana do Castelo (▷ 143) and Póvoa de Varzim (▷ 162), both packed and bustling in summer, but there is an endless choice of quieter places, where you can have a stretch of sand virtually to yourself. You need to leave the main N13 and take minor roads down to the sea to see the best of the area. A string of popular resorts, north of Porto, leads up to Póvoa, but north of here things are less developed, particularly the protected area south of the River Neiva, where you can still see traditional farms scraped out of the dunes.

Other villages worth seeing are Esposende, a low-key resort, and Mar, still a thriving fishing community with a sideline in seaweed gathering—the seaweed is used as fertilizer. North of Viana, dunes and pines run down to the sea; Afife and Carreço have great beaches, though you will find more facilities in Praia de Âncora. Bear in mind there is summer rain along this coastline, so expect a few cloudy days, rain or wind.

🚩 326 B3 ℹ️ Rua do Hospita Velho (off Praça da Erva), 4900-540 Viana do Castelo ☎ 258 822 620 🚉 Viana do Castelo

FREIXO DE ESPADA-À-CINTA
www.rt-nordeste.pt

In a fertile bowl surrounded by grim yet beautiful mountains, Freixo was founded by Dom Dinis in the late 13th century. The king is said to have cut an ash down on this spot, giving the town its name, which means 'tree of the sword'. The town's church is a late Gothic structure whose doorway is decorated with late 15th-century motifs in the shape of twisted columns and pinnacles. Inside, there's fine network vaulting and the chancel has a superb *retábulo* (altarpiece) by the great 16th-century artist Grão Vasco.

🚩 327 F4 ℹ️ Avenida do Emigrante, 5180-103 Freixo de Espada-à-Cinta ☎ 279 653 480

GUIMARÃES
▷ 134–135.

LINDOSO
www.adere-pg.pt

A true mountain village, Lindoso perches on granite slopes deep in the heart of the Parque Nacional da Peneda-Gerês (▷ 139–141). Despite the presence of a dam and some modern buildings, it is a traditional settlement. Like so many villages in the area it is dominated by a clutch of *espigueiros*, grain storehouses built on stilts in the 18th and 19th centuries. They all have roof crosses to bring blessings on the crops and are clustered together to make communal farming easier. Lindoso's Castelo (May–end Sep Tue–Fri 10–12.30, 2–6, Sat–Sun 10–12.30, 2–5; Oct–end Apr Tue–Fri 9.30–12.30, 2–5, Sat–Sun 10–12.30, 2–4.30) is a crenellated medieval keep whose little museum provides park information.

🚩 326 C2 ℹ️ Park office: ADERE Peneda-Gerês, Largo da Misericórdia 10, 4980-613 Ponte da Barca ☎ 258 452 250

Left *Many of the Costa Verde's fine beaches remain uncrowded*

GUIMARÃES

INFORMATION

www.guimaraesturismo.com

➕ 326 C3 ℹ️ Alameda de São Dâmaso 83, 4810-286 Guimarães and Praça de Santiago 37, 4810-300 Guimarães

☎ 253 412 450 or 253 518 790

🕐 Alameda office: Mon–Fri 9.30–12.30, 2–6.30; Praça de Santiago office: Mon–Fri 9.30–6.30, Sat 10–6, Sun 10–1

🚉 Guimarães

INTRODUCTION

The historic heart of Guimarães consists of tranquil squares linked by arcades and cobbled streets and lined with buildings painted in honey shades. The southern end is bordered by wide avenues surrounding the town gardens, while the castle and the Paço dos Duques de Bragança stand to the north.

Enter the old city at the southern end from the Largo República do Brasil. The Museu Alberto Sampaio is almost immediately on your right, while farther up, the street widens into the Largo da Oliveira, a square linked by arcades to the adjoining Praça de Santiago. From here, you can walk up Rua de Santa Maria to the castle and the palace. There are some stylish shops here, though there are more interesting ones along and around Rua Paio Galvā, outside the historic town to the west.

Guimarães was the birthplace of Afonso Henriques, who became the first king of Portugal in 1143. Although the capital was soon transferred to Coimbra (▷ 182–185), Guimarães has always retained its sense of historic pride, as evidenced by the city motto *Portugal nasceu aqui* ('Portugal was born here'). Today, this beautifully preserved city is surrounded by modern development. Home to the University of the Minho, it also has a thriving cultural scene and better-than-average nightlife.

WHAT TO SEE

PAÇO DOS DUQUES DE BRAGANÇA

This fortified palace, with its steep roof, crenellations and numerous chimneys, wouldn't look out of place in northern Europe. It was built in the early 15th century by Dom Afonso, Duke of Burgundy and the illegitimate son of João I, whose familiarity with French architecture is evident from the palace's exterior. Used as a royal residence for a century, the palace fell out of favour when the court moved to Vila Viçosa (▷ 247), and was restored only in the 1930s under the Salazar regime. It is still an official presidential residence. The interior is a procession of vast rooms, with fireplaces big enough to roast an ox, and hung with tapestries woven to cartoons by Rubens. The furniture, paintings, weapons and porcelain date mainly from the 17th and 18th centuries.

Above *The fortified Paço dos Duques de Bragança in French medieval style*

✉ Rua Conde D. Henrique, 4810-245 Guimarães ☎ 253 412 273 ⏰ Jul–end Aug Tue–Sun 9.30–6; rest of year Tue–Sun 9.30–12, 2–5 💶 €4, free Sun am

LARGO DA OLIVEIRA AND PRAÇA DE SANTIAGO

The Largo da Oliveira is dominated by two superbly contrasting buildings, the Igreja de Nossa Senhora da Oliveira (Our Lady of the Olive Tree) and the old council chambers, in an arcaded building remodelled in the 17th century. The church gets its name from a legendary olive tree, planted to provide oil for the church lamps. The tree died, but in 1342 it burst miraculously back into life after a cross was hung from one of its branches. The adjoining square, Praça de Santiago, with its old stone houses and wooden balconies, dates back to the 13th century. It was named after St. James who, according to legend, brought a statue of the Virgin to the spot to replace a pagan shrine.

MOSTEIRO DE SANTA MARINHA DA COSTA

On the slopes of the 617m (2,020ft) Penha, 2km (1 mile) to the southeast of Guimarães, stands this monastery, founded in 1154 by Queen Mafalda, Afonso Henriques' wife, in honour of Santa Marinha, the patron saint of pregnant women. The church's elaborate façade is rococo, but the interior is a beguiling mix of different architectural styles. The monastery was extensively damaged by fire in 1951, but was sensitively restored. It is now a hotel.
✉ 4810-011 Guimarães ⏰ Chapel: must be opened by the priest who lives next door

MUSEO ALBERTO SAMPAIO

This museum collection is beautifully presented in the cloisters and chapterhouse of the Oliveira. The highlight of the silver collection is a silver-gilt *Triptych of the Nativity*, said to have been looted by João I's troops after the Portuguese victory over the Castilians at Aljubarrota in 1385. Also here is the tunic worn by João I at the battle, a silver-gilt and enamel Gothic chalice and an ornate Manueline cross engraved with scenes from the Passion of Christ.
✉ Rua Alfredo Guimarães, 4800-407 Guimarães ☎ 253 423 910 ⏰ Jul–Aug Tue–Sun 10am–midnight, rest of year Tue–Sun 10–6 💶 €3.50, free Sun am

MORE TO SEE

CAPELA DE SÃO MIGUEL

This is a tiny 12th-century Romanesque chapel. Afonso Henriques is said to have been baptized here.
✉ Rua Conde D. Henrique, 4810-245 Guimarães ☎ 253 412 273 ⏰ Daily 9.30–12.30, 2–5 💶 Free

CASTELO

The 10th-century castle was extended by Afonso Henriques and restored in the 1940s. It's an impressive 28m (92ft) high, with seven towers and superb views.
✉ Rua Conde D. Henrique, 4810-245 Guimarães ☎ 253 412 273 ⏰ Daily 9.30–12.30, 2–5 💶 Free

IGREJA DE SÃO FRANCISCO

The chancel has beautiful 18th-century tile decoration. Look, too, for the elaborately painted panelled ceiling in the sacristy and the stately cloisters.
✉ Rua do Infante D. Henrique, 4835-001 Guimarães ⏰ Tue–Sat 9.30–12, 3–5, Sun 9.30 1 💶 Free

MUSEU ARQUEOLÓGICO MARTINS SARMENTO

The museum houses finds, dating from pre-Roman times, from archaeological digs around the cloisters of São Domingo.
✉ Rua Paio Galvão, 4814-509 Guimarães ☎ 253 414 011 ⏰ Tue–Sat 9.30–12, 2–5, Sun 10–12, 2–5 💶 €1.50

TIPS
» It is possible to see Guimarães in a day, but you will absorb more of the city's atmosphere if you stay overnight.
» Parking is difficult anywhere near the old part of town—use one of the underground parking areas outside the old city walls and walk from there.
» If you are planning to stay, reserve well in advance, particularly during the July and August festival period.

Below *The Castelo keep and two of the seven square towers*

Above *Miranda do Douro sits on the border with Spain, dominated by its beautiful Gothic cathedral*

MIRANDA DO DOURO

www.rt-nordeste.pt

The frontier town of Miranda do Douro faces the barren stony hills of Spain across a rocky gorge, a position that has made it strategically important for more than 600 years. In 1762 this role ended when an explosion during a Franco-Spanish attack destroyed 200 houses and much of the castle, and the town became a half-forgotten backwater. However, since 1955, when the Douro dam was built, the town has thrived and there is a steady stream of cross-border traffic attracted by the promise of low Portuguese prices. You will see evidence of this in the new town, which is packed with stores selling cut-price merchandise.

To sample the charm of Miranda, head for the old town, with its stately buildings and narrow cobbled streets lined with whitewashed, granite-trimmed houses. High on the list of things not to miss is the Sé (cathedral), for several centuries the main cathedral of the Trás-os-Montes. It was built as the result of Pope Paul III's response to a local request to make Miranda the seat of a bishopric. Work started in 1552. It's an austere and beautiful building, the Gothic interior full of light; the severity of its granite floor and walls contrasts with the fine gilding of the high altar, dedicated to the Assumption of the Virgin. The little statue of the infant Jesus to the right of the high altar, locally much venerated, comes with a full wardrobe of tiny suits, hats and shoes. Behind the Sé, you will see the ruins of the old episcopal palace. The *praça* (square) in front has superb views across to Spain.

Near here, in the Praça Dom João III, is the Museu da Terra de Miranda (tel 273 431 164; www.ipmuseus.pt; Jun–end Sep Tue–Sun 9.30–12.30, 2–6; rest of year Tue–Sun 9–12.30, 2–5.30; €2), a splendid collection of local bits and pieces that sheds light on the town and region. Look for the costumes worn by the *pauliteiros*, stick-dancers unique to the town, and for the thick woollen capes for which the region is traditionally famous.

➕ 327 G3 ℹ️ Largo do Menino Jesus da Cartolinha, 5210-191 Miranda do Douro ☎ 273 431 132

PARQUE NACIONAL DA PENEDA-GERÊS

▷ 138–141.

PARQUE NATURAL DO DOURO INTERNACIONAL

www.rt-nordeste.pt/douro.php

A fine example of international cooperation, the Parque Natural do Douro Internacional spans both the Spanish and Portuguese sides of the upper valley of the Douro. Established in 1998, the park covers a huge area running from Barca de Alva in the south up to Mirando do Douro in the north. Hidden for centuries beyond the Trás-os-Montes mountains, the entire region remained relatively untouched by 20th-century industry and agriculture, helping to preserve a huge variety of flora and fauna. With unemployment here among the highest in Portugal, the park authorities are particularly anxious to develop ecotourism in the area as well as encouraging sustainable low-key agriculture.

Meteorologically, the area has a Mediterranean microclimate, ensuring the survival of species that have vanished farther south. If you enjoy spending time in the great outdoors, the park has plenty to keep you occupied. It's particularly good for birdwatching, with more than 170 species, both resident and summer visitors, including Europe's largest group of Egyptian vultures. Botany enthusiasts should aim to visit in spring, when the hillsides are covered in almond blossom and there is an abundance of orchids, cistus and aromatic field plants. The main park office is in Mogadouro; the staff provide maps and advice on where to go and what to see, and will help you find guided tours or walks.

➕ 327 F3 ℹ️ Park office: Rua de Santa Marinha 4, 5200-241 Mogadouro ☎ 279 340 030

PARQUE NATURAL DE MONTESINHO

www.icn.pt

Covering more than 750sq km (290sq miles) between Bragança and the Spanish border, the Parque Natural de Montesinho is the only place in the Trás-os-Montes that remains untouched by rapid development. The population of around 8,000 is scattered among the park's 92 villages, where the way of life is traditional, hard and extremely basic.

The village of Rio de Onor, straddling the border, provides a fascinating insight into the local way of life, the subject of many anthropological studies. Spanish and Portuguese people have intermarried for generations, virtually creating their own autonomous state, with its own system of justice and mutual cooperation. Here, and in other villages, such as Guadramil, donkeys are a frequent means of transport and it is common to see women washing clothes in the river. The beautiful landscape, with rich woodlands and heather-clad moors, supports birds of prey and animals such as wild boar and wolves. Serious and well-equipped walkers can enjoy long-distance hikes between the villages, and there are plenty of shorter walks, bicycling trails and horseback-riding establishments to choose from. You can rent traditional houses by the week, and some villages have rooms for rent and simple cafés. Bragança itself (▷ 132) and the village of Vinhais to the west make the best bases for exploring the area.

✚ 327 E2 🚹 Park office: Rua Cónego Albano Falcão, Lote 5, Bairro Rubacar, 5300-044 Bragança ☎ 273 300 400 🕐 Mon–Fri 9–12.30, 2–5.30

PONTE DA BARCA
www.rtam.pt
The town gets its name from the boats that used to ferry passengers across the River Lima before the bridge here was built in the 15th century—this was a major crossing point for pilgrims on their way to Santiago de Compostela in Spain. Above the bridge, mansion-lined old streets lead past the town pillory and the 18th-century arcaded market, to a pleasant *praça* (square) and a couple of churches.

Walk or drive the 4km (2.5 miles) downriver to the hamlet of Bravães, where you will find one of Portugal's greatest architectural achievements, the Romanesque Igreja de São Salvador. This was built between the 12th and 13th centuries according to a French design, a style that had travelled down the Camino de Santiago—the pilgrim way of St. James that runs through here. Plain and stark, its granite solidity is offset by the carving around the remarkable doorway. It is sculpted with monkeys, doves and geometric motifs, while the tympanum (cross-stone) rests on the heads of two wide-horned cattle, still found in the Minho. Above this, two angels adore a Christ Pantocrator, a sculpted figure of the Glorious Christ, enclosed in a stone oval, with his hand raised in blessing. Inside the dark interior, lit by seven slit windows, are fine frescoes of St. Sebastian and the Madonna.

✚ 326 C2 🚹 Rua D. Manuel I, 4980-637 Ponte da Barca ☎ 258 452 899

PONTE DE LIMA
www.rtam.pt
Some 30km (20 miles) east from the coastal town of Viana do Castelo (▷ 143), this beautiful and peaceful little town is a beguiling mix of quiet old mansions, green shady gardens and riverside walks. It gets its name from the medieval stone bridge across the river, built to replace a Roman bridge that formed part of the military route from Astorga to Braga. Traces of the Roman occupation can still be seen in the form of five arches and a few milestones built into the bridge.

On the riverside, and just below the bridge, is the Largo Principal, a laid-back square surrounded by outdoor cafés, behind which lie the streets of the old town. Here you'll find buildings representing every era of vernacular architecture—Romanesque, Gothic, Manueline and baroque—along with churches, fountains and greenery. The Alameda, a tree-lined promenade, runs beside the river, which you cross to visit the Museu Rural (Tue–Sun 2–6; free), housing a collection of rural implements. Lima's other main site is the Igreja-Museu dos Terceiros (closed for renovation until early 2009; check with the tourist office for times and prices), a church and conventual complex with fine woodwork and 16th-century *azulejos* (tiles).

The countryside around is dotted with *solares* and *quintas*, both types of manor house. Many provide accommodation as well as producing the famous *vinho verde*, a slightly sparkling, dry white wine characteristic of the region.

✚ 326 C2 🚹 Paço do Marquês, 4990-063 Ponte de Lima ☎ 258 942 335

SOLAR DE MATEUS
▷ 142.

TORRE DE MONCORVO
www.cm-moncorvo.pt
The road from the south climbs steeply through the mountains to Moncorvo, a fortress-like town near the edge of a high plateau in the northeast of the Trás-os-Montes. Below are the fertile valleys of the Douro and Sabor rivers, while above the town arid mountains stretch towards Spain. To the east lie the hills of the Serra de Reboredo and around the town on the slopes the almond trees burst into white blossom in spring.

Legend has it that the trees were first planted to assuage the nostalgia of a northern princess. She had married a Moorish prince, and, though happy during summer, pined in winter for the snows of her native land. The prince hurried south to the Algarve and brought back hundreds of almond trees, whose blossom reminded her of the snow-covered hills of home. The town is still famous for both the trees and their fruit, attracting spring visitors to admire the spectacle and buy the locally produced sugared almonds.

Moncorvo's main monument is the Igreja Matriz. The largest church in the region, it was built between 1544 and 1650. The façade is dominated by a central tower and a Renaissance doorway, while inside you will find a fine 17th-century altar. Behind the church, a maze of medieval streets surrounds the central *praça* (square).

✚ 327 E4 🚹 Travessa Dr. Campos Monteiro, 5160-234 Torre de Moncorvo ☎ 279 252 289

Below *The medieval stone bridge gave Ponte de Lima its name*

INTRODUCTION

Portugal's only national park preserves a traditional way of life. A wilderness area, it's a paradise for walkers and outdoor enthusiasts. The Parque Nacional da Peneda-Gerês covers a crescent-shaped tract of land in the northern Minho, with its two arms encircling the southwest tip of the Spanish province of Orense. A staggering landscape of rock and scree, valleys and reservoirs, its separate mountain areas, the *serras* of Peneda, Soajo, Amarela and Gerês, are divided by three river valleys—the Lima, Homem and Cávado. Road access is restricted in certain areas and there are few north–south through routes; as a result, the quickest way for drivers to get from the northern Peneda section to the Gerês is through Spain. The western section of the Gerês *serra* is the wildest area, where roads skirt the southern edge of the massif.

To explore the southern section of the park, head for the spa town of Caldas do Gerês, where there is plenty of accommodation and some stunning local drives and walks. To head north, you need to backtrack to join the N101 to Ponte da Barca (▷ 137), from where a fairly good road leads up the Lima valley to the village of Lindoso (▷ 133) near the Spanish border. From here you could head through Spain and re-enter the park at Amejjoeira to explore the wild Serra da Peneda.

To make the most of the glorious scenery, though, it is best to do as much walking as you can—there is a huge range of hiking trails to choose from, of all lengths and standards. It's well worth consulting the park offices, as the staff there are very good at helping you to plan suitable routes. They also give out details of guided walks and can help you find a private guide, whose walking expertise and extensive local knowledge will help you search out the hidden highlights of the area.

INFORMATION
www.icnb.pt

PARK OFFICE
Braga Head Office
✠ 326 C2 🛈 Avenida António Macedo, 4704-538 Braga ☎ 253 203 480

ACCOMMODATION
Ponte da Barca
www.adere-pg.pt
✠ 326 C2 🛈 ADERE Peneda-Gerês, largo da Misericórdia 10, 4980-613 Ponte da Barca ☎ 258 452 250

INFORMATION POINTS
Caldas do Gerês
✠ 326 C2 🛈 Vidoeiro 99, 4845-081 Caldas do Gerês ☎ 253 390 110
🕐 Mon–Fri 9–12, 2–5.30

Above *The River Cávado flows through the park's heartland*
Opposite *Distinctive Minho cattle graze in the park*

TIPS

» Pick up walking leaflets in English at the information points and park offices—they have details of footpaths of all lengths from short strolls to three- to four-day hikes.

» Take warm and waterproof clothes, a compass, water and food if you are going on a long walk. Let someone know where you are going and what time you expect to be back.

» The weather can change suddenly in mountainous areas, while large areas of the park are buried in snow in winter.

» When driving, bear in mind that map distances are deceptive—the roads here are slow, steep and tortuous, so allow extra time.

Peneda-Gerês lies in the northern district of Braga, Viana do Castelo and Vila Real. Historically, this border country was one of the great through routes between Portugal and Spain, and the valleys and passes here are crisscrossed by footpaths that formed part of the Camino de Santiago, the great pilgrim route to the shrine of St. James at Santiago de Compostela in Galicia. The park itself was established in 1971 and covers 72,000ha (178,000 acres) of the countryside. In common with national parks in other countries, it aims not only to protect an area of outstanding natural beauty from the threat of development, but also to conserve the archaeological sites, plus the flora, fauna and bird life.

A considerable number of people live in the villages within the park, but such communities are dwindling and ageing, and traditional customs are consequently in danger of dying out. The park authorities are trying to strike a balance—protecting the environment and traditional way of life, while catering for the ever-increasing number of visitors that come to spend time in the park each year.

WHAT TO SEE
SERRA DO GERÊS

You must be prepared to do some hiking and climbing if you want to penetrate deeper into this dramatic mountain area, though it is possible to appreciate its scale from the Vale do Rio Cávado (▷ 143). Alternatively, start exploring from the Confluente de Caniçada, where there are two lakes formed by a dam some 10km (6 miles) to the west. From here, head for Caldas do Gerês, a relaxed

Right *Spa town Caldas do Gerês lies at the foot of a wooded gorge*
Below *Roadside orange sellers*

and faded little spa town at the bottom of a wooded gorge, whose waters are thought to aid in the treatment of liver and digestive disorders.

A hydrangea-lined road climbs steadily through the town, crossing the River Homem as it races through its rocky gorge, and continuing to the Spanish border. Just before, a track heading to Campo do Gerês crosses the Roman road that linked Braga and Astorga—you can still see the distance markers with their commemorative inscriptions. Below is the intense blue of the Represa de Vilarinha das Fumas, a superb reservoir in a rocky, wild landscape.

If you travel south from Gerês and turn right towards Campo do Gerês, there are stunning mountain views to be had, though the road is twisty. From its highest point you can walk to the Miradouro de Junceda, one of the area's most dramatic viewpoints. If you have time, continue on to the other end of the Vilarinha reservoir, perhaps taking the track from there to walk up and join the Roman road.

SERRA DA PENEDA

For a taste of the wild Peneda section of the park, you could enter at Lamas de Mouro and make an immediate detour to Castro Laboeiro, an ancient village that was once famous for its dogs, bred to protect sheep from wolves. The ruined castle has great views and there are some excellent walks around the village. Head south down a wooded valley and you will reach the Santuário de Nossa Senhora da Peneda, in Peneda. Set at the foot of a cliff, the pilgrimage site is modelled on Bom Jesus near Braga (▷ 129–131); in September, hundreds of pilgrims come to pay their respects here.

From here, the scenery gets wilder and wilder, with tiny fields hewn out of the landscape between great granite boulders. Keep an eye out for traditional espigueiros, granite grain stores, in the villages. There are some scattered in the terraced fields around Rouças, while farther on, Soajo has a superb group. From Soajo you can join the road running up the Lima valley to Lindoso (▷ 133).

Below *Traditional granite grain stores are a feature of the countryside*

INFORMATION

www.casademateus.com

➕ 326 D3 ✉ Fundacão da Casa de
Mateus, 5000 Vila Real ☎ 259 323 121
🕐 Jun–end Sep daily 9–7; rest of year
daily 9–6; guided tours only (maximum
ten visitors, only three tours at once), so
reserve ahead in summer 🖐 House and
garden: €7.50. Garden only: €4 🎫 All
visits are by guided tour (approx. 30 min)
and most guides speak some English
📖 No guidebooks; coffee-table book
available at €40 ☕ Small café selling
coffee, soft drinks and cakes 🏪 Shop
selling books, wine and jam

TIPS

» The *solar* is signposted 'Palácio
de Mateus' from the outskirts of Vila
Real—take the Bragança road out of
town and look for signs to Mateus.
» Arrive early in summer to avoid the
crowds and find a parking space.
» Both the Vila Real tourist office and the
solar have details of cultural events.

Above With its beautiful formal gardens
and elaborate façade, Solar de Mateus
is a triumph of Portuguese baroque
architectural style

SOLAR DE MATEUS

This perfect example of an 18th-century Portuguese manor house is set in
beautiful formal gardens. It is renowned worldwide as the symbol of Mateus
Rosé wine.

The Casa de Mateus was built in the 1740s by the third Margado de Mateus;
his descendants still live in one wing. The architect is thought to have been
Nicolau Nasoni, an Italian who had immense influence on the development of
Portuguese baroque.

THE FAÇADE

This is one of the finest examples of Portuguese baroque architecture. Its
central section is set back, with the main door at first-floor level. This is
flanked by two windows, approached by a double balustraded stairway and
surmounted by a tall emblazoned pediment with allegorical statues on either
side. Severe classical wings, topped by pinnacles, enclose a courtyard leading
to an archway beneath the main stairs. This leads to the inner courtyard,
with a further double staircase. To the left of the palace is a baroque chapel,
constructed in 1750.

THE INTERIOR

The hall, like many of the other rooms, has a fine chestnut carved ceiling. It
leads into the richly draped Four Seasons Room. From here, the Blue Room,
with its Chinese ceramics, leads to the Dining Room, with a rich collection of
silver and china. In the Four Corners Room, look for the Indo-Portuguese wood
and ivory portable desk.

Two rooms in the south wing have been converted into a museum, where
the highlight is the original printing plates made by Jean Fragonard to illustrate
an 1817 edition of *Os Lusíadas* by the poet Luís de Camões.

THE GARDENS

These were altered considerably in the 1930s, when the reflecting pool was
added. The parterres, planted with shrubs and flowers and surrounded by
topiary or box hedges, perfectly mirror the house's architecture. The planting
is dominated by camellias, hydrangeas and roses. Make sure to take the time
to explore the wisteria-hung pergola, the dense cedar tunnel, the three-tiered
pools and the adjoining old threshing floor, with its views to the Serra do Marão
and the famous vineyards stretching out in front.

VALE DO RIO CÁVADO

www.cm-braga.pt

For a superb mix of high mountains, wooded slopes, attractive villages and lake scenery, head for the upper valley of the River Cávado, which runs along the southern edge of the Serra do Gerês to Braga. Above Braga, the river cuts through and is enclosed by a rocky valley that was first dammed in 1946, creating a series of beautiful lakes, set in an upland landscape. There are seven dams in all, helping to generate enough waterpower to produce around 18 per cent of Portugal's hydroelectricity. The main road (N103) climbs east through a series of villages. Reservoir views open up below until you reach the plateau, where the vast expanse of the largest lake in the valley, the Barragem do Alto Rabagão, comes into view. There is little in the way of tourist development here, and the locals have managed to preserve their traditional way of life—you can still see primitive earth dams in the fields, designed to trap the water for summer grazing.

It's worth making a detour off the main road north to Montalegre, an ancient village with a ruined 14th-century castle that has breathtaking mountain views. Boticas and Vilarinho, unspoilt villages both on a minor road south of the reservoir, are also worth visiting.

✚ 326 D2 ℹ Avenida da Liberdade 1, 4710-305 Braga ☎ 253 262 550

VALENÇA DO MINHO

www.rtam.pt

The old town of Valença is a picturesque jumble of narrow cobbled streets, lined with splendid buildings and enclosed in a vast double fortress, itself enclosed in two massive linked fortresses overlooking the River Minho towards Spain. The fortress is largely 17th century, its star-shaped design and series of ramparts heavily influenced by the French military architect Vauban. A town grew up within the citadel, its two sections linked by a causeway across a dry moat. Enter through gates in either the south or east walls to wander around the streets and admire the views from the ramparts.

✚ 326 D2 ℹ Avenida de Espanha, 4930-677 Valença do Minho ☎ 251 823 374
🚊 Valença do Minho

VIANA DO CASTELO

www.rtam.pt

Within easy reach of one of northern Portugal's finest beaches, Viana do Castelo has a reputation for being one of the Minho's best resorts. Backed by the wooded Monte de Santa Luzia, crowned with an impressive basilica, there is plenty to explore and its elegant and historic heart is packed with good shops and restaurants. It comes alive during the August *romaria*, a three-day carnival with daily street parades, *gigantones* (giant figures), bands, fireworks and dancing in the streets.

Viana's history is entwined with the sea. Money from its maritime activities funded the town's fine buildings, seen at their best in and around the central square, the Praça da República. Here you will find the 1589 Misericórdia, a Flemish-Venetian-influenced almshouse whose façade is decorated with a massive colonnade and loggias. Near this is the 16th-century town hall, embellished with ground-level

arches and the town's caravel coat of arms.

Just off the square is the Igreja Matriz, a truly lovely church whose architectural shapes and detail are a happy mix of rounded, solid Romanesque forms and delicate Gothic touches. The Museu Municipal (tel 258 820 678; Jun–end Sep Tue–Sun 10–1, 3–7; Oct–end May Tue–Sun 10–1, 3–6; €2) was formerly an 18th-century palace. Its interior walls are covered with *azulejos* (tiles) depicting hunting and fishing scenes. It showcases a celebrated collection of superb glazed earthenware.

Southeast on the waterfront, ferries run across the Lima and the stylish marina is backed by pleasant gardens. Take the ferry to reach the Praia do Cabedelo, a curving expanse of smooth sand with good surf and summer watersports and bars. There's good walking on the slopes of Monte de Santa Luzia, where paths wind through eucalyptus woods with superb views—these are even better if you climb the steps to the dome of the basilica at the summit.

✚ 326 B2 ℹ Rua do Hospital Velho (off Praça da Erva), 4900-540 Viana do Castelo ☎ 258 822 620 🚊 Viana do Castelo

VILA REAL

www.cm-vilareal.pt

Vila Real lies above the River Corgo, with the ranges of the Marão and Alvão mountains behind. Seat of the region's university, the town is a pleasant base for a couple of nights, especially if you are car-less as it is the hub of the regional transport system. At its heart you will find some gracious buildings, including the town hall and the 15th-century Sé (cathedral), but its selling point is the lively atmosphere, best appreciated at the morning market and along the streets in the late afternoon. The town is the birthplace of explorer Diogo Cão, who discovered the Congo River in 1482.

✚ 326 D3 ℹ Avenida Carvalho Araújo 94, 5000-657 Vila Real ☎ 259 322 819
🚊 Vila Real

Below *Lively and elegant Vila Real de Santo Antonio is a good place to spend a few days while touring the Douro valley*

DRIVE

THROUGH THE DOURO VALLEY

This spectacular drive takes you through the best parts of the port-producing valley of the river Douro, where steep hillsides are clothed from top to bottom with terraced vineyards. You will have the chance to visit a wine lodge, taste and buy port, and enjoy the beauty of the famous Solar de Mateus and its glorious gardens.

THE DRIVE
Distance: 130km (80 miles)
Time: 4–5 hours
Start/end at: Vila Real

★ From Vila Real (▷ 143) take the IP4 towards Porto and Amarante. Follow this road for 24km (15 miles). At the sign for 'pousada', leave the main road and cross the river to reach the Pousada de São Gonçalo.

❶ The Pousada de São Gonçalo is a modern hotel, built as a base for visitors exploring the Serra de Marão mountains.

After leaving the pousada, turn left onto the N15, a minor road, and drive down through the pine forests of the Ovelha valley for 12km (7 miles) to Candemil.

❷ Candemil is in the heart of the Serra de Marão, a granite and shale mountain range whose

highest point is the Pico de Marão (1,415m/4,642ft). You should be able to pick this out from the road between São Gonçalo and Candemil. It's an extraordinary landscape, with the road descending through an enclosed gorge above the Ovelha, a river that is noted for its trout fishing.

Just after Candemil, turn left in a tiny hamlet onto a steeply climbing road signposted for Bustelo. This descends to join the N101, where you turn left. At this point you have effectively crossed the Serra de Marão, but the N101 now recrosses it, traversing a plateau with superb views of the mountains before dropping down through vineyards to the small town of Mesão Frio on the river Teixera.

❸ At Mesão Frio, cross the river, drive through town and you'll get your first view of the vine terraces

and the sweep of the River Douro far below. You're now right in the heart of the port country, where the steep valley sides have been painstakingly terraced into one of Europe's most fertile grape-growing areas. Carefully tended, the terraces themselves are a work of art; in the words of a local saying, 'God created Earth, but man created the Douro.'

At the intersection above the river turn left onto the N108 along the north bank of the Douro. Follow this road for 12km (7 miles) to Peso da Régua. Before the intersection, watch out for the Solar da Rede pousada, a fine old 18th-century manor house surrounded by 27ha (66 acres) of vineyards. It is a nice place to stop for a meal or to spend the night. You'll also drive through

Above *The beautiful formal gardens of Solar de Mateus are considered by many to be Portugal's finest*

the spa town of Caldas de Moledo, before reaching Peso da Régua.

❹ Peso da Régua, a thriving provincial town, was once dubbed the 'Capital of the Upper Douro', when it was the upriver focus of the port trade. All port still passes through here on its way downriver, but Régua's role as the trade's hub has been taken over by Pinhão to the east. There are still ornamental *barcos rabelos*, the traditional port cargo boats, moored on the river; you can visit the Quinta de São Domingos (▷ 168), where you can tour the lodge and sample port.

Cross the River Douro on the lower of the two bridges, keeping right to swing back under the bridge and emerge next to the river onto the N222. Follow this road for 25km (15 miles) to Pinhão.

❺ Pinhão is the main focus for quality port production, and several of the leading houses have *quintas* (wine lodges) here. The section of the drive leading to the town

is particularly attractive, running alongside the river with views of the terraced vineyards, olive groves and a steady procession of lodges, each with the name of the producer who owns it emblazoned on the hillside.

At Pinhão cross the Douro and return to the north bank. Leave Pinhão and take the N323 north, signposted for Sabrosa and Vila Real.

❻ Sabrosa is the birthplace of the explorer Ferdinand Magellan.

Turn left onto the N322 following the sign for Vila Real.

❼ The Solar de Mateus (▷ 142) is the highlight of this part of the tour. It is a magnificent country manor house whose outside is familiar from the labels on millions of bottles of Mateus Rosé wine.

Past here, turn right and follow the signs back to Vila Real.

WHERE TO EAT
Try the Pousada de São Gonçalo (open daily for lunch noon–2.30pm), just over halfway between Amarante and Vila Real, or the Pousada Solar da Rede (also open daily noon–2.30pm) in Peso da Régua. Both serve tasty regional food.

WHEN TO GO
The best times for this drive are late summer and autumn.

PLACES TO VISIT
SOLAR DE MATEUS
(▷ 142).

QUINTA DE SÃO DOMINGOS
✉ Juncal de Cima, 5050-244 Peso da Régua ☎ 254 320 260 ⏰ May–end Sep daily 9.30–6.30; rest of year daily 9–6 ✋ Free

QUINTA DO PANASCAL
✉ 5120-496 Valença do Douro ☎ 254 732 321 ⏰ Apr–end Oct daily 10–1, 2–6; rest of year Mon–Fri 10–1, 2–6 ✋ Free
A short detour up the Távora valley will take you to this port vineyard; audio-tours and vineyard walks are available.

Below *The Dão valley is the second most productive wine area in Portugal; most Dão wine is red*

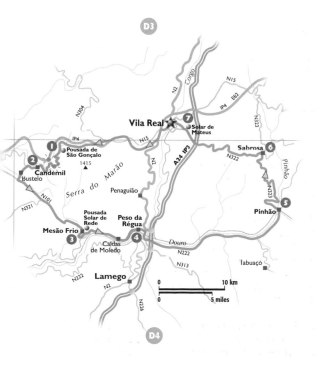

WHAT TO DO

BARCELOS

AMIGOS DA MONTANHA

www.amigosdamontanha.com

For hiking, bicycle riding or canoeing, the best company in town is surely Amigos de Montanha. It has a fixed calendar of events; for details or to arrange an activity, telephone or visit the office or go to the website.

✉ Rua Custódio José Gomes Vilas Boas 47, 4755-059 Barcelinhos, Barcelos ☎ 253 831 647, or mobile 960 486 617 🕐 Central office: Mon–Fri 6–8pm. Mobile phone lines: 9–7 👆 Mountain-biking €15, canoeing €20, paintball €15, white-water rafting €35; hiking information free 🚌 On the street leading to the medieval bridge

BARCELOS MARKET

This is one of the best ceramics markets in Portugal. Traditional earthenware and the ubiquitous red-, black- and white-painted cockerels are sold alongside basketware, hand-painted tin objects, household goods and fresh produce.

✉ Campo da República, 4750-275 Barcelos 🕐 Thu

CENTRO DE ARTESANATO DE BARCELOS

Within the 16th-century Torre da Menagem, this great craft shop offers both quality and good value. Two floors are crammed with a range of goods; perhaps most interesting of all are the comic green- and brown-glazed figurines fashioned by heirs of the famous Rosa Carvalho—the mother of Portuguese ceramicists.

✉ Largo da Porta Nova, 4750-329 Barcelos ☎ 253 812 135 🕐 Mar–end Oct Mon–Fri 9.30–6, Sat 10–12.30, 2.30–5.30, Sun 2.30–5.30; rest of year Mon–Fri 9.30–5.30, Sat 10–12.30, 2.30–5 🚌 From Praça da República, take Rua Dom António Barroso towards the river; it is in the same tower as the tourist office, opposite Santa Cruz church

BRAGA

BRAGA MARKET

The Braga weekly market sells the usual fare, but, thanks to its proximity to the northern shoe and textile factories, has a good selection of these. You can often find international brands at low prices.

✉ Parque de Exposições, 4705-104 Braga (near the São João bridge) 🕐 Tue

INSÓLITO

http://insolitobar.netfirms.com

Catering for Braga's student population, Insólito has three bar areas, the third of which, known as

Above Braga has both stylish fashion shops and an excellent market

the Grill, offers light snacks such as toasted sandwiches, burgers and hotdogs to replenish your strength for more dancing. Jazz, indie and house are the order of the evening, depending on the hour.

✉ Avenida Central 47, 4710-228 Braga ☎ 968 016 240 🕐 Mon–Sat 10pm–4am 👆 €3 Mon–Thu, €5 Fri–Sat

JOSÉ GONÇALVES

http://violeiro.no.sapo.pt

Among Braga's most important craft products are its fine folk guitars. This workshop near the Campo da Vinha specializes in classical guitars, the smaller *cavaquinhos, bandolinas* and *guitarras*.

✉ Rua da Boavista 69–71, 4700-416 Braga ☎ 253 612 428 🕐 Mon–Fri 10.30–1, 2–7, Sat 2–7

QUINTA PEDAGÓGICA DE BRAGA

For an insight into local agricultural customs take the children along to the Quinta Pedagógica, a traditional Minho farm which has been transformed into an educational facility promoting ancient farming and fishing methods as well as

environmental issues. The *quinta* is open to the public at the weekends, and is northwest of the city centre.
✉ Caminho dos Quatro Caminhos, Real (next to Chapel of S. Frutuoso), 4700-288 Braga ☎ 253 623 560 🕒 Sat–Sun and public holidays 2–6.30

SVBVRA – TABERNA ROMANA
http://tabernasubura.blogspot.com
Close to the Sé, Svbvra promotes live Portuguese music, art films, comedy, and provides a house guitar for anyone who feels inspired to share a song. Their much praised tapas-style snacks are available throughout the evening.
✉ Rua Frei Caetano Brandão 101, 4700-031 Braga ☎ 964 254 144 🕒 Daily 8pm–2am ✋ €5–€15 depending on snack/drink

BRAGANÇA
BRAGANÇA MARKET
In the west of town, this market sells all the usual products, including ceramics, household goods and fresh produce.
✉ Around Municipal Stadium, Avenida Abade de Baçal, 5300-068 Bragança ☎ 273 381 273 (tourist office) 🕒 3rd, 12th and 21st of month, or nearest Mon when these dates fall over weekends

MUNICIPAL MARKET
Worth a quick stop, the stalls here sell a selection of regional crafts, cured meats and cheeses, plus some less visitor-oriented foods, such as dried tripe for making your own sausages at home.
✉ Forte São João Deus, 5300-263 Bragança ☎ 273 325 474 🕒 Mon–Sat 7–7, Sun 8–1

PARQUE NATURAL DE MONTESINHO
www.icnb.pt
The wild reserve that stretches north of Bragança to the Spanish border is filled with heather- and broom-covered mountains and alder- and willow-filled valleys, creating a pleasurable terrain for hiking and walking. The park office has more detailed information.
✉ Park office: Bairro Rubacar, Rua Cónego Albano Falcão, Lote 5, Apartado 90, 5300-

044 Bragança ☎ 273 300 400 🕒 Mon–Fri 9–12.30, 2–5.30

ROSÁRIO AND JULIETA
To see two local ceramicists in action visit Rosário and Julieta, who produce, among other things, hand-painted plates and models of the local *pombais* (dovecotes). Don't be put off by the grim mall in which the workshop is housed.
✉ Shopping Loreto, Shop 26, Avenida Sá Carneiro, 5300-252 Bragança ☎ 919 130 366 or 919 130 346 🕒 Mon–Fri 9–7
🚌 The mall is on the ground floor of the tallest building on Avenida Sá Carneiro. Go up the main steps and, once inside, the shop is round to the left

CHAVES
CHAVES MARKET
This is a good place to buy local crafts, such as baskets made in the surrounding villages, or the distinctive black Chaves pottery, which is fired in an ash- and earth-covered pit to achieve its dark lustre.
✉ Next to stadium, Chaves ☎ 276 340 661 (tourist office) 🕒 Wed

NATURBARROSO
www.naturbarroso.net
Based approximately 35km (22 miles) to the northwest of Chaves, NaTurBarroso organizes outdoor activities emphasizing environmental and cultural preservation. There are themed walks including mushroom identification and collecting, virgin oak forest trails and medieval paths through the Barroso hills. English is spoken by the guides.
✉ Rua João Rodrigues Cabrilho 265, 5470-204 Montalegre, Chaves ☎ 276 518 125, 935 663 060, 965 663 068 🕒 Office Mon–Fri 9–5 ✋ Varies depending on activity. Walks €15–€20, minimum 10 people

NORTE AVENTURA
Norte Aventura provides qualified guides and instructors for all kinds of outdoor pursuits, such as hiking, mountain-biking and four-wheel driving, rock-climbing, canoeing, abseiling or white-water rafting.
✉ Turismo e Animação Lda, Largo de São Roque, Loja R/C Dt, 5400-504 Chaves

☎ 966 047 700 🕒 Office: Jun–end Oct Mon–Sat 10–1, 3–7.30; Nov–end May Sat 10–1, 3–7.30 ✋ Prices depend on activity

TERMAS DE CHAVES
http://termas.mj-multimedia.net
The natural spring here is one of the hottest in Europe, bubbling out of the ground at 71°C (160°F). The spa is generally full of elderly patients on extended courses of treatments, but casual visitors can take a swig from the waters.
✉ Largo das Caldas, 5400-460 Chaves ☎ 276 332 445 🕒 1 Mar–30 Nov daily 8–8 ✋ €4.70 daily treatments, up to €190 for 5-day package

VIDAGO PALACE GOLF CLUB
www.vidagopalace.com
For a game of golf, head 20km (12.5 miles) south of Chaves to the spa village of Vidago. The Palace Hotel has a hilly 18-hole course. The September competitions held here are well known to visitors from Lisbon and Porto. The clubhouse serves light meals.
✉ Parque de Vidago, 5425-307 Vidago 🕒 Check website for details
🚗 Southwest from Chaves on IP3 to Vidago, then signed

GUIMARÃES
A OFICINA
www.aoficina.pt
For a good selection of Guimarães' famous linens, including tablecloths, napkins and hand towels, try this municipal outlet, which was established to promote the town's artisans. Other regional crafts include fine gold- and silversmithing, embroidery and pottery.
✉ Rua Paio Galvão, 11, 4810-426 Guimarães ☎ 253 515 250 🕒 Mon–Sat 9–1, 3–7

GUIMARÃES MARKET
This market sells clothes, shoes and regional products, such as carved animal yokes, woven textiles, leatherware and pottery. Textiles are hand-spun, hand-woven and then embroidered; the quality is excellent.
✉ Praça de São Tiago and Largo da Oliveira 🕒 1st Sat of month

TERMAS DAS TAIPAS
www.termasdeportugal.pt
For a day of relaxed pampering, take the waters at one of Portugal's more traditional spas. Within a leafy park on the River Ave, the Termas das Taipas claims to help rheumatism, a range of skin allergies and respiratory problems.
✉ 4805-079 Caldas das Taipas ☎ 253 577 898 ◷ Mar–end Dec Mon–Fri 8–12, 4–7, Sat 8–12 ✋ €5–€32 according to which treatment you have

ULTIMATUM JAZZ CAFÉ
Playing a mix of classical, jazz and piano-bar tunes, the Ultimatum hosts jazz on Thursdays and puts on a disco on Fridays and Saturdays, starting at 1am and playing a blend of pop-rock and Latino sounds.
✉ Rua Rei do Pegú, 4810-025 Guimarães ☎ 253 415 294 ◷ Tue–Sat 8pm–2am ✋ Tue–Thu entry free, Fri–Sat €5 for women, €8 for men (includes drinks)

MIRANDA DO DOURO
ASSOCIAÇÃO PARA O ESTUDO E PROTECÇÃO DO GADO ASININO
www.aepga.pt
Created for the study and protection of donkeys and to promote their importance in traditional rural society, this sanctuary offers donkey rides through the Miranda plain, as well as educational farm tours. Reserve in advance.

Below *Canoeing on the Douro or another one of Portugal's many rivers can be a fun experience for everyone*

✉ Largo da Igreja, 5225-011 Atenor ☎ 273 739 307 or 960 173 863 ◷ Mon–Fri 9.30–12.30, 2.30–6 ✋ €30 for approximately 3-hour excursion 🚗 From Miranda da Douro head south to Sendim then 5km/3 miles northwest to Atenor

EUROPARQUES PORTUGAL
www.europarques.com
Miranda do Douro's most impressive sight is undoubtedly its dramatic river gorge and the dam standing 80m (264ft) high, which lies just east of town. You can take a one-hour cruise in the international waters of the river from the Parque Náutico, beside the dam on the Portuguese side of the river.
✉ Centro Ambiental Luso-Espanhol, Parque Náutico, Miranda do Douro ☎ 273 432 396 ◷ Boats leave Mon–Fri 4pm, Sat–Sun 11am and 4pm, also Aug Mon–Fri 11am ✋ €14

PARQUE NATURAL DO DOURO INTERNACIONAL
www.icnb.pt
The park encompasses the stretch of the River Douro that marks the frontier with Spain. It is outstandingly attractive, especially in late February and March when the steep river valley is covered in blossoming almond trees. Several hikes have been waymarked through the park, following ancient pathways, but they are not always easy to navigate. If you are visiting independently rather than taking a guided tour, contact the ICN office, which will provide directions, maps and details of the hike.
✉ ICN (Instituto da Conservação da Natureza), Rua do Convento, Palácio da Justiça, 5210 Miranda do Douro ☎ 273 431 457 ◷ ICN office: Mon–Fri 9–12.30, 2–5.30

SILBOTE
www.hrplanalto.pt
This company organizes daily hiking trips and mountain-bicycling in the Miranda. If you prefer a slower pace, donkey rides are available.
✉ Hotel Residencial Planalto, Rua 1 de Maio 25, 5210-191 Miranda do Douro ☎ 273 431 362 ◷ Daily

PONTE DE BARCA
MINHO ALEGRE
http://minhoalegre.no.sapo.pt
If you would like to hike in the area, but are worried about getting lost if you set out alone, why not take a trip with one of Minho Alegre's multilingual guides. As well as walks through the Gerês National Park, the company organizes canoeing, bicycling and horseback riding, all of which should be reserved at least three days in advance.
✉ Caixa Postal 47 4980, Ponte da Barca ☎ 258 455 500 or 966 129 218 ◷ Phone lines: 9am–10pm. There is no central office ✋ From €12, according to activity

PONTE DE LIMA
AXIS GOLFE DE PONTE DE LIMA
www.golfe-pontedelima.com
A short distance south of town, this 18-hole, par-71 course has great views. The modern clubhouse includes a restaurant, sauna and golf equipment shop.
✉ Quinta de Pias, Fornelos, 4990-620 Ponte de Lima ☎ 258 743 414 ◷ Daily 8.30–6.30 ✋ 18 holes €57; club rental €30; trolley €5 🍴 🚗 South of Ponte de Lima on EN307. Golf club is signposted

CLUB NÁUTICO
www.cnplima.com
Walk across the river to Arcozelo and turn left downstream. Near the N201 bridge is the Club Náutico, which rents kayaks and canoes.
✉ São Gonçalo Arcozelo, 4990-150 Ponte de Lima ☎ 258 944 899 ◷ Jul–end Sep daily 9.30–1, 2–8; Oct–end Jun Sat–Sun 10–12.30, 2–5.30 ✋ €3 for 1 hour

JOAQUIM CERQUEIRA DA SILVA
For an insight into the craft of artisan shoemaking, visit the workshop of Sr. Cerqueira da Silva, which specializes in *chinelas de lavradeiras*, wooden-soled clogs with finely embroidered uppers traditionally worn by women working in the fields. Best to call in advance to check if it is open.
✉ Lugar do Boudilhão, Moureira do Lima ☎ 966 721 154 ◷ Mon–Fri 10–6, but call in advance to visit 🚗 Head out of town on the EN202 towards Viana. Turn right at

sign for Moureira do Lima, and on reaching the village follow sign to Boudilhão. After the sign take the first left, first right and right again

PONTE DE LIMA MARKET
Given its charter in 1125, this is the country's oldest market. Every other Monday it spreads itself over the dry sandy river bed of the River Lima, selling everything from farm equipment and wine barrels to clothes and fresh bread.
☎ 258 942 335 (tourist office)
🕐 Alternate Mon

VIANA DO CASTELO
CAVALEIROS DO MAR
www.cavaleirosdomar.com
For outdoor activities in the coastal region of the Minho, this company offers plenty of choice. On-land options include archery, rock-climbing and paintball, or if qualified head out to sea for some diving.
✉ Avenida do Meio 726, 4900-834 Viana do Castelo ☎ 964 397 021/926 🕐 Office: Mon–Fri 10–1, 2.30–6. Phone lines: daily 10–8 💶 €15–€30 according to activity: canoeing, half-day, minimum 6 people, €30 per person inc. lunch; diving €25, rock-climbing €30, archery €15–€18, paintball €20

ISILDA PARENTE
www.rtam.pt
For fine embroidery typical of the Minho, it is worth heading out to the village of Perre, 5km (3 miles) east of Viana, and in particular to the shop of artisan Isilda Parente. Among other things, she specializes in the elaborately decorated local costumes of the north.
✉ Caminho do Mestre Parente 37, Perre 4925-582 Perre Viana do Castelo ☎ 258 841 047 🕐 Mon–Fri 9–12, 1–5; for weekend visits call in advance 🚗 East of Viana on the N202 to Santa Maria de Portuzelo. Turn left to Perre

KARTÓDROMO
www.kartodromodeviana.com
Next to the Praia da Amorosa, just to the south of Viana do Castelo, this is the largest go-cart track in Portugal. It consists of two tracks—468m (510 yards) and 1,117m (1,217 yards). The

FESTIVALS AND EVENTS

MAY
FESTA DAS CRUZES
This festival commemorates the 'miracle of the cross', when a 16th-century cobbler had a vision of a cross engraved in the ground. There are fireworks, dances, regional costumes and flowers strewn on the streets.
✉ Barcelos ☎ 253 811 882 (tourist office) 🕐 3 May

JUNE
FESTA DE SÃO PEDRO
The town's biggest and liveliest festival has bands, amusements and *farturas* (deep-fried, stick-shaped doughnuts). There is a large market—a good place to buy local black pottery and fine embroidery from surrounding villages.
✉ Vila Real ☎ 259 322 819 🕐 28–29 Jun

venue has hosted many national and international competitions.
✉ Praia da Amorosa, 4935-581 Chafé ☎ 258 320 080 🕐 Jul–end Aug daily 10–1, 2–midnight; rest of year Wed–Sun 9.30–1, 2–6.30 💶 €14–€30 depending on size of kart for 10 minutes 🚗 Leave IC1 at Castelo de Neiva exit At Castelo de Neiva head towards Praia da Amorosa. Kartódromo is signed

QUINTA DO SANTOINHO
www.avic.pt/santoinho
For a Minho extravaganza come to Santoinho, a huge rustic barn of a place dedicated to all things *minhoto*. The entry price covers a meal of limitless fresh sardines and *vinho verde* straight from the barrel, plus a show of traditional dancing to well-loved local tunes.
✉ Estrada Nacional 13, Darque ☎ 258 806 180 🕐 Aug Tue, Thu, Sat 8pm–1am; May–end Jul and Sep–end Nov Sat 8pm–1am 💶 Jul–end Sep and Nov: adult €15; May–end Jun and Oct: adult €13; child (4–10) €7 any month 🚗 5km (3 miles) from Viana, south on the EN13

AUGUST
FESTIVAL OF THE GUALTERIANAS
Celebrated since 1452, this is the most important festival in Guimarães, held in honour of São Gualter. For three days the town is filled with folk-dancing, rock concerts, fireworks and, on the Monday, a grand parade.
✉ Guimarães ☎ 253 412 450 (tourist office) 🕐 First weekend in Aug

DECEMBER
FESTAS DOS RAPAZES
This festival is rooted in ancient rites of passage, as unmarried men dressed in masks and rags leap bonfires and 'accost' young women—accompanied by the *pauliteiros* (stick-dancers).
✉ Miranda do Douro ☎ 273 431 132 (tourist office) 🕐 27–30 Dec

VIANA DO CASTELO MARKET
Held in the west of the town, Viana do Castelo's market sells all the usual things you would expect to find in a market, but specializes in an immense range of shoes and textiles produced in Portugal's northern factories. All items are sold at low prices.
✉ Campo da Agonia, Viana do Castelo ☎ 258 822 620 (tourist office) 🕐 Fri

VILA REAL
CENÁRIOS D'OURO
www.cenarios.pt
This company specializes in all kinds of activities along the River Douro. It also offers donkey and horseback rides, guided walks and horse and carriage trips
✉ Praceta Aureliano Barrigas 6, 1st floor, 5000-418 Vila Real ☎ 259 338 135 🕐 Office: Mon–Fri 9.30–1, 2.30–6.30 💶 Donkey rides (Castelo Rodrigo) €38.50 for 3 hours; horseback rides (Sabrosa) €20; carriage rides (Sabrosa and São Martinho da Anta) €20

EATING

PRICES AND SYMBOLS

The restaurants are listed alphabetically. The prices given are the average for a two-course lunch (L) and a three-course dinner (D) for one person, without drinks. The wine price is for the least expensive bottle. All the restaurants listed accept credit cards unless otherwise stated.

For a key to the symbols, ▷ 2.

BARCELOS
PEDRA FURADA

Regional Minho dishes are served here including the famous river Minho lampreys when in season, or the undisputed national favourite, *cozido à Portuguesa*, boiled meats, sausages and vegetables served in their own broth. There is also succulent roasted pork or kid.

✉ Lugar da Rua Nova, Pedra Furada, 4755-392 Barcelos ☎ 252 951 144 ◉ Tue–Sun 12–3, 7–10, Mon 12–3. Closed last week in Aug 👎 L €17, D €20, Wine €3.50 🚗 Take N306 south from Barcelos to Pedra Furada

BRAGA
ABADE DE PRISCOS

The restaurant serves regional food and dishes from farther afield, such as prawn or squid curry, Azorean beef, *galinha mourisca* (a chicken

dish dating from Moorish times seasoned with cinnamon), and rabbit with savoury herbs. To finish, you could try the region's most famous dessert: a sticky milk pudding made with eggs, lemon, cinnamon and ham called *abade de Priscos*. Credit cards are not accepted.

✉ Praça Mouzinho de Albuquerque 7, Campo Novo, 4710-301 Braga ☎ 253 276 650 ◉ Tue–Sat 12–3, 7.30–10, Mon 7.30–10. Closed Jun, 24–31 Dec 👎 L €15, D €20, Wine €7.50

CAFÉ VIANNA

A good place for a light snack, this art nouveau café in the heart of town serves excellent coffee and savoury pastries and cakes. Try a *prego* (fine slices of beef inside a bread roll) or an *empada de galinha* (small chicken pie). Sweet treats include *charutos de chila* (pastry tubes filled with sweet pumpkin), or *rabanadas* (cinnamon French toast). If Vianna is full, try the Astória next door.

✉ Praça da República, 4710-228 Braga ☎ 253 262 336 ◉ Daily 9–7 👎 Light snack and drink approx. €5 per person

CASA DAS ARTES

Rustic, with dark-wood dressers, the Casa das Artes focuses on game

dishes when in season. Year-long favourites include *arroz de polvo*, oven-baked octopus with rice. Finish with *abade de Priscos*, the local egg-and-milk pudding. There is an attractive terrace for outside dining.

✉ Rua Costa Gomes 353, Real, 4700-262 Braga ☎ 253 622 023 ◉ Mon–Sat 12–3, 7–12 👎 L €20, D €25, Wine €7.50 🚗 Take EN201 northwest out of Braga towards Ponte de Lima, following signs to Real. In Real the restaurant is signed

SAMEIRO 'MAIA'

With fantastic views this old dining room has been serving meals for more than 90 years. Try the delicious *bacalhau à Sameiro* (cod steak fried with onions and potato) or *bacalhau com natas* (cod with cream). Roast beef and duck with rice are two meat options. The house wine is a white *vinho verde*.

✉ Lugar de Sameiro, 4715-450 Braga ☎ 253 675 114 ◉ Tue–Sun 12–3, 7–10. Closed last week in Oct 👎 L €15, D €20, Wine €4 a pitcher 🚗 Take EN309 southeast out of Braga following signs to Sameiro for about 10km (6 miles). Restaurant is next to the Santuario de Sameiro

Above *Art nouveau Café Vianna in Braga serves excellent snacks*

BRAGANÇA

LÁ EM CASA
This congenial place showcases Trás-os-Montes cooking. Starters include local cheeses, sausages, and garlic and olive oil soup. For mains, choose from *arroz de polvo* (rice with octopus), roasted salt cod stuffed with air-cured ham, trout with ham, rabbit, partridge and wild boar. Apple or pumpkin tart make a good pudding.

✉ Rua Marquês do Pombal 7, 5300-197 Bragança ☎ 273 322 111 🕒 Daily 12–4, 7–11 🖐 L €12, D €16, Wine €6.50

O GEADAS
This place, with its slate interior, has views over the river. Starters are regional sausages such as spicy *salpicão* with capers, crêpes filled with wild mushrooms or a variety of soups including partridge broth. As a main course perhaps try the rice with wild hare or river trout, but leave room for the chestnut pudding.

✉ Rua do Loreto 32, 5300-189 Bragança ☎ 273 326 002 🕒 Daily 12–4, 7–11 🖐 L €20, D €30, Wine €8

SOLAR BRAGANÇANO
This 18th-century manor house in the middle of town has a garden terrace. The menu majors in regional cuisine with a strong emphasis on game. Try chestnut soup, braised wild boar with cabbage and fried apple, wild rabbit *'à monsenhor'*, or partridge with grapes.

✉ Praça da Sé 34, 5300-265 Bragança ☎ 273 323 875 🕒 Daily 12–3.30, 7–11. Closed Mon Nov–end Mar 🖐 L €14, D €20, Wine €8

CHAVES

ADEGA FAUSTINO
This no-frills restaurant serves an inexpensive but cracking meal. The menu, with little egg tarts, air-cured ham, home-made sausages, octopus and onion vinaigrette, stewed pork morsels, salt cod and so on, is great. The local red wine comes straight out of the barrels that line the walls.

✉ Travessa do Olival, 5400-423 Chaves ☎ 276 322 142 🕒 Mon–Sat 10am–midnight 🖐 L €10, D €16, Wine €4

GUIMARÃES

FLORÊNCIO
www.restauranteflorencio.com
The old wood-burning oven rules the roost, producing superb roasts, even though the starters could form a meal in themselves. Try *bacalhau*, octopus, lamb, kid, or beef with *leite creme* (crème brûlée) to finish. The *vinho verdes* are well worth trying.

✉ Madre de Deus, Azurém, 4800-022 Guimarães ☎ 253 415 820 🕒 Daily 12–11 🖐 L €15, D €20, Wine €6 🚗 Head north out of Guimarães to São Torcato. The restaurant is about 2km (1.5 miles) out of Guimarães on the left, next to a small chapel

SÃO GIÃO
Considered by one national paper to be the best restaurant in the Minho, this dining room is modern with elegant lines. The menu is vast, its roots firmly fixed in traditional Minho cuisine. There are spectacular meat, game and fish dishes and desserts, fine cheeses and first-rate wine list.

✉ Lugar das Vinhas, Moreira dos Cónegos, 4800-270 Guimarães ☎ 253 561 853 🕒 Tue–Sat 12–3.30, 7.30–10.30, Sun 12–3.30 🖐 L €20, D €26, Wine €8 🚗 Take the N105 south towards Santo Tirso. Moreira de Cónegos is on this road and the restaurant is next to the Moreirense Stadium

MIRANDA DO DOURO

CAPA D'HONRAS
This village house has a modern and bright interior. The menu leans heavily towards roasted and stewed meat dishes. The friendly owners take pride in their locally prized, home-made sausages and cured meats, produced from their own free-range pigs. There are some great salt-cod options too.

✉ Travessa do Castelo 1, 5210-324 Miranda do Douro ☎ 273 432 699 🕒 Daily 12–3, 7–10 🖐 L €14, D €17, Wine €4 🚗 Enter the old walled town and take the first right. Restaurant is on the right

PONTE DE LIMA

CARVALHEIRA
A rustic dining room with a log fire in winter, Carvalheira is sophisticated and offers the best in Minho cooking. Starters, such as broad beans with *chouriço*, *pataniscas* (cod fritters) and octopus vinaigrette, can be followed by *bacalhau com broa* (salt cod with maize bread), roast pork loin, or duck with rice. Service is attentive and the wine list is good.

✉ Arcozelo, 4990-231 Ponte de Lima ☎ 258 742 316 🕒 Tue–Sun 12–3, 7.15–10 🖐 L €16, D €22, Wine €12 🚗 In Ponte de Lima cross the new bridge and follow signs to Arcos de Valdevez. At the roundabout turn right. Restaurant is 700m (770 yards) past traffic lights on the right

VIANA DO CASTELO

TABERNA DO VALENTIM
This typical old Minho house, with granite walls and wooden ceiling, isn't much to look at but is renowned for only serving fish straight off the local fishing boats. On stormy days, if the boats cannot go to sea, the restaurant does not open. Their *chorinha* (fish soup) is much praised, as is their *caldeirada*, a hearty fish and potato stew. In season try the *sável frito*, a herring-like fish highly prized by locals, and finish off with a home-made *leite creme* (crème brûlée).

✉ Rua Monsenhor Daniel Machado 180, 4900-356 Viana do Castelo ☎ 258 827 505 🕒 Mon–Sat 12.30–3, 7.30–10 🖐 L €14, D €20, Wine €7

VILA REAL

PASSOS PERDIDOS
This gently lit restaurant is decorated in yellow, blue and terracotta, its tables dressed with rough linen cloths. The owners' vision is to promote traditional dishes, such as *porco no borralho* (grilled pork served with black-eyed beans and cabbage or with rice and chestnuts), pork marinated in garlic and red wine and cod with maize bread. They also serve a range of traditional Portuguese desserts.

✉ Casa da Coutada Vilarinho de Samardã, 5000-781 Vila Real ☎ 259 347 322 🕒 Tue–Sat 12–2.30, 7–10.30, Sun 12–2.30 🖐 L €18, D €22, Wine €5.50 🚗 Take N2 north out of town towards Chaves. After 10km (6 miles) turn off to Vilarinho de Samardã. The restaurant is signed at the far end of the village

STAYING

PRICES AND SYMBOLS

The prices are the lowest and highest for a double room for one night including breakfast, unless otherwise stated. All the hotels listed accept credit cards unless otherwise stated. Note that rates can vary widely throughout the year.

For a key to the symbols, ▷ 2.

BRAGA

HOTEL DO TEMPLO

Next to the church on the Bom Jesus hill, this 4-star hotel enjoys views over Braga and, on clear days, the sea. Totally renovated to cater for the Euro 2004 soccer competition, it now has modern (if characterless) rooms. It also has a health club, and, for those cooler days, an indoor pool. In summer months sit out on the terrace to make the best of the panoramic vistas.

✉ Monte do Bom Jesus, Tenões, 4710-455 Braga ☎ 253 603 610 💶 €80–€99 🛏 42 💲 🏊 Indoor 📺

POUSADA DE SANTA MARIA DO BOURO

www.pousadas.pt

This monumental granite *pousada*, northeast of Braga, was a Cistercian monastery, built in the 12th century.

An ingenious transformation in 1997 fused the plant-covered ruins with modern plate glass and wood, and converted monks' cells into contemporary bedrooms with fantastic views of the countryside. The huge granite water tank still feeds the system of channels that runs through the convent, including the monastery kitchens that now house a restaurant specializing in Minho cuisine. There are tennis courts on site.

✉ Santa Maria do Bouro, 4720-688 Amares ☎ 253 371 970 💶 €170–€270 🛏 30 rooms, 2 suites 💲 🏊 Outdoor 📺 From N101 north of Braga, turn right onto EN206 to Amares. Approximately 14km (9 miles) from Braga

BRAGANÇA

LAGOSTA PERDIDA

www.lagostaperdida.com

This hidden treasure, tucked away near the Spanish border in the Montesinho Park, is owned by an English/Dutch couple who have lovingly restored it to provide luxurious accommodation while retaining the original, rustic charm of the stone house. Rooms are sumptuous, with broadband Internet access and satellite TV. The gardens

Above *Many of Portugal's hotels have beautiful gardens*

are charming and there is a heated outdoor pool for the summer months, or alternatively borrow a bicycle and go exploring. For cooler days there is a library and a well-stocked games room.

✉ Aldeia de Montesinho, 5300-542 Bragança ☎ 273 919 031 💶 €90–€140 including breakfast and dinner (with wine and coffee) 🛏 6 💲 🏊 Outdoor 📺 From Bragança head north on the N103-7 towards the Spanish border and Puebla de Sanabria. Pass through Rabal and França then turn off left towards Montesinho

RESIDENCIAL TULIPA

Tulipa is simple but agreeable and offers extremely good value if you want to base yourself right in the heart of old Bragança. All the rooms are modern with bathroom and shower facilities, and some have balconies (though these are quite tiny). There is a regional restaurant on the ground floor that serves traditional northern dishes. Breakfast is also served.

✉ Rua Dr. Francisco Felgueiras 8–10, 5300-134 Bragança ☎ 273 331 675 💶 €35 excluding breakfast 🛏 28 💲

CHAVES

HOTEL FORTE DE SÃO FRANCISCO

www.forte-s-francisco-hoteis.pt
Head for the highest point in town to find the Forte de São Francisco, with its imposing stone walls and cannon; the hotel grounds occupy the whole of the fort's interior. The main hotel building is in the converted Franciscan monastery, where graceful modern structures have been built around ancient ruins. Rooms are well furnished in period style. Be sure to visit the chapel. There is tennis on site.
✉ Alto da Pedisqueira, 5400-435 Chaves ☎ 276 333 700 💶 €125–€165 🚪 53 rooms, 5 suites 🛗 🏊 Outdoor

GUIMARÃES

CASA DE SEZIM

www.sezim.pt
Casa de Sezim, an aristocratic 18th-century ochre home since 1376, is reached via a grand gateway, with an imposing coat of arms. Spacious salons are decorated with ancestral portraits, exquisite chandeliers and rare 19th-century wallpapers; some bedrooms have four-poster beds. Even the pool is surrounded by grass rather than concrete. The estate has produced wine since 1390 and provides tours for enthusiasts.
✉ Turismo de Habitação, Lugar de Santo Amaro, Nespereira, Guimarães ☎ 253 523 000 💶 €110 🚪 8 🏊 Outdoor 🚗 Head south from Guimarães on the N105 signed to Santo Tirso. In Covas turn right to Santo Amaro. The house is 1.5km (1 mile) after Santo Amaro on the left

POUSADA DA NOSSA SENHORA DA OLIVEIRA

www.pousadas.pt
In the middle of the historic old town (the so-called 'birthplace of Portuguese nationality'), this pousada was converted in 1973 from a row of 18th-century townhouses. Today, it is a welcoming place with low beamed ceilings, old floorboards, leather armchairs and, in the bedrooms, attractive soft furnishings and fine bed linen. In summer, the restaurant tables spill out on to the medieval square, and in winter an open fire blazes.
✉ Rua de Santa Maria, 4801-910 Guimarães ☎ 253 514 157 💶 €120–€198 🚪 10 rooms, 6 suites 🛗

POUSADA DE SANTA MARINHA

www.pousadas.pt
The monks made a good choice for the site of this 10th- to 12th-century monastery: on a hill with fine views over Guimarães. The reconstruction of the 17th-century buildings preserves monastic sobriety while providing modern comforts. Fine tiles, stone fountains and cloisters are just a few of the features. Some rooms in the old wing are former monks' cells, so are small, but well appointed. The restaurant serves high-quality Minho dishes.
✉ Largo Domingos Leite de Castro, 4810-011 Guimarães ☎ 253 511 259 💶 €150–€250 🚪 49 rooms, 2 suites 🛗 🏊 Outdoor

MESÃO FRIO

POUSADA DO SOLAR DA REDE

www.pousadas.pt
A baroque gateway leads to this beautiful palace and its spectacular 18th-century chapel, with fine tiles and a gilded altarpiece. Inside the *quinta* proper, there is a French influence in the opulent lounge and in the elaborate beds in the suites. There are other rooms in buildings in the garden.
✉ Santa Cristina, 5040-336 Mesão Frio ☎ 254 890 130 💶 €150–€250 🚪 19 rooms, 10 suites 🛗 🏊 Outdoor 🚗 On the N101 between Peso da Régua and Amarante

MIRANDA DO DOURO

ESTALAGEM DE SANTA CATARINA

www.estalagemsantacatarina.pt
This *estalagem* (inn) looks over the Miranda dam and Douro to Spain. Furnishings are dated, but from the windows and balconies there are breathtaking views. The restaurant serves Transmontano cuisine.
✉ Largo da Pousada, 5210-183 Miranda do Douro ☎ 273 431 005 💶 €92–€102 🚪 9 rooms, 3 suites 🛗

PINHÃO

HOTEL VINTAGE HOUSE

www.csvintagehouse.com
This idyllic place on the banks of the River Douro was once a port warehouse. The bedrooms still have original 18th-century features and each has a private balcony overlooking the river. The dining room serves traditional yet innovative dishes, and you can enjoy a glass of port on the shaded terrace. There is tennis on site.
✉ Lugar da Ponte, 5085-034 Pinhão ☎ 291 775 936 💶 €113–€161 🚪 37 rooms, 6 suites (non-smoking rooms available) 🛗 🏊 Outdoor

VIANA DO CASTELO

ESTALAGEM CASA MELO ALVIM

www.meloalvimhouse.com
The Melo Alvim was built in 1509 in the Manueline style, and is one of the oldest buildings of its type in Viana. Added to over the years, it has a lovely façade, a neo-baroque fountain and peaceful cloisters. In keeping with the original architecture, the modern interior is sober yet elegant. Bedrooms, reached by a stone staircase, are individually decorated.
✉ Avenida Conde Carreira 28, 4900-343 Viana do Castelo ☎ 258 808 200 💶 €115–€140 🚪 16 rooms, 4 suites 🛗

VILA REAL

CASA AGRÍCOLA DA LEVADA

www.casadalevada.com
A short distance out of Vila Real, this is a peaceful haven. There are four guest rooms in the main house, which dates from 1922 and has an attractive decorative façade; the apartments in the grounds were converted from outbuildings. In summer, enjoy breakfast on the patio and savour the homemade bread, jams and honey.
✉ Lugar da Timpeira, 5000-419 Vila Real ☎ 259 322 190 💶 €68–€80 🚪 4 rooms, 5 2-roomed apartments 🏊 Outdoor 🚗 Coming from Porto towards Vila Real on the IP4, turn off at Vila Real Norte. Turn left to 'centro' then left at the roundabout signed 'Mateus/ Sabrosa'. At second left look for 'Casa Agrícola/Turismo de Habitação' signs

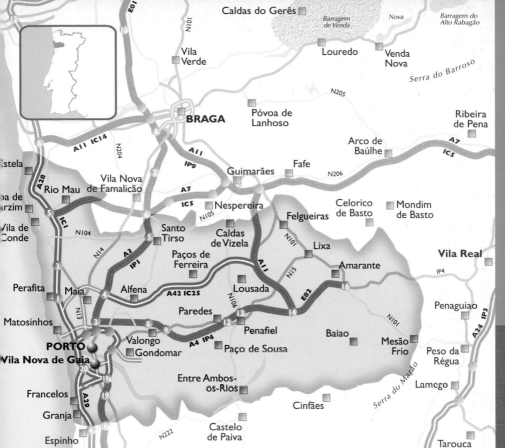

PORTO AND THE DOURO

It is said that while Lisbon plays and Braga prays, Porto works. Even the shortest stroll around its tightly packed and bustling streets will confirm this dictum. Many Portuguese also say that Porto is a dark city, a reputation not helped by the damp and sometimes dreary weather that rolls in from the Atlantic, but do not be put off by this. Porto is a city of treasures beginning with its glorious setting, tumbling down the steep valley to the gently flowing Douro below.

Architecturally there is something for all tastes from the 12th-century fortress cathedral, through the baroque Torre dos Clérigos and neoclassical stock exchange to the delightful simplicity of the art deco Casa Serralves and adjoining ultra-modern contemporary art museum. Culturally, Porto is thriving with its museums, traditional theatres, concert venues and avant-garde Casa da Música, home to the Porto National Orchestra. Explore its historic districts, beginning with the most ancient, Ribeira, a rambunctious maze of streets and lanes packed onto the waterfront; head then to the more formal streets and avenues of the commercial districts above or catch the tram down to Foz on the sea front.

Naturally, port should feature in any visit to the city; at the very least pop into the Port Wine institute for a glass, but if possible head across to Vila Nova de Gaia to one of the port lodges for an informative tour and tasting. Better still, take a river trip or drive up the idyllic Douro valley to see the precipitous terraces used to grow port grapes and visit one of the *quintas* where it is always possible to tastes their wares.

AMARANTE

www.amarante.pt
www.rtsmarao.pt

The beautiful old town of Amarante stands on the banks of the River Tâmega, a tributary of the Douro, in a scenic valley of wooded slopes and vines. This is wine country, birthplace of the light and sparkling *vinho verde*, and the surrounding countryside is dotted with fine old *solares* (manor houses), many of which are happy to provide accommodation for visitors.

Historically, Amarante's big moment came during the Peninsular War, when, in 1809, a heroic show of defence by the townspeople succeeded in halting Marshal Soult and his French forces as they retreated in the face of Beresford's advancing British columns. Amarante held out for two weeks, its inhabitants escaping to safety before the French planted explosives, blew up the defences and took the town. You can still see French bayonet marks in the paintings inside the church of São Gonçalo, the town's patron saint, made as the French feverishly searched for hidden treasure.

The church and former monastery dedicated to Gonçalo are Amarante's main sights, an interesting complex standing beside the graceful old bridge, which is now the Museu Municipal (tel 255 420 272; Tue–Sun 10–12, 2–5; €1). The museum is mainly devoted to the Cubist painter Amadeo de Souza Cardoso (1887–1918), who was born in the town and is one of the few Portuguese artists to have become famous worldwide.

Cross the bridge to reach Rua de Janeiro, lined with old buildings whose balconies hang over the Tâmega. The river is lined with waterside cafés and beaches, and you can rent boats and pedalos here. It is not always tranquil—look out for the plaques on buildings throughout town marking the high flood levels in record years—1909, 1939, 1962 and 2001. Downstream from the bridge, the Parque Florestal is green and cool in summer, while the swimming pool complex is great for kids. You'll find good local craft shops in town and the surrounding villages, while Amarante itself has a twice-weekly market (Wednesday and Saturday).

🕂 326 C3 🅹 Alameda Teixeira de Pascoaes, 4600-011 Amarante ☎ 255 420 246 🅻 Amarante

PAÇO DE SOUSA

www.cm-penafiel.pt

On the banks of the River Sousa, the village of Paço de Sousa is dominated by the monastic church of São Salvador, formerly the headquarters of the Benedictine order in Portugal. It was the Benedictine monks who initially terraced the valley slopes for vines, their other legacy being the fine Romanesque churches they left behind throughout the area. Their great medieval church at Paço has a simple façade with a rose window, while inside, the tomb of Egas Moniz, a Portuguese hero whose name is synonymous with loyalty, can be found in the right of the three shadowy aisles. In 1127 Egas negotiated peace with the King of Léon on behalf of his master, King Afonso Henriques, thus allowing the monarch to concentrate his military efforts on defeating the Moors in the south. Three years later, Afonso conveniently forgot the settlement and war again threatened. Egas journeyed to Toledo and offered up himself and his family for the punishment due to Afonso. His loyalty was rewarded when the Spanish monarch sent him home to Portugal unharmed.

🕂 326 C4 🅹 Avenida Sacadura Cabral 90, 4560-480 Penafiel ☎ 255 712 561

PENAFIEL

www.cm-penafiel.pt

Wine-lovers should head straight for Penafiel, the heart of the *vinho verde* wine country. A laid-back, relaxed little town, it has just one cultural sight, the Museu Municipal (tel 255 712 760; Mon–Fri 9.30–12, 2–5.30, Sat 9.30–12.30), with a small, well-presented collection of archaeological finds from the nearby Celtic settlement of Mozinho. Look for the exquisite gold jewellery.

There are plenty of opportunities to sample wine—the Quinta da Aveleda, just outside the town, is a good option, and the tourist office will advise where else you can try. Penafiel also makes a good base from which to track down some superb Romanesque churches—the ones in Abragão, Gandra and tiny Boelhe are within easy reach.

🕂 326 C4 🅹 Avenida Sacadura Cabral 90, 4560-480 Penafiel ☎ 255 712 561 🅻 Penafiel

Opposite *The abbey at Paço de Sousa, once the headquarters of the Benedictine order*
Below *The lovely town of Amarante overlooking the River Tâmega*

PORTO

INFORMATION

www.portoturismo.pt

➕ 326 B4

🔰 Rua Clube dos Fenianos 25, 4000-172 Porto ☎ 223 393 470 🕙 Mid-Jul to mid-Sep daily 9–7; rest of year Mon–Fri 9–5.30, Sat–Sun 9–4.30

🔰 Rua Infante D. Henrique 63, 4050-297 Porto ☎ 222 060 412 🕙 Mid-Jul to mid-Sep daily 9–7; rest of year Mon–Fri 9–5.30, Sat–Sun 9.30–4

🔰 Casa da Câmara, Terreiro da Sé, 4050-573 Porto ☎ 223 325 174 🕙 Mon–Fri 9–5.30

🚉 Estação de Campanhã, Estação de São Bento

Above *The cloisters, liberally decorated with 18th-century blue tiles, are a major feature of the cathedral*

INTRODUCTION

Porto is a big, sprawling city, but it is easy for visitors to get around as most of the main sights are clustered together. If you are touring, it makes sense to tackle the place before you pick up your car: There is a shortage of parking in the city, while the entire central area is a confusing grid of one-way streets.

Porto revolves round the Avenida dos Aliados, which ends at the Praça da Liberdade, a square that is the hub of the city's public transport system and only a couple of minutes from the Estação de São Bento, one of Porto's two mainline stations. South from here, the city's historic core tumbles down the hillside towards the Cais da Ribeira, the old waterfront, with the Sé (cathedral) complex looming above to the east. This is the most interesting quarter, so take time to explore it thoroughly before heading uphill via the Bolsa to the streets east of the Liberdade. Here you can climb the Clérigos tower for a bird's-eye view of the city.

Porto grew in importance during the Roman occupation, when two settlements developed on opposite banks of the River Douro. In 1095 the area passed to Henry of Burgundy by marriage. Under Afonso Henriques, it became the base for the Christian reconquest, and Porto eventually gave its name to the entire country. In 1387 Porto was the setting for the marriage of João I and Philippa of Lancaster, and their son, Henry the Navigator, was born in the city. Its harbour and shipbuilding industry rapidly developed and trading links were forged with many European nations—in particular England, through treaties signed in 1654 and 1703. During the Peninsular War, British troops under Wellington recaptured the city from its French occupiers in 1809; in 1820, Porto's citizens played a major part in forcing the adoption of a more liberal constitution for the whole country.

Today, Porto is Portugal's second city, a bustling, earthy mix of merging urban areas that for many years was so busy making money that its historic treasures were neglected and began to decay. Its naming as European City of Culture in 2001 was the spark for a massive urban renewal. The Ribeira quarter, a World Heritage Site, got a major face-lift, many buildings were restored, and streets and squares pedestrianized, creating a maritime promenade linking the heart of the city with the sea.

WHAT TO SEE

SÉ

There are expansive river views from the flagstoned Terreiro da Sé, the sweeping open space, complete with pillory, in front of Porto's cathedral. The Sé, like so many of Portugal's ancient cathedrals, is half-church, half-fortress, an austere but pleasing granite Romanesque building, founded in the 12th century by Dona Teresa, mother of Afonso Henriques. The interior was remodelled in the 18th century. Gleaming in the north transept to the left of the high altar is a superb silver altarpiece, dating from the mid-17th century.

More instantly appealing than the church are the cloisters, begun in 1385 and adorned with glowing panels of 18th-century *azulejos* (tiles). From here, a fine staircase designed by the Italian architect Nicolau Nasoni, who was responsible for introducing baroque architecture into the country between 1735 and 1748, leads to the chapterhouse and terrace—there are more great river and city views from here. Outside, pause to admire the classical façade of what was once the archbishop's palace, designed by Nasoni in 1772. Round the back, surrounded by a tranquil garden, is the Museu Guerra Junqueiro, Rua Dom Hugo 32 (tel 222 003 689; Tue–Sun 10–12, 2–5; €2). It houses a fine collection of Islamic Iberian art.

🔁 160 B3 ✉ Terreiro da Sé, 4050-573 Porto ☎ 222 059 028 ⏰ Cathedral: Apr–end Oct Mon–Sat 8.45–12.30, 2.30–7, Sun 8.30–12.30, 2.30–7; Nov–end Mar Mon–Sat 9–12.15, 2.30–5.15, Sun 8.30–12.30, 2.30–6. Cloisters: Apr–end Oct Mon–Sat 9–12.15, 2.30–6, Sun 2.30–6; Nov–end Mar Mon–Sat 9–12.15, 2.30–5.15, Sun 2.30–5.15 ♿ €3

RIBEIRA

From the Terreiro da Sé you plunge down into the heart of Porto's oldest district, a confusing maze of narrow streets, winding steps and alleyways. Despite a recent clean-up, it is still a resolutely raucous and vibrant area, revolving around the waterfront Cais da Ribeira, where you will find a lively weekday market. West of here, the Praça da Ribeira, lined with tall, rickety old houses, is the main square, from which precipitous streets run uphill towards the more modern parts of the city. There's a great view of the two-tiered Ponte Dom Luís I bridge—walk across the bottom level to reach the port warehouses of Vila Nova de Gaia (▷ 164–165). Head west from the Praça da Ribeira and up Rua da Alfândega to take in the Casa do Infante, said to be the birthplace of Prince Henry the Navigator in 1394.

🔁 160 B4 ✉ Cais da Ribeira, 4050-029 Porto 🏪 A good variety of general and craft shops

▷ 164–165

TIPS

» It is worth investing in the Porto Card, a 1- or 2- or 3-day discount card. This lets you travel free on public transport and gives you free or discounted admission to monuments and museums and discounts in shops, restaurants and on river cruises. It is available at tourist information offices (www.portoturismo.pt; 1-day €7.50, 2-day €11.50, 3-day €15.50).

» River cruises are the best way to see Porto's bridges and the Douro valley. Timings and services vary throughout the year, with few running during the winter months. Contact Barcadouro (tel 222 722 415; www.barcadouro.pt) or the tourist office for further details.

» Wear comfortable, flat shoes—Porto is very hilly, with steep cobbled streets in the historic areas.

Below *Houses in the Ribeira, Porto's oldest district*

TORRE DOS CLÉRIGOS AND IGREJA DOS CLÉRIGOS

A few minutes' walk west of the Praça da Liberdade, the baroque Torre dos Clérigos soars 75.6m (248ft) into the air. It was once the tallest structure in Portugal, and the bird's-eye view of the city and beyond from the top is excellent for getting your bearings. It, too, was designed by Nasoni. The Igreja dos Clérigos, right beside the tower, was the first oval-plan church to be built in Portugal, and is lavishly adorned with a riot of festoons and garlands.

✚ 160 B2 ✉ Rua São Felipe de Nery, 4050-546 Porto ☎ 222 001 729 🕐 Church: daily 8.45–12.30, 3.30–7. Tower: Aug daily 10–6.15; Apr–end Jul, Sep–end Oct daily 9.30–12.30, 2–6.15; Nov–end Mar daily 10–12.30, 2–4.30 ✋ Tower: €2 🚌 201, 302, 501 from Boavista

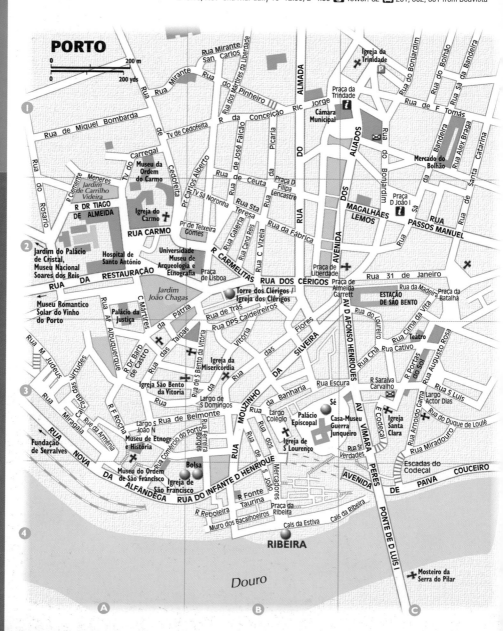

PORTO

0 ———— 200 m
0 ———— 200 yds

Rua Mirante San Carlos
Rua do Mártires da Liberdade
Rua Mirante
Rua de Miguel Bombarda
Carregal
Tv do
Tv de Cedofeita
Rua da Conceição
Ric
do Pinheiro III
Rua da Picaria
Rua Jorge
Igreja da Trindade
Praça da Trindade
Câmara Municipal

Museu da Ordem do Carmo
R Clemente Meneres
Jardim de Carrilho Videira
R DR TIAGO DE ALMEIDA
Igreja do Carmo
RUA CARMO
Pr Carlos Alberto
TV Sá Noronha
Rua de Ceuta
Praça D Filipa Lencastre
Mercado do Bolhão

Rua do Rosário
Jardim do Palácio de Cristal, Museu Nacional Soares dos Reis
Hospital de Santo António
RESTAURAÇÃO
Universidade Museu de Arqueologia e Etnografia
Praça de Lisboa
Pr de Teixeira Gomes
Rua Sta Teresa
Rua da Fábrica
MAGALHÃES LEMOS
Praça D João I
RUA PASSOS MANUEL

Museu Romântico Solar do Vinho do Porto
Palácio da Justiça
Jardim João Chagas
R CARMELITAS
Praça de Liberdade
RUA DOS CÉRIGOS
Praça de Almeida Garrett
Rua 31 de Janeiro
Praça da Batalha

Rua M Judeus
C Mártires
da Pátria
Torre dos Clérigos / Igreja dos Clérigos
Rua de Trás
ESTAÇÃO DE SÃO BENTO
Rua da Madeira

Rua das Taipas
R Dr Barb de Castro
Rua DPS Caldeireiros
Rua das Flores
AV D AFONSO HENRIQUES
Rua Cimo da Vila
Teatro
Rua Cativo

Rua Virtudes
R F Rocha
Igreja da Misericórdia
Igreja São Bento da Vitória
R Saraiva Carvalho
R Portas do Sol
Rua Augusto Rosa

Fundação de Serralves
RUA NOVA DA ALFÂNDEGA
Largo S. João N
Museu de Etnogr e História
Largo de S Domingos
MOUZINHO
Largo Colégio
Palácio Episcopal
Sé
Rua Escura
Casa-Museu Guerra Junqueiro
Rua S Luis
Largo Actor Dias

Bolsa
Museu do Ordem de São Francisco
Igreja de São Francisco
RUA DO INFANTE D HENRIQUE
Igreja de S Lourenço
Igreja Santa Clara
Rua Miradouro
Escadas do Codeçal

R Fonte Taurina
R Reboleira
Praça da Ribeira
Cais da Ribeira
AVENIDA PERES
PONTE DE D LUIS I
COUCEIRO

Muro dos Bacalhoeiros
Cais da Estiva
RIBEIRA

Douro
Mosteiro da Serra do Pilar

THE BOLSA

www.palaciodabolsa.pt

Up the hill and west of Ribeira is Porto's temple of commerce, the Stock Exchange, a building that typifies Porto's 19th-century commercial acumen and industry. Built to impress, its neoclassical façade is the perfect expression of financial solidity and probity. Designed and erected in 1834, it is elaborately decorated inside with a profusion of precious stone, marble and wood, seen at its most lavish in the wonderfully kitsch Arabian Hall, an amazing pastiche of Granada's Alhambra in Spain, complete with Moorish-style stuccowork, lavish stained glass and elaborately carved woodwork.

There is more ostentation next door in the Igreja de São Francisco (tel 222 662 100; Jul–end Sep daily 9–8; Mar–end Jun and Oct daily 9–7; rest of year daily 9–5.30; €3), which was built for the Franciscans and began life as a plain Gothic structure. The interior was reconstructed in the 18th century, and is now filled with golden rococo carving, the altars, walls and vaulting dripping with *putti* (cherubs), vines and depictions of wildlife. The clergy were so shocked by its extravagance when it was unveiled that the church was deconsecrated—it remains so. Don't miss the museum, beneath whose floor lies a vast *ossário*, or bone deposit, where thousands of bones were buried before public cemeteries were instituted in Portugal in 1845.

✚ 160 B4 ✉ Rua Ferreira Borges, 4050-253 Porto ☎ 226 399 000 ◷ Apr–end Oct daily 9–6.30; Nov–end Mar daily 9–12.30, 2–5.30 ✋ €5 🚌 500, 202 from station; 900 from centre

Above *Detail of the austere Romanesque cathedral exterior*
Below *Fishing boats moored on the Douro, with the graceful Ponte Dom Luís I in the background*

FUNDAÇÃO DE SERRALVES

www.serralves.com

Porto's modern art museum, the Fundação de Serralves, stands in a sculpture-dotted park a short distance west of the heart of the city. The permanent collection is focused on the relationship between Portuguese artists and their international counterparts from the late 1960s to the present day, and is displayed in a clean-cut ultra-modern building designed by renowned Portuguese architect Alvaro Siza. The museum also hosts temporary exhibitions in the 1930s art deco Casa de Serralves, which is part of the museum complex.

✚ Off map 160 A3 ✉ Rua Dom João de Castro 210, 4150-417 Porto ☎ 808 200 543 ◷ Apr–end Sep Tue–Fri 10–7, Sat–Sun 10–8; Oct–end Mar Tue–Sun 10–7 ✋ €5 🚌 201, 203, 207, 504 from centre, vintage bus and Portobus 🎁 Good art books and museum souvenirs

PÓVOA DE VARZIM

www.cm-pvarzim.pt/turismo

If what you want is a straightforward holiday resort with a real Portuguese twist, Póvoa de Varzim is a good option. With more than 7km (4.5 miles) of clean, pebble-and-sand beach, hotels and restaurants to suit every budget, and a clutch of traditional buildings, it is a good beach base for a few days. The long esplanade, dotted with fountains, is backed by high-rise hotels and apartments, but the town has enough atmosphere to outweigh what it lacks in style. At the southern end is the fishing harbour, a fine 18th-century fortress and the casino. Behind this strip are the vestiges of the original town, with some nice hidden streets and squares, good churches and the interesting small Museu Municipal (closed for refurbishment until early 2009; tel 252 090 002 for times and prices), which has archaeological displays and exhibits connected with local seafaring.

Póvoa has a procession of summer festivals, including a classical music event in July. To catch the best, try to be there on 15 August, the Feast of the Assumption of the Virgin, when there are processions to the fishing boats in honour of the Virgin, and spectacular fireworks.

✚ 326 B3 ℹ️ Praça Marquês de Pombal, 4490-442 Póvoa de Varzim ☎ 252 298 120

VILA DO CONDE

http://cmviladoconde.wiremaze.com

Around 30km (20 miles) north of Porto, the ancient port of Vila do Conde, a down-to-earth boat-building and fishing town that has retained its compact old quarter and some attractive buildings, makes a great contrast to neighbouring Póvoa. It's on the mouth of the Rio Ave, and you can still see fishing boats tied up alongside the riverbank with their fresh catches for sale, as well as the busy boatyard. It was here that a replica of the first caravel to round the Cape of Good Hope was built in 1987—it is now moored in South Africa where it finished its journey.

The area is dominated by the dome of the 17th-century Capela do Socorro, while the narrow cobbled streets are lined with a pleasing mix of simple whitewashed houses and fine mansions. You can't miss the huge bulk of the Convento de Santa Clara, now a reformatory, with its Gothic church and cloister. Behind it, you will find the remnants of the old aqueduct that supplied the convent with water. Walk downhill from here to reach the Igreja Matriz, a mixture of ornate Portuguese and more restrained Spanish styles—the result possibly of Basque workmen involved in the construction.

Vila has a couple of museums worth visiting: the Museu de Renda de Bilros (Mon–Fri 9–12, 2–6; free), where you can see the town's famous lace; and the Centro de Gência Viva (Tue–Sun 10–6; €2.50), a life science workshop with plenty of hands-on exhibits.

✚ 326 B3 ℹ️ Rua 25 de Abril 103, 4480-722 Vila do Conde ☎ 252 248 473

Above *Convento de Santa Clara is a landmark in Vila do Conde*
Opposite *Stained-glass window in Igreja Matriz, Vila do Conde*

INFORMATION

www.portoturismo.pt

326 B4 Avenida Diogo Leite 242, 4000-111 Vila Nova de Gaia or at Cais da Gaia, Loja 510, 4400-266 Vila Nova de Gaia 223 773 080 or 223 756 216

Jul–end Sep daily 9–7; Oct–end Jun Mon–Fri 9–5.30, Sat–Sun 9–4.30

There are 16 lodges open for tours

TIPS

» If time is short, join a tour from Porto: one takes in Porto and Gaia; the other is a mini-train trip from the Sé (cathedral) to Gaia—ask at Porto's tourist office.

» If you have a head for heights, approach Gaia by walking across the upper level of the Ponte Luís I, which has great views across to Gaia and back to the Ribeira waterfront.

» You can get top-quality port at good prices in Gaia.

Above *Wine lodges line the banks of the River Douro in Gaia*
Opposite *Port barrels*

INTRODUCTION

The heart of the centuries-old port trade, Vila Nova is famous for its wine lodges—the best places to learn about the history of this great fortified wine and sample a wide variety of vintages. It is easy to make your way across the river from Porto to visit Vila Nova de Gaia. Despite its close proximity to Porto, it's a city in its own right, usually known simply as Gaia. The wine lodges are in rows stretching back from the water's edge, so it's a case of choosing two or three to visit—though check with the tourist office for opening times first. Try to visit one of the large producers, such as Sandeman or Graham, and a smaller one like Barros or Ramos Pinto. For historical interest, Cockburn's, still British-owned and run, is well worth checking out, while Ferreira has one of the best tasting rooms, beautifully decorated with lovely *azulejos* (tiles). Take a stroll around the streets to soak up the historic atmosphere—if you are feeling energetic, you could climb up to the Mosteiro da Serra do Pilar for superb views of Gaia, Porto and the river. However, note that the monastery church is open only on Saturday and Sunday mornings.

Port's story as a recognized variety of wine dates back to the early 18th century, when English merchants based in Porto spread the word of its quality. It was an opportune moment—imports of French claret into England were impossible as the two countries were at war. In consequence, port drinking soon became all the rage, helped by the 1703 Methuen Treaty, which reduced the import duty on the wine. Profits were so high that many rogue producers passed off inferior wines as the genuine article. The port producers' response was to set up the Companhia General de Agricultura dos Vinhos do Alto Douro in 1756, which demarcated the port area and regulated how the wine was to be produced and then matured. Gaia had plenty of land for warehouses to mature the port and was perfectly positioned on the River Douro to take a leading role in the export trade. It maintains that role today.

WHAT TO SEE
THE PORT WINE LODGES
There are 16 wine lodges in Gaia that run tours and offer port tastings. Port's production area was the world's first demarcated wine zone; until 1987, the wine could be called port only if it had been matured in Vila Nova de Gaia. Traditionally, port was produced upriver and shipped down to Gaia; production still takes place on the *quintas* of the Douro valley, which are now also allowed to mature their port on site. The port producers are proud of their long history and welcome visitors into their lodges and warehouses.

HOW PORT IS MADE
Port is a fortified wine, which means that brandy is added to the grapes during production. This both strengthens the product and halts the fermentation, leaving half the natural grape sugar in the wine. The climate and geography of the valley play a key role: Temperatures are extreme, with broiling summers and bitter winters, and the soil is thin and poor, forcing the vines to root as deep as 6m (20ft) into the rock to find the moisture they need in order to grow and flourish.

The harvest takes place from mid-September to mid-October, when the grapes are picked, crushed and fermented at a controlled temperature, then stored upriver to settle and clear until the following spring. Once in Gaia, port is left to mature for as long as it takes to produce wines of the required quality and then is shipped all over the world.

There are several varieties of port: White, a subtly mellow yet dry wine mainly drunk chilled as an aperitif; ruby, a clear intense red; tawny, an older, more complex port; and late-bottled vintage and vintage port. Vintages are declared only in years when the quality is particularly high; the wine must then remain in cask for two more years before it can be bottled and left to mature.

THE WINE LODGES
Cálem
www.calem.pt
Cálem was founded in 1859. Its Tawny Port, Os Velhotes, is one of the best in Portugal. The visit includes a tasting.
✉ Avenida Diogo Leite 344, 4400-111 Vila Nova de Gaia ☎ 223 746 660
🕐 Mar–end Oct daily 10–7.15; rest of year daily 10–6.15 ✋ €3

Graham's
www.grahams-port.com
Founded in 1820, Graham's is a traditional working lodge. Free guided tours are preceded by a video, and you have the chance to taste the port.
✉ Rua Rei Ramiro 514, 4400-281 Vila Nova de Gaia ☎ 223 776 330
🕐 May–end Sep daily 9.30–6; rest of year Mon–Fri 9.30–1, 2–5.30

Ramos Pinto
www.ramospinto.pt
Ramos Pinto was founded in 1880 to supply the South American market. During a tour of the lodge you can sample some of the port. The lodge has a superb library and extensive vaulted cellars.
✉ Avenida Ramos Pinto 400, 4400-266 Vila Nova de Gaia ☎ 223 707 000
🕐 Jul–end Aug daily 10–5; Jun, Sep Mon–Sat 10–5; rest of year Mon–Fri 9–12, 2–4 ✋ €2

Sandeman
www.sandeman.com
This is the pick of the bunch if you want to visit a lodge, with guided tours of the cellars, tastings and a museum.
✉ Largo Miguel Bombarda 3, 4400-222 Vila Nova de Gaia ☎ 223 740 533
🕐 Mar–end Oct daily 10–12.30, 2–6; Nov–end Feb daily 9.30–12.30, 2–5.30
✋ €3 (redeemable against the price of a bottle of port)

Taylor's
www.taylor.pt
This lodge has been independent and family owned for the past 300 years. Long-lived vintage ports are their forte.
✉ Rua do Choupelo 250, 4400-088 Vila Nova de Gaia ☎ 223 742 800
🕐 Jul–end Aug 10–6.30 (last entry 1 hour before closing); Sep–end Jun Mon–Fri 10–6 ✋ Free

EXPLORING PORTO

This walk through the heart of Porto gives you a taste of the highly individual character of Portugal's vibrant second city and its wonderful old quarter. There is also the bonus of stopping off in some tempting cafés and bars for a breather along the way.

THE WALK

Distance: 2.6km (1.6 miles)
Time: 2 hours
Start/end at: Praça da Liberdade

★ Start at the southern end of Praça da Liberdade. Cross the road and head left to get to Porto's mainline station, Estação de São Bento.

❶ Estação de São Bento's booking hall is worth taking a look at for its fantastic *azulejos* (tiles). There are more than 20,000—all of them painted between 1905 and 1930 by artist Jorge Colaço and depicting historical landscapes and northern rural traditions.

With the station on your left, walk along Avenida Dom Afonso Henriques, crossing the road to turn down Rua Dom Hugo, along which you will find the Casa-Museu Guerra Junqueiro. Continue until you reach Porto's cathedral, the Sé (▷ 159).

❷ The Casa-Museu Guerra Junqueiro is a stunning collection of Islamic art assembled by the poet Abílio de Guerra Junqueiro (1850–1923).

Walk behind the Archbishop's Palace and plunge down to follow the steps and alleys through the atmospheric and medieval Bairro do Barredo to the Cais da Ribeira on the waterfront—as long as you keep heading downhill the exact route doesn't matter. This is the waterfront's main street, the home

to a weekday market. Turn right and walk alongside the river to Praça da Ribeira (▷ 159). From here head right and uphill along Rua dos Mercadores, and take the first left down Rua Infante Dom Henrique.

❸ Nos 47–53 Rua do Infante Dom Henrique is a striking medieval house donated by João I to the city merchants, eventually to become Porto's first stock exchange. Look, too, for the 18th-century English 'factory', designed by the British consul John Whitehead as a meeting place for English traders and port shippers. In the same street you'll

Above *Colourful buildings line the Praça da Ribeira, the Ribeira district's main square with shops and cafés*

also find the Igreja de São Francisco
(▷ 161) and the Bolsa (▷ 161).

Next to the church, turn down Rua
Ferreira Borges. Then go diagonally
right across Largo São Domingos
onto Rua das Flores.

❹ The Igreja da Misericórdia is on
your left, a 16th-century church with
a 17th-century façade designed
by Nasoni. Next door is the Santa
Casa da Misericórdia, which houses
the *Fons Vitae*, one of Porto's most
celebrated paintings.

Past the church take the second left
up Rua Trindade Coelho, then turn
left onto Rua dos Caldeireiros and
walk along to the Campo Mártires da
Pátria. Walk through the garden then
up to the Igreja do Carmo.

❺ The 18th-century Carmo is one of
Porto's most exuberant churches, its
1912 façade covered with *azulejos* of
deepest blue. Next to the Carmo is
the older Carmelitas church.

Leave the church and turn left
past the Livraria Lello & Irmão, a
famous bookshop with a fine interior

(▷ 169), and head down Rua das
Carmelitas to the Igreja
dos Clérigos and tower (▷ 160).
Return to Praça da Liberdade along
Rua dos Clérigos.

WHERE TO EAT
The Adega Vila Meã in Rua dos
Caldeireiros serves good no-frills
regional food (▷ 172).

WHEN TO GO
Either in the morning or mid-
afternoon when the streets are busy
and full of life.

PLACES TO VISIT
CASA-MUSEU GUERRA JUNQUEIRO
✉ Rua Dom Hugo 32, 4050-305 Porto
☎ 222 003 689 🕐 Tue–Sun 10–12, 2–5
💶 €2.06; free Sat–Sun 🚇 S. Bento

TIP
» Be prepared for walking up hills.

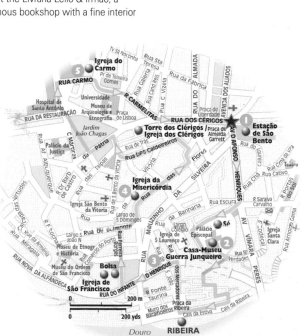

Above *Façade of the Igreja da Misericórdia
in Rua das Flores*

WHAT TO DO

AMARANTE

GOLF CLUB OF AMARANTE

www.portugalgolf.pt

Outside Amarante towards Fregim, this hilly course has 18 holes (par 68) and great views. Reserve a game on the website.

✉ Quinta da Deveza, 4600-593 Fregim ☎ 255 446 060 🕙 Tue–Fri 9–7, Sat–Sun 8–7 👋 18 holes Tue–Fri €50, Sat–Sun €75; club rental €30; hand trolleys €6 🍴 🍷

DOURO

QUINTA DO PANASCAL

www.fonseca.pt

There is no need to reserve ahead at this *quinta*, which has free tours of the vineyards and winery. Wine can be purchased in the winery shop (cash only).

✉ 5120-496 Valença do Douro ☎ 254 732 321 🕙 Apr–end Oct daily 10–1, 2–6; Nov–end Mar Mon–Fri 10–1, 2–6 👋 Free 🚌 From Régua take the N222 towards Pinhão. The estate is in the village of Valença do Douro

QUINTA DE SÃO DOMINGOS

www.castelinho-vinhos.com

This renovated *quinta* has one of the largest visitor facilities in the region. No reservation is required for their free tours and tastings of port and

Douro wines, which can be bought in the shop (cash only).

✉ Juncal de Cima, 5050-207 Peso da Régua ☎ 254 320 260 🕙 May–end Sep daily 9.30–6.30; rest of year daily 9–6 🚌 On the left on the road heading out towards Vila Real

PORTO

ANIKI BÓBÓ

This split-level club is a longstanding Ribeira landmark and attracts an arty, student crowd. In the lower part there is a dance floor, while upstairs the calmer bar area sometimes hosts live drama performances or art exhibitions on Thursdays.

✉ Rua da Fonte Taurina 36–38, Ribeira, 4050-269 Porto ☎ 223 324 619 🕙 Tue–Sat 10pm–4am 👋 €5

A PÉROLA DO BOLHÃO

For quality groceries, including superb cured sausages, try this place across from the market. The art nouveau building has a decorative façade with two blue-shawled oriental figures, intended to symbolize the places where its teas, coffees and spices originated.

✉ Rua Formosa 279, 4000-252 Porto ☎ 222 004 009 🕙 Mon–Fri 9.30–1, 3–7.30, Sat 9.30–1

Above *Porto's Estádio do Dragão stadium is home to FC Porto, and is part of the 'sport city' shopping complex*

ARCÁDIA

In business since 1933 this chocolate shop produces what many consider to be the best chocolates in town. Handmade with utmost care, using artisan recipes and 100 per cent natural ingredients, they come boxed in blue and white and tied with a golden ribbon, making an excellent gift.

✉ Rua do Alameda 63, 4050-036 Porto ☎ 222 001 518 🕙 Mon–Fri 9.30–7, Sat 9.30–1

ARMAZÉM DOS LINHOS

This great linen shop has been in business since the late 19th century. As well as embroidered and typical regional pieces, it also stocks the famous decorative printed cotton from Alcobaça.

✉ Rua de Passos Manuel 19, 4000-384 Porto ☎ 222 004 750 🕙 Mon–Thu 9.30–12.30, 2.30–7, Fri 10–12.30, 2.30–7, Sat 10–1

ARTE FACTO

In an elegant 18th-century building a block back from the river, this shop stocks a great selection of good-quality local crafts. It hosts frequent craft exhibitions and workshops.

✉ Rua da Reboleira 37, Ribeira, 4050-492 Porto ☎ 223 320 201 🕐 Mon–Fri 10–1, 2–6

CASA DA MÚSICA
www.casadamusica.com
The imposing Casa da Música was designed by Dutch architect Rem Koolhaas to mark Porto's nomination as European Capital of Culture in 2001. Home to several orchestras, including Porto's National Orchestra, it is one of the city's prime music and cultural venues.

✉ Avenida da Boavista 604–610, 4149-071 Porto ☎ 270 120 200 (9am–6pm) or 220 120 220 (call centre 10am–8pm) 🕐 Ticket office daily 10–8 and 30 min after show start on performance days 🖐 Varies depending on performance 🚌 201, 203, 502, 503, 504 🚇 Lines A, B, C and E Casa da Música

COLISEU DO PORTO
www.coliseudoporto.pt
This large theatre has attracted a variety of international stars over the years, and stages rock gigs, dance shows and classical concerts.

✉ Rua de Passos Manuel 137, 4000-385 Porto ☎ 223 394 940 🕐 Ticket office: Mon–Sat 2–8, 9–10 (show days); closed Aug 🖐 Tickets on average €15–€60 but can be much more depending on show 🚇 In auditorium 🅿

DIANA TOURS
www.dianatours.pt
This company offers a full range of city tours classified by themes. Don't be put off by the Tripeiro tour (tripeiro means tripe-eater), as it involves no tripe; the suspicious may opt for a rabelo river tour instead. Reservation required.

✉ Head office and reservations: Campo Grande 30B, 1700-093 Lisboa ☎ 217 998 540 🕐 All year, call for details 🖐 Prices start at €10 but vary depending on tour taken

ESTÁDIO DO DRAGÃO
www.fcporto.pt
Home to frequent national football champions FC Porto, this impressive stadium (picture ▷ 168)

was completed in 2003 to host the opening match of the 2004 European Football Championships. Seating 52,000, it is part of the 'sport city' complex of multipurpose pavilions, shops and housing. For match details see *Público* or *Jornal de Notícias*.

✉ FC Porto (club), Piso 3, Entrada Nascente, 4350-415 Porto ☎ 225 570 400 or 707 281 893 (club hotline) 🕐 Ticket office for matches: daily 10–1, 3–7 🖐 Tickets €15–€75 🚇 Antas 🚌 401 🚇 Lines A, B, C and E

FERNANDO S. DIAS DOS SANTOS
Amid several craft shops near the Torre dos Clérigos, this shop is one of the oldest, dating back to the 18th century. As well as the usual selection of pottery and textile goods, it also sells a great collection of national costumes as worn in different parts of the country.

✉ Rua dos Clérigos 45–47, 4050-205 Porto ☎ 222 006 053 🕐 May–end Sep daily 10–7; rest of year Mon–Fri 9.30–12.30, 2.30–5, Sat 9.30–1

FERREIRA
www.sogrape.pt
Ferreira is Portugal's best-selling port and remarkably the only major company to be founded by a native Douro family. Its founder, Dona Adalaide, began with a few vineyards, but success brought vineyards stretching from Porto to Spain. Come and taste the results for yourself.

✉ Avenida Ramos Pinto 70, 4400-082 Vila Nova de Gaia ☎ 223 746 107 🕐 Daily 10–12.30, 2–6 🖐 €3 including visit and tasting 🚌 Bus 900, 901, 904 from Rua Mouzinho da Silveira, just down from São Bento train station

GALERIA DE ARTESANATO 'O GALO'
In one of the roads leading down from São Bento station, this place attracts ceramics lovers with its shelves full of regional pottery, decorative plates and abstract artistic pieces. The permanent exhibitions display comical figurines by the descendants of the famous

Rosa Ramalho, along with pieces by Mistério and José Franco.

✉ Rua Mouzinho de Silveira 68, 4050-415 Porto ☎ 223 325 294 🕐 Mon–Fri 10–12.30, 1.30–7, Sat 10–1

GARRAFEIRA DO CARMO
Garrafeira do Carmo sells a variety of LBVs, tawnies and vintage ports—some dating back to 1900—as well as high-quality table wines at reasonable prices.

✉ Rua do Carmo 17, 4050-164 Porto ☎ 222 003 285 🕐 Mon–Fri 9–1, 2–7, Sat 9–1

GARRAFEIRA TIO PEPE
www.garrafeiratiopepe.pt
This giant wine emporium is an excellent place to stock up if you have a car with you (there's parking). Trained staff guide you through the huge range of ports and wines, and can offer advice.

✉ Rua Eng° Ferreira Dias 51, 4100-247 Porto ☎ 226 184 656 🕐 Mon–Fri 10.30–1.30, 3–8, Sat 10–1 🚌 302 from Avenida dos Aliados 🚇 Lines A, B, C or E Ramalde 🚗 Two streets over from the Avenida do Aeroporto, near the Nó de Francos roundabout (traffic circle)

HOT FIVE JAZZ AND BLUES CLUB
www.hotfive.eu
To experience some national jazz and blues, head to this cosy venue to hear some of the best. Check the website for performances. Thursdays are jamming days.

✉ Largo Actor Dias 51, 4000-192 Porto ☎ 919 015 374 🕐 Thu–Sun 10pm–3am 🖐 €5 on show days, otherwise free

LIVRARIA LELLO & IRMÃO
http://lelloprologolivreiro.com.sapo.pt
This neo-Gothic literary cathedral, with stained-glass ceiling and sweeping carved staircases, opened in 1906 and still justifiably claims to be the world's most palatial bookshop. Booklovers can browse through any of the 60,000 titles. It also sells books in English, French and German.

✉ Rua das Carmelitas 144, 4050-161 Porto ☎ 222 018 170 🕐 Mon–Fri 10–7.30, Sat 10–7

MERCADO DO BOLHÃO

Stalls in the market's open central courtyard and tiered verandas, busiest in the morning, sell everything from bread, cheeses and cured meats to household goods, pets and flowers. A selection of crafts, including ceramics and basketry, is also on sale.

✉ Rua Fernandez Tomás, 4000-214 Porto ☎ 223 326 024 🕐 Mon–Fri 8–5, Sat 8–1

OPORTO GOLF CLUBE

www.oportogolfclub.com

This is the oldest golf club in the country. The first of its 18 holes, a par 4, is cunningly set against the strong *nortada* (prevailing north winds), providing a challenge for any player. The clubhouse has good facilities, but the restaurant is open only to members.

✉ Paramos, 4500 Espinho ☎ 227 342 008 🕐 Tue–Sun 8am–sunset 🖐 18 holes €60; club rental €20; hand trolley €5 🚌 Take IC1 north for almost 20km (12.5 miles), leaving at Espinho exit. The course is just south of the town

Below *Barrels of port at Taylor's port lodge in Porto, which provides probably the best tour and tasting experience*

PAVILHÃO DA ÁGUA

www.pavilhaodaagua.blogspot.com

Created for Lisbon's Expo '98 this water pavilion was moved to Porto's Parque da Cidade in 2002. Its eye-catching cubic design houses a series of hands-on exhibits aimed at demonstrating the importance of water in our everyday lives, as a provider of energy and in the fields of technology and science.

✉ Parque da Cidade, Est. Circunvalação 15443, 4100-183 Porto ☎ 226 151 820 🕐 Jul–end Aug Tue–Sun 10–12.30, 2.30–5.30; rest of year Mon–Sat 9.30–12.30, 2–4.30 🖐 Adult €3.50, child (4–10) €2, family €8 🚌 501 from centre to northern entrance to park

ROTA DOS VINHOS VERDES

www.vinhoverde.pt

This organization suggests driving routes through the *vinho verde* region, taking in some of the most interesting *quintas*. Some tours providing English commentaries, offering the best wine-tastings with great places to eat, are singled out.

✉ Comissão de Viniculture da Região dos Vinhos Verdes, Rua da Restauração 318, 4050-501 Porto ☎ 226 077 300 🕐 Mon–Fri 9–12.30, 2–5.30

SHERATON PORTO SPA

www.sheratonporto.com

To recover from all those cobbles head to the Sheraton Spa. Complete with *hammam*, indoor pool, gym and saunas, the spa also offers a range of treatments including hot stone therapy, massage, facials, wraps and more.

✉ Rua Tenente Valdim 146, 4100-476 Porto ☎ 220 404 000 🖐 Prices start at €40 but vary depending on treatment

SOLAR DO VINHO DO PORTO

www.ivdp.pt

Situated near the Palácio de Cristal, this lovely *quinta* with graceful cloistered courtyard and superb views over the river offers by far the most genteel surroundings in which to taste a variety of the Douro's best ports, available by the glass.

✉ Quinta da Macieirinha, Rua de Entre Quintas 220, 4050-239 Porto ☎ 226 094 749 🕐 Mon–Thu 4–11, Fri–Sat 4–midnight 🖐 Varies depending on port chosen 🚌 200, 207, 302, 601

SWING

Off the Rotunda da Boavista is Porto's oldest club, which has remained fashionable since day one.

Music styles vary during the week from 1980s student nights to dance and commercial club, and attract a mixed crowd.

✉ Praçeta Engº Amaro da Costa 766, off Rua de Julio Dinis, Boavista, 4050-012 Porto ☎ 226 090 019 🕐 Wed–Sun midnight–7am 💶 €7.50, or €12.50 on special events nights (includes drinks) 🚌 201, 302, 501 🚇 Lines A, B, C and E, Casa da Música

TAYLOR'S
www.taylor.pt
Of all of the old English-run lodges this 300-year-old company probably provides the best tour and tasting of quality late-bottled vintage ports. Its good website gives plenty of useful information.

✉ Rua do Choupelo 250, 4400-088 Vila Nova de Gaia ☎ 223 742 800 🕐 Jul, Aug Mon–Fri 10–6.30; Sep- end Jun Mon–Fri 10–6 (last entry 1 hour before closing) 💶 Visit and tasting free 🚌 900, 901, 904 from Rua Mouzinho da Silveira, just down from São Bento train station

TEATRO NACIONAL DE SÃO JOÃO
www.tnsj.pt
Opened in 1798, this was gutted by fire and then turned into a sleazy cinema. It was bought by the government and restored. Reopened as the National Theatre of São João in 1995, it now hosts prestigious theatrical events.

✉ Praça da Batalha, 4000-102 Porto ☎ 223 401 900 🕐 Ticket office: Tue–Sat 1–7, show days 1–10 💶 €10–€50 🚫 In auditorium 🅿

VILA NOVA DE GAIA
BARCADOURO
www.barcadouro.pt
For the best views of the city, its river and bridges, hop aboard a river cruise. Options vary from an hour long tour of the city's bridges, to overnight cruises up the Douro to Régua and Barca de Alva. Shorter excursions depart daily throughout the year, numbers permitting. Advance booking is advised.

✉ Avenida Ramos Pinto, loja 240, Cais de Gaia, 4400-161 Vila Nova de Gaia ☎ 222 722 415

FEBRUARY–MARCH
FANTASPORTO
www.fantasporto.com
Porto's international arts film festival has been running since 1981 and is considered by many to be the world's top sci-fi and fantasy film forum. The festival also includes related events such as lectures, exhibitions and film workshops.
✉ Porto

APRIL
FESTIVAL INTERCÉLTICO DO PORTO
www.discantus.pt
The country's largest gathering of all things Celtic attracts groups from home and abroad, including Scottish and Irish bands.
✉ Rua Duque de Saldanha 97, 4300-464 Porto (information) ☎ 225 193 100 🕐 Early Apr

MAY
QUEIMA DAS FITAS
The end of the academic year and start of the examination period are marked by the Burning of the Ribbons, a week of rock concerts, beer-drinking and parties, culminating in a massive parade where final-year students dress up in their robes and top hats.
✉ Porto 🕐 Early May

JUNE
ROMARIA DE SÃO GONÇALO
São Gonçalo, associated with matchmaking and fertility, is remembered in Amarante's most important yearly festival, with bands, folk-dancing, processions and market stands. Saturday night is marked by a massive firework display on the river and Sunday by a solemn procession in honour of the saint.
✉ Amarante 🕐 First weekend in Jun

FESTAS DA CIDADE—SÃO JOÃO
On the night of São João, crowds take to the streets, often in carnival costume, to enjoy sardinhadas (sardine barbecues), parades and dances. Watch out for the plastic hammers that are used to hit passers-by on the head, supposedly wishing them good fortune.
✉ Porto 🕐 23–24 Jun

JULY
JAZZ NO PARQUE
www.serralves.com
Both home-grown and international musicians perform in the glorious surroundings of Serralves gardens.
✉ Fundação de Serralves, Rua D. João de Castro 210, 4150-417 Porto ☎ 808 200 543 or 226 156 500 🕐 Second, third and fourth weekend in Jul 💶 €10 🚌 203 from central Porto

AUGUST
NOITES RITUAL ROCK
www.noitesritual.com
Held in the Crystal Palace Gardens, this is the place for Portuguese rock bands to get some exposure.
✉ Rua Dom Manuel II, 4050-346 Porto ☎ 222 089 925

FESTAS DE SÃO BARTOLOMEU
A unique festival that takes place in the old fishing village of Foz do Douro. People dress up in imaginative, multi-hued paper costumes to parade through the streets before taking a symbolic cleansing plunge into the ocean.
✉ Foz do Douro 🕐 Sun following 24 Aug

OCTOBER–DECEMBER
CARTOON WORLD FESTIVAL
This unusual festival was launched in 1900 by the National Printing Museum with the aim of putting Porto firmly on the world cartoon map and has proved to be extremely successful. It hosts exhibitions of cartoons from around the world and live sessions with famous international cartoonists.
✉ Museu Nacional de Imprensa, EN108, 206, Freixo, 4300-316 Porto ☎ 225 300 648 or 225 304 966 💶 Free

EATING

PRICES AND SYMBOLS

The restaurants are listed alphabetically. The prices given are the average for a two-course lunch (L) and a three-course dinner (D) for one person, without drinks. The wine price is for the least expensive bottle. All the restaurants listed accept credit cards unless otherwise stated.

For a key to the symbols, ▷ 2.

AMARANTE

TASQUINHA DA PONTE

The Tasquinha caters not so much for visitors, but for locals in search of hearty, regional food, and serves substantial amounts of authentic dishes, full of flavour.

✉ Rua 31 de Janeiro, 4600-043 Amarante ☎ 255 433 715 🕐 Tue–Sun 9am–midnight ✋ L €10, D €12, Wine €3.50

PORTO

For all restaurants in Foz do Douro, either take the bus or tram from the middle of the city, or a taxi, which will cost approximately €12.

ADEGA VILA MEÃ

This not-to-be-missed *adega* (wine cellar) serves unadorned regional food in massive portions *à moda antiga* (as in the old days). Ask for

a quarter-portion if you are on your own. Daily specials are (Monday to Friday): salt-cod fritters, roast octopus, braised pork, *cozido à Portuguesa* (boiled meats and vegetables), roast veal and kid.

✉ Rua dos Caldeireiros 62, 4050-137 Porto ☎ 222 082 967 🕐 Mon–Sat 12–3, 7–10 ✋ L €15, D €20, Wine €7.50

BULL AND BEAR

Acclaimed in the national press, this is one of Porto's most popular restaurants. Its menu—a fusion of tradition and innovation—changes with the seasons. There is foie gras terrine served with 10-year-old port, roe and beer blinis, hake in olives and maize bread, duck and truffle pie, and more than 400 wines to choose from. Chef Miguel Castro e Silva is one of Portugal's best known.

✉ Avenida da Boavista 3431, Boavista, 4149-017 Porto ☎ 226 107 669 🕐 Mon–Fri 12.30–3, 8–11, Sat 8–12 ✋ L €25, D €35, Wine €12 🚌 502

CAFEÍNA

www.cafeina.pt

This landmark restaurant has dark green walls and modern art panels. It is known for its fine steaks, and there are French and Italian

Above *Dom Tonho restaurant in Porto is set in a converted salt-cod warehouse*

influences, as seen in the foie gras with bacon and mushroom, truffle tagliolini and grilled bream risotto. The desserts include pear and almond tart with vanilla ice cream.

✉ Rua do Padrão 100, Foz do Douro, 4150-557 Porto ☎ 226 108 059 🕐 Daily 12–6, 7.30–1.30 ✋ L €20, D €30, Wine €12 🚌 500

CAFÉ MAJESTIC

www.cafemajestic.com

This luxurious art nouveau coffee house opened in 1921, complete with cherubs, chandeliers, leather upholstery, marble floors and Antwerp mirrors. It is an ideal place for a coffee and pastry or light meal.

✉ Rua de Santa Catarina 112, 4000-442 Porto ☎ 222 003 887 🕐 Mon–Sat 9.30am–midnight ✋ Light snack and drink €9 per person

CASA AGRÍCOLA

www.casa-agricola.com

Inside an 18th-century building, the first-floor Casa Agrícola, with its ox-blood walls and wooden floors, is an elegant place. It has a choice of grilled fish, meats (including duck

and succulent peppered steaks) and, unusually for Portugal, a vegetarian menu. There is a fixed lunch menu for under €10. For dessert, try port pudding with mango ice cream.
✉ Rua do Bom Sucesso 241–243, 4150-150 Porto ☎ 226 053 350 ◷ Mon–Sat 12–3, 8–11 ✋ L €23, D €30, Wine €7

O COMERCIAL
Monumental granite pillars and fine old tiles grace the floors and walls. Chestnut and onion soup, and *pataniscas de bacalhau* (cod and potato fritters) make great starters, followed by salt cod with broad beans and sweet potato, sautéed monkfish with mustard sauce and chocolate fondue with fresh fruits.
✉ Rua Ferreira Borges, Palácio da Bolsa, 4050-252 Porto ☎ 223 399 000 ◷ Mon–Fri 12.30–3, 7.30–10.30, Sat 7.30–10.30 ✋ L €15, D €20, Wine €6.50 🚌 500, 900

DOM TONHO
www.dtonho.com
This salt-cod warehouse looks over the Douro. Recipes are traditional and full of flavour; they include beef or kid roasted in a wood-burning oven, baked octopus and salt-cod fritters. There are two daily specials.
✉ Cais da Ribeira 13 -15, Ribeira, 4050-509 Porto ☎ 222 004 307 ◷ Daily 12.30–2.45, 7.30–11.15 ✋ L €25, D €35, Wine €12

ESCONDIDINHO
Perfectly prepared French food is on offer in a country house setting. All manner of fish is served. Dessert includes *folhada de maçã* (apple tart).
✉ Rua Pasos Manuel 144, 4000-302 Porto ☎ 222 001 079 ◷ Mon–Sat 12–3, 7–10.30 ✋ L €20, D €35, Wine €8

FILHA DA MÃE PRETA
This traditional eatery serves good home cooking, such as tripe or fillets of bream and tender roast beef or pork loin. A lavish dessert made with dried and fresh fruits and ice cream is aptly named 'end of the world.'
✉ Cais da Ribeira 40, Ribeira, 4050-510 Porto ☎ 222 086 066 ◷ Mon–Sat 12–3, 7–10 ✋ L €15, D €20, Wine €8

FOZ VELHA
www.fozvelha.com
This is one of Porto's hippest restaurants. You can eat à la carte or choose fixed menus. The dishes include foie gras with glacé pears in puff pastry and grilled beef with *queijo da serra* (ewe's-milk cheese).
✉ Esplanada do Castelo 141, Foz do Douro, 4150-141 Porto ☎ 226 154 178 ◷ Tue–Sat 12.30–3, 7.30–midnight, Mon 7.30–midnight ✋ L €25, D €35, Wine €12

HOMEN DO LEME
Sit on the terrace, or in the simple modern interior, warmed by an open fire. Come here for a quick drink and snack, or for a full meal of pâté, prawn crêpes, freshly grilled fish, mango mousse and orange cake, and enjoy the stunning sunsets.
✉ Avenida de Montevideu, Foz do Douro, 4150-516 Porto ☎ 226 181 847 ◷ Daily 9am–2am ✋ L €15, D €25, Wine €10
🏖 On the Homen do Leme beach, below the statue *Fisherman at the Helm*

MERCEARIA
On the riverfront, this place was once the local grocery store. Given the location, Mercearia's focuses on fresh grilled fish and seafood, but meat lovers are also catered for. Dishes include grilled rabbit and the much-prized *bife mirandesa* (high-quality breed of beef cattle).
✉ Cais da Ribeira 323/33, 4050-510 Porto ☎ 222 004 389 ◷ Daily 12–4, 7–12 ✋ L €15, D €27, Wine €8

MUSEU DOS PRESUNTOS
Set on a narrow street in the old part of Foz, here you can try prime beef on a skewer, or home-made sausages, black-eyed bean vinaigrette, and air-cured ham.
✉ Rua Padre Luís Cabral 1070, Foz do Douro, 4150-461 Porto ☎ 226 106 965 ◷ Tue–Sat 7pm–4am, Sun 7pm–2am ✋ D €25, Wine €6.50

PEIXES E COMPANHIA
Fresh bream, bass, mullet and monkfish grilled, baked or boiled, accompanied by sautéed vegetables and *batatas a murro* (literally, 'bashed potatoes') are specialities

here. Finish with fresh tropical fruit, almond tart or *chocolate brigadeiros*.
✉ Rua do Ouro 133–135, Foz do Douro, 4150-552 Porto ☎ 226 185 655 ◷ Mon–Sat 12–3.30, 7.30–11.30. Closed Mon in Aug ✋ L €17, D €25, Wine €10

PRAIA DA LUZ
www.praiadaluz.pt
Sit in the chic, glassed-in dining room or outside on the deck looking out to sea. A variety of pasta dishes and more traditional options, such as baked salt cod, is available, while light snacks are served all day.
✉ Avenida do Brasil, Foz do Douro, 4150-153 Porto ☎ 226 173 234 ◷ Daily 9am–2am ✋ L €10, D €25, Wine €12.50

RESTAURANTE CAFETARIA DA FUNDAÇÃO DE SERRALVES
Art deco architecture and views of the park make this a privileged spot. There is a lunch-time buffet and a fine selection of puddings, while dinner is a sophisticated affair, produced by Michelin-starred chefs.
✉ Rua Dom Joao de Castro 210, 4150-417 Porto ☎ 226 170 355 ◷ Lunch: Apr–end Sep Mon–Fri 12–7, Sat 10-7, Sun 10–8; rest of year Mon–Fri 12–7, Sat–Sun 10–7. Dinner: Tue–Sat 8–midnight ✋ L €12, D €25, Wine €12.50

SESSENTA SETENTA
A Porto landmark, with glorious views over the Douro valley, this place serves innovative dishes. Be tempted by fresh oysters with pineapple and soy sauce; crab with cream of avocado; or sea bass with cream potato. Then try glacé pears.
✉ Rua Sobre o Douro 1A, 4050-592 Porto Just off Rua da Restauração ☎ 223 406 093 ◷ Mon–Fri 12.45–2.30, 8–12, Sat 8–12. Closed first 2 weeks of Jan and Aug ✋ L €25, D €35, Wine €10

SURIBACHI
This flower-filled vegetarian restaurant has a small waterfall and fish pond. Macrobiotic meals are served. Try the seaweed soup or the tofu dishes, or the seafood stew.
✉ Rua do Bonfim 134–140, 4300-066 Porto ☎ 225 106 700 ◷ Mon–Sat 12–3, 7–10 ✋ L €10, D €15, Wine €6

STAYING

PRICES AND SYMBOLS

The prices are the lowest and highest for a double room for one night including breakfast, unless otherwise stated. All the hotels listed accept credit cards unless otherwise stated. Note that rates can vary widely throughout the year.

For a key to the symbols, ▷ 2.

AMARANTE
CASA DA CALÇADA
www.casadacalcada.com

This imposing building, painted in highly individual yellow, is one of the loveliest places to stay in Portugal. Sitting on the banks of the River Tâmega, overlooking Amarante's church and baroque bridge, the hotel is furnished with a harmonious blend of period and contemporary pieces. Warm and sumptuous tones fill the public spaces and rooms, and the luxurious fabrics, graceful ornaments and flowers make the rooms seem like those of a private house. The fine garden has age-old camellias, a granite water tank with a fountain, and a tennis court. The elegant restaurant serves national and international cuisine.

✉ Largo do Paço 6, 4600-017 Amarante ☎ 255 410 830 💶 €170–€220 ① 30

rooms, 3 suites, 1 presidential suite 🕙 🏊 Outdoor 🏠 The hotel is a conspicuous yellow building in the middle of town

POUSADA DE SÃO GONÇALO
www.pousadas.pt

This *pousada* is not in an historic building, but it has outstanding views of the River Tâmega and Serra do Marão, and is just 20km (12.5 miles) from Amarante. All the rooms enjoy valley views and have been refurbished in country style; the dark wooden furniture and tasteful bedspreads make them welcoming and comfortable. The restaurant serves high-standard regional fare.

✉ Curva do Lancete, Ansiães, 4604-038 Amarante ☎ 255 461 113 💶 €120–€198 ① 14 rooms, 1 suite 🕙 🏠 Leave Amarante on IP4, and go east towards Vila Real. Turn right at the sign to the *pousada*

PORTO
ALBERGARIA MIRADOURO

This slim 13-storey hotel with its 1950s–1960s feel seems uninspiring, until you see the views. Spread out beneath it are the city and River Douro with the Gaia port warehouses on the opposite bank. Many of the rooms are large and

Above Hotel da Bolsa, near the Ribeira in Porto, was built on the site of the old São Francisco monastery

well appointed; the corner rooms with dual aspect are the best. Day or night, enjoy a sunny breakfast or leisurely dinner in the highly acclaimed Restaurante Portucale.

✉ Rua da Alegria 598, 4000-037 Porto ☎ 225 370 717 💶 €50–€75 ① 30 🕙

CASTELO DE SANTA CATARINA
www.castelosantacatarina.com.pt

This flamboyant Gothic Revival villa is surrounded by palms and covered in tiles depicting scenes from Portuguese history. Built in the 1920s a short distance from the heart of the town, the hotel's interior is a warren of stucco and chandeliers, gilt mirrors and fine faded salons. Art nouveau bathroom fittings, reproduction beds and wardrobes, and bright carpets grace the bedrooms. The villa is ostentatious and possibly gaudy, but mostly a stay here is an unforgettable experience.

✉ Rua de Santa Catarina 1347, 4000-457 Porto ☎ 225 095 599 💶 €48–€70 ① 23 rooms, 3 suites 🕙

HOTEL BOA VISTA

www.hotelboavista.com

This classic hotel was purpose-built during Porto's heyday at the end of the 19th century, and its position, looking over the river mouth and the Atlantic, could not be better. The elegant architecture, typical of that era, has in no way been compromised by the renovations, which added a modern wing and rooftop swimming pool to the villa. The views from some of the bedrooms, the restaurant and the pleasant rooftop terrace are really quite stunning.

✉ Esplanada do Castelo 58, 4150-196 Foz do Douro ☎ 225 320 020 ✋ €80–€92 ⓘ 67 rooms, 4 suites ⬟ ⩉ Outdoor ⬟ From the middle of Porto, follow the riverside road all the way to Foz at the mouth of the river. The hotel is up behind the fort on the right

HOTEL DA BOLSA

www.hoteldabolsa.com

Down towards the Ribeira, right next to the fine stock exchange building and close to the Port Wine Institute, the Hotel da Bolsa was built on the site of the old São Francisco monastery. Its archetypal 19th-century façade with decorative

Below Castelo de Santa Catarina's extravagant Gothic Revival façade

lintels and arched windows gives way to a modern and comfortable interior. The bedrooms, though largely unexceptional, have all the facilities you would expect of a 3-star hotel.

✉ Rua Ferreira Borges 101, 4050-253 Porto ☎ 222 026 768 ✋ €72–€87 ⓘ 36 ⬟

HOTEL INFANTE SAGRES

www.hotelinfantesagres.pt

Built by a wealthy industrialist in the 1950s, this city landmark is just off the Avenida dos Aliados. Its sumptuous furnishings, draped fabrics and 17th-century Chinese porcelain recall a lost age of elegance. The delicate and sinuous wrought-iron staircase is worthy of special attention, as is the interior courtyard, which is used for alfresco meals as well as being a sun trap in the summer. Rooms have period-style furniture. The opulent dining room serves international and Portuguese cuisine and there's also an intimate cocktail bar.

✉ Praça Dona Felipa de Lencastre 62, 4050-259 Porto ☎ 223 398 500 ✋ €195 ⓘ 72 rooms, 9 suites ⬟

HOTEL MERCURE BATALHA

www.mercure.com

A couple of minutes up from the Baixa, right in the middle of Porto's main commercial district and just opposite the national theatre, the Mercure offers quality surroundings and service. The rooms are large and modern, yet traditional in style. The restaurant serves good regional Portuguese dishes.

✉ Praça da Batalha 116, 4049-028 Porto ☎ 222 043 300 ✋ €110 excluding breakfast (€7.50) ⓘ 140 rooms, 9 suites (non-smoking available) ⬟

RESIDENCIAL DOS ALIADOS

www.residencialaliados.com

This residencial is great value for money. It is conveniently located in the heart of town, and the service is friendly. Rooms are simply but adequately furnished and all have their own bathroom. Some have small balconies and overlook the

Avenida; the ones at the back are slightly smaller, but are generally much quieter.

✉ Rua Elísio de Melo 27, 4000-196 Porto ☎ 222 004 853 ✋ €50–€95 ⓘ 38 ⬟

RESIDENCIAL REX

On the north side of one of the most attractive garden squares in the city is the Rex, providing low-cost accommodation amid the faded grandeur of yesteryear. The art nouveau exterior is decorated with beautiful emerald-green tiles, while an impressive marble staircase leads up to the reception area. Inside, the public rooms are equally grand, with intricate stucco ceilings. The bedrooms, though fairly basic, are furnished with a well-judged mix of modern and antique pieces.

✉ Praça da República 117, 4050-497 Porto ☎ 222 074 590 ✋ €40–€45 ⓘ 20 ⬟

SHERATON PORTO HOTEL AND SPA

www.sheraton.com/porto

For a little state-of-the-art pampering check in to this new 5-star hotel and spa in Boavista. Rooms are slick and modern with lots of wood and glass, plasma screens and luxurious bathrooms. Take advantage of the spa's indoor pool, relaxation area, special treatments or unwind in the hammam or sauna. For refreshment, head to the Juice Bar for a thirst-quenching fruit smoothie or for a vegetarian sandwich.

✉ Rua Tenente Valadim 146, 4100-476 Porto ☎ 220 404 000 ✋ €165–€220 ⓘ 241 rooms, 25 suites ⬟ ⩉ Outdoor ⬟

VILA DO CONDE

www.forte.com.pt

This 18th-century fortress has been converted into a delightful small hotel. The bedrooms have soft goose-feather pillows, cosy bathrobes and candles, and the paintings, by young Portuguese artists, are for sale.

✉ Forte de São João, Avenida Brasil, 4480-659 Vila do Conde ☎ 252 240 600 ✋ €100–€150 ⓘ 7 suites ⬟

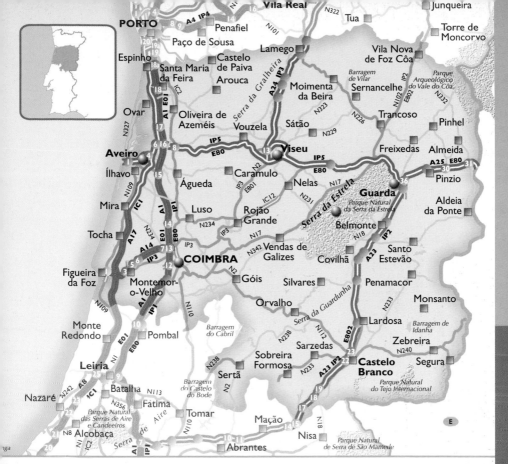

THE BEIRAS

This region offers great variety as it stretches from the Atlantic coast, east over the mountains, to the border with Spain. Its geographical features include lagoons and salt marshes, best visited by boat out of Aveiro and still navigated by the traditional flat-bottomed *molicieros;* the vast national forest of Buçaco, home to more than 700 species; and the majestic scenery of the Serra da Estrela with mainland Portugal's highest peaks. The Beiras also possesses fine examples of ancient civilizations best seen near the river Côa, where unique Palaeolithic art extends for some 17km (10.5 miles) down the rocky valley; and at the much excavated Celtic settlement of Conímbriga.

Its largest city is Coimbra, home to the country's oldest university. The historical university buildings, dating primarily from the 17th and 18th centuries, sit high above the Mondego and are open to visitors. In the busy streets below there are some fine museums, churches and good shopping; in the hours after dark its student population lends it a vibrant atmosphere as they pack the many bars and cafés.

For a slightly slower pace, set out to explore the regions' smaller towns. Medieval Guarda is Portugal's highest town and can feel somewhat inhospitable due to its isolation, bitter winds and austere cathedral; Viseu is at the heart of the Dão wine region and home to an outstanding collection of paintings by the Portuguese master Grão Vasco; and Figueira da Foz has some great family beaches. Perhaps the highlights, however, are the fortified hilltop villages of Sortelha, Monsanto and Belmonte which sit like medieval sentries above the plains and the 18th-century fortifications of Almeida, fought over during the Peninsular Wars.

ALMEIDA

www.cm-almeida.pt

Tucked away in barren upland country in the east of the mountain Beiras and only 15km (9.5 miles) from the Spanish border, Almeida is a compact border town entirely enclosed within the star-shaped walls of a military fortification built in the 18th century. The Dutch design was heavily influenced by the work of the French military architect Vauban, and consists of a twelve-pointed star with six bastions and six curtain walls pierced by two superb double gates whose tunnels run under the grass-topped outer walls. Almeida played a key part in the Peninsular Wars, falling twice to the French, who were eventually thrown out by Wellington in 1811; plaques in the town commemorate Lord Beresford, one of Wellington's chief subordinates and organizer of the Portuguese forces. The Casamatas were once home to 5,000 troops; for a great overview, take the 4km (2.5-mile) trail along the grass-covered walls.

Park outside the walls and walk through the approach tunnels into the town. Built in the 18th century, the harmonious streets and squares have a logical layout, filled with homogeneous buildings. These open up as you head towards the ruins of the castle, destroyed by the French.
✚ 329 E5 🚹 Praça de Liberdade, 6350-130 Almeida ☎ 271 570 020

AROUCA

www.cm-arouca.pt

The monastic settlement of Arouca sits in a small green valley surrounded by agricultural terraces and wooded hills. The huge Convento da Arouca was founded in the eighth century AD and what you see today is baroque laid over late-medieval foundations. The single-naved abbey church is rich with silver and precious wood. This is the burial place of Queen Mafalda,

daughter of Sancho I, who retired here after the death of her husband, Dom Henriques I de Castilha. Some of Mafalda's possessions are in the Museu de Arte Sacra here, notably a 13th-century silver diptych, as well as Portuguese primitive paintings from the 15th and 16th centuries.
✚ 328 C4 🚹 Rua Alfredo Vaz Pinto, 4540-118 Arouca ☎ 256 943 575

AVEIRO

▷ 180–181.

BELMONTE

www.cm-belmonte.pt

The little agricultural town of Belmonte was established between the 11th and 12th centuries as a stronghold against the Moors. It is dominated by its castle, gifted by Afonso V in the 15th century to the Cabral family, who transformed it into a fortified manor house. Pedro Alvares Cabral, the discoverer of Brazil, is said to have been born in the castle—a statue of the Virgin that accompanied him on his voyages is in the Igreja Matriz, down the hill. South from here is the Jewish quarter, a warren of ancient alleys with more than 120 resident Jewish families. There has been a Jewish community in Belmonte since at least the 13th century. For more history, take in the ancient Romanesque church of Santiago, transformed in the 15th century as a burial place for the Cabrals—Pedro Alvares is buried here.

✚ 329 E6 🚹 Praça da República, 6250-048 Belmonte ☎ 275 911 488

BUÇACO

www.jtluso-bucaco.pt

The northernmost peak of the Serra do Buçaco is crowned by the *Mata Nacional* (National Forest), a 105ha (250-acre) wood, best appreciated on foot (▷ 197). This beautiful forest is encircled by stone walls and planted with native and exotic trees and shrubs, and there are splashing fountains, lakes and rushing water.

Benedictine monks established the first hermitage here in the sixth century AD. The wall was built around the forest in 1622 when women were forbidden entry on pain of excommunication according to the rule of the Barefoot Carmelite order. Nearby, you can still see the remains of the 17th-century Carmelite convent. The Carmelites also planted a huge variety of trees, a tradition that was continued after the religious orders were abolished in 1834. The woods now contain around 400 native tree species, 300 or more non-natives, banks of camellias, rhododendrons, magnolias and superb tree ferns.

Between 1888 and 1907 King Carlos built a palatial hunting lodge here. A pastiche of Manueline style, it is now a luxury hotel. You can park here to walk in the forest.
✚ 328 C6 🚹 Avenida Emídio Navarro 136, 3050-902 Luso ☎ 231 939 133 🚉 Luso (3km/2 miles from Buçaco)

Opposite The hotel at Buçaco, once a royal hunting lodge

Right Part of Almeida's defensive walls

INFORMATION

www.rotadaluz.pt

⊞ 328 B5 ⓘ Rua João Mendonça 8, 3810-200 Aveiro ☎ 234 420 760 or 234 423 680 Ⓓ Jun–end Sep daily 9–8; Oct–end May Mon–Sat 9–7; ⊞ Aveiro

INTRODUCTION

A thriving city in a unique canal and lagoon setting, Aveiro offers excellent shopping and dining with easy access to some superb beaches. Begin by strolling around the narrow streets that back the Rossio, central Aveiro's attractive palm-fringed square. The streets all lead to the fish market, close to a canal inlet. Walk back to the Praça Humberto Delgado and the main bridge. The shallow lagoon led to the development of the *moliceiros*, flat-bottomed boats beautifully painted with traditional designs. Their numbers are declining, but you are sure to see some moored on the canal—the best place to find them is below the main bridge and Praça Humberto Delgado. Cross the central canal to visit the Misericórdia, then head northeast along Rua Homem Cristo, one of Aveiro's main shopping streets. At the next bridge you could cross and turn left to take in the city's main market, or head right along Avenida 5 de Outubro to the Convento de Jesus and the museum. After visiting the collections, stroll around the fine buildings, spacious streets and pleasant green spaces in the area. Leave time to take a trip on the lagoon, the best way to catch a glimpse of life in Aveiro. There are superb beaches to the north and south of the town.

Aveiro was an important fishing port throughout the Middle Ages until disaster struck. In 1575, a storm altered the course of the River Vouga and the harbour silted up as a result. It was not until 1808, when a breakwater was built to open up a new passage from the lagoon to the sea, that Aveiro's fishing industry was reborn. A ceramic industry was also established; the new money flooding into Aveiro paid for many of its finest buildings. Today, Aveiro is still primarily a fishing port, its catches coming from both its lagoon and the sea. It is also Portugal's third-largest industrial town, dedicated to shipping, fish

Above *Waterfront buildings reflected in the Canal do São Roque at night*

processing, engineering, and iron and steel production. Traditional industries also survive, including salt farming from the lagoon, the production of fertilizer utilizing the local seaweed, and rice-growing.

WHAT TO SEE

THE OLD QUARTER

The huddle of streets on the north side of the main canal makes up Aveiro's old quarter. Admire the *moliceiros* along the waterside before exploring the backstreets, where rows of neatly tiled houses face each other. In the evening this area throngs with people drinking in the lively bars before they head off to eat in the many excellent fish restaurants.

CONVENTO DE JESUS

www.ipmuseus.pt

The Convento de Jesus (Museu de Aveiro), built between the 15th and 17th centuries, and with a baroque façade added in the 18th, is now Portugal's second-largest museum after the Museu Nacional de Arte Antiga in Lisbon (▷ 79). The richness of the collections owes much to the Infanta Joana, daughter of Afonso V, who lived in the convent from 1471 until her death 18 years later. Some time after she died, the convent's church was sumptuously decorated as a fitting place for her tomb, and now forms part of the museum. The exuberant chancel is covered in intricately carved gilt wood, while the *azulejos* (tiles) decorating the walls depict scenes from Joana's life. The chancel contains her tomb, carved by João Antunes in the early 18th century.

From the church you can visit the Renaissance-style cloisters, whose highlight is the distinctive side chapel containing fine Renaissance tombs—off here, the refectory is entirely covered with flower-strown 17th-century *azulejos*. The museum proper has other remembrances of Joana, notably her portrait, attributed to Nuno Gonçalves, and an oratory in the room where she died. Other highlights on show include primitive Portuguese paintings, wooden baroque statues, rich church vestments and delicate porcelain and ceramics.
✉ Avenida Santa Joana Princesa, 3810-379 Aveiro ☎ 234 423 297 🕐 Tue–Sun 10–1, 2–5.30 💷 Free

THE RIA DE AVEIRO AND THE BEACHES

The tidal lagoon known as the Ria de Aveiro is best explored on a boat trip from Aveiro. It is bordered by salt marshes, woods and small villages, while to the west, a narrow strip of land separates it from the sea. This is some of Europe's most spectacular dune land, and you can explore the habitat and learn about the area's flora and fauna at the Reserva Natural das Dunas de São Jacinto.

On the landward side, the settlements vary in size from small fishing ports like Bico and São Jacinto to bigger towns such as Ílhavo, where you will find a good fishing museum, and Vista Alegre, with its famous china factory and museum, the perfect place to watch craftsmen at work and buy the product direct. If you are looking for a beach, try Praia da Barra, Costa Nova or Torreira.

MORE TO SEE

IGREJA DA MISERICÓRDIA

The church with a lovely tiled façade and 17th-century doorway has more decorative tiles inside and an interesting church wardens' pew. The church is best known for its 18th-century organ pipes.
✉ Rua Coimbra, 3810-086 Aveiro 🕐 Daily 10–12.30, 2.30–5.30 💷 Free

SÉ

Once part of a convent, Aveiro's cathedral has a baroque façade but a stylistically mixed interior.
✉ Rua Batalhão Caçadores, 3810-064 Aveiro 🕐 Daily 8.30–7 💷 Free

TIPS
» If you are driving, the IP5 takes you straight into the city.
» City parking is difficult. There is limited parking by the Canal das Pirâmides just off the IP5, otherwise head through the town towards the N109 or N1.
» Outside the peak season between July and September, it is still possible to rent a boat to tour the Ria de Aveiro—ask at the tourist office.

COIMBRA

INFORMATION

www.cm-coimbra.pt
www.turismo-centro.pt

➕ 328 C6 ℹ️ Largo da Portagem, 3000-337 Coimbra; Largo Dom Dinis, 3000-143 Coimbra; or Praça da República, 3000-343 Coimbra ☎ 239 488 120, 239 832 591 or 239 833 202 🕐 Easter week and mid-Jun to mid-Sep Mon–Fri 9–8, Sat–Sun 9.30–1, 2.30–6; rest of year Mon–Fri 9.30–5.30, Sat–Sun 10–1, 2.30–5.30

🚢 Basófias River Tours: Parque Dr. Manuel Braga, tel 239 912 444 or 969 830 664; www.basofias.com; Apr–end Sep daily 4–5 departures; Oct–end Mar daily 1–3 departures; €6 🚉 Coimbra A, Coimbra B, Coimbra Parque

Above *The courtyard and clock tower of the old university*

Opposite *An elegant loggia outside the Museu Nacional Machado de Castro*

INTRODUCTION

Coimbra is a vibrant and historic city and Portugal's oldest university town, with plenty of good shopping, splendid monuments and museums, and a buzzing, student-oriented nightlife. The nucleus of old Coimbra spreads down a steep hill towards the River Mondego, the university buildings crowning the summit. Most of the highlights are in this relatively small area, which has always been traditionally divided into A Cidade Alta, the upper town that is home to the university and religious buildings, and A Cidade Baixa, the lower area, with excellent shops along pleasant pedestrianized streets.

The best place to start exploring Coimbra is at the university—it is the easiest place to find and the splendid views will give you a chance to get your bearings. After visiting the university buildings and the nearby Sé Velha (Old Cathedral), make your way through the maze of ancient cobbled streets downhill towards the lower town. Here, the Praça do Comercio is the hub—the main shopping streets, Rua Visconde da Luz and Rua Ferreira Borges, run just east of the square into the Largo da Portagem. From here, you can cross the river over the Ponte Santa Clara, which has great views back over the old city. On the other side of the river are the two Conventos de Santa Clara, as well as the Portugal dos Pequenitos (Portugal for the Little Ones) theme park.

Coimbra is an ancient city, once inhabited by the Romans and occupied by the Moors. The historic university traces its origins back to 1290. João III donated a palace to it in 1537 and it was the country's only university until 1911. Perhaps because of lack of competition, the university had a chequered history of corruption until 1772, when the Marquês de Pombal introduced reforms as well as commissioning some of its most beautiful buildings. The university has always been associated with political activism, its students opposing the Salazar regime from the 1950s. After the 1974 revolution, it expanded. Today it remains the country's most prestigious seat of learning.

WHAT TO SEE

VELHA UNIVERSIDADE

The old university buildings, once part of the royal palace, lie around the Patio das Escolas, or Paço dos Estudos. Little has changed here since 1540, when João III donated the buildings. Step through the Porta Férrea on the east side, though, and you are definitely back in the mid-20th century, surrounded by unstylish concrete buildings, the unfortunate outcome of a Salazar-inspired modernization in the monumental style typical of his era. Rather, concentrate on the harmonious architectural ensemble around the patio, beginning by admiring the views over the city and river from the front of the terrace, approached on the right by a wonderfully complicated flight of zigzag, terraced steps, before turning round to face the square. Towering above the other buildings looms a 1733 clock tower, once used to summon the students to lectures and affectionately nicknamed *A Cabra* (The Goat).

On the left is the Capela de São Miguel, a Manueline chapel, while on the right is the elegant façade of the university lecture rooms and offices, pierced by the 17th-century *porta férrea* (iron gate), the main entrance to the university courtyard. Linking these two wings is the Paços da Universidade, the original palace building, with its late 18th-century colonnade, known as the Via Latina. ✚ 185 B2 ✉ Largo da Porta Férrea, 3000-451 Coimbra ☎ 239 859 800 🕐 Apr–end Oct daily 8.30–7 (tickets), 9–7.30 (guided tours); Nov–end Mar Mon–Fri 9–5, Sat–Sun 10–4 (tickets), Mon–Fri 9.30–5.30, Sat–Sun 10.30–4.30 (guided tours) 📖 Library, chapel and Sala dos Capelos: adult €6, over-65s €4.20, under-12s free. Library only: adult €3.50, concessions €2.45. Chapel only: adult €3.50

SALA DOS CAPELOS

To the right of the central range of the main university complex is the Sala dos Capelos, which gets its name from the *capelos* (caps) given to students on graduation. The huge hall, hung with portraits of Portuguese monarchs, is still the venue for graduation ceremonies. It has a fine painted Manuelino ceiling, as does the adjoining examination room. The building also contains lecture halls and tutorial rooms—you can usually peek in or get behind the scenes down in the basement at the students' bar.

BIBLIOTECA JOANINA

The undisputed highlight of the university is its old library, the Biblioteca Joanina, behind the right-hand wing. It was gifted to Coimbra in 1724 by João V, and consists of three rooms richly decorated in the baroque style. Look for the *trompe l'oeil* design, which draws the eye towards the donor's portrait in the final room. The opulent gilding and lacquerwork are heavily influenced by Chinese decorative techniques and style. The library contains more than 30,000 books arranged on two levels with ladders for reaching the higher shelves. Back on the main Patio das Escolas is the entrance to the Capela de São Miguel, an elaborately decorated church with painted ceiling, *azulejos* (tiles) and intricately twisted columns—the gilding and decoration of the organ is particularly extravagant.

TIPS

» Most of the streets in the heart of the city are pedestrianized, so driving in Coimbra can be a nightmare. Use one of the signposted parking areas–you will need to arrive early in the day to get a space. Alternatively, park across the river and walk into town.

» May, the end of the academic year, is a great time to visit. There are concerts, parades and student ceremonies all over the old city, and the streets are wonderfully vibrant and busy.

» Old Coimbra is very steep—wear flat, comfortable shoes to cope with the cobbles, or take a No. 1 tram from the Largo da Portagem to avoid the climb.

» Take a river trip on the Mondego—a great way to relax after a morning spent walking.

THE REPUBLICS AND STUDENT LIFE

There are around 20,000 students at Coimbra University, some of whom live in unique establishments known as republics. These were devised at the end of the 18th century to emulate some of the ideals of the French Revolution, notably *liberté, égalité, fraternité* (freedom, equality, brotherhood). Over the years they evolved into communes and today the republics generally consist of between 15 and 20 students, who rent huge apartments and pool their living expenses. A maid who prepares the communal meals is usually included in the budget.

You can identify the republics in the old town by the flags hanging from their façades. It is quite common, too, to see the students clad in their voluminous black capes, which are fringed with ribbons to identify the faculty to which they belong: blue for arts, yellow for medicine and red for law. Some of the capes are distinctly ragged, the cuts round the hems denoting the number of times the owner has been rejected by a loved one.

SÉ VELHA

Forbidding yet serene, the superb Romanesque Sé Velha (Old Cathedral) squats halfway up the hill on a sloping square. Commissioned by Afonso Henriques and built between 1140 and 1175, this is Portugal's oldest cathedral and one of the country's most important Romanesque buildings. Once standing at the frontier of the Christian and Moorish worlds, it has a fortress-like appearance little altered over the centuries. It is modelled on Cluny and other churches in the Auvergne, the probable birthplace of Bernard and Robert, the cathedral's two French architects, and has remained untouched, the simplicity of the overall design accentuated by a few flourishes.

One of these flourishes is the north doorway, added in 1530. Despite being a relatively recent part of the building, it is in worse condition than other older areas. Also admire the tower on the east side, with its beautifully integrated arcaded gallery. Inside, the sense of solidity continues, the simplicity of the plain design of the nave highlighted by a wide gallery above the aisles. The rich, gilt Gothic altarpiece, carved by the Flemish masters Olivier de Ghent and Jean d'Ypres, stands out.

To the right of the chancel, the Capela do Sacramento (Chapel of the Sacrament) contains another altarpiece by Tomé Velho, a pupil of Coimbra's famous sculptor, João de Ruão, who was responsible for the Renaissance-Manueline font to the front of the cathedral. You can enter the late 13th-century Gothic cloisters from the south aisle—the chapterhouse, off to one side, is the burial place of Dom Sesnando, the first Christian governor of Coimbra. He was reputedly a Moor who converted to Christianity.

✚ 185 B2 ✉ Largo da Sé Velha, 3000-291 Coimbra ☎ 239 825 273 🕐 Mon–Thu and Sat 10–1, 2–6, Fri 10–1. Visits not allowed during prayer times 🖐 Free

MOSTEIRO DE SANTA CRUZ

Santa Cruz is an excellent place to admire the work of three of Coimbra's major 16th-century sculptors: Nicolas Chanterene, João de Ruão and João de Castilho. Though their work on the porch has sadly deteriorated, the detailed carving of the pulpit inside the church is a superb example of the Coimbra school. The sculptors also worked on the tombs of Afonso Henriques and Sancho I on either side of the high altar, rich with early Renaissance decoration.

Just off the church is the Claustro do Silêncio (Cloister of Silence). Designed by Marcos Pires in 1524, its airy arches and elaborate stonework are acknowledged to be some of the purest examples of the Manueline style. The low-relief sculptures illustrate scenes from the Passion of Christ, while the *azulejos* (tiles) date from the 16th and 17th centuries.

✚ 185 A1 ✉ Praça 8 de Maio, 3000-300 Coimbra ☎ 239 822 941 🕐 Mon–Sat 9–12, 2–5, Sun 4–5.30 🖐 Cloister: €2.50

MORE TO SEE

CONVENTO DE SANTA CLARA-A-NOVA

The convent was built in 1560. The church, a good example of Portuguese baroque, contains the original 14th-century tomb of Queen Isabel as well as her 17th-century silver replica tomb in the chancel.

✚ Off map 185 B3 ✉ Santa Clara, 3000-340 Coimbra ☎ 239 441 674 🕐 Church: daily 8.30–6.30. Cloisters: daily 8.30–6.30 🖐 €2

JARDIM BOTÂNICO

www.uc.pt/jardimbotanico

These terraced botanical gardens were once among the most important in Europe; this is where new plant discoveries were acclimatized. There are also many rare tropical trees.

✚ 185 C3 ✉ Calçada Martim de Freitas, 3000-393 Coimbra ☎ 239 855 233 🕐 Greenhouses Mon–Fri 9–12, 2.30–5; gardens Mon–Fri 9–5.30 🖐 €2

MUSEU ACADÉMICO

A museum that concentrates on university life and traditions.

🚩 185 C1 ✉ Praça de Dom Dinis, 3001-401 Coimbra ☎ 239 857 000 🕐 Mon–Fri 9–12, 2–5 ✋ €1

MUSEU NACIONAL MACHADO DE CASTRO

www.impmuseus.pt

A superb museum in the old episcopal palace.

🚩 185 B1 ✉ Largo Dr. José Rodrigues, 3000-236 Coimbra ☎ 239 828 727 🕐 Check with tourist office for opening times and prices

PORTUGAL DOS PEQUENITOS

www.fbb.pt

A theme park containing scale models of great Portuguese buildings plus examples of vernacular and colonial architecture.

🚩 Off map 185 B3 ✉ Rossio de Santa Clara, 3040-256 Coimbra ☎ 239 801 170 🕐 Jun to mid-Sep daily 9–8; Mar–end May and mid-Sep to mid-Oct daily 9–7; mid-Oct to end Dec and Feb daily 10–5 ✋ Easter and Jun to mid-Sep adult €9, child (6–13) €4.50, under-6s free; rest of year adult €6, child (6–13) €3, under-6s free

SÉ NOVA

The cathedral was built by the Jesuits in 1598; the niches in the façade contain statues of Jesuit saints. The one vast nave has a barrel vault topped by a lantern. The main altar and side chapels are baroque; note the gilt wooden altarpiece and silver throne.

🚩 185 B1 ✉ Largo da Se Nova, 3000 Coimbra ☎ 239 823 138 🕐 Tue–Sat 0.30 12, 2 6 ✋ Free

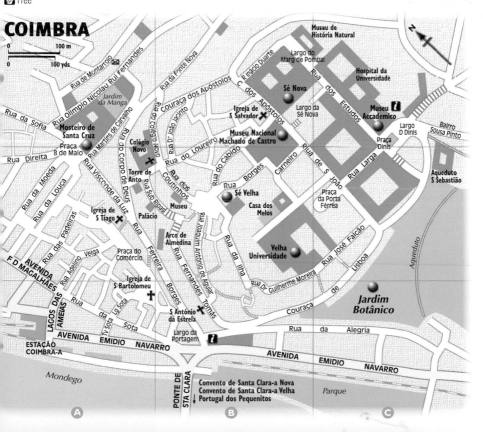

COIMBRA

0 ▬▬▬ 100 m
0 ▬▬▬ 100 yds

CARAMULO

www.turismodaolafoes.com
Walkers will love this magnificent upland country, a verdant mountain area scattered with tiny villages and rich in thickets of rhododendrons, azaleas and hydrangeas. The town of Caramulo, at 800m (2,620ft), is a good base from which to explore the Serra do Caramulo and its main peak, Caramulino (1,075m/3,520ft). It is also a spa town, laid out amid parks and gardens, with a couple of good museums. The Museu do Caramulo (Jul–end Sep daily 10–1, 2–6; Oct–end Jun daily 10–1, 2–5, www.museu-caramulo. net; €6 includes entry to Museu do Automóvel) has a rich art collection—Tournai 16th-century tapestries of the Portuguese arrival in India, furniture and porcelain, and some 20th-century art, including works by Picasso and Dalí and a portrait of Queen Elizabeth II by Graham Sutherland, donated in recognition of the centuries-old alliance between England and Portugal. More specialized is the nearby Museu do Automóvel (Apr–end Oct daily 10–1, 2–6; rest of year daily 10–1, 2–5; €6 includes entry to Museu do Caramulo and several other exhibits), a collection of vintage cars and motorcycles. The oldest exhibit is an 1899 Peugeot, and there is a large group of shiny 1950s Harley-Davidsons.
328 C5 Avenida Abel Lacerda, 3475-031 Caramulo 232 861 437

CASTELO BRANCO

www.cm-castelobranco.pt
The capital of the Beira Baixa, Castelo Branco, a frontier town guarded over by an ancient Templar castle high above the town, is only 18km (11 miles) from the Spanish border. Centuries of invasion, particularly by Napoleon's troops in 1807, have ensured that little remains of the castle and old town, but it is worth heading up the hill to take in the sweeping views from the Miradouro de São Gens, a flower-decked esplanade to the left of the castle ruins.

Below the medieval city are the broad streets and shady squares of modern Castelo, a buzzing and wealthy agricultural hub—local cheese and honey bring in the money, and the olive oil is considered to be some of the best in Portugal. Civic pride is also in evidence in the 17th-century Palácio Episcopal and its surrounding buildings, now the Museu Tavares Proença Júnior (tel 272 344 277; Tue–Sun 10–12.30, 2–5.30; €2), with a local collection of intricate *colchas* (bedspreads) for which the town is famous. These striking embroideries are still traditionally made by young girls for their trousseau—the clothes and linens collected together by a bride before her wedding day.

Next to the palace, and once solely reserved for the bishop, is the Jardim do Antigo Paço Episcopal, a 17th-century formal parterre garden—a pleasant surprise in this remote eastern corner of the country. The flower beds are approached from an elegant double stairway, decorated with *azulejos* (tiles), a splendid mix of statuary, brilliant flowers, water and fountains.
329 D7 Praço do Município, 6000-458 Castelo Branco 272 330 339
Castelo Branco

COIMBRA
▷ 182–185.

CONÍMBRIGA

www.conimbriga.pt
Conímbriga, an ancient settlement 16km (10 miles) from the modern city of Coimbra, was founded by the Celts and later flourished as a Roman city between the second and fourth centuries AD. The archaeological site here is the most important example of a Roman settlement in Portugal, largely because Conímbriga, a major staging post on the route between Lisbon and Braga, was abandoned in the 460s and thus stayed untouched rather than being fought over.

Before they fled the threat of the barbarian Suevi, the Roman inhabitants constructed a massive wall right through the heart of the city in an attempt to keep out the invaders. To build this, houses were pulled down for use as construction materials, and you can see pillars, stone blocks and bricks taken from the dwellings still embedded in the wall as it survives today. Most of the excavations lie around the wall, and it will take you an hour or so to explore them. One of the highlights is the ruins of the Casa de Cantaber, with its central atrium (an inner open courtyard), arcaded porticoes, pools and private baths. Opposite is the Casa dos Repuxos, a second-century AD house with an atrium and a *triclinium* (dining room). Its superb mosaic floors have been well preserved along with the original fountains that have now been restored to working order.

Elsewhere there are remnants of the aqueduct that supplied the town with water, the forum and the baths. A museum of finds from the site is laid out thematically and according to location. Highlights here are jade jewellery, surgeons' instruments and delicate glass. It is worth buying the guidebook, as the exhibits are labelled only in Portuguese.
328 C6 Museu Monográfico de Condeixa, 3150 Condeixa-a-Nova Ruins: Jun–end Sep daily 9–8; Oct–end May daily 10–6. Museum: Jun–end Sep Tue–Sun 10–8; Oct–end May Tue–Sun 10–6 €3

Below *Fine topiary in Castelo's Jardim do Antigo Paço Episcopal*

FIGUEIRA DA FOZ

www.figueiraturismo.com

Figueira da Foz—'Fig Tree at the Mouth of the River'—stands at the mouth of the Mondego. It is an important deep-sea fishing port and a major resort. Don't expect anything picturesque; this is a modern and unpretentious town, with more than a touch of industry on the outskirts and a long promenade backed by modern apartment blocks. What Figueira does have, though, is two superb beaches, great restaurants, bars, a casino and clubs. It also has a couple of small museums: the Casa do Paço in Largo Prof. Vítor Guerra No. 4 (tel 233 402 840; Mon–Fri 9.30–12.30, 2–5.30; free), whose walls are completely covered with Delft wall tiles, part of a ship's cargo that arrived in Figueira in the 17th century; and the Museu Municipal in the Rua Calouste Gulbenkian (tel 233 402 840; Jun to mid-Sep Tue–Fri 9.30–5.15, Sat–Sun 2–7; mid-Sep–end May Tue–Fri 9.30–5.15, Sat 2–5; €1.30), which focuses on local archaeology.

➕ 328 B6 ℹ️ Avenida 25 de Abril, 3080-501 Figueira da Foz ☎ 233 402 610 🕐 Jul and Aug daily 9–midnight; Sep and Jun Mon–Fri 9–12.30, 2–5.30, Sat Sun 10–12.30, 2.30–6.30 🚉 Figueira da Foz

LAMEGO

www.douro-turismo.pt

Wealthy Lamego is isolated in the Beira hills, its riches based on wine and its position on major trade routes. The elegant and prosperous old part of town is scattered with beautiful patrician buildings and dominated by the splendid Sé (cathedral), predominantly Renaissance in style, but still retaining its 13th-century Romanesque bell-tower and tranquil cloister. Facing this across the spacious Largo de Camões is the town's museum (tel 254 600 230; Tue–Sun 10–12.30, 2–5; €2)–the star attraction is five panels from an altarpiece by Grão Vasco. To the northwest, down a tiny street lined with shops, loom the walls of the ancient citadel—walk through to the

castle, which dates from the 12th and 13th centuries.

Back in the heart of town, allow time to wander round the hidden corners and stately mansions. The tree-lined Avenida Dr. A. de Sousa draws the eye west to Lamego's great shrine of Nossa Senhora dos Remédios, approached by a magnificent 18th-century baroque stairway, embellished with statues, fountains and chapels, and modelled on Bom Jesus (▷ 129–131). This is one of Portugal's most important pilgrimage sites and thousands of sick people visit it every year. The main pilgrimage takes place during early September.

➕ 326 D4 ℹ️ Avenida Visconde Guedes Teixeira, 5100-074 Lamego ☎ 254 612 005

LUSO

www.jtluso-bucaco.pt

Luso, just 3km (2 miles) down the hill from the National Forest at Buçaco (▷ 197), is a spa town, its health-giving waters bottled and sold all over Portugal. It's a lovely place to escape from the summer heat, with a gentle pace of life and easy access to the attractive countryside.

The town is dotted with turn-of-the-20th-century spa buildings and elegant villas, and there are some evocative 19th-century-style

tea rooms and a rather restrained casino. Most people come to take the waters—it's easy to book, and you can have hydrotherapy, massage and other treatments, or swim in a pool fed by the mineral springs.

➕ 328 C6 ℹ️ Avenida Emídio Navarro, 3050-902 Luso ☎ 231 939 133 🚉 Luso

MONSANTO

Ancient Monsanto clings to the foot of a granite outcrop in the middle of a plain. Founded in prehistory, it was occupied by the Romans and in 1165 handed over to the Knights Templar, who built the impregnable citadel, its ruins now half-lost amid the boulders. Up here, in the Beira Baixa hills near the Spanish border, the views are immense, on clear days stretching even as far as the Serra da Estrela (▷ 191). Beneath the fort and the ruined chapel of São Miguel, the granite houses huddle between massive boulders along streets seemingly hewn from the living rock, and you may meet the occasional pig or chicken in the narrow alleys. The town attracts a large number of tourists, so come early or late to see it at its best.

➕ 329 E6 ℹ️ Rua Marques da Graciosa, 6060-091 Monsanto ☎ 277 314 642 🕐 Apr–end Oct daily 10–1, 2–6; Nov–end Mar daily 9.30–1, 2–5.30 🚉 Monsanto

Above *The ruined citadel of the Knights Templar lies amid boulders at Monsanto in the Beira Baixa hills, near the border with Spain*

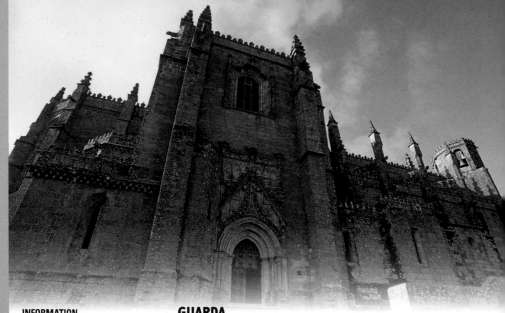

INFORMATION

www.mun-guarda.pt/turismo
✚ 329 E5 ℹ Praça Luís de Camões,
6300-725 Guarda ☎ 271 205 530
🕐 Daily 9–12.30, 2–5.30 🚉 Guarda

TIPS

» Guarda is a confusing city to drive through—come early or during the siesta hours, when there is less traffic.
» The Serra da Estrela has its own information office, about 100m (110 yards) from the tourist office, at Rua Dom Sancho I (tel 271 225 454).

GUARDA

Cold, windswept and forbidding, Guarda is the highest town in Portugal (1,056m/3,465ft), a dour mountain place where bitter winters are the norm. During the second half of the 20th century the town expanded down the hill and the student population swelled as well, bringing a touch of liveliness to this old settlement which has remained largely unspoilt through history. There is plenty to keep you occupied, with a maze of old streets to explore and a good choice of restaurants for lunch.

SÉ

The weighty stone cathedral in the Praça Luís de Camões (Apr–end Oct Tue–Sun 10–1.30, 3–6.30; Nov–end Mar Tue–Sun 9–12.30, 2–5.30; free) dominates Guarda's central square, its castellated façade flanked by heavy octagonal towers. It took so long to complete that it is virtually an architectural textbook, with Gothic, Renaissance and Manueline elements all in evidence. Construction started in the 14th century and was finally completed in 1540. The main façade is pure Gothic, with a Manueline window inserted later, but the side elevations are altogether lighter, with soaring pinnacles, flying buttresses and grotesque gargoyles.

Step inside, and you will find yourself in a lofty space, the twisted pillars and arched vaulting heavily influenced by the Manueline style. Gleaming out of the gloom at the far end of the cathedral is the superb *retábulo* (altarpiece), a Renaissance masterpiece of white, marble-like Ança stone from Coimbra province, gilded in the 18th century. The high-relief figures, 100 in all carved in the 1530s, are the work of João de Ruão, a leading light in the Coimbra sculpture school during the 16th century.

For a bird's-eye view of the town and its surroundings, climb the staircase in the south transept to reach the cathedral's roof.

MUSEU DA GUARDA

This museum in the Rua Alves Roçadas (tel 271 213 460; http://museudaguarda.imc-ip.pt; Tue–Sun 10–12.30, 2–5.30; €2) is in the old bishop's palace outside the original fortifications. Here you can see local archaeological finds, art and sculpture, as well as everyday objects spanning the centuries—an interesting retreat from the wind on chilly days.

Above *Guarda's cathedral towers above the central square*

MONTEMOR-O-VELHO

www.turismo-centro.pt

It is impossible to miss the dramatic, crenellated silhouette of Montemor-o-Velho as you approach Coimbra from the west along the flatlands of the Mondego valley. Montemor has a chequered past—founded by the Romans, the town passed several times from the Moors to the Christians and back again until finally it was secured by the Christians in 1064. The castle became a strategic outpost in the push south against the Moors, and by the 13th century it was the royal residence of choice.

Today, you can wander round the medieval nucleus and take in the views over the valley. The ancient church of Santa Maria da Alcáçova was founded in 1095. Inside, twisted columns support an intricate wooden ceiling, and there are Moorish-style *azulejos* (tiles) and architectural Manueline touches.

There is a twice-monthly market on Wednesday, when local delicacies on sale include duck, lamprey and eels. A walk in the fields should yield some sightings of storks; bird enthusiasts can book a birdwatching afternoon (tel 239 980 500).

✠ 328 B6 ⓘ Castelo de Montemor, Paço das Infantas, 3140-258 Montemor-o-Velho ☎ 239 680 380 🚊 Montemor

PARQUE ARQUEOLÓGICO DO VALE DO CÔA

www.ipa.min-cultura.pt/coa

In 1992 archaeologists discovered a cache of Palaeolithic outdoor art in what is now known as the Parque Arqueológico do Vale do Côa. The biggest such find made in Europe, it contains 28 different areas that extend for 17km (10 miles) along the steep, rocky river valley. New discoveries are still being made—depictions of horses, deer, the extinct ox-like auroch and goats etched into the rock. These 20,000-year-old carvings are unique.

Vale do Côa also contains later rock art spanning the Neolithic era, Bronze Age and Iron Age. There are even some 17th- and 18th-century rock engravings. When the carvings

were discovered, the site was under threat from EDP, Portugal's national electricity company, which wanted to build a dam to generate hydroelectric power. Archaeologists, environmentalists, art historians and locals joined forces to fight against the dam. Their campaign was successful and in 1995 the plan was abandoned. The area became a World Heritage Site in 1998.

Four sites are accessible by guided tour, led by archaeology students. Canada do Inferno, No Rasto dos Caçadores Páleolíticos, Penascosa and Ribeiro de Piscos all have interpretation offices, clarifying the site area and its art, from where you can take a tour of the site in an eight-seater 4WD vehicle. Advance reservation is compulsory—well ahead in summer—and the tours involve walking in difficult terrain. Wear boots and waterproofs in winter, and take a sun hat and plenty of water in summer; temperatures in the valley can exceed 40°C (104°F) in the hottest months.

If you have time to take only one tour, Penascoso is probably the best bet—the engravings here are the most legible. Try to go in the afternoon when the angle of the light is best, and look in particular for the vivid depiction of horses.

✠ 327 E4 ⓘ Avenida Gago Coutinho e Sacadura Cabral 19A, 5150-610 Vila Nova de Foz Côa ☎ 279 768 260 information and booking

PINHEL

www.cm-pinhel.pt

Remote Pinhel is a quintessential Beira Alta town, where sightings of foreign visitors are rare and the pace of life is snail-like compared with that of the cities. This is all part of the region's contrasting charm.

In the old part of town, superb mansions, decorated with coats of arms and fronted by delicate wrought-iron balconies, are evidence of Pinhel's wealth in days gone by. Walk through the main street to find the best examples, set around the beautifully planted central square and lining the adjoining streets.

Farther on, the narrow alleys of the oldest part of town run down the hill from the ruins of the old castle, a forbidding tower enlivened by a Manueline window.

Pinhel lies at the heart of an olive oil and wine area, and you can sample the excellent red made by the local co-operative.

✠ 329 E5 ⓘ Câmara Municipal, Rua Silva Gouveia 1, 6400-455 Pinhel ☎ 271 410 000

SANTA MARIA DA FEIRA

www.cm-feira.pt

Feira, as it's mostly known, has two contrasting attractions—an old castle and Portugal's biggest science museum, packed with interactive, state-of-the-art displays.

Head first for Castelo da Feira (tel 256 372 248; www.castelodafeira.com; Apr–end Oct Tue–Fri 9.30–12.30, 1.30–6, Sat–Sun 10–12.30, 1.30–6.30; rest of year Tue–Fri 9.30–12.30, 1–5, Sat–Sun 9.30–12.30, 1–5.30; €3), standing on a wooded height facing the main town. It was built in the 15th century; the keep has pepperpot turrets and hefty perimeter walls. A sunken gateway leads into the castle proper, whose highlight is a vast Gothic hall. Climb up from here for great views from the upper platform—you can see the Ria de Aveiro (▷ 181) in the distance. From the keep a heavily fortified tunnel links the two parts of the castle—look for the narrow arrow slits and hidden entrances. Then move on to the science park.

Grandly named Europarque Visionarium (www.visionarium.pt; Mon–Fri 9–6, Sat–Sun 2–8; adult €6.50, under-14s €5) is a complete contrast with its distinctly 21st-century feel. It is an architecturally stunning museum that brings science to life. The visit starts with an audio-visual introduction, which fills you in on all the exhibits and displays. The emphasis is on Portugal, with excellent material on the great voyages of discovery, but everything is accessible in English as well as Portuguese.

✠ 328 C4 ⓘ Praça da República, 4524-909 Santa Maria da Feira ☎ 256 370 802

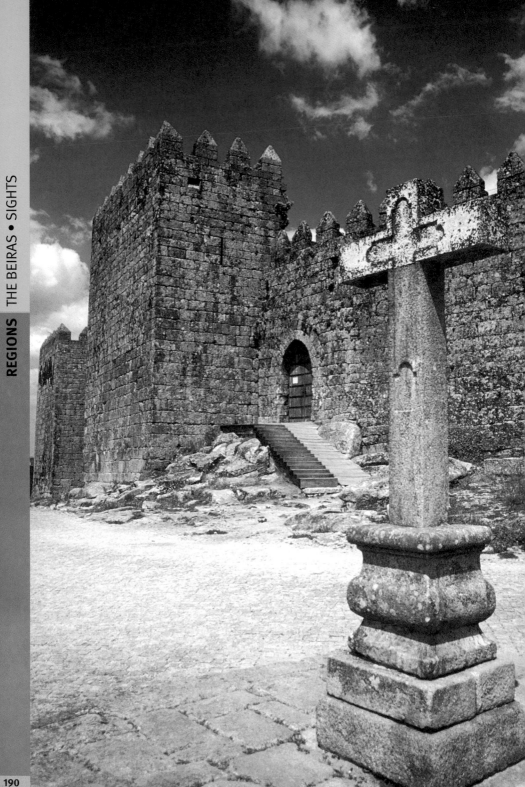

SERRA DA ESTRELA

Majestic scenery and untouched villages characterize this high granite massif, home to mainland Portugal's highest peak. The Serra da Estrela is the westernmost of the high *serras* that spread across the Iberian peninsula. It's a granite massif containing some of Portugal's most imposing peaks, including Torre (1,993m/6,538ft), the highest on the mainland. Much of it is a high plateau cut by valleys, in two of which rise two major rivers, the Mondego and the Zêzere. The high tops are a forbidding jumble of rocks and scree; the lower slopes are forested. The crops in the valleys vie for space with the local sheep, whose wool has long been the backbone of the area's economy. Visitors can enjoy outdoor activities all year round. The weather can deteriorate rapidly, so wear sensible footwear and clothing.

THE SOUTHERN SERRA

You can cross the entire mountain range from Covilhã to Seia during the summer, a beautiful drive that takes in the full range of mountain scenery in the park as well as Torre and some attractive villages. Follow the N339 uphill through Penhas de Saúde, then branch left to follow the road to Torre—you can drive right to the top for superb views over the mountains.

En route in a desolate area of worn granite, you will pass the imposing statue of Our Lady of the Holy Star. In August every year this is the scene of a lavish religious procession.

Northeast of Torro, look for the narrow rock cone known as the Cântaro Magro (Slender Pitcher), which conceals the source of the Zêzere. The scenery here is extraordinary, a wilderness of granite and lakes—the largest is Lagoa Comprida. From here, the road drops rapidly into the Mondego valley and the village of Sabugeira, where you can taste and buy the local rye bread, spicy sausage and *Queijo da Serra*, the strong local sheep's cheese that is also a national favourite.

THE NORTHERN SERRA

You will see the best of the *serra* by driving from Covilhã to Caldas de Manteigas (▷ 194–195), but, if you head northwest from Manteigas on the N232 to Gouveia, you will get a taster. The town has lost its isolated atmosphere, but there are some fine buildings to explore. Linhares to the north is a traditional village overlooking the Mondego with a castle and some superb paintings in the church. Animals live in the heart of the settlement, and donkeys are still the main transport.

INFORMATION

Manteigas—Main office for Parque Natural da Serra da Estrela
www.icnb.pt
✚ 329 D6 🛈 Rua 1° de Maio 2, 6260-101 Manteigas ☎ 275 980 060 🕙 Mon–Fri 9–12.30, 2–5.30

Regional Offices
Gouveia
www.icnb.pt
✚ 329 D5 🛈 Casa da Torre, Avenida Bombeiros Voluntários 8, 6290-520 Gouveia ☎ 238 492 411 🕙 Mon–Fri 9–12.30, 2–5.30

Guarda
www.icnb.pt
✚ 329 E5 🛈 Rua D. Sancho 1.3, 6300-548 Guarda ☎ 271 225 454 🕙 Mon–Fri 9–12.30, 2–5.30

Seia
www.icnb.pt
✚ 329 D6 🛈 Praça da República 28, 6270-496 Seia ☎ 238 310 440 🕙 Mon–Fri 9–12.30, 2–5.30

TIP
» If you want to walk here, take a good map, a compass, and food and water with you. Let someone know where you are going and when you expect to be back.

Above *A fabulous view from Torre*
Opposite *The squat old fortress walls at Trancoso (▷ 192)*

SERNANCELHE

www.cm-sernancelhe.pt

High in the Serra de Lapa, in the dour upland country typical of the Beira Alta, stands the plain old granite town of Sernancelhe. The town is an agricultural hub that brings together people, mules and donkeys from far and wide for its weekly Thursday market.

In the old part of town, the main *praça* (square) is ringed with fine stone mansions, many dating from the 16th and 17th centuries and embellished with coats of arms. This pleasing ensemble is dominated by the Igreja Matriz, a beautiful Romanesque church whose façade is decorated by three free-standing statues set in niches on either side of the door—art historians maintain they are the only examples of such statues in Portugal.

Sernancelhe had many Jewish residents in the Middle Ages. You can still wander round the old Jewish quarter of the town—look for houses with a pair of unequal-sized doors, a wide one for use by tradespeople and a narrower one reserved for the exclusive use of the immediate family.

✚ 329 D4 ℹ️ Rua Dr. oliveira Serrão, 3640-240 Sernancelhe ☎ 254 598 300

TRANCOSO

www.cm-transcoso.pt

www.rt-serradaestrela.pt

Trancoso feels a long way from anywhere, an atmospheric fortress town on the boulder-strewn *planalto* (high plateau) of the Beiras. It was captured by the Moors in the 10th century, whose legacy is evident in the squat design of the castle, its sturdy battlements echoing those on top of the town gates. By the 12th century Trancoso was in Christian hands, and it was here, in 1282, that the marriage of Dom Dinis to St. Isabel took place. Wander round the town's walls, perhaps bypassing the main gates and ducking through one of the narrow entrance passages to enter its heart, where you will find a collection of churches, chapels and fine mansions. There are echoes of the Peninsular War at the Quartel do General Beresford—a house named after one of Wellington's leading generals and organizer of the Portuguese forces in the struggle against Napoleon—and a clutch of beguiling squares.

Trancoso has a Friday market and shops selling local produce such as cheese, ham and sausage.

✚ 329 E5 ℹ️ Avenida Herois de S. Marcos, 6420-003 Trancoso ☎ 271 811 147

VILA NOVA DE FOZ CÔA

www.cm-fozcoa.pt

If you are planning several visits to the Parque Arqueológico do Vale do Côa (▷ 189), Vila Nova de Foz Côa is a good base. It is a pleasant little town, remarkably unaffected by its close proximity to a renowned World Heritage Site.

The town's main attraction is the 16th-century Igreja Matriz, fronted by the town pillory from the same period. The church's granite façade is a remarkable example of Manueline decoration, with pilasters around the door, itself topped by an archivolt below a beautiful limestone Pietà. Inside, the three naves are covered by a painted wooden ceiling, the leaning columns giving the impression that the building is open to the sky. The pillory, with its ropework decoration, statues and columns, is also a classic example of the Manueline style.

✚ 327 E4 ℹ️ Avenida Cidade Nova-Centro Cultural, 5150-642 Vila Nova de Foz Côa ☎ 279 760 329

Below *Vila Nova de Foz Côa's square is dominated by the 16th-century church and town pillory*

VISEU

Modern Viseu, prosperous capital of the Beira Alta, stands on the site of a Roman settlement, built close to the camp of Viriatus, leader of the Lusitanian rebels against Rome. The ruins of this camp lie to the north—it was there that Viriatus fought his last battle. The town prospered on agriculture in the Middle Ages, the wealth funding the building of the cathedral, churches and fine mansions, all of which were enclosed within the city's stout defensive walls. Today, Viseu is the regional capital. It is also the heart of the Dão wine area, producer of excellent reds exported worldwide.

MUSEU DE GRÃO VASCO

As its name implies, Viseu's star turn alongside the cathedral in the Praça da Sé (tel 232 422 049; www.ipmuseus.pt; Tue 2–6, Wed–Sun 10–6; €4, free Sun am) is mainly devoted to the art of the great Portuguese painter Vasco Fernandes, who earned the nickname Grão Vasco (the Great Vasco). Vasco lived from 1480 to around 1543. It is the only place in Portugal where you can see a large and representative collection of his work.

The museum's collection was originally distributed around the cathedral, the episcopal palace and other churches in the region. Gathering the works together has given art historians the chance to trace the evolution of Vasco's style and learn more in general about Portuguese art of the period. The pictures you will see here were originally panels that made up a series of large altarpieces designed for the cathedral in Viseu and other churches in the region. Concentrate on the pictures that once hung in the chancel of Viseu's Sé (cathedral), which depict detailed scenes from the life of Christ.

SÉ

The Sé, remodelled between the 16th and 18th centuries, is Romanesque, and has retained its weighty twin towers, though the façade was altered in the 17th century. The vast hall-church has a wonderful Manueline roof of intricate ropework supported on Gothic pillars. Shining through the dimness is a glittering 18th-century baroque altarpiece, with a serene 14th-century Madonna as its focus. There is also a fine gallery and a restrained Renaissance cloister, decorated with 18th-century *azulejos* (tiles). The first floor is home to the cathedral's small museum.

INFORMATION

www.cm-viseu.pt
www.turismodaolafoes.pt
329 D5
Avenida Calouste Gulbenkian, 3500-055 Viseu 232 420 950 May–end Sep Mon–Fri 9.30–12.30, 2–6, Sat 9.30–12.30, 2.30–5.30, Sun 9.30–12.30; rest of year Mon–Fri 9.30–12.30, 2–6, Sat 9.30–12.30

TIP

» Driving into Viseu is quite confusing; head for the heart of the city and park before trying to get your bearings.

THE VISEU SCHOOL

Like Lisbon, Viseu had a flourishing school of painting during the 16th century, led by Gaspar Vaz, who died around 1568, and Vasco Fernandes (Grão Vasco). Vaz studied in Lisbon, where he was much influenced by Flemish artists, particularly Van Eyck, though his work is distinctly Portuguese in style. Grão Vasco is one of Portugal's finest painters. He combines a great sense of composition and drama with rich shades, fine detail and a gift for realism inspired by local people and landscapes.

Above *The Misericórdia's Romanesque twin bell towers are a distinctive feature of the city of Viseu*

DRIVE

THROUGH THE SERRA DA ESTRELA

This is a high-altitude drive into the heart of the Serra da Estrela, Portugal's highest mainland mountain range. The route takes you up to Portugal's only ski area before following a dramatic glacial valley through the mountains and out into the fertile land below.

THE DRIVE
Distance: 38km (24 miles)
Time: 1.5 hours without detours
Start at: Covilhã
End at: Belmonte

★ Covilhã, a textile town sprawled across the lower slopes of the *serra*, is popular all year with Portuguese visitors to the Parque Natural da Serra da Estrela (▷ 191). An old town, whose steep streets give glimpses of the plain below, it was the birthplace of the explorer Pêro de Covilhã, who reached India via the Cape of Good Hope in 1498.

Follow the brown signs marked 'Centro Historico' and 'Serra da Estrela' uphill through the town—keep your eyes open as the signs are few and far between. In the main square, Praça do Município, veer right to make a right turn (unsigned) along a busy shopping street and out of town. The street is

steep and rapidly becomes steeper. Over the next 8km (5 miles) you'll gain a lot of altitude, so be prepared for a steep, twisting road, with plenty of hairpin bends and drops; although the road is relatively wide, it's not for the nervous.

The first 3km (2 miles) are lined with eucalyptus and acacia, but, once past the 1,200m (3,937ft) sign, which marks the start of the natural park, the trees thin out and you emerge onto a high, arid landscape, dotted with scrubby pines and littered with vast granite slabs and outcrops. Continue into Penhas de Saúde.

❶ Penhas da Saúde is a low-key mountain ski resort with a scattering of alpine-style chalets, hotels and cafés. This is where most of the accommodation is to be found for Portugal's only ski area. It is also a summer base for long-distance hiking in the *serra*.

The road climbs through the village and past a reservoir; ahead you'll see the peak of Torre, at 1,993m (6,537ft) the highest point in mainland Portugal. At the intersection, turn right onto the N338 but, in summer, it's worth taking a short detour to the left to take in Torre itself. In winter, however, it is best to avoid this road.

❷ Torre is named after the tower on its summit, added in the 19th century to bring the mountain's height up to a round figure. You can drive right to the top, passing a huge rock statue of Nossa Senhora da Boa Estrela, the focus of a huge pilgrimage each August.

If you have made the Torre detour, return to the intersection. The N338 descends from the heights into the Zêzere valley. Near the top is a series of stopping places where you can admire the views.

❸ The Zêzere valley is a textbook example of a glacial geological feature. From the viewpoints along the road, you can see the spectacular valley encircled by dramatic mountains, with the road carved out of sheer walls of rock and scree. Tumbling streams run down the slopes.

Continue your descent. Once back below the treeline, you'll see stands of pine and beech, plus heather and broom.

❹ The lower reaches of the valley still have the remnants of the cultivated terraces that once provided a subsistence living for the locals. You'll also notice the last remaining traditional stone houses with their primitive thatched roofs.

The first settlement you'll come to is Caldas de Manteigas.

❺ Caldas do Manteigas, a lovely spa village with a gushing stream, merges into the small town of Manteigas. Set above the river Zêzere, Manteigas is home to the main office of the Parque Natural da Serra da Estrela, a good source of information if you're planning a stay. The town itself is a pleasant place to pause for a wander.

Take the N232 out of Manteigas towards Belmonte. From here, the road passes through a gentler valley, heavily forested with the river Zêzere at the bottom.

❻ The valley between Manteigas and Belmonte gives a great feeling of being deep in mountain territory, with the hills all round, the clear fast-flowing river, the little patches of cabbages, and tiny, isolated villages such as Sameiro.

As you lose altitude, the valley continues to open up, until you

Opposite The glaciated valley of the Zêzere
Right Waterfalls tumble over the rocky slopes into the Zêzere river

eventually cross the river. Continue along this road until you reach the fortress town of Belmonte (▷ 179) where the drive ends.

WHERE TO EAT
In Covilhã, there's the Cozinha da Avó in the country club at Quinta do Covelo. There's also the Hotel Serra da Estrela in Penhas de Saúde, the Pousada de São Lourenço at Manteigas and, in Belmonte, the Pousada do Convento.

WHEN TO GO
The landscape is at its best in spring and autumn, while the cool mountain air is refreshing during the summer months.

PLACES TO VISIT
MANTEIGAS
🛈 Information Office, Parque Natural de Serra da Estrela 2, Rua 1º de Maio, 6260-101 Manteigas ☎ 275 980 060
🕐 Mon–Fri 9–12.30, 2–5.30

CASTELO DE BELMONTE
✉ 6250-048 Belmonte ☎ 275 913 901
🕐 Daily 10–12.30, 2–5

TIP
▸ If you're intending to drive this tour in the winter or early spring, check the status of the roads. They may be closed due to snow blockage. Even if open, they may be treacherously slippery in icy or snowy conditions. Check at the tourist offices, or on the boards at the bottom of the access road.

A CIRCULAR WALK FROM MANTEIGAS

This straightforward walk from the village of Manteigas takes in a waterfall and swimming hole deep in the Parque Natural da Serra da Estrela.

THE WALK
Distance: 10.7km (6.6 miles)
Time: 3–4 hours without stops
Start/end at: Manteigas

★ Start in the middle of Manteigas, outside the park information office. Cross the road to the Galp service station and take the steep track on the right of the main road behind the tourist office. Follow this downhill, bearing right past the houses until you come to a bridge over the River Zêzere. Cross this and bear left past the factory at São Gabriel. Continue left, watch closely for the yellow waymark arrows leading into the woods. These markers will take you all the way to the Poço do Inferno waterfall. The name is Portuguese for 'Hell's Well.'

❶ Poço do Inferno is a waterfall in an idyllic situation. It's a good place

Above Manteigas village nestles in the Serra da Estrela mountains

for a picnic and even a swim—but take care as the water is glacially cold. En route to the falls, you'll climb around 300m (1,000ft) as you walk through some fine woodland of pine, beech and birch. At the right times of year, particularly in spring, there are also some lovely wild flowers to spot.

Pick up the surfaced road that winds its way around the mountain and into the valley of the Zêzere river.

❷ As you come into more open country you'll see flocks of sheep; their milk is used to make the local cheese, *Queijo da Serra*, which is famous all over Portugal. You might also catch sight of one of the celebrated Serra da Estrela dogs, a unique breed that was developed to guard the sheep of the area.

Follow the road down to join the N338. Turn right to descend to Caldas de Manteigas.

❸ Caldas de Manteigas, a little spa town that spreads along the river valley, is now more or less part of Manteigas itself. It has two hot springs, both sulphurous, which are used to treat rheumatism and skin and lung diseases.

Follow the road downward back to central Manteigas.

WHERE TO EAT
Take a picnic, or, in Manteigas, try the Pousada de São Lourenço.

WHEN TO GO
Choose a clear, settled day any time between May and September. It's inadvisable to attempt the walk after snow, or in bad weather.

TIP
» Although this is a popular excursion, it is a mountain walk. This means being prepared, with stout footwear, suitable clothes (including waterproofs), and something to eat and drink.

WALK

IN THE NATIONAL FOREST OF BUÇACO

On this shady walk in Portugal's best-known and best-loved woodland, you can see many varieties of shrubs and trees—it is estimated that there are around 700 varieties of trees here, some native and others exotic. The forest also harbours intriguing follies and water features.

THE WALK

Distance: 2.6km (1.6 miles)
Time: 50 minutes with no stops
Start/end at: Main parking area below Palace Hotel do Bussaco
Parking: Leave your car in the main parking area below the hotel

★ Look for the path on the right, signed *'Fonte Fria'*. Follow the steps leading down the hill, ignoring the turning to the left. Keep to the path that circles a hut, continuing until you reach the top of the Fonte Fria.

① Fonte Fria is a water staircase with a series of steps on either side of a central cascade. The tumbling water forms a succession of pools and water terraces, all connected by the main stream. Once you get to the bottom, there's a great view back up from the pool with its focal tree fern (if you don't want to do the full walk, you can access this directly from the road to the hotel).

Turn left near the pool, signposted *'Vale dos Fretos'*.

② The Vale dos Fretos is an avenue planted with pines, sequoias and superb tree ferns, huge specimens as tall as 4–5m (13–16ft). The water running alongside the path feeds two lakes, while the area is planted with camellias and rhododendrons.

Keep on the left side of the second, larger lake and turn left up the steps, then right at the intersection. About 220m (240 yards) farther on, you'll come to a fork; take the wide dirt track on the left uphill. Fork left again, climbing steadily, and then swing right onto a wide path. At the next intersection you'll see the first of a series of fascinating follies.

③ The little building decorated with pebbles is the Porta Pedron. Keeping this on your left, turn right along a wide path to reach the Porta de Siloa, a double-arched folly. Walk through this and turn left through the second arch, up the steps, and then along a wide avenue, where you'll find another folly at the top.

Turn left along a wide level track near the last building. The track crosses a stream and continues uphill; at the next intersection bear right, then right again, continuing upwards. This path will take you back to your starting point in the parking area.

WHERE TO EAT
Palace Hotel do Bussaco (▷ 206) also sells maps of the forest.

WHEN TO GO
Good at any time in dry weather.

TIP
» The paths are a mixture of gravel, soft footing and steps, so wear sensible shoes.

Above *Tree ferns in the Vale dos Fretos*

DRIVE

FROM FIGUEIRA DA FOZ TO MEALHADA

A varied route that takes you from the typically Portuguese holiday resort of Figueira da Foz into the hills, with a great selection of places to visit along the way, including picturesque Montemor, historic Coimbra and the national forest of Buçaco.

THE DRIVE

Distance: 100km (62 miles)
Time: 2–3 hours' straight driving, 1–2 days if visiting everything
Start at: Figueira da Foz
End at: Mealhada
Overnight stop: Coimbra

★ Stroll along the lovely beach at Buarcos, on the northern outskirts of Figueira da Foz (▷ 187), before starting your drive at the central roundabout. Follow the brown signs for *outras direcções* (other directions) along the waterfront until you see the lighthouse and the deep-water fishing port ahead. Follow the road round to the left, keeping the old castle on your right, and continue upriver.

❶ On your right is the marina, the departure point for boat trips. You'll notice the older part of Figueira to your left, set around the leafy greenery of the municipal gardens.

Follow the blue A1/A14 sign to Lisboa, Porto, Coimbra and Viseu past the port and under the cantilevered motorway bridge. At the roundabout turn left following the A14 Coimbra and Viseu signs, then fork right towards Coimbra and Viseu. Stay on this highway for 14km (8.6 miles) until you reach exit 4.

❷ This stretch of the route runs through pine and eucalyptus woods above the Mondego estuary. The Mondego is one of Portugal's loveliest rivers, rising in the Serra da Estrela and running for much of its course through wooded country scattered with picturesque hamlets. The lower reaches are noted for waders and over-wintering seabirds. Look for herons and egrets feeding, and for storks' nests on chimneys and poles.

Take exit 4 to Montemor-o-Velho (▷ 189), which you'll see on a

hill above the salt flats. Leaving Montemor, follow the signs to Soure round two roundabouts—the road crosses the river, and then the railway. Immediately after this, turn right, again following the signs to Soure. Drive up the hill and turn left at a T-junction signed 'Soure 14'. At the next roundabout follow the signs to Condeixa, crossing the railway again, then turn left onto the Granja road at the next roundabout.

❸ You're now following the Mondego upstream along the south bank on a wonderfully rural road that crosses fertile alluvial agricultural land. The road undulates to give views left to the river and runs through a string of untouched farming villages. These give a real glimpse of traditional country life, where farms are little more than smallholdings growing a range of crops and supporting just a few animals. Farmers aim to be largely self-sufficient, growing food to feed their families and bartering or selling the surplus. From the economic standpoint, this system of agriculture is inefficient, but it adds to the area's charm for visitors.

At the intersection with the major road, follow the signs on the wide, modern N341 towards Coimbra.

Above The Palace Hotel do Bussaco was once a royal hunting lodge

❹ Coimbra (▷ 182–184) has Portugal's oldest university and many historic buildings. If you're not visiting the city, skirt it on the ring road to pick up the IC2 and then the IP3.

Leave Coimbra on the IC2 and head north, turning off at exit 8 to join the IP3, a good road that runs over beautiful wooded hills. After 13km (8.6 miles) take the N235 left towards Luso.

From here, you climb steadily up through gentle hill country on a shady road planted with eucalyptus on either side. The clearings are filled with olives, and you'll spot the terraces—once heavily cultivated and still used for grazing and food crops—that the locals created to make best use of the pockets of fertile soil. Tiny settlements, dripping with geraniums and ringed by orange groves, lie along the road—a

landscape that's characteristically rural Portuguese.

❺ Look for the start of a high stone wall to your right; this rings the Mata Nacional (National Forest) of Buçaco (▷ 197), which you enter through the main gate. At the hotel you can park to stretch your legs or go for a walk in the woods (▷ 197). It is worth allowing time for the latter, since the forest is one of Portugal's most important natural treasures.

❻ Drive downhill to the spa town of Luso (▷ 187).

Take the N234 west to Mealhada, a pretty drive that drops through the woods.

❼ Mealhada is famous for its *leitão*, which is considered to be the most delicious roast suckling pig served in Portugal.

The town is just five minutes from the A1, for the drive back to Figueira.

WHERE TO EAT

In Montemor-o-Velho, try Ramalhão in the Rua Tenente Valadim, which is renowned for its desserts. Buçaco has the Palace Hotel do Bussaco, where regional and international cuisine are served (▷ 206).

WHEN TO GO

Early summer or autumn are great times for this drive, as the weather should be settled, the countryside is at its best, and Coimbra itself will be relatively crowd-free. High summer is both busier and hotter.

TIP

» It makes sense to spend a night in Coimbra, which deserves at least a couple of hours' exploration. Leave the next morning for the second half of the drive, and plenty of time for a walk in the Buçaco forest.

REGIONS · THE BEIRAS · DRIVE

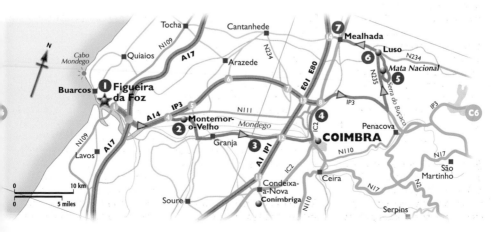

AVEIRO

AVEIROSUB
www.aveirosub.com
Outside Aveiro towards Praia da Barra, this place offers scuba-diving lessons and organizes diving trips either in the lagoon or open sea. Introductory lessons, including trial dives, are available for beginners.
✉ Avenida José Estevão 681, 3830-555 Gafanha da Nazaré ☎ 234 367 666 ◉ Phone lines: Mon–Sat 9–12.30, 2–7 🖐 Day's diving (2 dives) €50; dive course (17 theory lessons, 7 pool lessons, 5 open sea lessons) €400; introductory dive €35

BUGA
BUGA (Bicicleta de Utilização Gratuíta de Aveiro) is Aveiro's free bicycle scheme. Head for the shop at the Forum shopping mall, hand in your ID, then take the bicycle and use it within the city limits, returning it to the shop when finished.
✉ Centro Comercial Forum, 3800 Aveiro ☎ 967 050 441 ◉ BUGA shop: daily 9–7

CLUB 8
www.club8aveiro.com
Aveiro's biggest nightclub, south of the central canal. The terrace overlooks the river and two floors play house, drum 'n' bass and a

few hits from the 1980s and 1990s. Thursday is student night.
✉ Cais do Paraíso 19, 3810-146 Aveiro ☎ 917 753 861 ◉ Wed–Sat midnight–4am 🖐 Wed–Thu free, Fri–Sat €5 (includes drink)

ECO RIA
Eco Ria offers regular boat trips in launches as well as in *moliceiros* from May to the end of September. Weather permitting and depending on numbers, they will also operate throughout the year.
✉ Rua Cândido dos Reis 59B, 3800-098 Aveiro ☎ 967 088 183 or 234 425 563 ◉ Office: Mon–Fri 9–12.30, 2–5.30. *Moliceiro* trips: Jun–end Sep daily 10–6, every hour. Motor launch trips: Jun–end Aug daily, depart 12.30 return 2.30 🖐 *Moliceiro* trips €5 per person, minimum 8 people; motor launch trips €20 per person including lunch €4 (reserve 2–3 days in advance); (times subject to change; call to confirm)

FÁBRICA VISTA ALEGRE
www.vistaalegre.pt
Some 6km (4 miles) south of Aveiro, the village of Vista Alegre is home to this prestigious porcelain works. The museum records its history.
✉ Vista Alegre, 3830-292 Ílhavo ☎ 234 324 223 ◉ Museum: Tue–Fri 10–6,

Above *Figueira da Foz is a great place for windsurfing and other watersports*

Sat–Sun 10–12.30, 2–5. Shop: Mon–Sat 9.30–6.30 🖐 Museum: €1.50 🚌 Take the N109 south out of Aveiro, past Ílhavo

MARIA DA APRESENTAÇÃO DA CRUZ
Aveiro's most famous food is its *ovos moles*, literally 'soft eggs', sweet cakes that this family store has been producing according to a closely guarded recipe since 1882. They are sold in traditional wooden painted barrels.
✉ Rua D. Jorge de Lencastre 37, 3800-142 Aveiro ☎ 234 422 323 ◉ Mon–Sat 9–8, Sun 9.30–1

COIMBRA

A CAMPONESA
This long-established wine store, with an ancient (and still functioning) cash register and a large gilt clock fitted among the original wooden shelves and counters, stocks a great selection of port and wines from several of Portugal's wine-producing regions. You can come and take a look even if you don't want to buy.
✉ Rua da Louça 80, 3000-243 Coimbra ☎ 239 827 947 ◉ Mon–Fri 9–7, Sat 9–1

A CAPELLA
www.acapella.com.pt
Housed in a 14th-century chapel, this unusual bar has daily live *fado* shows from March to October and sometimes during the winter.

✉ Capela Nossa Senhora da Vitória, Rua Corpo de Deus, Largo da Vitória, 3000-111 Coimbra ☎ 239 833 985 🕙 Daily *fado* shows from 10pm 💶 €10 (advisable to reserve during Jul and Aug)

BASÓFIAS
www.basofias.com
Basófias runs boat trips on the River Mondego, departing from beside the Parque Dr. Manuel Braga. Along the way you'll get great views of the historic buildings on the far bank.

✉ Parque Dr. Manuel Braga, Coimbra ☎ 239 912 444 or 969 830 664 🕙 Apr–end Sep daily 3, 4, 5, 6, 7; rest of year daily 3, 4, 5 💶 €6

GOLF QUINTA DAS LÁGRIMAS
www.quintadaslagrimas.pt
The golf academy at Quinta das Lágrimas, on the banks of the River Mondego, has a nine-hole pitch-and-putt course, plus a driving range, putting and chipping greens.

✉ Rua António Augusto Gonçalves Santa Clara, 3041-901 Coimbra ☎ 239 002 388 🕙 Tue–Sun 10–7 💶 Daily green fee €12.50; club rental free 🚌 Cross the Santa Clara bridge, turn left then right at the sign

O CANTINHO DA ANITA
Behind the medieval-looking exterior is a fine craft shop selling traditional Coimbra ceramics, imitation 17th-century Viuva Lamêgo tiles, and cotton embroidery and weavings.

✉ Rua Sargento Mor 2, 3000-382 Coimbra ☎ 239 827 415 🕙 Jul–Aug Mon–Fri 9–7, Sat 9–1; rest of year Mon–Fri 9–1, 3–7, Sat 9–1

O PIONEIRO DO MONDEGO
www.opioneirodomondego.com
Rent a kayak for a trip on the River Mondego between Penacova and Coimbra. Paddling up to 25km (16 miles) takes around four hours, but there are shorter options. A minibus collects you at the eastern corner of Parque D. Manuel Braga at 10am.

✉ Rua da Calçada 21, 3360-184 Penacova ☎ 239 478 385 🕙 Phone lines: Jun–end Sep daily 8–10, 1–3, 8–10 💶 €20 including transportation

PORTUGAL DOS PEQUENITOS
www.fbb.pt
This theme park is Coimbra's most-visited attraction (though a little overrated). It provides family fun, with child-size models of Portugal's most famous monuments, and areas dedicated to the former colonies.

✉ Rossio de Santa Clara, 3040-256 Coimbra ☎ 239 801 170 🕙 Jun to mid-Sep daily 9–8; Mar–end May and mid-Sep to mid-Oct daily 9–7; mid-Oct to end Dec and Feb daily 10–5; closed Jan 💶 Easter week and Jun to mid-Sep: adult €9, child (under 14) €4.50; rest of year: adult €6, child (under 14) €3, under-6s free

TEATRO ACADÉMICO GIL VICENTE
www.uc.pt/tagv
The theatre hosts a varied selection of shows and events, including music, dance, cinema and plays.

✉ Praça da República, 3000-343 Coimbra ☎ 239 855 630 🕙 Ticket office: Mon–Sat 5–10, Sun (on show days) 5–10 💶 €10–€30 🎭 In auditorium 🍷

TERMAS DA CURIA
www.termasdacuria.com
The thermal spa at Curia has been going since the 19th century, when the curative properties of its waters were internationally recognized. There's also a hotel, bicycles, mini-golf and swimming pools.

✉ Curia, 3780-541 Tamengos ☎ 231 519 825 🕙 Mon–Sat 8–12.30, 4.30–7, Sun 8–12.30 💶 €7–€110 according to which treatments you take 🚌 Take the IC2 north out of Coimbra. Turn left at the sign to Curia and follow signs for *'Termas'*, 25km (16 miles) north of Coimbra

VIA LATINA
Just off the Praça da República, this is one of the city's most popular clubs, especially among the student crowd. During the week there are often university parties, and at the weekend national and international DJs play mainly house and dance.

✉ Rua Almeida Garrett 1, 3000-021 Coimbra ☎ 239 820 293 🕙 Mon–Sat midnight–6am 💶 €5 (includes drink)

FIGUEIRA DA FOZ
BAR HAVANA
With its Latin theme, Little Havana brings a taste of Cuba to the Atlantic coast. Palm trees, vibrant tones and free-flowing margaritas and *mojitos* are enhanced by live bands playing salsa and Latin American tunes.

✉ Rua Cândido dos Reis 86A, 3080-155 Figueira da Foz ☎ 233 434 899 (tourist office) 🕙 Tue–Sun 9pm–2am 💶 Free

CAPITÃO DUREZA
www.capitaodureza.com
Qualified instructors and the latest equipment are provided for white-water rafting, paintballing, canoeing, kayaking, canyoning, abseiling and other sports and events.

✉ Rua Principal 64C, Telhado, 3360-062 Penacova ☎ 239 918 148 or 918 315 357 🕙 Phone lines: Mon–Fri 9.30–8.30 💶 €18–€97 according to activity

CASINO DA FIGUEIRA DA FOZ
www.casinofigueira.pt
From the beginning of the 20th century, this casino attracted Portugal's aristocracy. The elegant gaming rooms now sit inside an ultra-modern glass and foil façade alongside slot machines, a restaurant, nightclub and show girls.

✉ Rua Dr. Calado 1, 3080-153 Figueira da Foz ☎ 233 408 400 🕙 Jul–Aug daily 4pm–4am; rest of year daily 3pm–3am. Shows: Wed–Thu 10.30, Fri 11, Sun 4 💶 Entry free

CENTRO DE ARTES E ESPECTÁCULOS DA FIGUEIRA DA FOZ
Figueira's main venue for drama, music and dance was built in white concrete and glass in 2000. Inside is an 800-seat auditorium, a small cinema, an exhibition hall, and there's an outdoor amphitheatre.

✉ Rua Abade Pedro, 3080-081 Figueira da Foz ☎ 233 407 200 🕙 Ticket office: Mon–Fri 9–7, Sat 10–8, Sun 10–9.30 (on show days open until 11pm). 💶 €10–€40 🎭 In auditorium 🖥

JOGOS DE PRAIA

During July and August the beaches of Figueira come alive with the *Jogos da Praia*, literally 'beach games'. There is beach volleyball, aerobics classes and fashion shows.
✉ Figueira da Foz ☎ 233 422 610 (tourist office)

PERFUMARIA PUB

With two floors, gentle lighting and unobtrusive music, this pub-like bar is one of Figueira's oldest and is an ideal place for a quiet drink. Beware of the tight spiral staircase.
✉ Rua Dr. Calado 37, 3080-081 Figueira da Foz ☎ 233 426 442 🕐 Daily 9.30pm–6am
⛟ Free

TOURADA

On weekends in August, the municipal bullring, just off Rua do Viso, hosts an impressive line-up of top *talento taurino* (bullfighting talent). For more details, contact the tourist office.
✉ Praça de Touros, Figueira da Foz ☎ 233 422 610 (tourist office) ⛟ €15–€60 according to the status of the bullfighters

GUARDA

A CATEDRAL

The best bars in Guarda are dotted around the old town in townhouses, and so all of them are quite small inside. This bar, decorated with religious themed paintings from which it gets its name, is one of the most popular. Because of this, be aware that it can get quite cramped.
✉ Rua dos Cavaleiros 22, 6300-675 Guarda ☎ 271 223 386 🕐 Tue–Sat 10pm–3am

CASA ESPIGADO

Founded in 1916, this shop is packed with copper, stainless steel, wrought iron and tin items, both the practical and the curious.
✉ Rua da Torre 21, 6300-768 Guarda ☎ 271 212 269 🕐 Mon–Fri 9.30–1, 3–7, Sat 9.30–1

O PECADO DO REI

This homelike bar, just off the Rua D. Francisco de Passos, mainly attracts a student crowd. It has five rooms whose stone walls

are decorated with a collection of stringed instruments. Although quiet during the week, it comes to life at weekends, with karaoke and bands.
✉ Rua D. Dinis 9, 6300-546 Guarda ☎ 271 215 170 🕐 Mon–Sat 8pm–2am

UNIVERSO TT

www.universott.pt
For exciting Land Rover excursions through the Mondego valley or Malcate Serra, or along themed frontier castle, wool or cheese routes, try this company. It also organizes outdoor activities, such as hiking and hot-air balloon flights.
✉ Rua Almirante Gago Coutinho 10, 2nd floor, right-hand door, 6300-507 Guarda ☎ 271 084 400 or 967 949 196 🕐 Daily 10–7. Phone lines: daily 9–9 ⛟ Half-, 1- and 2-day trips available from €35

LUSO

TERMAS DO LUSO

www.termasdoluso.com
The medicinal properties of the waters were decorated in the late 1700s, with the first spa opening in the 1850s. Facilities include a swimming pool, a high-powered Vichy shower, and massage.
✉ 3050-902 Luso ☎ 231 937 910 🕐 2 May–31 Oct Mon–Sat 8–12, 4–7 ⛟ €7–€75 depending on treatment; advance booking advised in Jul and Aug

VISEU

CASA DA RIBEIRA

Viseu is known for basketware and lace, both of which can be found here. You can see craftspeople working, while items on sale include glassware, pottery and textiles.
✉ Largo da Nossa Senhora de Conceição, 3500-198 Viseu ☎ 232 427 400 🕐 Tue–Sat 9–12.30, 2–5.30

CENTRO HÍPICO MONTEBELO

www.centrohipicomontebelo.pt
This equestrian centre is 10 minutes' drive from Viseu. It has covered and outdoor arenas, paddocks and a clubhouse. Horses can be rented by the hour. It's best to call day before to confirm availability and times.
✉ Farminhão, 3510-643 Viseu ☎ 232 856 474 🕐 Tue–Sun 9–8 ⛟ €20 per hour

Above *The cities and towns of the Beiras have a lot to offer in the evenings*

🚌 Take the IP3 south out of Viseu. Turn off at São Miguel de Outeiro/ Sabugosa. The centre is signed

GOLFE MONTEBELO

www.golfemontebelo.pt
This hilly course has the magnificent Serra da Estrela and Serra do Caramulo as a backdrop. The 18 holes are set around pines, oaks and clumps of gorse with frequent dog-legs, streams and lakes.
✉ Farminhão, 3510-643 Viseu ☎ 232 856 464 🕐 May–end Sep 8–8; Oct–end Apr 8–7 ⛟ 18 holes Mon–Fri €41, Sat–Sun €54; club rental €25; buggy €27 weekdays, €34 weekends 🚌 Take the IP3 south out of Viseu. Turn off at São Miguel de Outeiro/ Sabugosa. The golf course is signed

MTM TEAM

www.mtm-team.com
For the adventurous, this company, located to the north of Viseu, offers white-water rafting, bungee jumping, canyoning, canoeing and much more in the idyllic setting of the Paiva river valley.
✉ Sete Pães, Vale de Matos, 3600 Castro D'Aire ☎ 936 933 111 or 938 460 246 🕐 Phone lines daily 9–6 ⛟ Depend on activity chosen

OBVIAMENTE

This bar is quiet until 11pm then plays dance and 1980s music to a young crowd. It serves snacks late, which can be a lifesaver for hungry dancers near dawn.

✉ Largo do Pintor Gata 26, 3500-136 Viseu
☎ 232 426 635 ⏰ Mon–Sat 8.30pm–4am
🎫 Free

PALÁCIO DO GELO SHOPPING
www.palaciodogelo.pt
This gigantic complex offers shops, restaurants, cinemas, health club, sports facilities and ice-skating. The largest shopping venue in the region houses all the expected chains plus a huge hypermarket and 7-screen cinema complex. Portugal's largest ice-skating rink is also here. Skates are available to rent. A health club offers a sauna, whirlpool bath, Scottish bath, hydro-massage, solarium and relaxation room. Prices vary according to treatment.
✉ Quinta da Alagoa, 3500-606 Viseu
☎ 232 483 900 ⏰ Daily 10am–11pm
🚗 On the EN231 just to the south of town

TERMAS ALCAFACHE
www.termasdealcafache.pt
This tranquil spa in the pine forests of the Dão valley offers medicinal treatments for joint and respiratory complaints and hydro-massage.
✉ Rua do Balneáreo, 3530-026 Alcafache
☎ 232 479 797 ⏰ Apr–end Nov
🎫 €3–€75 according to treatment 🚗 From Viseu take the EN231 south. Then take EM594 left to Alcafache, 8km (5 miles) from Viseu

TERMAS DE SÃO PEDRO DO SUL
www.termas-spsul.com
In use for medicinal purposes since before Roman times, these hot springs are the most popular in the country, receiving some 25,000 visitors a year. The healing waters here are believed by many people to relieve respiratory, rheumatic and muscular complaints.
✉ Praça Dr Antonio José de Almeida, Termas de São Pedro do Sul, 3660-692 Varzea ☎ 232 720 300 ⏰ D. Afonso Henriques Baths daily 8–1, 4–7; Rainha D. Amelia Baths Mon–Fri 7–1, 3–9, Sat–Sun 7–1, 4–8 🎫 €3–€97 depending on treatment and time of year 🚗 Head northwest out of Viseu on the N16 until you reach São Pedro Sul. There pick up the N16 towards Vouzela. Springs are on this road after approximately 2km (1.2 miles)

JANUARY
FESTA DE SÃO GONÇALINHO
The old town is lavishly decorated in honour of São Gonçalo. Special loaves of bread known as cavacas are thrown to the crowds from the top of a chapel in thanks for the safe return of the town's fishermen.
✉ Aveiro ☎ 234 423 680 (tourist office) ⏰ First or second week in Jan

FEBRUARY
CARNAVAL
Exotic Rio-style parades on carnival Saturday and Shrove Tuesday feature decorated floats, glitzy costumes, and parading soap stars are the main attractions.
✉ Figueira da Foz ☎ 233 422 610 (tourist office)

MARCH/APRIL
FEIRA DE MARÇO
Held since the mid-15th century, the fair has folk-dancing, street parties and, at weekends, lavish parades and processions.
✉ Aveiro ☎ 234 423 680 (tourist office) ⏰ Late Mar–late Apr

MAY
FESTA DE SANTA JOANA
Held in honour of Santa Joana, the beatified daughter of Afonso V who lived in an Aveiro convent for 20 years. The most important day is 12 May, with its procession in honour of the saint.
✉ Aveiro ☎ 234 423 680 (tourist office) ⏰ 12 May

QUEIMA DAS FITAS
www.queimadasfitas.org
Celebrated in Coimbra since 1899, this student festival marks the end of the academic year and, for finalists, the end of their student career. There are dances, open-air concerts and ceremonies and the colourful faculty parades. Check with tourist office for dates.
✉ Coimbra ☎ 239 488 120 (tourist office) ⏰ Mid-May

JUNE
FESTAS DA VILA
Held in honour of São João, the patron saint of Figueira, this festival has regional crafts, gastronomic delicacies and concerts. On 24 June there is a parade of folk-dancing and costumes.
✉ Figueira da Foz ☎ 233 422 610 (tourist office) ⏰ 13–24 Jun

FESTA MEDIEVAL
This one-day festa features street performances and medieval-looking stands selling traditional foods. Telephone the tourist office to check the date.
✉ Coimbra ☎ 239 488 120 (tourist office)

JULY–AUGUST
FESTA DA RIA
This important festival celebrates the canals and the moliceiros (boats) which compete to be the best decorated. Regattas are held.
✉ Aveiro ☎ 234 423 600 (tourist office) ⏰ Mid-Jul

AUGUST–SEPTEMBER
FEIRA DE SÃO MATEUS
Held yearly at the Campo de Feira de São Mateus, this festival honours St. Matthew with folk music, dancing and fireworks, and an agricultural and crafts market.
✉ Viseu ☎ 232 470 950 (tourist office) ⏰ 14 Aug–21 Sep

DECEMBER
MAGUSTO DA VELHA
The Magusto da Velha (literally 'Old Lady's Roasted Chestnuts') celebrations began after an old lady left instructions in her will that each year 50kg (110 lb) of chestnuts should be roasted and tossed from the church tower every Boxing Day.
✉ Guarda ☎ 271 205 530 (tourist office) ⏰ 26 Dec 🚗 Take the EN16 west, then north, out of Guarda. Take the road to Aldeia Viçosa signed to the left after about 15km (9 miles)

EATING

PRICES AND SYMBOLS

The restaurants are listed alphabetically. The prices given are the average for a two-course lunch (L) and a three-course dinner (D) for one person, without drinks. The wine price is for the least expensive bottle. All the restaurants listed accept credit cards unless otherwise stated.

For a key to the symbols, ▷ 2.

AVEIRO

SALPOENTE

www.salpoente.com
On the ground floor of this traditional restaurant is a display of regional costumes and salt-gathering implements; upstairs there are views of the salt flats. The menu concentrates on fish and seafood cooked in copper *cataplanas* and (when in season) the local eels.
✉ Canal de São Roque 83, 3800-256 Aveiro
☎ 234 382 674 🕐 Sun 12–2.30, Tue–Sat 12–2.30, 7.30–10.30 ✋ L €18, D €22, Wine €8

A TASCA DO CONFRADE

This restaurant has a true Beiras theme, with wine barrels on the counter, typical terracotta crockery and slightly comic regionally costumed mannequins. The wood panelling of the bar complements the panels depicting daily activities. The menu consists of *petiscos* (tapas), local dishes and a daily set menu. Worth trying are baked octopus, monkfish with rice and prawns, or roast kid.
✉ Rua dos Marnotos 34, 3800-220 Aveiro
☎ 234 386 381 🕐 Tue–Sat 12–3, 7–11, Sun 12–3 ✋ L €14, D €18, Wine €8
🚌 Next to the fish market in the Rossio

COIMBRA

ARCADAS DA CAPELA

www.quintadaslagrimas.pt
The restaurant in this famous palace-hotel successfully combines refined surroundings with excellent service and Michelin-starred menu. The international menu changes every season but may include lobster with avocado, breast of wild pigeon stuffed with meats and foie gras with coffee sauce. Finish with chocolate pudding with cinnamon ice cream.
✉ Hotel Quinta das Lágrimas, Rua António Augusto Gonçalces, Santa Clara, 3041-901 Coimbra ☎ 239 802 380 🕐 Jul–end Sep daily 7.30–10.30; rest of year daily 12.30–2.30. Call for reservation ✋ L €40, D €50, Wine €15 🚌 Cross the Santa Clara bridge, turning left then right at the sign

Above *Salpoente restaurant in Aveiro specializes in fresh fish dishes*

CAFÉ SANTA CRUZ

This is the most famous and imposing coffee house in town. Housed in a 15th- to 16th-century chapel next to the cathedral, it has a heavy, dark-wood panelled interior with old mirrors. A constant flow of students, professors and visitors passes through its Manueline doorway—there's no better place to stop for a coffee and snack.
✉ Praça 8 de Maio, 3000-300 Coimbra
☎ 239 833 617 🕐 Mon–Sat 7pm–2am
✋ Drink and snack €5 per person

A TABERNA

All the food in this small restaurant comes out of the wood-burning oven or off the charcoal grill—both of which are in full view. The home-baked bread is a treat, as is the chargrilled octopus served with spring greens and *batatas a murro* ('bashed' potatoes). The roast kid and casseroled beef are also much praised. To finish, there is *leite creme* (crème brûlée) or crêpes.
✉ Rua dos Combatentes da Grande Guerra 86, 3030-181 Coimbra ☎ 239 716 265
🕐 Tue–Sat 12.30–3, 7.30–10, Sun 12.30–3

L €20, D €25, Wine €6.50 🚌 Between the university and the football stadium, southeast of the heart of the city

ZÉ CARIOCA RESTAURANTE

Try out this Brazilian restaurant between the Praça da República and the Avenida shopping mall. They recommend fillets of grouper with a prawn sauce, *rodizio de picanha* (cuts of grilled meat) and *feijoada à Brasileira* (typical black-bean stew). Live music is played nightly.

✉ Avenida Sá de Bandeira 89, 3000-351 Coimbra ☎ 239 835 450 🕐 Daily 12–3, 7–10.30 🖐 L €14, D €18, Wine €7

FIGUEIRA DA FOZ

CAÇAROLA

Near the casino, this restaurant may not win any interior decorating prizes with its mix of nautical memorabilia and plastic plants, but the food is superb. It specializes in fish and seafood, which is simply prepared.

✉ Rua Cândido dos Reis 65, 3080-155 Figueira da Foz 📠 233 424 861 🖐 Daily 10am–5am 🖐 L €12, €D €15, Wine €5.50

GUARDA

CASAS DO BRAGAL

www.casasdobragal.com
A couple of kilometres to the east of Guarda this restaurant has won several national gastronomy awards. Start with their selection of *'coisinhas boas'* (good things), such as broad beans with home-made sausage, blood sausage with apple or rabbit in green sauce. Main courses include acclaimed oven-roasted dishes like lamb with rosemary, pork, beef, octopus, kid, cod and suckling pig.

✉ João Bragal de Baixo ☎ 271 963 396 🕐 Thu–Mon 12.30–3, 7.30–10, Wed 7.30–10 🖐 L€20, D€25, Wine €8

O BULE

Up from the cathedral square, these tea rooms decorated in warm tones, with wood panelling and framed engravings, are just right for morning coffee or afternoon tea. It's hard to resist the counter full of freshly made cakes and local delicacies, such as *pão lô de ovar* (light sponge

made with eggs). Credit cards are not accepted.

✉ Rua Dom Miguel de Alarcão 25–27, 6300-684 Guarda ☎ 271 214 392 🕐 Daily 8–8 🖐 Coffee and cake €3.50 per person

RESTAURANTE BELO HORIZONTE

For true northern cooking, come to the Belo Horizonte, on the corner down from the cathedral square, and with an austere stone façade and white linen curtains in the door. Here, friendly staff will serve you any number of regional dishes, including roasted, grilled and stewed meats and fresh fish. The restaurant's *pièce de résistance*, though, is *bucho recheado*, a huge home-made sausage big enough for four.

✉ Largo de São Vicente 2, 6300-600 Guarda ☎ 271 211 454 🕐 Sun–Fri 12.30–2.30, 7.30–10 🖐 L €14, D €18, Wine €6

SORTELHA

RESTAURANTE DOM SANCHO I

The fortified hamlet of Sortelha, perched on its massive boulders, is a fantastic place, and a meal at Dom Sancho will serve to add to the experience. The restaurant is up a flight of stone steps in one of the tiny village houses, its bare granite walls softened by low beamed ceilings and rustic cabinets. The menu is divided into 'stewed' (lamb and kid), 'grilled' (cod, lamb or pork) or 'game' (hare, boar, venison). Various regional desserts are displayed on the dresser. Credit cards are not accepted.

✉ Largo do Corro, 6320-536 Sortelha ☎ 271 388 267 🕐 Tue–Sat 10–2.30, 7–9.30, Sun 10–2.30 🖐 L €16, D €20, Wine €6 🚌 Go through the main gateway and the restaurant is on the right

VISEU

CLUBE DE CAÇADORES

As its name suggests, this restaurant is attached to a hunting/shooting club next to the practice range. Its three dining rooms each have their own open hearth, and walls are lined with fine bottles of red wine and—as suits the nature of the club—several trophies lovingly

preserved by local taxidermists. The game theme continues, with rabbit salad, hare and rice, wild duck with pine nuts and partridge with onions appearing on the menu regularly.

✉ Muna, Lordosa, 3500-000 Viseu ☎ 232 450 401 🕐 Thu–Tue 12–3, 7–10 🖐 L €15 D €20, Wine €7 🚌 Take EN2 north out of Viseu towards Lamego. After 10km (6 miles) follow signs to *'autódromo'*. Restaurant is next to the *autódromo*

O CORTIÇO

www.restaurantecortico.com
Owned by the same family for 35 years, this is the restaurant that many locals recommend for a memorable and not too expensive meal. The food is simple, hearty and, above all, delicious. Some dishes are given slightly humorous names, such as *bacalhau podre* (stale salt cod) and *coelho bêbado* (drunken rabbit), but there is no need to worry. The rest are standard regional dishes, including roast kid, fried *chouriço* (smoked sausage), cheeses and air-cured ham. Cottage cheese served with pumpkin jam makes a superb dessert.

✉ Rua Augusto Hilário 45–47, 3500-089 Viseu ☎ 232 423 853 🕐 Daily 12–3, 7–11 🖐 L €15, D €20, Wine €6 🚌 In middle of town next to the Dom Duarte statue

MURALHA DA SÉ

Down to the left of the Misericórdia church, Muralha da Sé serves great regional food. The interior is granite with terracotta floors and red drapes, which highlight the dark red window frames. In summer there is seating on the terrace. During winter months, the *menu desgustação*, the special tasting menu that showcases the best the restaurant has to offer, is the one to go for, provided you are hungry enough to do it justice. Dishes that appear on the menu regularly include fish fritters, pork chops and fried octopus.

✉ Adro da Sé 24, 3500-195 Viseu ☎ 232 437 777 🕐 Tue–Sat 12.30–2.30, 7.30–10.30, Sun 12.30–2.30 🖐 L €14, D €20, Wine €7

PRICES AND SYMBOLS

The prices are the lowest and highest for a double room for one night including breakfast, unless otherwise stated. All the hotels listed accept credit cards unless otherwise stated. Note that rates can vary widely throughout the year.

For a key to the symbols, ▷ 2.

AVEIRO
HOTEL MERCURE

www.mercure.com

This imposing 1930s townhouse was formerly known as the Hotel Paloma Blanca. Bought by the Accor Group, it has thankfully retained its charm and individuality. An attractive tiled stairwell with a stained-glass window leads to the large bedrooms, decorated in gentle tones. Some rooms overlook the goldfish pond and an attractive conservatory has a garden view.
✉ Rua Luís Gomes de Carvalho 23, 3800-211 Aveiro ☎ 234 404 400 ✋ €68–€95 excluding breakfast (€8) ⓘ 49 ⑤

HOTEL MOLICEIRO

www.hotelmoliceiro.com

In the middle of the old town, in front of the main canal, this modern hotel has elegant lodgings along

with a family atmosphere and personal service. Public areas have polished wood and marble, while large bedrooms have wrought-iron beds and views over Aveiro's old quarter. The best rooms are on the top floor in a 'penthouse' style and have small balconies. Port and *ovos moles* (traditional cakes) are served on arrival, and there's complimentary tea and biscuits.
✉ Rua Barbosa de Magalhães 15–17, 3800-154 Aveiro ☎ 234 377 400 ✋ €98–€115 ⓘ 49 ⑤

BELMONTE
POUSADA DO CONVENTO DE BELMONTE

www.pousadas.pt

South of Belmonte, this *pousada*, one of Portugal's most attractive hotels, was built on the ruins of a 13th-century Franciscan monastery. The granite chapel and sacristy are now home to a snug, rustic-style bar and lounge, with antiques. The individually designed bedrooms have panoramic views of the Zêzere valley and the Serra de Estrela, and the restaurant serves local recipes.
✉ Convento de Belmonte, 6250-073 ☎ 275 910 300 ✋ €170–€250 ⓘ 23 rooms, 1 suite ⑤ ⛰ Outdoor

Above *Palace Hotel do Bussaco has fabulous neo-Manueline architecture*

BUÇACO
PALACE HOTEL DO BUSSACO

www.almeidahotels.com

This outstanding building, created as a hunting lodge for the Portuguese royal family, shows neo-Manueline architect Manini at his best. Set in protected forest, it became a hotel in 1917 after the fall of the monarchy. Its profusion of carved stone, wood panelling, painted tiles and priceless furnishings is overwhelming. The restaurant serves Portuguese-French cuisine and has a fine wine list.
✉ Mata do Buçaco, 3050-261 Luso ☎ 231 937 970 ✋ €90–€205 ⓘ 60 rooms, 4 suites

COIMBRA
HOTEL ASTÓRIA

www.almeidahotels.com

The wedge-shaped Astória, with its distinctive cupola, has provided fine service since 1926. Restored in 1990, it has kept its original charm. The period elevator—oldest in the city—takes guests from the marble-and-wood lobby to art deco bedrooms. The dining room has wooden floors and panelling.

✉ Avenida Emídio Navarro 21, 3000-150 Coimbra ☎ 239 853 020 ✋ €90–€110 🛏 60 rooms, 2 suites ♿

HOTEL QUINTA DAS LÁGRIMAS
www.quintadaslagrimas.pt
Across the river from the heart of the town, this wonderful 17th-century palace with its double-staired entrance is now a luxury hotel. The delicately hand-painted breakfast rooms and impressive library are particularly noteworthy; the latter opens out onto the gardens packed with rare plants. The new wing houses the cheaper rooms and a spa but does (along with surrounding high-rises) detract somewhat from the otherwise romantic atmosphere.
✉ Rua António Augusto Gonçalves, Santa Clara, 3041-901 Coimbra ☎ 239 802 380 ✋ €153–€219 🛏 48 rooms, 5 suites (non-smoking available) ♿ 🏊 Outdoor and indoor 🍴 🅿 Cross the Santa Clara bridge, turn left, then turn right at the sign

PENSÃO LAR BELO
For an inexpensive and central choice, try Lar Belo, on the west side of the old town of Coimbra. Rooms have plain, somewhat dated furniture, but they are clean and all have private facilities. The front rooms have views of the river Mondego and are double-glazed. Bedrooms are on the first to third floors; there's no elevator. Credit cards are not accepted.
✉ Largo da Portagem 33, 3000-337 Coimbra ☎ 239 829 092 ✋ €35–€45 excluding breakfast (€2.50) 🛏 17

FIGUEIRA DA FOZ
CASA DA AZENHA VELHA
With its outdoor pool, tennis courts, horses and bicycles, this is a great place for children. The bedrooms are in beautiful outbuildings, with breakfast served in the main house. There is a comfortable lounge plus a good restaurant. Credit cards are not accepted.
✉ Turismo Rural, Caceira de Cima, 3080-390 Alhadas ☎ 233 425 041 ✋ €75–€100 🛏 6 rooms, 1 suite ♿ 🏊 Outdoor 🅿 From Coimbra, take N111 to Figueira

da Foz. Shortly before Figueira turn towards Caceira, then immediately left following signs 'Turismo Rural'. After 2km (1.25 miles) turn right for 500m (550 yards); the house is on the left

GUARDA
CASAS DO CÔRO
www.assec.pt/casa-do-coro
Fine fabrics, hand-embroidered sheets, pastels and rich hues sit among a fusion of classic and contemporary furniture to provide the guest with every luxury in these restored cottages. After a breakfast of freshly baked bread, cakes, apple pie and home-made jams, make the most of one of the walking or bicycle trails before relaxing in the whirlpool bath, sauna or heated outdoor pool.
✉ Marialva Mêda, 6430-081 Guarda ☎ 271 590 003 ✋ €135–€700 (many different combinations available—check website for details) 🛏 5 rooms, 1 suite, 6 cottages with 2–4 bedrooms ♿ 🏊 Outdoor 🅿 North out of Guarda on the N102, after 20km (12 miles) turn off left at Marialva and follow signs

QUINTA DA PONTE
www.quintadaponte.com
In the main house (dating from the 18th century) are two bedrooms plus an attractive salon with a fine Italianate painted ceiling. Five apartments are housed in a modern building overlooking the pool. All have a lounge, log fire, small kitchen, double room and bathroom. Tennis is available on site. It is closed from October to Easter.
✉ Faia, 6300-095 Guarda ☎ 271 010 005 ✋ Rooms €90, apartments €100 🛏 2 rooms, 5 apartments ♿ 🏊 Outdoor 🅿 Leave IP5 at exit 26. Join EN16 for Porto da Carne. The house is signed 'Turismo de Habitação' to the right

RESIDENCIAL SANTOS
www.residencialsantos.com
This residencial is excellent value and well worth a visit just for its architecture. The modern multilevelled interior has been expertly constructed around medieval features and granite

boulders. Rooms are simple, with matching fabrics; breakfast is served in a bright and cheerful room on the top floor.
✉ Rua Tenente Valdim 14, 6300-764 Guarda ☎ 271 205 400 ✋ €35–€45 🛏 27 rooms, 1 suite ♿ Some rooms

MONSANTO
DIVINO MONSANTO
www.divinomonsanto.pt
In what has been called the 'most Portuguese village in Portugal', this estalagem has a modern exterior. For a view over the countryside, ask for the corner room upstairs. The restaurant serves a selection of regional dishes.
✉ Rua da Capela 3, 6060-091 Monsanto ☎ 277 314 471 ✋ €70–€80 🛏 10 ♿

VISEU
ALBERGARIA JOSÉ ALBERTO
Set in an elegant building, the inside of this guesthouse has been completely remodelled with clean, minimalist lines and furnished with modern pieces. Some of the rooms have the additional benefit of their own balcony and all are comfortable and well equipped with private bathrooms. Just 500m (550 yards) from the Rossio (main square) and with its own parking this makes an ideal spot to stop off for the night if touring the area.
✉ Rua Cândido dos Reis 42–48, 3510-056 Viseu ☎ 232 467 310 ✋ €50 🛏 30 rooms, 2 suites ♿

HOTEL AVENIDA
www.hotelavenida.com.pt
Located just off the Rossio (main square), this very friendly, family-run hotel has employed the courageous use of rich, bright tones, so often lacking in Portuguese interior design. The first-floor lounge is a welcoming mix of deep green walls, comfortable sofas and an open fire in winter, while the stylish bedrooms are decorated in warmer tones. This hotel is extremely good value for money.
✉ Avenida Alberto Sampaio 1, 3500-030 Viseu ☎ 232 423 432 ✋ €40–€50 🛏 29 rooms, 2 suites ♿

ESTREMADURA
AND THE RIBATEJO

To the north of Lisbon, this region is home to Portugal's most famous religious monuments. The churches of Batalha and Alcobaça exhibit magnificently ornate stone work, statuary, flying buttresses and vaulted Gothic interiors and some fine Manueline details; the shrine of Fátima inspires tourist and pilgrim alike thanks to its vast esplanade and neoclassical Basilica; and the 12th-century Romanesque Convento de Cristo at Tomar, home to the Order of the Knights Templar, is most impressive thanks to decorative additions made to the exterior, considered to be one of the finest examples of Manueline ornamentation in the country.

The regions' towns are relatively small and provincial, often sidestepped by visitors, and as such offer a privileged insight into true Portuguese life. Abrantes, Leiria and Ourém all retain interesting historic centres, while Santarém is famous for its bulls and gastronomy festival. Epicureans will also not want to miss the chocolate festival held yearly in the picturesque, hilltop village of Óbidos; the fresh fish and seafood straight off the boat at Ericiera, Peniche or Nazaré; or a glass of *ginginha* cherry liqueur.

There are several less publicized attractions in the area. Don't miss a visit to the Serra de Aire hills, riddled with cavernous grottoes, several of which have been illuminated to created maximum impact; or Almourol which stands guard like a fairytale castle on an island in the middle of the Tagus; or a boat trip to the reserve-island of Berlenga, fabulous for its birds and scuba-diving.

For the shopper there are ceramics bargains to be had at factory outlets in Caldas da Rainha and Alcobaça and some exceptional glassware in Marinha Grande.

ABRANTES

www.cm-abrantes.pt

Abrantes, set high on a hill above the Tejo, is historically renowned for its role as a defensive outpost. Romans and Moors established strongholds here, though today's castle dates from the early 14th century. It later fell into disrepair and was partly ruined by the time it was taken by the French in 1807 during the Peninsular War. General Wellesley, later to be the Duke of Wellington, then recaptured it and made it his headquarters for a brief period in 1809. Climb up through the narrow, flower-hung streets to the castle, where there are great views along the river and south over a landscape planted with olives and dotted with white villages. Inside the fortress you can visit the Igreja de Santa Maria, now the town's archaeological museum. Highlights of the small collection are some rare 16th-century Hispano-Moorish *azulejos* (tiles) and a beautiful 15th-century statue of the Virgin and Child. The two large white churches visible from the battlements are the Igreja da Misericórdia and the Igreja de São João Baptista, both remodelled in the 16th century.

✚ 330 C8 🏠 Largo 1º de Maio, 2200-320 Abrantes ☎ 241 362 555 🚉 Abrantes

ALCOBAÇA

> 212–213.

BATALHA

> 214–216.

CALDAS DA RAINHA

www.rt-oeste.pt

Caldas da Rainha is a bustling spa and market town, a good stopping-off point en route to Alcobaça (> 212–213). It got its name, meaning 'Queen's Hot Springs', in 1484, when Queen Leonor, the wife of João II, was intrigued by the sight of peasants bathing in sulphurous-smelling waters by the side of the road. The locals explained that the waters were good for treating rheumatism and Leonor decided to try them for herself. She funded a hospital here, and for the next four centuries Caldas was popular as a bathing retreat with royalty and the nobility. Its zenith came in the 19th century, but the spa still continues to attract visitors. Caldas is also noted for its ceramics, some of the quirkiest in the country, in the shape of mythical beasts and peculiar vegetation. You can see examples of these in the Museu de Cerâmica (tel 262 840 280; Tue–Sun 10–12.30, 2–5; €2). Take time, too, to enjoy the lovely town park and the market, held daily in the Praça da República.

✚ 330 A8 🏠 Rua Engº Duarte Pacheco, 2500-110 Caldas da Rainha ☎ 262 839 700 🚉 Caldas da Rainha

CASTELO DE ALMOUROL

www.castelodealmourol.com

The fairy-tale castle of Almourol crowns the slopes of an island in the middle of the Tejo. This commanding site was probably fortified in pre-Roman times and may have been used by the Moors—documents show that a castle stood here as early as 1129. In 1171 Gualdin Pais, Master of the Templars from Tomar (> 118), built the existing castle, a copy-book design that was new to Portugal, with double perimeter walls, a tall square keep—85 steps take you to the top—and nine small towers around the walls. The castle was never tested during conflict, but it was the setting for many romantic tales, such as Francesco de Morais' *Palmeirim de Inglaterra* (Palmeirim of England), a story crammed with fights and duels around the castle. You reach the castle by ferry, a romantic approach to what is an enchanting building.

✚ 330 C8 🏠 Centro Cultural Vila Nova da Barquinha, Castelo de Almourol ☎ 249 720 358 🕐 May–end Sep daily 10–7; Oct–end Apr daily 10–5 ✋ Entrance: free. 🚢 From landing stage on north bank of river €1.25; larger boat from village of Tancos €2

ERICEIRA

www.ericeira.net

North along the coast from Lisbon, perched on a cliff facing the Atlantic, is the resort town and fishing port of Ericeira. To see the fishing boats setting off or returning to be hauled up the beach, head for the Largo das Ribas, a lively square that overlooks the fishermen's beach, sheltered by a long jetty and the surrounding cliffs. From here, walk through the narrow cobbled alleys, lined with white houses, to the main town square, Praça da República, for the short stroll to the Igreja Matriz, filled with blue-tiled decoration.

Ericeira has great fish restaurants and two bathing beaches to the north and south of the fishing beach. To escape the weekend crowds, walk north along the coast to Praia do São Sebastião, a stretch of unspoilt sand with crashing surf. The beach of Ribeira D'Ilhas is known as one of Europe's best surf spots.

✚ 330 A9 🏠 Rua Dr. Eduardo Burnay 46, 2655-370 Ericeira ☎ 261 863 122

Opposite The Castelo de Almourol, with its nine towers, was built in 1171
Below Waves pound the rocks below the fishing port of Ericeira

ALCOBAÇA

INFORMATION

www.ippar.pt

➕ 330 B8 ℹ️ Praça 25 de Abril, 2460-018 Alcobaça ☎ 262 582 377

✉️ Mosteiro de Alcobaça, 2460-018 Alcobaça ☎ 262 505 120 🕐 Apr–end Sep daily 9–7; Oct–end Mar daily 9–5 ✋ Entrance to church: free. Monastery complex: adult €4.50, under-14s free; Sun 9–2 free 📖 Good English-language pamphlet €1; also available in Portuguese, French, Spanish and German 🏛️ Small shop selling postcards, books and expensive museum souvenirs but very little relevant to Alcobaça itself

Above *Monks performed their ablutions in the hexagonal 14th-century lavabo in the monastery of Alcobaça*

INTRODUCTION

It is difficult to park near the monastery; instead, park on the town's outskirts and stroll through the streets to reach the church. Walking to the monastery will give you an idea of the sheer scale of the building; pause in the square outside to marvel at the 18th-century façade, flanked by its two wings. Entry to the cloisters and monastic buildings is through a door just inside the church and to the left. Take in the church, then explore the rest of the monastery. Allow one to two hours for a visit. Climb the hill overlooking the town for fine views of the monastery complex. Alcobaça makes a good overnight stop, with the bonus of seeing the church ahead of the day trippers.

The monastery owes its existence to Afonso Henriques, first king of Portugal, who is said to have vowed that he would found a monastery here if he captured Santarém from the Moors. Building started in 1178, the church was completed in 1253 and, by the end of the century, Alcobaça was the richest and most powerful monastery in Portugal. It continued to thrive, and soon more than 900 monks were in residence, celebrating Mass and chanting their prayers around the clock.

By the 18th century, however, Alcobaça was more famed for the profligacy of its monks' lifestyle than for its spirituality, though the monastery's hospitality and charity remained bywords, with visitors being plied with the best of food and wine. The place was also famous for its superb library and for the Royal

Pantheon, the burial place of Portugal's kings and queens. In 1834, Portugal abolished the religious orders, the monks left and Alcobaça's collections were broken up to go into museums in Portugal or sold. Alcobaça was designated a World Heritage Site in 1985.

WHAT TO SEE

THE CHURCH

Filled with light, the lofty interior of the church is a supreme example of the uncluttered style of pure Gothic architecture, a contrast to the fussiness of the façade, which was reworked in the baroque style. The church is divided into a central nave with two side aisles, which are separated by solid pillars supporting magnificent vaulting. The aisles are nearly as long as they are high, giving the church a unique perspective. The crossing transept is backed by the high altar with a superb ambulatory behind. It contains the 14th-century tombs of Dom Pedro and Dona Inês de Castro, the ill-fated protagonists of one of the most tragic of all medieval love stories.

Inês was the daughter of a Galician nobleman and thus considered politically unsuitable to be the wife of Dom Pedro, the eldest son of Afonso IV and so heir to the Portuguese throne. When Pedro's first wife died, he married Inês in secret at remote Bragança, and installed her at Coimbra, provoking his father to such a rage that he had her murdered in 1355. When Afonso died two years later, Pedro immediately had the assassins killed and in 1361 ordered Inês' exhumation. Her corpse was crowned before being buried at Alcobaça. Pedro is buried opposite her, the tombs, on his orders, lying foot to foot, so that the two can rise and face each other on Judgement Day.

Inês, supported by six angels, reclines upon her tomb, which is carved with a plethora of biblical scenes, animals, heraldic symbols and ornate decoration. At the foot, a dragon, representing Hell, consumes the damned, her murderers among them. Pedro's equally fine sepulchre has a wheel of fortune at the head and scenes from his life and death. Touchingly, the tombs are inscribed with the epitaph 'Até ao Fim do Mundo' ('To the End of the World').

THE ABBEY BUILDINGS

You enter the monastic buildings through the Sala dos Reis (Royal Hall), built in the 18th century, and decorated with statues of Portuguese kings carved by the monks and blue *azulejos* (tiles) telling the story of the monastery's foundation. This opens into the Claustro do Silêncio (Cloister of Silence), commissioned by Dom Dinis in the 14th century. The traceried windows contrast with the plain arches of the upper storey, added 299 years later. The small hexagonal building jutting out on the east side of the cloister was the *lavatorium* for pre-meal handwashing, positioned, as was customary, opposite the entrance to the refectory, a vaulted hall with a simple reader's lectern, from where the monks were entertained with readings during mealtimes. Off here is the large kitchen, whose size gives a clue as to why the monastery had a reputation for good living. The huge room has a vast chimney and a stream running through. This not only provided water for the cooks, but also delivered fish straight to the kitchen from the ponds outside. Back in the cloister, take the narrow stairs up to the left to a monks' dormitory. The one you see, another grandiose space 60m (195ft) long, is one of the many original sleeping areas. The tour finishes in the chapterhouse.

GINGINHA

Apart from the monastery, Alcobaça is best known for *ginginha*, a cherry liqueur, made from locally grown fruit—you can sample and buy it at many places in town. The Museu da Junta Nacional do Vinho, outside town on the Leiria road, tells you more about how it is made. Look, too, for the attractive blue pottery that is made in and around Alcobaça.

TIP
» For a superb contrast, combine Alcobaça with a visit to Batalha, 20km (12.5 miles) to the north (▷ 214–216).

Below *The monastic buildings of Alcobaça are some of the finest examples of Gothic architecture*

BATALHA

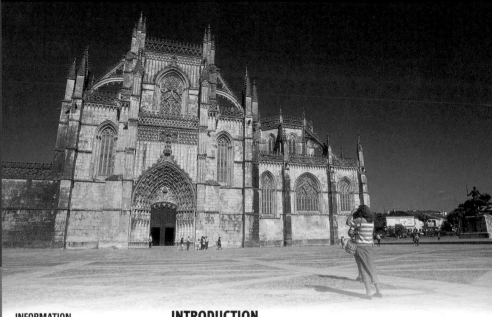

INFORMATION

www.ippar.pt

⊞ 328 B7 ✉ Mosteiro de Santa Maria da Vitória, 2440-109 Batalha ☎ 244 765 497 🕓 Apr–end Sep daily 9–6; rest of year daily 9–5 🖐 Church: free. Monastery complex: adult €5, under-14s free; Sun 9–2 free 📖 Good English-language pamphlet €1.50; also available in Portuguese, French, Spanish and German 🎫 Small shop selling postcards, books and expensive museum souvenirs

INTRODUCTION

Apart from the abbey itself, there is little to see at Batalha, so concentrate on this magnificent building. If driving, you should be able to park without difficulty within easy walking distance. Start your visit by tackling the church and the Capela do Fundador (Founder's Chapel), before moving into the cloisters, chapterhouse and monastic buildings. To visit the Capelas Imperfeitas (Unfinished Chapels), you have to exit the main complex and walk round to the east end of the church.

In 1383, the death of Dom Fernando, the last ruler of the House of Burgundy, marked the start of a period of feverish political intrigue as rivals tried to secure the throne. Fernando's widow, strongly pro-Spanish, betrothed her daughter to Juan I of Castile, the dead king's nephew, but João, Grand Master of the Order of Avis, also laid claim to the throne.

On 13 August 1385, the armies of the two pretenders clashed at Aljubarrota south of Batalha. The odds were firmly stacked against João, who, knowing that defeat would mean Spanish domination of Portugal, vowed to the Virgin Mary that he would build her a great church if she brought him victory. She seemingly heard his prayers, because the Spanish were defeated and Portuguese independence was consequently secured for almost 200 years.

In 1386 work started on the building of Batalha under the Portuguese architect Afonso Domingues; it continued from 1402 to 1438 under a Catalonian, Huguet. It was he who designed the Capela do Fundador and started work on the Capelas Imperfeitas. Afonso V had the cloisters built and there was further work done on the capelas. They were never completed, however, as Batalha was abandoned by João III for his new Mosteiro dos Jerónimos in Lisbon (▷ 74).

Batalha's monastery, named for Our Lady of Victories, quickly fell into disrepair following its dissolution in 1834. In 1840 restoration began, but pollution has taken its toll on the soft limestone used to build the monastery, which is also threatened by the vibration caused by the constant heavy traffic on the nearby N1. Batalha was named a World Heritage Site in 1983.

Above *The entrance to the Capela do Fundador, one of the glories of the great abbey at Batalha*

WHAT TO SEE

THE CHURCH

The exterior of this soft yellow abbey church is a profusion of pinnacles, flying buttresses, spires, parapets and towers, the ultimate expression of a peculiarly ornate form of French Gothic. Most of it was built between 1388 and 1434, with later 15th- and early 16th-century additions in the Portuguese Manueline style. The interior is plain, its strong vertical lines soaring up from solid pilasters to accentuate the vaulting in a manner reminiscent of British cathedrals of the time, such as York and Winchester. The chancel is lit by stained-glass windows, used here for the first time in Portugal and designed and installed by craftsmen from Flanders and Germany.

THE CAPELA DO FUNDADOR

From the right-hand aisle you enter the Capela do Fundador, a square chamber surmounted by an octagonal lantern topped by a cupola. Beneath the lantern are the tombs of Dom João I and Philippa of Lancaster; their four younger sons (the eldest, Duarte, is interred in the sanctuary) are buried in recessed and ornamented bays along the south and west walls. Second from the right is the canopied tomb of Prince Henry the Navigator, the driving force behind the development of Portuguese navigational techniques and a key player during the great age of discoveries. The beginning of this momentous era coincided with the building of Batalha, and consequently the abbey reflects Portugal's growing national self-confidence and wealth.

THE CLAUSTRO REAL AND THE SALA DO CAPÍTULO

The Claustro Real (Royal Cloister) was originally a simple Gothic construction, but, during the reigns of Afonso V and Manuel, it was completely revamped with a triumphantly successful series of Manueline flourishes, notably the stone tracery added to the original plain windows. These grilles are considered a high point of Manueline decoration. They are adorned with distinctive crosses, symbols of the Order of Christ, and armillary spheres, similar to those at Tomar (▷ 220–222), while the columns are decorated with elaborate ropework, pearls and shells.

TIPS

» Avoid visiting on 12–13 May and 12–13 October, the most important pilgrimage days in nearby Fátima, when thousands of pilgrims also make the day trip to Batalha.
» Accommodation is limited, so it is best to visit Batalha as a day trip—Leiria, Fátima and Nazaré are within easy distance, or it's feasible to travel from Lisbon.
» Combine a visit to Batalha with a trip to contrasting Alcobaça, 20km (12.5 miles) to the south (▷ 212–213).

Left *Light filters through the stained-glass windows into Capela do Fundador*
Below *Elaborate exterior detail adds to the grandeur*

AN OLD ALLIANCE

A contingent of English longbowmen fought at the battle of Aljubarrota in 1385, and English architects and builders were involved in the construction of Batalha. The latter had accompanied Philippa of Lancaster to Portugal for her marriage to João in 1386, a union that was part of the terms of the Treaty of Windsor, 'an inviolable, solid, perpetual and true league of friendship' between the two countries. It's a friendship that's continued ever since, strengthened by Charles II's marriage to Catherine of Bragança in 1661 and then by the Methuen Treaty of 1703.

At 600 years plus, the alliance is the longest-standing in Europe. It enabled the British to establish military bases in the Azores during World War II, though Portugal was officially neutral. The Portuguese offered the British facilities in the Azores again during the 1982 Falklands War.

Below *The Capela do Fundador was the first building in Portugal to have stained-glass windows*

THE CHAPTERHOUSE

Opening off the east side of the cloister is the chapterhouse, an early 15th-century innovative vaulted structure, whose unsupported ceiling spans 20m (65ft) or more. It was a radical design when it was built, and there were great fears that the roof would collapse. Construction was considered so dangerous that only criminals condemned to death worked on it, and the architect slept there for a night to allay fears after the scaffolding came down. Today, it's a national shrine containing Portugal's Tomb of the Unknown Soldiers (there are two of them), guarded day and night by the Portuguese army. There is a museum in memory of Portuguese soldiers who have died in war, in the refectory on the other side of the cloister.

THE CAPELAS IMPERFEITAS

At the east end of the church are the Capelas Imperfeitas (Unfinished Chapels). Commissioned in 1437 by Dom Duarte, eldest son of João and Philippa, as a royal mausoleum, they were totally remodelled by Dom Manuel's architects. This is Manueline at its most flamboyant, a riot of stone decoration. The doorway, around 15m (50ft) high, which gave access to the east end of the church, is a superb example of the style, its arches and pillars heavily carved with strange vegetation and animals. The tombs of Dom Duarte and his queen, Leonor of Aragon, lie side by side in one of the seven hexagonal chapels that surround the central octagonal space.

MORE TO SEE

CLAUSTRO DE DOM AFONSO V

These fine and restrained Gothic cloisters, built during the reign of Afonso V, contrast with the flamboyance of the Claustro Real.

LAVABO

This is a beautiful structure in the northwest corner of the Claustro Real, opposite the refectory, which was used by the monks for ablutions before their meals. The focal point of the washroom is a superbly ornate three-tiered fountain and the exterior arches are decorated with exquisite examples of Manueline ropework.

FÁTIMA

On 13 May 1917, three peasant children, Francisco, Jacinta and Lúcia, were watching over their parents' sheep near Fátima when they saw a flash of lightning and 'a lady brighter than the sun' standing in the branches of an oak tree. She asked them to return on the same day monthly for six months, at the end of which she would tell them who she was and what she wanted. Although only the children could see the Virgin, and Lúcia was the only one who could hear her speak, the crowds swelled. By that October more than 70,000 were present.

The Virgin, so it is said, revealed three secrets to Lúcia. The first was a prophesy of peace, the second predicted the coming of Communism in Russia and the third foretold the 1981 assassination attempt on Pope John Paul II. Over the following years the cult grew, and the Basílica was completed in 1953. Francisco and Jacinta died shortly after the last apparition; Lúcia died in 2005. Today, the shrine attracts thousands of pilgrims, the crowds thickest and the atmosphere most charged on the 12th and 13th of every month.

THE ESPLANADE AND BASÍLICA

The Esplanade can hold up to a million people. It measures 540m by 160m (1,772ft by 525ft), sweeping down a slope and up to the Basílica at the far end. Twice the size of St. Peter's Square in Rome, the proportions are such that you only grasp its size once you realize how long it takes to walk from one end to the other. The neoclassical Basílica, with its open altar in front and a vast tower, has a semi-circular peristyle curving round from each side. It can accommodate more than 300,000 people. Francisco, Jacinta and Lúcia are buried inside.

CAPELA DAS APARIÇÕES

The Capela das Aparições (Chapel of the Apparitions) is far more compact in comparison to the surrounding expanses. It is built on the spot where the Virgin is said to have appeared, a simple, clean-cut modern structure, with plain benches occupied by devoted pilgrims. A constant stream of them wait to light candles before the statue of Our Lady of Fátima. Nearby stands an oak; it replaces the original tree, which was destroyed by early pilgrims in search of souvenirs.

INFORMATION

www.santuario-fatima.pt
www.rt-leiriafatima.pt
🗺 328 R7 🛈 Avenida Dom José Correia da Silva, 2495-402 Fátima
☎ 249 531 139

TIPS

» To appreciate Fátima fully, visit it when the shrine is packed with thousands of fervent devotees. There are celebrations on the 13th of every month, but the biggest are on 13 May and 13 October.
» From May to October there's a candlelit procession every evening at dusk.

Above *Religious souvenirs are on sale everywhere in Fátima*

LEIRIA

www.rt-leiriafatima.pt

Leiria, at the confluence of the rivers Liz and Lena, is an inland town with easy access to the beautiful Pinhal de Leiria, an extensive pine forest that stands high on the cliffs above some of Estremadura's most beautiful and unspoilt beaches. Penetrate the unprepossessing outskirts to the graceful old town, where you will find fine squares and cobbled streets dotted with gardens. Leiria's main attraction is its Castelo (tel 244 813 982; Apr–end Sep Tue–Sun 10–6, rest of year Tue–Sun 9.30–5.30; castle €1.18, castle and museum €2.37), which occupies a commanding site that made it strategically important. It was captured from the Moors by Afonso Henriques in 1135, and rebuilt during the 14th and 15th centuries.

Within the walls you will find the keep and a royal palace built by Dom Dinis for Queen Isabel, his beloved queen for whom he also built the castle of Óbidos. It is fronted by a superb loggia overlooking the town. Lower down from here, head for the spacious Praça Rodrigues Lobo, the heart of the old town, lined with arcaded buildings, from which a tangle of pretty streets radiates.

Leiria is particularly noted for its lively festivals and wide range of folk arts. Local wares include bright pottery and glass, woven textiles and willow baskets.

✚ 328 B7 ℹ Jardim Luís de Camões, 2401-801 Leiria ☎ 244 848 770 🚉 Leiria

NAZARÉ

www.rt-leiriafatima.pt

Despite the huge influx of summer visitors, Nazaré just about manages to hang on to its original role as a picturesque fishing village—there's still a harbour, and you will see boats drawn up on the beach and women stalking regally along with trays of fish on their heads. But summer brings big crowds, here for the superb beaches and buzzing restaurants serving fish.

The main town beach—the safest place to swim on this dangerous coast—is backed by a wide esplanade. This opens up into a couple of laid-back squares, lined with bars and scattered with outdoor cafés. For a change of scene take the funicular (Jul–end Aug daily 7am–2am; rest of year 7am–midnight; may be closed in Mar for maintenance; 90¢) up to the Sítio headland, 110m (360ft) above the town. This was the site of the original settlement, out of the reach of marauding pirates, and it's home to the church of Nossa Senhora da Nazaré, a 17th-century building decorated with azulejos (tiles). They commemorate the legend of Dom Fuas Roupinho, a long-ago knight who was saved from tumbling over the cliff in pursuit of a deer in the mist by a vision of the Virgin Mary warning him of the danger.

✚ 328 B7 ℹ Avenida da República, 2450 Nazaré ☎ 262 561 194

ÓBIDOS

www.cm-obidos.pt; www.rt-oeste.pt

Postcard-pretty Óbidos attracts coachloads of visitors every day, so you may want to arrive early, visit out of season or spend the night to best appreciate it. The town, surrounded by its medieval walls, stood on the edge of the sea until the 15th century, while Peniche (▷ 219), 23km (14 miles) to the west and now on the coast, was an island. From 1282 the town was the traditional wedding gift of the kings of Portugal to their wives; the first donor, Dom Dinis, built the massive castle here, now one of Portugal's most celebrated pousadas.

A long central street cuts through the town, from where steep alleyways, flights of steps and tiny cobbled squares open up, all dripping with flowers and lined with brilliantly white-washed buildings. It is a pleasure to explore the network of streets and squares, and you can also walk right around the town's perimeter walls, admiring the surrounding countryside and catching glimpses of life behind the tourist façade as you go—aim to stay until dusk, when there is sensitive floodlighting.

The Igreja de Santa Maria, on a small praça (square) shaded by trees, was where the ten-year-old Afonso V married his eight-year-old cousin, Isabel, in 1444. Inside, the Renaissance church is lined with 17th-century blue azulejos (tiles).

✚ 330 A8 ℹ Parque de Estacionamento da Porta da Vila, 2510-089 Óbidos ☎ 262 959 231 🚉 Óbidos

Below *Medieval walls straddling the hillside surround pretty Óbidos*

Above *The castle at Ourém was destroyed by Napoleonic troops but is now restored*

OURÉM

If you are on the way from Tomar
(▷ 220–222) to Fátima (▷ 217),
Ourém makes a pleasant place to
pause and stretch your legs. Ignore
the workaday and modern section
of the town, the Vila Nova, and head
up the hill to the fortified medieval
area, home to a ruined castle,
collegiate church and an attractive
village. The castle courtyard still
retains the old Moorish cisterns
dating from the ninth century AD,
but Ourém's heyday was in the 15th
century, when Dom Afonso, son of
the Duke of Bragança, converted the
existing castle into a palace and built
several grand monuments—Afonso
is buried in the crypt of the church.
Destroyed by Napoleon's troops
during the Peninsular War, the castle
has now been restored, with fine
views west to Fátima and north to
Pinhel (▷ 189).

✚ 328 B7 🛈 Rua Beato Simão Lopes,
Nª Sª das Misericórdias, Castelo de Ourém,
2490-473 Ourém ☎ 249 544 654

PALMELA

www.costa-azul.rts.pt

In Portuguese minds the pretty
town of Palmela is associated with
one thing—wine. By the middle of
the 18th century wine was being
produced here on a large scale, and
the town's September grape festival
is the big date in the local calendar.
The red and white wines from the
area are noted for their distinctive
taste and full body, the Periquita
grape variety producing a deep

red and the Fernão Pires a smooth
white. *Adegas* (wine cellars) around
the town run tours and tastings.

The town stands on a spur of
the Arrábida hills, its huge castle
dominating the horizon. After several
attempts, it was finally taken from
the Moors in 1196 and became a
stronghold of the Knights of St.
James, a military order involved
in the reconquest. The castle is a
mixture of styles and eras, dating
from the 14th to 18th centuries, its
main attraction being the *pousada*
in the conventual buildings and the
superb panoramic view from the top
of the keep—worth every one of the
64 steps. Near the castle, too, is the
church of São Tiago (St. James), its
clean Romanesque and Gothic lines
accentuated by the *azulejos* (tiles) on
the walls. There are more tiles in the
church of São Pedro below.

✚ 330 B10 🛈 Castelo de Palmela, 2950-
221 Palmela ☎ 212 332 122

PARQUE NATURAL DAS SERRAS DE AIRE E CANDEEIROS

The undulating upland limestone
country between Fátima and
Batalha has been designated a
natural park to preserve both the
landscape and way of life. It's a
good mix of rugged hills and high
farmland, with some well-marked
hiking trails and interesting and
beautiful flora in spring and early
summer. Most visitors head here
to visit the network of spectacular
underground caves in the chalk of
these limestone hills, most of which

were discovered in the second half
of the 20th century.

The caves are open to the public
and the stalactites and stalagmites
are floodlit. The best-known and
most easily accessed cave is the
Grutas de Mira de Aire (tel 244 440
322; www.grutasmiradaire.com;
Jul–end Aug daily 9.30–7.30; Jun,
Sep daily 9.30–7; Apr–end May daily
9.30–6; Oct–end Mar daily 9.30–5.30
€5), a labyrinthine system crammed
with dramatically lit rock formations
and an underground lake. There are
more caves at Santo António, São
Mamede, Alvados and Moeda.

✚ 330 B8

PENICHE

Until the 15th century, Peniche was
an island, but the sands slowly
seeped in and it's now joined to
the mainland by a narrow isthmus
fringed by shelving beaches. It's an
active fishing port where traditional
boat building still goes on, and you
can stroll along the waterfront to get
a glimpse of the boatyards at work.
The old town, huddled inside its
walls, is dominated by the vast 16th-
century *fortaleza*, one of Portugal's
most notorious political jails under
the Salazar regime. It is now a
small museum.

Drive north along the coast and
you will reach Cabo Carvoeiro, a
peninsula with some extraordinary
flat laminated rock formations.
From here, there are views across
the sea to the Ilha Berlenga, the
main island of a tiny archipelago
that's now a nature reserve. Its
coastline, indented with inlets and
grottoes, is one of the best places
for scuba diving in Portugal. If you
are interested in birds, this is a great
place to see cormorants, puffins
and gulls, or you can take a boat trip
to explore the best of the island's
coastline (boats run 15 May–15
Sep; crossing time is about an hour.
(Contact Viamar, tel 262 785 646 for
reservations; www.viamar-berlenga.
com; €18 round trip). Visitors are
limited to 300 daily.

✚ 330 A8 🛈 Rua Alexandre Herculano,
2520-273 Peniche ☎ 262 789 571

TOMAR

INFORMATION
www.rtt.ipt.pt

✚ 328 C7 ℹ Avenida Dr. Cândido
Madureira, 2300-351 Tomar; Rua Serpa
Pinto 1, 2300-592 Tomar ☎ 249 329 000
🚉 Tomar

INTRODUCTION

Most of what's worth seeing lies on the west bank of the river, an attractive grid of streets, some running parallel with the river and others running down to it. Above looms the spectacular Convento de Cristo on a hill that provides excellent views of the town and its surroundings. If time is short, concentrate your energies here—you should allow at least an hour, and more likely two, to explore the church and the castle. You could then make your way downhill past the church of Nossa Senhora da Conceição to the Praça da República, a good point to start a tour round the town. Don't miss taking a stroll along the river, taking in the Parque do Mouchão, Tomar's town park on a river island.

The Order of the Knights Templar, forerunners of the Order of Christ, was founded in Jerusalem shortly after the creation of the Crusader Latin Kingdom of Jerusalem in 1118. The knights' remit was to guard the holy places, and their beliefs were shrouded in mystery and secrecy—some said they had searched for and found the Ark of the Covenant and the Holy Grail, others that they had discovered how to turn base metals into gold through the use of the legendary philosopher's stone. Whatever the truth, the Order was formally established in 1128, creating an independent organization of knight-monks, answerable only to the popes. The Templars prospered rapidly, accruing property, riches and power to such an extent that they were seen as a threat by Europe's temporal rulers. In contrast, the Portuguese kings saw them as an essential tool in consolidating the Christian reconquest, and hence their role became entwined with the drive to expel the Moors. They established their headquarters at Tomar in 1158, and the building of their castle and church there started two years later. In 1312, Philip IV of France, determined to put an end to the Templars' power, disbanded the order. In 1319, Dom Dinis, following the French example, created his own new order, the Order of Christ, to which he transferred all the Templars' possessions and privileges. Tomar was kept as the order's headquarters, and ultimately the order became involved in the country's overseas expansion, answerable only to Portugal's monarchs. It continued to build at Tomar, adding to the Templar structures to create the existing castle.

Every four years or so Tomar celebrates the *Festa dos Tabuleiros*—literally, the Festival of the Platters. It keeps alive a tradition started by the saintly

Above *The Charola at Tomar, built by the Knights Templar, is modelled on the Church of the Holy Sepulchre in Jerusalem*

Queen Isabel in the 14th century as a way of distributing bread, wine and meat to the poor. Today's celebration takes place over five days, when more than 400 young women and their partners process through the streets. Each girl, dressed in white, carries an immense edifice on her head as tall as herself. This *tabuleiro* is constructed of 30 small loaves, entwined with flowers and leaves and threaded on vertical canes. It is surmounted by a white dove, the symbol of the Holy Spirit, and weighs up to 15kg (33lb)—hence the need for the accompanying young man to steady the load. The festival also includes dancing in the streets, feasting, drinking and fireworks. The next festival will be in 2011.

WHAT TO SEE
CONVENTO DE CRISTO
www.ippar.pt

The Convento de Cristo is an architectural *tour de force* that embodies in its grandeur the religious, political and military power of a medieval knightly order. In 1834, when the Portuguese religious orders were abolished, the Convento de Cristo ceased to be occupied by the Order of Christ. Afterwards it was variously used as a residence of the counts of Tomar and a religious seminary. It became a national monument in 1910 and a UNESCO World Heritage Site in 1983.

THE CHAROLA
The term *charola* is used to describe the round structures that were at the heart of Templar worship. Like all circular churches, the one at Tomar is modelled on the Church of the Holy Sepulchre in Jerusalem, for whose protection the Knights Templar were founded. From here, the knights drew their spiritual strength, attending Mass on horseback, and passing solitary nights of vigil before their initiation. Tomar's Charola is a Romanesque 12th-century construction, an eight-sided building that contains the high altar of the church, which stretches to the west. It was ornately decorated during the 16th century with paintings and polychrome wooden statues. The central temple stands in a virtually circular 16-sided chapel, which acts as a cloister.

THE CHURCH AND CHAPTERHOUSE
In 1492 Dom Manuel, later Manuel I, became Grand Master of the Order and instigated a series of alterations that radically changed the building. He extended the convent by building a nave westwards from the Charola, enlarging the church and creating two different levels. The upper one was to serve as the church's choir, the lower as the chapterhouse.

Internally, these plain vaulted extensions contrast admirably with the excesses of the Charola, but it's the exterior decoration that's impressive. The doorway, and particularly the window, is considered to be a crowning example of Portuguese Manueline ornamentation, liberally embellished with maritime motifs. The ropework, so typical of the style, is prominent, but look, too, for the seaweed, coral, cables and anchor chains as well as Manuel's armillary spheres—navigational instruments that were the monarch's personal emblem.

THE MAIN CLOISTER
João III was responsible for the next big building project between 1557 and 1566. He transformed the place from the purely political headquarters of the order into a monastic complex, adding dormitories, kitchens and no fewer than four new cloisters, making a total of seven. The grandest by far is the two-floor Main Cloister to the southwest of the church and Charola. João turned his back on the home-grown Manueline style, and looked to Italy for inspiration. The Main Cloister is thus an example of pure Renaissance classicism, with Ionic and Tuscan columns influenced by the ideas and principles of the Italian architect Andrea Palladio. The rounded arches, balustrades and alternating

TIPS

» When visiting the Convento de Cristo you have the choice of two routes, marked by red or blue arrows at infrequent intervals throughout the building. The red route will take you to the highlights; the blue covers everything there is to see.

» Tomar has a large market every Friday, spread out on either side of the river.

» During summer, a tourist train trundles round Tomar, dropping off visitors at all the main sites. Departures from Praça da República currently run at 11, 4 and 6, but are subject to change. Contact the tourist office for details.

Below *Some fine examples of Manueline decoration are to be seen on the exterior of the Convento de Cristo*

square and round apertures are perfectly balanced, while the spiral stairways in the corners add a quirky twist. These lead to the second floor and up to roof level, giving views of the whole Convento de Cristo. It is a good vantage point from which to admire the cloister's fountain.

ADDITIONAL CLOISTERS, CELLS AND CONVENT BUILDINGS

Take your time exploring the rest of the complex, a compelling labyrinth of cloisters, corridors, kitchens and monks' cells, surrounded by terraced gardens, with decorative *azulejos* (tiles). Each of the cloisters is different—particularly beautiful are Santa Barbara, with its squat arches; the verdant Cemetery Cloister, with its Gothic pointed arches; and the Washing Cloister, lined with *azulejos*, where the domestic laundry was carried out. Both of the latter cloisters were commissioned by Henry the Navigator, who was Grand Master, and thus head, of the Order of Christ between 1417 and 1460. On the third floor, a corridor cuts through the building from north to south, with another branching off at right angles. Both are lined with surprisingly well-appointed and spacious monks' cells; there's a small chapel at the crossing, designed for the use of monks who were unable to get to the main church to pray.

✉ Castelo dos Templários, 2300-303 Tomar ☎ 249 313 481 🕐 Jun–end Sep daily 9–6; rest of year daily 9–5; last entry 1 hour before closing ✋ Adult €5, under-14s free; Sun 9–2 free

MORE TO SEE

CAPELA DE NOSSA SENHORA DA CONCEIÇÃO

Standing on its own down the hill to the north of the Convento de Cristo, this serene little 16th-century Renaissance church was begun by João de Castilho and finished by Diogo de Torralva. It has three vaulted aisles.

✉ Rua Convento de Cristo, 2300-322 Tomar 🕐 Usually closed to the public, but the custodian is willing to open for visits (tel 249 313 481 or contact the tourist office)

IGREJA SANTA MARIA DOS OLIVAIS

This 13th-century church stands on the site of the original church built for the Templars as part of their foundation. Gothic in style, it has a fine rose window and an interior remodelled in the 16th century. It is the burial place of Gualdim Pais, the founder of the Templar castle, and during the age of discoveries was the mother church for all the churches the Portuguese founded overseas.

✉ Rua Aquiles da Mota, 2300-455 Tomar 🕐 Jul–end Sep daily 10–6; Oct–end Jun daily 10–5 except during Mass ✋ Free

IGREJA DE SÃO JOÃO BAPTISTA

Standing on the east of Tomar's main *praça* (square), the Gothic church of São João Baptista has some nice Manueline elements, most notably the belfry with its beautiful and flamboyant door. The interior features fine pictures and good-quality *azulejos* (tiles).

✉ Praça da República, 2300-550 Tomar 🕐 Jul–end Sep Tue–Sun 10–6; Oct–end Jun Tue–Sun 10–7 ✋ Free

MUSEU DOS FÓSFOROS

This unusual museum claims to have Europe's largest matchbox collection.

✉ Convento de São Francisco, Várzea Grande, 2300-535 Tomar ☎ 249 329 814 🕐 Daily 10–5 ✋ Free

SINAGOGA

Tomar's early 15th-century synagogue is the oldest in Portugal, its domed ceiling suppported by free-standing columns. Closed after the expulsion of the Jews in 1496, it somehow survived. The Museu Luso-Hebraico Abraão Zacuto contains a collection of 13th- to 14th-century Hebrew inscriptions.

✉ Rua Joaquim Jacinto 73, 2300-577 Tomar ☎ 249 329 814 🕐 Daily 10–1, 2–6 ✋ Free

Above *The Igreja de São João Baptista is on the east side of the main square*
Below *The two-floor Main Cloister is overshadowed by the bell tower*

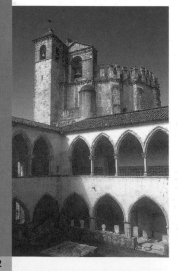

Above *Portinho da Arrábida village lies in a bay with white sands on the edge of the Serra da Arrábida*

QUINTA DA BACALHOA
www.azeitao.net
www.bacalhoa.eu

For a contrast to the wild beauty of the Serra de Arrábida, make a point of stopping at the Quinta da Bacalhoa, a villa with a classic Renaissance garden and wine estate on the Setúbal road. It was built in the 1550s by the son of Afonso de Albuquerque, a viceroy of India and great seaman. Afonso the younger visited Italy, where he saw the great gardens laid out by the ducal families and absorbed stylistic ideas that he was to blend with Indian and Moorish inspiration at Bacalhoa. From the villa's loggias and balconies a series of geometric parterres opens up, delineated and planted with box hedging and dotted with fountains and topiary. One of the most important design elements is the reflecting pool, an idea borrowed from India. There is no floral planting, but additional shades are supplied by the *azulejos* (tiles) in the loggias, patios and buildings.

✚ 330 B10 ℹ️ Quinta da Bacalhoa, Vila Nogueira Azeitão ☎ 212 180 011
⏰ Tue–Sat 9–5

SANTARÉM
www.cult.pt/turismo.pt

Santarém, capital of the Ribatejo, sits high on a hill on the north bank of the Tejo at the heart of the region's flat plains and bull-rearing country, which stretches out to the south and east. The quiet streets of the old town wind up to the Portas do Sol, a splendid *miradouro* (viewpoint) with sweeping views over the town and surrounding landscape. From here, head downhill to the two main churches: the Igreja da Marvila, with its Manueline doorway and stunningly tiled interior; and the 14th-century Igreja de Graça, with a rose window and unfussy nave. Santarém is famous for festivals. The best are *Feira Nacional da Agricultura* in June, and November's gastronomy festival, which celebrates the best of traditional Portuguese cooking.

✚ 330 B8 ℹ️ Rua Capelo e Ivens 63, 2000-039 Santarém ☎ 243 304 437
🚉 Santarém

SERRA DA ARRÁBIDA
www.visitcostaazul.com

The Serra da Arrábida is a range of mountainous hills, stretching some 35km (21 miles) along the coast from Sesimbra (▷ 110) to Setúbal. It's a beautiful area, its landscape and vegetation more Mediterranean than Atlantic, with scented undergrowth, cypresses, pines and dramatic cliffs running down to sheltered coves. Away from the sea on the northern side of the hills, the land is fertile and dotted with vineyards, olive trees and orchards, the villages prosperous and the country scattered with long-established *quintas* (estates). Since 1976 much of the area has been a natural park, formed to protect the landscape, flora and fauna, buildings and traditional way of life.

The N379/N10 across the hills and along the coast runs through Portinho da Arrábida, a coastal village on a white-sand bay guarded by a 17th-century fort, and along a corniche road on the crest of the *serra*, with great views north and

south over the landscape to the coast. The Convento da Arrábida (by appointment only, tel 212 197 620; Wed–Sun 3–4; €3), a Franciscan foundation, is along the same road.
✚ 330 B10 ℹ️ Travessa Frei Gaspar 10, 2900-388 Setúbal and Praça do Quebeda, 2900-575 Setúbal ☎ 265 539 120 or 265 534 402

SETÚBAL
www.mun-setubal.pt

Setúbal, Portugal's third-largest port and a major industrial town, doesn't pretend to be a prime tourist destination, but if you are heading south from Lisbon it makes a good stop. This honest maritime city has a beguiling old town, good shopping and some interesting monuments and museums. It's also an excellent place if you are interested in outdoor activities—from the port, you can explore the Sado estuary and go dolphin-watching or snorkelling, while the tourist office will fill you in on walking, jeep safaris and hot-air ballooning in the area. Setúbal's greatest building is the extraordinary Igreja de Jesus in the Rua Acácio Barradas (Tue–Sat 9–12, 2–5; free), designed in 1491 by the architect Boytac—Portugal's first building with Manueline decoration. The essentially late-Gothic interior, approached through a flamboyant doorway, is embellished by extraordinary columns of twisted granite that support the spiral vaulting ribs. The town's less-than-riveting museum (Tue–Sat 9–12, 1.30–5.30; €1.50) is next to the church; other low-key museums include the Museu Arqueológico in the Avenida Luisa Todi (Tue–Sat 9–12.30, 2–5.30; free), where you will find displays on the fishing trade, and the Museu Michel Giacometti in the Largo Defensores da República (Tue–Sat 9.30–6; €1.50), a large ethnographical collection.
✚ 330 B10 ℹ️ Avenida Luisa Todi 466–468, 2900-456 Setúbal ☎ 936 515 845
🚉 Setúbal

TOMAR
▷ 220–222.

A COASTAL DRIVE FROM ALCOBAÇA TO FÁTIMA

Starting at Alcobaça, home to a superb monastic complex, this drive takes in the fishing village and resort of Nazaré, a stretch of little-known coast and aromatic pinewoods, and the magnificent abbey of Batalha, before reaching Fátima, the so-called 'altar of Portugal' which is one of the world's most celebrated Catholic shrines.

THE DRIVE
Distance: 80km (50 miles)
Time: 2 hours' straight driving, 2–6 hours with stops at Nazaré, beaches in the Pinhal, Leiria and Batalha
Start at: Alcobaça
End at: Fátima

★ In Alcobaça (▷ 212–213) follow the Nazaré signs out of town to the roundabout (traffic circle), where you'll pick up the signs to the A8, which will take you on to the N8-5. This road crosses a wide fertile plain, planted with fruit trees, bordered by rolling hills to the left.

After 5km (3 miles) you'll come to a roundabout; follow the brown signs for Nazaré and climb up through pines to the village of Tedeneira and on to Nazaré. Drive downhill,

following the signs marked 'Centro' to the heart of the town. There, turn right along the waterfront.

❶ Nazaré (▷ 218) is a lively resort, a good place to stop and stretch your legs. The original fishing village has been all but swamped by holiday apartment buildings and the town bathing beach is likely to be packed, but there are fine stretches of sandy beach to the north and south. Note, though, that these beaches are dangerous for bathing.

Leave town following the signs uphill to Sítio and the N242 to Leiria. Look for a left turn above Sítio— ignoring the N242—towards Falor, Miradouro and Hospital; the orange sign marked 'Parque Aquatico' is useful here. A sign marked 'Praia da

Légua', to the right, takes you onto the coastal road running north.

❷ The coastal road runs peacefully through the Pinhal de Leiria, a 700-year-old pine forest originally planted by Dom Dinis to protect the arable land from the encroaching dunes. Miles of aromatic trees are crisscrossed by sandy tracks, and side roads lead off to beaches and tiny holiday settlements. It's worth considering taking a detour to explore some of these—little Légua is particularly pleasant.

The main road drops right down to the sea at the lovely beach at Esteleira.

Above *The main square of Marinha Grande, a town on the route*

Left *The village of Reguengo do Fatal, on the edge of the Serra de Aire*

WHERE TO EAT

In Nazaré, there's the A Celeste in the Avenida da República, in Batalha the Pousada Mestre Afonso Domingues, and in Fátima the Tia Alice in the Rua do Adro (▷ 231).

WHEN TO GO

Avoid high summer; it will be hot and places of interest crowded.

PLACES TO VISIT

NAZARÉ
(▷ 218).

LEIRIA
(▷ 218).

BATALHA
(▷ 214–216).

TIP

» You could continue to Tomar (▷ 220–222) via Ourém (▷ 219), an attractive drive through unspoilt hill country sprinkled with tiny farms.

❸ Esteleira makes a good stop for a swim in the clear, clean sea, but bear in mind that these beaches are steeply shelving and currents and tides can be dangerous. There's another great beach farther north at Polvoeira, a more developed place with holiday apartments and villas.

Past here, and 30km (18 miles) from the start of the drive, turn right at the easy-to-miss sign to Marinha Grande along a road running inland through the woods. After 4km (2.5 miles), go straight over the crossroads across open, scrubby country towards Marinha. Bear right at the next intersection, then bear right again into Marinha Grande itself. At the roundabout in the middle of town, follow the signs to the A8 and Leiria, then, at the intersection with the A8/IC1, continue straight on to join the N242, a good shady road planted with pines and eucalyptus. Unless you intend to visit Leiria (▷ 218), take the slip road signed for Lisboa and Batalha (IC2 N1); you'll soon pick up the brown tourist signs for Batalha and Fátima. Batalha (▷ 214–216) is 8km (5 miles) farther on.

❹ Batalha, with its glorious Gothic/Manueline church, is visible from the busy road well before you reach it. Indeed, the church's outer fabric is beginning to suffer deterioration due to the proximity of the N1, with its polluting fumes from the constant heavy traffic.

Leave on the N356 for Fátima and turn left at the roundabout.

❺ The drive from Batalha to Fátima is a lovely section of the route, running across the northern tip of the Serra de Aire and passing through upland country scattered with villages and smallholdings. At the intersection with the N357, follow the signs to 'Santuario' to reach Fátima (▷ 217).

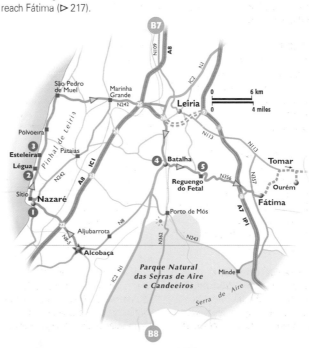

WHAT TO DO

ALCOBAÇA

ATLANTIS CRISTAIS DE ALCOBAÇA, S. A.

www.atlantis-cristais-de-alcobaca.pt
Founded in 1945, Atlantis is Portugal's best-known manufacturer of fine lead crystal. Made with the purest sand, potash and litharge (lead monoxide), its crystal pieces vary from tableware to figurines and vases. You can visit the working factory, explore the small historical museum and buy some crystal to take home from the shop.

✉ Casal da Areia, Cós, 2460-392 Alcobaça ☎ 262 540 200 ◑ Factory and museum visits: Tue–Sat 9–6 (every 30 min), final visit at 5. Closed for two weeks in Aug (dates vary) and last 2 weeks in Dec. Shop: Mon–Sat 9.30–6.30 ✋ Adult €2.60, under-10s free 🚍 Take the N8-4 north out of Alcobaça. Turn right to Maiorga and Cós

MONUMENTO NATURAL DAS PEGADAS DE DINOSSÁURIOS

www.pegadasdedinossaurios.org
If you or your children are looking for a break from monuments and museums, you may be interested in seeing the fossilized dinosaur prints to the south of Fátima. The trails are believed to date from the Jurassic period, some 175 million years ago. Leaflets and information panels explain how the trails were formed and describe how they are now being preserved.

✉ Estrada de Fátima, Bairro, 2490-216 Ourém ☎ 249 530 160 ◑ Mid-Mar to mid-Sep Tue–Fri 10–12.30, 2–7, Sat–Sun 10–12.30, 2–8; rest of year Tue–Sun 10–12.30, 2–7 ✋ Adult €2, child (6–10) €1, under-6s free

SPAL

www.spal.pt
For fine porcelains and everyday china, pop into the factory store of this highly regarded producer. Here you will find that the prices are significantly cheaper than those on offer in the manufacturer's retail store outlets.

✉ Ponte da Torre, Valado dos Frades, 2561-956 Alcobaça ☎ 262 580 498 ◑ Mon–Fri 10–1.30, 3–7, Sat 10–7

Above *Stalactites and stalagmites in part of the Grutas de Mira de Aire extensive cave system*

CALDAS DA RAINHA

MOLDE

www.molde.com.pt
For quality ceramics in tasteful designs visit the Molde factory shop on the industrial estate to the west of Caldas. Don't miss the bargain tables where many pieces sell for as little as a euro.

✉ Rua Inácio Perdigão 10, Zona Industrial, 2504-913 Caldas de Rainha ☎ 262 889 120 ◑ Mon–Fri 9–1, 2–6, Sat 10–1, 3–6

FÁTIMA

FUNPARQUE

www.funpark.pt
This outdoor adventure park offers a range of activities designed to appeal to all ages. There is a go-cart track of 1,130m (1,230 yards), rough-terrain kartbugs, paintballing, abseiling, mountain-bicycling and lots more. When you want to take a break, there is a restaurant and, if

you prefer to cook your own food, a park which has designated barbecue areas.

✉ Boleiros, 2495-326 Fátima ☎ 249 521 030 🕐 Jul–end Aug daily 10–8; Sep–end May Tue–Fri 10–7, Sat–Sun 9–7 ♨ Go-carts €15 for 15 min, €27.50 for 30 min 🚗 At the Pastorinhos roundabout, head south on the EN360, following signs to FunParque and the Kartódromo

GRUTAS DE MIRA DE AIRE
www.grutasmiradaire.com
Portugal's largest cave system stretches for 4km (2.5 miles), though the guided tours cover only about 700m (760 yards). The final cave in the system, complete with artificial fountains and waterfalls, has an elevator to take visitors back to the surface.

✉ Avenida Dr. Luciano Justo Ramos, 2485-050 Mira de Aire ☎ 244 440 322 🕐 Jul, Aug daily 9.30–7.30; Apr, May daily 9.30–6; Jun, Sep daily 9.30–7; Oct–end Mar daily 9.30–5.30 ♨ €5 🚗 Take the N360 south out of Fátima, then turn left onto the N243 towards Porto de Mós. The caves are on the left

GRUTAS DA MOEDA
www.grutasmoeda.com
These caves, about 3km (2 miles) from Fátima, were discovered unexpectedly in 1971 by two hunters. The huge galleries stretch for 350m (380 yards) and are endowed with emerald-green lakes and spectacular stone formations, including a limestone column believed to be around 30,000 years old.

✉ São Mamede, 2495-326 Fátima ☎ 244 704 302 🕐 Jul–end Sep 9–7; Apr–end Jun 9–6; Oct–end Mar 9–5 ♨ €5 🚗 From Fátima's northern roundabout follow signs to the A1. Just before joining the A1 turn right. The caves are signed

LEIRIA
PARQUE AQUÁTICO-MARIPARQUE
Great for a day out with the kids, this water park is about 25km (18 miles) north of Leiria. Situated on the beachfront at Praia da Vieira, the complex includes chutes, rapids,

twisting toboggans and junior pools. There are bars and a restaurant that provide refreshments.

✉ Avenida Marginal, Praia da Vieira Aptdo 62, 2430-696 Vieira de Leiria ☎ 244 440 700 🕐 Jun to mid-Sep (weather permitting) daily 10–7.30 ♨ Adult €4.90–€6.20, child €3.20–€4.90 (half- and full day) 🍴🚻🚗 Take the IC1 north out of Leiria. Turn left to Monte Real/Vieira de Leiria and then follow signs to Praia da Vieira

MARINHA GRANDE
JASMIM-VICRIMAG
www.jasmimglass.com
One of many glass producers in the area, Jasmim opened in 1996 with the aims of reviving ancient hand-blown glass-making methods using environmentally friendly materials. Visitors can watch the artists at work and there are English-speaking experts available to answer any questions about the craft.

✉ Estrada de Leiria 227, Apt. 87, 2431-901 Marinha Grande ☎ 244 575 590 🕐 Daily 10–7

MUSEU DO VIDRO
This museum was opened in 1998 to commemorate 250 years of glass production in Marinha Grande. Its stunning glass collections are housed in the 18th-century Palácio Stephens, named after the Englishman who re-established glass-making in the town in 1769.

✉ Palácio Stephens, 2430-960 Marinha Grande ☎ 244 573 377 🕐 Jun–end Sep daily 10–7; Oct–end May Tue–Sun 10–6 ♨ €1.50

ÓBIDOS
ABRIGO DA BIQUINHA
One of the town's oldest and best-loved bars is set on a series of levels, the small rooms giving the place a homelike feel. Be sure to try the local *ginginha de Óbidos* (cherry brandy), along with their excellent *linguiça* (spicy sausage).

✉ Rua da Biquinha, 2510-046 Óbidos ☎ 262 959 449 🕐 Daily noon–2am

CASA DOS SABORES D'ÓBIDOS
Part cake and wine shop, and part café, here you can try the

delicious cherry *ginginha* served in a chocolate cup, then eat the cup. Be sure to buy a bottle to take with you or, if you prefer, choose from the good selection of port wine.

✉ Rua Direita 66, 2510-060 Óbidos ☎ 262 959 729 🕐 Apr–end Oct daily 9–7; Nov–end Mar daily 9–6

GOLFE DA PRAIA D'EL REY
www.praia-del-rey.com
www.portugalgolf.pt
This golf course, part of the 5-star Praia d'El Rey Golf and Country Club, has 18 championship holes (par 72). The clubhouse has a health club, restaurant and indoor pool.

✉ Vale de Janelas, 2510-451 Óbidos ☎ 262 905 005 🕐 Apr–end Oct daily 8–8; Nov–end Mar 8–5.30 ♨ 18 holes Mar–end Oct Mon–Fri €100, Sat–Sun and national holidays €125; Nov–end Feb Mon–Fri €75, Sat–Sun and national holidays €93.75; club rental €39, electric trolley €20, cart €45 🍴🚗 Indoor 🚗 Take the EN114 west out of Óbidos. Turn right at Serra d'El Rei and follow signs to the resort

ÓBIDOS TUR
www.obidostur.pt
Among other activities, this company organizes horse-drawn buggy and carriage rides to local places of interest. Trips last between 10 and 60 minutes. A couple of the drivers speak English; there is a route information board at the departure point.

✉ Animação Turística Ltd, Casal de Soitão, 2510 Óbidos ☎ 969 052 148 🕐 May–end Sep daily 9–6.30 ♨ Routes and prices include: aqueduct €20, village of Pinhal €25, Igreja da Pedra €35, Roman excavations and Rio Arnóia €60 🚗 Departures are from the Óbidos car park at the entrance to the town

RUA DIREITA
This street is full of small shops selling an assortment of curios and souvenirs. It is worth looking around for a while as it is possible to find some interesting examples of tasteful regional crafts among the trinkets. The town's weekly market is on Saturday.

✉ 2510-001 Óbidos

PENICHE

BALEAL SURF CAMP

www.balealsurfcamp.com

This company organizes individual surfing lessons and week-long surf camps. It also rents equipment and arranges basic accommodation.

✉ Rua dos Amigos do Baleal 2, Praia do Baleal, 2520-052 Ferrel Baleal ☎ 963 982 899 or 262 769 277 ⏰ Apr–end Oct daily 10–8; Nov–end May daily, call to arrange times ✋ 2-hour lesson €30; 1-week course Mon–Fri with 2 hours of lessons a day €130; 1-week surf camp including lessons as above plus equipment, insurance and accommodation in dormitory room €325–€465, private room €395–€545

BERLENGA ISLANDS TOURS

These clear-watered islands are designated bird sanctuaries. You can visit the largest island, but are restricted to waymarked paths. Five-hour trips are available from several companies at the harbour.

✉ Largo da Ribeira, 2520 Peniche ☎ 918 619 311 or 917 601 114 ⏰ Daily 9–8 ✋ Berlenga trips €18 per person, minimum 10 people, or €180 for boat. Departures weather dependent

DANAU BAR

This surfer-style hangout, just north of Peniche at the Baleal beach, is one of the most happening bars in town. It often features live bands and there is usually karaoke on offer at weekends.

✉ Praia do Baleal, 2520 Baleal Ferrel ☎ 262 709 818 ⏰ Jun–end Sep Sun–Thu 9am–midnight, Fri–Sat 9am–4am; rest of year Sun–Thu 10am–midnight, Fri–Sat 10am–4am 🚌 Praia do Baleal is to the north of Peniche. The all-wooden Danau is at the right-hand end of the beach

ESCOLA DE RENDAS DA CAMARA MUNICIPAL DE PENICHE

Peniche is famous for its bobbin lace. The tourist office is also home to the town's lace school, which demonstrates how bobbin lace is made here.

✉ Rua Alexandre Herculano, 2520-273 Peniche ☎ 262 789 571 ⏰ Mon–Fri 9–12.30, 2–5.30

HALIOTIS, AVENTURAS SUBMERSAS

www.haliotis.pt

This company organizes great scuba-diving trips around the Berlenga islands as well as offering PADI courses. Check the company's website for dive dates.

✉ Hotel Praia Norte, Avenida Monsenhor Manuel Bastos, 2520-206 Peniche ☎ 262 781 160 or 913 054 926 ⏰ Office daily 9–6.30 ✋ €31.50 for a 1-dive excursion, €70 for a 2-dive excursion

MERCADO MUNICIPAL

If you would like to to stock up for a picnic or self-catering in the region this market is packed with a great selection of locally grown fresh produce. It is also fantastic for well-priced fresh fish, straight off the boat at Peniche.

✉ Rua Architecto Paulino Montez ⏰ Mon–Sat 7–2

NAUTIPESCA

This outfit organizes coastal and open-sea fishing, providing all the necessary equipment. Nautipesca also organizes visits to the Berlenga islands. These trips take place from May to the end of September.

✉ Largo da Ribeira Velha, Office A1, 2520 Peniche ☎ 917 588 358 or 262 789 648 ⏰ Office: Jun–end Sep daily 9–7. Phone lines operate daily 9–9. Trips run daily at any pre-arranged time, depending on the weather ✋ Coastal trip Mon–Fri €60, Sat–Sun €80; pre-booked fishing trip €400 per boat

TASCA DO JOEL

www.tascadojoel.com

In addition to the restaurant, this establishment now boasts an

excellent wine shop. In addition to an impressive collection of national wines they also stock accessories for the wine connoisseur and a selection of gourmet delicacies to accompany the wines. Their hams, jams and pâtés and cheeses are of excellent quality.

✉ Rua do Lapadusso 73, 2520-370 Peniche ☎ 262 782 945 ⏰ Tue–Sat 10–4, 6–midnight

TOMAR

PRAIA FLUVIAL DA CASTANHEIRA

Some 15km (9 miles) to the northeast of Tomar, off the N238, these floating pools are a great place to take the children on a hot afternoon. There is also a bar and terrace serving light snacks, and a restaurant.

✉ Castanheira, Lagoa Azul, 2240 Ferreira do Zêzere ☎ 249 360 150 ⏰ Jul–end Sep daily ✋ Free

TEMPLARIOS AVENTURA

www.templar.online.pt
Canoeing, mountain-bicycling, archery, hiking and abseiling are organized by Templar, plus a range of watersports, such as diving, water-skiing and boardsailing.

✉ Rua Dr Joaquim Jacinto 103, Tomar ☎ 249 323 414 ⏰ Mon–Fri 2–5.30 ✋ Prices vary according to the activity chosen

VIA AVENTURA

www.via-aventura.com
In the summer, rent a canoe or a bicycle here. Via Aventura also organizes canyoning excursions through the year.

✉ Rua Principal 45D, 2305-406 Carvalhal Pequeno, Tomar ☎ 939 641 425 or 919 641 425 ⏰ Daily ✋ Bicycle rental including helmets €15; canoeing, including all equipment €15; canyoning trips (3–4.5 hours) €40. Reserve by phone

Opposite *There are many opportunites for kayaking and other outdoor activities in Estremadura and the Ribatejo*

FESTIVALS AND EVENTS

EASTER
SEMANA SANTA
The most important religious and cultural event in Óbidos is its Easter celebration, attracting thousands of visitors and pilgrims from all over the country. Saints and images are taken out of their churches and paraded through the streets. The *Via Sacra* procession re-enacts Christ's last hours.

✉ Óbidos ☎ 262 959 231 (tourist office)

MAY
PILGRIMAGES
The pilgrimages mark the alleged first and last appearances of the Virgin Mary to three shepherd children (▷ 217). Though it is always busy, Fátima is transformed during these days as literally thousands of road-weary pilgrims from across the country and around the world crawl the last kilometre up to the Basilica on their knees.

✉ Fátima ⏰ 12–13 May (see also October)

JULY
FESTA DOS TABULEIROS
The unique Festival of the Trays honours both the Holy Spirit and the saintly Dona Isabel (married to Dom Dinis, a medieval king of Portugal). It is particularly famous for the massive headdresses of bread and paper flowers topped with a white dove—the *tabuleiros*—which the women of the town wear as they take part in processions through the streets. Next in 2011.

✉ Tomar ☎ 249 322 427 ⏰ Runs for 10 days leading up to final parade on the second Sun of Jul

FESTA DA LAGOA
Promoting the *Lagoa de Óbidos* (Óbidos Lagoon) and those whose livelihood depends upon it, this festival includes live music and gastronomical delights made exclusively from seafood caught in the lake. Head towards the *ribeira*

(waterfront) to sample some of these local specialities.

✉ Óbidos ☎ 262 959 231 (tourist office) ⏰ Last weekend in Jul

JULY–AUGUST
SEMANA INTERNACIONAL DE PIANO
www.pianobidos.org
Held in several locations in Óbidos, including the Auditório da Casa da Música, this piano festival brings international names to the concert stage. In addition to concerts, the maestros give master classes and lectures, which culminate with the students' concert on the festival's last day.

✉ Óbidos ☎ 262 959 231 ⏰ Last week Jul–first week Aug

AUGUST
FESTA DE NOSSA SENHORA DA BOA VIAGEM
The highlight of the Festival of Our Lady of the Good Voyage—patron saint of Peniche's fishermen—is on the Saturday night when a statue of the Virgin Mary is carried down to the ocean and taken by a procession of illuminated trawlers out to Cabo Carvoeiro.

✉ Peniche ☎ 262 789 571 (tourist office) ⏰ First Fri in Aug for 4 days

OCTOBER
PILGRIMAGES
✉ Fátima ⏰ 12–13 Oct (see also May)

NOVEMBER
FESTIVAL INTERNACIONAL DO CHOCOLATE
A must for chocoholics, this festival brings national and international chocolate chefs to Óbidos. Prizes are awarded for Best International Chocolate Recipe, Chocolatier of the Year and Artistic Pieces in Chocolate. There are also exhibitions, demonstrations and free samples.

✉ Óbidos ☎ 262 959 231 (tourist office) ⏰ Early Nov

PRICES AND SYMBOLS

The restaurants are listed alphabetically. The prices given are the average for a two-course lunch (L) and a three-course dinner (D) for one person, without drinks. The wine price is for the least expensive bottle. All the restaurants listed accept credit cards unless otherwise stated.

For a key to the symbols, ▷ 2.

ALCOBAÇA
ANTÓNIO PADEIRO

After walking around the convent this makes an ideal place to sit and refuel. The dishes are traditional and hearty. For something really local try the *Frango na púcara à moda de Alcobaça* a chicken dish served in a rustic earthenware pot and to finish, the very sweet egg-based *doces conventuais* for which the restaurant is justly famed. The fluffy *pão de ló* sponge is a less sweet but no less delicious alternative.
✉ Rua Dr. Maur Cocheril 27, 2460-032 Alcobaça ☎ 262 582 295 🕔 Daily 12–4.30, 7–11.30 ✋ L €14, D €17, Wine €7

TRINDADE

Thanks to its hearty food and central location in a tree-shaded square near the monastery, this little eatery often gets packed with visitors. It serves a great *frango na púcara* (chicken stew), grilled fish such as sole and bream, roast chicken and rabbit. There are also light snacks, such as toasted sandwiches and pastries. The crush is relieved in the summer by extra tables that are set out in the shady square.
✉ Praça Dom Afonso Henriques 22, 2460-030 Alcobaça ☎ 262 582 397 🕔 Daily 12–4, 7–10 ✋ L €12, D €18, Wine €8

BATALHA
VINHO EM QUALQUER CIRCUNSTÂNCIA

This bar, cum shop, cum restaurant, began life as a wine bar dedicated in its entirety to wine tasting and serving only light tapas-style snacks to complement the drinking. Its popularity grew and customers began demanding more substantial meals which are still limited but of good quality. Their salt-cod comes recommended. The shop is a great place to get advice on Portuguese wines before buying.
✉ Estrada de Fátima 15, 2440-901 Batalha ☎ 244 768 777 🕔 Mon–Thu 5–11.30, Fri 5–1am, Sat 12–1am, Sun 12–4 ✋ L €18, D €22, Wine €8

Above *Estelas restaurant in Peniche serves excellent fish and seafood dishes, many specialities of the region*

CALDAS DA RAINHA
ADEGA DO ALBERTINO

With its checked tablecloths, beamed ceilings and rustic arches this place has a homely feel. Its main courses are traditionally hearty; try the grilled prawn and squid kebab, lamb stew or pork with honey, wine and almonds. Leave room for the local rocha pear stewed in quality red wine and served with the prized *trouxas de ovos* (sticky egg-based sweet).
✉ Rua Júlio Sousa 7, Imaginário, 2500-312 Caldas de Rainha ☎ 262 835 152 🕔 Tue–Sat 12–3, 7–10, Sun 12–3 ✋ L €16, D €20, Wine €7.50

CARTAXO
CONDESTÁVEL

www.condestaveldeluissuspiro.net
Known across the region for its fine dining, Condestável is a place to take time over a meal. Chef Luís Suspiro presents innovative and contemporary dishes while keeping within Portuguese tradition. Specialities include, duck risotto with chanterelle mushrooms, partridge

stuffed with white Ribatejo truffles and mouth-watering, sautéed strawberries in flaked pastry. A selection of quality coffees is available for you to choose from. They are freshly ground and served with the house *aguardente*.

✉ Travessa do Olival, Ereira, 2070-326 Cartaxo ☎ 243 719 786 🕐 Mon, Wed–Sat 1–3, 8–10 Sun 1–3 ✋ L €25, D €37, Wine €12

FÁTIMA
TIA ALICE

Tia Alice opened in 1988 inside a humble townhouse next to Fátima's parish church. The bare stone walls have been left as they were and gentle lighting added to give a relaxed feel. Thanks to its wood-oven-baked bread, excellent soups, roasts and *açordas* (bread stews), the reputation of its fine Serra de Aire cooking has spread the length and breadth of the country. There are only 12 tables, so be sure to reserve in advance.

✉ Rua do Adro 152, 2495-557 Fátima ☎ 249 531 737 🕐 Tue–Sat 12–3, 7.30–10, Sun 12–3. Closed Jul ✋ L €27, D €40, Wine €12 🚗 Leave the Fátima sanctuary on the EN356 towards Tomar. Restaurant is on right-hand side by the parish church

LEIRIA
PUTTANESCA

As the name would indicate, this is an Italian restaurant but it also serves Spanish-style tapas, ideal for a light lunch. For something more substantial try the kid or lamb simply but succulently roasted in the wood-burning oven. The house forte, however, is said to lie in the caramel desserts and home-made ice cream. Interesting photographic prints decorate the walls.

✉ Rua da Escola 463, Planalto Leiria, 2400-321 Leiria ☎ 244 856 180 🕐 Mon–Sat 12–3, 6–midnight ✋ L €15, D €20, Wine €8

TROMBA RIJA

www.trombarija.com
People come from all over the country to eat in this renowned restaurant. One of the two fixed-price menus offers a choice of 50 starters from the buffet: cheeses, home-made sausages, octopus, chickpeas (*grão de bico*), salt-cod salads and more. If you are still hungry, you can order one of the main courses from a tempting selection of regional dishes on the à la carte menu.

✉ Rua Professore Portelas 22, Marrazes, 2415-534 Leiria ☎ 244 852 277 🕐 Mon–Sat 1–3.30, 8–10, Sun 1–3.30 ✋ Executive (à la carte) menu Tue–Thu lunch and dinner, Fri lunch. Flavours of Portugal (buffet) menu Fri dinner, Sat lunch and dinner, Sun lunch €32.50; à la carte wine €10 🚗 Take Figueira da Foz exit from the A1 highway. Follow signs to Marrazes

ÓBIDOS
A ILUSTRE CASA DE RAMIRO

Inside the ancient town walls, this rustic split-level dining room is painted in pink terracotta throughout. It has a medieval atmosphere, with its solid pillars, deep arches and alcoves filled with giant ceramic pots. The food is regional, with special dishes such as garlic fried prawns, stuffed squid, grilled grouper kebabs and duck with rice. The extensive wine list includes wines from all over the country. Finish with *crêpes à Ilustre*.

✉ Rua Porta do Vale, 2510-084 Óbidos ☎ 262 959 194 🕐 Sat–Wed 12.30–3, 7–10.30, Thu–Fri 7–10.30 ✋ L €25, D €30, Wine €7

COZINHA DAS RAINHAS

www.senhorasrainhas.com
Found within the stylish hotel Casa das Senhoras Rainhas, this quiet restaurant looks straight out onto the medieval walls of Óbidos; in warmer months it is possible to dine on the garden terrace. All dishes are home-made on the premises and for this reason, quality is consistently high. Try the fish soup followed by black pork with chestnut purée, accompanied by one of the excellent Estremadura wines on offer.

✉ Rua Padre Nunes Tavares 6, 2510-999 Óbidos ☎ 262 955 360 🕐 Daily 12.30–2.30, 7.30–10 ✋ L €18, D €26, Wine €10

PENICHE
ESTELAS

One of the best dishes here is the steamed lobster Peniche-style, which must be ordered in advance; or try *sequinho de cherne*, a grouper fish dish invented by the local fishermen. Other dishes include *caldeiradas* (mixed fish and seafood stew), plain grilled fish and a variety of fresh seafood.

✉ Rua Arquitecto Paulino Montez 21, 2520-294 Peniche ☎ 262 782 435 🕐 Thu–Tue 12–3, 7–12. Closed second 2 weeks in Aug ✋ L €18, D €25, Wine €9 🚗 Next to the municipal market and courthouse

SANTARÉM
TABERNA DO QUINZENA

www.quinzena.com
In business for almost 140 years, this tavern is a Santarém landmark, decorated with bullfighting posters—nothing too gory so don't be put off. Food is served in generous portions on traditional glazed earthenware. Each day is designated its own particular dish, running from duck rice, through *cozido* (a substantial Portuguese stew, not for the faint-hearted), roast kid, leg of pork and 'wild bull' stewed in wine.

✉ Rua Pedro de Santarém 93–94, 2000-223 Santarém ☎ 243 322 804 🕐 Mon–Sat 12–10 ✋ L €10, D €13, Wine €6.50

TOMAR
CHICO ELIAS

People come to Tomar just to eat at this fine restaurant. Chickpea broth, pumpkin stuffed with rabbit, salt cod with *presunto* and corn bread are just some of the delights on offer at Chico Elias. Reserve and order in advance to give them time to marinate food overnight. Credit cards are not accepted.

✉ Rua Principal 70, Algarvias, 2300-302 Tomar ☎ 249 311 067 🕐 Wed–Sat, Mon 12.30–3.30, 7–10.30, Sun 12.30–3.30. Closed second 2 weeks in Jul and first 2 weeks in Sep ✋ L €23, D €27, Wine €12 🚗 Take Torres Novas road out of Tomar. Restaurant is 1.5km (1 mile) on the left

PRICES AND SYMBOLS

The prices are the lowest and highest for a double room for one night including breakfast, unless otherwise stated. All the hotels listed accept credit cards unless otherwise stated. Note that rates can vary widely throughout the year.

For a key to the symbols, ▷ 2.

ALCOBAÇA
CASA DO VALE
www.casadovale.net

A somewhat eclectic décor, defined by the owner as 'refined rustic', gives this guesthouse a homely feel. Its Provence-style kitchen is used in winter months as a dining room while in warmer months guests eat under the porch overlooking the verdant valley and fruit orchards. There is a good-sized infinity pool and hammocks in quiet garden nooks for relaxing. Meals are available on request. Credit cards are not accepted.

✉ Travessa dos Guedes Reis, Cela, 2460-355 Alcobaça ☎ 919 384 292 or 262 500 243 ✋ €65–€85 ❶ 3 ⛲ Outdoor

HOTEL SANTA MARIA

This is the best of Alcobaça's modern hotels. In a quiet corner

of the old town, just next to the monastery, its rooms are relatively small but are spotlessly clean. Several of them have small balconies looking over the flower-filled square. The hotel is ideally placed for exploring the town. It has underground parking and, although it has no restaurant of its own, there are several good eateries nearby.

✉ Rua Francisco Zagalo 20–22, 2460-041 Alcobaça ☎ 262 590 160 ✋ €50–€75 ❶ 78 rooms, 2 suites ⛲

FÁTIMA
DOM GONÇALO HOTEL AND SPA
www.hoteldg.com

The Sanctuary of Our Lady of Fátima is visited by thousands of pilgrims every year, yet accommodation in the area is uninspiring. The best is the recently renovated Dom Gonçalo, set some 400m (440 yards) from the Basilica precinct. The rooms have all modern amenities, with the modern wing offering 'designer' accommodation and spa facilities. The restaurant is known for its traditional cuisine and extensive selection of regional wines.

✉ Rua Jacinta Marto 100, 4295-450 Fátima ☎ 249 539 330 ✋ €65–€95 ❶ 67 rooms, 4 suites ⛲

Above *Creepers adorn the walls around the entrance to the* pousada *at Óbidos*

ÓBIDOS
CASA D'ÓBIDOS
www.casadobidos.com

Built by 19th-century railway engineers, and with great views up to the fortified town of Óbidos, this *casa* offers the choice of double rooms and cottages with kitchens. Rooms in the main house are classically furnished with attractive printed fabrics, while those in the annexe and cottages are more country in style. There isn't a restaurant on site, but there are several within 10 minutes' walk. Tennis is available on site.

✉ Turismo de Habitação, Quinta de São José, 2510-135 Óbidos ☎ 262 950 924 ✋ €80 rooms including breakfast, €80–€160 cottages excluding breakfast ❶ 6 rooms, 3 garden cottages ⛲ Outdoor

CASA DAS SENHORAS RAINHAS
www.senhorasrainhas.com

Sitting inside the medieval walls of Óbidos this small hotel has been carefully renovated to offer very comfortable lodgings while maintaining traditional architectural details. Rooms all have small verandas or for a special occasion reserve the large tower room overlooking the monumental church of Jesus da Pedra. A delicious breakfast is included in the price and in summer months is served out on the terrace. Parking nearby is limited so bags may need to be carried along cobbled streets.

✉ Rua Padre Nunes Tavares 6, 2510-999 Óbidos ☎ 262 955 360 ♨ €163–€179 ⓘ 9 rooms, 1 tower suite

HOTEL REAL D'ÓBIDOS
www.hotelrealdobidos.com
The oldest part of this hotel is believed to date from the 14th century, although its most outstanding feature is the imposing façade, added in the 1700s. Rooms are named after Portuguese kings and queens, and decorated in the style of the appropriate era. The sitting room is rustic, with a big granite fireplace and old beams; outdoors there is a heated pool and a sun terrace overlooking the village.

✉ Rua Dom João de Ornelas, 2510-074 Óbidos ☎ 262 955 090 ♨ €120–€140 ⓘ 15 rooms, 2 suites 💺 ♒ Outdoor saltwater

POUSADA DO CASTELO
www.pousadas.pt
The *pousada* at Óbidos, within the town's medieval castle, was the first to be converted from a historic building classified as a national monument. The main entrance and windows are noteworthy examples of Manueline carving. The best rooms are the duplex suites in the towers, which have medieval furniture and four-poster beds. Standard rooms are more modest but still comfortable. The limited number of rooms makes advance booking essential.

✉ Rua do Castelo, 2510-999 Óbidos ☎ 262 955 080 ♨ €190–€320 ⓘ 9 rooms, 3 duplex suites 💺

PRAIA D'EL REY MARRIOTT GOLF AND BEACH RESORT
www.marriottpraiadelrey.com
A few minutes from Óbidos, the resort of Praia D'El Rey offers 5-star

accommodation and is an ideal spot to spend a few days unwinding after touring the area. A comprehensive range of resort activities is available including horseback riding, jet-skiing, scuba-diving and golf, while at the end of the day, the onsite spa offers respite to aching muscles. A number of packages are available to include combinations of golf, spa, different meal-plans and airport transfers. See the website or call for details.

✉ Avenida D. Inês de Castro 1, Vale de Janelas, 2510-451 Amoreira, Óbidos ☎ 262 905 100 🌐 €135–€195 ⓘ 179 rooms, 9 suites 💺 ♒ Indoor and outdoor 🚗

OURÉM
CASA ALTA
www.casaaltaroyallodge.com
For something a little different in the Fátima area, try this former royal lodge; Catherine of Braganza spent her last night here before leaving to marry Charles II. Packed with antiques and old-world charm, the rooms have spectacular views over the surrounding countryside. Both have wood-burning fireplaces, embroidered linen sheets, duvets and fresh flowers. Father Mariani provides free transportation to the shrine of Fátima daily.

✉ Castelo de Ourém, 2400 000 Ourém ☎ 249 543 515 ♨ €120–€200 ⓘ 1 room, 1 suite

CASA DA ALCAIDARIA-MOR
www.quintaalcaidaria-mor.pt
A couple of kilometres outside Ourém on the road to Tomar, this 17th-century manor house offers in-house bed-and-breakfast accommodation and self-catering cottages within the grounds. Built for the king's personal physician, the house boasts fine wood-panelled ceilings, ancestral paintings and antiques, and a historic 14th-century chapel. There is a hedged pool in the well-kept garden and horseback riding can be arranged with a qualified instructor.

✉ 2490-799 Ourém ☎ 249 542 231 ♨ Rooms €90–€115, self-catering cottages €85–€130 ⓘ 6 rooms, 5 2-bedroom cottages

SANTARÉM
CASA DA ALCÁÇOVA
www.alcacova.com
This manor house, right inside the castle walls, provides unparalleled views over the Tagus plains below. Rooms are classically furnished, many with four-poster or canopied beds, fine linens and Jacuzzis. There is a fitness room and outdoor pool nestled below the ramparts.

✉ Largo da Alcáçova 3, Portas do Sol, 2000-110 Santarém ☎ 243 304 030 ♨ €95–€180 ⓘ 8 ♒ Outdoor 🚗

TOMAR
CASA DA AVÓ GENOVEVA
www.avogenoveva.com
This 17th-century country house, with a pink façade and palm trees, provides a quiet retreat. The cobbled courtyard leads to a series of public rooms—the music room, library and snooker room, small bar, dining room and lounge, where you can see the family photos. Bedrooms, in the main house or in the apartments in the converted granary, are decorated with wood-panelled ceilings, antiques and oil paintings. Tennis is available on site.

✉ Rua 25 de Abril 16, Curvaceiras, 2305-509 Tomar ☎ 249 982 219 ♨ €75; apartment €85 for 2 people, €140 for 4 people ⓘ 3 rooms, 2 apartments ♒ Outdoor 🚗 Head south out of Tomar on N110. Turn right onto N358 to the village of Curvaceiras

ESTALAGEM DE SANTA IRIA
Although dwarfed by the luxurious Hotel dos Templários nearby, this inn, with its ancient water-wheel, has much more character. It sits on a wooded island in the river Nabão, peacefully removed from the hustle and bustle of the nearby town of Tomar. The bedrooms are unpretentious, light and airy, and look out onto the park or across the river. Almost all have balconies that are large enough to sit out on and enjoy a drink or two. The restaurant serves typical regional dishes.

✉ Parque do Mouchão, 2300-536 Tomar ☎ 249 313 326 ♨ €58–€85 ⓘ 13 rooms, 1 suite

Leiria

Fátima

Proença-a-Nova

Perdigão

Parque Natural do Tejo Internacional

Tomar

Alcobaça

Tolosa

Marvão

Barragem da Póvoa

Abrantes

Portalegre

Santarém

Ponte de Sôr

Crato

Parque Natural de Serra de São Mamede

Barragem de Montargil

Barragem do Maranhão

Fronteira

Avis

Monforte

Coruche

Estremoz

Barragem do Caia

Alverca do Ribatejo

Sintra

Sacavém

Arraiolos

Elvas

Estoril

LISBOA

Azaruja

Vila Viçosa

Cascais

Montemor-o-Novo

Évora

Setúbal

São Cristóvão

Reguengos de Monsaraz

Monsaraz

Sesimbra

Torrão

Barragem do Alvito

Barragem do Alqueva

Alcácer do Sal

Vidigueira

Grândola

Moura

Santiago do Cacém

Santa Margarida do Sado

Beja

Barrancos

Cabo de Sines

Ermidas

Barragem do Roxo

Serpa

Sines

Cercal

Torre Vã

Albornoa

Parque Natural do Vale do Guadiana

Vila Nova de Milfontes

Santa Luzia

Entradas

Mértola

Tolheiro

Ourique

Odeceixe

Barragem de Santa Clara

Dogueno

São Marcos da Serra

Messines de Baixo

Odeleite

Alfambras

Silves

Barranco do Velho

THE ALENTEJO

Alentejo *(além do Tejo),* literally means 'beyond the Tagus' and encompasses everything south of the river, with the exception of the Ribatejo ('banks of the Tagus') and the Algarve in the far south. The region is characterized by undulating plains, scattered with cork oaks, grazing cattle and megalithic remains; fertile soil grows olives, wheat and grapes. Its coastline is unadulterated and pristine, its hinterlands agricultural. Spring brings new life and swathes of wild flowers; summer is so hot that life seems to come to a halt as the country dries; autumn is serene and bathed in orange light, winter can be bitter.

Straddling the northern tip of the Alto Alentejo, is the protected Serra de São Mamede; a mountainous natural park, great for walking thanks to its diverse flora and fauna. Watch for wild boar and dear in the chestnut and holm-oak forests; spot griffon vultures and Bonellis eagles overhead; and be prepared for rapid and extreme weather changes. Also within the park are the hilltop villages of Castelo de Vide, with its medieval and Jewish quarters, and Marvão perched high on a rocky outcrop offering breathtaking views over to Spain.

Farther south is Évora, the regional capital and hub of activity. Tourists flock to see its Roman temple, churches and stately mansions. Quieter, but no less interesting, is the town of Estremoz with its famed Saturday market; Elvas, one of Portugal's most impressive frontier posts; and Vila Viçosa the seat of the House of Bragança and home to an impressive ducal palace. For carpets, visitors should head to Arraiolos, for plums to Elvas, for cheese to Serpa, and for excellent wines head just about anywhere.

ALCÁCER DO SAL

www.cm-alcacerdosal.pt

Laid-back and slightly scruffy, Alcácer do Sal is at the head of the estuary of the River Sado, a vast wetland nature reserve. The town runs along the banks of the river and up the hill behind, looking towards the paddy fields and salt flats that have ensured local prosperity. The Moors built a castle here, high above the river, which was temporarily taken in 1158 during Afonso Henrique's first big push south, finally becoming Christian in 1217. The town has since quietly prospered, with salt, bulls and horses making the money.

Stroll along the riverfront promenade, where you'll find local ladies ladling out freshly boiled shrimps—the town's delicacy—before heading into the medieval warren of narrow streets. Climb up to the castle, now a pousada, for a good view over the roofs, their chimneys crowned with the nests of Alcácer's resident stork population. If you're interested in nature, it's worth heading into the Sado estuary to see more storks, herons, marsh harriers and flamingos—you can even view the lagoons from a hot-air balloon (contact the tourist office).

✚ 330 B10 ℹ Praça Pedro Nunes, Edificio o Revês 1, R/c, 7580-125 Alcácer do Sal ☎ 265 610 070

ARRAIOLOS

www.cm-arraiolos.pt

If you want to visit a typical Alentejo town head for Arraiolos, perched on a hill above the rolling plain. Sparkling white houses, picked out with blue or yellow trim, line the cobbled streets leading up to the old walls that enclose the castle and its surrounding dwellings and church. You'll notice the large number of shops selling carpets—these have been manufactured here since the 17th century, when an industry was set up to make hemp-and-linen embroidered rugs, which were used as wallhangings and table and chest covers. The patterns originally followed Persian and Indian designs, using animal and plant motifs, but this intricacy gradually gave way to something simpler and more geometric, with yellow and blue the dominant shades. If they appeal, buy them here—prices are high, but you won't find them less expensive anywhere else.

The surrounding countryside has a desolate beauty, the huge wheat fields scattered with holm oak and cork, while other areas are dedicated to wine production. From Arraiolos, you can follow the circular wine route from village to village; pick up a leaflet at the tourist office.

✚ 330 C9 ℹ Praça Lima Brito, 7040-027 Arraiolos ☎ 266 490 254

AVIS

www.rtsm.pt

After the long slog across the Alentejan plateau, with only cork and olive trees for interest, Avis comes as a welcome sight and a good place for a break. It's an old settlement, retaining traces of its ramparts and medieval towers—you'll get a good view of these as you approach on the N244. This road crosses the vast lake at the confluence of the Seda and Avis rivers, formed when a hydro-electric dam was built 15km (9 miles) downstream.

Backwater it may seem now, but Avis played a significant role in shaping Portuguese history. It was here, in the early 13th century, that the Order of Avis, the oldest order of chivalry in Europe, was founded by Afonso Henriques to fight the Moors. In 1385, the Grand Master of the Order, João, was proclaimed king, the first monarch of the House of Avis, which was to rule Portugal until 1580. João I was one of Portugal's great rulers; in 1387 he married Philippa of Lancaster, so strengthening the Anglo-Portuguese alliance further.

✚ 331 D9 ℹ Câmara Municipal, Largo Serpa Pinto 1, 7480-122 Avis ☎ 242 412 024

BEJA

www.rt-planiciedourada.pt

Beja, the capital of the Baixa Alentejo, lies in the heart of this southern region and makes a good stopping-off point. First Roman, then Visigothic, Moorish and finally Christian, it's a prosperous agricultural town, neatly laid out on a rise in the plains. Its main sights all lie within the old part of town.

Head first for the Convento de Nossa Senhora da Conceição in the Rua Conde de Boavista, now home to the Museu Regional (tel 284 323 351; www.museuregionaldebeja. net; Tue–Sun 9.30–12.30, 2–5.15; €2, free on Sun 9.30–12.30). The convent's Manueline architectural flourishes attest to its 15th-century foundation, while the interior highlights include a cloister and chapterhouse totally covered with bright azulejos (tiles) and an over-the-top rococo chapel, complete with flying gilded cherubs. The exhibits fight to compete with this, but provide an insight into Beja's past.

From the convent, take a pleasant stroll through the heart of the town to the Castelo, whose tower has good views. The nearby Igreja Santo Amaro, now an archaeological museum, is a rare reminder of Visigothic Portugal; parts of this basilica date back as far as the sixth century AD.

✚ 333 D11 ℹ Rua Capitão João Francisco de Sousa 25, 7800-451 Beja ☎ 284 311 913 🚉 Beja

Opposite *Castelo walls at Beja*
Below *Inside the chapterhouse of Beja's convent, now a museum*

CASTELO DE VIDE

www.rtsm.pt

www.cm-castelo-vide.pt

The hills of the Serra de São Mamede are where you will find a pair of picturesque hilltop villages, Marvão and Castelo de Vide. Castelo de Vide's streets huddle along the hillside from the spacious main square, an elegant expanse with a church and some fine 17th-century buildings. Behind the church, dive into the maze of narrow streets of the Judiaria, the old Jewish quarter. Winding, flower-hung alleys are lined with white houses, many retaining their Gothic doorways and windows. Steep streets climb towards the castle—one leads past a fine granite Renaissance fountain to the 13th-century synagogue, the oldest surviving in Portugal. The castle squats firmly within the fortified walls of the original medieval settlement—head for the room with the Gothic cupola and cistern, for a glimpse of the wonderful view of the village below.

✚ 331 E8 ℹ Praça Dom Pedro V, 7320-113 Castelo de Vide ☎ 245 901 361

CRATO

www.rtsm.pt

www.cm-crato.pt

Crato is an ancient agricultural town on the plateau to the west of Portalegre (▷ 245). It was a textile boom town in the 16th century and its surviving monuments date mainly from that time. There are three fine churches and a clutch of mansions, though the most interesting structure is the Varanda do Grão Prior in the main square, a type of loggia built for the outdoor celebration of Mass. Far older than all this was the castle, now an overgrown ruin but once the seat of a priory of the Knights Hospitallers of St. John of Jerusalem, a military religious order that was to evolve into the Knights of Malta.

The village of Flôr de Rosa is only 2km (1 mile) away. The highlight here is the beautifully restored *mosteiro* once owned by the Knights of Malta—it's now a *pousada*.

The village manufactures its own distinctive pottery—if you buy a *caçoila*, a round cooking pot, be aware that they are fragile and will need careful packing.

✚ 331 D8 ℹ Rua D. Nuno Álvares Pereira 58, 7430-221 Flôr da Rosa ☎ 245 997 341

CROMELEQUE DO ALMENDRES

West of Évora (▷ 240–243) is an area rich in megalithic monuments—cromlechs, dolmens and caves, all dating from between 4000 and 2000BC. Almendres is extremely easy to visit—take the N114 towards Montemor-o-Novo and after 10km (6 miles) bear left to the village of Guadalupe and follow the signs. You will find a 2.5m-high (8ft) menhir near the village, while the impressive stone circle, composed of 95 granite monoliths, is farther along the rough road. It stands in a clearing among the cork oaks, a 60m by 30m (197ft by 98ft) oval that's best explored on foot.

Nobody really knows the significance of these stone circles—they probably had a religious or astronomical purpose.

It's a lovely area, rich in bird life—look out for hoopoes in spring and early summer. In wet weather, leave the car as the road can be extremely muddy.

✚ 330 C10 ℹ Details on the sites from the Évora Tourist Information Office, Praça do Giraldo 73, 7000-508 Évora ☎ 266 777 071

ELVAS

www.rtsm.pt

www.cm-elvas.pt

If you visit only one of the Alentejan fortified towns, it should be Elvas, one of Portugal's mightiest frontier posts, whose star-shaped walls and forts make it one of Europe's most complex military fortifications, though little remains of its earliest walls. Wrested from the Moors in 1230, its later history was shaped by incessant friction with Spain that culminated in a massive 17th-century defensive building scheme under the French military architect Vauban. This incorporated the existing defences into the complex

system of forts, walls and bastions that still surrounds the town.

Begin exploring in the Praça da República, dominated by the stylistically eclectic church of Nossa Senhora da Assunção (Mon–Fri 10–12.30, 3–5.30, Sun for mass; times can vary), the town's cathedral until 1882 when the bishopric moved. It was designed by Arruda, who was also responsible for the town's Aqueduto da Amoreira. Up the hill is the Nossa Senhora da Consolação (Tue–Sun 9–12.30, 2–5.30; times may vary), an octagonal church of immense interior beauty, modelled on a Knights Templar design. Inside, its walls and eight-sided ceiling are covered with yellow-and-blue 17th-century *azulejos* (tiles), and there's a superb pulpit, fronted by a graceful iron balustrade. Outside in the Largo de Santa Clara stands the town's pillory, still topped by metal shackles. Walk farther up the hill to explore the Castelo (Mon–Fri 9.30–12.30–5.30; €1.50), built by the Moors on a Roman site—with views towards Spain.

✚ 331 E9 ℹ Praça da República, 7350-126 Elvas ☎ 268 622 236 🚉 Elvas

Below *The Judiaria was the Jewish quarter of Castelo de Vide*

Above *Marvão's 13th-century castle was built to guard the frontier with Spain*

ESTREMOZ
www.cm-estremoz.pt
www.visitevora.pt

Estremoz stands at the heart of a marble-quarrying area, a pleasing city whose Saturday market is one of Portugal's biggest and liveliest—a great place to buy the bright local pottery, made here since the 16th century, sometimes decorated with marble chips.

The town is neatly divided into two, the lower quarter focused round the huge marketplace, the Rossio, lined with cafés and the marble-faced former Câmara Municipal. It's also where you will find the Museu Rural (tel 963 004 79; Tue–Sat 10–12.30, 2–5.30; €1), a good place to see the full range of local pottery, as well as displays of Alentejan tools, textiles and objects. For religious art and artefacts try the Museu de Arte Sacra at Rossio Marquês de Pombal (tel 967 528 98; Mon–Fri 9–12.30, 2–5.30, Sun –5.30; €1).

You can walk from the Rossio up the hill to the Vila Velha (Old Town), once one of Portugal's major fortified citadels and a splendid contrast to the 'new' town below. Bulky walls surround the nucleus of this historic heart, whose focus is a harmonious open square around which stand Gothic and Manueline buildings. The eye-catching 13th-century Torre de Menagem is now one of Portugal's most famous *pousadas*. Go inside and climb the main tower for views of the town below and surrounding

countryside. Don't miss the Capela da Rainha Santa Isabel to the right behind the *pousada*, a beautiful chapel with *azulejos* (tiles) depicting stories from the life of the saintly queen. One tells of the Miracle of the Roses, when a skirtful of bread she was taking to the poor against her husband's wishes miraculously turned to roses when he demanded to see what she was carrying. Near here, the fine old almshouses are now the Museu Municipal (tel 268 333 608; Tue–Sun 10–12.30, 2–5.30; €2.50), with displays of historic pottery figures.

🖼 331 D9 🛈 Praça da República 26, 7100-505 Estremoz ☎ 268 333 541

ÉVORA
▷ 240–243.

ÉVORAMONTE
www.visitevora.pt

If you are driving north from Évora on the E802, you will pass through rolling country, dotted with whitewashed villages and softened by stands of cork oaks and olive groves. Some 15km (9 miles) southwest of Estremoz is a castle surrounded by walls and battlemented towers. This is Évoramonte, a historic, fortified medieval town and castle on a steep 474m-high (1,558ft) hill. The Romans were the first to fortify the site and, as elsewhere, they were followed by the Moors, who were evicted by Afonso III. Dom Dinis ringed the hilltop with walls in the

1200s, but the castle gained its present appearance when João III reconstructed it after an earthquake in the 16th century. He built the solid rounded towers at the corners, and added the huge ropework course to the outer walls. The knots are Bragança dynasty symbols derived from a play on words on their motto *'Despois vós, nós'* ('After you, us'); *'nós'* can mean both 'us' and 'knots'. There's not much to see inside but, if the weather's clear, it's worth climbing the battlements, from where you are supposed to be able to see from one side of Portugal to the other.

🖼 331 D9 🛈 Rua de Santa Maria, 7100-314 Évoramonte ☎ 268 959 227

MARVÃO
www.cm-marvao.pt
www.rtsm.pt

Perched high on the eastern frontier, little Marvão is a compact fortified town with a superb castle and some of the finest panoramas over mountainous border country in the Alentejo. For the best views, stay the night and get up early to see dawn breaking over Spain.

Encircled Marvão was settled by the Romans, Visigoths and Moors, fell to the Christians in 1166 and got its castle under Dom Dinis in 1229. From then on it was a key border fort, but, isolated, windy and waterless, it was always difficult to keep manned. The garrison was often made up of exiled soldiers and malcontents, who chose service here rather than face prison.

In the town, pop into the old church of Santa Maria, now the tourist office and a small museum (tel 245 909 132; daily 9–12.30, 2–5.30; €1), and look out for the Manueline doors and wrought-iron balconies that adorn many buildings. The castle has fortified gates, parapet walkways, crenellated watchtowers and an underground cistern, which provided catchment water for the medieval garrison.

🖼 331 E8 🛈 Posto de Turismo, Largo de Santa Maria, 7330-101 Marvão ☎ 245 909 131

INFORMATION

www.cm-evora.pt/guiaturistico
www.visitevora.pt
☩ 331 D10 🛈 Praça do Giraldo
73, 7004-508 Évora ☎ 266 777 071
🕓 Apr–end Oct daily 9–7; Nov–end Mar
daily 9–6 🚊 Évora

INTRODUCTION

Aim to spend a night in Évora to give yourself enough time to explore the city properly and for the pleasure of enjoying it after dark, when many of the buildings are floodlit. Alternatively arrive early in the day and allow the whole morning to see the main sights. Whatever your schedule, you'll probably have to leave your car outside the city walls, so start by walking up the hill to the Praça do Giraldo, the main square, where you can drop into the tourist office for local information. From here, head up one of the steepish streets to the top of the hill, where you'll find most of Évora's main sights—the Sé (cathedral), the Templo Romano and the museum. After visiting these, head back down, perhaps stopping for a drink in an outdoor café in the Giraldo.

South of here, and down the hill from the left-hand corner of the Praça do Giraldo, is the church of São Francisco and the extraordinary Capela dos Ossos. If you would like to spend some time shopping, the best streets are Rua da República, Rua dos Mercadores and Rua João de Deus. All three streets run off the Praça do Giraldo.

Évora was an important city in Roman times, when it was the political heart of Iberia. When Rome fell, the city declined, its fortunes reviving only during four centuries of Moorish occupation. It became an important agricultural and trading hub, a tangle of typically Moorish streets growing up around the old Roman core. By the mid-12th century, internal squabbles were weakening the Muslims, prompting Afonso Henriques to attack. In 1165 the town became the seat of the royal House of Avis and remained the capital of choice through to the 16th century. Scholars, writers, architects and artists flocked to the court, enriching Évora with churches, monuments and stately mansions. In 1559 Dom Henriques founded a prestigious Jesuit university, but this proved to be the final flowering of Évora's golden age as in 1580 Portugal was annexed by Spain.

Although the country regained its independence in 1640, later monarchs moved the court closer to Lisbon, the university closed, and Évora became a backwater. It was this obscurity that preserved Évora until the 20th century, when intensive restoration began, culminating in the city becoming a World Heritage Site in 1986. The university reopened in the 1970s, and Évora is once again a successful regional capital, a university city and an agricultural hub.

Above *The dramatic hilltop Templo Romano is incredibly well preserved*

WHAT TO SEE

TEMPLO ROMANO

For a chronological tour, start at the Templo Romano, just west of the Sé on top of the hill. This architectural fragment is the best-preserved Roman ruin in Portugal. The temple was probably built in the second or third centuries AD for worshipping Jupiter—though locals believe it was a temple to the goddess Diana. What's left comprises 14 elegant columns raised on a high plinth, the carving of the marble Corinthian capitals being wonderfully preserved. It comes into its own at night when floodlights bring drama to the ruins.

✚ 243 B2

SÉ

The Sé is a fortress-like construction that, with its rounded arches, is typical of the Portuguese Romanesque style. Building started around 1185 on the site of the former mosque and continued into the 13th century. The result was a church that combines Romanesque and Gothic elements, as on the main façade where the plain and solid towers flank an intricate doorway, carved with figures of the Apostles by late 13th-century French and Portuguese sculptors.

Inside, Gothic features dominate in the high nave, with its barrel vaulting and beautiful transept dome, while there are Romanesque echoes in the clerestory arcade running high above the nave and behind the apse. Don't miss the rose windows—the north one shows the Morning Star and the south the Mystic Rose. Elsewhere in the cathedral, be sure to take in the Gothic cloister, built between 1322 and 1340, where the elegant tracery contrasts with the solid granite stonework. You will get a good view of the bell tower, pure Romanesque, from the southwest corner, and it's also worth visiting the terrace for views of the town.

An even better townscape opens up from the terrace over the main door, which you'll cross on your way to the Museu de Arte Sacra and the choir in the gallery. Pause to examine the choir stalls with their lively carvings of agricultural scenes before tackling the museum. This is crammed with rich textiles, vestments and a mass of ecclesiastical silver, jewellery and statues—look out for the mind-boggling solid gold rosary and the chalice studded with emeralds and diamonds.

✚ 243 B2 ✉ Largo Marquês de Marialva, 7000-809 Évora ☎ 266 759 330 🕐 Sé: Jul–end Aug daily 9–5; rest of year daily 9–12.15, 2–4.45. Museum: Jul–end Aug Tue–Sun 9–4.30; rest of year Tue–Sun 9–12, 2–4.30 💶 Sé: €1; Sé and Cloister: €1.50; Sé, Cloister and Museum €3

Below *The cathedral's façade, a mix of Romanesque and Gothic styles*

» Do not drive into the middle of Évora outside the winter; instead, use one of the numerous well-signposted parking areas outside the walls of the old city.

» Évora has a particularly lively *passeio* (early evening promenade), when it seems as if the whole city is out on the streets. See this at its best in and around the Praça do Giraldo.

IGREJA/CONVENTO DOS LOIOS

The Convento dos Loios, a church and monastery dedicated to St. John the Baptist, dates from 1585. It was owned by the dukes of Cadaval, and is now one of Portugal's most appealing *pousadas*, so, unless you're staying, it's off-limits. You can, however, visit the convent's church, rebuilt after the 1755 earthquake, whose nave is totally covered from floor to ceiling with *azulejos* (tiles) telling the story of St. Laurence Justinian, Patriarch of Venice. The nave contains some fine Renaissance tombs and you can peer through a floor grille to the ossuary which contains the bones of the monks who lived and died in the monastery.

✚ 243 B2 ✉ Largo do Conde de Vila Flor, 7000-804 Évora ☎ 266 704 714 🕐 Tue–Sun 9–12.30, 2–6 (sometimes closed without notice) ✋ €3

IGREJA DE SÃO FRANCISCO

South of the Praça do Giraldo you will find Évora's other main attraction, the church of São Francisco and its gruesome adjunct, the Capela dos Ossos (Chapel of Bones). The Franciscan church was built in the early 16th century and is fronted by an unusual portico, whose diversely shaped arches—pointed, rounded and horseshoe—are crowned with battlements and pinnacles. The lofty building is typical of the Franciscan style; the order's churches were used for preaching, so there had to be room for the crowds who came to hear Mass from miles around.

✚ 243 B3 ✉ Praça 1° de Maio, 7000-650 Évora ☎ 266 704 521 🕐 Daily 9–12.30, 2.30–5.15 ✋ Free

CAPELA DOS OSSOS

The chapterhouse of the Igreja de São Francisco gives access to the Capela dos Ossos, built between 1460 and 1510 for the bones of more than 5,000 monks, collected from various resting places across Évora, where they were taking up valuable space. Walls and columns are entirely covered with neatly arranged tibias, femurs, vertebrae and skulls, a macabre design highlighted by the welcoming inscription over the door, which reads *'Nós ossos, que aqui estamos, Pelos vossos esperamos'* ('We bones here are waiting for your bones'). There's a certain grimness, too, in the braids of hair hung about the entrance, left here by young women as good-luck offerings before they embarked on marriage.

✚ 243 B3 ✉ Praça 1° de Maio, 7000-650 Évora ☎ 266 744 307 🕐 Daily 9–12.45, 2.30–5.45 ✋ €1.50

MORE TO SEE

ANTIGA UNIVERSIDADE

These university buildings have a lovely inner courtyard and a fine 16th-century cloister with an attractively arched gallery.

✚ 243 C2 ✉ Largo dos Colegiais, 7004-516 Évora ☎ 266 740 800 🕐 Mon–Fri 8–9, Sat 10–2, 3–6 ✋ €1.25 Sat 3–6 (rest of week free)

AQUEDUTO DA AGUA PRATA

This magnificent medieval aqueduct runs into the city from the northwest—walk west from the Giraldo along Rua do Cano to traverse it and admire the houses that have been built in its arches.

✚ 243 A1 ✉ 7000-708 Évora

LARGO DA PORTA DE MOURA

Évora's most picturesque square is divided into two unequal-sized sections, the larger one containing a Renaissance fountain. The whole square is bordered by fine 16th-century houses with Manueline-Moorish arcades.

✚ 243 C2 ✉ 7000-708 Évora

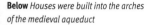

Below *Houses were built into the arches of the medieval aqueduct*

MOURARIA

The name was coined to define the old Moorish quarter to the north of the cathedral complex. It consists of picturesque cobbled alleys and tiny squares.
✚ 243 B1 ✉ 7000 Évora

PRAÇA DO GIRALDO

This beautiful central square, with its arcaded shops, lies at the heart of the city. The fountain standing on the site of the Roman triumphal arch dates from the 18th century.
✚ 243 B2 ✉ Praça do Giraldo, 7000-508 Évora

Above *The interior of the macabre Capela dos Ossos in the Igreja de São Francisco*

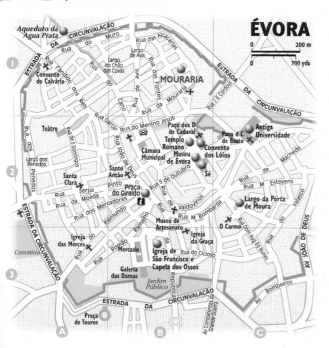

Above *The Igreja Matriz in Mértola was once a mosque*

Right *Cobbled street in tiny Monsaraz*

MÉRTOLA

www.rt-planiciedourada.pt

www.cm-mertola.pt

Mértola stands at the confluence of the Guadiana and Oeiras rivers. Here, the river valley breaks the monotony of the plains, with the little white town rising on the slopes above. At the highest point stands the 12th-century castle—it's partly ruined but excavations around it are slowly revealing traces of a Roman and Moorish past.

For more insight, visit the small Museu de Mértola (Jul to mid-Sep Tue–Sun 9.30–12.30, 2–6; rest of year Tue–Sun 9–12.30, 2–5.30; €2 for each collection or €5 for all collections), which has a nicely presented collection of local finds. Also don't miss the Igreja Matriz, the parish church, which started life as a mosque. It's a wonderful building, virtually square, with a typically Moorish forest of columns supporting the central space. Behind the high altar you'll see the *mihrab,* the old prayer niche.

✚ 333 D12 🛈 Rua da Igreja 31, 7750-338 Mértola ☎ 286 610 109

MONSARAZ

The Alentejo is scattered with villages and it's hard to choose which to visit. Don't miss Marvão (▷ 239) or Monsaraz though.

Monsaraz has a superb hilltop settlement with a castle encircled by walls. It has just four streets, all cobbled, but it's a great place to wander. Walk up the Rua Direita to see the best of the village houses, many dating from the 16th and 17th centuries and adorned with the exterior staircases and wrought-iron balconies that are typical of the Alentjo area. On the way you will pass the Igreja Matriz, with a 14th-century carved tomb, and the Antigo Tribunal, once the town's courthouse—on the left, with pointed arches over the doors and windows. At the end, the street widens into a square, with an 18th-century pillory.

The castle was built by Dom Dinis in the 14th century, some 200 years after Monsaraz was captured from the Moors and became a Knights Templar fortress. Part of the Templar fort has been turned into a bullring, but time is better spent admiring the incredible views of the surrounding landscape dotted with cork stands and olive groves.

✚ 331 E10 🛈 Largo Dom Nuno Álvares Pereira, 7200-175 Monsaraz

✉ 266 557 136

MOURA

www.rt-planiciedourada.pt

Moura, surrounded by silvery-grey olive groves, is a pretty, low-key spa town, its clutch of mansions and monuments testifying to a wealthy past. It's named after a Moorish girl, who threw herself in despair from the castle after her lover was slain by Christian knights who went on to occupy the town. The Moors were here from the eighth century AD up to 1233, and the Mouraria quarter, all narrow streets and low houses decorated with tiles, is the oldest part of town.

More elegant is the spacious pedestrian main square, home to a fine Câmara Municipal, which stands facing the Gothic church of São João Baptista. As you enter the church through the lovely Manueline doorway you are met by twisted white marble columns and soaring vaulting, the simplicity lifted by the vivid tiles in the chapels to either side of the high altar.

Outside, to the right, is the entrance to the thermal baths, nestling in a pretty garden. The waters are recommended for the treatment of rheumatism.

✚ 333 D11 🛈 Largo Santa Clara, 7860-204 Moura ☎ 285 251 375

PORTALEGRE

www.cm-portalegre.pt
www.rtsm.pt
Capital of the Alto Alentejo,
Portalegre crouches in the shadow
of the Serra de São Mamede. It's an
attractive town, whose mansions,
the legacy of its 17th- and 18th-
century industrial heyday, give the
historic heart of the place an air of
faded elegance that has survived
even the incursions of modern
traffic. Portalegre built its wealth on
textiles, concentrating on intricate
tapestry and fine silk, and the
surviving Fábrica Real de Tapeçarias
still takes tapestry commissions
from all over Europe, knotting more
than 5,000 shades of wool 250,000
times for each square metre. You can
see some of the historic products in
the Museu da Tapecaria do Guy Fino
in the Rua da Figueira (tel 245 307
530; Tue–Sun 9.30–12.10, 2.30–5.30;
€2). To see what the fruits of 17th-
century industry built, walk up the
Rua 10 de Junho, a narrow and now
sadly traffic-clogged street that's
lined with splendid mansions. This
leads to the Largo da Sé and the
16th- to 18th-century cathedral.
The square is overlooked by the
former seminary. This now houses
the Museu Municipal (tel 245 300
120 ext 344; Tue–Sun 9.30–12.30,
2–6; €2), an eclectic collection of
religious art, ivories, ceramics and
some examples of early carpets
from Arraiolos (▷ 237).
✚ 333 E8 ℹ Rua Guilherme Gomes
Fernandes 28, 7300-186 Portalegre ☎ 245
307 445 ☎ Portalegre

SANTIAGO DO CACÉM

www.visitcostaazul.com
www.cm-santiago-do-cacem.pt
Heading south through the Alentejo
from Lisbon, Santiago do Cacém
makes a good stop. It's a pleasant
town with a highly impressive
Moorish castle, a laid-back
atmosphere and easy access to
one of Portugal's most compelling
Roman sites. Begin by heading
up to the castle, rebuilt by the
Knights Templar and encircled with
battlements—with superb views.
Wander round the old lower town
and visit the Museu Municipal in the
Praça de Municipio (Tue–Fri 10–12,
2–4.30, Sat 12–6, Sun 2.30–5; free),
an excellent regional museum
housed in what was one of the
Salazar regime's most notorious
prisons. One of the cells has been
preserved, but of more appeal are
the mock-ups of Alentejan interiors.
From here head out to Miróbriga,
the ruins of a Roman town that
thrived between the first and fourth
centuries AD. It's a romantic grassy
site, where you can follow what
was a Roman road from the Temple
of Jupiter and the Forum, at the
highest point, to the baths, where
the heating systems and the water
channels are still visible.
✚ 332 B11 ℹ Praça do Mercado, 7540-
135 Santiago do Cacém ☎ 269 826 696

SERPA

www.rt-planiciedourada.pt
Serpa, overlooking a classic
Alentejan landscape of vast rolling
wheatfields dotted with cork oaks
and planted with olives and vines,
has all the classic ingredients of a
plains' market town—a walled heart
around a castle and narrow streets.
It's a good stop if you are heading
south to the Algarve.
To see the best of Serpa, walk
through the fortified gate in the
ramparts into the middle of town,
where you will find the main square
and parish church. Turn down to the
right to reach the mainly Moorish
castle—climb up to the sentry
path for splendid views. You can
learn more about Serpa's past
in the Museu Etnográfico In the
Largo do Corro (Tue–Sun 9–12.30,
2–5.30; free), where agricultural and
domestic implements, costumes
and craft exhibits illustrate aspects
of the local story.
✚ 333 D11 ℹ Largo Dom Jorge de Melo
2/3, 7830-382 Serpa ☎ 284 544 727

Below *Elegant Portalegre is still attractive
despite modern traffic*

REGIONS THE ALENTEJO • SIGHTS

SERRA DE SÃO MAMEDE

www.icnb.pt

Tucked up against the Spanish border, the Serra de São Mamede, a green and hilly oasis, comes as a welcome relief after the flatlands to the south. This rocky lump is a geological aberration, the altitude, granite and impermeable soil creating sufficient humidity for a lush range of green vegetation to thrive. You can explore the entire range in two to three hours by car, stopping to enjoy the fresh, clear mountain air and take in the picturesque villages of Marvão (▷ 239) and Castelo de Vide (▷ 238) along the way.

The road climbs steeply from Portalegre (▷ 245), through chestnut and cork oak to reach an undulating plateau where you will see irrigated fields, olives, vines and timeless hamlets, along with pigs, chickens

and mules. The highest point is São Mamede (1,025m/ 3,336ft), signposted off the main road, from where there are incredible views over the Alentejo and eastwards towards the Spanish *sierras*.

The whole area is tiny, a miniature mountain wilderness with good walking on well-marked trails. Most of the walks are circular and vary from around 8 to 18km (5 to 11 miles)—pick up a leaflet at any of the local tourist offices.

✚ 331 F8 🚹 Rua Guilherme Gomes Fernandes 22, 7300-954 Portalegre ☎ 245 307 445 🚹 Praça Dom Pedro V, Castelo de Vide ☎ 245 901 361 🚹 Largo de Santa Maria, Marvão ☎ 245 909 131

VILA NOVA DE MILFONTES

www.vnmilfontes.net

www.cm-odemira.pt

The southern Alentejo coast is popular with Portuguese

Above *Vila Nova de Milfontes, the Alentejo's liveliest tourist resort, clusters round the Mira's sandy estuary*

holidaymakers, many of whom spend their summer vacations at Vila Nova, a good-value, no-frills seaside town on the sandy estuary of the River Mira. It's the Alentejo's liveliest and most crowded resort, with a wide range of modern hotels, good restaurants and some far funkier clubs than you might expect in this largely rural region.

It's still essentially Portuguese, with an old heart and a castle, giving it a more genuine atmosphere than resorts in the Algarve. Escape the crowded beaches in high summer by heading southward down the coast, where the sea and scenery are wilder.

✚ 332 B12 🚹 Rua António Mantas, 7645 221 Vila Nova de Milfontes ☎ 283 996 599

VILA VIÇOSA

The seat of the Bragança dynasty and site of their last palace, Vila Viçosa is a prosperous and attractive town with an ancient hilltop castle and walled village. The dukes of Bragança established their seat at Vila Viçosa in the 15th century. It was the fourth duke who began work on the ducal palace, and with building under way, the town became the base for a burgeoning court.

The Braganças eventually moved on to grander palaces in Lisbon (▷ 63–105), Mafra (▷ 110), Queluz (▷ 110) and Sintra (▷ 112–115), stripping their original seat of many of its treasures. But they retained a fondness for the place, often returning to hunt from their simple country home. Portugal's last two kings, Dom Carlos 1 and Manuel II, were particularly fond of Vila Viçosa. Manuel's will established the Fundação da Casa de Bragança, and the doors of the palace opened to the public in the 1940s.

THE PAÇO DUCAL

Situated in the aptly named Terreiro do Paço, the Paço Ducal sprawls over two wings and three floors of an elegant, flat-fronted building set back from a spacious square with an equestrian statue of João IV.

Before you go in, admire the Porta dos Nós, a splendid gateway that's one of the last remnants of the original 16th-century wall—its Manueline knots are a play on the Bragança motto *'Despois vós, nós'* ('After you, us'). Knots were chosen as the family's emblem because *'nós'* can mean 'us', 'we' and 'knots'. Inside, the tour takes you through a series of lavishly decorated rooms. Of these, the Sala dos Duques stands out, both for its gilded and painted ceiling showing the Bragança dukes and the splendid 17th-century tapestries, designed by Rubens. Far more evocative, though, are the private apartments of Dom Carlos I and his wife Maria-Amélia, left virtually untouched since the couple left for Lisbon on 1 February 1908. The king was assassinated that same afternoon.

The huge porcelain collection mostly dates from the 17th to 19th centuries. It's particularly strong on Chinese ware, but fine examples from all the major European manufacturers include Meissen, Limoges, Worcester, Dresden and Delft. From here, move to the Coach Museum in what were the royal stables—more than 70 beautifully maintained and venerable vehicles are housed here.
✉ Terreiro do Paço, 7160-251 Vila Viçosa ☎ 268 980 659 🕐 Apr–end Sep Tue 2.30–5.30, Wed–Fri 10–1, 2.30–5.30, Sat–Sun 9.30–1, 2.30–6; rest of year Tue 2–5, Wed 10–1, 2–5, Thu–Sun 9.30–1, 2–5. Guided tours only; last tours leave 60 min before closing. The treasury is only open Oct–May; guided visits at 12.15 and 3.30 ✋ Palace: €6. Armoury: €2.50. Coach Museum: €1.50. Chinese Porcelain Collection: €2.50. Treasury: €2.50. Castle €3. Child (under 10) free

INFORMATION

www.cm-vilavicosa.pt
✚ 331 E9 🛈 Praça da República, 7160-207 Vila Viçosa ☎ 268 881 101
🕐 Apr–end Oct Mon–Fri 9–12.30, 2–9; rest of year Mon–Fri 9–12.30, 2–6

TIPS

» Allow an hour for the main palace, 45 minutes to an hour for the armoury, 30 minutes for the coach collection, and the same for the Chinese porcelain and treasury respectively.

» Apart from a couple of expensive options, there's little accommodation in the town, so it's best to visit for the day from Évora or Estremoz.

Below *The impressive frontage of the Paço Ducale*

THE LOWER ALENTEJO

This drive takes you through the lonely country of the Baixo Alentejo, where villages and towns are few and far between and the landscape has a special and unique beauty—a real taste of the undiscovered Portugal many visitors miss.

THE DRIVE

Distance: 222km (138 miles)
Time: 4–5 hours
Start/end at: Mértola

★ Leave Mértola (▷ 244) by crossing the River Guadiana to join the N265 towards Serpa. You'll get a good view back towards the town as you cross the bridge. The road climbs through an area that's designated as the Parque Natural do Vale do Guadiana.

❶ The Parque Natural do Vale do Guadiana is good for birds. Watch out for storks, azure-winged magpies, and egrets in the wetter areas. Once you've gained altitude, the road runs through shady avenues of eucalyptus, introduced here from the southern hemisphere in the early 20th century.

After 17km (10.5 miles) you'll come to the Barragem da Tapada reservoir,

and the old copper-mining town of Mina de São Domingos. You're less than 5km (3 miles) from the Spanish border here, although there's no crossing point.

❷ Mina de São Domingos has been the focus of mining from Roman times right up to the 1960s. The small Casa-Museu do Mineiro in São Domingos traces the impact of more than 2,000 years of industrialization on the landscape. The site is well worth visiting, especially if you're interested in industrial archaeology. Guided visits can be arranged through the museum (tel 286 647 534).

Continue north on the N265 for 37km (23 miles) until you get to the sign for Serpa. Before entering the town, it's worth making a quick detour. Follow the *pousada* signs up the hill to take in the fine views over the plain. Also visit the little

whitewashed chapel of Nossa Senhora da Guadalupe.

❸ Serpa (▷ 245) is found at the end of a stretch of road that passes through some classic Alentejan landscape. It's an undulating country made up of huge wheat fields, dotted with cork oaks and interspersed with sheep pastures and olive groves. It has a beauty all of its own, partly because it is virtually uninhabited. Santa Iria, just across the river Limas, relieves the monotony; it's a farming village that makes its living from olive and orange groves.

Leave Serpa on the N255, signposted to Espanha.

❹ Pias is the first village on this lovely road. It's worth a stop here to see the frescoes in the Igreja de Santa Luzia and to sample the local red wine.

Opposite *Mértola stands at the confluence of the Guadiana and Oeiras rivers*
Below *Serpa town and castle*

From here, stay on the N255 through olive groves and vineyards until you reach Moura (▷ 244).

❺ Moura is a thermal spa town with Moorish roots. Its name, meaning 'Moorish Maiden', relates to a legendary tale of a Moorish girl who threw herself to her death from the tower of the castle when Christian knights killed her fiancé and captured the town on her wedding day.

Leave Moura on the N255. Just after crossing the river Ardila, turn left onto the N233 towards Alqueva and Portel. The Alqueva dam will soon come into view.

❻ The Alqueva dam is the result of a huge and contentious EU-funded project to dam the river Guadiana, with what could be hugely detrimental effects on the ecosystem of the whole area. Despite worldwide opposition from environmentalists, the dam gates closed and the reservoir started to fill in 2002. Now full, it is Europe's largest reservoir, with a total surface area of 250sq km (155sq miles) and perimeter of 1,200km (746 miles). Campaigners hope that by stopping the fill at this level many of the threatened trees and wildlife habitats will be safeguarded

Follow the N384 to Portel then turn left onto the IP2 towards Beja (▷ 237), a pleasant town at the heart of the Alentejo's southern plains.

❼ Beja's story goes back to Roman times. Its name is a corruption of the Latin *pax* (peace), given to the town in celebration of a peace treaty agreed here between Julius Caesar and the Lusitanians in 48BC.

Leave Beja on the IP2 south. After 15km (9 miles) turn onto the N122 for the journey back to Mértola.

WHERE TO EAT
In Serpa, there's Molha o Bico in Rua Quente, in Pias the Restaurante O Lagar in the Estrada de Brinches, and in Moura there is O Trilho on Rua 5 Outubro. In Beja, you could try A Esquina in Rua Infante D. Henrique, or, for something a little more sophisticated, the Pousada de São Francisco (▷ 256), which serves regional cuisine.

WHEN TO GO
Spring or autumn are the best times for this drive; avoid high summer, when the heat can be unbearable in this exposed countryside.

PLACES TO VISIT
SERPA
(▷ 245).

MOURA
(▷ 244).

BEJA
(▷ 237).

Above *Shops around Évora's main square, Praça do Giraldo*

ALQUEVA
BARRAGEM DE ALQUEVA
Having taken four years to fill, Alqueva is now Western Europe's largest reservoir, providing irrigation and hydro-electric power for the region. Its floodgates, between the village of Alqueva and town of Moura, are an impressive sight.
✉ Alqueva ☎ 285 251 375 (tourist office at Barragem)

ALTER DO CHÃO
COUDELARIA REAL
www.snc.min-agricultura.pt
The Royal Stud at Alter was founded in 1748 by João V to breed and train horses for the House of Bragança. Pure Andalucian stock was used to breed the now world-famous performing Lusitanians, which can be seen during training sessions.
✉ 7440-152 Alter do Chão ☎ 245 610 060 ⏰ Visits: Tue–Fri 10, 11.30, 2, 3.30, Sat–Sun 10.30, 3 🖐 Guided visits €3.80 🚌 4km (2.5 miles) northwest of Alter do Chão; follow signs to the Coudelaria

ARRAIOLOS
CALIFA
www.freewebs.com/califa
Founded in 1916, Califa is the oldest rug manufacturer in Arraiolos.

Its showrooms, furnished with antiques, have fantastic displays of traditional handcrafted rugs, while in the studio you can see the craftspeople at work on the intricate and individual designs. A shipping service is available.
✉ Rua Alexandre Herculano 34, 7040-029 Arraiolos ☎ 965 538 829 ⏰ Mon–Fri 9–1, 2–6

BEJA
CAFÉ LUIS DA ROCHA
The Alentejo is renowned for its *doces conventuais* (sweet eggy desserts, traditionally made by local nuns), and this art deco-style shop is one of the best places to buy them. Also try unique *porquinhos doces* (sweet pigs), made with marzipan, eggs and squash.
✉ Rua Capitão João Francisco de Sousa 63, 7800-451 Beja ☎ 284 323 179 ⏰ Jul–end Sep Mon–Sat 8am–11pm; rest of year daily 8am–11pm

CASA DE CHÁ MALTESINHAS
This tea house specializes in *doces conventuais*, but deliberately limits what it makes to typical Beja recipes handed down from the nearby convents. Try *toucinho do céu*, a fine pastry with a rich almond filling, or

queijinhos de hóstia, made with a sweet egg custard.
✉ Rua dos Açoutados 35, 7800-493 Beja ☎ 284 321 500 ⏰ Mon–Sat 9–7.30

IGREJA DA MISERICORDIA
For the best selection of crafts in town, this converted church is now dedicated to promoting the work of artisans of the southern Alentejo region. Don't miss the delicate linen embroideries, considered to be Beja's strong point.
✉ Praça da República, 7800-427 Beja ⏰ Daily 9.30–12.30, 2–5.30

CASTELO DE VIDE
CASA DA VILA
Near the 16th-century marble fountain, this ceramics shop sells pottery, most of which is hand-painted on site. If you are staying in the area for a while, ask about decorating your choice of plain pieces, which can then be fired and collected a few days later.
✉ Largo Dr. José Frederico Laranja 4, Fonte da Vila, 7320-110 Castelo de Vide ☎ 245 919 169 ⏰ Apr–end Oct daily 9–7; Nov–end Mar daily 9–6

PARQUE NATURAL DA SERRA DE SÃO MAMEDE

For a hike in the Serra de São Mamede, start at the park office, which has information on flora and fauna and semi-reliable maps of marked trails, often along medieval cobbleways, tracks and paths.

✉ Centro de Interpretação do Parque de São Mamede, Praça Dom Pedro V, 7320-177 Castelo de Vide ☎ 245 901 306
🕐 Mon–Fri 9.30–12.30, 2–5.30 🚪 In same building as tourist office

ELVAS

AMEIXAS D'ELVAS

Ameixas d'Elvas (Elvas plums) have been produced in the region of Elvas since the 15th century. These sugar plums are in fact greengages. Despite the misnomer they make an excellent gift and are best served with the local *sericaia* dessert. Pick up both at any of the town's *pastelarias* such as Pastelaria Cantarinha (Rua da Cadeia 41-A, 7350-146 Elvas; tel 268 624 241).

ESTREMOZ

JOÃO PORTUGAL RAMOS-VINHOS, S. A.

www.vinhosdoalentejo.pt
www.jportugalramos.com

A stop along one of the three wine routes in the region, the João Portugal Ramos winery uses a selection of noble grape varieties, such as Aragonez, Trincadeira and Antão Vaz. Reserve a day ahead for a tour and tasting.

✉ Monte da Caldeira, 7100-149 Estremoz ☎ 268 339 910 🕐 Reception/shop: Mon–Fri 9–6.30, Sat 10–6; visits/tastings Mon–Fri 9.30–12.30, 2.30–4.30, Sat 10–4.30 🍷 Visit free; wine tasting €5.50 🚪 Head out of town on the EN4 towards Montemor. The winery is signed about 1.5km (1 mile) after the Galp fuel station.

MERCADO TRADICIONAL

Held along the southern side of the Rossio, Estremoz's market is especially noted for its crafts, rustic antiques and unglazed earthenware pottery, including typical Estremoz terracotta figurines. It is also good for goat's- and ewe's-milk cheese.

✉ Rossio do Marquês de Pombal, 7100-513 Estremoz ☎ 268 333 541 (tourist office)
🕐 Sat 8–1

ÉVORA

A CHAPELARIA

Under the arches in the main square, this hat store is the only shop in Évora to have preserved its traditional interior. Ceilings are decorated with stucco reliefs and the walls are lined with old wooden cabinets displaying a huge range of hats for all tastes.

✉ Rua da República 7–9, 7000-656 Évora
🕐 Mon–Fri 9.30–1.30, 3–7, Sat 9.30–1

ARTESANATO DIANA

For a selection of good-quality regional crafts, try this shop to the east of Praça do Giraldo. As well as leather, cork and sheepskin items, it also sells the typical Alentejan *capotes*: heavy woollen capes with fur collars, that are ideal for winter.

✉ Rua 5 de Outubro 48, 7000-054 Évora
📠 266 704 600 🕐 Daily 9.30–1, 3–7

CONCERTOS DE MUSICA CLÁSSICA

Promoted by the Duchess of Cadaval, these classical concerts are held outdoors in the Jardim do Paço or in the Loios church and are the highlight of Évora's cultural calendar. For tickets and information, contact the tourist office.

☎ 266 777 071 (tourist office) 🕐 Evenings in July

LIVRARIA NAZARETH

Opposite the tourist office in the main square, this bookshop has been in business since 1890 and, while most publications are in Portuguese, they do stock some English language coffee-table books which make great gifts and mementos. They also sell maps.

✉ Praça do Giraldo 46, 7000-508 Évora
☎ 266 702 221 🕐 Mon–Fri 9–1, 3–7, Sat 9–1

MARKETS

Évora's main market is held on the second Tuesday of each month at the Rossio de São Brás. Its endless stands sell everything from shoes and clothes to agricultural hardware and fresh produce. On the second Sunday of the month there is an antiques market at the Largo do Chão das Covas near the aqueduct.

☎ 226 777 071 (tourist office)

OFICINA BAR

Just off Praça Giraldo and playing a mix of music—jazz, blues and Lou Reed—this friendly bar attracts all ages; especially student and artist types who browse newspapers, check emails and enjoy the fabulous *shoarma* (spit-roasted lamb), which is served late into the evening.

✉ Rua da Moeda 27, 7000-513 Évora
☎ 266 707 312 🕐 Tue–Fri 8pm–2am, Sat 9pm–2am

OFICINA DA TERRA

www.oficinadaterra.com

If you are interested in ceramics, it's well worth visiting this gallery and workshop off the western side of the Praça do Giraldo. The handmade ceramics, especially the terracotta character figures made by Tiago Cabeça, have won national prizes.

✉ Travessa do Sertório 26, 7000-561 Évora (just off Praça Municipal) ☎ 266 746 049 🕐 Mon–Sat 10–7, Sun and national holidays 1–6

PASTELARIA PÃO DE RALA

This tile-panelled cake shop is the best place in Évora to buy *doces conventuais*. As well as trying the *pão de rala*, made with marzipan, almond and squash, don't miss the less sweet *cerica*, a dense cinnamon-flavoured sponge.

✉ Rua do Cicioso 47, 7000-658 Évora
☎ 266 707 778 🕐 Daily 7.30am–8pm

PISCINAS MUNICIPAIS

These municipal pools have something for everyone. There is a baby and toddler pool, a pool for people learning to swim, a diving pool and an Olympic-size pool.

✉ Avenida Eng. Arantes e Oliveira, Évora
☎ 266 777 186 🕐 Jul to mid-Sep Sun–Mon 1–8, Tue–Sat 9–8 🍷 €2.50
🚪 Outside the town walls; follow signs to *'Piscinas Municipais'*

ROTA DOS VINHOS DO ALENTEJO

www.vinhosdoalentejo.pt

Contact this establishment for information, driving instructions and lists of wineries on the area's three wine routes: the São Mamede route, the Historic route and the Guadiana route.

✉ Praça Joaquim António de Aguiar 20–21, 7000-510 Évora ☎ 266 746 498 or 266 746 609 🕐 Mon–Fri 9–12.30, 2–5.30

SCOOTBIKE

Bicycling is a great way to explore Évora's narrow cobbled streets. Scootbike is right next to the Câmara Municipal (municipality building); they rent out bicycles either by the hour or the day. Safety helmets are included in the rental price.

✉ Praça do Sertório 6, 7000-509 Évora ☎ 266 731 666 🕐 Mon–Sat 9–1, 3–7 ✋ €3 for 1 hour, €5 for 2 hours, €20 for 24 hours, helmets included

Below *Colourful locally made pottery for sale at the Mercado Tradicional in Estremoz*

TURAVENTUR

www.turaventur.com

Based just outside Évora (they will pick you up in town), this company organizes canoeing, mountain bicycling, and 4x4 trips to archaeological sites.

✉ Quinta do Serrado, Senhor dos Aflitos, 7000-173 Évora ☎ 266 743 134 or 966 758 940 🕐 Office: Mon–Fri 9.30–6 ✋ €25–€100 according to activity

MARVÃO

AMMAIA CLUBE DE GOLF DO MARVÃO

www.portugalgolf.pt
www.marvaogolfe.com

Nestling below the medieval fortified village of Marvão, this 18-hole, par-72 course has water hazards and some challenging steep sections.

✉ Quinta do Prado, São Salvador de Aramenha, 7330-330 Marvão ☎ 245 993 755 ✋ Due to reopen in 2009; call for information 🚗 From Marvão, go down to the bottom of the hill. In Portagem, turn right just before the main intersection; the golf club is on the left. From Castelo de Vide,

follow directions to Marvão, then turn left where signed

MONSARAZ

LOJA DA LIZETTE

This is a wonderful little store producing *mantas alente-janas* (heavy loom-woven blankets) in traditional and modern patterns. These blankets make great gifts to take home.

✉ Rua dos Celeiros, 7200-175 Monsaraz ☎ 266 557 159 🕐 Apr–end Oct Mon–Fri 9.30–1, 2.30–7, Sat–Sun 10–1, 2.30–8; Nov–end Mar Mon–Fri 9–1, 2.30–6, Sat–Sun 10–1, 2.30–6

OLARIA CARTAXO

In the most important pottery area in the region, Olaria Cartaxo is a good place to purchase traditionally patterned or plain plates, pots and floor tiles.

✉ Rua da Primavera 23, São Pedro do Corval, 7200-175 Reguengos de Monsaraz ☎ 266 549 681 🕐 Daily 8–12, 1–5 🚗 5km (3 miles) northeast of Reguengos de Monsaraz

PORTALEGRE

ADEGA COOPERATIVA DE PORTALEGRE
www.adegaportalegre.pt
Founded in 1955, the wine cooperative of Portalegre produces a wide range of wines grown in the hills of the Serra de São Mamede. Telephone a day in advance to reserve a tasting at this state-of-the-art winery.
✉ Apartado 126, Tebaida, 7301-901 Portalegre ☎ 245 300 530 🕙 Mon–Fri 9–12.30, 2–5 💷 Visit: free. Tastings: prices vary considerably depending on wines chosen 🚗 Take southeasterly road out of Portalegre towards Alegrete and watch for Adega Cooperativa/Quinta da Cabaça

SANTIAGO DO CACÉM

BADOCA SAFARI PARK
www.badoca.com
To the north of Santiago de Cacém you will find the Badoca safari adventure park. Here you can ride through enclosures of giraffe, zebra, impala and gnu and perhaps take in one of the reptile or bird shows. Thrill-seeking visitors can pluck up courage to ride the 'African Rapids' or the 7m (23 feet) harnessed trampoline. A great day out for all the family.
✉ Herdade da Badoca, Apartado 170, 7501-909 Vila Nova de Santo André ☎ 269 708 850 🕙 Mar–end Oct daily 9–8 or dusk 💷 Adult €16, child (4–10) €12, under-4s free

VIDIGUEIRA

QUINTA DA FÉ
www.quintadafe.com
Around 3km (2 miles) outside Vidigueira, this beautiful estate offers horseback-riding lessons at various levels as well as rides through surrounding countryside. The owner is a qualified horseback-riding instructor and has dedicated himself and the riding centre to the famous Lusitanian horses. Bed-and-breakfast accommodation is available.
✉ Estrada de Alcaria, Taipinhas, 7960 Vidigueira ☎ 284 434 105/284 434 148 💷 €27.50 for 1 hour horseback riding. Reserve well in advance

FESTIVALS AND EVENTS

FEBRUARY

FEIRA DO QUEIJO SERPA
Held in the Pavilhão de Multiusos on the road into Serpa, this yearly fair showcases the highly prized Alentejo cheeses. Come for tastings, regional crafts and gastronomy and folk bands.
✉ Serpa ☎ 284 544 727 (tourist office) 🕙 End Feb

APRIL–MAY

FEIRA INTERNACIONAL DE ARTESANATO E AGRO-PECUÁRIA DE ESTREMOZ (FIAPE)
www.fiape.estremozmarca.com
This is Estremoz's biggest yearly event and is of great importance to the northern Alentejo region, as it promotes livestock and breeders from across the area. In addition to agricultural events, festivities include themed parties such as Fado Night and Spanish Night.
✉ Estremoz ☎ 268 333 541 (tourist office) 🕙 Late Apr–early May

OVIBEJA
www.ovibeja.com
The biggest fair south of the Rio Tejo is held yearly at the Parque de Feiras e Exposições. Originally a livestock market, it has grown to include fishing contests, equestrian events, bullfights and displays of regional crafts, dance and music.
✉ Beja ☎ 284 310 350 or 284 311 913 (tourist office) 🕙 End Apr/beginning May

JUNE–JULY

FEIRA DE SÃO JOÃO
The Fair of St. John, celebrated since 1569, is one of the Alentejo's biggest and best festivals. Traditionally agricultural, it now includes folk-dancing, crafts, fairground rides, food stands, music and bullfights, which take place from 24 to 29 June.
✉ Évora ☎ 266 777 071 (tourist office) 🕙 22 or 23 Jun–1 or 2 Jul

AUGUST

FESTIVAL INTERNACIONAL DE FOLCLORE DOS POVOS DO MUNDO
Usually held in the Praça da República, this international folklore festival hosts dance and musical groups from as far afield as Peru and Russia, plus national groups.
✉ Elvas ☎ 268 622 236 (tourist office) 🕙 First 2 weekends in Aug

SEPTEMBER

FESTAS DAS FLORES DE CAMPO MAIOR
This festival is held every four years if the inhabitants of Campo Maior decide to organize it. It is worth a detour to see the streets carpeted with handmade and real flowers. The next festival is due in 2012.
✉ Campo Maior (20km/12.5 miles north of Elvas on N373), Elvas ☎ 268 622 236 (tourist office) 🕙 Sep

FESTAS DO SENHOR DA PIEDADE E DE SÃO MATEUS
Held in the Parque de Piedade, in honour of Our Lord of Mercy and St. Matthew, this is by far Elvas' biggest annual festival. In addition to elaborate religious processions, there are bullfights, folk-dancing, street performances, craft displays with examples of the crafts for sale, and food pavilions serving a huge range of local delicacies. Reserve accommodation in advance.
✉ Elvas ☎ 268 622 236 (tourist office) 🕙 Last 2 weeks in Sep

NOVEMBER

FEIRA DA CASTANHA MARVÃO
Running for more than 25 years, the chestnut festival of Marvão draws crowds from across the region. In addition to all things chestnut, medieval-style stands are set up within the castle selling basketware and other regional crafts.
✉ Marvão ☎ 245 909 131 (tourist office) 🕙 Early Nov

PRICES AND SYMBOLS

The restaurants are listed alphabetically. The prices given are the average for a two-course lunch (L) and a three-course dinner (D) for one person, without drinks. The wine price is for the least expensive bottle. All the restaurants listed accept credit cards unless otherwise stated.

For a key to the symbols, ▷ 2.

ELVAS
A BOLOTA CASTANHA

Terracotta floors, wooden latticework and dressers holding regional ceramic plates give this place a country feel. Tables are simple yet refined, with linen cloths and fine tableware, and staff are happy to offer advice. Either stick with the delicious starters, such as spinach with prawns, salt cod with asparagus, and mint and partridge soup, or move on to one of the superb main courses, such as wild boar with chestnut purée or duck stuffed with raspberries.
✉ Quinta das Janelas Verdes, Terrugem, 7350-491 Elvas ☎ 268 657 401
⏰ Tue–Sat 12–4, 7–11, Sun 12–4
✋ L €25, D €35, Wine €11 🚗 Terrugem is just off the N4 between Elvas and Estremoz. The *quinta* is well signposted

TABERNA DO ADRO

For a snack, a light tapas-style lunch or a main meal, try this *taberna*. Its rustic interior, with green stained-wood panelling, is crammed with regional ceramics of every shape and size. Roasted red peppers, spicy sausages, cheese and cured meats are just a few of the *petiscos* (tapas) on offer. For something more substantial, order a tasty fish stew with coriander (cilantro) or the succulent casseroled lamb, but leave room for one of the convent desserts, which are generously drowned in *ginginha*, the Portuguese cherry brandy. Credit cards are not accepted.
✉ Largo João Dias de Deus 1, Vila Fernando, 7350-511 Elvas ☎ 268 661 194
⏰ Thu–Tue 12.30–2, 7–9.30 ✋ L €14, D €20, Wine €6 🚗 From the western roundabout, by the Hotel Dom Luís, take the EN372 following signs to Vila Fernando (14km/8 miles from Elvas)

ESTREMOZ
SÃO ROSAS

São Rosas is located within the medieval walls in a modest townhouse next to the *pousada*. It has a country feel thanks to its whitewashed walls, wood-beamed

Above *Tasquinha do Oliveira in Évora serves innovative and original dishes*

ceilings and the solid wooden chairs with which it is furnished. Bread comes wrapped in linen and pâté is served in individual little pots. In season, wild asparagus and mushrooms feature prominently on the menu. Also try partridge pie or the pork loin with plums, choosing one of the fine regional wines on offer to accompany them. Reserve ahead at weekends.
✉ Largo Dom Dinis 11, 7100-509 Estremoz ☎ 268 333 345 ⏰ Tue–Sun 12.30–3.30, 7.30–10.30. Closed first 2 weeks in Jan and first 2 weeks in Jul ✋ L €25, D €35, Wine €14

ÉVORA
CAFÉ ALENTEJO

This old tavern, now painted in vivid orange, has one of the best selections of regional *petiscos* (tapas) in the area and offers a great way to savour various dishes at one sitting. Their main courses are also not to be missed, however, and include ox-tail stewed in red wine, and *migas de esparragos* (asparagus with fried breadcrumbs). If you missed out on *fado* in Lisbon or

Coimbra, pop in here on a Thursday for their show.

✉ Rua do Raimundo 5, 7000-661 Évora
☎ 266 706 296 🕐 Mon–Sat 12.30–3, 7.30–10 ♿ L €15, D €20, Wine €8

BOTEQUIM DA MOURARIA

This family eatery is in the Moorish quarter; it has no outside sign other than its street number, so you need to look carefully for it. The interior is tiny, but it serves some of the best food in town. Try a selection of the cured meat and cheese appetizers, then one of the soups or *açordas* followed by roast lamb. Finish with a home-made dessert.

✉ Rua da Mouraria 16A, 7000-585 Évora
☎ 266 746 775 🕐 Mon–Fri 12–3, 7–10, Sat 12–3. Closed Aug ♿ L €15, D €25, Wine €8

O FIALHO

A landmark among Alentejo restaurants and one of the best places to experience the local cuisine, Fialho attracts customers from far and wide. Owned by the same family since 1945, its forte is the huge number of starters it offers, which you will see on display in the front dining room. There is octopus vinaigrette, stuffed mushrooms, prawns, beans, peppers and many more. The daily specials include all the usual Alentejan delicacies, along with superb wines as well as deliciously sweet and sticky desserts.

✉ Travessa Mascarenhas 14–16, 7000-557 Évora ☎ 266 703 079 🕐 Tue–Sun 12–12. Closed 1–15 Sep, 23 Dec–2 Jan ♿ L €25, D €35, Wine €11 🚌 In a narrow lane near the Garcia de Resende theatre

O MOINHO

Part of a working mill, this cottage-like restaurant near the Campo do Juventude to the south of the city hub was once a grocery store. Its small dining rooms, with rough terracotta floor tiles, wood-beamed ceilings and blue gingham tablecloths, are decorated with interesting collections of copper cooking pots, pottery and other local craft items of interest. All the usual

Alentejo dishes are on the menu, including a great pork loin with *migas de batata*, a mix of tomato with potatoes typical of the area. The wine list is stunning.

✉ Rua Santo André 2A, Bairro Nossa Senhora do Carmo, 7005-401 Évora
☎ 266 771 060 🕐 Mon–Sat 12–3, 7–10 ♿ L €15, D €20, Wine €6 🚌 Head south out of town towards the Ibis hotel. After the hotel turn right. The restaurant is just past the Campo do Juventude

TASQUINHA DO OLIVEIRA

This place is noted for its innovative and original cooking, and has numerous newspaper accolades and local gastronomy awards decorating its walls. Cold starters include artichokes with ham or stuffed crab, or, on colder days, try prawn soufflé with spinach, or chickpea and mint stew. In season, there is usually partridge or rabbit, or, if not, the more traditional roast lamb. There is a wide selection of wines to complement the food and the owner is only too happy to suggest which goes best with what. Reserve ahead at weekends.

✉ Rua Cândido dos Reis 45A, 7000-582 Évora ☎ 266 744 841 🕐 Mon–Sat 12.30–3, 7.30–10. Closed first 2 weeks in Aug ♿ L €25, D €35, Wine €10

MARVÃO
POUSADA DE SANTA MARIA
www.pousadas.pt
Marvão is an obligatory stop on any tour of the fortified hill towns, and this *pousada* affords a magnificent viewpoint. The regional food here is wonderful, especially the cream of pea soup and the excellent local cheeses. The tables dressed with printed fabrics are attractive, and the staff are friendly, but the lasting impression is that of the marvellous views that open up before you, looking far out across the groves of olive trees and the cork oaks typical of the Alentejo. (For accommodation details ▷ 257.)

✉ Rua 24 de Janeiro 7, 7330-122 Marvão
☎ 245 993 201 🕐 Daily 1–3, 7.30–10 ♿ L €25, D €30, Wine €12 🚌 At the double-gated town entrance follow signs to

the *pousada*—down to left if in car or up to right if walking

REGUENGOS DE MONSARAZ
GALERIA DO ESPORÃO
www.esporao.com
If you are touring the Alentejo wine region, the Esporão winery is an ideal place to stop for a tour of the estate (reserving an appointment in advance is preferred) rounded off by a hearty lunch. The genteel arched dining room serves quality regional cuisine and is often busy at the weekend so be sure to make a reservation here too. Start with a soup, maybe partridge broth or cream of green asparagus, then choose from one of the speciality game dishes such as rabbit, venison or wild boar with creamed spinach and chestnut purée. For dessert you may like to try the Elvas plums with *sericaia* (a moist egg-based cake flavoured with cinnamon).

✉ Herdade do Esporão, 7200 000 Reguengos de Monsaraz ☎ 266 509 280 🕐 Daily 12.30–3.30 ♿ L €40, Wine €15

VILA VIÇOSA
POUSADA DOM JOÃO IV
www.pousadas.pt
Inside the main *pousada* building, this welcoming dining room with its polished terracotta floors and decorative latticed shutters has wood-panelled ceilings and high frescoed vaulting. It serves traditional yet inventive culinary creations that are all delivered with an appealing combination of professionalism and flair. Pheasant with port and chestnut purée, cabbage stuffed with lamb and potatoes, and roast lamb encased in a pastry crust with artichokes and pine nuts are among the establishment's signature dishes. In the summer there is the option of alfresco dining on the *pousada*'s outdoor terrace. (For accommodation details ▷ 257.)

✉ Terreiro do Paço, 7160-251 Vila Viçosa
☎ 268 980 742 🕐 Daily 1–3, 7.30–10 ♿ L €25, D €30, Wine €12 🚌 Next to the Paço Ducal

PRICES AND SYMBOLS

The prices are the lowest and highest for a double room for one night including breakfast, unless otherwise stated. All the hotels listed accept credit cards unless otherwise stated. Note that rates can vary widely throughout the year.

For a key to the symbols, ▷ 2.

ARRAIOLOS
TEMBO BED AND BREAKFAST

www.tembo-alentejo.com
This fantastic little hideaway set amid the boulder-strewn plains of the Alentejo has five different accommodation options. Choose between the Suite with its two double beds and Moroccan-style whirlpool bath; the Loft, with great free-standing bath; the Duo, a secluded stone house and wood cabin with outside kitchen, barbecue, extra outdoor bathroom and private pool (sleeps 4); or the Colonial or Bali. All guests have access to a living room and fully equipped kitchen should they want to self-cater; there is a large swimming pool in the grounds. Credit cards are not accepted.
✉ Posto de Correio, 7040-641 Vimieiro, Arraiolos ☎ 966 883 842 ✋ €95–€140;

Duo suite €200 for 4 persons ⓘ 4 rooms, 1 suite (summer only as no heating)
⛱ Outdoor ⊟ From Arraiolos head east on N4 to Vimieiro. At Vimieiro take N251 towards Pavia. Tembo is between km 88 and 87

BEJA
POUSADA DE SÃO FRANCISCO

www.pousadas.pt
In the heart of the old town, this former 13th-century Franciscan convent is an impressive *pousada*. Note the fine frescoed vaulting in the former chapter room, which now serves as a public lounge. Appropriately, the old refectory houses the restaurant, which serves acclaimed regional cuisine. The bedrooms, with their locally produced carpets, are stylishly furnished and many look out over the swimming pool and palm-filled gardens. Tennis is available.
✉ Largo Nuno Álvares Pereira, 7801-901 Beja ☎ 284 313 580 ✋ €150–€225 ⓘ 34 rooms, 1 suite ✿ ⛱ Outdoor

CASTELO DE VIDE
ALBERGARIA EL REI DOM MIGUEL

One of the Alentejo's most attractive hilltop towns, Castelo de Vide

Above Pousada Flor da Rosa in Crato occupies a 14th-century castle monastery

makes a good base from which to explore the area. On the town's main street, this village house has been converted into a family-run inn. The owner's passion for antiques is demonstrated in the lounge and passages, while bedrooms are more contemporary with plentiful use of coordinated fabrics.
✉ Rua Bartolomeu Álvares da Santa 45, 7320-117 Castelo de Vide ☎ 245 919 191 ✋ €50–€60 ⓘ 7 ✿

CRATO
POUSADA FLOR DA ROSA

www.pousadas.pt
Built in the 14th century as the headquarters of the warrior knights of Malta, this restored castle monastery, with cloisters and superb brick vaulting, has managed to maintain the feel of an ancient ruin while providing modern and elegant lodgings. A surprisingly unobtrusive extension contains large minimalist rooms with panoramic windows looking out across the olive groves. Bedrooms in the old part are smaller, yet more atmospheric. The elegant restaurant serves local cuisine.

Mosteiro da Santa Maria de Flor da ... osa, 7430-999 Crato ☎ 245 997 210 ✋ €170–€270 ① 24 🅱 🏊 Outdoor 🚗 From Castelo de Vide take the N246 to ...lpalhão, then N245 to Crato. Flor da Rosa ...nd the *pousada* are signed right

ESTREMOZ
MONTE DA FORNALHA
...ww.montedafornalha.com
...ime-washed walls and fine linen ...ive the rooms of this converted ...lacksmith's house a Mediterranean ...eel. The public areas are large and ...iry in summer and warmed by large ...res in winter. As with the rest of ...he house, the guest rooms are ...imple yet attractively decorated in ...varm, natural tones beneath wood-...eamed ceilings. Credit cards are ...ot accepted.
✉ Turismo Rural, A. Maria Ruiva, Arcos, 100 Estremoz ☎ 935 792 330 ✋ €95–135 ① 3 rooms, 3 suites 🏊 Outdoor 🚗 Turn off the A6 at the Estremoz/ Borba ...xit. Follow signs to Estremoz. After 500m ...50 yards), look for the sign to the right

ÉVORA
POUSADA DOS LÓIOS
...ww.pousadas.pt
...his fine *pousada* is one of Évora's ...nost impressive buildings. Originally ... 15th-century monastery, it ...encompasses several architectural ...tyles; as is fitting, furnishings are ...ombre and classical. Rooms on the ...irst floor, most of which have been ...expertly converted from the original ...nonks' cells, are reached by way ...f an impressive marble staircase. ...egional cuisine is served in the old ...efectory or in the glassed-in cloister. ...Note, too, the ornately painted walls ...nd ceilings in the main lounge.
✉ Largo Conde de Vila Flor, 7000-804 Évora ☎ 266 730 070 ✋ €150–€250 ① 30 ...ooms, 2 suites 🅱 🏊 Outdoor 🚗 Follow ...igns to *centro histórico* and Templo de ...Diana. The *pousada* is in the same square ...s the temple

RESIDENCIAL RIVIERA
...ww.riviera-evora.com
...his guest house is on one of ...he prettiest streets in Évora, just ...down the cobbled hill from the

cathedral. The rooms are bright, clean and airy (although not always well coordinated), and each has a big spotless bathroom. Service is professional and they serve a good breakfast. Originally a private house, it retains many of its design features, such as stone window frames, decorative ironwork and attractive tiling in the entrance hall.
✉ Rua 5 de Outubro 49, 7000-854 Évora ☎ 266 737 210 ✋ €66–€77 ① 21 🅱

SOLAR DE MONFALIM
www.monfalimtur.pt
In a jacaranda-lined square in the heart of Évora, this 16th-century building has been receiving paying guests since 1892. Its arched first-floor arcade and coat of arms make it easy to recognize; a solid granite staircase leads from the cobbled street to reception. Bedrooms have old wrought-iron and brass bedsteads. Breakfast is served in the dining room, or on the terrace.
✉ Largo da Misericórdia 1, 7000-646 Évora ☎ 266 750 000 ✋ €70–€85 ① 26 🅱

MARVÃO
POUSADA DE SANTA MARIA
www.pousadas.pt
This is one of the snuggest *pousadas* in the country, and has some of the most magnificent views. Built within a group of medieval village houses, it is warm and welcoming and the staff are eager to please. The bedrooms have Alentejan hand-painted beds.
✉ Rua 24 de Janeiro 7, 7330-112 Marvão ☎ 245 993 201 ✋ €120–€198 ① 28 rooms, 3 suites 🅱 🚗 At double-gated entrance follow signs to the *pousada*. Take the left fork if driving, the right fork if on foot

MONSARAZ
ESTALAGEM DE MONSARAZ
www.estalagemdemonsaraz.com
This small, whitewashed and blue-trimmed village inn is near the main entry point to the medieval cobbled village of Monsaraz. The public lounge area has a rustic, lived-in look, with mock-leather sofas, heavy archways and a large fireplace. All the bedrooms have private

bathrooms. The pool and sun terrace have spectacular views. There is also a restaurant.
✉ Largo de São Bartolomeu 5, 7200-175 Monsaraz ☎ 266 557 112 ✋ €84–€90 ① 15 rooms, 4 suites 🅱 🏊 Outdoor

MOURA
HORTA DE TORREJAIS
www.hortadetorrejais.com
This property has been acclaimed in the national press for its exceptional renovation using traditional techniques and materials. Whitewashed exteriors lead into split levels which follow the natural contours of the land. The bedrooms are homely and tastefully decorated, with wrought-iron beds. Be sure to note the fine brick-vaulting in the dining room. Down through the olive grove is a large outdoor pool. Credit cards are not accepted.
✉ Estrada da Barca, Apartado 116, 7860-909 Moura ☎ 285 253 658 or 963 272 562 ✋ €70 ① 5 🏊 Outdoor

SANTIAGO DE CACÉM
CAMINHOS DE SANTIAGO
www.hotelcaminhosdesantiago.pt
Opened in 2008, this ultra-modern hotel was a former *pousada*, though only three of the original rooms remain. Most accommodation is now in a minimalist new wing where boutique-style rooms use local marble, slate, cork and textiles.
✉ Rua Cidade de Beja, 7540-163 Santiago do Cacém ☎ 269 825 350 ✋ €115–€150 🅱 🏊 Outdoor

VILA VIÇOSA
POUSADA DE DOM JOÃO IV
www.pousadas.pt
This converted 16th-century convent, next to the ducal palace, has been a *pousada* since 1996. Public areas are furnished with 16th- and 17th-century pieces, while the large bedrooms have embroidered bedspreads and regional Arraiolos carpets. The restaurant serves traditional Portuguese cuisine.
✉ Convento das Chagas, Terreiro do Paço, 7160-251 Vila Viçosa ☎ 268 980 742 ✋ €150–€250 ① 32 rooms, 7 suites 🅱 🏊 Outdoor 🍴

THE ALGARVE

Cut off from the rest of the country by a series of low mountain ranges, the Algarve has developed at a pace and in a style all of its own. Long sandy beaches, sheltered coves and rocky headlands, originally the domain of local fishermen, have now been appropriated by the international tourist set, enticed further by its amenable climate.

As more visitors have poured in, so development has increased, often in an ad hoc manner, with little thought to long-term sustainability. Thankfully, recent years have seen a slowing in the construction of high-rise, low-cost resorts as Portuguese and foreign investors attempt to attract the more discerning customer. Luxury hotels and spas perch on clifftops, designer retreats nestle unobtrusively in the hills and golf courses are attempting to be more ecological in their approach.

Amid the frenzy, however, it is comforting to know that the 'real' Algarve is still attainable and waiting to be discovered by those willing to search. Bustling tourist destinations such as Faro, Tavira and Lagos contain hidden treasures in their historic centres; working towns like Olhão, with its large fishing fleet, give an insight into local life; and the hills beyond the coast are dotted with sleepy villages, nestled amid almond, citrus and olive trees and unchanged for centuries. For empty beaches and great surf, head around to the wild Atlantic seaboard; for indigenous and migratory birds visit the dunes and marshlands of the Ria Formosa. It is also possible to savour the 'real' Algarve: on the coast, fresh fish, grilled in the open air over hot coals; up in the hills heavier pork and game dishes; a shot of medronho liqueur to finish.

ALBUFEIRA

www.cm-albufeira.pt

Since the 1960s, when it was still essentially a fishing village, Albufeira has changed beyond recognition, evolving into one of the most popular package-tour destinations in the Algarve. There's little left today of the traditional way of life, and the old village, nestling between two headlands, is virtually swamped by high-rise apartments and hotels, while development creeps farther inland every year.

Despite this, you can still see the fishermen on their beach in the early morning, and Albufeira manages to hang on to some of its charm. This is best seen in the steep cobbled streets and distinctive architecture of the old town, revolving around the main square, Largo Duarte Pacheco. This is the hub of the town, lined with outdoor cafés and bars, where you can eat an English breakfast or drink a pint of Guinness.

From here the main street leads towards the sea, plunging through a tunnel to reach a terrace above the town beach, with its high cliffs and smooth sand. Wander along a corniche-type street above the main beach to reach the Gruta do Xorino, a sea-cave with crystal waters.

For a change of pace, the town has a couple of churches. A good time to hit the old town, particularly Rua Candido dos Reis, is the early evening when the shops are open, the bars are buzzing, and the whole town is gearing up for eating, drinking and dancing. Most bars stay open well after midnight, while summer clubs along Montchoro are open until around 6am.

✚ 332 C13 🅷 Rua 5 de Outubro, 8200-109 Albufeira ☎ 289 585 279

ALMANCIL

www.portugal-info.net

On the eastern outskirts of Almancil (Almansil), a service town on the N125, is the church of São Lourenço (Tue–Sat 10–12.30, 2–6, Sun 2–6; €2), whose interior is one of Portugal's most outstanding examples of 18th-century tilework.

Every inch of the walls and ceiling is covered with glowing blue-and-white *azulejos* (tiles) depicting stories from the life of the martyr, St. Laurence. The tiles were painted in 1730 by Policarpo de Oliveira Bernardes, who is acknowledged to be one of the country's finest artists. Look for the background details of local life in the big panels and also the wonderful *trompe l'oeil* colonnades on the ceiling.

✚ 332 C13

ALTE

www.visitalgarve.pt

Head inland from Albufeira and you will soon be in unspoilt countryside, where almond trees, citrus trees and olive groves cover the hillsides, and where village life remains largely untouched by tourism. One of the prettiest of these villages is Alte, a bus tour stop and a popular weekend destination for locals—to see it at its best, avoid these times.

The well-tended village nestles in the limestone hills of the area known as the Barrocal and sprawls along a hillside, its narrow cobbled streets crammed with hidden corners, whitewashed houses with colourful window surrounds and plenty of excellent photo opportunities. The exhibition in the tourist office will fill you in on local history—from here head uphill to explore the town and take in the Igreja Matriz. The church was built in the 16th century and features a fine Manueline doorway as well as a wealth of 18th-century woodwork

and *azulejos* (tiles). There are also two Manueline fonts and several fine 17th- and 18th-century statues.

From the heart of the village it's a five-minute walk out to a couple of natural springs, the Fonte Pequena and Fonte Grande, a local beauty spot where picnic tables are set under the trees beside a series of shallow canals. For the more energetic there's a good waymarked walk through the hills west to São Bartolomeu de Messines. This path is part of what is ultimately intended to be a trans-Algarve hiking trail.

✚ 332 C13 🅷 Estrada da Ponte 17, 8100-021 Alte ☎ 289 478 666

CACELA VELHA

www.visitalgarve.pt

To get a taste of what the eastern Algarve once looked like, head for Cacela Velha, a tiny whitewashed village on a dead end road 10km (6 miles) east of Tavira (▷ 270). Perched on a bluff above the eastern end of the Parque Natural da Ria Formosa (▷ 267), Cacela Velha is little more than a handful of cottages, a church and an 18th-century fort.

Below the village lies the lagoon and beach—you can walk down through the dunes and olive trees to wade out to the barrier island at low tide, or you can catch the ferry at the hamlet of Fábrica. At sea level, beaches stretch east along the coast for miles; even in high summer a short walk should get you away from the crowds in the better-known resorts and on their beaches.

✚ 333 D13

Opposite *Façade of the 18th-century São Lourenço church in Almancil*
Below *Local fishing boats on the fishermen's beach at Albufeira*

INTRODUCTION

The Algarve's capital has a picturesque old quarter, an atmospheric harbour filled with yachts and fishing boats, fabulous shopping and a buzzing nightlife. Most visitors flying into Faro bypass the town, but it makes an ideal stopover for a night or so if you're arriving late or leaving on an early morning flight. Head first for the harbour, from where you can explore the historic old town before strolling through the pedestrianized shopping streets to the Museu Regional. From here it's a 10- to 15-minute walk northwest to the churches.

The Faro area was colonized by the Romans, based at Milreu. Ultimately control passed to the Moors, for whom it was a major port. It was reconquered by Afonso III for the Christians in 1249 and thrived, emerging by the 15th century as one of the most important towns in southern Portugal.

In 1580 Philip II of Spain usurped the Portuguese throne, giving the English the perfect excuse to attack the Algarve, which was now nominally part of Spain. The Earl of Essex landed in Faro in 1596, sacking the city and looting the bishop's palace, which he then made his headquarters. The contents of the library were sent back to England as a gift for Essex's friend Thomas Bodley, founder of the Bodleian Library in Oxford. Essex eventually withdrew, setting fire to the city as a parting gesture. The devastation that resulted was matched by that caused by serious earthquakes in 1722 and 1755, which destroyed

INFORMATION

www.cm-faro.pt
www.visitalgarve.pt
✚ 333 D13 ℹ️ Rua da Misericórdia 8, 8000-269 Faro ☎ 289 803 604, 808 781 212 (national tourist line) 🕓 May–end Sep daily 9.30–7; Oct–end Apr daily 9.30–5.30 🚆 Faro

Above *The Largo da Sé in the heart of the old town of Faro*
Opposite *Cloister at Convento Nossa Senhora da Assunção, which houses the Museu Arqueológico*

what little was left of old Faro. By 1776, when Faro became the regional capital much of the town had been rebuilt.

The town got an extra boost with the opening of the Lisbon–Faro railway in 1889, with holiday visitors starting to arrive as a result. But, though there was some low-key tourism in the first half of the 20th century, it was only with the construction of the airport in 1965 that Faro and the Algarve really took off as a holiday destination. Today, nearly 5 million tourists pass through the airport annually and mass tourism has brought increasing prosperity to the city and the surrounding area.

WHAT TO SEE

CIDADE VELHA

Faro's old town is still completely enclosed within walls, a dense complex of narrow streets and ancient houses with the majestic Largo da Sé and cathedral (May–end Sep Sun–Fri 10–6, Sat 10–12; rest of year Sun–Fri 10–5.30, Sat 10–12; €3) at its heart. Walk up through the Arco da Vila, the 19th-century town gate designed by the Italian Francisco Fabri, to the harmonious cathedral square, planted with orange trees and lined with 18th-century buildings, one of which was the episcopal palace. The cathedral is a hybrid of Gothic, Renaissance and baroque architecture, the result of rebuilding after the 1755 earthquake. The interior is richly gilded and there's a fine old organ and some fine examples of 18th-century *azulejos* (tiles). Climb the tower for superb views over the town.

Behind the Largo da Sé is the Largo Dom Afonso III, dominated by a statue of Afonso III, where you will find the Museu Arqueológico (May–end Sep Tue–Fri 12.30–midnight, Sat–Sun 5.30–midnight; rest of year Tue–Sun 10–5.30; €2). The museum, the Algarve's oldest, is in the 16th-century Convento de Nossa Senhora da Assunção, an elegant building with an airy internal courtyard. The museum concentrates on Roman and medieval finds, many from the excavations at Estói (▷ 266). Look for the statues from the site. Don't miss the star turn, a superb third-century AD mosaic showing Neptune and the four winds, found near Faro station. Take a different route back to the Arco da Vila for a glimpse of everyday life in this picturesque district.

✚ 265 A3

THE HARBOUR AREA

Sleek yachts are moored in Faro's harbour, the focus of a bustling area that buzzes throughout the day and into the evening. The harbour is backed by attractive gardens and cafés. Two child-friendly attractions are located here the Museu Marítimo (Capitania do Porto do Faro, Rua da Comunidade Lusiada; tel 289 894 990; Mon–Fri 9–12, 2–5; €1), and the Centro Ciência Viva in the Rua Comandante Francisco Manuel (tel 289 890 920; Jun to mid-Sep Tue–Sun 10–8, rest of year Tue–Fri 10–5, Sat–Sun 11–6; adult €4, child (under 12) €2, family €8) The former concentrates on model boats and fishing, while the science exhibit along the waterfront, is more ambitious, with plenty of interactive action. Don't miss the flight simulator.

Take a stroll beside the sea and railway before cutting up into the old town, or perhaps catching a ferry to one of the offshore beaches. Alternatively, head inland from the Jardim Manuel Bivar into Faro's shopping area, an attractive spread of pedestrianized streets where you'll find the best of the international chain stores alongside some highly individual and typically Portuguese shops.

THE BEACHES

The beaches mostly fall inside the eastern end of the Parque Natural da Ria Formosa and are long and low sandbars, reached through marshy channels. Ferries run from the jetty in Faro harbour to both Farol, on the Ilha da Culatra, and the Ilha Deserta (or Ilha da Barreta), the most southerly point in mainland

Portugal, with watersports, restaurants and bars. Farol tends to be quieter, but the best time to visit both is during the week rather than at weekends. Outside high season, there are not many people around during mid-week, so, if you are planning a beach day, this is a good time to go.

If you have a couple of hours to spare before a flight, the Praia de Faro, close to the airport, is worth investigating. It's another typical lagoon stretch, with a sweep of beautiful sand and a sheltered inland side. Out of season it's quiet, but far more developed than the offshore beaches, with bars, restaurants and holiday houses.

MORE TO SEE

IGREJA DE NOSSA SENHORA DO CARMO
An early 18th-century baroque church with a carved, gilt high altar, the main attraction is the Capela dos Ossos (Chapel of the Bones). This side chapel is lined with decorative displays of monks' bones—these were disinterred from a cemetery in the 19th century and displayed to act as a reminder of mortality.
➕ 265 A2 ✉ Largo do Carmo, 8000-148 Faro 🕐 May–end Sep Mon–Fri 10–1, 3–6, Sat 10–1; rest of year Mon–Fri 10–1, 3–5.30, Sat 10–1 ✋ Church: free. Capela dos Ossos: €1

IGREJA DE SÃO PEDRO
This beautiful 16th-century church is decorated with a frieze of polychrome *azulejos*. The side chapels have more blue-and-white tiles and gilt altarpieces.
➕ 265 A2 ✉ Largo de São Pedro, 8000-145 Faro 🕐 Mon–Fri 9–5.30, Sat 9–4, Sun 9–1 (these times may vary) ✋ Free

IGREJA DE SÃO FRANCISCO
Opened by the monks from the adjacent monastery for late afternoon visits, this medieval church was all but destroyed by fire before being rebuilt in the 19th century. It boasts a fine baroque bell tower and 18th-century statuary.
➕ 265 B3 ✉ Largo de São Francisco, 8000-142 Faro 🕐 Daily 5–7.30 ✋ Free

Above *The gateway to the old town*
Below *Faro harbour has many attractions, and is still a fishing port*

CARVOEIRO

www.carvoeiro.com

A narrow fertile valley leads down to the sea from the inland wine town of Lagoa to Carvoeiro, once an unspoilt fishing village, now a resort on the package-tour circuit. To see it at its best means coming out of season, when the tiny triangular beach is empty and the old streets on either side of the cove, lined with painted houses, are crowd-free.

In summer, Carvoeiro is heaving with visitors, many based in the sprawl of apartment blocks and villa complexes either side of the old town, and you will be pushed to park or find a peaceful spot on the beach. The best bet is to hop on one of the fishingboat ferries that ply the coast, dropping visitors off at a series of sandy coves, many with spectacular cliffs and rock formations. The pick of these is Algar Seco, where winds and tides have chiselled away at the cliffs, forming grottoes and pinnacles. The clear water makes it ideal for snorkelling. Other nearby beaches include the Praia do Paraiso, just west of the village; Centianes; Benagil, still largely unspoilt; and Marinha, a beautiful and relatively undeveloped spot. Be warned that signposting to the beaches is generally inadequate, and parking difficult everywhere in high summer.

Above *Sandy coves and rugged rock formations characterize the coastline near Carvoeiro*

➕ 332 C13 ℹ️ Praia do Carvoeiro, 8400-517 Lagoa ☎ 282 357 728

CASTRO MARIM

www.cm-castromarim.pt

Two castles bear witness to the past strategic importance of Castro Marim, a little village on a hill overlooking the marshlands of the River Guadiana, which here acts as the border between Portugal and Spain. The main castle, to the north of the town, was built in 1319 as the headquarters of the Order of Christ, the successors to the Knights Templar, and remained their base until the order moved north to Tomar (▷ 220–222) in 1334.

The castle was built on an earlier 12th-century Moorish fortification,

which you can still see within the main walls; it's now a small archaeological museum. The walls themselves were erected in the 17th century and are topped with ramparts, from where you'll get great views of the river, the shimmering salt flats, the roofs of the town below and the sea to the south. Here, too, you can pick up information on the surrounding Reserva Natural do Sapal, a nature reserve that protects the wetlands around the town and along the river. It's a varied habitat, with more than 150 species of birds, including flamingos, storks, avocets, ducks and waders. Across the town are the remnants of the 17th-century fort of São Sebastião, another great lookout point.

➕ 333 D13 ℹ️ Rua José Afonso Moreira 2–4, 8950-138 Castro Marim ☎ 281 531 232

ESTÓI

www.portugalvirtual.pt

The sugar-pink Palácio d'Estói is a real Sleeping Beauty's palace. The

building and its garden date from the 1740s, when the Conde de Cavalhal constructed a miniature version of the royal rococo palace of Queluz (▷ 110) here. Today, both palace and gardens have undergone a multi-million euro facelift, turning the palace into a luxury *pousada* (due to open in early 2009). Sections of the hotel are off-limits (unless you are a hotel guest) but pop in for a drink or lunch and step outside to explore the gardens.

Palm and orange trees line the approach avenue, at the end of which a double stairway, decorated with tiles and statuary, leads to the reflecting pool and terrace in front of the palace. There are statues, busts, huge vases and pots dotted around, and the air is perfumed with the scents of oranges and aromatic plants. The village is also worth a quick inspection, particularly the Igreja Matriz on the main square—it was built after the 1755 earthquake and designed by Fabri, who worked in Faro.

➕ 333 D13

FARO
▷ 262–265.

LAGOS
www.cm-lagos.pt
The biggest town in the western Algarve, Lagos is a vibrant place packed with history, making it a good base for a couple of nights if you want a buzz of life that the smaller western villages don't provide. The area has been settled since Phoenician times, but it won European fame in the 15th century when the port was the departure point for Henry the Navigator's explorers as they set off on the great voyages of discovery. Lagos is on the River Bensafrim, with most sights found inside the medieval walls encircling the old town.

Start your visit at the waterfront, backed by gardens and guarded at the sea end by the trim little 17th-century Forte da Ponte da Bandeira. Walk upriver from here beside the solid town walls to reach a square, the Praça Infante Dom Henrique, with its fine bronze statue of Henry the Navigator. The old custom house is also here. Its small arcade was once the site of Europe's first slave market, from 1444 to 1756.

From here, walk through to the Museu Municipal in the Rua General Alberto da Silveira (tel 282 762 301; Tue–Sun 9.30–12.30, 2–5; €3). Exhibits include much of local interest, including a model Algarve village, but also such curiosities as an eight-legged goat. The superb church of Santo António, a riot of baroque gilding built between 1710 and 1720, is part of the museum.

East from here are shopping streets and a huge range of bars, cafés and restaurants. The best of these are around two mosaic-paved squares, the Praça Luis de Camões and the Praça Gil Eanes. For a change of pace, you could take the half-hour boat trip to the Ponta da Piedade (Bridge of Piety), a spectacular rock formation with stacks, arches and grottoes. Near here, a string of delightful cove beaches is enclosed by headlands. East of Lagos, across the river, the Meia Praia is a 4km (2.5-mile) stretch of soft sand. Kids will enjoy a trip to Lagos Zoo (www.zoolagos.com; Apr–end Sep daily 10–7; Oct–end Mar daily 10–5; adult €10, under-12s €6, family €26), an environmentally conscious zoo for small mammals, birds and farm animals.
✚ 332 B13 🛈 Rua Belchoir Moreira Barbudo, 8600-772 Lagos ☎ 282 763 031
🚃 Lagos

OLHÃO
www.cm-olhao.pt
Down-to-earth Olhão is the biggest fishing port in the Algarve, and a good base from which to explore the Parque Natural da Ria Formosa. Its highlights are the waterfront and harbour area, with superb fish and produce markets and tranquil gardens, and the Praça da Restauração, reached through the warren of twisting streets that makes up the fishermen's quarter. Climb up the tower of the early 18th-century Igreja Matriz for terrific views over the roof terraces of the whitewashed cube houses, reminiscent of North African buildings and reflecting Olhão's old trading links.
✚ 333 D13 🛈 Largo Sebastião M. Mestre 8A, 8700-349 Olhão ☎ 289 713 936
🚃 Olhão

PARQUE NATURAL DA RIA FORMOSA
www.icnb.pt
Just west of Faro towards Manta Rota is the Parque Natural da Ria Formosa, established in 1987 to protect the barrier islands and lagoons that run along the east end of the Algarve. The lagoons, riddled with tidal flats, islets, channels and salt marshes, form what is a unique ecological environment and an important bird nesting area. Residents, overwintering and migratory birds all feed here, while the dunes and marshlands themselves support rich vegetation.

Around 7,500 people live within the park, most working in lagoon-related activities—nearly 80 per cent of Portuguese clams and other shellfish come from here. During the summer the population triples, and the park authorities have the task of balancing environmental needs with the demands of tourism.

To promote this work, the Environmental Education Centre was set up near Olhão. Other attractions include a traditional water mill powered by the tides and a lagoon on which an old tuna fishing boat sails filled with visitors who want to explore this fascinating place further. Don't miss the Portuguese water dogs, a unique web-toed species bred for work with fishing boats.
✚ 333 D14 🛈 Centro de Educação Ambiental de Marim, Quinta do Marim, Quelfes, 8700 Olhão ☎ 289 700 210
🕐 Park: daily 10.30–6. Office: Mon–Fri 9–12.30, 2–5.30

Left The whitewashed buildings of the fishermen's quarter of Olhão, seen from the tower of the 18th-century Igreja Matriz

PORTIMÃO

www.cm-portimao.pt

Romans and Moors inhabited the Portimão area, but the present city on the banks of the River Arade was established by charter in 1463, flourishing during the era of the great voyages of discovery. The 1755 earthquake destroyed much of the town and the subsequent economic decline was halted only towards the end of the 19th century, when fishing and fish-canning took off here.

Today, Portimão is thriving, a mainly modern town that's the second largest in the Algarve. Its economy is now driven by tourism, canning and construction, with the traditional fishing industry playing an increasingly minor role. The famous open-air sardine restaurants along the riverfront, grilling fish fresh off the boats, have been moved, with a smart marina taking their place. The area behind Rua Serpa Pinto is still probably the pleasantest part of town, with its shady gardens, bars and restaurants. The marina and quayside area are also the departure point for boat excursions, which cruise both east and west along the coast or up the river valley to historic Silves (▷ 270).

West from the quayside area is the heart of town, its largely pedestrianized streets and good shops pulling in the crowds– Portimão also has several out-of-town malls. The town's main church of Nossa Senhora de Conceição is situated a few blocks back from the water; its Manueline doorway dates from the 15th century, but much of the rest of the building post-dates the 1755 earthquake.

✚ 332 B13 ℹ Avenida Zeca Afonso, 8500-516 Portimão ☎ 282 470 717
🚆 Portimão

PRAIA DA ROCHA

www.cm-portimao.pt

Praia da Rocha is the oldest-established Algarve resort, popular from the start of the 20th century. It was home to a largely British colony of writers and artists from the 1930s to the 1950s and boomed in the following two decades, when it became known as the 'Queen of the Algarve'. Now this famous holiday resort is largely given over to high-rise hotels, faceless apartment blocks, home-from-home bars and noisy nightclubs.

Nothing, however, can detract from the dramatic rock formations and the glorious beach, the widest cliff-backed stretch of sand in Europe. It was created artificially in 1969 when a million tonnes of sand were moved here, pushing the sea back some 150m (490ft) and leaving the rock stacks, formerly lapped by water, high and dry.

Access to the beach is from various points along the Avenida Tomas Cabreira, which runs along the clifftop from the Fortaleza de Santa Caterina. Built in 1691 to protect the river mouth, the fort is a great place from which to watch the fishing boats come into port, or to take in the sunset. Walk down the avenue to admire the remaining turn-of-the-20th-century villas, relics of when Praia da Rocha was a hotbed of international partying.

✚ 332 B13 ℹ Avenida Tomás Cabreira, 8500-802 Portimão ☎ 282 419 132

QUARTEIRA

www.portugal-info.net

Nowadays, Quarteira, the first of the Algarve resorts to be developed in the 1970s, comes in for a lot of criticism. It's big, its high-rise buildings are ugly and the town is often noisy during the summer high season, but it's blessed with a long, gently shelving beach, perfect for little ones to play, paddle and swim safely. The resort's other main selling points are its relaxed family atmosphere and realistic prices.

The glorious beach is fronted by a palm-lined promenade, with a small fishing harbour at the west end. The streets are buzzing with life, there's a good daily market, and on Wednesdays the town plays host to one of the biggest and liveliest gypsy markets in the Algarve.

✚ 332 C13 ℹ Praça do Mar, 8125-156 Quarteira ☎ 289 389 209

QUINTA DO LAGO

www.quintadolago.com

The quiet roads of Quinta do Lago are lined with villas hidden by trees, expensive luxury hotels and country clubs. This purpose-built resort caters for the rich, who pay for privacy, exclusivity and access to the best golf courses in the Algarve. If you are staying at one of the hotels, the resort office will fill you in on what's happening; if you are visiting for the day, head down to the beach at the western end of the Parque Natural da Ria Formosa.

Take the walkway across the lagoon and mudflats to reach the superb beach or head out along one of the nature trails to explore the marshlands, lakes and woods. Here you can take a look at the salting tanks dating from Roman times, or you can do some birdwatching—it's a good place to spot flamingos. Golf, tennis or riding are all on offer in the resort, but if you prefer to shop, the complex also has some of the region's classiest designer stores.

✚ 332 C13 ℹ Quinta do Lago, 8135-024 Almansil ☎ 289 351 900

Below *Looking across the Arade from Portimão to the old fort*

SAGRES AND CABO DE SÃO VICENTE

This old fort dating from the time of Henry the Navigator and the great age of discoveries is a must-see along a stretch of magnificent coastal scenery.

Known to the Romans as the Promontorium Sacrum (Sacred Promontory) and to ancient Portuguese mariners as O Fim do Mundo (End of the World), Cabo de Sao Vicente is the southwesternmost point of mainland Europe.

Prince Henry the Navigator set up his celebrated School of Navigation at Sagres in 1415. Henry gathered the best astronomers, cartographers and navigational instrument-makers of the day around him to launch the great age of discoveries; the revolutionary ocean-going caravel was also designed and subsequently developed here.

FORTALEZA DE SAGRES

www.ippar.pt

It's generally agreed that Henry's School of Navigation occupied the headland at Sagres, though his fort was sacked by Sir Francis Drake in 1587. The present one dates from 1793. The entire area is surrounded by massive walls and bastions. Walk through and you will find yourself in a vast and windswept space, with a range of modern buildings ahead and the tiny church of Nossa Senhora da Graça, where Henry certainly worshipped, to the right.

Before visiting the church, climb the ramp to the right of the entrance for an overview of the area—below is the outline of the 39m-diameter (127ft) *Rosa dos Ventos*, a wind, or compass, rose thought to have been used to help teach navigation. Unearthed by accident in 1921, it certainly dates from Henry's time, but how it worked is still a mystery.

✉ 8650-360 Sagres ☎ 282 620 140 🕐 May–end Sep daily 9.30–8; rest of year daily 9.30–5.30 (last entry 15 min before closing) ✋ €3

CABO DE SÃO VICENTE

Whatever the weather, mainland Europe's remotest point has great views, fresh air and wild sea. You can walk into the lighthouse complex—once a fortress—and peer down to the rocks and pounding surf, or photograph the superb views up and down the coast. The lighthouse's lamp is the most powerful in Europe. The place is not officially open to the public, but the keeper sometimes gives tours.

INFORMATION

www.visitalgarve.pt
www.sagres.net
✚ 332 B13 ℹ Rua Comandante Matoso, 8650 367 Sagres ☎ 202 624 873 🕐 Mon–Sat 9.30–1, 2–5.30

TIPS

❯❯ Cabo de São Vicente can get very crowded with day trippers in the summer.
❯❯ If you take a tour of the lighthouse, tip the keeper when he's finished.

Above *A spectacular sunset at remote Cabo de São Vicente*

SERRA DE MONCHIQUE

www.cm-monchique.pt

Just 25km (15 miles) from the teeming coast, the hills of Serra de Monchique are a different world—this is rural Portugal, with unspoilt countryside and small traditional villages that are untouched by the commercialization found along much of the coast. The hills are mainly wooded, with almonds, olives and mimosa giving way to eucalyptus and pine trees on the higher slopes. Above the tree line are the peaks of Fóia, at 902m (2,960ft) the highest point in the Algarve, and Picota, 774m (2,540ft). You can drive to the top of each to enjoy the magnificent views over the western Algarve, but this is excellent walking country and it's quite feasible to hike up them.

The main settlement and start point for walks in the *serra* is Monchique, a small hill town that's renowned for its handicrafts and its fine 16th-century church. A few miles below is the tiny spa settlement of Caldas de Monchique, where the mineral-rich waters gush out at 32°C (90°F). Popular in the 19th century, the spa retains a faded *fin-de-siècle* elegance; the waters are used to treat rheumatism and respiratory illnesses. From the hills, west towards Aljezur, a magnificent drive takes you on a twisting road down to the wild west coast.

✚ 332 B13 🅸 Largo de São Sebastião, 8550 Monchique ☎ 282 911 189

SILVES

www.cm-silves.pt

Silves, known to the Moors as Xelb, is historically the Algarve's most important city. It was the Islamic capital of Al-Gharb, a major fortress, river port on the Arade and a trading hub, whose wealth and influence were renowned all over Europe. After the 13th-century expulsion of the Moors, the town declined, the river silted up and by the 16th century Silves was a forgotten backwater, its population, once 30,000, shrinking to 150.

Cork processing revived the town in the 19th century, and today Silves thrives on citrus growing, farming and tourism, with thousands visiting the city walls and castle, one of Portugal's best-preserved Moorish monuments. You will have to climb steeply uphill to reach the castle (daily 9–5; €1.25), now little more than a shell, with magnificent views from the walls. Just outside is the Sé (daily 8.30–6.30; times may vary; free), a fine twin-towered Gothic cathedral built on the site of the Moorish mosque. It was the Algarve's most important church until the bishopric moved to Faro in 1577.

Downhill from here is the Museu Arqueológico (tel 282 444 832; Mon–Sat 9.30–5.30; €1.50), whose displays trace local history through Phoenician, Roman and Moorish times. There is more history in the town's one-time cork factory, the Fábrica do Inglês (tel 282 440 480; www.fabrica-do-ingles.pt; Jul–end Aug daily 9am–midnight; rest of year Tue–Sat 9am–10pm (times may vary); museum May–end Sep daily 9.30–12.45, 2–8.45; rest of year daily 9.30–12.45, 2–6.15), which has been revamped as a cultural and leisure venue. There's a morning market.

✚ 332 C13 🅸 Rua 25 de Abril 26–28, 8300-184 Silves ☎ 282 442 255

TAVIRA

www.cm-tavira.pt

Tavira, on the banks of the River Gilão, is a prosperous town that made its money from tuna fishing 300 years ago and has managed to withstand the impact of 20th-century mass tourism. It can no longer be described as undiscovered, but it has kept its soul and retained its fine buildings, narrow streets, old-fashioned shops, cafés and traditional way of life. From the river, spanned by a 'Roman' bridge that's actually 17th century, you can explore the heart of town, a tangle of narrow streets and old houses that contrast with broad riverside avenues. Tavira is rich in churches, with more than 25 to view; pick of the bunch are the beautiful Igreja da Misericórdia, built between 1541 and 1551 by Pilarté, a mason who worked at Belém, and Santa Maria do Castelo, famous for the tombs of seven Christian knights slain by the Moors. The killings were the catalyst for the Christian revolt that expelled the Muslims.

The Moorish castle ruins, set in immaculate gardens, lie just up the hill, a good place for a pause, as are the riverside gardens that run down from the main Praça da República. From here, a miniature train runs seawards to the ferry departure point for the Ilha de Tavira, where there's a superb sandy beach with good walking through the dunes.

✚ 333 D13 🅸 Rua da Galeria 9, 8800-329 Tavira ☎ 281 322 511 🆁 Tavira

Left *Tavira, on the River Gilão, prospered because of its tuna fishing in the 1700s*

VALE DO LOBO

www.valedolobo.com

Like Quinta do Lago (▷ 268), Vale de Lobo caters for the rich, who come here to play golf and relax in secluded and well-heeled surroundings. Similar in style to Quinta do Lago, Vale de Lobo has a wonderful beach, which may be worth investigating in high season—the resort villas all have their own pools, which usually means that the beach is uncrowded.

Golfers should enquire at the resort office about playing, but note that green fees are high, the courses exclusive and advance reservation a must. The resort has several classy hotels and country clubs, and is well served by international-style restaurants, bars and shops—if you're staying here, there seems hardly any need to venture out at all.

✚ 332 C13

VILA REAL DE SANTO ANTÓNIO

www.cm-vrsa.pt

For a taste of successful 18th-century rationalism, head for Vila Real de Santo António on the banks of the River Guadiana, opposite Spanish Ayamonte. Founded in 1773 to replace an earlier settlement swallowed up by waves and shifting sand, it was the brain-child of the Marquês de Pombal, who was also responsible for rebuilding Lisbon's Baixa district (▷ 77). A grid design was drawn up, pre-cut stone was shipped in and the entire town was virtually completed in six months. Arrow-straight streets of wonderfully homogeneous buildings converge on the central square, the Praça Marquês de Pombal, with its church, town hall and former barracks. Stroll around the town and along the riverbank, or hop on the ferry and enjoy a few hours in Spain. Boats cruise upriver, too, through undulating countryside. Vila Real's stores are popular with Spanish shoppers looking for bargains.

✚ 333 D13　ℹ Centro Cultural António Aleixo, Rua Teófilo Braga, 8900-303 Vila Real de Santo António ☎ 281 510 045　🚉 Vila Real de Santo António

Above *Vilamoura's marina is one of the largest in Europe and is a centre for watersports, as well as shopping, entertainment and nightlife*

VILA ROMANA DE MILREU

www.ippar.pt

Just down the hill from the palace at Estói (▷ 266) are the ruins of Milreu, a first- to third-century AD villa and bath complex that's the Algarve's most important Roman excavation. You will need a little imagination to work out the site, most of which is occupied by what was a huge third century AD country house, complete with a central pool and garden backed by a colonnaded peristyle. Surrounding this are the fragments of an extensive bath complex, which still retains the original tubs and heating furnaces.

The sheer numbers of changing rooms and pools have given rise to the theory that Milreu was once a spa and temple complex—it has been proved that a large sanctuary was built here during the fourth century AD.

It is all somewhat confusing, so concentrate on the lively mosaics scattered throughout the villa, all that's left of its archaeological treasures, most of which are now in museums in Faro and Lagos. The mosaics accurately and creatively depict dolphins, many varieties of fish, shells and seaweed. Some scholars think this concentration may provide a clue to the villa's owner, who could have been a fish-processor with a factory on the coast. Be sure to peek inside the 16th-century house built on top of part of the ruins, a fine example of vernacular architecture incorporating Roman masonry.

✚ 333 D13　ℹ Ruínas de Milreu, Estói, 8000 Faro ☎ 289 997 823　◷ Apr–end Sep Tue–Sun 9.30–12.30, 2–6; rest of year Tue–Sun 9.30–12.30, 2–5 ♿ €2

VILAMOURA

www.vilamoura.net

Hotels, shops, a casino, restaurants and bars surround the huge marina here in Vilamoura. The resort's story dates back to the 1970s, when visitors began to flock to the Algarve. Vilamoura continues to expand, with villa and hotel developments radiating ever farther inland.

The resort's main attraction is golf; there are five courses, all challenging and all beautifully maintained. The marina is the hub for all watersports activities, with everything from jet skiing to big-game fishing, while inland there's horseback riding and tennis. Northwest of the marina is the Museu Cerro da Vila (tel 289 312 153; May–end Oct daily 10–1, 4–9; rest of year daily 9.30–12.30, 2–6; €2), a Roman archaeological site with an adjoining small museum housing a variety of local finds.

Vilamoura has two great beaches, the 3km (2-mile) long Praia de Marinha and Falésia. The latter, Falésia, is reached via a walkway over an inlet and consequently is usually less crowded.

✚ 332 C13

INTO THE HIGH ALGARVE FROM PORTIMÃO

This drive runs inland from bustling Portimão to the historic town of Silves before taking you, via some attractive villages, to the Algarve's highest point for some tremendous views.

THE DRIVE

Distance: 80km (50 miles)
Time: 2 hours without stops, 3–5 hours with stops
Start /end at: Portimão

★ Leave Portimão (▷ 268) on the N124 signposted for Monchique. (If you're accessing the road from the N125, take the slip road off the N125 in the northern outskirts of Portimão.) Head north for 6km (3.5 miles), then take a right turn at Porto de Lagos, continuing on the N124 towards Silves. The road runs along the fertile Arade valley, an area of rolling citrus orchards. The local smallholders set up stands outside their houses where you can buy

freshly picked fruit for about €1.50 per 2kg (4.4 lb) bag.

❶ Silves (▷ 270), once a Moorish royal capital famed throughout the Islamic world, is worth a long stop. Park the car and explore the town on foot. Many old buildings were destroyed by the earthquake of 1755, but the great red sandstone fortress, symbol of Moorish dominance, remains.

On leaving Silves, retrace your route to the intersection with the N266 (same road, new number) and turn right along the valley of the river Boina to head up towards the town of Monchique.

❷ The Boina valley is traced by a shady, wooded road, where acacia (mimosa) and eucalyptus predominate—a scented sea of soft yellow in early spring. Both these southern hemisphere species were discovered by the botanist Sir Joseph Banks, who accompanied Captain Cook on his epic Pacific voyage in 1770. Both trees adapted to life in Europe and there are large areas of the Algarve where they predominate over the native species. They are, however, a fire hazard, particularly the eucalyptus, which has high levels of natural oils.

After 11km (7 miles) look for the tiny slip road down to the spa village of Caldas de Monchique (▷ 270). Continue uphill to Monchique itself (▷ 270).

❸ Monchique holds a big market on the second Friday of the month, where you can buy the famous local ham, *presunto de Monchique*, and—if you're brave enough—some *medronho*, the powerful local spirit distilled from the fruit of the arbutus, also called the strawberry tree. Look, too, for the traditional stools made to a design that originated with Roman furniture makers.

In the main square, turn steeply left uphill to leave town on the N266-3 towards the summit of Fóia—watch for the signs.

❹ Fóia, at 902m (2,959ft), is the highest point in the Algarve, so on a clear day it's worth getting out a map at the summit to identify the landmarks that will be spread out at your feet. The whole of the southwestern tip of Portugal, with the sprawl of Portimão (▷ 268) and Lagos (▷ 267), should be visible to the south, with wild Cabo de São

Vicente (▷ 269) at the farthest point. Fóia is a popular tour destination, so arrive early, or, better still, late—it's a great place for sunsets.

Leave the summit and retrace your route to Portimão. As an alternative,

turn left onto the N267 south of Monchique and continue to the tiny village of Casais, where you take the unclassified road that runs south via Montes de Cima. After about 3km (1 mile) you can either turn right to rejoin the N266 or continue south to hit the N125 to the west of Portimão.

WHERE TO EAT

For light snacks in Silves, try the Café Inglês, Escadas do Castelo (▷ 287), and, in Caldas, the restaurant in the spa complex. Just beyond Monchique on the Fóia road, there's the Jardim das Oliveiras (▷ 287) with its hearty mountain cooking and pretty terrace.

WHEN TO GO

This is a particularly appealing drive in late winter, when the almond blossom is out and the road between Silves and Caldas de Monchique is a sheet of mimosa. In summer, it's a great way to escape the crowds on the coast.

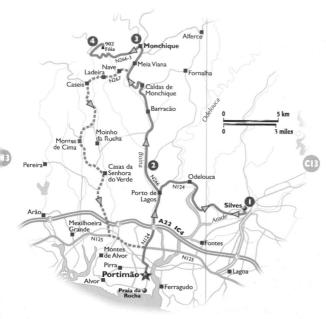

Above *The main square in Silves*
Opposite *The Gothic cathedral towers above the red-tiled roofs of Silves*

REGIONS THE ALGARVE ● DRIVE

273

IN THE SERRA DE MONCHIQUE FOOTHILLS

On this lovely walk in the wooded foothills of the Algarve's Serra de Monchique you can escape from the crowds on the coast into a quieter, calmer world.

THE WALK
Distance: 7.5km (4.5 miles)
Time: 2–3 hours
Start/end at: Caldas de Monchique

★ Set off from the red telephone box in Caldas de Monchique (▷ 270) and walk downhill through the village to the water bottling plant. The mineral water produced here is considered the best in Portugal. It's sweet-tasting and high in minerals. Keeping the bottling plant on your left, turn right off the road onto a track that leads steeply downhill.

❶ The path is lined with acacia trees; in late winter they're covered in fluffy yellow blossom. The river is below you to the right as you walk.

Continue until you come to a bridge across the river. Walk over the bridge—take care if it has been raining as it may be slippery—and turn left along a narrow path that runs alongside the water.

❷ In these hills, the greenery is lush during late winter and spring, with almond and acacia blossom. A small bush has clusters of red fruit that vaguely resemble strawberries. This is *Arbutus unedo* whose fruit is used to make the Algarve's best-known spirit, *medronho*. This ranges from a 40°-proof version for tourist sale to a brain-numbing moonshine with a staggering 70°- to 90°-proof punch that's still brewed in the hills.

Continue on the riverside path, passing a bridge on your left, and walk on until you see tiny fields above the river, planted with citrus trees, and a large house on the opposite bank. At the fork in the path, take the right branch uphill, away from the water. This path drops down to become a wide track, which runs fairly steeply uphill. Follow this as far as an intersection where another track comes in from the left. Turn right here and stay on this track for around 25 to 30 minutes.

❸ Bright Bermuda buttercups carpet the ground in late winter and spring, while the scents of lavender, thyme, rosemary and oregano fill the air during the hotter months.

When you reach a right-hand turn where the path climbs slightly before levelling off, take it—you'll be able to enjoy a fine view down to Caldas de Monchique below. Follow the track steeply downhill, passing a small white house on the left at the bottom. The track bears right and you'll soon see the bridge over the stream that you took near the start of the walk. Cross it and retrace the route into Caldas.

WHERE TO EAT
There is nowhere to eat on this walk, so take a picnic with you. It's well worth carrying a bottle of water, especially in summer.

Above *Caldas de Monchique lies in the foothills of the Serra de Monchique*

WALK

EXPLORING THE HIGH ALGARVE

Good tracks and paths take you from the heart of the one time Moorish capital of the Algarve, through smallholdings into the countryside, with lovely views along the way.

THE WALK

Distance: 7.5km (4.5 miles)
Time: 2–2.5 hours
Start/end at: Silves

★ Start in Largo do Município in Silves (▷ 270). Head up Rua da Sé to the cathedral. Just past the cathedral, turn right and skirt the castle remains. Keeping the castle to the left, head straight downhill. After about 10 minutes, you'll come to an intersection. Here, turn left, then right onto a track running alongside an orange grove. This leads to a *levada*, a concreted water channel. Cross the footbridge and turn right, walking alongside the water channel. Follow the path left towards houses, where you turn left, then sharp right at the next intersection. To reach the ruined windmill, head for the aqueduct and walk underneath it, before immediately turning left at the intersection of several tracks and then right where the new track forks up to the ruins through groves of almond and fig trees and past attractive traditional whitewashed cottages. In late winter, the ground is yellow with Bermuda buttercups, and strongly scented wild narcissi.

❶ Windmills are a common sight all over Portugal, and are mainly used for pumping water. Here, few traces remain of the original superstructure, except for the solid stonework of the tower. It is a good place to pause and take in the superb views back towards Silves, down to Portimão (▷ 268) and into the hills of the Serra de Monchique (▷ 270). Look for pink, white and purple cistus and dense clusters of lavender. In spring, orchids should be in bloom—the tiny green-winged orchid is a rarity.

With your back to the sea, follow the ridge north to the end; the valley ahead on the right is the Bastos. Turn left downhill. At the bottom, turn right onto the lower track, then, shortly ahead, left at an intersection.

Follow this path above a wooded valley, eventually dropping down to where several paths meet. Here, turn left onto the main track and follow this south downhill.

❷ As you walk south, the landscape is one of olives and eucalyptus. These soon give way to vegetables, almond and citrus trees, lavender, rosemary, cistus and the curry plant.

Turn left when you reach the main track, which becomes a surfaced road as you approach the outskirts of Silves. Keep right at the first houses, then turn left and climb the steps. Turn left at the top of the steps, then right to the water channel, the footbridge, and your starting point.

WHERE TO EAT
You can take a picnic or try the Café Inglês, in the Escadas do Castelo (▷ 287), for snacks and meals.

Above *View from the ruined windmill*

EXPLORING THE BARROCAL HILLS

This round trip north from Loulé takes in the fertile rolling hills of central Algarve, an unspoilt rural area known as the garden of the Algarve, rich in almond and orange groves.

THE DRIVE

Distance: 50km (30 miles)
Time: 2–3 hours without stops
Start/end at: Loulé

★ Loulé is a thriving market town. Lying inland and northwest of Faro, it was an important place long before the development of the coastal towns. Today, it is the administrative capital of the area. The old part is a grid of whitewashed, cobbled alleyways focused on the 13th-century Gothic Igreja Matriz. The earlier bell tower was once the minaret of a Moorish mosque, the only part of the Islamic building to survive. Round here are numerous craft shops, many devoted to

copperware and handmade lace. The castle ruins are home to an archaeological museum and you can climb the castle walls for fine views over the old town. Loulé has an excellent produce market, held in an eye-catching, domed Moorish-style building near the heart of town.

Follow the signs out of town for Querença/Ameixial onto the N396. After about 8km (5 miles) you'll see a fine old arched bridge and a sign marked *'fonte'* (spring). Turn left (signed to Querença), then left again up into the heart of the village.

❶ Unspoilt Querença is a pleasant stop. You could have a peep into

the church or enjoy a drink at a characterful bar. If the local sausage is available, it's really worth trying —it's so well known that the village feast day in January is devoted to its celebration.

Drive back down the hill and turn left to join the N524. About 3km (2 miles) along, you could park and take the short walk up to the Fonte da Benémola (▷ 280). Otherwise, continue left towards Salir (signposted).

❷ The road to Salir passes through typical Barrocal countryside. The land here is intensely fertile and farmed by smallholders, many of whom

Left *The road winds its way past the remains of Salir's Moorish castle*
Opposite *Salir, where the Moors once had a stronghold*

PLACES TO VISIT
LOULÉ
🛈 Rua 25 de Abril 9, 8100-506 Loulé
☎ 289 463 900 or 808 781 212 (information number) 🕐 Jul–end Sep Mon–Sat 9.30–7; rest of year Mon–Sat 9.30–5.30

MUSEU ARQUEOLÓGICO, LOULÉ CASTLE
✉ Largo Dom Pedro 1, 8100-519 Loulé
☎ 289 400 642 🕐 Museum: Mon–Fri 9–5.30, Sat 10–2

stick fervently to the historic ways of their peasant ancestors. Donkeys are still used for transportation, for instance, and you may even see older people proudly wearing traditional local costume. The main crops, apart from vegetables, are oranges, almonds, carobs and figs, and you'll also see plenty of cork oak stands. More than 50 per cent of the world's supply of cork oak comes from the inland Algarve and the Alentejo, the tree's spongy bark being harvested every nine years.

At the intersection with the N124 turn left to Salir, and follow the road steeply uphill into the middle of the village.

❸ Salir is another traditional farming village, where you can stroll from the former church along flower-hung white alleys to the remains of the Moorish castle. There's not much to see, but the position is glorious, with fine views over the village and the valley beyond.

Leave Salir and take the unclassified road south for 16km (10 miles) back to Loulé.

WHERE TO EAT
Just out of central Loulé, on the Clareanes/Querença road, is the Casa Paixanito (▷ 287). In Querença, try De Querença in the church square, and in Salir try the Mouro Bar Castelo by the castle.

WHEN TO GO
This pleasant drive is best in the spring when the almond trees are in blossom.

TIP
» Make sure that you have plenty of fuel as service stations are few and far between.

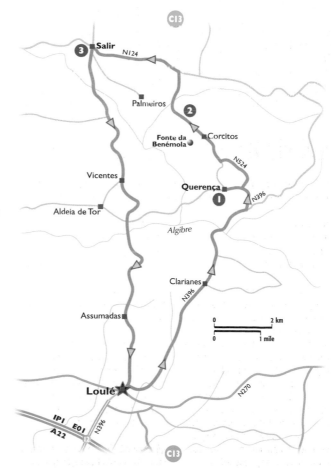

A TRIP ROUND THE WESTERN ALGARVE

In the undiscovered and undeveloped far western Algarve, you'll drive along deserted hill roads and experience the grandeur of the magnificent cliffs and wild scenery of the dramatic Atlantic coast.

THE DRIVE

Distance: 153km (95 miles)
Time: 3 hours' straight driving, or 5–7 hours with stops and detours
Start/end at: Lagos

★ Leave Lagos (▷ 267) on the busy N125 and head west to Vila do Bispo.

❶ Vila do Bispo is a typical Algarve agricultural village, virtually untouched by modern tourism. While you are here, visit the ornate 17th-century parish church within the central core of whitewashed houses. Next, you could head west across the hills for 5km (3 miles) to Praia do Castelejo, a huge sandy beach at the foot of dramatic, forbidding cliffs.

Leaving Vila do Bispo, turn left and follow the N268 south to Sagres (▷ 269). On the way into Sagres you will pass Surf Planet if you fancy hitting the waves (▷ 285).

❷ Sagres is believed to be the place where Prince Henry the Navigator established his headquarters when he became Governor of the Algarve in 1419. His settlement, known as Vila do Infante (Prince's Town), may have been on the site of Sagre's *fortaleza* (fortress).

From Sagres, go north along the coast for 6km (3.5 miles) to Cabo de São Vicente (▷ 269).

❸ Wild Cabo de São Vicente, is the site of Europe's second most powerful lighthouse. The lighthouse is not officially open to the public, but the keeper may allow visitors.

Return to Sagres, and retrace the route to the intersection with the N125 at Vila do Bispo. Turn left here and take the N268 north to Carrapateira.

❹ The road north from Vila do Bispo passes through a lusher landscape, with gently rolling hills, patches of eucalyptus and acacia, and neatly tended smallholdings. Little side roads off the N268 give access to superb beaches. For a real treat, take the turn-off to Praia do Amado, just south of Carrapateira. This broad sandy bay, backed by low hills and renowned for its excellent surf, has the bonus of being relatively quiet even in summer.

In Carrapateira turn left onto the loop road that runs round the headland and down to Praia da Bordeira.

❺ Praia da Bordeira is an unusual beach for the area. A broad stretch of sand, backed by dunes and a little river valley, it provides a pleasing contrast to the precipitous cliffs elsewhere on this coast.

Return to the main road (N268) and continue north to the intersection with the N120. Turn left in the direction of Aljezur.

To explore more beaches, you could make a detour after approximately 1.8km (1 mile). Turn left onto an unclassified road signed 'arrifana'. Continue north through Vale da Telha to Praia de Monte Clérigo (great for families) and return up the river valley to the N120. Turn left and drive north to Aljezur.

⑥ Aljezur, little more than a large village, is the largest settlement on the western Algarve coast. Park in the modern lower town, where you'll find most of the shops and restaurants, and walk up the steep cobbled streets of the old town to reach the ruins of the 10th-century Moorish castle, from where there are views over the town and the surrounding countryside. There are also a couple of local museums.

At Aljezur turn right onto the N267 and continue for 10km (6 miles), before turning right down a minor road to Corsino and the Barragem da Bravura. This hilly road runs through lovely countryside between the western edge of the lower Serra de Monchique (▷ 270) and the Serra do Espinhaço de Cão. Follow the signs to the Barragem da Bravura on the N125-9.

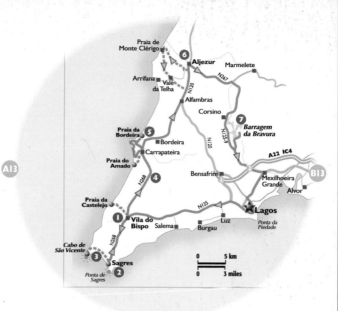

⑦ The Bravura reservoir is one of the finest in the Algarve, a smooth stretch of deep, green water backed by wooded hills. You can walk across the dam and along a track, or simply relax at the café.

Head south on the N125-9 to the N125. Turn right to return to Lagos.

WHERE TO EAT
In Sagres, there's A Tasca at Praia da Baleeira (▷ 286–287). Praia da Bordeira has Sítio do Rio, which serves great charcoal grills (▷ 286), and Praia de Monte Clérigo has the Casa de Pasto O Zé and the Snack Bar a Rede. You can choose from several beachside bars in Praia do Amado, while in Aljezur itself there's the Restaurante Ruth in Rua 25 de Abril.

WHEN TO GO
Both Sagres and Cabo de São Vicente are popular tourist stops in summer, so aim to arrive early in the day to avoid the crowds.

TIP
» The sea is much colder here than it is along the southern Algarve and currents and tides also can be treacherous. Take particular care if bathing.

Left *The colourful marina at Lagos*
Opposite *Rugged Cabo de São Vicente and its lighthouse*

A WALK IN THE BARROCAL HILLS

This cool, leafy walk, with varied trees, shrubs and wild flowers along the way, takes you down a gentle valley to a little-known beauty spot.

THE WALK
Distance: 5km (3 miles)
Time: 1 hour
Start/end at: 3km (2 miles) north of Querença on N524, at the sign *'Fonte de Benémola, circulo pedestre'*
Parking: Off the road next to the ruined house on the left at the start of the track

★ Start walking at the sign marked *'circulo pedestre'* and follow the track—there's only one—for about 1km (half a mile). At the fork, head left and follow the signs to the *fonte* (spring) across a small bridge.

❶ Along this stretch you'll see two types of vegetation: well-ordered fields of crops, fruit and olive trees, and vegetables; and the *matos* (scrubland) to the right, rich in orchids, rosemary, lavender, thyme and juniper.

Turn left beyond the bridge, then left again, keeping the river on your left. Here you're in a verdant haven.

❷ The sound of running water and the scent of orange, lemon and carob trees assault your senses here. You may be able to hear, if not spot, warblers and other birds, while, after rain, there may be otter prints in the soft earth beside the water. The otters feed on the tiny fish in the river.

Walk on for about five minutes to reach the Fonte de Benémola itself.

❸ The Fonte de Benémola spring is rich in minerals and there's a tradition of bathing in the water for health reasons—it's considered good for arthritic conditions. There are picnic tables in a clearing here. You can explore farther upstream, where you'll find caves as the river passes through a rocky ravine.

Cross the river on the stepping stones and turn immediately left, following the water downstream and keeping it on your left.

❹ A basketmaker's hut is a few minutes' walk farther along the river. The craftsman sells a variety of traditional baskets.

Continue through a stand of cork oaks until you get back to the N124; turn left, cross the bridge and follow the road back to where you parked.

WHERE TO EAT
Take a picnic, or try De Querença back in the town in the Largo da Igreja before or after the walk.

TIPS
» If the river is high, the stepping stones at the farthest point of the walk will be submerged and you'll have to retrace your steps.
» You'll see a variety of signs to the spring or red, white and yellow paint marks on walls and trees. Though locals drive down to the spring—the track is just wide enough to take a car—it's not recommended.

Above *The cultivated Barrocal countryside*

THE CLIFFS OF LAGOS AND PRAIA DA LUZ

This invigorating clifftop walk encompasses a quintessential stretch of the western Algarve coastline. En route, you'll enjoy superb views of the coastal rock formations and the open Atlantic.

THE WALK
Distance: 6km (3.5 miles)
Time: 2.5–3 hours
Start at: Lagos
End at: Praia da Luz

★ Start on the riverside in Lagos (▷ 267), where the palm-shaded Avenida dos Descobrimentos runs alongside the River Bensafrim. Walk to the end of the promenade to the Forte da Ponta da Bandeira.

❶ The 17th-century Forte da Ponta da Bandeira was built to guard the harbour entrance. Go inside the fort to enjoy the views; just below you is Praia da Batata, a sandy cove.

Continue up the hill out of town until you reach the viewpoint, with its conspicuous stone monument.

❷ The monument at the viewpoint commemorates São Gonçalo, a local fisherman's son who became a monk and the patron saint of Lagos.

At the top of the hill look for a sign to the left marked *'Praia do Pinhão'* and follow the path. It leads along the cliffs past tiny, sheltered Pinhão beach to Praia de Dona Ana.

❸ Praia de Dona Ana has gently shelving sands and the rocks, sea stacks and caves so typical of this stretch of the coast. The clifftops are covered with with hotels, cafés and apartment blocks but, out of season or late in the day, it's a delight.

Cross the beach and car park above it and make your way back up to the cliffs. There's a plethora of narrow tracks, but keep the sea on your left and you can't go wrong. The next cove is the Praia do Camilo, a classic but less crowded beach. Continue to Ponta da Piedade.

❹ Ponta da Piedade is a series of spectacular, red rock stacks rising from crystal-clear water and riddled with grottoes. In summer, fishermen

run trips to them. Past the lighthouse are good coastal views.

Keep the sea on your left and continue along the cliffs. At Praia de Porto de Mós the path drops down to the sea. From here, follow the path uphill for 40 minutes or so. An obelisk, at 109m (358ft) is the highest point on the walk. Go through the gap in the bushes on the left and scramble down the slope to a cobbled path that leads onto the beach at Praia da Luz.

❺ Praia da Luz is an attractive, low-key resort with a pleasant promenade, a clutch of bars and restaurants, and a Portuguese heart.

There are regular buses to Lagos.

WHERE TO EAT
Locals recommend the Restaurante Paraíso in Praia da Luz.

Above *The beach at Praia de Dona Ana*

WHAT TO DO

ALBUFEIRA

AQUALAND
www.aqualand.pt
North of Albufeira, Aqualand has wave pools and gentle rapids, twisting water slides or, for the intrepid, a 92m (300ft) kamikaze chute and a 23m (75ft) death drop.
✉ Apartado 11, 8365-908 Alcantarilha
☎ 282 320 230 🕐 May to mid-Sep daily 10–6 👋 Adult €18.50, child (4–12) €15
🚌 Just off the EN125 at Alcantarilha

MARKET
This twice-monthly market north of town near the new bus station sells mainly clothes and shoes, but, during summer, extra stands along the main shopping streets sell jewellery, ceramics, copper, leatherwear and souvenirs.
☎ 289 585 279 (tourist office) 🕐 First and third Tue of month

RUA CÂNDIDO DOS REIS
This street off the Largo Engenheiro Duarte Pacheco is full of craft and souvenir shops. Among the best are Infante Dom Henrique (No. 40), which sells quality ceramics, and La Lojas (Nos 20–22), which has lead crystal and fine porcelain.
✉ Albufeira 🕐 Mon–Sat 10–8

ZEBRA SAFARI
www.zebraincentives.com
This outdoor pursuits company, with its convoy of distinctive zebra-patterned 4x4s, organizes guided day trips (9–5) to monuments, unspoilt hill country and local craftspeople. It also provides a seemingly endless list of activities.
✉ Apt. 836, Arcadas de São João, Areias de São João, 8201-911 Albufeira ☎ 289 583 300 🕐 Office: Mon–Fri 9–1, 3–7, Sat 4–6 👋 1-day 4x4 tour €47.50 including lunch 🚌 From Albufeira follow signs to Areias de São João. The office is on the main street next to the Caixa General de Depósitos bank

ZOOMARINE
www.zoomarine.com
At this oceanographic theme park the emphasis is on environmental conservation and education. A marine museum and cinema complement the large aquarium; daily attractions include the sea-lion and the dolphin show. There is also the chance to swim with bottle-nose dolphins.
✉ On the EN125 (km 65), Guia junction, 8200-864 Albufeira ☎ 289 560 300
🕐 Jun–6 Sep daily 10–7.30; Apr–end May and 7 Sep–end Oct daily 10–6; rest

Above *The Algarve has some of Europe's best golf courses*

of year Tue–Sun 10–5 👋 Adult €23, child (5–10) €14; swimming with dolphins €145
🚌 Just off the EN125 between Guia and Alcantarilha

ALMANCIL

GRIFFIN BOOKSHOP
www.griffinbookshop.com
This is probably the best place to find English-language books in the Algarve. It sells a wide selection of fiction, non-fiction, children's and second-hand books.
✉ Rua 5 de Outubro 206-A, 8135-103 Almancil ☎ 289 393 904 🕐 Mon–Fri 9.30–6, Sat 9.30–2

KARTING ALMANCIL
www.mundokarting.pt
This 760m (828-yard) track is a replica of a former Brazilian Formula 1 circuit and attracts more than 250,000 visitors a year. Set in a Western-style theme park, it has a saloon café, bar and restaurant, and a children's circuit.
✉ Sitio das Pereiras, 8135-022 Almancil
☎ 289 399 899 🕐 Jul–end Aug daily 10–midnight; Sep daily 10–8; Feb–end May and Oct–end Dec Tue 3–6, Wed–Fri 10–6,

Sat–Sun 10–7 🏍 €15 for 160cc, €22.50 for 390cc 🚌 Take Almancil turning off the EN125. Karting Almancil is on the right

FARO
FORUM ALGARVE
www.forumalgarve.net
This shopping mall on the outskirts of town has more than 120 shops, including well-known international chains. It makes a good wet-weather option, as its shopping, cinemas, restaurants, snack bars and parking are all housed under one roof.
✉ On the EN125, Pontes de Marfil
☎ 789 889 300 🕐 Jun–end Sep and Dec daily 10am–midnight; Jan–end May and Oct–end Nov Sun–Thu 10am–11pm, Fri–Sat 10am–midnight 🚌 Minibus No. 1 runs Mon–Fri 8–8 every 15 min from several central pick-up points 🚌 The mall is at km 103 of the N125 on the western side of town

O ATELIER
This shop has three rooms crammed with farm furniture, paintings, books, silverware, faïence ceramics, postcards and some impressive antique watches.
✉ Rua Brites de Almeida 32, 8000-234 Faro
☎ 289 821 777 🕐 Mon–Fri 9–1, 3–7, Sat 10–1

LAGOA
OLARIAS DE PORCHES
The village of Porches, to the east of Lagoa, is one of the few places in the region that sells genuine Algarve pottery, as opposed to imported Alentejo wares. It is best known for its good-quality, blue-and-green Mallorcan-style ceramics, which are usually decorated with naïve hand-painted motifs of sweeping leaves, fruits, birds and flowers.
✉ On the EN125, Porches

SLIDE & SPLASH
www.slidesplash.com
This is Portugal's largest water park, with around 6.5ha (16 acres) of children's pools, waves, rapids, twisting shoots and, for the more adventurous, the thrilling Kamikaze or the dark drop of the Black Hole. For the less crazy, there are great lawns for sunbathing.

✉ On the EN125, Vale de Deus, Estombar, 8401-901 Lagoa ☎ 282 340 800
🕐 Easter–end Oct daily 10–5/5.30/6
🏊 Adult €18, child (5–10) €14.50 🚌 Go west from Lagoa on the EN125 towards Portimão. At a roundabout (traffic circle) turn off to Estombar; after 0.5km (0.25 mile) Slide & Splash is signed to the left

LAGOS
BOM DIA
www.bomdia.info
This company organizes excursions along the Algarve coast in traditional Portuguese sailing ships. The multilingual crews sail the schooners down to Sagres for lunch, or offer shorter trips to explore the grottoes at Ponta da Piedade.
✉ Marina de Lagos, shop 10, 8600-780 Lagos ☎ 282 087 587 🕐 Jul–end Sep daily departures 10–5; Oct, Nov and Feb–end Jun daily departures 10–3 🏊 5-hour grotto and barbecue trip adult €49, child (5–10) €24.50; 3-hour family fishing trip adult €39, child (5–10) €29; 2-hour grotto trip adult €25, child (5–10) €12.50 🚌 Follow signs to the marina

CENTRO CULTURAL DE LAGOS
A cultural venue hosting art and photographic exhibitions, music recitals and theatre performances. The snack bar also serves a great-value prato do dia (dish of the day) at lunchtime.
✉ Rua Lançarote de Freitas 7, 8600-605 Lagos ☎ 282 770 450 🕐 Mid-Jun to mid-Sep daily 1pm–midnight; rest of year Mon–Sat 10–8 🏊 €2.50–€30 according to exhibition and performance 🔲 🖥

DOLPHIN SEAFARIS
www.dolphinseafaris.com
Based at the Lagos marina, this company organizes dolphin-watching excursions from a RIB (rigid inflatable boat); there is, they say, an 85 per cent chance of actually spotting some dolphins.
✉ Marina de Lagos, 8600-780 Lagos
☎ 282 799 209 or 918 704 267
🕐 Jun–end Aug daily 8.30, 10, 11.30, 1 and 3; rest of year call for times 🏊 Adult €40, under-11s €30 🚌 The office is well signposted within the Centro Comercial da Marinha at Lagos marina

MARKET
Lagos's covered market has a good selection of fruit and vegetables, fresh bread and unusual cheeses. On the first Saturday of every month, there is an open-air gypsy market selling mainly shoes, clothes and textiles.
✉ Rua das Portas de Portugal, 8600-657 Lagos 🕐 Mon–Sat 8–1

MOTORENT
www.motorent.pt
One of the best ways to explore the narrow streets of Lagos's old town is by bicycle. Alternatively, head off to the hills behind the town on a motorcycle. Both engine- and leg-powered versions can be rented.
✉ Rua Victor Costa e Silva, Ed. Vasco da Gama, loja 8b, 8600-764 Lagos ☎ 282 769 716 🕐 Daily 9–1, 2–7 🏊 Bicycle rental €13 per day (plus €50 deposit); helmet €2.50; child seat €2.50; motorcycle rental: €28–€80 depending on type; quad bikes €80; delivery to hotel

PARQUE ZOOLÓGICO DE LAGOS
www.zoolagos.com
This small zoo is home to about 120 animals, but the emphasis is on birds, which can be observed in a 60m (65-yard) walk-through aviary. There is a good farm for children.
✉ Quinta Figueiras, Sítio do Medronhal, Barão de S. João, 8600-013 Lagos
☎ 282 680 100 🕐 Apr–end Sep daily 10–7; Oct–end Mar daily 10–5 🏊 Adult €10, child (4–11) €6 🚌 Take the EN120 northwest out of Lagos to Bensafrim. In Bensafrim turn left at the signs

TIFFANY'S
www.valegrifo.com
Instead of kitting you out with diamonds, this Tiffany's organizes riding holidays and day rides.
✉ Vale Grifo, Almádena, Luz, 8600-102 Lagos ☎ 282 697 395 🕐 Apr–end Sep daily 9–1, 3–7; Oct–end Mar daily 9–1, 3–5
🏊 1-hour country jaunt €30; Breakfast at Tiffany's (a 1.5-hour ride followed by breakfast) €50; 5-hour adventure ride €125 🚌 Head west out of Lagos on the EN125 towards Sagres. After passing through Espiche, watch for signs on the right to Tiffany's before Almádena

LOULÉ

CENTRO DE ARTESANATO

This centre has a good collection of lace, leather goods, pottery and copper ware, plus fine displays of model wooden caravels.

✉ Rua da Barbaça 11–13, Loulé ☎ 289 412 190 ◉ Daily 9.30–7

MARKETS

Loulé's daily market (Mon–Fri 8–1) at the Praça da República sells tasty produce and traditional crafts. The weekly market, held on a Saturday morning on the western side of the town, has clothes, shoes and inexpensive souvenirs.

☎ 289 463 900 (tourist office)

MEGASPORT

www.megasport.pt

For every type of bicycle rental, Megasport is the place to go. Their range of bicycles includes mountain, ladies', racing, downhill and bicycles of all sizes for children. They also have guides who will take you on escorted tours.

✉ Estrada Nacional 125, Quatro Estrados, 8100-321 Loulé ☎ 289 393 044 ◉ Daily 9–1, 3–7 ✋ 1-day rental adult bicycle €9–€30 depending on type, child bicycle €9; guided tandem tours €30 per hour; helmet €2; child seat €3

MONCHIQUE

ALTERNATIV TOUR

www.alternativtour.com

The wooded hills of Monchique are great for hiking and bicycling. If you prefer to take a guide, contact Alternativ, whose staff are experts on the region. They also provide information on independent routes and will arrange canoeing trips. Telephone lines for making reservations are open daily all year round. There is no central office; instead staff arrange appropriate meeting places individually with cyclists and hikers.

✉ Sitio das Relvinhas, 8550-909 Monchique ☎ 282 913 204 or 965 004 337 ✋ Guided walking tours €30 including picnic lunch; bicycle tours €37 including lunch; independent bicycle tours with maps provided €15; canoeing €30

MONCHIQUE MARKET

Monchique's monthly market is a good place to buy local crafts such as wooden items, cork and basketware. Particularly attractive are the naïve hand-painted children's chairs and folding X-shaped scissor-stools, a design thought by some to be of Roman origin.

☎ 282 911 189 (tourist office) ◉ Second Fri of the month

TERMAS DE MONCHIQUE

www.monchiquetermas.com

Since Roman times, these hot springs have been used to help treat ailments. You can taste the waters free of charge; there is also a therapeutic spa clinic, which treats skin, digestive and rheumatic complaints. For something stronger, try a *medronho*, the local brandy, at one of the bars outside.

✉ Caldas de Monchique, 8550-232 Monchique ☎ 282 910 910 ◉ Wed–Mon 9–7, Tue 10.30–7 ✋ €25–€195 depending on treatment

OLHÃO

MARKET

The town is not geared to tourism, but its market gives a rare insight into day-to-day Algarve life. It is the biggest covered market in the region, with two enormous Moorish-style halls. One sells fresh fruit and vegetables, the other fish and meat.

✉ Avenida 5 de Outubro, 8700 Olhão ◉ Mon–Sat 8–1

PARQUE NATURAL DA RIA FORMOSA

www.icnb.pt

This unspoilt natural park is home to many wetland birds, including rare nesting gallinules. It consists of lagoons, marshes, beaches and dunes, and is good for hiking. For maps and information on paths, contact the park office.

✉ Centro de Educação Ambiental de Marim, Quinta do Marim, Quelfes, 8700 Olhão ☎ 289 700 210 ◉ Daily 10.30–6 (park); Mon–Fri 9–12.30, 2–5.30 (offices) 🚗 Take EN125 east out of Olhão. Turn right at Cepsa fuel station. The office is 1km (0.75 mile) down the road towards the sea

PORTIMÃO

DOLPHIN SEAFARIS

www.dolphinseafaris.com

This company, which also operates from the marina in Lagos (▷ 283), organizes dolphin-watching excursions from Portimão marina.

✉ Marina de Portimão, 8500 Portimão ☎ 282 799 209 or 918 704 267 ◉ Jun–end Aug 9, 10.30, 12, 1.30, 3.30; rest of year call for times ✋ Adult €40, child (under 11) €30 🚗 The office is next to Pizza Hut within the Centro Comercial da Marinha at Portimão marina

O AQUÁRIO

These central shops have a great selection of copper, brass and ceramics. They stock the highly regarded Atlantis full-lead crystal from Alcobaça, north of Lisbon (▷ 226), and the classically designed Vista Alegre porcelain.

✉ Rua Vasco da Gama 42–46, and Praça da República 42–46, 8500 Portimão ☎ 282 426 673 ◉ Mon–Fri 9.30–1, 3–7, Sat 9.30–1

PRAINHA THALGO

www.prainha.net

This Thalgo thalassotherapy clinic offers a range of sea-water treatments and health, beauty and relaxation therapies. Enjoy a relaxing seaweed poultice before being pummelled and then invigorated in a Scottish shower, or take it easy in the Turkish baths, Jacuzzis or hydro-massage tubs.

✉ Prainha dos 3 Iramãos, 8500-072 Alvor Portimão ☎ 282 480 000 ◉ Mon–Sat 9am–10pm ✋ €15–€195 according to treatment 🚗 Leave Portimão in the direction of Alvor. Follow Prainha signs. The club is next to Hotel Prainha

QUINTA DO LAGO

GOLF QUINTA DO LAGO

www.portugalgolf.pt
www.quintadolagogolf.com

Quinta do Lago has four immaculately maintained nine-hole golf courses dotted with umbrella pines looking out over the Ria Formosa Natural Park. The lake at the sixth on 'C' course collects some 1,000 balls a week.

✉ Quinta do Lago, 8135-024 Almancil
☎ 289 390 700 🕐 Daily 7–7 ⛳ 18 holes
€160; club rental €40; trolley €6; buggy €50
🚗 From the EN125, take the Vale do Lobo
turn at Almancil. Turn left at the sign for
the course

CENTRO HÍPICO QUINTA DO LAGO
In addition to renting out horses
by the hour for riding within the
school, the centre offers escorted
hacks through the countryside. At
full moon you can go on a two-hour
night ride around the lagoons and
forests. Children are well looked
after, with half-hour escorted pony
rides and half-day practical courses,
and a daily pony camp.
✉ Lote Hípico, Avenida Ayrton Senna,
Quinta do Lago, 8135-161 Almancil ☎ 289
396 099 🕐 Apr–end Sep daily 7–12, 4–9;
Oct–end Mar daily 8–12, 2–6 ⛳ Adult €35
per hour, €60 for 2-hour group trek to beach;
child €20 for half-hour ride, €25 for half-day
activities, €65 for children's daily pony camp
🚗 Head out of town towards the N125. At
the second roundabout turn right then look
for signs

SAGRES
SURF PLANET
www.surfplanet.pt.com
This shop is close to the Costa
Vicentina and has everything
a surfing fanatic might need:
surfboards, bodyboards and
skimboards, fins, wetsuits and
even surf-themed accessories and
street wear. It also organizes surfing
lessons at nearby beaches.
✉ EN268, 268, Vila do Bispo, 8650-355
Sagres ☎ 282 624 815 🕐 Mon–Sat
9.30–7

TAVIRA
FERRIES
To get to the beaches of the Parque
Natural da Ria Formosa around
Tavira take a boat to the sand spits.
Aquataxis has various pick-up points
for rides to Tavira.
☎ 281 322 511 (tourist office) 🕐 From
city centre Jul to mid-Sep daily 8–8 (€1.80
return); from Quatro Águas Jul to mid-Sep
daily 8am–midnight; rest of year daily 8.30–
dusk (€1.30 return. For private watertaxi

EASTER
CARNAVAL DE LOULÉ
Loulé comes to life at Carnaval
time, putting on the most
impressive show in the Algarve.
Costumed parades, samba dancers,
live music, dancing, fireworks
and themed tractor-drawn floats
entertain the crowds.
✉ Loulé ☎ 289 463 900 (tourist office)
🕐 Late Feb–early Mar

JUNE
FESTA DA CIDADE
Tavira's biggest yearly celebration
is held in June, when the town's
streets are lavishly decorated with
paper flowers and myrtle leaves.
Sardines are grilled and served free
in the streets.
✉ Tavira ☎ 281 322 511 (tourist office)
🕐 24–25 Jun

contact Aquataxis at the quay in town or at
Quatro Águas or call 917 035 207

RENT-A-BIKE
Rent-a-Bike offers four-hour guided
bicycling trips and one- or two-hour
hikes to the Parque Natural da Ria
Formosa or around Tavira, with
English-speaking guides.
✉ Rua do Forno 33, Tavira ☎ 281 321
973 🕐 Daily 9–5 ⛳ Bicycle trip €25
per person; hikes €6–€10 🚗 Just off the
bottom end of Rua Infante Dom Henrique

VILAMOURA
CASINO DE VILAMOURA
www.solverde.pt
Vilamoura's casino offers 350 slot
machines and 14 gaming tables.
In addition to bars and a restaurant,
there are floor shows and a
nightclub.
✉ Praça do Casino, Vilamoura, 8125-410
Quarteira ☎ 289 310 000 🕐 Daily
4pm–3am ⛳ Entrance to gaming tables
€4 🚗 On the east side of the Vilamoura
marina, between the Hotel Atlantis and
Hotel Marina

JULY
CONCENTRAÇÃO INTERNACIONAL DE MOTOS DO ALGARVE
www.motoclubefaro.pt
This rally attracts more than 30,000
bikers to Faro waterfront for rock
concerts and accessory stands.
✉ Moto Clube de Faro, Sítio Vale da
Amoreira 328A, 8005-334 Faro ☎ 289 823
845 🕐 Three days in Jul

AUGUST
FESTIVAL DO MARISCO
This seafood festival attracts almost
100,000 people to its stands, which
sell lobsters, prawns and other
kinds of shellfish. The eating is
enhanced by live stage shows.
✉ Jardim Pescador Olhanense, 8700
Olhão ☎ 289 713 936 (tourist office)
🕐 Second week in Aug

ILLUMINATI CAFÉ
This welcoming bar near the
Vilamoura cinema is a great place
to start off the night. It plays
mainly commercial pop and it often
organizes themed parties in the
summer months.
✉ Praça do Cinema, Edifício Pirâmides,
8125-432 Vilamoura ☎ 289 316 272
🕐 Tue–Sun 8pm–2am

THE OLD COURSE
www.portugalgolf.pt
Listed among Europe's top 100
courses, the Old Course, with its
English school design, winds its
way gently through umbrella-pine
woods. The par-3 fourth hole, played
over a small lake, and the back
par-5 16th are considered to be the
course's highlights.
✉ 8125-507 Vilamoura ☎ 289 310 333
🕐 May–end Sep daily 7am–8pm; Oct–end
Apr daily 7–4.30 ⛳ 18 holes €140; club
rental €27.50; trolley €5; buggy €50
🚗 From the EN125 take the Vilamoura exit.
Turn right and continue to the sign for the
course on the left

PRICES AND SYMBOLS

The restaurants are listed alphabetically. The prices given are the average for a two-course lunch (L) and a three-course dinner (D) for one person, without drinks. The wine price is for the least expensive bottle. All the restaurants listed accept credit cards unless otherwise stated.

For a key to the symbols, ▷ 2.

ALBUFEIRA
A RUÍNA

www.restaurante-ruina.com
Set into the cliff face of Praia dos Pescadores, where the old castle once stood, this restaurant has a beach terrace, a dining room on the middle floor and a rooftop patio. The fare is straightforward and unpretentious, but it's all top quality. Fresh fish is seasoned with sea salt and plainly grilled, while there is a good choice of other seafood. ✉ Praia dos Pescadores, Largo Cais Herculano, 8200-061 Albufeira ☎ 289 512 094 ⊙ Daily 12–2.30, 7–11 ✋ L €20, D €30, Wine €12

ALJEZUR
SÍTIO DO RIO

Bream, bass, mullet, beef, pork or kid are all expertly cooked over

the hot coals. Salads are dressed simply with fine olive oil and vinegar; all vegetables come from the restaurant's garden and the chickens are all free range. Credit cards are not accepted. ✉ Praia Bordeira, Carrapateira, 8670-230 Aljezur ☎ 282 973 119 ⊙ Wed–Mon 12–10. Closed Nov–end Jan ✋ L €15, D €18, Wine €6 🚗 Take N125 to Vila do Bispo, then north on N268 to Carrapateira. Just after Carrapateira, turn left to beaches. Restaurant is last building on the right before the beach

ALMANCIL
AUX BONS ENFANTS

Whether you eat in the charming dining room or on the pleasant terrace, this candlelit restaurant serves some of the best French cuisine in the Algarve and has a wine list to match. Snails or fresh foie gras are good starters, followed by Chateaubriand steak in pepper sauce and *confit de canard*. There is a mouthwatering list of desserts and, most agreeably, port is available by the glass. ✉ Sítio das Areias, 8135-000 Almancil ☎ 289 396 840 ⊙ Mon–Sat 7–10 ✋ D €40, Wine €16 🚗 Take the Quinta do Lago road out of Almancil. About 1km (0.75

Above Fresh sardines are one of the regional specialities of the Algarve

miles) outside Almancil turn left; Aux Bons Enfants is down on the right

VINCENT

In summer, reserve ahead for a table on the lovely terrace or in the light and airy dining room, with huge Algarvian curved fireplace. Once known as the Tradicional, this place was taken over by legendary Vincent Nas and Willemina Zuydervelt (formerly of the famous Ermitage). As before, Vincent cooks while Willemina looks after the guests. Vincent recommends the foie gras terrine, beef with goose liver sauce, and offers an outstanding wine list. ✉ Estrada da Fonte Santa, Escanxinas, 8135-016 Almancil ☎ 289 399 093 ⊙ Jul–end Aug Mon–Sat 7–10.30; rest of year Tue–Sat 7–10.30. Closed 13 Dec–1 Feb ✋ D €55, Wine €18 🚗 Head south out of Almancil towards Vale do Lobo. Restaurant is next to Avia fuel station

FARO
A TASKA

Not far from the Largo do Carmo, this no-frills Portuguese eatery is popular among locals. Dining rooms

are split between two floors and there is an open fire in winter. The walls are decorated with the work of local artists and with verses by António Aleixo, a popular 20th-century Algarvian poet. The kitchen serves up regional food in healthy sized portions, including bean rice with razor fish, prawn curry, fried squid and much more. Credit cards are not accepted.
✉ Rua Alportel 38, 8000-293 Faro ☎ 289 824 739 ⊙ Mon–Sat 12.30–3, 7.30–11.30 🖐 L €12, D €16, Wine €5

LOULÉ
CASA PAIXANITO
Passed down from father to son for decades, this place has a friendly atmosphere, its beamed ceilings and yellow walls enlivened by bright framed prints. Choose from a large variety of tapas, such as octopus salad, pâté, home made sausages, cured meats and more; or from some notable main courses, such as the house's wild boar, venison, roast duck or lamb dishes. The partridge in red wine marinade is also highly praised. Credit cards are not accepted.
✉ Estrada Querença, 8100-129 Loulé ☎ 289 412 775 ⊙ Jul–end Aug daily 7–10.30; rest of year daily 12–3, 7–10.30 🖐 L €30, D €40, Wine €9 🚍 Take the Clareanes/Querença road north. The restaurant is 2km (1.5 miles) on the right, just after the Centro de Saúde

MONCHIQUE
JARDIM DAS OLIVEIRAS
For some hearty mountain fare, come up to Monchique and visit this rustic little eatery where you can savour some of the region's best. Start off with stuffed aubergines (eggplants) or a cottage cheese and chestnut salad followed by oven-roasted kid with plums. Try their local medronho, made from the fruits of the strawberry tree. In good weather you can sit on the terrace.
✉ Sítio do Porto Escuro, 8550-351 Monchique ☎ 282 912 874 ⊙ Daily 12–10 🖐 L €15, D €20, Wine €8 🚍 Head west out of Monchique on the Fóia road and restaurant is signed on right

PORTIMÃO
DONA BARCA
In the middle of town behind the sardine quay, this place is great value for money. Fish is brought directly from the quay to the terrace grill, so the prato do dia (dish of the day) is always super-fresh.
✉ Largo da Barca 9, 8500-527 Portimão ☎ 282 484 189 ⊙ Daily 12–3, 6–10.30. Closed 2 weeks in Jan 🖐 L €10, D €14, Wine €5.50

SAGRES
A TASCA
Overlooking the marina, this place has a slightly eccentric feel. Its walls are covered with a profusion of bottles, pebbles and ceramic plates set decoratively into the plaster, in stark contrast to the black-painted tables and chairs. Alternatively, try the terrace. The service is friendly and the food, though simple, is of a high quality. Try the grilled oysters, lobster, crab, tuna fish stew, squid kebabs or fresh grilled fish, with almond or orange tart to finish.
✉ Praia da Baleeira, Sagres ☎ 282 624 177 ⊙ Daily 12–3.30, 6–10 🖐 L €15, D €20, Wine €12 🚍 At the fishing port of Sagres

SILVES
CAFÉ INGLÊS
Behind the cathedral, on the steps below the castle, this elegant 1920s house is now a popular English-run café and restaurant, which makes a good place to stop off on a day's sightseeing. Sit inside or outside on the terrace for a mid-morning reviver of fine coffee and a slice of cake from the home-made selection. For something bigger, choose from the salads, pastas, pizzas or traditional Portuguese dishes on offer.
✉ Escadas do Castelo 11, 8300-144 Silves ☎ 282 442 585 ⊙ May–end Oct Tue–Sun 9am–midnight, Mon 9am–6pm; rest of year Tue–Sat 9am–10pm, Sun–Mon 9–6 🖐 L €12, D €18, Wine €7

TAVIRA
AQUASUL
Aquasul has a fresh and cheerful, southern European feel to it.

The cuisine is mainly Italian and Mediterranean. Diners can choose from a variety of fresh, crisp leafy salads, vegetarian dishes and pizza straight from the wood-fired oven. There is a magnificent white chocolate tart that comes highly recommended for dessert. Credit cards are not accepted.
✉ Rua Dr. A. Silva Carvalho 13, 8000-324 Tavira ☎ 281 325 166 ⊙ Tue–Sat 7pm–10.30pm 🖐 D €18, Wine €7.50 🚍 From the Roman bridge head down the pedestrian street. Aquasul is just down the pedestrian street on the left

O PÁTIO
Winner of several local prestigious gastronomy awards, O Pátio serves hearty regional food, cooked beautifully. House specials include fish or seafood cataplana (stew cooked in large copper pans), prawns fried in cognac and chicken with almonds. Finish your meal with the delicious toasted almond cake and a tot of aguardente, a local fig and wild strawberry liqueur.
✉ Rua António Cabreira 30-1°, 880-344 Tavira ☎ 281 323 008 ⊙ Mon–Sat 7–11.30 🖐 L €12, D €17, Wine €8 🚍 Near the Roman bridge in the old town of Tavira

VALE DO LOBO
SÃO GABRIEL
www.sao-gabriel.com
Less formal than some of its competitors, São Gabriel is one of the top restaurants in the area and holder of a Michelin star. French, Italian and Swiss influences have long been the mainstay of São Gabriel's cooking. However, these have been joined in recent years by lighter Mediterranean dishes, such as lobster with fresh vegetables and lemon sauce, and sautéed sole with asparagus. There is a non-smoking section in the restaurant.
✉ Estrada Quinta do Lago, Vale de Lobo, 8135-107 Almancil ☎ 289 394 521 ⊙ Tue–Sun 7–12. Closed Jan to mid-Mar 🖐 D €65, Wine €18.50 🚍 From Vale do Lobo take the road to Quinta do Lago. The restaurant is 2km (1.5 miles) down this road on the left

STAYING

PRICES AND SYMBOLS

The prices are the lowest and highest for a double room for one night including breakfast, unless otherwise stated. All the hotels listed accept credit cards unless otherwise stated. Note that rates can vary widely throughout the year.

For a key to the symbols, ▷ 2.

ALBUFEIRA
MONTE DAS CORTELHAS

www.montecortelhas.com
This attractive farmhouse to the northwest of Albufeira is surrounded by protected agricultural land. Single-storey and whitewashed, with traditional light blue trim, it sits among shady gardens and cobbled courtyards filled with palms and trellises. Rooms are rustic and simple, with terracotta floors, rough wooden beams and patches of bright paint and fabrics. Just minutes away from popular beaches, this is a tranquil haven, with its views of the Serra de Monchique. Credit cards are not accepted.
✉ Caminho do Monte, Guia, 8200-413 Albufeira ☎ 289 561 487 💰 €75–€85
🛏 4 rooms, 1 apartment ➹ Outdoor
🚗 From Albufeira take the EN125 west towards Guia. At the traffic lights in Guia

follow signs to Portimão. Monte das Cortelhas is signed about 500m (550 yards) after the lights

SHERATON ALGARVE HOTEL AT PINE CLIFFS RESORT

www.pinecliffs.com
Standing on a cliff top overlooking the Atlantic Ocean, the Sheraton Algarve is surrounded by pine trees and is part of the impressive Pine Cliffs Resort. The hotel overlooks miles of unspoilt beaches and clear blue seas. The Moorish-influenced architecture results in airy interiors, open patios and gardens, with well-equipped bedrooms and excellent services—just as you would expect from a world-class hotel chain. A health club, children's village, mini golf and tennis are complemented by several 18-hole PGA gold courses nearby and the hotel's own nine-hole golf course and academy. No fewer than six restaurants and bars cater for your every need, from snacks by the pool to cocktail bars and a gourmet meal accompanied by fine wines.
✉ Pinhal do Concelho, 8200-912 Albufeira ☎ 289 500 100 💰 €130–€400 🛏 215
🌀 3 outdoor, 1 indoor 🚗 In Albufeira, follow the blue Sheraton signs

Above *Vila Joya, west of Albufeira, is exclusive, elegant and exquisite*

VILA JOYA

www.vilajoya.com
The most exclusive hotel in the Algarve, this Moorish-style villa is perched on a bluff above the ocean west of Albufeira. Its gardens, shaded by palms, bougainvillea and agaves, lead into sumptuous bedrooms. The keynote here is formal elegance. Richly hued, tile-clad bathrooms, reminiscent of Arab bath houses, exquisite bedlinens and fine furnishings all contribute to the understated luxury. The terrace is home to one of Portugal's best restaurants, and the resort has its own tennis courts.
✉ Praia da Galé, 8201-902 Guia Albufeira ☎ 289 591 795 💰 €390–€700 including breakfast and lunch or dinner 🛏 6 rooms, 7 suites 🌀 ➹ Outdoor 🚗 Praia da Galé is 10km (6 miles) west of Albufeira towards Armação de Pêra. Follow signs to Praia da Galé; the hotel is signed

BOLEQUEIME
QUINTA DA CEBOLA VERMELHA

www.quintadacebolavermelha.com
This low-lying, terracotta *quinta* is 1km (0.6 miles) outside Bolequeime

and 11km (7 miles) west of Loulé. Its rooms are decorated simply with warm shades and attractive fabrics. In summer they are shaded by the surrounding fruit and olive trees, and, in winter, made extra warm by the under-floor heating. Most of the year, breakfast is served on the shady terrace, lunch is available at the poolside and three times a week a delicious three-course dinner is available for €29.50 per person. Bicycles are available.

✉ Campina, 8100-908 Boliqueime ☎ 289 363 680 ♨ €115 🛈 6 🏊 Outdoor saltwater

CARRAPATEIRA
MONTE VELHO
www.wonderfulland.com

This simple, informal hotel stands in the Costa Vicentina Natural Park between the beaches of Amado and Carrapateira. It is powered by wind and solar energy and the decoration is simple and bright. Bedrooms are painted in warm tones, with mosquito nets protecting the beds and hammocks on the porch. In warm weather, breakfast is served outside; otherwise it is taken in the vivid yellow dining room with fun fish paintings on the walls. Credit cards are not accepted.

✉ Carrapateira, 8670-230 Bordeira ☎ 282 973 207 ♨ €100–€120 (rooms), €120–€160 (suites) 🛈 2 rooms, 7 suites 🚗 From Carrapateira head south following the signs to Vilarinha; watch for a right turn signed 'Monte Velho'

ESTÓI
MONTE DO CASAL
www.montedocasal.pt

Excellent accommodation and intimate surroundings are found here. The restaurant serves French-influenced meals, on the patio in warm weather surrounded by palms, bougainvillea and honeysuckle. Breakfast is served on bedroom balconies and terraces. All rooms are attractively decorated. There are great sun decks, swimming pools and fountains in the gardens.

✉ Cerro do Lobo, Estói, 8005-436 Faro ☎ 289 991 503 ♨ €155–€360 lunch and dinner by request 🛈 18 rooms, 6 suites 🏊 Outdoor (heated) 🚗 Take Estói turning off IP1 or N125. Head towards the market, which is on the right-hand side. On the left is a sign to Monte do Casal

ESTÔMBAR
CASA DO RIO ARADE
www.rioarade-accommodation.com

This 18th-century manor house is a great choice if you want a central location. Some of the best beaches in the Algarve are on its doorstep and there are reportedly 10 top golf courses within a 20km (12-mile) radius of the house. The busy town of Portimão is 15 minutes away. Rooms in the house are fresh and airy and the communal rooms are comfortable yet retain a touch of rustic charm.

✉ Rua D. João II 33, 8400-092 Mexilhoeira da Carregação, Estombar ☎ 282 423 202 ♨ €59–€125 🛈 9 🏊 Outdoor 🚗 Leave A22 at junction 6 (Lagoa/Silves). Take third exit off round-about to Estômbar. Follow signs to Estômbar. At roundabout (traffic circle) turn right to Mexilhoeira da Carregação. House is 350m (380 yards) farther on, on left

LAGOS
CASA DA MOURA
www.casadamoura.com

Inside the medieval walls and five minutes' walk from the town centre, this is an ideal spot if wanting to stay in town. As the name suggests, there is a North African feel to this place with its Moroccan glass lanterns, rugs and mosaic wrought-iron tables. All the rooms are decorated in warm shades and the apartments have kitchenettes. Breakfast is served on the terrace.

✉ Rua Cardeal Neto 10, 8600 Lagos ☎ 282 770 730 ♨ €60–€149 🛈 8 1-bedroom apartments 🏊 Outdoor

QUINTA DAS ACHADAS
www.algarveholiday.net

The rooms and apartments here are all named after flowers, inspired by the lush setting. They have wooden ceilings, are simply decorated with modern art on the walls, and are furnished with rural antiques;

all have terraces overlooking the landscaped gardens. Apartments have a small kitchen; the restaurant serves international cuisine.

✉ Estrada da Barragem, Odiáxere, 8600-251 Lagos ☎ 282 798 425 ♨ Rooms €80–€110, apartments €360–€1,050, (3-day minimum stay in apartments) 🛈 2 rooms, 3 self-catering apartments 🏊 Outdoor 🚗 Exit IP1 at junction 3, signed to Odiáxere and Mexilhoeira. Go straight across first roundabout, then at second roundabout take first exit right to Odiáxere. In Odiáxere turn right at traffic lights. Follow road for 1.3km (1 mile); the quinta is signed on the right

LOULÉ
LOULÉ JARDIM
www.loulejardimhotel.com

This attractive building on the corner of a square has been refurbished to provide excellent accommodation within the historic heart of Loulé. The white-and-yellow Loulé Jardim has simple, modern rooms. The ones on the fourth floor have balconies that overlook the town, as does the pool terrace and bar.

✉ Praça Manuel de Arriaga, 8100-665 Loulé ☎ 289 413 094 ♨ €50–€78 🛈 52 🏊 🚗 From the tourist office go left along Rua 5 de Outubro, then left into Rua Vasco da Gama. The hotel is on the corner of the Praça Manuel de Arriaga

QUINTA DO CORAÇÃO
www.algarveparadise.com

To get a taste of the real Algarve head up into the hills, north of Loulé. Surrounded by wild flowers, birds and fruit trees, this small, eco-friendly guest house offers tranquillity, ideal for nature lovers and hikers. During the warmer months, breakfast (including freshly baked bread, free range eggs and fresh orange juice) is served on the terrace with fantastic views down the valley. Dinner can be ordered in advance and options include vegetarian dishes. Credit cards are not accepted.

✉ Carrasqueiro, 8100-202 Salir ☎ 289 489 959 ♨ €50 including breakfast (studio €55, cottage €59 breakfast not included) 🛈 2 bedrooms, 1 studio, 1 self-contained cottage (minimum stay 2 nights)

MONCHIQUE

ESTALAGEM D. LOURENÇO
VILLA TERMAL DAS CALDAS DE MONCHIQUE

www.monchiquetermas.com

The originally Roman spa at Monchique was at its most fashionable back in the 19th century, when the rich and famous flocked to it from all over the country. Today, it is enjoying a new lease of life as spas once again become popular. Part of a hotel chain, this one is probably the pick of the bunch, with stylish rooms and a good restaurant that, in winter, has a log fire.

✉ Caldas de Monchique, 8550-233 Monchique ☎ 282 910 910 🖐 €90–€130 ⓘ 12 🅿 🚗 Take the N266 towards Monchique. The spa is just before the village, and the hotel is signed

QUINTA DA CORTE

www.quintadacorte.com

This quiet retreat, 7km (4 miles) from Monchique and set in unspoilt hill country, is a hiker's paradise. It offers four rooms in a modern building, each with panoramic windows leading out to private verandas with views of the mountains and, in the distance, the ocean. The style is modern-rustic, each bed dressed with colourful patchwork quilts and warm woollen blankets provided for cool evenings outdoors. To ensure peace and quiet there are no televisions on site. Dinner is available on request.

✉ Corte Grande, 8550-909 Monchique ☎ 282 911 290/919 002 827 🖐 €80–€90

Below *Caldas de Monchique is famous for its spas and retreats*

ⓘ 4 🚗 Take N266 towards Monchique. Just after the golf course turn right to Alferce. At crossroads turn left up into the hills. At the top turn left towards Picota and Monchique, then follow signs to *quinta*

OLHÃO

PEDRAS VERDES GUESTHOUSE

www.pedrasverdes.com

If you want to stay somewhere that is unquestionably cool, you should try Pedras Verdes. The minimalist rooms of this trendy guest house take the themes of Asia, Africa, Arabia, the baroque and Zen as their decorative inspirations. Simple but with flashes of rich tones, they all have up-to-the-minute bathrooms and walk-in shower areas with pebble or slatted-wood floors. The low, Moorish-style building is surrounded by olive trees, and has outdoor terracing.

✉ Sitio da Boavista 658T, Quelfes, 8700 Olhão ☎ 963 364 252 🖐 €65–€95 ⓘ 6 🅿 🚗 Take the Olhão/Quelfes exit from the IP1, then the N398 south. Follow signs for Quelfes. On entering the village, take a sharp right turn at the grocery store and continue for 1.5km (1 mile)

PORCHES

HOTEL VILA VITA PARC

www.vilavita.com

A luxury resort with every conceivable facility, the Vila Vita Parc is expensive, but what you get compensates. The clifftop gardens have steps to the beach and are home to a seawater spa, tennis, squash, swimming pools and a nine-hole pitch-and-putt golf course. The elegant rooms are in the main building, or in Moorish-style bungalows and villas in the grounds.

✉ Alporchinhos, 8400-450 Porches ☎ 282 310 200 🖐 €190–€555 ⓘ 84 rooms, 86 suites, 12 apartments 🅿 🚗 Indoor and outdoor 🚗 🚗 At Porches take Alporchinhos/ Armação de Pêra turn off N125. Follow signs to Vila Vita Parc

PORTIMÃO

QUINTA DAS FLORES

This delightful Algarvian villa is carefully planned, with swaying palms, a pretty pool, shady corners and bougainvillea trellises. The interior design features warm tones of yellow, bright printed fabrics and lively paintings, which are often African in theme. There are tennis courts on site, too. Credit cards are not accepted.

✉ Vale de Pega, Mexilhoeira Grande, 8500-132 Portimão ☎ 282 968 649 🖐 Rooms €85–€95, cottage €120 per night (€800 per week, minimum 3 nights) ⓘ 1 room, 1 self-catering studio, 1 self-catering cottage (sleeps 4) 🚗 Outdoor 🚗 Take the Figueira turning off the N125 between Portimão and Lagos. Pass the church and take the right turn just before Café Célia

SAGRES

POUSADA DO INFANTE

www.pousadas.pt

Strategically positioned on the rugged cliffs above the Atlantic, this *pousada*'s decoration is themed around early discoveries. Guest rooms have balconies or terraces overlooking the ocean. The building is attractive; long, low and whitewashed, with a red-tiled roof, arched colonnades and decorative chimneys. The restaurant serves regional Portuguese cuisine.

✉ Ponta da Atalaia, 8650-385 Sagres ☎ 282 620 240 🖐 €120–€198 ⓘ 50 rooms, 1 suite 🅿 🚗 Outdoor 🚗 In Sagres, follow signs leading to the *pousada*

TAVIRA

QUINTA DA LUA

www.quintadalua.com.pt

The lasting impression of this peaceful haven is of the quality of the service provided by the friendly hosts, Miguel and Vimal. The rooms are a very harmonious mix of simple rustic furniture and boutique-style chic. Outside, shady gardens, bamboo-covered decks for alfresco breakfasts and saltwater pool complete the picture. No children. Credit cards are not accepted.

✉ Bernardinho 1662-x, Santo Estevão, 8800-513 Tavira ☎ 281 961 070 🖐 €155 ⓘ 6 rooms, 2 suites (all non-smoking) 🚗 Outdoor 🚗 From Tavira take the N125 towards Olhão. Turn right to Santo Estevão, then first left and next right. Look for the arched entrance

PRACTICALITIES

Practicalities gives you all the important practical information you will need during your visit from money matters to emergency phone numbers.

WEATHER

CLIMATE

Despite its Atlantic position, Portugal's climate is predominantly Mediterranean, with the characteristic warm, dry summers and mild, wet winters. Its geographic position on Europe's western edge ensures that the average rainfall is far higher than that of Spain to the east, which means that north of Lisbon, the landscape is verdant year-round. Much of the rain falls between November and April, with levels increasing as you move north; showers are possible throughout the year in the far north, particularly in the higher areas of the Douro and Trás-os-Montes. Winters in the latter can be bitter, with low temperatures and snow. In central and southern Portugal, especially on the coast, it's mild throughout the year, though it is often cloudy in winter. Summers are hot and sunny all over the country, the high temperatures pleasantly tempered by cooling breezes along the coast.

WHEN TO GO

Most seasoned visitors to Portugal agree that spring and autumn are the best times to go; the weather is at its best and you'll escape the huge influx of high-summer tourists. In late spring the whole country looks superb, with sheets of brilliant wild flowers. Autumn is warm but not too hot. It is a particularly good time to visit the Douro and the wine-producing areas as the grape harvest is in full swing and the red and gold shades of the season are at their best.

July and August are prime vacation time, with millions of foreign visitors flocking into the country and many Portuguese themselves on holiday. The Algarve, in particular, is at its busiest: Prices are at their peak, and bars, shops and beaches are packed to bursting point. This time of year is ideal for exploring northern Portugal, however, as the days are hot and sunny and there's less chance of rain than during the rest of the year.

Lisbon and the southern third of the country have mild winters, so this is an excellent time to explore the capital, the Alentejo and the Algarve. A few tourist facilities may be closed, but there's the huge advantage of dramatically reduced prices and few other visitors. The Algarve, in particular, feels like a different place without the crowds, and the hillsides pink and yellow with almond blossom and acacia.

LISBON
TEMPERATURE

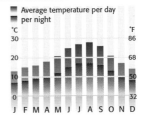

RAINFALL

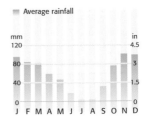

Opposite Costa de Caparica benefits from cooling Atlantic breezes in summer

WEATHER REPORTS

BBC World news and CNN have websites and broadcast regular global weather updates in English, and the Weather Channel and the Met Office in the UK also have global weather websites:
www.bbc.co.uk/weather
www.CNN.com
www.weather.com
www.metoffice.com

WHAT TO TAKE

» Clothing requirements will differ depending on the time of year and where you're going. It is advisable to take lightweight cotton and linen clothing to wear during the summer, with some type of light wool garment or a cotton jacket for cooler evenings in the north. Waterproofs and an umbrella are essential for winter and make sense if you're in northern Portugal at any time of the year.

» If you intend to visit churches or other religious buildings, take some clothes that cover your shoulders and knees.

» Casual clothing is the norm during the day, but take more formal clothes for the evening, particularly for Lisbon, Porto and the classier Algarve resorts.

» Comfortable shoes are essential for sightseeing.

» Take emergency contact telephone numbers and addresses, the numbers of your travellers' cheques in case of loss or theft, the numbers of credit/debit cards, and registration numbers of mobile phones, cameras or expensive equipment (in case you need to report their loss or theft to the police or insurance company).

» Carry your travel insurance details; you will need to clear any medical emergency payments with your insurers, and to notify them immediately in case of theft or loss.

» If you are taking any prescribed medication, bring enough for the duration of your trip. If you do need to replace medicine, you should have a note of the pharmaceutical name of your medication, as trade names may differ in Portugal.

» If you forget to take anything, you should be able to buy most things you are likely to need in Portugal, although the choice may be somewhat limited in the more remote areas.

TIME ZONES		
CITY	**TIME DIFFERENCE**	**TIME AT 12 NOON IN PORTUGAL**
Auckland	+12	midnight
Berlin	+1	1pm
Brussels	+1	1pm
Chicago	-6	6am
Dublin	0	noon
Johannesburg	+2	2pm
London	0	noon
Madrid	+1	1pm
Montreal	-5	7am
New York	-5	7am
Paris	+1	1pm
San Francisco	-8	4am
Sydney	+10	10pm
Tokyo	+9	9pm

Portugal uses GMT in winter, moving the clocks forward one hour between the last Sunday in March and the last Sunday in October. The 24-hour clock is generally used in Portugal.

COIMBRA
TEMPERATURE

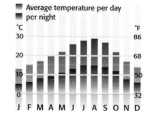

FARO
TEMPERATURE

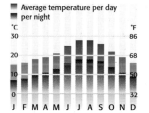

PORTO
TEMPERATURE

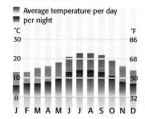

RAINFALL

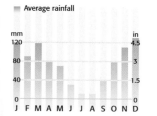

RAINFALL

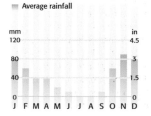

RAINFALL

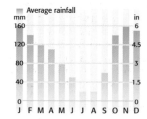

REMEMBER TO PACK

» Waterproofs and a folding umbrella.
» A secure bag for daily use, large enough to hold camera, books, maps, etc.
» Your driver's licence.
» Your address book.
» A torch (flashlight) and binoculars.
» Sunscreen and a first-aid kit, including plasters (Band Aids), antiseptic and antihistamine creams, and painkillers.
» A Portuguese phrasebook—any efforts to speak Portuguese are much appreciated; English may not be spoken in the remoter rural areas (▷ 322–323).

DOCUMENTS

PASSPORTS AND VISAS

» All visitors to Portugal must carry a valid passport or identity card at all times.
» UK citizens need a passport to enter Portugal, but visitors from other EU countries need only an identity card. No visa is necessary if you're from the EU, and there is no time limit to your stay.
» US, Canadian, Australian and New Zealand visitors need a passport valid for a further six months from the date of entry into Portugal. Visitors from those countries can stay for up to 90 days without a visa.
» US, Canadian, Australian and New Zealand visitors can extend their stay by obtaining an extension from district police headquarters or a branch of Servico de Estrangeiros e Fronteiras (Foreigner's Registration Service), which has offices in the most popular tourist areas. Applications for an extension should be made at least a week before the entry permit runs out. Applicants should be prepared to offer proof that they can support themselves without working.
» Visa rules can change at short notice and you should check with the Portuguese embassy in your home country.

TRAVEL AND HEALTH INSURANCE

» Take out travel insurance as soon as you book your trip to ensure you will be covered for cancellations and delays.
» Make certain your policy includes repatriation, medical expenses, baggage and money loss, accident compensation and personal liability.
» Keep all receipts in case you need to make an insurance claim.
» Report losses or theft to the police and make sure you obtain a written report from them. No insurers will consider your claim without this.
» If you have private medical coverage, check your policy, as you may be covered while you are away.
» If you travel a lot, consider taking out an annual travel insurance policy.

DUTY-FREE GUIDELINES

Duty-free allowances for US citizens

You may take home up to $800 of duty-free goods, providing you have been out of the country for at least 48 hours and have not made an international trip within the previous 30 days. This limit applies to each member of the family regardless of age, and allowances may be pooled. For the most up-to-date information, see the US Department of Homeland Security's website: www.dhs.gov

» 1 litre of alcohol	» 1 bottle perfume
» 100 cigars (non-Cuban)	(if trademarked in the US)
» 200 cigarettes	

Duty-free guidelines for EU citizens

You cannot buy goods duty-free if you are journeying within the EU. You can take home unlimited amounts of duty-paid goods, as long as they are for your personal use. For UK visitors, anything more than the following is considered to be for commercial use:

» 3,200 cigarettes	» 10 litres of spirits
» 3kg of tobacco	» 90 litres of wine
» 400 cigarillos	» 20 litres of fortified wine
» 200 cigars	(such as port or sherry)
» 110 litres of beer	

Whatever your entitlement, you may not bring back goods for payment (including payment in kind) or for resale. For the most up-to-date information, see the H. M. Revenue & Customs website: www.hmrc.gov.uk

PORTUGUESE EMBASSIES AND CONSULATES ABROAD

COUNTRY	ADDRESS AND TELEPHONE NUMBER	WEBSITE
Australia	Level 9, 30 Clarence Street, Sydney, NSW 2000, tel 926 221 99/1572/1071	www.consulportugalsydney.org.au
Canada	645 Island Park Drive, Ottawa K1Y 0B8, tel 613/729-0883	www.embportugal-ottawa.org
Ireland	Knocksinna House, Knocksinna, Fox Rock, Dublin 18, tel 01 289 4416	www.pt.embassyinformation.com
New Zealand	16 Fisher Crescent, Mt Wellington, PO Box 305, Auckland, tel 09 259 4014	
	PO Box 1024, Suite 1, 1st Floor, 21 Marion Street, Wellington, tel 04 382 7655	www.pt.embassyinformation.com
South Africa	1006 Main Tower, Suite 1005, 10th Floor, Standard Bank Centre, Hertzog Boulevard, 8001 Cape Town, tel 4180080	
UK	11 Belgrave Square, London SW1X 8PP, tel 020 7235 5331	www.pt.embassyinformation.com
USA	2125 Kalorama Road NW, Washington DC 20008, tel 202-328 8610	www.pt.embassyinformation.com

MONEY

Like many other EU countries, Portugal has adopted the euro as its official currency. Outside larger cities and the main tourist areas, cash is still widely used, although the majority of hotels will accept credit and debit cards. You will need cash to pay for small transactions, and market traders don't accept credit cards. It's a good idea to carry some euros on arrival, although larger hotels will change money for you.

A combination of cash, travellers' cheques and credit cards is better than relying on one form of payment. Before departure, check with your bank that you can withdraw cash from cash machines (ATMs) in Portugal. Ask what charge is made for this service and note an emergency telephone number to call if your card is lost or stolen.

Travellers' cheques are by far the safest way of carrying money, because you are insured against loss. Remember to keep a separate note of the cheque numbers and the telephone number you need to call if they are stolen. You will need to show your passport when cashing travellers' cheques.

ATMS

Cash machines, called *multibancos*, are the easiest way of withdrawing cash in Portugal. You'll find ATMs in even the most remote places and

Below *Many shops accept payment by credit card, but look for the logo in the window*

you can withdraw up to €200 a day with a national *multibanco* card or €200 in a single transaction (which can then be repeated) if using an accepted international credit card. They are accessible 24 hours a day and most have onscreen instructions in English and other languages.

Check with your bank that you will be able to use your debit card for transactions in Portugal, and make certain that you have a 4-digit PIN. You will normally be charged a cash-handling fee on credit card withdrawals as well as the usual currency conversion charge. This may be high so it is worth checking with your bank before travelling.

BANKS

There are *bancos* (banks) in most towns, normally open Monday to Friday 8.30–3, but in Lisbon and some Algarve resorts they may also be open in the evening. Commission rates for changing money stand at around €3–€5; some banks have automatic exchange machines. Commission rates for changing travellers' cheques in a bank can be exceptionally high—it's better to head for a *caixa* (savings bank) or a *câmbio* (exchange bureau).

BUREAUX DE CHANGE

There are *câmbios* (exchange bureaux) in all cities and resort areas; the commission for changing travellers' cheques will be lower than that charged by a bank.

CREDIT CARDS

American Express, MasterCard and Visa are the most widely used credit cards, but are not accepted by smaller establishments or for small purchases. Look for credit card logos in shop and restaurant windows, or check with staff before making your purchase. You can use your credit card to withdraw cash, although your card issuer will charge it as a cash advance. Check charges before leaving home. Make sure you have a 4-digit PIN to use this service. Banks will also advance cash against your credit card at the counters.

LOST/STOLEN CREDIT CARDS

American Express	800 205 598
www.americanexpress.com	
Diners Club	213 159 856
www.dinersclub.com	
MasterCard	800 811 272
www.mastercard.com	
Visa	800 811 824
www.visa.com	

TAX REFUNDS

Sales tax or VAT (known in Portugal as IVA) is added to prices in Portugal; it is non-refundable to EU residents. US visitors can claim it back on goods purchased from participating shops. Keep receipts and fill in the claims form at the departure airport.

WIRING MONEY

You can have money wired from your home country in an emergency, but this can be expensive and may entail lengthy telephoning. The main agents are Western Union (www.westernunion.com) and Moneygram (www.moneygram.com).

10 EVERYDAY ITEMS AND HOW MUCH THEY COST

Sandwich	€2.50
Bottle of water	50¢
Cup of tea or coffee	€1–€3
0.5 litre of beer	€1–€3
Glass of wine	60¢–€4.50
Daily newspaper	€1–€1.50
Roll of camera film	€4
20 cigarettes	€3.30
An ice cream cone	€1–€2
A litre of petrol (gas)	€1.52

TIPPING

The Portuguese do not tip heavily, though service is rarely included in your hotel or restaurant bill. It is therefore usual to leave a little extra if the service has been particularly good. The following is a general guide:

Bars and cafés:	round up to the nearest euro
Restaurants:	10%
Taxis:	round up to the nearest euro
Porters and chambermaids:	50¢–€1 per day
Cloakroom attendants:	20¢–50¢

HEALTH

BEFORE YOU GO

» If you are likely to need a repeat prescription during your trip, apply for this well before you travel. Also ask your doctor to give you a note of the pharmaceutical name of any medications you are taking in case your medicine goes missing. Trade names for various medicines may differ in Portugal.

» If you are planning a long visit, it is advisable to have a health check, an eye test and a dental check-up before you leave home.

» No inoculations are required for visiting Portugal, although it is a good idea to check the date of your last tetanus shot and have a booster if necessary.

INSURANCE

» As part of the European Union, Portugal has free reciprocal health agreements with other member states. To take advantage of this, UK citizens should carry their EHIC (European Health Insurance Card), which came into use from January 2006. (The old E111 is no longer valid.) This card can be applied for online or by post and is valid for between 3 and 5 years. It entitles the holder to reduced-cost medical (including hospital) treatment while you are in Portugal. The reduced fee, however, must be paid, plus part of the cost of any prescribed medicines. For more information,

MEDICAL ASSISTANCE

Ambulance (emergencies)
112

call 020 7210 4850 in the UK or see www.dh.gov.uk/travellers.

» In some parts of Portugal, public health care lags behind that of other European countries and you are strongly advised to take out insurance to cover the cost of private treatment. This is essential for US citizens, who must pay for all medical treatment in Portugal. Check to see if your existing health cover is valid when abroad.

» For up-to-date information, see the Department of Health's website on www.doh.gov.uk (in the UK) or the National Center for Infectious Diseases on www.cdc.gov/travel (in the US).

» If you need treatment, take your insurance documents to the doctor or hospital—they may be able to bill your insurance company direct.

» You may need to contact your insurance company for clearance before treatment, so make sure you have their 24-hour emergency number.

» If you have to pay for treatment or medicines, keep all receipts for your insurance claim.

WHAT TO TAKE WITH YOU

» Mosquitoes can be prevalent in Portugal, so stock up with insect

Above *Pharmacies display a list of late-opening* farmácias *on their doors*

repellent. Coils or electric zappers for use in bedrooms at night are readily available in Portugal.

» A small first-aid box is a good idea, particularly if you have children with you. This should include painkillers (Paracetamol or Tylenol), antiseptic and antihistamine cream, sunburn lotion and plasters (Band Aids).

» A spare pair of glasses or contact lenses (if worn).

» Prescription medication.

FINDING A DOCTOR OR GETTING HOSPITAL TREATMENT

» Go to the local *centro de saúde* (health clinic) closest to where you are staying. You'll find one in every town, and some provide a 24-hour emergency service, called SAP/ CATUS.

SUNBURN INDEX

SKIN TYPE

Index	Fair, burns	Fair, tans	Brown skin	Black skin
1/2	Low	Low	Low	Low
3/4	Medium	Low	Low	Low
5	High	Medium	Low	Low
6	Very high	Medium	Medium	Low
7	Very high	High	Medium	Medium
8	Very high	High	Medium	Medium
9	Very high	High	Medium	Medium
10	Very high	High	High	Medium

Low risk: The sun is not likely to harm you but you should still use sunscreen.

Medium risk: Do not stay in direct sunlight for more than 1–2 hours.

High risk: You could burn in 30–60 minutes. Avoid direct sunlight, cover up and use sunscreen of SPF 15+.

Very high risk: You could burn in 20–30 minutes. Avoid direct sunlight, cover up and use sunscreen of SPF 15+.

SELECTED HOSPITALS WITH EMERGENCY DEPARTMENTS

CITY	ADDRESS	TELEPHONE
Lisbon	Hospital de Santa Maria, Avenida Prof. Egas Moniz, 1649-035 Lisboa	217 805 111
Porto	Hospital Santo António, Largo Prof. Abel Salazar, 4099-001 Porto	222 077 500
Coimbra	Hospital de Universidade de Coimbra, Praça Prof. Mota Pinto, 3004-561 Coimbra	239 400 400
Lagos	Hospital Distrital, Rua do Castelo dos Governadores, 8600-563 Lagos	282 770 100
Portimão	Centro Hospitalar do Barlavento Algarvio, Sítio do Poço Seco, 8500–338 Portimão	282 450 300

» Ask at the local *farmácia* (pharmacy).

» Ask your hotel to call a *médico* (doctor) for you.

» For an ambulance call 112.

PHARMACIES

» Pharmacies *(farmácias)* are designated by a green cross on a white background.

» They are generally open 9–1 and 3–7 Monday to Friday and 9–1 on Saturdays.

» Every *farmácia* displays a notice in its window or on its door giving the address of the nearest pharmacy with a 24-hour service, and a list of those open until 10pm. Alternatively call 800 202 134 for pharmacy information.

» Portuguese pharmacists are highly trained and can give medical advice and dispense drugs, such as antibiotics, that normally would be available only on prescription in many countries.

» For many minor ailments it is worth consulting a pharmacist before looking for a doctor; many speak English.

WATER

» Portugal's tap water is generally safe to drink, but be careful in small or remote villages.

ALTERNATIVE MEDICAL TREATMENTS

Portugal has no tradition of complementary medicine, apart from the widespread use of traditional herbal remedies in rural areas. Alternative medicine is only now starting to catch on, with a growing interest in homoeopathic and holistic treatments. The best way to track down practitioners is to look in the Yellow Pages under *Homeopatia*.

» You'll see roadside fountains all over Portugal, where people fill bottles with local spring water; if you follow suit, always fill your container from the running water just below the spring itself.

» Bottled water is cheap in Portugal; it comes *com gás* (sparkling) or *sem gás* (still).

» If you're out and about, always make sure you have a supply of bottled water with you—and make sure you drink it regularly when temperatures soar. Sugary drinks, coffee and alcohol are diuretics and will add to, rather than quench, your thirst.

» If you're feeling thirsty, it's a sign you're already mildly dehydrated.

SUMMER HAZARDS

Portugal is extremely hot in summer, so you will need to protect yourself against the heat and the sun.

» Dress in loose clothing, keep the back of your neck covered and wear a sunhat.

» Apply high-factor (SPF 15+) sun cream at frequent intervals.

» Drink about 2 litres (4 US pints) of water a day during hot weather.

» Keep out of the sun when it's at its strongest—between midday and 3.30pm.

HEALTHY FLYING

» People visiting Portugal from places like the US, Australia or New Zealand may be concerned about the effect of long-haul flights on their health. The most widely publicized concern is deep vein thrombosis, or DVT. Misleadingly called 'economy class syndrome', DVT is the forming of a blood clot in the body's deep veins, particularly in the legs. The clot can move around the bloodstream and could be fatal.

» Those most at risk include the elderly, pregnant women and those using the contraceptive pill, smokers and the overweight. If you are at increased risk of DVT, see your doctor before departing. Flying increases the likelihood of DVT because passengers are often seated in a cramped position for long periods of time and may become dehydrated.

To minimize risk:
Drink water (not alcohol)
Don't stay immobile for hours at a time
Stretch and exercise your legs periodically
Do wear elastic flight socks, which support veins and reduce the chances of a clot forming

Exercises

1 ankle rotations	2 calf stretches	3 knee lifts
Lift feet off the floor. Draw a circle with the toes, moving one foot clockwise and the other counterclockwise	Start with heel on the floor and point foot upward as high as you can. Then lift heels high keeping balls of feet on the floor	Lift leg with knee bent while contracting your thigh muscle. Then straighten leg pressing foot flat to the floor

Other health hazards for flyers are airborne diseases and bugs spread by the plane's air-conditioning system. These are largely unavoidable, but seek advice from a doctor before flying if you have a serious medical condition.

BASICS

ELECTRICITY

» Electricity in Portugal is 220/380 volts. Electric sockets follow European regulations and take plugs with two round pins. If your appliances are manufactured for 240 volts, you will need a plug adaptor, which is best bought before you leave home.

» North American visitors, whose voltage is different, will also need to bring a transformer; this should be bought before leaving home, as they are hard to find in Portugal.

LAUNDRY

Many middle- to top-range hotels have a laundry service, where your clothes are collected from your room and returned there, and the (often high) charge added to your bill. There aren't many self-service launderettes, but *lavandarias* are common. These provide a *roupa branca* (general laundry service), which includes overnight washing, ironing and mending (if necessary) at a relatively low cost, or *limpeza*

a seco (dry cleaning). Some *lavandarias* do only dry cleaning.

PUBLIC TOILETS

You'll find the most hygienic facilities in museums, restaurants and shopping malls. Otherwise, public toilets are few and far between and hygiene levels may leave a lot to be desired. It's acceptable to use the toilets in bars, and they are usually fairly clean. Look for signs saying *Lavabos* or WC; once inside, it's *homens* or *cabalheiros* for men and *senhoras* or *mulheres* for women. Ask for a *casa de banho* or *serviços* if in doubt.

SMOKING

» Smoking is now prohibited in indoor public places in Portugal. Some restaurants may still offer a smoking section.

» Smoking is not permitted in museums, inside airport buildings, or on public transportation.

» You can buy cigarettes at tobacconists, or from vending machines in bars and cafés.

CONVERSION CHART

From	To	Multiply by
Inches	Centimetres	2.54
Centimetres	Inches	0.3937
Feet	Metres	0.3048
Metres	Feet	3.2810
Yards	Metres	0.9144
Metres	Yards	1.0940
Miles	Kilometres	1.6090
Kilometres	Miles	0.6214
Acres	Hectares	0.4047
Hectares	Acres	2.4710
Gallons	Litres	4.5460
Litres	Gallons	0.2200
Ounces	Grams	28.35
Grams	Ounces	0.0353
Pounds	Grams	453.6
Grams	Pounds	0.0022
Pounds	Kilograms	0.4536
Kilograms	Pounds	2.205
Tons	Tonnes	1.0160
Tonnes	Tons	0.9842

VISITING PORTUGAL WITH CHILDREN

You should have no serious problems if you are on a package holiday, as these are organized by foreign tour operators with their own nationals in mind. Independent holidaymakers in Portugal with children may find the following pointers useful.

» Like many other southern Europeans, the Portuguese adore children and are tolerant towards them, fussing over them everywhere and welcoming them into bars and restaurants.

» Despite this, facilities such as changing rooms, high chairs and special children's menus are not always available.

» Portuguese children stay up late—if parents are eating out, the kids go too. This means that most hotels do not have a babysitting/listening service.

» In summer, adjust to the local routines, making sure your children have a quiet time out of the heat during the afternoon siesta hours.

» Most hotels, if notified in advance, will put up to three or four beds in a room so families can stay together; there is usually no charge for children under 6 sharing their parents' room, while discounts for kids aged between 6 and 12 can be as much as 50 per cent.

» Disposable nappies (diapers) and other baby requisites are available everywhere, but if you are bottle-feeding your baby you might want to bring your usual formula with you. *Leite do dia* (fresh milk) is sold in larger shops and supermarkets only. You can buy *fraldas* (nappies/diapers) in supermarkets and pharmacies (*farmácias*).

» Children aged between 5 and 11 qualify for a 50 per cent discount on trains, but must pay full fare on buses and metros; under-5s go free.

» Museums and most sights are usually free for small children.

» Pushchairs (strollers) can be hard work on cobbled streets.

» In traffic-heavy areas, keep a close eye on your children; Portuguese drivers sometimes ignore people using pedestrian crossings.

» Remember the strength of the sun in Portugal; use a high-factor sun cream and keep the children covered up until they acclimatize. Get them to stay in the shade during the middle of the day when the sun is at its hottest, and if they're swimming, persuade them to cover up—better a wet T-shirt than a sunburned and miserable child.

» Don't be surprised if total strangers talk to your children. This is quite normal in Portugal.

VISITORS WITH DISABILITIES

» Portugal's facilities for visitors with disabilities are not extensive and you should not expect standards as high as those at home. However, the situation is slowly improving, and major hotels in the main cities and visitor areas usually provide good access, as do official buildings, including some museums.

» Portuguese national tourist offices abroad can supply lists of wheelchair-accessible hotels.

» Airports and major railway stations generally have good facilities for people with disabilities.

» The Portuguese will often go out of their way to help make your visit problem-free.

Contact Addresses

» Secretariado Nacional Para a Reabilitação e Integração das Pessas com Deficiência in Portugal is an organization that produces a comprehensive, accessible tourism guide, with good hotel and restaurant listings and much more (Avenida Conde Valbom 63, 1069-178 Lisboa, tel 217 929 500, www.inr.pt).

» Holiday Care is a UK-based organization that publishes information about accessibility for holidaymakers with disabilities (Tourism for All, The Hawkins Suite, Enham Place, Enham Alamein, Andover SP11 6JS, tel 0845 124 9971, www.holidaycare.org.uk).

» In the US, SATH (the Society for Accessible Travel and Hospitality) has lots of tips for holidaymakers with visual impairment or poor mobility (347 5th Avenue, Suite 605,

New York, NY 10016, tel 212/447-7284, www.sath.org).

PLACES OF WORSHIP

You will find Catholic churches in even the smallest towns and villages, and there are some famous pilgrimage sites to track down. Numerous religious festivals are celebrated all over the country throughout the year, and tourist offices can give details about local places of worship and service times. With its large expatriate communities, the Algarve is also well served with places of worship for other religions and religious denominations, and you'll be able to get details at tourist offices and in the foreign-language local press. The following are places of worship in Lisbon:

Anglican
St. George's Church
Rua São Jorge, Jardim de Estrela
tel 214 602 303
www.lisbonanglicans.org

Baptist
Igreja Evangélica Baptista da Graça
Rua Capitão Humberto Ataíde 28,
Santa Apolónia, 1170-072 Lisboa
tel 218 132 889

Islamic
Mesquita Central de Lisboa
Avenida José Malhôa, Praça de Espanha, 1070-158 Lisboa
tel 213 874 142
www.comunidadeislamica.pt.

Jewish
Comunidade Israelita de Lisboa
Rua Alexandre Herculano 59, Rato,
1250-101 Lisboa
tel 213 931 130
www.cilisboa.org

Ismaeli
Centro Cultural Ismaili
Avenida Lusíada, 1600-001 Lisboa
tel 217 229 002
www.fakp.pt

PRACTICALITIES   ESSENTIAL INFORMATION

FINDING HELP

PERSONAL SECURITY

Although Portugal is a safe country with low levels of crime, particularly against visitors, you should still take common-sense precautions.

» Take care around main railway stations, on public transportation in cities, and in areas full of visitors in larger towns, which pickpockets and bag-snatchers may frequent. Be especially aware of pickpockets on the tourist tram routes in Lisbon (No. 28 and No. 12).

» Beware of thieves operating in pairs; one may try to distract you with a question or remark while the other robs you.

» Never carry more cash than you need and keep passports, credit cards and travel tickets separate from your money.

» Never carry a wallet, money or credit cards in a back pocket.

» Place valuables in a hotel safe-deposit box.

» Wear your bag or camera slung diagonally across your chest, rather than hanging loose from one shoulder; knapsack-type bags are also good.

» Always lock your car, even if leaving it for only a short time, and make sure luggage and other valuables are kept securely out of sight in the boot (trunk).

» Take especial care if your journey includes a night train, as thieves sometimes target sleeping passengers. If you are travelling with a companion, take it in turns to watch the luggage. Keep an eye on suitcases during daytime journeys as well.

» Never leave valuables on a bar, a restaurant table or hanging from the back of a chair.

» Leave valuable jewellery at home.

» Stick to brightly lit main thoroughfares at night.

» If you are robbed, whatever you do, don't resist.

LOST PROPERTY

» If you lose money or other items, inform the police and contact your insurance company as soon as possible.

» If your travellers' cheques are stolen, notify the issuing company, quoting the numbers of the first and last cheque and the numbers of those you have already cashed.

» If your debit or credit card is stolen, report it to the police and phone your bank/credit card emergency number to cancel the card. Emergency lines are open 24 hours a day and have English-speaking staff.

» If you want to make an insurance claim for theft, you will have to get a written report from the police. This can be a time-consuming business, so it's not usually worth reporting the loss of inexpensive items or small amounts of money.

LOSING A PASSPORT

» If you lose your passport or it is stolen, report it to the police and then contact your embassy or consulate for assistance (see panel below).

» Keep a separate note of your passport number and a photocopy of the page that carries your personal details.

EMERGENCY NUMBERS

From anywhere in Portugal	112

Dial this number and ask for the emergency service you need—*Polícia* (the police), *Ambulância* (ambulance), or *Bombeiros* (fire service)

POLICE

There are four different types of police force in Portugal. Note that Portuguese police sometimes retain authoritarian attitudes that were common during the Salazar dictatorship. If you are stopped by them for any reason, don't argue, and treat the police with courtesy. Politeness should always ensure that you will be on your way as quickly as possible.

» The PSP (Polícia de Segurança Pública) wear blue uniforms and police the cities. Among other duties, they are responsible for incidents and crimes involving visitors.

» The GNR (Guarda Nacional Republicana) wear blue-grey uniforms and knee-high boots; they operate in rural areas and patrol the roads and motorways for traffic offenders.

» The PJ (Polícia Judiciária) often wear plain-clothes and are responsible for investigating serious crime.

» The Serviço de Estrangeiros e Fronteiras is a specialist police force dealing with foreign and border affairs, such as work permits.

» The Polícia Municipal operates in major cities and deals with minor local incidents.

FIRE

» When checking into your room, read the fire instructions that should be posted on the back of the door and check where the nearest fire escapes are.

» Never use lifts (elevators) during a fire emergency.

» If you are trapped in your room, block the bottom of the door with wet towels and remember that the air closest to the floor will be relatively smoke free.

EMBASSIES AND CONSULATES

Australian Embassy	Avenida da Liberdade 200, 2nd Floor, 1250-147 Lisbon, tel 213 101 500, www.portugal.embassy.gov.au. Consulate services at same address
Canadian Embassy	Avenida da Liberdade 200, 3rd Floor, 1269-121 Lisbon, tel 213 164 600, www.dfait-maeci.gc.ca. Consulate services at same address
Irish Embassy	Rua da Imprensa a Estrela 1-4, 1200-684 Lisbon, tel 213 929 440, fax 213 977 363. Consulate services at same address
UK Embassy	Rua de São Bernardo 33, 1249-082 Lisbon, tel 213 9240 00. www.fco.gov.uk. Consulate services at same address
USA Embassy	Avenida das Forças Armadas, 1600-081 Lisbon, tel 217 273 300. www.american-embassy.pt. Consulate services at same address

OPENING TIMES AND TICKETS

Most shops and businesses in Portugal close during the siesta period, usually from around 12.30pm to 2.30 or 3pm.

BANKS

Banks are open Monday to Friday 8.30am–3pm. Branches in large towns may stay open until 6pm.

BARS

Bars open around 8.30am and close any time between 10pm and 2am. Opening hours may vary in rural areas or holiday resorts. In summer they may be open until 3 or 5am.

CAFÉS

These are usually open from about 7am onwards.

CHURCHES

Most churches open early in the morning for Mass, though some are kept locked and can be visited only by prior arrangement with the caretaker. Others have specific opening times and may charge a fee for entry to their cloisters or treasuries. Churches that open regularly will close for a couple of hours in the middle of the day, opening again between 3 and 6pm. Check the Sights section of this book for specific times, or contact the church concerned.

MUSEUMS AND GALLERIES

Museums and monuments are normally open from 10–12.30 and 2–6, though times vary according to the season and location. Check the Sights section of this book, or contact the museum, gallery, or local tourist office. Almost all museums are closed on Mondays, and national palaces on Wednesdays.

OFFICES

Opening hours are usually 9–12.30 and 2.30–6.

POST OFFICES

Post offices are normally open 8.30–6 Monday to Friday; larger ones may also be open on Saturdays, and the main offices in Lisbon and Porto have much longer opening hours.

SHOPS

Shops are generally open between 9 and 1 and again from 3 to 7. Outside larger towns and cities they often close on Saturday afternoons and Sundays. Shopping malls stay open seven days a week, often until midnight, and large supermarkets are open every day from 9am to 10pm (1pm or 5pm on Sundays).

PHARMACIES

Pharmacies are open from 9 to 1 and 3 to 7 Monday to Friday, 9 to 1 on Saturdays. Every *farmácia* displays a card giving the address of the nearest pharmacy with a 24-hour service and a list of those open until 10pm.

RESTAURANTS

Restaurants that serve lunch open from noon and may close for a while during the afternoon. They open for dinner at around 7pm, staying open until 10 or 11; in remote or rural areas they may close earlier. Restaurants catering for visitors in the Algarve are often open throughout the day. Most restaurants in Portugal are closed on one evening during the week—often Sunday or Monday.

ENTRANCE FEES

Many sights, museums and galleries charge admission fees, but these are generally moderate or inexpensive. Recreational facilities aimed at holidaymakers, such as waterparks in the Algarve, are more expensive.

COMBINED TICKETS

Lisbon, Porto and Braga have combined tickets—the Lisboa Card, the Porto Card and the Braga Card—giving free access to public transportation and reduced admission charges or free entry to museums, monuments and places of interest. If you intend to do a lot of sightseeing, the cards are good value and well worth purchasing.

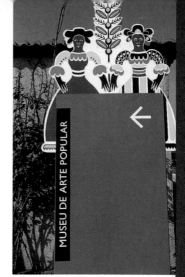

Above *A bright sign points the way to the Museu de Arte Popular in Lisbon*

DISCOUNTS

Discounts on travel and entrance to museums, galleries and other sights of interest are often available to both students and senior citizens. It's always worth showing your senior citizen's card or passport or International Student ID Card when asking for tickets. Offers include 50 per cent off the cost of the *bilhete turístico* (tourist ticket) rail pass, and discounts of up to 35 per cent on seasonal promotions at the *pousadas*.

NATIONAL HOLIDAYS	
On public holidays almost everything is closed and transportation services are reduced.	
1 Jan	New Year's Day
Mar/Apr	Good Friday
25 Apr	Liberty Day (commemorating 1974 Revolution)
1 May	Labour Day
Late May/ early Jun	Corpus Christi
10 Jun	Camões Day
15 Aug	Feast of the Assumption
5 Oct	Republic Day
1 Nov	All Saints' Day
1 Dec	Independence Day (from Spain in 1640)
8 Dec	Immaculate Conception
25 Dec	Christmas Day

TOURIST OFFICES

Cities, towns and villages all over Portugal have tourist offices—look for the word *turismo*—and even in the smallest places there will usually be at least one English-speaking staff member. They can supply local information as well as help to find accommodation; some offices will make reservations, while others simply supply accommodation lists. In addition, they should have up-to-date information about opening hours of local museums and sights (which can fluctuate), town plans and various brochures about the local area. The national tourist telephone line is 808 781 212.

Tourist offices in the big towns and major resorts have longer opening hours than those in remoter areas: They generally open all day, while rural offices will normally close for a couple of hours in the middle of the day and may be closed at weekends.

The Portuguese National Tourist Board operates an excellent tourist freephone telephone number *(Linha Verde Turista*, tel 808 781 212), which operates daily 8–7. English-speaking operators have information about everything from transportation and accommodation to museum opening times and the whereabouts of English-speaking doctors.

You will find that the information provided by different tourist offices varies immensely. Some places have an excellent range of good, free information, while others apparently have little on offer. If the latter is the case, persevere—a smile and a few words of Portuguese may produce a plethora of maps, brochures and leaflets from under the counter.

OVERSEAS TOURIST OFFICES

Australia
Suite 507/147A, King Street, Sydney NSW-2000
Tel (02) 9221 9866

Canada
60 Bloor Street West, Suite 1005, Toronto, Ontario M4W 3B8
Tel 416/921-7376

Republic of Ireland
54 Dawson Street, Dublin 2
Tel 01 670 9133 or 1800 943 131

New Zealand
The office in Sydney, Australia (see above) is responsible also for New Zealand

UK
Portuguese Embassy, 11 Belgrave Square, London SW1X 8PP
Tel 0845 355 1212

USA
4th Floor, 590 Fifth Avenue, New York, NY 10036-4704
Tel 646/723 0200

TOURIST OFFICES

Albufeira
Rua 5 de Outubro,
tel 289 585 279

Alcobaça
Praça 25 de Abril,
tel 262 582 377

Amarante
Alameda Teixeira
Pascoaes, tel 255 420 246

Arraiolos
Praça Lima e Brito,
tel 266 490 524

Aveiro
Rua João Mendonça 8,
tel 234 420 760

Beja
Rua Capitão João Francisco
de Sousa 25,
tel 284 311 913

Braga
Avenida da Liberdade 1,
tel 253 262 550

Bragança
Avenida Cidade de Zamora,
tel 273 381 273

Cascais
Avenida Visconde da Luz
14, tel 214 868 204

Castelo Branco
Praça do Municipio,
tel 272 330 339

Castelo de Vide
Praça Dom Pedro V,
tel 245 901 361

Coimbra
Largo da Portagem,
tel 239 488 120,
Largo Dom Dinis,
tel 239 832 591,
Praça de República,
tel 239 833 202

Elvas
Praça de República,
tel 268 622 236

Estoril
Arcadas do Parque Poente,
tel 214 663 813

Estremoz
Praça de República 26,
tel 268 333 451

Évora
Praça do Giraldo 73,
tel 266 777 071

Faro
Rua da Misericórdia 8,
tel 289 803 604

Fátima
Avenida Dom José Correia
da Silva, tel 249 531 139

Guarda
Praça Luís de Camões, tel
271 205 530

Guimarães
Alameda de São Dâmasa
86, tel 253 412 450,
Praça de Santiago,
tel 253 518 790

Lagos
Rua Belchoir Moreira
Barbudo, tel 282 959 231

Lamego
Avenida Visconde Guedes
Teixera, tel 254 612 005

Leiria
Jardim Luís de Camões,
tel 244 848 770

Lisboa
Praça do Comércio, tel 210
312 810; Palácio Foz,
Praça dos Restauradores,
tel 213 463 314

Mafra
Palácio Nacional de Mafra,
tel 261 817 170

Marvão
Largo de Santa Maria,
tel 245 909 131

Miranda do Douro
Largo do Menino Jesus da
Cartolinha, tel 273 431 132

Monsaraz
Largo Dom Nuno Alvares
Pereira, tel 266 557 136

Nazaré
Avenida da República,
tel 262 561 194

Óbidos
Rua de Estacionamento da
Porta da Vila,
tel 262 959 231

Peniche
Rua Alexandre Herculano,
tel 262 789 571

Ponte de Lima
Paço do Marquês,
tel 258 942 335

Portalegre
Rua Guilherme Gomes
Fernandes 28,
tel 245 307 445

Portimão
Avenida Zeca Afonso,
tel 282 470 717

Porto
Rua Clube dos Fenianos 25,
tel 223 393 470,
Rua Infante Dom Henrique,
tel 222 060 412

Sagres
Rua Comandante Matoso,
tel 282 624 873

Santiago do Cacém
Praça do Mercado,
tel 269 826 696

Sesimbra
Largo da Marinha,
tel 212 288 540

Setúbal
Casa do Corpo Santo, Praça
do Quebedo,
tel 265 534 402

Sintra
Praça da República 23,
tel 219 231 157

Tavira
Rua da Galeria 9,
tel 281 322 511

Tomar
Avenida Dr. Cândido
Madureira, tel 249 322 427

Valença do Minho
Avenida de Espanha,
tel 251 823 374

Viana do Castelo
Rua do Hospita Velho, t
el 258 822 620

Vila Nova de Gaia
Avenida Diogo Leite 242,
tel 223 773 080

Vila Viçosa
Praça da República,
tel 268 881 101

Viseu
Avenida Calouste Gulben-
kian, tel 232 420 950

USEFUL WEBSITES

TOURISM

www.visitportugal.com
Main tourist board site.
www.portugal.org
Tourist board site, aimed at US.
www.portugalvirtual.pt
Information for Portuguese regions.
www.orderportugal.com
Brochure ordering online for North Americans.
www.obrigado.com
General independent site.

REGIONAL TOURISM

www.visitlisboa.com
Lisbon.
www.costa-azul.rts.pt
Costa Azul, south of Lisbon.
www.rt-leiriafatima.pt
Leiria and around; includes Alcobaça, Fátima and Batalha.
www.rt-oeste.pt
North of Lisbon.
www.mafra.net
Mafra.
www.estorilcoast-tourism.com
Estoril and around; includes Mafra and Sintra.
www.rt-atb.pt
www.brancanet.pt
Both cover northeast Portugal; the latter in Portuguese only.
www.rt-nordeste.pt
Trás-os-Montes.
www.rtam.pt
Alto Minho.
www.rtvm.pt
Verde Minho northeast of Porto.
www.guimaraesturismo.com
Guimarães.
www.douro-turismo.pt
Douro.
www.portoturismo.pt
Porto.
www.cm-gaia.pt
Vila Nova de Gaia.
www.rotadaluz.pt
Aveiro and around.
www.turismo-centro.pt
Coimbra and around.
www.rtdaolafoes.com
Viseu area; in Portuguese only.
www.rt-serradaestrela.pt
Serra da Estrela.
www.cm-covilha.pt
Covilhã and Serra da Estrela.

www.mun-guarda.pt
Guarda.
www.rttemplarios.pt
Tomar and surrounding area.
www.rtribatejo.org
Ribatejo, north of Lisbon.
www.rtsm.pt
Northern Alentejo.
www.visitevora.pt
Évora; in Portuguese only.
www.rt-planiciedourada.pt
Southern Alentejo.
www.visitalgarve.pt
Algarve.

TRANSPORTATION

www.ana-aeroportos.pt
Airports.
www.tap.pt
TAP Air Portugal.
www.cp.pt
Portuguese trains.
www.rede-expressos.pt
Countrywide express bus services.
www.rodonorte.pt
Express bus services in northern and central Portugal.
www.carris.pt
Lisbon public transportation.
www.metrolisboa.pt
Lisbon metro system.
www.eva-bus.com
Bus travel to and in the Algarve.
www.transtejo.pt
Ferries and cruises on the Tejo.
www.stcp.pt
Porto public transportation.

ACCOMMODATION

www.maisturismo.pt
Hotel booking site.
www.pousadas.pt
Pousada booking site.

www.roteiro-campista.pt
Campsite booking site.

SPECIAL INTEREST

www.icnb.pt
National parks and nature reserves. Portuguese only.
www.ippar.pt
Portuguese National Trust.
www.ipmuseus.pt
Museum site, in Portuguese only.
www.termasdeportugal.pt
Portuguese spas site.
www.vinhoverde.com
Vinho verde site.
www.ivp.pt
Port and Douro region site.
www.wannasurf.com
Surfing information.
www.beachcam.pt
Webcams with wave reports in Portuguese.
www.portugalgolf.pt
www.golfportugal.com
Both golf tourism.

GENERAL

www.fco.gov.uk
www.travel.state.gov

MAJOR SIGHTS QUICK WEBSITE FINDER

SIGHT	WEBSITE	PAGE
Braga	www.cm-braga.pt	129
Porto	www.portoturismo.pt	158
Aveiro	www.rotadaluz.pt	180
Coimbra	www.cm-coimbra.pt	182
Alcobaça	www.ippar.pt	212
Batalha	www.ippar.pt	214
Fátima	www.santuario-fatima.pt	217
Tomar	www.rttemplarios.pt	220
Lisbon	www.visitlisboa.com	70
Sintra	www.cm-sintra.pt	112

COMMUNICATIONS

TELEPHONING

» All calls are most easily made using card-operated *credifones* or with your credit card, although they also take coins.

» Cards are available from post offices, newspaper shops, kiosks and tobacconists, and come in denominations of €5 and €10.

» You'll find *credifones* on the street, in bars and cafés and in some tourist information offices.

» Main post offices also have telephone cabins where you can make your call and pay afterwards. The clerk will assign you a cabin.

» The cheap rate for national and international calls runs from 9pm to 9am Monday to Friday and all day at weekends and on public holidays.

» Hotel charges for telephoning from your room are high.

» You can make a reverse-charge (collect) call *(chamada a cobrar ao destinatório)* from any telephone via an operator. Dial 120 for a European connection and 172 for the rest of the world. (For direct reverse-charge calls ▷ 305.)

» Dial 800 210 520 for general customer service.

» If you have problems, dial 179 to speak to an operator.

MOBILE PHONES

» It can be expensive to use your mobile phone abroad as you will often be charged for receiving as well as making calls.

» If your mobile phone SIM card is removable, it makes sense to remove it and replace it with a local card on arrival. You will then be able to use the Portuguese mobile telephone system and pay at local rates.

» Text messages are often a cheaper alternative, but check the charge for messaging with your provider before you leave home.

» US visitors will require a Triband phone for it to work in Portugal without changing the SIM card.

SENDING A LETTER

» *Selos* (stamps) can be bought at *correios* (post offices), kiosks, tobacconists, automatic dispensing machines and anywhere that has the sign of a white horse on a red background and the words *'Correio de Portugal'*.

» There are two levels of mail service: *correio azul* (blue mail) for urgent letters, which must be weighed and posted in a blue box; and regular mail, which is collected from red boxes. Letters to destinations within the EU will normally arrive in 4 to 8 days, and to the USA in 10 to 14 days.

POST OFFICES

» Post offices are normally open 9–6 Monday to Friday; larger offices may

AREA CODES FOR MAJOR CITIES

Aveiro	234
Beja	284
Braga	253
Bragança	273
Coimbra	239
Évora	266
Faro	289
Guarda	271
Leiria	244
Lisbon	21
Portimão	282
Porto	22

To call from outside Portugal, dial the international access code + 351 + the 9-digit number.

USEFUL TELEPHONE NUMBERS

Emergency services	112
International operator-assisted service	171
Directory enquiries (directory assistance)	118
International directory enquiries	177
Speaking clock	12151
Tourist enquiries (freephone)	800 781 212

Below *You can use a* credifone, *cash or credit cards to make a call on a public phone*

Left *Blue post boxes are for urgent mail, red ones for regular post, national and international*

POSTAGE RATES

Within Portugal	30¢
Within Europe	61¢
To America	75¢
To Africa	75¢
To Asia	75¢
To Australia	75¢

COURIERS

DHL	707 505 606
Federal Express	800 244 144
UPS	707 232 323
EMS–International	707 262 626

REVERSE-CHARGE CALLS ABROAD

To make direct reverse-charge (collect) calls to the UK from Portugal, dial 800 800 440 + the area code (omitting the first 0) + the number.
To call the USA from Portugal, dial 800 800 + your telephone company's US code + the area code + the number.

LAPTOPS

If you intend to use your own laptop computer in Portugal, remember to bring a power converter for re-charging and a plug socket adaptor. You will also need an adaptor for the telephone socket, and it's also a good idea to bring a surge protector.

also be open on Saturdays, while the main post offices in Lisbon and Porto have longer opening hours.
» You can have mail delivered *poste restante* (general delivery) to yourself at any post office in Portugal. You will need to go to the counter marked *Encomendas* and show your passport. Filing may be erratic, so get the clerk to check under all your initials or other possible letters when you collect mail. There is a small charge (about €1) for the service. *Encomendas* letters should be addressed as follows:
LAST NAME first name
Posta Restante
Correios Portugal
Address of post office

INTERNET ACCESS AND CAFÉS

» Internet cafés can be found in larger towns and resorts. Most charge around €2.50–€4 per hour.

INTERNATIONAL DIALLING CODES

To call home from Portugal, dial the international access code (00) followed by the country code (see below), the area code (omitting the 0), then the number:

Australia	61
Canada	1
New Zealand	64
Republic of Ireland	353
UK	44
US	1

» It may be cheaper to buy a debit card for use at Internet stations available in some post offices; these give you up to 3 hours' access for around €5.50.
» You'll need a web-based email account if you want to send or receive email from abroad (Hotmail, Yahoo, etc.)
» The netcafes.com website lists Internet cafés in Portugal and around the world.
» Remember to log out when you've finished and close the browser to dump your session cookies (temporary files). These are shared computers and you don't want someone else reading your emails, or accessing your personal information.
» If you have Bluetooth technology you can access the Internet using your mobile phone.

USING A COIN-OPERATED PHONE

1 Lift the receiver and listen for the dial tone.
2 Insert phone card or coins. The coin drops as soon as you insert it.
3 Dial or press the number.
4 If you want to cancel the call before it is answered, or if the call does not connect, press the coin release lever or hang up and take the coins from the coin return.
5 Once your call is answered, the display will show how much money or units you have left. Unused coins will be returned after the call.

MEDIA

NEWSPAPERS

If you read Portuguese, there's a wide choice of newspapers available. Even if your command of the language is less than perfect, local papers can be a good way to find out what's on in the way of entertainment. Portugal's main daily papers include:

» *Público*: A quality daily with comprehensive coverage; good on international news, and Friday guide to the arts (www.publico.clix.pt).

» *Diário de Notícias*: A long-established Lisbon-based paper, a big seller and noted for its classified ads (www.dn.sapo.pt).

» *Jornal de Notícias*: Sister paper to the *Diário*, published in Porto. It produces local sections for virtually every area of the country. (http://jn.sapo.pt).

» *Diário Económico*: A national daily business paper that also covers international finance (http://diarioeconomico.com).

» *Expresso*: Weekly, multi-sectioned paper that summarizes the week's news. Its political analysis is considered good and it runs excellent cultural listings. (http://aeiou.expresso.pt).

» *A Bola*, *Record* and *O Jogo*: A trio of sports dailies that concentrate on the Portuguese obsession with soccer—although some other sports news does creep in. Each is packed with photos and graphics and concentrates respectively on Benfica, Sporting (the two Lisbon soccer teams) and Porto (www.abola.pt, www.record.pt, www.ojogo.pt).

ENGLISH-LANGUAGE NEWSPAPERS

There are a few local English-language newspapers for Portugal's expatriate communities. *The News* is published in the Algarve and re-hashes national and foreign events, with individual sections for Porto and the north, Lisbon and the Algarve (http://thenews.net). It's good for listings and residents swear by the classified ads. *The Algarve*

Resident is a free monthly paper aimed at resident Britons, with both Algarve and Lisbon editions (www.portugalresident.com).

You'll find international newspapers on sale in Lisbon, Porto and some other major cities, and on the Algarve, though the quality papers usually arrive a day or more late. Tabloids, such as the UK's *Sun*, *Daily Mirror* and *Daily Mail*, are published in Spain, and are normally on sale the same day on the Algarve. *The International Herald Tribune* and *USA Today* are available in Lisbon, Porto and major towns.

MAGAZINES

On Portuguese newsstands and kiosks, television and gossip magazines dominate the magazine genre. The immensely popular *TV Mais* comes out weekly, presenting news of schedules and gossip; *Caras* is another popular weekly with plenty of gossip and pictures. Quality publications include *Visão*, a respected news weekly similar to *Time* or *Newsweek*, and *Grande Reportagem*, which, despite its glossy looks, is a serious monthly magazine with similar coverage. *Happy* and *Cosmopolitan* are aimed at women and cover fashion and beauty, while *Boa Mesa*, *Caras Decoração* and *Casa Claudia* concentrate on food, home and interior design.

For a real taste of TV obsessiveness, take a look at *Telenovelas*, which is entirely devoted to the super-popular Portuguese and Brazilian soaps.

Disney publishes no fewer than four titles aimed at younger readers.

TELEVISION

Portugal has two state-run television channels, RTP1 and RTP2, and two private channels, SIC and TV1.

The public-service channels have strong news reporting and investigative journalism, and also show imported US and UK shows, which are subtitled in Portuguese rather than dubbed. This also applies to all films shown on television.

SIC and TV1 are unashamedly lowbrow, the former devoting hours to Brazilian *telenovelas* (soap operas) and ludicrous game shows—riveting viewing even if you don't understand a word. Cable and satellite channels in bars and restaurants are mostly tuned to sport, but better hotels will generally have CNN and BBC World available.

RADIO

Portuguese radio concentrates on music, with the occasional bursts of news, soccer and traffic reports. Rádio Cidade (107.2FM) gives a good taste of what's popular in music, and you'll hear international hits alternating with distinctive Latin American and local sounds. The church-owned Rádio Renascença has a huge following for its talk shows; there's also a 24-hour news channel, TSF (89.5FM). The BBC World Service broadcasts on 648KHz medium wave and 15.00MHz short wave, and the Voice of America is on 553KHz to 1700KHz.

BOOKS, MAPS AND FILMS

BOOKS

Reading enriches your knowledge of a country and its history, people and culture, and the following suggestions may help whet your appetite before you go to Portugal, or answer a few questions and amuse you once you're there.

» *Backwards Out of the Big World*—Paul Hyland. A journey through Portugal by an author who knows the country as few other foreigners do.

» *The Portuguese: the Land and its People*—Marion Kaplan. Excellent overview of every aspect of the country

» *Journey to Portugal*—José Saramago. Story of a journey round Portugal in the 1990s by Portugal's Nobel prize-winning author.

» *Ricardo Reis*—José Saramago. Saramago's easiest-to-read novel focuses on the pre-Salazar years.

» *Portugal: A Companion History*—José Hermano Saraiva. Excellent, concise and up-to-date history written for non-specialist foreign readers.

» *The Lusiads*—Luís de Camões. Portugal's great 16th-century epic poem celebrating Vasco da Gama's voyage to India.

» *The Wines and Vineyards of Portugal*—Richard Mayson. All you need to know about what's best to drink.

» *The Taste of Portugal*—Edite Vieira. A lovely cookery and food history book that will have you reaching for your knives and pans.

» *Living in Portugal*—Anne de Stoop. A beautiful picture book to whet your appetite or bring back memories.

» *A Small Death in Lisbon*—Robert Wilson. A contemporary murder mystery, set in Lisbon and Cascais, by a British author resident in Portugal.

MAPS

An atlas can be found at the back of this book, and there are other maps integrated throughout the

text. The Portuguese National Tourist Board and *turismos* in larger towns can give you a useful free map of the whole country, with main topographical features, railways, motorways (expressways) and main roads clearly marked. You'll be able to augment this from local *turismos*, which will have regional maps and plans, though these are often less than detailed.

It's worth looking at http://snig.igeo/pt for its satellite and aerial images, as well as maps of virtually all of Portugal.

If you plan to hike, ask at local visitor information offices, or contact the Instituto Geográfico do Exercito, Avenida Dr. Alfredo Bemsaúde, Olivais Norte, 1849-014 Lisboa (tel 218 505 300, www.igeoe.pt), but be warned that many of their maps, though excellently detailed, are out of date. Publishing dates vary so check each area map for a date; look for the Serie M888.

FILMS

Portuguese films rarely reach a wide international audience, and there are few films that have made it onto the big screen overseas. The genre tends to reflect political concerns dating from the 1974 revolution and—oddly in this light-drenched country—there's a distinct emphasis on gloomy interiors and shadowy landscapes.

Portugal's big-name director is Manoel de Oliveira, whose work spans 70 years of the 20th century. His debut feature film, *Aniki-Bóbó* (1942), is a delicate story of poor children in Porto, which was panned by Portuguese critics but highly praised abroad. Unable to work for much of the Salazar era, he became the standard-bearer for Portuguese cinema with *Amor de Perdição* (Love of Perdition) in 1978. The 1990s saw the release of *O Convento* (The Convent), starring Catherine Deneuve and John Malkovich, and *Viagem ao Princípio do Mundo* (Journey to the Beginning of the World), the Italian actor Marcello Mastroianni's last film.

On a lighter note, Portugal occasionally makes an appearance in mainstream commercial movies, notably a couple of the James Bond epics.

WHAT TO DO

SHOPPING

Until Portugal joined the European Union in 1986, shopping was confined largely to small specialist stores, with only Lisbon and Porto offering much besides. That's all changed now, and most larger towns have malls on their outskirts with a vast range of goods on offer. Lisbon and Porto still rule the luxury market, but other towns are catching up, particularly in the heavily populated north and the prosperous Algarve. A plethora of tiny, specialist stores still exists, alongside the larger outlets, in towns and cities, while remote villages have some wonderful general stores catering for the needs of the locals.

DEPARTMENT STORES AND SHOPPING MALLS

Department stores are virtually non-existent in Portugal, where the emphasis has always been on individual, specialist retail. If you're visiting Lisbon or Porto, El Corte Inglés, the giant Spanish chain store, has branches there. Another is planned for Cascais, west of Lisbon.

Since 1987, when the Amoreiras shopping mall, Portugal's first, opened in Lisbon, the Portuguese have fallen in love with huge shopping complexes that are as much day-out destinations as retail outlets. These all have branches of Portuguese and international chain stores—which you often won't find in traditional downtown locations. They have longer opening hours than the shops in the heart of the city, and there's normally a supermarket or hypermarket attached. In addition to food, they sell clothes, white goods and electronic equipment. The main chains are Continente, Jumbo and the smaller Pingo Doce.

OPENING HOURS

Small shops open around 10, close between 12 and 2, and re-open until around 6 or 7. Outside large cities, shops tend to close for the weekend at Saturday lunchtime.

Traditional shops may have random closing times; a *volto já* (back soon) sign on the door should be taken with a pinch of salt. Small shops sometimes close for a month in summer.

PAYMENT

Credit cards are increasingly accepted in shops, though not for small transactions or on the same scale as in other European countries. Market traders are always paid in cash. Personal cheques are not generally accepted.

TAX REFUNDS AND SALES
Residents of non-EU countries can claim back IVA (VAT) for goods purchased at shops that are part of the tax-free scheme. Such stores will have a sticker displayed in the window. Claims are made by filling in a form available at the tax-free counter at the airport when you are departing the country.

HANDICRAFTS
Portugal has a very strong and flourishing tradition of handicrafts and artisan work, best seen at the weekly markets all over the country and in particular the big fairs. You'll also find specialist outlets for different handicrafts in their location of manufacture.

CERAMICS AND POTTERY
Ceramics generally are excellent value. *Azulejos* (decorated tiles) are a major Portuguese product, and retailers will be able to arrange shipping if you're buying in bulk.

Portugal's main porcelain manufacturer is Vista Alegre, whose high-quality products are exported worldwide. Selection and prices are better in Portugal than overseas, and a visit to their factory near Aveiro is well worthwhile.

TEXTILES
Portugal produces superb textiles, many of whose designs are traditionally associated with a particular place. Lace and embroidery are often used as decoration on textile products, with the finest lace coming from the coastal areas. The silk-embroidered linen *colchas* (bedspreads) from Castelo Branco are among the best-known and loveliest textiles in Portugal, while Arraiolos is famous for its excellent linen-based wool-embroidered carpets.

LEATHER
Shoes and leather goods are major industries. Prices are extremely competitive, but check for quality if they seem too good to be true.

JEWELLERY
Portugal has a tradition of filigree work, and you'll find intricate pieces made from fine gold wire in different shapes. Brooches and earrings are both good buys.

WOODWORK AND BASKETWARE
Wooden cupboards, chairs and trays are made in different regions, often beautifully decorated in bright designs. Easier to transport is basketwork, and you'll find finely made baskets in a variety of shapes and sizes on sale in markets and shops all over the country.

FOOD AND WINE
Every region in Portugal has its own special foods and wines, which you'll find in markets, at food shops and at local delicatessens. You can also buy wine and olive oil direct from many producers—look for signs or ask at the local tourist information office.

Opposite *Armazens do Chiados shopping mall in Lisbon*
Below *Pottery is exported worldwide*

ENTERTAINMENT AND NIGHTLIFE

If you're looking for a break from sightseeing or lazy beach days, you'll find a good range of entertainment on offer in Portugal. Lisbon is the main live performance arena, but Porto and other large provincial cities have a variety of theatre and concerts. Don't miss the chance to hear some *fado*, Portugal's soul music, or to take in some regional music, often performed on traditional instruments unique to the country. Nightlife in Lisbon and Porto is up there with the best in Europe, with a plethora of late bars and clubs offering something for every taste. Outside these two main cities (with the exception of the university city of Coimbra during term time) you'll find things quieter during the week, when choice will be limited to a couple of music bars, but there'll be something on offer at the weekends. The Algarve is packed with night-time options, and you'll find plenty to choose from at other popular summertime coastal resorts. Don't miss the chance to participate in local celebrations, when small communities let their hair down in uniquely Portuguese style.

CINEMA

Multiplexes have proliferated all over the country in recent years, many of them located in major shopping malls. If you don't speak Portuguese the big bonus is that all films are shown in their original language, so you'll be able to catch the latest international blockbusters almost everywhere, as well as art-house films from all over the world in the bigger cities. Prices are low (around €5.50), with further reductions on Mondays. Online film listings and ticket sales are available at www.iol. pt, http://cinema.sapo.pt and www.lusomundo.pt, though you'll need some knowledge of Portuguese to negotiate the sites.

Details of films are shown in weekend or Friday newspapers, and in weekly and monthly listings magazines.

CLASSICAL MUSIC, BALLET AND DANCE

There is usually a good selection of classical music concerts during the main season, which runs from October to May. Lisbon has three orchestras, which perform in the city and at venues across the country. Concerts are often staged in historic settings, such as monasteries, cathedrals, palaces and castles, so it's worth finding out what's on simply to enjoy fine music in beautiful surroundings.

Portugal's national ballet company, the Companhia Nacional de Bailado, performs classical ballet during the winter months, while the Sintra Music and Dance Festival (June–July) brings in international ballet companies.

Opposite *An azulejo (tile) depicting* fado
Below *The Teatro Nacional de Dona Maria in Lisbon*

Modern dance fans should try to catch a performance by companies like the Companhia Portuguesa de Bailado Contemporâneo, which stages highly theatrical works that include an impressive dash of African influence.

FADO
This is Portugal's soul music, an urban invention involving singer and guitar, and expressing the uniquely Portuguese concept of *saudade*, a sadness or yearning that has a beauty all of its own. There are two *fado* traditions, from Lisbon and Coimbra respectively, so you'll hear the best in either of these cities.

Lisbon's version is purely vocal and can be sung by men and women, while Coimbra's includes guitar pieces as well as song, and is performed exclusively by men.

You'll hear *fado* at specialist clubs, where eating and drinking are very much part of the proceedings. Some clubs are expensive, some real tourist traps, and there's no real way of knowing whom or what you'll hear on a given night. That said, in Lisbon, some well-known *fadistas* run their own clubs. The music is performed by a solo singer, usually accompanied by the *guitarra* (despite its name, not a guitar but a type of six-stringed 18th-century cittern) and the *viola de fado* (similar to the Spanish guitar). For the Portuguese, the words are an essential part of *fado*, but even if you don't speak the language, the combination of voice and instruments can be truly spine-tingling. In Lisbon, head for the Bairro Alto for a good range of *fado* clubs; in Coimbra, it's associated with the university.

CONTEMPORARY LIVE MUSIC
International bands and stars tend to concentrate on Lisbon and Porto, where they often perform in stadiums and large concert halls. Artists include big names from Brazil, giving a chance to hear something not normally on offer in other European cities. Portugal's main cities, too, are places to hear a wide range of musical styles, often fuelled by a steady supply of African, Cape Verde and Brazilian musicians. Concerts are advertised in listings magazines, by posters and by flyers in bars—or ask at tourist offices. Local rock music is performed all over the country, and jazz takes the stage at some of the summer music festivals.

FOLK AND REGIONAL MUSIC
Characteristic songs, ensembles and instruments survive in each region, and tend to be at their best in rural inland areas such as the Trás-os-Montes, the Beiras and the Alentejo.

Many towns and villages have their own *ranchos folclóricos*, troupes who perform at festivals and keep the old traditions going. They often play uniquely Portuguese instruments, such as the *gaita-de-foles* (bagpipes) in the Trás-os-Montes and Minho, the *flauta pastoril* (whistle), and drums, such as the *adufe* (square drum), *bombo* (bass drum) and *caixa* (snare drum). Ask at local tourist information offices about performances or check out the website www.attambur. com for festival listings and music samples you can download.

THEATRE
Unless you are a Portuguese-speaker, you are unlikely to want to go to the theatre in Portugal. Many places, however, double up as venues for music or dance, so in the bigger cities check listings or ask at the tourist office.

LISTINGS IN LISBON
The best listings magazine is the Agenda Cultural, a free monthly that's published in Portuguese only, though much of the information also appears in the *Follow me Lisboa* booklet (in English) produced by the tourist board; you can pick up both at city tourist offices. Both the Gulbenkian and the Belém Cultural Centre publish a schedule of their concerts, exhibitions and events, which you can collect from their reception desks. Two newspapers, the *Diário de Notícias* and *O Independente*, publish Friday supplements with full listings.

LISTINGS IN PORTO
Listings can be found in the free quarterly arts listings booklet *Agenda do Porto* (www.cm-porto. pt), available from tourist information offices. The newspaper *Público* publishes a listings supplement on Fridays and you can also find information in the *Jornal de Notícias*, Porto's leading paper.

LISTINGS IN THE ALGARVE
There are entertainment listings in the free monthly papers *Welcome to the Algarve* and the *Algarve Guide*.

LISTINGS ELSEWHERE
In other towns and cities, check the listings in the local newspapers, particularly for late-night music events and for the club scene. In smaller places, contact the tourist information office or pick up flyers.

TICKETING IN LISBON
Reserve ahead for events at these outlets:

ABEP (Agência de Bilhetes para Espectáculos Públicos)
✉ Praça dos Restauradores, 1250-188 Lisboa ☎ 213 425 360 🕐 Mon–Sat 10–7.30 🚇 Restauradores

Agência de Bilhetes Alvalade
✉ Praça de Alvalade 6, Edifício Centro Comercial Alvalade, Loja 43, Alvalade, 1700-036 Lisboa ☎ 217 955 859 🕐 Mon–Sat 11am–11.30pm, Sun 12.30–8.30 🚇 Alvalade

FNAC Centro Comercial Colombo
✉ Avenida Lusíada, Loja (shop) A-103, 1500-392 Lisboa ☎ 760 309 330 (ticket line) 🕐 Daily 10am–midnight 🚇 Colegio Militar

FNAC Chiado Armazéns do Chiado
www.fnac.pt
✉ Rua do Carmo 2, Loja 407, 1200-094 Lisboa ☎ 760 309 330 (ticket line) 🕐 Daily 10–10 🚇 Baixa-Chiado

BARS AND NIGHTCLUBS
There's a fair amount of crossover between bars and clubs, with many bars hosting live music some nights of the week. Most bars open around 8pm, with things getting going near midnight and continuing until 2am or later. Clubs open around 10pm–midnight, and get going about 2am. Lisbon and Porto can be packed all night at weekends with clubbers moving on from one venue to another.

In Lisbon, the traditional place for night-time action has always been the Bairro Alto, though this area now concentrates more on late bars than dance venues. You'll find the best, brashest and most exciting of these by the waterside, notably around Santa Apolónia and the Doca de Santo Amaro beneath the Ponte 25 de Abril. Lisbon's other hot spots are around the Avenida 24 de Julho and in Alcântara.

In Porto, many of the main dance venues are outside the heart of the city, though you'll find late music bars and some clubs clustered around the Ribeiro waterfront. Across the river, there's clubbing to be done in Vila Nova de Gaia, while summer sees the scene shifting towards the beach-side clubs at Foz do Douro.

If you're in the Algarve, you'll find clubs and bars of every type, ranging from the packed discos of Albufeira to pricey and romantic music bars in the more sophisticated resorts.

Check with local tourist information offices or listings magazines (▷ 311) for the latest news and opening times, and keep an eye out for posters and flyers in bars.

Many clubs operate what's known as the *consumo mínimo* system, specifying a minimum amount that you have to spend while in the club. In other words, it's a disguised admission charge, though it includes the price of one or more drinks. On entering you are handed a card, which is stamped every time you order a drink. On the way out you pay the minimum *consumo* stamped on the card—even if you've had nothing to drink. In a few very exclusive clubs, the *consumo mínimo* can vary hugely from person to person (from €10 to €250) as it is used to deter less 'desirable' or less 'well-dressed' customers.

In the listings in this guide, the *consumo mínimo* is treated as an admission charge.

GAY AND LESBIAN NIGHTLIFE
Over the last decade or so attitudes to gay and lesbian people have lightened up considerably in what is still a conservative society.

Lisbon has long been a gay-friendly city, and the Algarve, too, offers a relaxed welcome at clubs and bars, though it's best to keep a low profile in conservative, church-going country places.

To check out what's on, pick up a copy of the quarterly gay men's magazine *Korpus* or, for women, *Zona Livre*, available in newspaper shops in Lisbon and the Algarve.

In Lisbon, most gay bars and clubs are found in the Bairro Alto and Príncipe Real. The Centro Comunitário Gay e Lesbico de Lisboa (tel 218 873 918) is a good starting point for contacts and information.

It's also worth checking out the English-language website www.portugalgay.pt for information on what's on.

Below *Lisbon has a plethora of late-night cafés, bars and nightclubs*

SPORTS AND ACTIVITIES

Portugal has some of Europe's finest year-round facilities, seen at their best in the superb golf courses and tennis complexes in the Algarve. There's a great number of activities visitors can take part in; in the cities, too, leisure and sports facilities are burgeoning. Soccer is Portugal's most popular spectator sport. Roller-hockey is another popular spectator sport, with the Portuguese women's team winning the world championships in 2003.

BULLFIGHTING
The heart of bullfighting in Portugal is the Ribatejo, where the animals are bred. Portuguese bullfighting differs from the Spanish version in that the bull is not killed in the ring, but wrestled to the ground. The season runs from April to October, with *festas* at Vila Franca de Xira and Santarém. Other Ribatejo towns and villages also stage bull-running through their streets, similar to that at Pamplona in Spain.

FISHING
Portugal's northern rivers are rich in trout, with those of the Minho offering the best fishing. If you're interested, you'll need a permit, available from local town halls.

GOLF
Portugal has some of Europe's finest golf courses. The pick of the bunch are found all along the Algarve coast, particularly at Vilamoura, Quinta do Lago and Vale de Lobo. Farther north, you'll find courses in the Lisbon area. The Portuguese Open Championships are held in the Algarve during April. For further information, see www.portugalgolfe.com or www.portugalgolf.pt.

GYMS AND FITNESS
It's rare to see people jogging, even in the larger cities, but gyms are all the rage. Local tourist offices should be able to advise. Gyms in Lisbon and Porto are normally open from around 7am to 10pm Monday to Friday (shorter hours at weekends).

HORSEBACK RIDING
Companies organizing riding excursions or holidays can be found all over the country. You may even get the chance to ride the Lusitanos, Portugal's famous breed of horse. Ask for details at local tourist information offices.

ROLLER-HOCKEY
Portugal excels at this fast-moving sport. National league matches are played on Saturday or Sunday; ask at local tourist offices if you want to catch a match. The season runs from September until June.

SOCCER
The staging of the European Football Championships in 2004 put Portuguese *futebol* (soccer) on the map. Soccer is dominated by two Lisbon teams, Benfica and Sporting Lisbon, and FC Porto from Porto. The league season runs from September until May, and matches are played on Sunday. Tickets are generally inexpensive (€3–€30). Matches are prominently advertised in the sporting press, particularly *Bola* or *Jogo*, or you can catch the latest news at www.portuguesesoccer.com or www.infordesporto.sapo.pt.

SPAS
You'll find spas all over the country. Some are of the five-star health-farm type, others are more traditional. Note, though, that some are well off the beaten track. If you want to alleviate a medical condition, you'll need to see a doctor on arrival, who will work out the regime best suited to your needs. If you just want to wallow in a steaming hot tub, make a reservation and lie back and enjoy.

Portuguese spas are overseen by an umbrella organization, the Termas de Portugal (Avenida Miguel Bombard 110, 2nd floor, 1050-167 Lisbon, tel 217 940 574, 217 940 505, fax: 217 938 233, www.termasdeportugal.pt)

SURFING AND WINDSURFING
Portugal has superb surfing year-round. Windsurfing is also an option; you can rent boards at many places in the Algarve, at the bigger resorts in the north and around Lisbon. Popular locations are Guincho, north of Lisbon, and Ericeira, farther north up the coast. Several companies offer surfing holidays with tuition. For general information, go to www.surf-experience.com or www.purevacations.com/surf/portugal.

SWIMMING AND WATERSPORTS
The Algarve, with its year-round balmy climate, is the top draw for swimmers. Farther north, sea swimming is more of a summertime activity, and you could find the water off the northern coast cold. Popular beaches are manned by lifeguards, but still be aware of strong currents. Larger resorts offer jet-ski and motor-boat rental, and you may be able to rent a small sailing boat. Scuba-diving is well catered for in the clear waters of the Algarve.

TENNIS
Many hotels and villa complexes have their own tennis courts, and you'll find tennis clubs in larger towns and cities. In the south, coaching and holidays can be organized by clubs in the central Algarve, notably at Quinta do Lago and Vale de Lobo.

WALKING AND HIKING
Walking as a recreational pursuit is still a relatively new concept in Portugal. The best way to undertake serious walking is with a specialist company. Local companies offer day walks, while some tourist offices can provide leaflets detailing safe walking routes.

FOR CHILDREN

Children are very much part of the mainstream of life in Portugal, fussed over by people of all ages, and happily participating in most everyday activities. This means that adult tolerance levels are high, but the downside is that there are relatively few child-specific facilities and amusements. Nor should you expect too much in the way of child concessions, baby-changing facilities or children's menus. There's plenty for kids to do, though, particularly on the coast and in the larger cities, where there are museums and other attractions. Older children might appreciate Portugal's great outdoors, with its opportunities for walking, horseback riding, quad-biking and watersports.

FAMILY-FRIENDLY AREAS
If you're visiting with younger children, a beach holiday makes sense, with the Algarve and its many attractions heading the list. Resorts here are well geared to children, there's a wide range of types of beach to choose from, and there are waterparks and other attractions for a change of pace. The balmy climate allows for year-round holidaying; visiting outside the high-season summer months means that you will pay less and also benefit by escaping the high temperatures that small children will find hard to tolerate.

Also bordered by wonderful sandy beaches, the west coast has lively resorts where there are more opportunities for children to experience real Portuguese life.

Bear in mind, though, that sea temperatures are lower here than in the south, and some rain is almost inevitable, even in summer.

For older children, a judicious mix of sightseeing and country and seaside activities can work wonders—the Beira Alta, the Trás-os-Montes and the Minho might well appeal to those in their early teens.

BEACHES
Seaside resorts everywhere are busy throughout the peak holiday period of July and August, with the Algarve's season lasting a bit longer, from May until October.

Small children will be happy in the eastern Algarve, where there are miles and miles of gently shelving sandy beaches, beach games and playgrounds. Older children may well prefer more scenic areas, such as the coves and cliffs of the western Algarve and southern Alentejo.

If you're planning a beach holiday farther north, bear in mind that the water can be cold and that there are dangerous currents and undertows in many places. Because of this it's best to stick to busier beaches, even if your children are strong swimmers. Boat trips are often popular with children of all ages—ask at local tourist offices.

THEME PARKS
Portugal's biggest and best waterparks are in the Algarve, but you'll also find adventure and theme parks in other regions, though not on the same scale as in many other European countries. Ask at tourist information offices for details of children's attractions.

CITIES
Portuguese cities don't usually have the wealth of children's indoor attractions that other European cities offer, but Lisbon has plenty to keep them entertained. Getting around, by tram, funicular, open-top bus or ferry, is fun, while the Parque das Nações has plenty to keep most children busy.

Elsewhere, holidaying in cities with children can be hard work, but shopping malls often have amusements, and films and cartoons are shown in English throughout the country. Tourist offices will advise on where to go for child-oriented attractions.

Left *Thrills and spills at Slide and Splash waterpark, Estombar*

FESTIVALS AND EVENTS

Like many European countries, Portugal stages arts festivals throughout the year. There is also a huge number of local, traditionally Portuguese festivals, which can range from tiny but exuberant village celebrations to huge week-long fairs and pilgrimages that draw thousands. Most reflect important themes in Portuguese life, and there's no better way of experiencing what makes the country tick than mingling with the crowds. Ask at tourist offices for up-to-the-minute information or keep an eye out for posters.

RELIGIOUS
Religious festivals are linked both to the great feasts of the Church calendar and to religious shrines, many devoted to the Virgin Mary. Of these, Fátima (▷ 217) tops the list, with those in Viana do Castelo in the Minho and Lamego in the Beiras mixing let your-hair-down celebration with religious fervour. The festivals of Santo António and São João are similar, and the minor festivals in smaller towns and villages are a highly enjoyable blend of religion and party time.

TRADITIONAL
Some of Portugal's most lively celebrations are the *feiras* (festivals), which combine the best of traditional country fairs with serious festivities. At one of these you can experience an exciting blend of agricultural show, folk festival and amusement park, with eating and drinking high on the agenda.

ARTS FESTIVALS
Many of Portugal's major arts festivals take place in and around Lisbon and Porto, and feature classical music, jazz and film. Ask at any local tourist information office for details of what's on where and when.

THE BIGGEST AND BEST
Carnaval
Celebrates the start of Lent with street processions in towns all over Portugal; see the best in Lisbon and the major resorts along the Algarve (Feb–early Mar).

Queima das Fitas (Coimbra)
Marks the end of the academic year in Coimbra with traditional customs, partying and plenty of Coimbra-style *fado* (mid-May, ▷ 203).

Fátima
Portugal's most famous pilgrimage in honour of the Virgin Mary (13 May). A second major pilgrimage takes place in October.

Feira Nacional da Agricultura (Santarém)
A huge country show with the accent on traditional farming, bullfighting and dancing (10 days from first Fri in Jun).

Santos Popularos
Celebrations all over Portugal in honour of St. Anthony (12–23 Jun), St. John (23–24 Jun) and St. Peter (28–29 Jun). Lisbon focuses on St. Anthony, Porto on St John.

Romaria da Nossa Senhora da Agonía (Viana do Castelo)
Weekend-long pilgrimage and festivities with dancing, music parades and fireworks (nearest weekend to 20 Aug).

Romaria da Nossa Senhora dos Remédios (Lamego)
Pilgrimage and *festa* with religious processions, parades, car-racing, rock music and non-stop partying (pilgrimage 6–8 Sep, but other events take place over a fortnight).

Feiras Novas (Ponte de Lima)
Huge market and fair—music, *gigantones* (carnival figures), fairground and bands (second and third weekend in Sep).

Feira Nacional do Cavalo (Golegã)
Portugal's biggest horse fair, with mounted parades of magnificent beasts, bull-running and lively street partying (second week in Nov; www.horsefairlusitano.org).

Below *A procession at the Festa das Cruzes, Barcelos, typical of religious festivals throughout the country*

EATING

The range of foods on offer reflects Portugal's history and culture, with the accent firmly on fresh, seasonal, local produce. The Moors, the Spanish and the British all left their mark on the country's food and drink, while the coast and great sea voyages of discovery produced a passion for fish and seafood, spices and ingredients from across the globe. Cooking is intensely regional, with every area having its own special dishes.

MEALS AND MEALTIMES

Pequeno-almoço (breakfast) is usually eaten between 8am and 9am by the Portuguese, often at a café or *pasteleria* (pastry shop), where some sort of cake or pastry is washed down by a cup of coffee. In remote areas you may still be served bread and soup for breakfast, or simply a hefty bread roll and a pat of butter.

Almoço (lunch) starts with bread, served with a selection of pâtés, olives, cheese and other titbits and perhaps soup. This is followed by a meat dish served with fries and rice and usually a simple salad of lettuce, tomato and onion, or fish served with boiled potatoes and vegetables. Puddings are generally quite sweet and simple.

Jantar (dinner) normally starts around 7.30pm. Outside major cities and tourist resorts, it is not available much after 9.30pm; in rural areas it may well be served earlier.

Menus will sometimes advertise the *ementa turística;* this is not a tourist menu, but the set meal of the day. The price includes two courses plus beer or wine, and can be excellent value.

WHERE TO EAT AND WHAT TO EXPECT

The best and most typical food is often found in seemingly unpretentious eating establishments. These are the places to go to sample local dishes. Only the more expensive restaurants in larger cities and tourist areas take reservations. Reserve ahead in the peak season and at weekends.

» *Restaurantes* are straightforward restaurants, where you'll be served a two- or three-course meal. They're normally open from 12am to 3pm for lunch and 7pm to 10pm for dinner. They may open longer in tourist areas or at peak season.

» A *casa de pasto* is an inexpensive, often family-run, local dining room, offering budget three-course meals, mainly at lunchtime only. They're excellent value for money.

» *Tascas* are small, inexpensive, family-run eateries. Expect huge portions of stews, grilled sardines, chicken and bean soups.

» A *marisqueira* is a seafood restaurant, where both shellfish and fish are served. You can pick your own from the display, which will be cooked to order. Menu prices are in kilos, and will add up fast, so expect a fairly hefty bill.

» Lunch at a shared table in a *taberna* is a real Portuguese experience. Many serve a different regional dish daily. Service is fast and friendly.

» *Churrasqueiras* specialize in *frango no churrasco* (chargrilled chicken) with *batatas fritas* (fries), though they serve other types of grilled food too.

» *Cervejarias* primarily serve beer and snacks, and are open all day and late into the evening.

» *Pousadas*, the nationwide chain of deluxe hotels, all have restaurants serving regional food and wine, though standards vary.

» A restaurante *típico* serves regional food and wine and has, by law, to offer traditional entertainment and display local objects. Standards vary considerably, but it's worth looking at the menu.

LOCAL CUSTOMS

» Once you are seated, bread and nibbles will be placed on the table. These range from fish pâté and olives to cheese, *chouriço* (spicy sausage) and more elaborate dishes. You will be charged for what you eat (*couvert* on the bill).

» Smoking is no longer allowed in restaurants.

» Some restaurants will have a television playing.

» In simple *restaurantes* it's quite acceptable to ask for a *meia dose* (half-portion); Portuguese servings are large.

» If you share a table with people who are already eating, they may ask you *E servido?* (Have you been served?), meaning 'Would you like some of ours?' Just say politely *Não, muito obrigado* (No thank you)—it's just a way of saying 'Enjoy your meal.'

PAYING THE BILL

Ask for a *conta* (the bill) and check to see whether *serviço* (a service charge) has been included, as occasionally happens in more expensive restaurants. If not, it's customary to leave a 5–10 per cent tip.

» Quite a few restaurants are cash only; check in advance to find out if they take credit cards (*Aceita cartões de crédito?*).

» Many restaurants are closed all day Sunday, or on Sunday afternoon and evening or on Mondays.

CAFÉS

Cafés are open from early morning until late. Prices are sometimes higher if you sit down, so, if you just want a quick coffee, it's less expensive to drink it standing at the bar. Cafés also serve a wide variety of snacks, ranging from breakfast pastries to lunchtime specials, which can be anything from simple fare such as *prego no pão* (steak sandwich) to *pastéis de bacalhau* (salt-cod fishcakes).

TEA ROOMS

Casas de chá (tea rooms) serve a range of excellent teas, including herbal infusions, as well as coffee and a sometimes overwhelming range of sweet cakes and other indulgences. These are the places you need to go to when you are trying to track down *doces regional* or *doces conventuais*, the ultra sweet sugar-and-egg-yolk confections that were originally made by nuns in the convents. Savoury snacks are also often served at lunchtime.

INTERNATIONAL CUISINE

Major Portuguese cities have French, Italian and other national restaurants, including a good selection serving South American—particularly Brazilian—food. Chinese restaurants also exist in larger towns and tourist resorts. As you would expect, the widest choice of international restaurants are to be found in Lisbon and Porto, and in places in the Algarve.

SPECIAL REQUIREMENTS

Vegetarians may find eating out difficult, as even seemingly suitable soups, rice and bean dishes will be based on meat stock, or enlivened with small pieces of bacon or sausage. You will probably find that even seemingly straightforward vegetable dishes may contain pork fat. If you eat fish there's no problem, but otherwise you may find there's little you can eat on the menu, except for cheese, an omelette or salad.

WHAT TO DRINK

» Coffee (*café*) in Portugal is excellent and inexpensive. It's served in cafés, *casas de chá* and bars. The most popular varieties are *bica* or *café*, a short black espresso, *garoto*, an espresso with a dash of milk, and *meia de leite*, a larger, milky coffee.

» *Chá* (tea) is popular in Portugal and is normally served relatively weak without milk. If you like milk ask for a *chá com leite*; *chá com limão* is tea with a slice of lemon.

» Fruit juice can be *sumo de laranja natural* (freshly squeezed orange juice), or one of the bottled varieties. Soft drink brands to look out for are Tri Naranjus and Sumol.

» *Cerveja* (beer) is widely drunk. The main brands are Sagres, popular in central and southern Portugal, and Super Bock, northern Portugal's favourite. Draft beer comes as *um imperial* (200ml/7fl oz), the less common *principe* (330ml/12fl oz) or *uma canoca* (500ml/18fl oz). The alcohol content is 5–6 per cent, depending on the brand.

» *Vinho da casa* (house wine) is usually good value, but it's worth paying more to sample some better wines. This is especially true as there is such a wide range to choose from, many of which are unavailable outside Portugal. The country is divided into eight wine regions; which region your wine comes from will be specified on the bottle. The DOC specification is a more specific guarantee of the provenance of the wine.

» Portugal's own spirit is *aguardente*, a variety of brandy. Types to look out for include *medronho*, made from the fruit of the strawberry tree, *aguardente de figo* (fig spirit) and *ginginha* (cherry spirit).

» Port (*vinho do Porto*) makes a superb after-dinner drink; but don't miss the chance to try chilled *porto branco* (white port), not often available outside Portugal, as an aperitif.

» Madeira (*vinho da Madeira*) is another delicious aperitif or after-dinner tipple.

PRACTICALITIES EATING

Left A selection of pastéis *(tarts) makes a delicious snack*

Fiambre........................cooked ham
Frango...................................chicken
Javalí................................wild boar
Lebre...hare
Morcelas...................blood sausage
Novilho.....................................veal
Pato...duck
Peru......................................turkey
Porco..pork
Presunto...........air-dried cured ham
Toucinho..............................bacon

PEIXES FISH

Alabote................................halibut
Arenque/sável.....................herring
Arinca............................... haddock
Atum...tuna
Bacalhau................dried salted cod
Dourada...............bream/John Dory
Espardate.......................swordfish
Linguado....................................sole
Peixe-espada.............. scabbard fish
Pescada............................whiting
Pescadinha.......................whitebait
Pregado/rodovalho...............turbot
Raia...ray
Robalo....................................bass
Salmão...............................salmon
Salmonete.......................red mullet
Sardinha........................ sardines
Solha.......................flounder/plaice
Tamboril.........................monkfish
Truta...trout

MARISCOS E FRUTOS DO MAR
SEAFOOD AND SHELLFISH

Ameijoas................................clams
Anchova...........................anchovies
Camarão/gambas..shrimps/prawns
Chocos...........................cuttlefish
Enguia...eel
Lagosta............................lobster
Lulas...squid
Mexilhões.........................mussels
Ostras.................................oysters
Perceves....................... barnacles
Polvo...................................octopus
Sapateira.................................crab
Vieira...................................scallops

The best way to enjoy fine Portuguese cuisine is to venture off the tourist trail in favour of restaurants where the locals go. If you don't speak Portuguese this may seem a daunting prospect, but the knowledge of a few key words and names will help you track down regional dishes all over the country. Below is a menu reader to help you translate common words, get to grips with dishes and ingredients, and order the meals you are likely to see on a Portuguese menu.

COURSES AND THE MENU

Entradas e acepipes.... starters and
hors d'oeuvres
Sopas.......................................soups
Peixes...fish
Marisco e frutos do mar.... shellfish
and seafood
Aves e caça..........poultry and game
Carnes................................... meat
Acompanhamento........side dishes
Pratos completas.. complete dishes
Sobremesas e doces.........pudding,
desserts

Fruta...fruit
Lista de vinhos................. wine list
Por pessoa..................... per person
2 pessoas..........dish for two people
Especialidades da casa special dish
Prato do dia..............dish of the day
Meia dose.....................half-portion
Cozido.... boiled, stewed or poached
Assado...................................roasted
Frito.. fried
Grelhado................................grilled
À casa.................. in the house style
À moda da, a região..............in the
regional style
Pão e manteiga..... bread and butter

CARNES MEAT

Alheiras...............................sausages
Bife..steak
Borrego/cordeiro.....................lamb
Cabrito.......................................kid
Carne de vaca......................... beef
Carneiro.............................. mutton
Chouriços...........smoked sausages
Coelho....................................rabbit
Cordoniz.............................. quail
Costeletas................................cutlets
Farinheiras.......... pork-fat sausages

HORTALIÇAS VEGETABLES

Abacate....................... avocado pear
Abóbora..............................pumpkin
Aipo...celery
Alcachofra .... artichoke
Alface ....lettuce
Alho... garlic
Alho-Francês ....leek
Arroz ....rice
Azeitona .... olives
Batata .... potato
Beringel.............aubergine/eggplant
Beterreba ....beetroot
Bróculos............................ broccoli
Cebola...................................onion
Cenoura .... carrot
Cogumelos .... mushroom
Corgete ....courgette/zucchini
Couve .... cabbage
Couve...............Galega Galician kale
Ervilhas....................................peas
Espargos......................... asparagus
Favas ....broad beans
Feijão ....beans
Feijão verde ....green beans
Grão de bico ....chickpeas
Lontilha..................................lontilo
Nabos.................................... turnip
Pepino ....cucumber
Pimento verde........... green pepper/
capsicum
Pimento vermelho .... red pepper/
capsicum
Piri-piri ....chilli
Salada .... salad
Tomate.................................. tomato

DOCES E PASTÉIS
SWEETS AND PASTRIES

Arroz doce ....rice pudding
Bolos....................................... cakes
Doce..jam
Doces de amêndoa.......... marzipan
sweets, often shaped as fruit
Doces conventuais ....sweet
desserts, originally made by nuns
Doces de ovos .... egg-yolk sweets
Figos cheios dried figs with almonds
Fios de ovos .... sweetened egg-yolk
threads
Gelado ....ice cream
Leite crème..............crème caramel
Mel ....honey
Ovos moles ... sweetened egg yolks
Pão-de-ló .... sponge cake
Pastéis de nata........... custard tarts

Queijadas...........sweet cheese tarts
Toucinho do céu........sweet almond
and cinnamon cake

FRUTA FRUIT

Ameixa.....................................plum
Ananás............................ pineapple
Cereja....................................cherry
Damasco/alperce.................apricot
Figo ....fig
Framboesa...................... raspberry
Laranja ....orange
Limão ....lemon
Maçã ....apple
Melão ....melon
Mirtilo .... blueberry
Morango .... strawberry
Pêra ....pear
Pêssego .... peach
Romã .... pomegranate
Salada de frutas.............. fruit salad
Tâmaras................................dates
Quiejo .... cheese
Queijo de Azeitão ....cured
sheep's-milk cheese from Setúbal
Queijo de cabra..... fresh goat's-milk
cheese
Queijo da ilha........island cow's milk
cheese from the Azores
Quiejo do Monte.............................
sheep- and cow's-milk cheese from
the Trás-os-Montes
Queijo de ovelha..........sheep's-milk
cheese
Queijo da Serra/Estrela.................
sheep's-milk cheese fermented with
cardo thistles

ESPECIALIDADES
SPECIAL DISHES

Açorda ....bread soup
Arroz ...complete rice dishes cooked
with seafood, duck or goat
Bacalhau.................... dried salt cod
Bolo Rei .... (King's Bread) spiced
bread with dried and crystallized fruit
eaten during Christmas season
Caldo verde ....Galician kale and
potato soup
Canja de Galinha chicken broth with
rice and lemon
Carne de porco à Alentejano ...pork
cooked with clams
Cozida à Portuguesa...............stew
with meat, offal, sausages, green
vegetables, rice and potatoes

Empadas de galinha .. small chicken
pies
Feijoada ....bean stew with lamb,
seafood, pork or rabbit
Frango no Churrasco/Piri-piri ....
charcoal-grilled chicken with chilli
sauce
Polvo assado ....baked octopus
Sardinhas grelhadas grilled sardines

TEMPEROS FLAVOURINGS

Açúcar.....................................sugar
Alho... garlic
Azeite...................................olive oil
Caril .... curry
Especiaries .... spices
Mostarda .... mustard
Pimenta .... pepper
Piri-piri .... chilli sauce
Sal ....salt
Vinagre .... vinegar

BEBIDAS DRINKS

Água fresca ..... water served chilled
Água mineral com/sem gás fizzy or
still mineral water
Água ....natural water served
at room temperature
Aguardente............brandy-like spirit
Bica, ... café small, black coffee
Café.......................................coffee
Café descafeinado .....decaffeinated
coffee
Cerveja.................................... beer
Chá..tea
Chá com leite ....tea with milk
Chá com lima ....tea with lemon
Garoto.................. short coffee with
dash of milk
Galão or meia de leite .... long milky
coffee
Gelo..ice
Sumo de laranja...........orange juice
Sumo de maçã...............apple juice
Vinho branco.................white wine
Vinho doce ....sweet wine
Vinho da Madeira ..... fortified white
wine from the island of Madeira
Vinho do Porto........................ port
Vinho seco.........................dry wine
Vinho tinto ....red wine
Vinho verde......light white sparkling
wine

There is a wide range of accommodation all over Portugal. For budget travellers, there is plenty of choice in the shape of clean, simple pensions and a wealth of self-catering options. Accommodation overall is excellent value, and even top-notch options cost appreciably less than elsewhere in Europe. Expect to pay more in Lisbon and the Algarve in high season, but even then you may be pleasantly surprised by how far your money goes.

TYPES OF ACCOMMODATION

Pousadas, a chain of more than 40 nationwide luxury hotels, provide levels of comfort you won't find elsewhere. Prices vary considerably, and they run seasonal promotions, while over-65s can get discounts of as much as 35 per cent.

Hotels in Portugal are graded from between one and five stars. It's acceptable to ask to see the room before you take it; the official price list (which includes IVA—the equivalent of VAT) must be displayed inside the door. Extra beds can normally be provided for a small charge, but children under four years can usually stay free in their parents' room. Simpler hotels are often quite basic and have little in the way of heating in winter.

Pensões and **residenciais** are a good budget choice. *Residenciais* are unlikely to serve meals other than breakfast. They are classified from one to three stars. A 3-star *pensão* costs roughly the same as a 1-star hotel. Not all rooms have private bathrooms, but the accommodation will be simple, clean and reasonably comfortable. **Hospedarias** are very similar in style, with even lower prices.

Privately owned country and manor houses provide superb accommodation at varying prices, and are ideal if you are touring outside the cities. Promoted and inspected by the government tourist office, they vary from simple farmhouses *(casas rústicas)* to country manor houses *(quintas)* and even palaces *(casas antigas)*. Rooms and facilities must meet certain standards and are categorized on a scale of A–C. You can make bookings through the various marketing companies. **Country guest houses** are classified as *turismo rural*. They are government-inspected and awarded a green tree symbol.

VILLAS AND SELF-CATERING

Self-catering options are available all over Portugal. They range from simple one-room, studio-type apartments to luxurious houses with a pool, gardens and maid service. It's advisable to reserve ahead, using one of the many specialist holiday or tour operators. You can often get all-in packages that include flights and car rental. You can arrange to rent a property yourself—a much less expensive option—either by obtaining a list of properties from the local tourist board or by checking websites devoted to private rentals.

CAMPSITES

There are official campsites *(parques de campismo)* all over Portugal, many open year round. The pick of the bunch are operated by Orbitur and can be huge; these also have spaces for camper vans (RVs) and caravans, and some have permanent caravans and bungalows you can rent. They can be crowded during the summer months, particularly in the Algarve—be aware that theft is becoming an increasing problem.

YOUTH HOSTELS

Portugal has around 30 youth hostels *(pousadas de juventude)*, though those in Lisbon, Porto and the Algarve are more expensive. They're clean, safe and friendly, with dormitory-style accommodation. Most have a curfew (11pm or midnight) and all require a valid Hostelling International card.

FINDING A ROOM

Advance reservation is vital in July and August or if your stay coincides with local festivals or pilgrimages.
» If you haven't reserved, start by asking at the tourist office; they will have lists of accommodation and may be willing to reserve for you.
» You'll be asked to leave your passport when you check in; don't forget to collect it later.
» In larger towns and cities there's plenty of *pensão* accommodation, as well as pricier hotels.
» Many hotels in rural area and some in coastal areas may be closed out of season.
» Check-out time is normally noon, but some hotels will keep luggage until the end of the day.
In smaller places, pay your bill the night before to make an early start.
» Many hotels and self-catering apartments in the Algarve are block-booked by travel operators in the summer, so reserve well ahead.

PRICING

Rates vary according to season, by as much as 40 per cent.
» Agree a price before you make a reservation, and ask for written confirmation if calling from home.
» Hotels will often quote their most expensive rates; ask if they have cheaper rooms.

ACCOMMODATION INFORMATION

HOTELS

The following are quick, efficient, online booking sites for hotel accommodation and all-in holidays across Portugal, offering good value for money and a wide range of options.
www.hotelopia.co.uk
www.strawberry-world.net

POUSADAS

✉ Rua Soares de Passos 3, Alto de Santo Amaro, 1300-314 Lisboa
☎ 218 442 001
✉ Keytel, 402 Edgware Road, London W2 1ED, UK ☎ 020 7616 0300; www.keytel.co.uk
✉ Marketing Ahead, 381 Park Avenue South, Suite 718, New York, NY 10016 ☎ 800-223-1356, 212/686-9213; www.marketingahead.com
or try www.pousadas.pt

COUNTRY HOUSE ACCOMMODATION

✉ Solares de Portugal, Praça da República, 4990-062 Ponte de Lima
☎ 250 741 072;
www.solares-de-portugal.com
✉ Privetur, Largo das Pereiras, 4990-047 Ponte de Lima ☎ 258 743 923 or 020 7096 0210 (UK); www.privetur.co.uk
✉ CENTER, Praça da República, 4990-062 Ponte de Lima ☎ 258 931 750; www.center.pt

SELF-CATERING AND VILLA HOLIDAYS

✉ CV Travel, Skyline House, 200 Union Street, 2nd Floor, London SE1 0LX, UK
☎ 020 7401 1035; www.cvtravel.co.uk; specialists in luxury villas
✉ The Villa Holiday Centre, 12 Headlands Business Park, Blashford, Ringwood, Hampshire BH24 3PD, UK
☎ 01425 484430; www.villaholidaycentre. co.uk; a wide selection of villas around Carvoeiro in the Algarve
✉ Holidaylets.Net, Unit 30B, Innovation Centre, Cranfield Technology Park, Cranfield, Bedfordshire MK43 0BT, UK
☎ 01234 756940; www.holidaylets.net; a good selection of privately owned villas and apartments all over Portugal
✉ Selfcatering Hols, Pinetrees, Old Road, Wrinehill, Crewe CW3 9BW, UK
☎ 01234 480012; www.selfcateringhols. com; villas and apartments in the Algarve and northern Portugal

www.portugalvirtual.pt/_lodging; a comprehensive site with self-catering options all over Portugal

CAMPING

The booklet *Roteiro Campista* (€6.50) is available from tourist offices, bookshops and newsstands, or from *Roteiro Campista*, Apartado 3168, 1301-902 Lisboa; www. roteiro-campista.pt
✉ Orbitur, Rua Diogo Couto 1–8, 1149-024 Lisboa; www.orbitur.pt; operates campsites all over Portugal

You can get an international camping carnet from:
UK
✉ Camping and Caravanning Club, Greenfields House, Westwood Way, Coventry CV4 8JH
☎ 0845 130 7631;
www.campingandcaravanningclub.co.uk
✉ The AA; www.theAA.com
USA
✉ Family Campers and RVers, 4804 Transit Road, Building 2, Depew, NY 14043
☎ 800/245-9755; www.frcv.org

YOUTH HOSTELS

✉ Movijovem, Rua Lúcio de Azevedo 27, 1600-146 Lisboa
☎ 217 232 100;
www.pousadasdejuventude.pt
UK
✉ YHA, Trevelyan House, 8 Dimple Road, Matlock, Derbyshire DE4 3YH
☎ 01629 592700; www.yha.org.uk
✉ SYHA, 7 Gelbe Crescent, Stirling, Scotland FK8 2JA
☎ 0870 155 3255;
www.syha.org.uk
USA
✉ HI-AYH, 8401 Colesville Road, Suite 600, Silver Spring, MD 20910
☎ 301/495 1240; www.hiayh.org

Even if you're far from fluent, it is always a good idea to try to speak a few words of Portuguese. The words and phrases on the following pages should help you with the basics, from ordering a meal to dealing with emergencies.

CONVERSATION

I don't speak Portuguese.
Não falo português.
Do you speak English?
Fala inglês?
I don't understand.
Não compreendo.
My name is ...
Chamo-me ...
Hello, pleased to meet you.
Olá, prazer em conhecê-lo(a).
I'm on holiday.
Estou de férias.
I live in ... Vívo em ...
Good morning..................Bom dia.
Good afternoon............ Boa tarde.
Good evening/night.......Boa noite.
Goodbye..........................Adeus.
See you later................... Até logo.
May I/Can I?...................... Posso?
How are you?..............Como está?
I'm sorry.........................Desculpe.
Excuse me................. Com licença.

SHOPPING

Could you help me, please?
Podia ajudar-me, por favor?
How much is this?
Quanto custa isto?
I'm looking for ...
Preciso de ...
This isn't what I want.
Não é isto que eu queria.
When does the store open/close?
Quando é que a loja abre/fecha?
I'm just looking, thank you.
Estou só a ver, obrigado(a).
Do you accept credit cards?
Aceitam cartões de crédito?
This is the right size.
Este é o tamanho certo.
Do you have anything less expensive/smaller/larger?
Tem algo mais barato/mais pequeno/maior?

I'll take this.
Levo este(a).
Do you have a bag for this?
Tem um saco para isto?
I'd like ... grams please.
Queria ... gramas, por favor.
I'd like a kilo of ...
Queria um quilo de ...
What does this contain?
O que é que isto contém?
I'd like ... slices of that.
Queria ... fatias disto.
bakery............................... padaria
bookshop...........................livraria
chemist........................... farmácia
market.............................mercado

NUMBERS

1..um
2... dois
3...três
4...quatro
5... cinco
6.. seis
7..sete
8..oito
9... nove
10... dez
11... onze
12... doze
13...treze
14... catorze
15... quinze
16.. dezasseis
17..dezassete
18... dezoito
19...dezanove
20.. vinte
21.................................vinte e um
30...trinta
40...quarenta
50....................................... cinquenta
60... sessenta
70..setenta
80..oitenta
90... noventa
100...cem
1000.. mil

USEFUL WORDS

yes.. sim
no.. não
there... ali

here................................... aqui
where...................................onde
who....................................quem
when................................ quando
why....................................porquê
how....................................como
later...............................mais tarde
now................................... agora
open...................................aberto
closed.............................. fechado
please...........................por favor
thank you.................... obrigado(a)

HOTELS

Do you have a room?
Tem um quarto?
I have made a reservation for ... nights.
Fiz uma reserva para ... noites.
How much each night?
Quanto é por noite?
double room
quarto de casal
twin room
quarto duplo
single room
quarto individual
with bath/shower/toilet
com banho/duche/sanita
Is there a lift in the hotel?
O hotel tem elevador?
Is the room air-conditioned/heated?
O quarto tem ar condicionado/aquecimento?
Is breakfast/lunch/dinner included in the cost?
O pequeno-almoço/almoço/ jantar está incluído no preço?
Is room service available?
Tem serviço de quarto?
When do you serve breakfast?
Quando servem o pequeno-almoço?
May I have breakfast in my room?
Posso tomar o pequeno-almoço no quarto?
Do you serve evening meals?
Servem jantares?
The room is too hot/cold.
O quarto está demasiado quente/frio.
May I see the room?
Posso ver o quarto?

May I have my room key?
Pode dar-me a chave do quarto?
Where can I park my car?
Onde posso estacionar o carro?
Please can I pay my bill?
Posso pagar a conta?
swimming pool
piscina

RESTAURANTS
**I'd like to reserve a table for ...
people at ...**
Gostaria de reservar uma mesa para
... pessoas às ....
A table for ..., please.
Uma mesa para ..., por favor.
We have/haven't reserved.
Temos reserva/não temos reserva.
Is this table taken?
Esta mesa está ocupada?
**Could we see the menu/
wine list?**
Pode trazer-nos a ementa/lista dos
vinhos?
Are there tables outside?
Há mesas lá fora?
Where are the toilets?
Onde ficam as casas de banho?
We'd like something to drink.
Gostávamos de tomar uma bebida.
**Could I have bottled still/
sparkling water?**
Pode trazer-me uma garrafa de água
sem gás/com gás, por favor?
**I can't eat wheat/sugar/salt/
pork/beef/dairy.**
Não posso comer trigo/
açúcar/sal/carne de porco/carne de
vaca/lacticínios.
I am a vegetarian.
Sou vegetariano(a).
The bill, please.
A conta por favor.
Is service included?
A taxa de serviço está
incluída?

FOOD AND DRINK
breakfast .... pequeno-almoço
lunch .... almoço
dinner .... jantar
starters .... entradas
main course .... prato principal
dessert .... sobremsa
knife .... faca
fork .... garfo
spoon .... colher

salt .... sal
pepper .... pimenta
bread .... pão
sugar .... açúcar
cheese .... queijo
soups .... sopas
sandwich .... sanduíche
cod .... bacalhau
sardines .... sardinhas
wine list .... lista de vinhos

GETTING AROUND
Where is the information desk?
Onde é o balcão das
informações?
Where is the timetable?
Onde está o horário?
Does this train/bus go to ...?
Este comboio/autocarro vai para ...?
Do you have a metro/bus map?
Tem um mapa do metro/dos
autocarros?
train/bus/metro station
estação de comboios/terminal dos
auto carros/ estação de metro
Where can I buy a ticket?
Onde posso comprar bilhete?
Where can I reserve a seat?
Onde posso reservar um lugar?
**Please can I have a single/
round-trip ticket to ...?**
Pode dar-me um bilhete/bilhete de
ida e volta para ...?
Where can I find a taxi?
Onde posso encontrar um táxi?
How much is the journey?
Quanto é a viagem?
I'd like to rent a car.
Gostaria de alugar um carro.
no parking
estacionamento proibido
I'm lost.
Estou perdido(a).
Is this the way to ...?
É este o caminho para ...?
Go straight on.
Vá sempre em frente.
Turn left.
Vire à esquerda.
Turn right.
Vire à direita.
traffic lights
semáforos
intersection
cruzamento
corner
esquina

DAYS/MONTHS/TIMES
Monday .... segunda-feira
Tuesday ....,............... terça-feira
Wednesday .... quarta-feira
Thursday .... quinta-feira
Friday .... sexta-feira
Saturday .... sábado
Sunday .... domingo
January .... janeiro
February .... fevereiro
March .... março
April .... abril
May .... maio
June .... junho
July .... julho
August .... agosto
September .... setembro
October .... outubro
November .... novembro
December .... dezembro
spring .... primavera
summer .... verão
autumn .... outono
winter .... inverno
Easter .... Páscoa
Christmas .... Natal
morning .... manhã
afternoon .... tarde
evening .... fim da tarde
night .... noite
today .... hoje
yesterday .... ontem
tomorrow .... amanhã
day .... dia
month .... mês
year .... ano

MONEY
**Is there a bank/currency exchange
office nearby?**
Há um banco/uma agência de
câmbio aqui perto?
Can I cash this here?
Posso levantar isto aqui?
**I'd like to change sterling/dollars
into euros.**
Gostaria de cambiar libras/dólares
para euros.
**Can I use my credit card to
withdraw cash?**
Posso usar o meu cartão de crédito
para levantar dinheiro?
What is the exchange rate today?
Qual é a taxa de câmbio hoje?

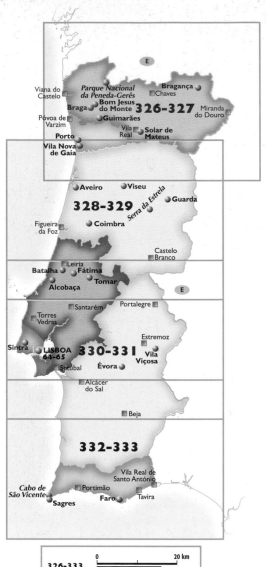

E

Viana do
Castelo
Parque Nacional
da Peneda-Gerês
Bragança
Chaves
Braga
Bom Jesus
do Monte
326-327
Miranda
do Douro
Póvoa de
Varzim
Guimarães
Vila
Real
Solar de
Mateus
Porto
Vila Nova
de Gaia

Aveiro
Viseu
328-329
Guarda
Serra da Estrela
Figueira
da Foz
Coimbra
Castelo
Branco

Leiria
Batalha
Fátima
Tomar
Alcobaça
E

Santarém
Portalegre
Torres
Vedras
Estremoz
Sintra
LISBOA
64-65
330-331
Vila
Viçosa
Setúbal
Évora
Alcácer
do Sal
Beja

332-333

Vila Real de
Santo António
Cabo de
São Vicente
Portimão
Sagres
Faro
Tavira

326-333

0		20 km
0	10 miles	

Toll motorway (Turnpike)

Motorway (Expressway)

Motorway junction with
and without number

National road

Regional road

Railway

International boundary

Administrative region boundary

Built-up area

■ City / Town

National park

Featured place of interest

✈ Airport

621
▲ Height in metres

Viewpoint

Mountain pass

MAPS

Map references for the sights refer to the atlas pages within this section or to the individual town plans within the regions. For example, Coimbra has the reference 328 C6, indicating the page on which the map is found (328) and the grid square in which Coimbra sits (C6).

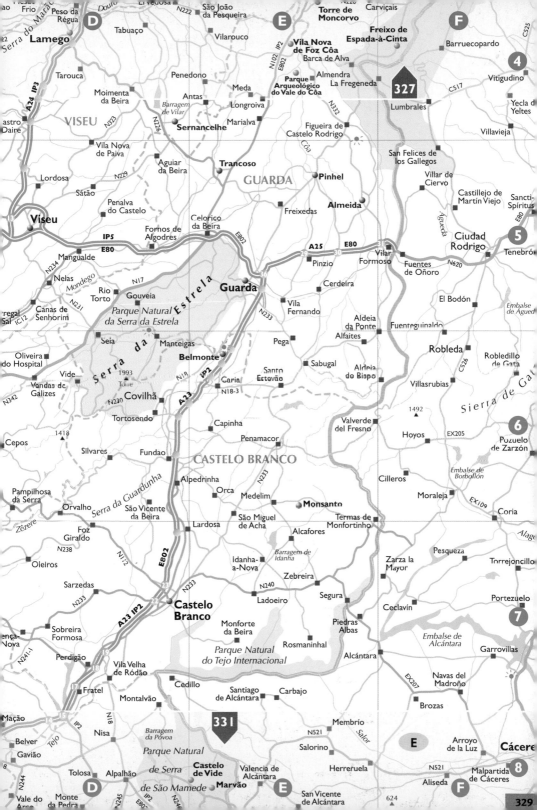

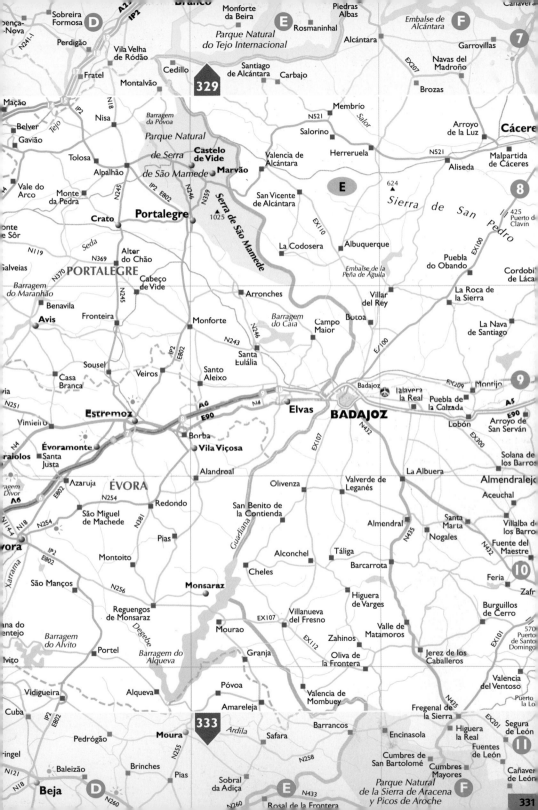

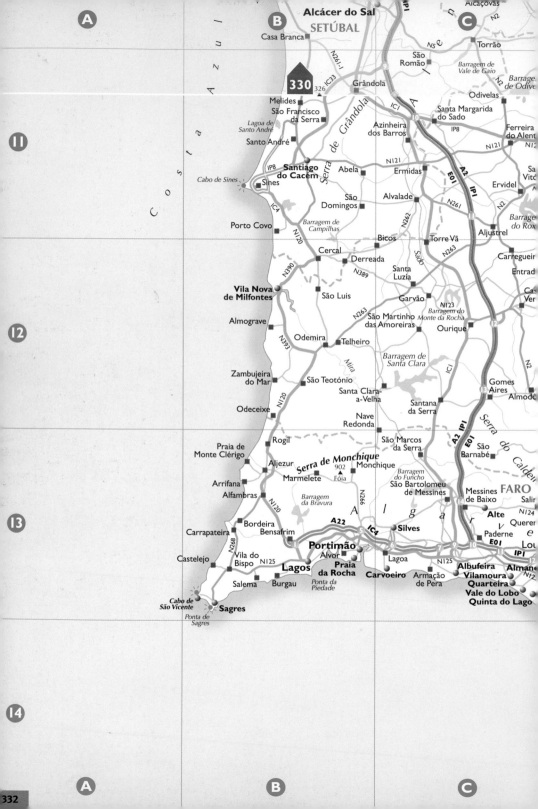

MAPS INDEX

Place	Page	Grid
Foz Giraldo	329	D7
Francelos	326	B4
Fratel	329	D7
Freixedas	329	E5
Freixianda	328	C7
Freixo de Espada-à-Cinta	327	F4
Fronteira	331	D9
Fundão	329	D6
Furadouro	328	B4
Fuzeta	333	D13
Gafanha da Nazaré	328	B5
Galveias	331	C8
Gândara	328	C6
Garvão	332	C12
Gavião	331	D8
Góis	328	C6
Golegã	330	C8
Gomes Aires	332	C12
Gondomar	326	C4
Gouveia	329	D5
Gralhos	326	D2
Grândola	330	B11
Granja	326	B4
Granja	331	E10
Guarda	329	E5
Guimarães	326	C3
Idanha-a-Nova	329	F7
Ílhavo	328	B5
Infantado	330	B9
Izeda	327	F3
Junqueira	327	E4
Ladoeiro	329	E7
Lagoa	332	C13
Lagos	332	B13
Lamarosa	330	C9
Lamas do Vouga	328	C5
Lamego	326	D4
Landedo	327	E2
Lanhelas	326	B2
Lardosa	329	E7
Lavos	328	B6
Lavre	330	C9
Leiria	328	B7
Leirosa	328	B6
Lindoso	326	C2
Lisboa	330	A9
Lixa	326	C3
Longroiva	327	E4
Lordosa	329	D5
Loulé	332	C13
Louredo	326	C3
Loures	330	A9
Lourical	328	B6
Lourinhã	330	A8
Lousa	330	A9
Lousã	328	C6
Lousada	326	C4
Luso	328	C6
Mação	331	D8
Macedo de Cavaleiros	327	E3
Mafra	330	A9
Maia	326	B4
Malhadas	327	F3
Malveira	330	A9
Mamarrosa	328	B5
Mangualde	329	D5
Manteigas	329	D6
Marateca	330	B10
Marialva	329	E4
Marianos	330	C8
Marinha Grande	328	B7
Marinhais	330	B9
Marmelete	332	B13
Martim Longo	333	D12
Marvão	331	E8
Matosinhos	326	B4
Mealhada	328	C6
Meda	327	F4
Medelim	329	E6
Melgaço	326	C2
Melides	332	B11
Mértola	333	D12
Mesão Frio	326	D4
Messines de Baixo	332	C13
Mina de São Domingos	333	D12
Mira	328	B5
Miranda do Corvo	328	C6
Miranda do Douro	327	G3
Mirandela	327	E3
Mogadouro	327	F3
Moimenta da Beira	326	D4
Moita	330	B10
Moledo	326	B2
Monção	326	C2
Moncarapacho	333	D13
Monchique	332	B13
Mondim de Basto	326	D3
Monforte	331	E9
Monforte da Beira	329	E7
Monsanto	329	E6
Monsaraz	331	E10
Montalegre	326	D2
Montalvão	329	D7
Montalvo	330	B10
Montargil	330	C9
Monte da Pedra	331	D8
Monte Gordo	333	D13
Montelaver	330	A9
Montemor-o-Novo	330	C10
Montemor-o-Velho	328	B6
Monte Redondo	328	B7
Montijo	330	B9
Montoito	331	D10
Mora	330	C9
Moura	333	D11
Mourao	331	E10
Muge	330	B9
Murça	327	E3
Murtosa	328	B5
Nave Redonda	332	C12
Nazaré	328	B7
Nelas	329	D5
Nespereira	326	C3
Nisa	331	D8
Nossa Senhora do Cabo	330	A10
Óbidos	330	A8
Odeceixe	332	B12
Odeleite	333	D13
Odemira	332	B12
Odivelas	332	C11
Odivelas	330	A9
Ofir326		D3
Oiã328		C5
Oleiros	329	D7
Olhão	333	D13
Oliveira de Azeméis	328	C5
Oliveira de Frades	328	C5
Oliveira do Bairro	328	C5
Oliveira do Hospital	329	D6
Orca	329	F6
Orvalho	329	D6
Oura	326	D3
Ourém	328	B7
Ourique	332	C12
Ovar	328	B4
Paço de Sousa	326	C4
Paços de Ferreira	326	C3
Paderne	332	C13
Padrógão Grande	328	C7
Palmela	330	B10
Pampilhosa da Serra	329	D6
Paradela	326	D2
Paredes	326	C4
Paredes de Coura	326	C2
Pavia	331	C9
Pedrógão	333	D11
Pedrógão	328	B7
Pega	329	E6
Pegões	330	B10
Penacova	328	C6
Penafiel	326	C4
Penaguiao	326	D4
Penalva do Castelo	329	D5
Penamacor	329	E6
Penedono	327	E4
Penela	328	C6
Peniche	330	A8
Perafita	326	B4
Perdigão	329	D7
Peredo	327	E3
Pereiro	333	D12
Pernacha de Cima	330	C8
Pernes	330	B8
Peso da Régua	326	D4
Pias	333	D11
Pias	331	D10
Pinhel	329	E5
Pinzio	329	E5
Poceirao	330	B10
Podence	327	E3
Pombal	328	B7
Pontão	320	C7
Ponte da Barca	326	C2
Ponte de Lima	326	C2
Ponto do Sôr	331	C0
Portalegre	331	D8
Portel	331	D10
Portelo	327	F2
Portimão	332	B13
Portinho da Arrábida	330	B10
Porto	326	B4
Porto Alto	330	B9
Porto Covo	332	B11
Porto de Mós	328	B7
Porto Novo	330	A8
Portos dos Fusos	333	D13
Póvoa	331	E11
Póvoa de Lanhoso	326	C3
Póvoa de Varzim	326	B3
Praia da Rocha	332	B13
Praia da Vieira	328	B7
Praia de Mira	328	B5
Praia de Monte Clérigo	332	B13
Praia de Santa Cruz	330	A8
Praia Grande	330	A9
Praias-Sado	330	B10
Proença-a-Nova	329	D7
Quarteira	332	C13
Quebradas	330	B8
Querença	332	C13
Quiaios	328	B6

PICTURES

The Automobile Association would like to thank the following photographers, companies and picture libraries for their assistance in the preparation of this book.

Abbreviations for the pictures credits are as follows – (t) top;
(b) bottom;
(c) centre;
(l) left;
(r) right;
(AA) AA World Travel Library.

Cover Pat Behnke/Alamy;
Spine AA/C Jones;
Back Cover AA/T Harris

4 AA/M Wells;
5 AA/A Mockford & N Bonetti6 AA/P Wilson;
7l AA/A Mockford & N Bonetti;
7r AA/T Harris;
8 AA/A Mockford & N Bonetti;
9 AA/A Mockford & N Bonetti;
10 AA/M Wells;
11 AA/T Harris;
10t AA/C Jones;
12b AA/A Kouprianoff;
13 AA/T Harris;
14 AA/A Kouprianoff;
15l Jose Pedro Fernandes/Alamy;
15r AA/M Wells;
16 AA;
17l Jean-Christophe Verhaegen/AFP/Getty Images;
17r Butchofsky-Houser/Corbis;
18 AA;
19l Pinto/ASP Europe;
19r AA/M Chaplow;
20 Serra Fernandes;
21t Editorial Caminho;
21b Eric Fougere/Corbis;
22 AA/M Wells;
23l Metro Porto;
23r AA/J Edmanson;
24 Kevin George/Alamy;
25l World Pictures/Photoshot;
25r AA/P Wilson;
26l Stuart Franklin/Bongarts/Getty Images;
26r AA/A Kouprianoff;
27 AA/A Kouprianoff;
28 AA/A Kouprianoff;
29l AA/A Mockford & N Bonetti;
29r AA/C Jones;
30 AA;
31l AA/M Chaplow;
31r AA/A Mockford & N Bonetti;
32 British Library Board/The Bridgeman Art Library;

33l AA/J Edmanson;
33r AA/C Jones;
34 Museo del Prado/Giraudon/The Bridgeman Art Library;
35l AA/A Kouprianoff;
35r AA/I Burgum;
36 AA/A Mockford & N Bonetti;
37l AA/M Wells;
37r AA/A Mockford & N Bonetti;
38 Mary Evans Picture Library/Mary Evans ILN Pictures;
39l AA/T Harris;
39r Keystone/Getty Images;
40 Fred Bridgland/Getty Images;
41l Rex Features Ltd.;
41r AA/J Tims;
42l AA/A Mockford & N Bonetti;
42r AA/T Harris;
43 AA/C Jones;
46 AA/M Wells;
47 AA/A Mockford & N Bonetti;
48 AA/M Wells;
50t Communicarta/Robin Woods;
50b AA/A Mockford & N Bonetti;
52 AA/A Mockford & N Bonetti;
55 AA/C Jones;
60 Wheeling Around the Algarve;
61 AA/A Mockford & N Bonetti;
62 AA/A Mockford & N Bonetti;
68 AA/A Mockford & N Bonetti;
69l AA/A Kouprianoff;
69r AA/A Mockford & N Bonetti;
70 AA/M Wells;
71 AA/A Mockford & N Bonetti;
72 AA/A Kouprianoff;
73 AA/M Wells;
74 AA/M Wells;
75 AA/M Wells;
76 AA/A Kouprianoff;
77 AA/A Mockford & N Bonetti;
78 AA/M Wells;
79 AA/A Kouprianoff;
80 Fundação Calouste Gulbenkian;
81 Fundação Calouste Gulbenkian;
83 AA/A Kouprianoff;
84 AA/M Wells;
85t AA/A Mockford & N Bonetti;
86 AA/A Mockford & N Bonetti;
87t AA/T Harris;
87b AA/M Wells;
88 AA/A Kouprianoff;
89 AA/A Kouprianoff;
90 AA/A Mockford & N Bonetti;
91 AA/T Harris;
92 Coliseu Lisboa;
95 AA/M Wells;

97 Moda Lisboa/Rui Vasco;
98 AA/M Wells;
102 AA/A Mockford & N Bonetti;
105 AA/A Mockford & N Bonetti;
106 AA/T Harris;
108 AA/A Mockford & N Bonetti;
109 AA/A Mockford & N Bonetti;
110 AA/A Mockford & N Bonetti;
111 AA/A Mockford & N Bonetti;
112 AA/T Harris;
113l AA/A Mockford & N Bonetti;
113r AA/A Kouprianoff;
114l AA/A Kouprianoff;
114r AA/A Mockford & N Bonetti;
115t AA/T Harris;
115b AA/A Kouprianoff;
116 AA/P Wilson;
117l Jose Manuel;
117r Jose Manuel;
118 AA/A Mockford & N Bonetti;
120 AA/A Mockford & N Bonetti;
122 AA/A Mockford & N Bonetti;
124 AA/P Wilson;
126 AA/A Mockford & N Bonetti;
127 AA/A Kouprianoff;
128 AA/A Mockford & N Bonetti;
129 AA/A Mockford & N Bonetti;
130 AA/A Mockford & N Bonetti;
131t AA/P Wilson;
131b AA;
132 AA/A Mockford & N Bonetti;
133 AA/A Mockford & N Bonetti;
134 AA;
135 AA;
136 AA;
137 World Pictures/Photoshot;
138 AA/T Harris;
139 AA/A Mockford & N Bonetti;
140l AA/T Harris;
140r AA/A Mockford & N Bonetti;
141 AA/A Kouprianoff;
142 AA/T Harris;
143 AA/J Edmanson;
144 AA/T Harris;
145 AA/T Harris;
146 AA/A Mockford & N Bonetti;
148 Cavaleiros do Mar;
150 AA/A Mockford & N Bonetti;
152 AA/A Mockford & N Bonetti;
154 AA/T Harris;
156 AA/A Mockford & N Bonetti;
157 AA/A Mockford & N Bonetti;158 AA/A Mockford & N Bonetti;
159 AA/A Mockford & N Bonetti;
160 AA/A Mockford & N Bonetti;
161t AA/A Mockford & N Bonetti;
161b AA/A Kouprianoff;
162 AA/A Mockford & N Bonetti;
163 AA/A Mockford & N Bonetti;
164 AA/A Mockford & N Bonetti;
165 AA/T Harris;
166 AA/A Mockford & N Bonetti;
167 AA/A Mockford & N Bonetti;
168 AA/A Mockford & N Bonetti;
170 AA/T Harris;
172 AA/A Mockford & N Bonetti;
174 AA/A Mockford & N Bonetti;
175 AA/A Mockford & N Bonetti;
176 AA/T Harris;
178 AA/A Kouprianoff;
179 Bob Krist/Corbis;
180 AA/A Mockford & N Bonetti;
182 Aflo Co. Ltd./Alamy;
183 AA/A Kouprianoff;
185 AA/A Kouprianoff;
186 AA/A Mockford & N Bonetti;
187 edo loi/Alamy;
188 AA/A Kouprianoff;
190 AA/A Mockford & N Bonetti;
191 AA/T Harris;
192 AA/A Mockford & N Bonetti;
193 AA;
194 AA/A Mockford & N Bonetti;
195 AA/A Mockford & N Bonetti;
196 AA/T Harris;
197 AA/A Mockford & N Bonetti;
198 AA;
199 AA/A Kouprianoff;
200 AA/A Kouprianoff;
202 AA/A Mockford & N Bonetti;
204 AA/A Mockford & N Bonetti;
206 AA/A Mockford & N Bonetti;
208 AA/A Mockford & N Bonetti;
210 AA/A Kouprianoff;
211 Kevin Schafer/Corbis;
212 AA/A Kouprianoff;
213 AA/A Kouprianoff;
214 AA;
215l AA/A Kouprianoff;
215r AA/A Kouprianoff;
216 AA/A Kouprianoff;
217 AA/A Kouprianoff;
218 AA/A Kouprianoff;
219 AA/A Mockford & N Bonetti;
220 AA/A Kouprianoff;
221 AA/A Kouprianoff;
222t AA/T Harris;
222b AA/A Kouprianoff;
223 AA/A Mockford & N Bonetti;
224 AA/A Mockford & N Bonetti;
225 AA/A Mockford & N Bonetti;
226 AA/A Mockford & N Bonetti;
228 AA/M Langford;
230 AA/A Mockford & N Bonetti;

232 AA/A Kouprianoff;
234 AA/A Mockford & N Bonetti;
236 AA/A Kouprianoff;
237 AA/A Kouprianoff;
238 AA/A Mockford & N Bonetti;
239 AA/A Kouprianoff;
240 AA/A Mockford & N Bonetti;
241 AA/J Edmanson;
242 AA/A Mockford & N Bonetti;
243 AA/P Wilson;
244l AA/P Wilson;
244r AA/A Kouprianoff;
245 AA/A Kouprianoff;
246 AA/P Wilson;
247 AA/A Mockford & N Bonetti;
248 AA/A Kouprianoff;
249 AA;
250 AA/A Mockford & N Bonetti;
252 AA/A Kouprianoff;
254 AA/A Mockford & N Bonetti;
256 AA/A Mockford & N Bonetti;
258 AA/A Mockford & N Bonetti;
260 AA/M Chaplow;
261 AA/ C Jones;
262 AA/ C Jones;
263 AA/ C Jones;
265t AA/ C Jones;
265 AA/ C Jones;
266 AA/ C Jones;
267 AA/ C Jones;
268 AA/ C Jones;
269 AA/A Kouprianoff;
270 AA/ C Jones;
271 AA/ C Jones;
272 AA/M Chaplow;
273 AA/M Chaplow;
274 AA/M Chaplow;
275 AA/A Mockford & N Bonetti;
276 AA/M Chaplow;
277 AA/M Chaplow;
278 AA/ C Jones;
279 AA/ C Jones;
280 AA/M Chaplow;
281 AA/M Chaplow;
282 AA/ C Jones;
286 AA/ C Jones;
288 Vila Joya Hotel;
290 AA/J Edmanson;
291 AA/ C Jones;
292 AA/A Mockford & N Bonetti;
295 AA/M Wells;
296 AA/A Mockford & N Bonetti;
297 AA/A Mockford & N Bonetti;
301 AA/A Kouprianoff;
303 Stockbyte;
304 AA/T Harris;
305t AA/M Wells;

305b AA/A Mockford & N Bonetti;
306 AA/M Wells;
307 AA/A Mockford & N Bonetti;
308 AA/M Wells;
309 AA/ C Jones;
310 AA/A Mockford & N Bonetti;
311 AA/M Wells;
312 AA/M Wells;
314 AA/ C Jones;
315 AA/P Wilson;
316 AA/ C Jones;
318 AA/M Wells;
320 AA/M Chaplow;
325 AA/A Mockford & N Bonetti.

Every effort has been made to trace the copyright
holders, and we apologise in advance for any accidental
errors. We would be happy to apply any corrections in
the following edition of this publication

CREDITS

Managing editor
Sheila Hawkins

Project editor
Lodestone Publishing Ltd

Design
Drew Jones, pentacorbig

Picture research
Susana Vazquez Fernandez

Image retouching etc
Sarah Montgomery

Main contributors
Emma Rowley-Ruas, Jo Chapman,
Charlotte Eimer, Sally Roy

Updater
Emma Rowley-Ruas

Production
Karen Gibson

Published by AA Publishing, a trading name of AA Media Limited, whose registered office is
Fanum House, Basing View, Basingstoke, RG21 4EA. Registered number 06112600.
A CIP catalogue record for this book is available from the British Library.

ISBN 978-0-7495-6235-9

KeyGuide is a registered trademark in Australia and is used under license.
Style with plastic section dividers by permission of AA Publishing.
Colour separation by Keenes, Andover, UK
Printed and bound by Leo Paper Products, China

We believe the contents of this book are correct at the time of printing. However, some details, particularly prices, opening times and
telephone numbers do change. We do not accept responsibility for any consequences arising from the use of this book.
This does not affect your statutory rights. We would be grateful if readers would advise us of any inaccuracies they may encounter, or any
suggestions they might like to make to improve the book. There is a form provided at the back of the book for this purpose, or you can email us
at Keyguides@theaa.com

A03807
Maps in this title produced from mapping © MAIRDUMONT / Falk Verlag 2009 and with reference to mapping
© ISTITUTO GEOGRAFICO DE AGOSTINI S.p.A., NOVARA 2008
Transport map © Communicarta Ltd, UK
Weather chart statistics supplied by Weatherbase © Copyright 2004 Canty and Associates, LLC.

Find out more about AA Publishing and the wide range of travel publications and services the AA provides by visiting our website at
www.theAA.com/bookshop

READER RESPONSE

Thank you for buying this KeyGuide. Your comments and opinions are very important to us, so please help us to improve our travel guides by taking a few minutes to complete this questionnaire.

You do not need a stamp (unless posted outside the UK). If you do not want to cut this page from your guide, then photocopy it or write your answers on a plain sheet of paper.

Send to: **KeyGuide Editor, AA World Travel Guides**
FREEPOST SCE 4598, Basingstoke RG21 4GY

Find out more about AA Publishing and the wide range of travel publications the AA provides by visiting our website at www.theAA.com/bookshop

ABOUT THIS GUIDE

Which KeyGuide did you buy? ....

Where did you buy it? ....

When? ....month .... year

Why did you choose this AA KeyGuide?
☐ Price ☐ AA Publication
☐ Used this series before;
title
☐ Cover ☐ Other (please state)

Please let us know how helpful the following features of the guide were to you by circling the appropriate category: very helpful (VH), helpful (H) or little help (LH)

Size	VH	H	LH
Layout	VH	H	LH
Photos	VH	H	LH
Excursions	VH	H	LH
Entertainment	VH	H	LH
Hotels	VH	H	LH
Maps	VH	H	LH
Practical info	VH	H	LH
Restaurants	VH	H	LH
Shopping	VH	H	LH
Walks	VH	H	LH
Sights	VH	H	LH
Transport info	VH	H	LH

What was your favourite sight, attraction or feature listed in the guide?

Page................. Please give your reason ....
....

Which features in the guide could be changed or improved? Or are there any other comments you would like to make?

ABOUT YOU

Name (Mr/Mrs/Ms)...

Address ....
....
....
....
Postcode.. Daytime tel nos...

Email..
Please only give us your mobile phone number/email if you wish to hear from us about other products and services from the AA and partners by text or mms.

Which age group are you in?
Under 25 ☐   25–34 ☐   35–44 ☐   45–54 ☐   55+ ☐

How many trips do you make a year?
Less than1 ☐   1 ☐   2 ☐   3 or more ☐

ABOUT YOUR TRIP

Are you an AA member?   Yes ☐ No ☐

When did you book?............. month................ year

When did you travel?.............month................ year

Reason for your trip?   Business ☐ Leisure ☐

How many nights did you stay? ....

How did you travel?   Individual ☐ Couple ☐ Family ☐ Group ☐

Did you buy any other travel guides for your trip? ....

If yes, which ones?..

Thank you for taking the time to complete this questionnaire. Please send it to us as soon as possible, and remember, you do not need a stamp (unless posted outside the UK).
AA Travel Insurance call 0800 072 4168 or visit www.theaa.com

Titles in the KeyGuide series:
Australia, Barcelona, Britain, Brittany, Canada, China, Costa Rica, Croatia, Florence and Tuscany, France, Germany, Ireland, Italy, London, Mallorca, Mexico, New York, New Zealand, Normandy, Paris, Portugal, Prague, Provence and the Côte d'Azur, Rome, Scotland, South Africa, Spain, Thailand, Venice, Vietnam, Western European Cities.
Published in July 2009: Berlin

The information we hold about you will be used to provide the products and services requested and for identification, account administration, analysis, and fraud/loss prevention purposes. More details about how that information is used is in our privacy statement, which you'll find under the heading "Personal Information" in our terms and conditions and on our website: www.theAA.com. Copies are also available from us by post, by contacting the Data Protection Manager at AA, Fanum House, Basing View, Basingstoke, Hampshire RG21 4EA.

We may want to contact you about other products and services provided by us, or our partners (by mail, telephone, email) but please tick the box if you DO NOT wish to hear about such products and services from us. ☐

AA Travel Insurance call 0800 072 4168 or visit www.theaa.com